PIPES
VENTS ETC
DETAIL
1.

STOCK
METAL.
NOZZLES

STOCK
METAL
PIECE.

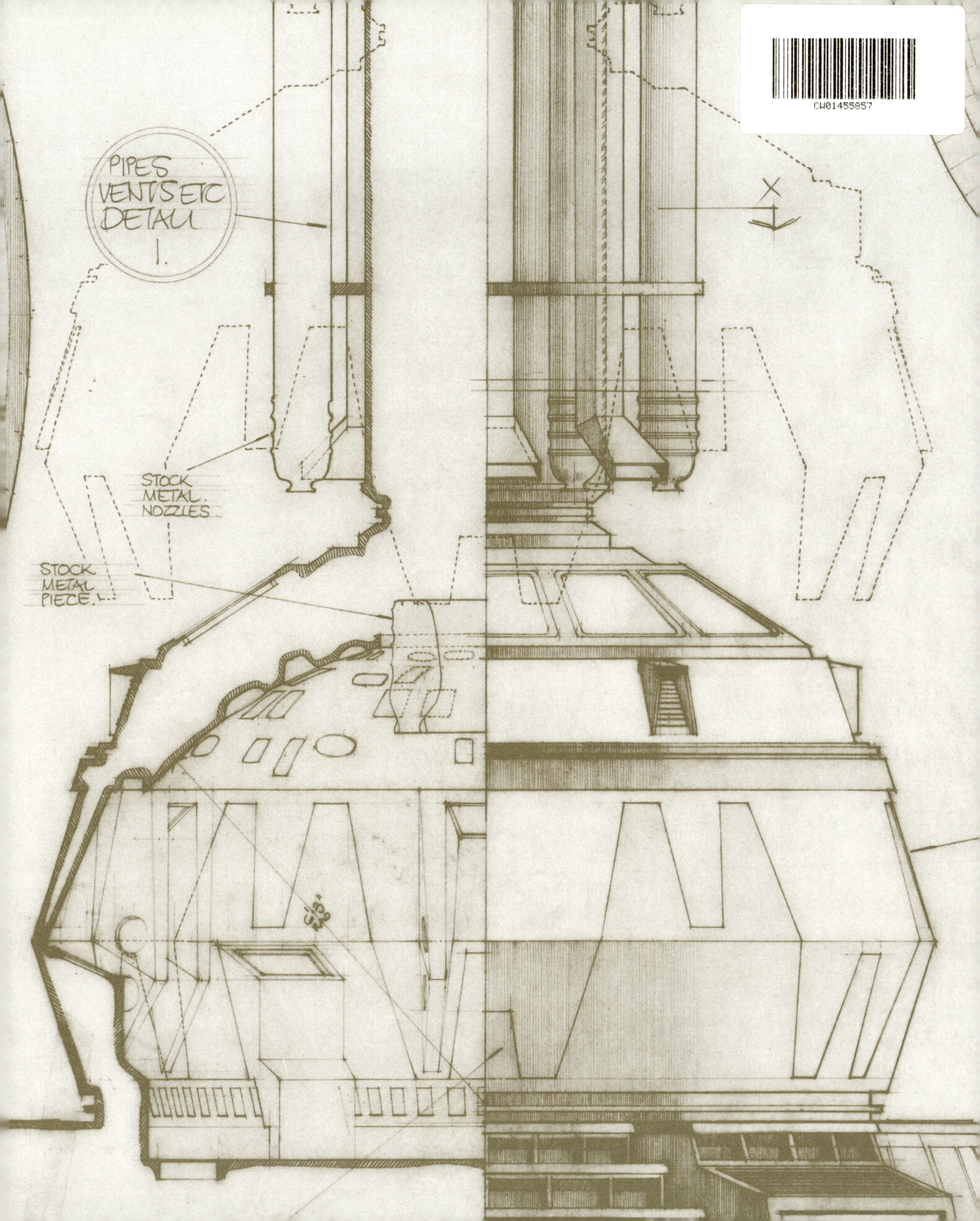

STAR WARS™

THE BLUEPRINTS

DESIGNS AND ARTWORK FROM THE SKYWALKER SAGA

J.W. RINZLER

PABLO HIDALGO

DK | Penguin Random House

Project Editor Frankie Hallam
Senior Designer Nathan Martin
Production Editor Siu Yin Chan
Senior Production Controller Mary Slater
Managing Editor Emma Grange
Managing Art Editor Vicky Short
Publisher Paula Regan
Art Director Charlotte Coulais
Managing Director Mark Searle

Edited by Simon Beecroft
Designed by Office of Craig
Cover concept by Office of Craig

For Lucasfilm
Senior Editor Brett Rector
Creative Director Michael Siglain
Art Director Troy Alders
Story Group Leland Chee, Kate Izquierdo
Creative Art Manager Phil Szostak
Asset Management Chris Argyropoulos, Allison Bird, Jackey Cabrera, Elinor De La Torre, Gabrielle Levenson, Nick Miano, Bryce Pinkos, Sarah Williams

Dorling Kindersley would like to thank: Chelsea Alon, Angela Grief, Shana Highfield, Rima Simonian, and Thomas Wang at Disney; David Fentiman and Matt Jones for editorial assistance; Jen Murray for DTP support; Kath Hill for proofreading, and Michael Goldstein for indexing.

First published in Great Britain in 2025 by
Dorling Kindersley Limited
20 Vauxhall Bridge Road,
London SW1V 2SA

The authorised representative in the EEA is
Dorling Kindersley Verlag GmbH. Arnulfstr. 124,
80636 Munich, Germany

Copyright © 2025 Dorling Kindersley Limited
A Penguin Random House Company
10 9 8 7 6 5 4 3 2 1
001–349690–Oct/2025

© & TM 2025 LUCASFILM LTD.

A CIP catalogue record for this book
is available from the British Library.
ISBN: 978-0-2417-4160-3

Printed and bound in China

www.dk.com
www.starwars.com

MIX
Paper | Supporting
responsible forestry
FSC™ C018179

This book was made with Forest Stewardship Council™ certified paper – one small step in DK's commitment to a sustainable future. **Learn more at www.dk.com/uk/information/sustainability**

Original dedications from J.W. Rinzler

Dedicated to those art department crew who have passed away: Ivor Beddoes,
Reg Bream, Richard J. Dawking, George Djurkovic, Michael Lamont, Harry Lange,
Elliot Scott, Bill Welch...

...to John Barry, a visionary...

...to Fred Hole, one of the brightest lights of four *Star Wars* art departments,

...to Irvin Kershner, a Renaissance man,

...and to Ralph McQuarrie, a sublimely patient and beautiful soul.

↑ A photo of Stage 1 at Elstree Studios, in England, taken during the making of The Empire Strikes Back circa March 1979, shows the exterior wood structures of the ice corridor and Medical Center sets (note the circular opening in the latter's roof), with other structures in various stages of seemingly chaotic construction.

↑ A photo taken during the making of *Revenge of the Sith* on Stage 1 of Fox Studios in Sydney, Australia, circa July 2003, shows the bridge of General Grievous's Trade Federation cruiser as it is being constructed on a rostrum; the final set would have at least a dozen illuminated screens.

CONTENTS

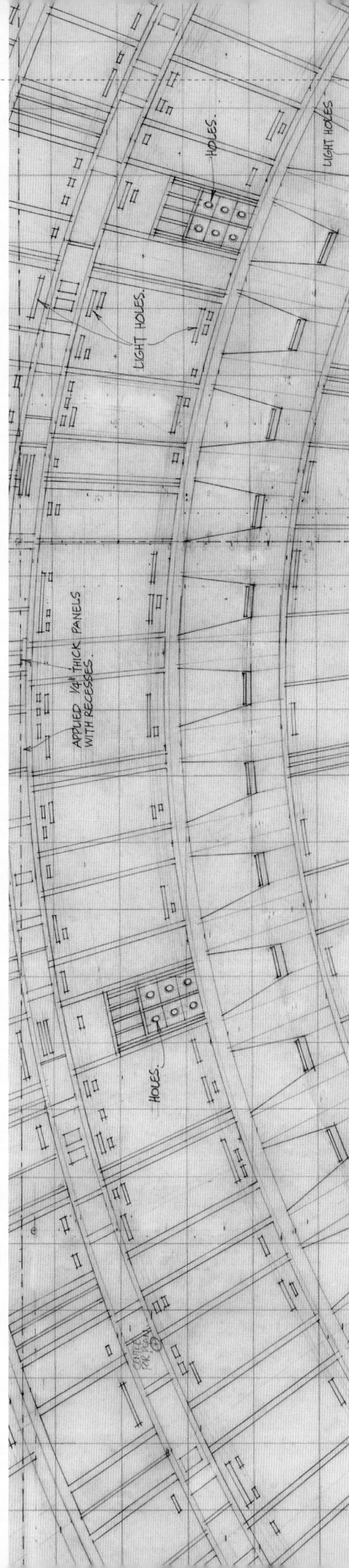

→ The detail is from Ted Ambrose's technical drawing of the gantry built backing from *The Empire Strikes Back*, March 1979.

It was *Revenge of the Sith* that changed everything. Though I knew J.W. Rinzler prior to that, the nature of our work—he as an editor on Lucasfilm's publishing team and me as a content developer on Lucasfilm's online team—only really meant the occasional emails regarding posting news of Jonathan's upcoming titles on StarWars.com. But as Episode III launched into production in the middle of 2003, our remarkable paths through *Star Wars* became entwined.

I had been given the audacious task of blogging from the set every day as it lensed in Sydney, Australia; he was the editor of the movie's *Making Of* book. By odd occurrence, the author originally slated to write the book became suddenly unavailable, requiring Jonathan to voyage Down Under and take the reins of the project. Jonathan and I were in constant contact during the making of this movie, comparing notes and assembling as complete a picture as we could. We both sat ringside to the making of Episode III in a capacity that gave us unprecedented contact with George Lucas, Rick McCallum, key creatives at Industrial Light & Magic, and other prominent figures vital to the completion of the film. We earned the friendship and trust of many of these people we regarded as legends.

This contact was reciprocated in kind, in welcome ways. For me, it exposed the fact that my deep knowledge of *Star Wars* minutia could be a benefit to production teams, a role that has only grown. For Jonathan, it revealed to the crew—and George Lucas in particular—his passion for the art and craft of filmmaking and his dogged dedication to chronicling the people and processes with an unerring journalistic eye. Jonathan was devoted to preserving these stories for future generations. George and Jonathan clicked in a way few authors ever did. Jonathan became his trusted witness, his embedded journalist, digging through the history of Lucasfilm.

Aside from the sizable tragedy of losing a friend, it was also a deep loss to *Star Wars* when Jonathan passed in 2021. It meant this new era of production would not get the same level of in-depth coverage as the past did. We endeavor to live up to his example, but it will take many, many writers to equal what Jonathan covered in his far too brief time.

Pablo Hidalgo
March 2025

INTRODUCTION TO THE ORIGINAL EDITION

Star Wars: The Blueprints gives a voice to the *Star Wars* studio art departments who, film after film, laid the groundwork and built the structures of many of the most iconic sets in the history of cinema.

There have been many art of *Star Wars* books, usually consisting of fantastic concept illustrations, sketches, and storyboards. Often these artworks are juxtaposed with final frames from the film, unintentionally conveying the idea that concept drawings were translated directly into finished sets. But the fact is that an interim "stage" existed: the blueprint, or technical drawing. Occasionally these same books have even reproduced a few blueprints, but almost always too small to be read, studied, or fully appreciated. (There was a very early set of 15 blueprints published by Ballantine Books in 1977, with no supporting text.) And yet during principal photography for all six films, actors have worked on very real, very detailed creations. From the Rebel Blockade Runner hallway and the cockpit of the *Millennium Falcon* to the bridge of General Grievous' flagship, Jabba the Hutt's Palace, the Death Star, and the Tatooine homestead—all of these places and hundreds more had to be designed, built, painted, and dressed, with technical drawings showing the way.

One of the reasons, perhaps, for the relative neglect of blueprints is that their progeny, these sets and full-sized vehicles, existed only briefly, wisps of artistry constructed from wood, plaster, metal, foam, fiberglass, and other materials; cut, sawed, measured, and hammered into form by teams of craftspeople and used just long enough for the days needed— before being smashed to pieces and thrown into a junk pile to make room for the next one. The number of stages was always limited, while the number of sets multiplied as the imagination of George Lucas, creator of the *Star Wars* saga, expanded in proportion to growing budgets and progressively modernized effects.

Many of these illusory interiors and exteriors for the original trilogy came from concepts worked up in conjunction with Lucas by the now-legendary Ralph McQuarrie. Lucas would explain his ideas in broad strokes, sometimes supplying reference material, and then McQuarrie would make sketches on the subject until Lucas was satisfied; McQuarrie would then produce a color study and finally a finished painting. Vehicles were generally under the purview of the visual effects art director at Industrial Light & Magic (ILM), Joe Johnston. For the prequel trilogy, Lucas made use of a team of artists under the supervision of Doug Chiang, Ryan Church, and Erik Tiemens. But in all cases, every practical set was eventually turned over to the film's production designers: John Barry (Episode IV), Norman Reynolds (Episodes V and VI), and Gavin Bocquet (Episodes I, II, and III).

With his team of art directors, assistant art directors, draftspeople, set dressers, and set modelers, the production designer would work out how to translate blue-sky concepts into nuts-and-bolts sets. Not only would they have to solve many conceptual problems, they would also have to do it as cheaply and effectively as possible, while often considering how one set might be revamped and used as another to further economize time and money.

Lost in most of the literature about *Star Wars* is that, particularly for the first film, the production designer conceptualized many sets from the ground up, literally. Luke's garage, the Cantina bar, the white corridor of the Rebel Blockade Runner, many interiors of the Death Star, the *Falcon* cockpit—nearly all of the sets, really—stemmed from the collaboration of Lucas with veteran production designer John Barry. It is not for nothing that Lucas to this day refers to Barry as a "genius."

Indeed, each film in the saga contains indelible marks left by the studio art departments. The seemingly disparate parts of these six *Star Wars* art departments came together from a relatively small pool of talent fostered in English film studios. Nurtured on the movies of Sir David Lean, Sir Carol Reed, Richard Lester, Ken Annakin (who directed many films for Walt Disney), and others, they trained with the great production designers of their time, including John Box, Ken Adam, and Charles Bishop. Some of the art department crew, such as art director Alan Tomkins and construction manager Bill Welch, came from the "class of *2001*," having worked on Kubrick's groundbreaking, mind-bending film of 1968, *2001: A Space Odyssey*.

After having labored on one, two, or all three of the original trilogy *Star Wars* films, the different men of the art departments split off and reformed for the *Indiana Jones* trilogy, *Alien*, *James Bond* and *Monty Python* films, and many other movies. They would reappear as Academy Award® winners on *Titanic* in 1998, production designers and art directors of the *Harry Potter* series, and so on. The family tree of this core group would show a pedigree that more or less dominated production design in the United Kingdom, and to some extent the United States, for 30-odd years.

The unsung heroes of the original trilogy art departments are the draftspeople, who drew in collaboration with their respective art department heads, but who also added their own ideas. They worked quickly and creatively, almost always under difficult deadlines. Their blueprints are often not as sexy as concept work, but they have an attribute that concept art lacks—a sense of the real. In fact, blueprints had to be more worldly and team-oriented works, something that the construction, paint, and plaster departments could use and that other key figures in the creation of the movie could consult, from the director of photography to the set dresser.

Generally the draftsperson's artistry lies within their discipline; in another age, draftspeople would have belonged to a guild. Like their forebears, members of the art department earn their spots and promotions thanks to years of training and apprenticeship, as they become familiar with a host of materials. A draftsperson might work on a dozen films or more before becoming an assistant art director; very few would ever become production designers. And then there's Reg Bream, by all accounts the superlative draftsperson of the original trilogy, fast and unmatched, who seems to have had no other ambition than to create one fantastic drawing after the next.

My privilege during the research and writing of this book was getting to hear their stories and the larger narratives of the successive art department chiefs. Norman Reynolds not only consented to several hours of interviews over a period of weeks, but also responded to dozens of emails. Talking to *Star Wars* set dresser Roger Christian was a valuable lesson in the earliest days of the first film's aesthetic revolution and allowed me to add his memories and experiences to the amalgamating history of the groundbreaking first film (his original interview with Charles Lippincott from 1976 is lost, and so his crucial part was not told in *The Making of Star Wars*—but is fortunately now included in this book). Christian was also very patient, responding to many questions via email. He is working on a book about his experiences on *Star Wars*, *Alien*, and his other films, and I can't wait to read it.

Alan Tomkins was a big help, as were former draftsmen Ted Ambrose, Michael Boone, Steve Cooper, Peter Childs, and Fred Hole, who is the only draftsperson to work on both trilogies and is widely admired as having a beautiful "hand" (and who, sadly, passed away in February 2011). Indeed, Gavin Bocquet told me how much he had learned from Hole as a junior draftsman during the several films they worked on together. Of course, Bocquet's participation was essential to the book and, luckily, he found time to talk while working in England on another film—even pulling in his supervising art director on the prequel trilogy, Peter Russell, who had essential insights on the technical drawings. Indeed it was great fun seeing Gavin and Peter again (thanks to Skype), as I hadn't seen them since I was at Fox Studios in Sydney, Australia, chronicling their efforts in my book, *The Making of Star Wars: Revenge of the Sith*.

Writing *Star Wars: The Blueprints* has been an adventure into the past that I hope will endure and that readers will enjoy. My sincere wish is that *Star Wars: The Blueprints* will preserve the efforts of the magnificently trained and inspired men and women who contributed so much to the art of cinema.

J. W. Rinzler
Skywalker Ranch

INTRODUCTION
EPISODES IV, V, VI: THE ORIGINAL TRILOGY

A REVITALIZED INDUSTRY

In 1973, George Lucas began toying with the concept of a space-fantasy film in the tradition of *Flash Gordon* and *Buck Rogers* (both originally 1930s comic strips and movie serials). Instead of aliens or humanoids from the future uniformly dressed in streamlined costumes, sitting on brand-new identical chairs, and using improbable laser guns, Lucas would clothe his characters in realistic garments, place them in a lived-in world, and equip them with a tremendous variety of familiar-looking weapons and tools. These characters would come to life in a future past that was established on-screen in the now famous line, "A long time ago, in a galaxy far, far away…." This fairy-tale mindset was light years away from the science-fiction films that had been made up to that time.

In 1975, Lucas and 20th Century Fox, the studio that was considering financing *Star Wars*, estimated the movie would make, with luck, $12 to $16 million at the box office. The studio proposed a tight budget for production: $4 million for all departments, including sets, camera crew, and travel. But working in Hollywood would cost about $8 million to realize Lucas' vision. A London-based Fox executive named Pete Beale, whose job was to encourage the making of films in Britain, told Lucas that they could do it for half price there. At that time, the once-thriving British film industry was at an all-time low. Television was in the ascendant and studios were closing. Elstree Studios was virtually empty, enabling Fox to make an amazing deal, renting the entire facility at a bargain.

Lucas had made his first two low-budget independent films, *THX 1138* (1971) and *American Graffiti* (1973), for under a million dollars with tiny crews and on locations in Northern California in order to be far away from Hollywood, of which he was extremely wary, and to have control over his productions. The UK is even farther away and Lucas came to learn that he would also be making use of the UK's skilled craftspeople, who had grown up in a system that consistently generated some of the most talented and disciplined behind-the-scenes professionals. If it were not for the success of *American Graffiti*, the studio would never have agreed to even consider backing his movie. Fox was therefore dithering about whether or not to finance *Star Wars*, so Lucas used his profits from *Graffiti* to pay for several key aspects of pre-production.

↑ Lucas directs Peter Cushing (who would be filmed only from the waist up that day) and an Imperial officer in a Barry-designed tulip-shaped Death Star work station on Stage 2, circa spring 1976.

Lucas received several recommendations to hire John Barry as a production designer. Previously, he had worked on Brian G. Hutton's war comedy *Kelly's Heroes* (1970) and Stanley Kubrick's *A Clockwork Orange* (1971). Lucas' friends Gloria and Willard Huyck were on location in Guaymas, Mexico, writing scenes for director Stanley Donen's *Lucky Lady* (1975), for which Barry was also designing sets. Over the Fourth of July weekend of 1975, Lucas and producer Gary Kurtz flew down to Mexico to meet with Barry and set dresser Roger Christian.

"George talked to me about the sets," Christian said "I was excited, because I had always hated science-fiction films before, just the look of them, because they were so unreal. We realized that we shared a common philosophy about spaceships, that they should look like they were in your garage and they had been repaired and had oil dripping from them and all of these things."

From that trip, Lucas and Kurtz began to assemble a production art department. They hired Barry as production designer, Christian as set dresser, Bill Welch as construction manager and Les Dilley as assistant art director.

"The reason they went with me was because I didn't actually sort of reel and fold up when they told me about their film," said Barry. "Because there were some really quite mind-blowing problems they were into." Many of those problems were in realizing Lucas' ambitious ideas within the shrinking time frame. Barry estimated that he would need about seven months to plan, design, and build the sets, which was just the amount of time that remained. But Fox had still not committed to the film and was negotiating hard with Lucas. At the time, therefore, the agreements between these key players were only handshake deals.

"I certainly thought the movie had enormous potential," said Barry. "And I took the movie because of George, because of his film, *American Graffiti*. I thought of the things in it that were all down to George, which I would be happy to be associated with."

Finding space at Lee Studios in West London, John Barry, Roger Christian, Les Dilley, Bill Welch, sketch artist Harry Lange (who was uncredited in the actual film), carpenter Bill Harman, sculptor Liz Moore, production manager Robert Watts, and production buyer Peter Dunlop, who came on part-time, began work on *Star Wars*.

"Lee Studios was really a sort of warehouse that didn't have much going for it, but it sufficed for us," said Dilley. "We were in these little sheds,

↑ Barry and Lucas examine a maquette of what appears to be Mos Eisley streets.

small stages they called them, but we were using them as workshops while doing the development stuff with George. We were a pretty closely knit bunch. If George didn't like something, he told you; and if he did like it, he told you that, too. So, it was pretty good."

As Fox delayed further, Christian and the others had to find a way to dovetail Lucas' vision with their projected budget. "I kept thinking and thinking," Christian said. "And I had been doing something a bit on *Lucky Lady*, using scrap for sets and stuff, so I kind of talked it through with John Barry. I said, 'Look, I've done this on other things, and I think we should do my dressing out of airplane junk and scrap,' which at that time cost nothing, because it was sold by weight."

Lucas finally received the green light from Fox on December 13, 1975, when there was only about three months left before shooting would begin on location in Tunisia. The film involved many sets, most of which depicted otherworldly environments. Barry had to hire a crack team to help him sort out the film's myriad problems: art director Norman Reynolds, whose work on *The Incredible Sarah* (1976) would be nominated for an Academy Award® for Best Art Direction; draftspeople Michael Lamont, Ted Ambrose, Michael Boone, Alan Roderick-Jones, and Reg Bream; storyboard artist Ivor Beddoes; and others. "Something like two weeks before Christmas, John

rang me and asked me if I wanted to work on this science-fiction film, called 'Star something or other,'" said Reynolds. "So I did. It sounded interesting and John was quite excited." Reynolds' first day at the "office" was December 22, 1975. The other members of the *Star Wars* art department, which gathered in the tiny, ramshackle rooms of Elstree in the winter of 1975–76, were veterans of the film business.

The art department at Elstree was the nerve center for several other departments, as evidenced by the graphic box that sits on the corner of every blueprint. By making check marks, the draftspeople could designate which department crew would be needed to construct the set designated by that technical drawing: carpenters, scenic/paint shop, metal shop, drapes, special effects, electrical, plasterers' shop, studio stage space. (These working technical drawings are referred to as "blueprints" in the US) All departments had to be aware of what was coming down the pipeline. For example, the studio managers needed to know which stage each set was to be built on in order to arrange safety and fire protection, and so on. A mistake in the technical drawing could mean costly errors.

Lucas was an unofficial member of the art department. As such, he tried to maintain a hands-on approach but was inevitably buffeted by the problems of his unprecedented film and those inherent in any big production. "George had never worked with a production designer, which was a real problem for him," said Barry. "Of course, it's a problem for anybody. I'll tell you what the problem is: You cannot control it. And it drives people mad, particularly [directors] like Stanley Kubrick, who likes to feel he's doing it himself. I mean, you can dictate what the letter is going to say, but it's going to come out in somebody else's handwriting, because the million decisions, from minute to minute to minute, all make a difference. That's the sort of situation. And George is very aware of watchable images. So that's what worries him about having a picture designed for him."

"When I first met George, it was a strange experience in some ways, because on all the films I've worked on, I'd never seen the director every day," Reynolds remembered with astonishment. "I mean, George came to the art department *every* day, which was very unusual. He was around all the time. He was like part of the art department, really, and he was just—what can I say? I think you use the expression 'a regular guy,' don't you?"

In Los Angeles, production illustrator Ralph McQuarrie had done a number of paintings in consultation with Lucas to start off the conceptual journey that would lead to the sets of *Star Wars*; but with Barry on board, conceptual design had crossed the Atlantic in mid-1975. By January 1976, nearly the entirety of the sets had been dreamed up by Barry with Lucas in the UK, from the Cantina, the streets of Mos Eisley, and the homestead, to

the Death Star interiors and the Throne Room. The vehicles, on the other hand, had mainly been designed by visual effects art director Joe Johnston, who worked at Lucas' facility, Industrial Light & Magic (ILM), in Van Nuys, north of Hollywood.

"John was a brilliant designer, a brilliant mind, and, unusually for a production designer in movies, he was actually a trained architect, as well," said Watts of Barry. "He had a wonderful eye in everything, and the combination of him and Ralph McQuarrie was unbeatable. But Ralph was establishing more on what I call the wardrobe side: the costumes, the uniforms, stormtroopers, Darth Vader; all of that kind of look. John was a designer. John Barry was going to direct the design of the movie."

"We had three months for this huge, monster epic, really, to be put together," said Christian. "So, we were winging it every day." Indeed, it was now a very short schedule of just 12 weeks before the first day of principal photography was due to commence. "I was very concerned about getting things done, like the landspeeder and the Death Star; lots and lots of stuff, really," said Reynolds. "I was really immersed with things. The way that an art department tends to work is that the designer comes up with good ideas—a good designer will always accept other ideas from his assistants, but it really emanates from the designer. So I have to say that ninety percent of the stuff was, in my book, down to John."

As the technical drawings came pouring out,

and as they were modified and approved by Lucas, it became apparent that Barry was a master of recycling parts of one set for another—and had become a fearless innovator. "Another thing that we did which was very useful and made the picture much cheaper than it would have otherwise been, and quicker: we used a lot of junk," said Barry. "George had a lot of the spaceships that he'd designed, and the model makers had basically used the same premise that they'd used on *2001: A Space Odyssey* [1968]. They were using model kit parts to make the basic models look interesting. But I had to build full-scale seventy-feet-across versions of these things. So, it sort of dawned on me that the kit parts represented things like crank shafts and other parts in miniature—so I went back to the originals that the kit parts represented and used those. We bought thousands of pounds worth of aircraft junk and took it to pieces."

"Without being able to think differently, I could never have tackled *Star Wars*, as it meant inventing an entirely revolutionary and new way of set dressing, using junked airplane scrap, office machinery, anything I could lay my hands on," said Christian. "I was lucky because they'd closed down a telephone exchange, so I had the buyer purchase everything. It was a treasure trove of set dressing materials."

"I think one of the reasons why we were able to do so much so quickly was because, unlike at Universal or Warner Bros. Studios, Elstree was small," said Reynolds. "It was almost like one department. The construction manager, Bill Welch, was in the art department all the time. The construction manager is employed by the production designer, he's one of his lieutenants, really, and Bill almost lived in the art department. So, the lines of communication were very, very short. And the set dresser is part of the art department, so it was a very tight ship."

"On one occasion George said to me, 'You know, if people don't have quite enough time, you really get great value for the money, you get a better job, and I think it's really good all around,'" said Barry. "I think what he was implying is that, because you're in a corner, you get the maximum effort out of everybody."

The results were fantastic, and when *Star Wars* debuted on May 25, 1977, crowds all over the world went wild. "We didn't know that would happen, and whoever says they did is a little bit devious," Reynolds said. "I don't think any of us realized quite the magnitude of that film. In my case, I had been more concerned just about getting things

↑ Lightning in a bottle: set dresser Roger Christian, assistant art director Les Dilley, production designer John Barry, construction supervisor Bill Welch, and art director Norman Reynolds—in the Elstree art department, early 1976.

done on time. Hearing some of these strange names, 'Obi-Wan Kenobi' and the like, I didn't have time to be thinking about it."

At the Academy Awards® ceremony in 1978, the Elstree art department received its due: an Oscar for Best Art Direction, which was given to John Barry, Roger Christian, Les Dilley, and Norman Reynolds. John Dykstra, Richard Edlund, Grant McCune, and Robbie Blalack at ILM, with John Stears, also won an award for Best Visual Effects.

"We watched all the special-effects boys going up and they were all dancing around on stage and thanking their dogs and their aunties," said Christian. "I said, 'John, why don't you just say something that's a bit more dignified?' And he said, 'Yes, okay.' So John got up when it was our turn, went to the microphone, and said, 'Every single frame of this film belongs to that man down there, George Lucas.' And I think that summed up our attitude."

STRIKING BACK

After the phenomenal success of *Star Wars*, Lucas planned a bigger budget sequel, which was eventually titled *The Empire Strikes Back*. This was an even more ambitious production than the first: deeper characterizations, more visual effects—and larger, more complex, and more numerous sets. So many, and so huge, in fact, that Lucas authorized and paid for the construction of a new stage at Elstree Studios: the *Star Wars* Stage.

Given his long-held desire to write and direct, John Barry relinquished the role of production designer for the next *Star Wars* film. He would act as consultant on the sequel, allowing more time to helm *Saturn 3* (1980). "Robert Watts asked me if I would go to Finse, Norway, on a location scout for the next *Star Wars* whilst they were sort of looking for a production designer," said Reynolds. "We went to Oslo, then up by train to Finse, and it seemed to be ideal. And then that night or the next day, when we got back to Oslo, Robert sort of sprang it on me when we were in the men's room together, as chaps do: he said, 'You know, I was wondering whether you might want to design the film?' And I said, 'Serious? You can't be serious.' And he said, 'Yeah. George thought it might be quite a good idea.'"

Another change was that Michael Ford took over set dressing from Christian, as the latter had gone back to film school to become a director. As was now a tradition, Ford scoured salvage yards, airports, and manufacturing companies, and then filled the cavernous prop room with a

↑ McQuarrie, Kurtz, Reynolds, and director of photography Peter Suschitzky examine a maquette of the rebel hangar on Hoth.

mass of interesting pieces. The art department would then be able to choose and build selections into props and sets. For the draftspeople, these found objects were invaluable.

Back in the States, Lucas rehired Ralph McQuarrie and Joe Johnston. The former would tackle even more chores, doing conceptual artwork for nearly every set and creature, while the latter would once again handle vehicle design. Lucas also moved ILM to the San Francisco Bay Area from Southern California.

In the UK, Reynolds hired his art directors and draftspeople. Some *Star Wars* veterans would return, including Harry Lange, Reg Bream, Steve Cooper, Ivor Beddoes, and Ted Ambrose, among others; and a couple of new people were brought on, including Michael Boone (draftsperson), Fred Hole and Michael Lamont (assistant art directors), and Alan Tomkins (art director).

In the fall and winter of 1978, the art department swung into high gear preparing for the spring 1979 shoot. "We had extensive models built and we made all kinds of special finders to view them," said Irvin Kershner in 1979, whom Lucas had hired to direct the sequel. After the exhausting process of making *Star Wars*, Lucas was giving up his on-set chores, though executive producing and financing the film himself. "I found myself on my knees three or four hours a day looking over the

tops of tables into miniature sets. We made a huge book of every major sequence, shot by shot."

The art department experienced an awful setback, however, when Stage 3 at Elstree Studios burned to the ground. "Stanley Kubrick had built a hotel for *The Shining* [1980] and they kept on covering it with salt [used to simulate snow], which was melting, so the studio was a real mess," said Reynolds. "And it was cold and it was just dreary, really dreary. And then the hotel set caught fire and the stage burned to the ground. It was a tough time, actually."

At this point, Watts, Reynolds, and Bill Welch, who returned as construction manager, had to put their heads together and figure out solutions to this new physical conundrum, because the projected number of sets now simply outnumbered the stages. It didn't help that the UK was having its coldest winter in years, which forced many of the workers on the *Star Wars* Stage to seek shelter from the freezing winds near the one completed wall, eat hot soup during their breaks, and, inevitably, fall behind schedule.

"I'm not sure if I would have done the film had I realized that it would involve working for almost a year every day, every weekend," said Reynolds. "It actually took over my life. But it seemed to me to demand that sort of attention; you had to be aware and know what was happening everywhere. Seven

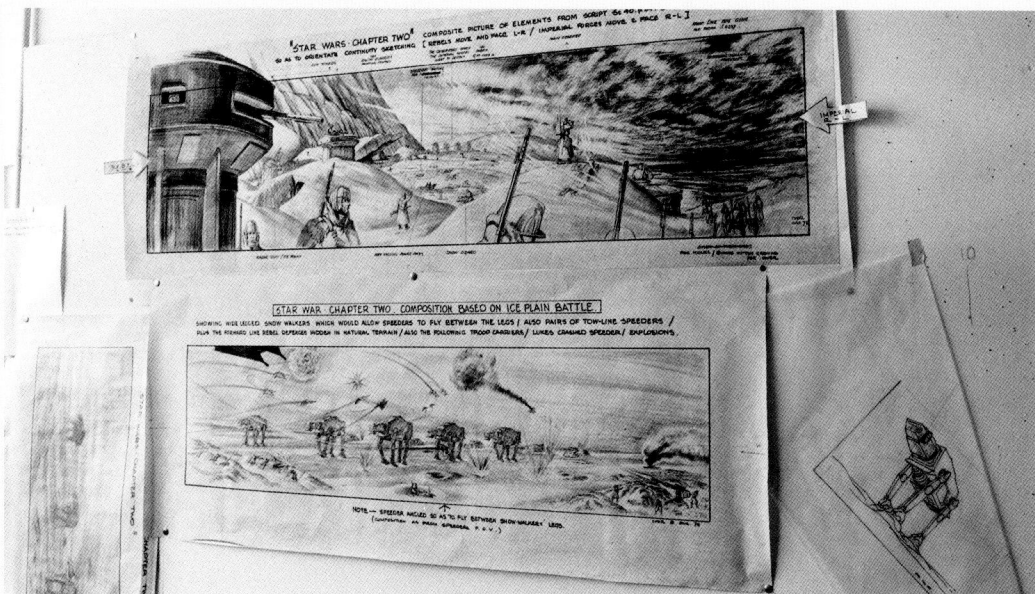

↑ Blow-ups of sketch artist Ivor Beddoes' storyboards pinned to the wall of the art department.

days a week for months and months and months, that was my introduction to production design."

"Because of the fire on Stage 3, it was very, very difficult having nowhere to work," said construction supervisor Bill Welch in 1979. "So, if I could find an area as big as an office anywhere, suddenly you'd find two carpenters in there trying to make something."

"Robert Watts and I worked very well together, I have to say," added Reynolds. "He would tell me how long he would need the stage, so then part of the equation would be to see how long it would take to either revamp the set or change it or use part of it or whatever. So, we evolved a way of doing that. The moment they were finished shooting on the set and the dailies had been cleared, then Bill Welch would jump on it. We would set about dismantling them and rebuilding and so on, in time for the next phase of the shooting. Of course, the public is totally unaware of that process, but it's a juggling act."

Fortunately, Kershner and Reynolds also worked well together, with the latter making sure that the sets would suit the director's needs. Kershner also consulted closely with Ivor Beddoes, as he storyboarded the choreography of the action scenes. "Kersh had a mischievous sense of humor," said Reynolds. "But once I got to know him and once he trusted me, it was really a delight to work with him. I think that one or two people weren't too happy, because it did go over budget a bit and over schedule, but as far as I was concerned, he was a great chap to work with who was very helpful and very enlightened. I think he gave *Empire* a dimension that perhaps it might not have had had he not directed it."

As John Barry did before with Lucas, Norman Reynolds would walk the set with Kershner the evening before filming. Unlike Lucas, however, Kershner would sometimes change his mind as to what was the best shot the following morning. "He would arrive on a new set and he would consider all the possibilities: What would the first shot be—on a long lens high up or whatever—and I think he had a slight problem deciding which would be the best way of approaching a set. It's a huge decision for a director, but once he had made that decision and was resolved in what he was going to do, he would move along. As a result of that, he may have wanted to add things that he hadn't thought of previously because he hadn't considered going down a particular road. But he was never difficult."

Yet production did become bogged down and so, as they soldiered on, a competent second unit director became needed to complete work Kershner was unable to direct himself. In an unforeseen turn, John Barry became available when his film, *Saturn 3*, was taken away from him.

In short, *Lucky Lady*—a comedy-drama set in the prohibition era—had been a disaster, a box office flop for director Stanley Donen, who was therefore reportedly looking for a way back to success. *Saturn 3* was Barry's first time in the director's chair, which is often a delicate moment—and in this case the star of the movie, Kirk Douglas, agreed with Donen to take Barry off the film, so that Donen could direct it. (Barry did receive "story credit.")

"Stanley Donen was the producer and basically he didn't like the way John was doing it and he fired him," said Robert Watts. "I think it was just the chemistry didn't work. I'm sure it must have been terrible [for Barry]. If one puts it contextually into one's own life, how would anyone feel?"

What nobody knew at the time was that Barry was also suffering from a deadly infection—and about two weeks after he started work on *The Empire Strikes Back* he collapsed and had to be taken to a hospital. A matter of hours later he was dead; it was June 1, 1979.

"It was just beyond belief," said Reynolds. "I saw Robert in the morning, and he said John had come in and had a cup of coffee and a little chat with him, because it was new to him. He hadn't done much second unit. When I saw Robert later on, he said that John wasn't feeling too well, and then, after lunch I think it was, he said, 'He's really not at all well. He's going to hospital.' So, they sent him to the local hospital, and he died during the night. I could not believe that. It was just horrendous."

"Sadly, one day John showed up in my office and said, 'I don't feel very well,'" said Watts. "I got our doctor to look at him. He had a temperature of 104, so I sent him home, and his local doctor recognized it and took him into the hospital. He had a thing called meningococcal meningitis, and he was dead that night. It was a real shock."

As several daily papers wrote at the time, the crew, actors, and director kept their composure despite the tragedy. Lucas flew over from the US, producer Gary Kurtz stepped in as interim second unit director until Harley Cokeliss was hired as a permanent replacement, and the film, though over budget, was completed. The result has since been hailed as a masterpiece of cinema, with all departments on both sides of the Atlantic excelling at their tasks.

"We soldiered on and it came to an end finally," said Reynolds. "I had survived my first film as production designer." Although it didn't win, *Empire* was nominated for an Academy Award® for Art Direction. "I think what added to the film was that it was so varied, from the planet Hoth to the swamp planet to Cloud City," Reynolds explained. "And I think what Kershner did with the film was really interesting."

WRAPPING THE TRILOGY

Before principal photography began on *Return of the Jedi*, a little movie came out in the summer of 1981, *Raiders of the Lost Ark*. Lucas had laid out the groundwork for this film with Steven Spielberg back in 1977: he would executive produce and write the story, which would feature an adventurer-archaeologist named Indiana Jones, while his friend would direct. In late 1979, many of the Elstree art department simply transitioned from

Empire to *Raiders* after the former wrapped, including production designer Norman Reynolds, master plasterer Ken Clarke, Les Dilley, Fred Hole, and Michael Lamont, among others. With his creative drive, Lucas was keeping this core group of artists and craftspeople employed almost single-handedly.

Lucas and Spielberg's *Raiders of the Lost Ark* was of course the beginning of another epic cinematic saga and a huge box-office success—not to mention another Academy Award® for Best Art Direction going to Norman Reynolds and Les Dilley, and a first to set dresser Michael Ford, in 1982. By that time, however, the art department was well into the next Lucasfilm project. Among the returnees were Reynolds, Hole, Ford, Lamont, Bream, Lange, Ambrose, Welch, and Clarke. A new junior artist was Gavin Bocquet, who had come into the film business with production designer Stuart Craig on his first feature film, the ill-fated *Saturn 3*. In fact, Bocquet was a rare hybrid in those days, a concept artist/draftsperson. Coming out of the product design school at the Royal College of Art in London, he was not able to enter immediately into one of the unions and therefore the film business; instead Craig gave him a role that was then relatively new.

"These days there's an awful lot of concept designers; they're a very big part of the film business and art departments," Bocquet explained in 2010. "Well, in the early 1980s, those sorts of people didn't really exist as a name. You had concept illustrators and production illustrators, but they weren't dedicated concept designers. Probably George, with Joe Johnston, was one of the first people to take product designers or outside designers into the film business and introduce that sort of facility. *Star Wars* was Stuart's inspiration for taking somebody like me directly from school to do that sort of job on *Saturn 3*. I was called a 'space equipment deviser,' bizarrely. But when I think back on that, I was probably more or less a concept designer, doing props, gadgets, control panels, and dressing pieces, as well as some drafting work."

Bocquet stayed in Craig's orbit for two more films: David Lynch's *Elephant Man* (1980) and Mel Brookes' *History of the World, Part I* (1981). "But when he was going off to do [Richard Attenborough's] *Gandhi* [1982] as his fourth film, I was too low down the pecking order to go on location," Bocquet said. "So, he introduced me to Norman Reynolds, who was looking for a draftsman on *Jedi*. Although the title was draftsman, I was then given the opportunity to go and do things like the deck gun on Jabba's barge and all those mechanical things that were pulling the robots apart. That was my introduction into George's world of *Star Wars*."

The other new kid on the block was higher up the pecking order, director Richard Marquand, whom Lucas hired to complete the trilogy. Lucas was determined not to face the gut-wrenching experiences of the first two *Star Wars* films: *Jedi* was going to come in on schedule and on budget, as *Raiders* had. To that end, he replaced Kurtz with producer Howard Kazanjian and promoted Robert Watts to co-producer; the latter would deal primarily with work in the UK and the former

↑ Marquand and Harrison Ford talk over a scene.

would take care of production in the United States, where the location filming would also take place this time around.

In retrospect, it's easy to see that Marquand was the odd man out; nearly everyone else working on the film at that level was an old hand. Early on, because he was under pressure to move quickly, it was clear that Marquand's dailies were not looking as good as those of *Empire*. Marquand and his DP, Alan Hume, came mainly from television and were lighting *Jedi* equivalently in order to stay on the hectic schedule.

"Richard was more conventional, a charming man, very thorough, and he worked closely with George," said Reynolds. "He was very easy to work with, but more predictable. I do believe he was a bit intimidated by George, because *Star Wars* and *Empire* were such a huge thing by then."

After principal photography was completed and ILM polished off *Jedi*, the story of Luke and Anakin Skywalker, Han Solo and Leia Organa, Chewbacca and the droids, and the fall of the Empire was complete. Not surprisingly, but to their credit, the Elstree art department was nominated in 1984 for yet another Academy Award® for Art Direction. And while Lucas had completed his space fantasy, and *Star Wars* productions would go on hiatus for more than a decade, Indiana Jones was being prepped for his second adventure.

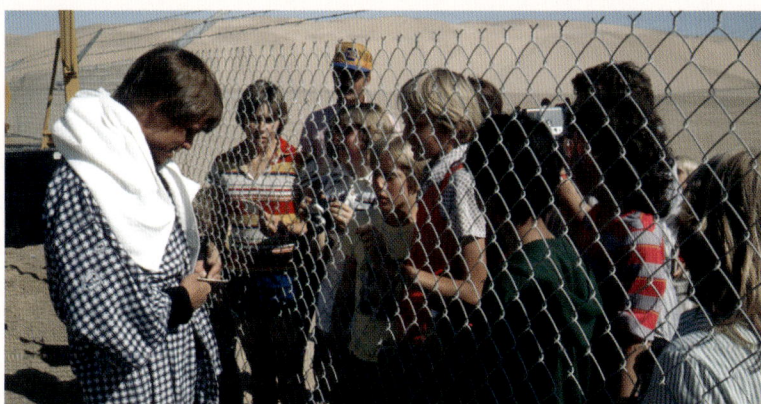

→ Mark Hamill signs autographs at the "high-security" fence.

REBEL BLOCKADE RUNNER

The opening shot of *Star Wars* has become legend. But after the two starships burst onto the silver screen, courtesy of ILM, the film moves to a soundstage at Elstree Studios, where the first set—the white corridor of the Rebel Blockade Runner, or "rebel spacefighter"— has also become iconic. But the reality is that this production design came very late in the game. As the blueprint (no. 317) title attests, it was an addition, built on Stage 9 next to an existing set.

"I looked at the revamped set about a week or so before shooting, and I said, 'I can't possibly shoot the sequence on this set,'" said Lucas in a 1977 interview. "The original set was the little alleyway with the Princess and the robots. That was all we had. And I just realized I couldn't shoot a battle, five pages of dialogue, all these people running around, and have it all take place in one little hallway. So I said, 'John, you have to build another big hallway next to this little hallway'—and that created a whole big ruckus with Fox and everybody, because it cost a lot more money. I got a lot of flak—everybody came down on me. There was a lot of screaming and yelling. We had a lot of problems with that, but eventually John, who is a genius, did it."

"One set we changed quite a bit was the interior of the first spaceship," said Barry of the corridor. "In fact, we added a great white chunk [corridor] to it 'cos the rest of it was a revamp of the interior of the *Millennium Falcon*, which we'd changed into the rebel ship. But George figured that it wasn't going to give him enough,

because it was quite a long scene, that opening scene. Also, I think he wanted, and I think it was a good idea, he wanted it to look at first sight like you are in your conventional all-white interior, a *2001*-type spaceship—and then the door blows down and in comes Darth Vader. I think it's an amusing little joke."

"*Star Wars* was very different from *2001*, which was the only other piece of science fiction I had ever been involved in," said Robert Watts, who was a production manager on the Kubrick film. "This was very, very different. *2001* was very factual and Stanley insisted that everything was to be precisely as known at the time and an intelligent conjecture of what would be, whereas *Star Wars* didn't obey rules like that. It had spaceships that leaked oil, which was way out of the convention of normal science fiction."

Designed by John Barry and technically drawn by Ted Ambrose, the white corridor made ample use of vacuum-formed shapes as it was very quickly built. Lucas directed the entrance of Darth Vader, preceded by his stormtroopers, in July 1976.

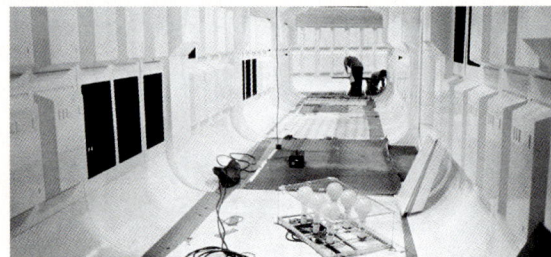

→ The crew is building the rebel corridor set addition at Elstree Studios, during the first week of July 1976.

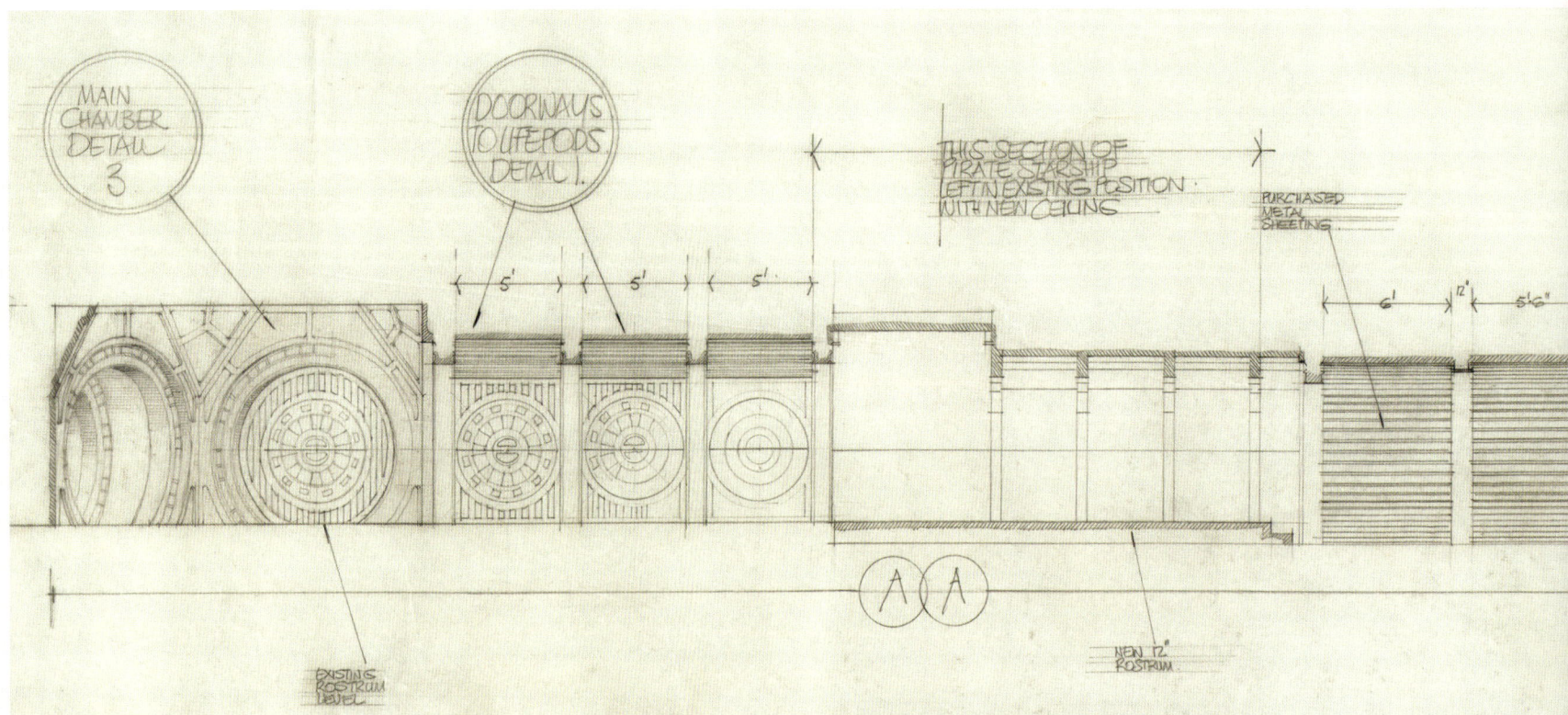

↓ Production illustrator Ralph McQuarrie painted "Laser Duel" on February 14 and 15, 1975. In it, Jedi Deak Starkiller battles Darth Vader on the rebel ship. The starship set was designed primarily to convey character concepts and costumes and is filled in only to minimal extent. Production designer John Barry and his art department would build on McQuarrie's interior designs to create the set in all of its myriad detail at Elstree Studios.

↑ Lucas is behind the camera directing the *Star Wars* opening live-action scenes on July 9, 1976.

← John Barry would make quick sketches on occasion to guide his draftspeople. His 1975 drawing featured wider and longer corridors as based on early designs for the rebel ship; his revised 1976 drawing is closer to Ted Ambrose's technical drawing (no. 317 on pages 16 and 17) of the corridor created that June 28. The late revision came about when Lucas realized he needed another set on which to shoot all of the opening scenes.

← Bream's blueprint drawing exhibits the revamp of the *Falcon*, "existing from pirate starship," which became the part of the rebel spacefighter where Princess Leia (Carrie Fisher) gives the Death Star plans to R2-D2. The revamped section was recycled from the *Falcon*'s main hold, left "in existing position" on Stage 9, "with new ceiling." Another recycled part of the rebel spacefighter set consisted of the flanking engine-like parts, probably recycled from a real jet engine, which had already been used overhead for the power trench set (see pages 56 to 59). Purchased metal sheeting was also used for dressing, while plastic pallets, a mainstay of *Star Wars* production design, were used as the floor. Older than most of those in the art department, Reg (or Reginald, as he's sometimes credited) Bream was employed on a permanent basis at MGM/Elstree by Elliot Scott. Before entering the film industry, Bream had worked for an interior design company that created hotels in London. "Reg worked on many films at MGM," said Reynolds. "I can't tell you an awful lot about him other than the fact that he was just a brilliant sort of guy; very well-read, very rounded, and extremely capable."

"Reg Bream was so brilliant at drafting and drawing," said Les Dilley. "He had a unique style where he managed to get just about everything on one sheet of paper, including the full-size details."

SET	REBEL SPACEFIGHTER
DETAIL	PLAN & ELEVATIONS
DRG. NO.	282
DATE	MAY 10 1970
DRAWN BY	REG BREAM

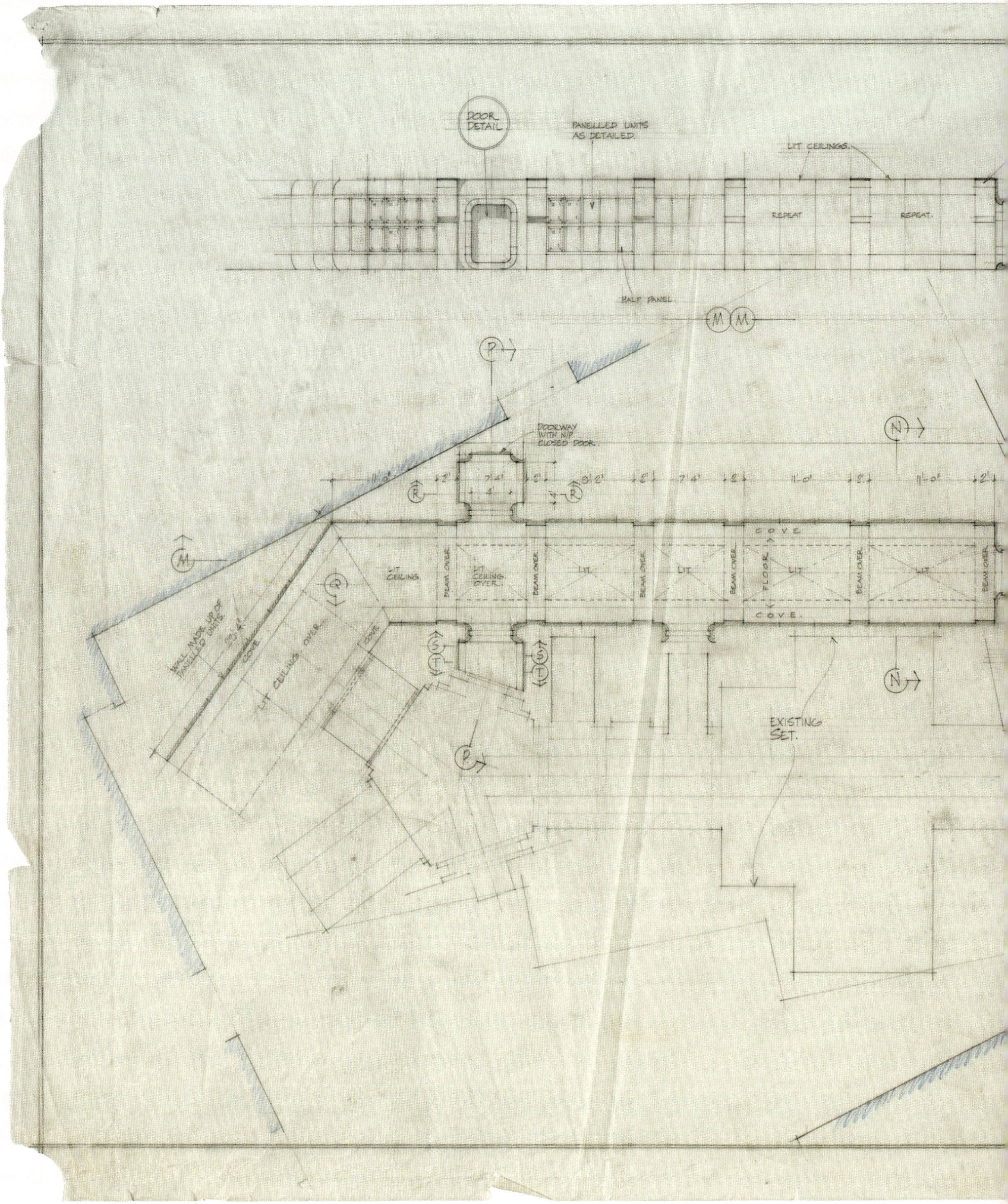

DOOR
DETAIL

PANELLED UNITS
AS DETAILED.

LIT CEILINGS.

REPEAT

REPEAT.

HALF PANEL.

DOORWAY
WITH N/P
CLOSED DOOR.

LIT
CEILING

LIT
CEILING
OVER.

BEAM OVER.

LIT

BEAM OVER.

LIT

BEAM OVER.

COVE.

FLOOR

LIT

BEAM OVER.

LIT

BEAM OVER.

COVE.

WALL MADE UP OF
PANELLED UNITS

COVE

LIT CEILING OVER.

COVE

EXISTING
SET.

SET	REBEL SPACEFIGHTER	DATE	JUNE 28 1976
DETAIL	ADDITIONAL CORRIDOR	DRAWN BY	TED AMBROSE
DRG. NO.	317		

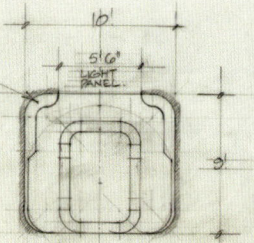

AMS & ARCHES
DETAILED.

16'

5'6"
LIGHT
PANEL.

7'10½"

EXISTING
SET.

N N

P P

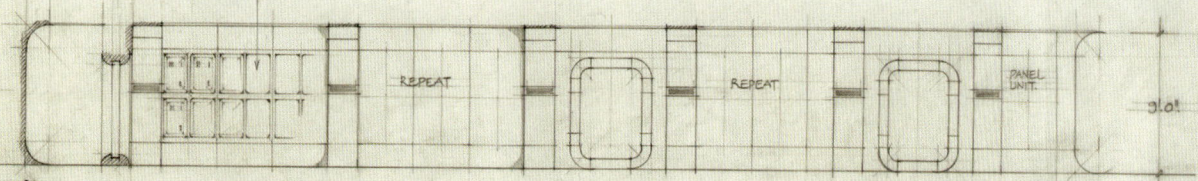

PANELLED UNITS
AS DETAILED.

REPEAT

REPEAT

PANEL
UNIT.

3'0"

M
Q

4'6"

WALL

Q Q

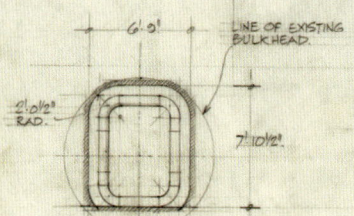

6'0'

LINE OF EXISTING
BULKHEAD.

2'0½"
RAD.

7'10½"

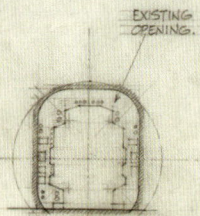

EXISTING
OPENING.

R R

T T

S S

STAGE 9.

20 CENTURY FOX LTD.		PROD.Nº
THE STAR WARS		E76/1
SET INT. REBEL SPACEFIGHTER.		SET Nº
DETAILS ADDITIONAL CORRIDOR P & E.		SCALE ¼"

DRAWN T.A	Capps	Metal	Const	X	DRG Nº
DATE 28.6.76	Paint	X SFX			317.
	Plaster	M			

(317)

EARLY PODCAST

A lifepod drawing from 1975 (no. 513)—with approximate pilot size and position, boarding procedures, a side view of landing gear, and thruster location—shows humans instead of droids inside the capsule. Early scripts had several uses for the pods, one of which was to transport the film's heroes from the *Falcon* to the secret rebel base on Yavin 4:

"130. EXT. SPACE AROUND FOURTH MOON OF YAVIN

Two small lifepods jettison away from the starship and slowly drift toward the awesome deep green surface of the moon. Retro-rockets automatically kick in and slow the pods. The two tiny craft break through the light cloud cover and disappear in the dense, steaming jungles of Yavin's fourth moon.

131. EXT. FOURTH MOON OF YAVIN—VINE JUNGLE

One of the lifepods has come to rest in the middle of a small clearing. Han, Luke, and Threepio emerge from the capsule into a forest of gargantuan trees shrouded in an eerie mist. The air is heavy with the fantastic cries of unimaginable creatures."

Steve Gawley was originally hired by ILM art director Joe Johnston to do orthographic drawings in order to help model builders and set builders translate 2D vehicle concepts into 3D miniatures and full-sized sets. "I basically saw this drawing and I thought, *God, that's just like a paint bucket*," said model maker Lorne Peterson. "And so we enlarged the model and lengthened the thing. After I got the basic shapes in there and the panels and everything, then Joe all of a sudden came down the stairs. He and I went *Thwack*! and put the thing together. I probably worked on it for four days by myself and then Joe came down and we added all the details and the rockets and everything."

By the time of shooting, budget and time constraints meant that only droids would ever use a lifepod, as its later scenes had all been excised.

↑ A storyboard from the summer of 1975 by Joe Johnston shows an early concept of how the lifepod would be tracked by an Imperial gunner aboard a Star Destroyer.

↑ Joe Johnston drew hundreds of storyboards for *Star Wars*, including this one of the lifepod being jettisoned from the rebel ship.

← A touched-up marketing still of the lifepod heading for the planet Tatooine was created for the *Star Wars* launch campaign of 1977.

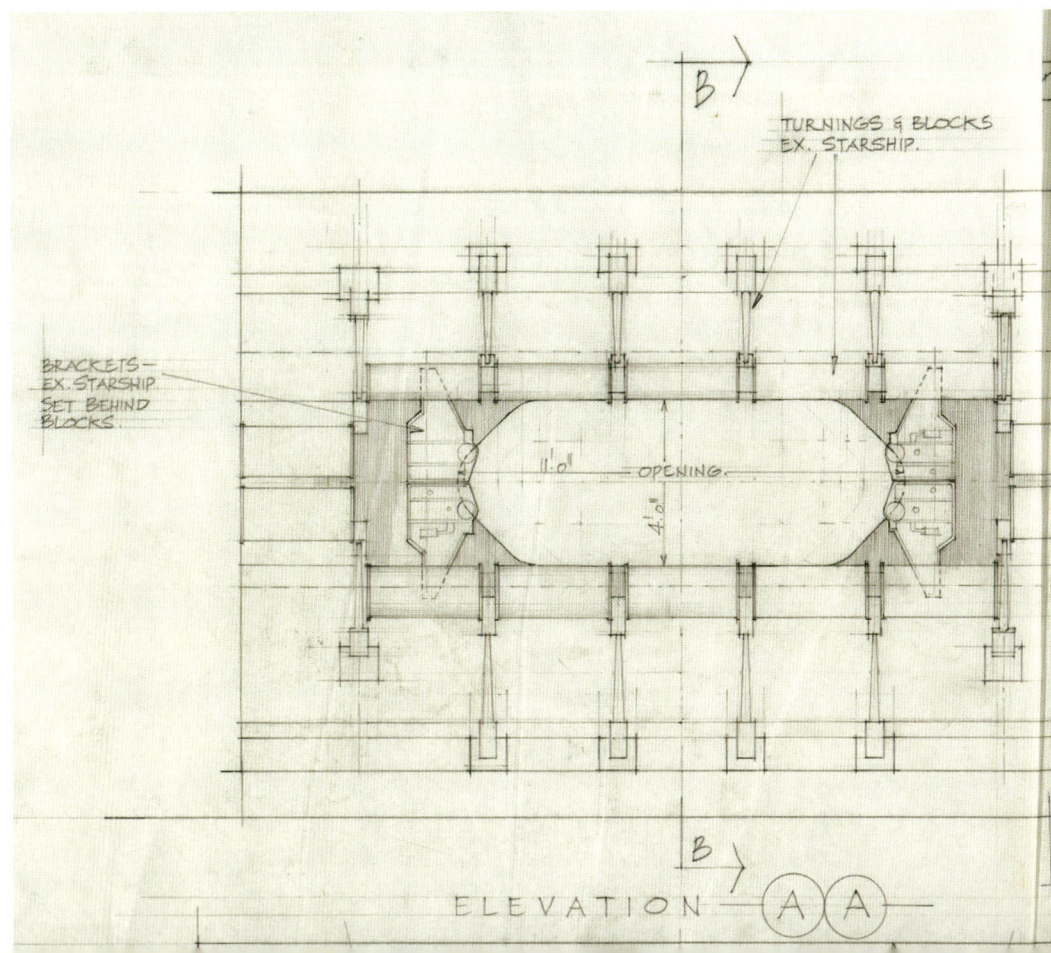

SET	IMPERIAL STARSHIP COCKPIT
DETAIL	PLAN & ELEVATIONS
DRG. NO.	319
DATE	JULY 2 1976
DRAWN BY	TED AMBROSE

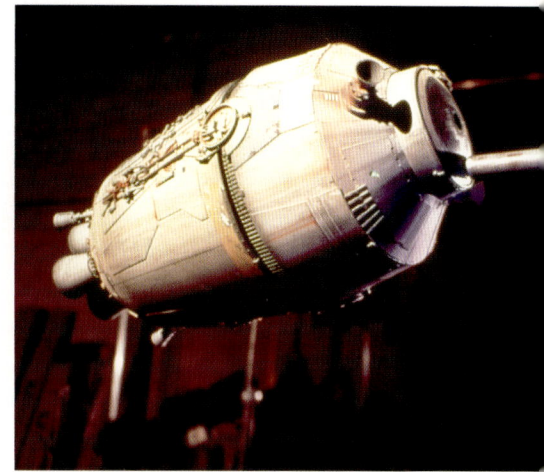

↑ Shown is the lifepod miniature.

↓ The exteriors of Star Destroyers are seen several times in *Star Wars*, all models made at ILM, but only a single shot of their interior is seen, when gunners spy a lifepod ejected from the rebel ship. They read no life-forms and give it a pass; of course, C-3PO and R2-D2 are hidden there. The blueprint makes note of "black velvet for sfx" beyond the window, where ILM would later composite in a shot of the lifepod falling toward Tatooine. It also notes "prop-made gun-sights to rotate by hand"; camera placement, important because of the effect to be added; and that this small set was to be recycled from parts of previous sets.

SET	LIFEPOD OF A PIRATE SHIP
DETAIL	FRONT, TOP, & BOTTOM
DRG. NO.	513
DATE	SEPTEMBER 26 1975
DRAWN BY	STEVE GAWLEY

R2-D2

"As I remember, Artoo-Detoo came from this tiny little sketch that Ralph McQuarrie did," said Lorne Peterson. "A couple of brush strokes, a round thing, and a little bit of blue."

In fact, McQuarrie did a few paintings and drawings of the feisty little droid, Harpo to C-3PO's fussy butler persona, but it was up to the art department at Elstree to make R2-D2 a physical reality; they would have to fill in a hundred variables naturally left by McQuarrie's airy if brilliant design work. In turn, the art department would work hand-in-hand with John Stears, who headed up the mechanical effects department. (Much to Lucas' disappointment, R2 never functioned properly.)

R2-D2 began at Lee Studios, where Christian hired carpenter Bill Harman and together they built the droid prototype out of wood. Because *Star Wars* wasn't given a green light until December 13, final preparations couldn't begin until January, the date of this blueprint, which also indicates that separate drawings would be made for the "mechanical arm arrangement; head assembly, leg assembly." The construction of the R2 body was assigned to an outside fabricator, while its original design and realization were influenced by three little robots seen in the 1972 film directed by Douglas Trumbull, *Silent Running*: Huey, Dewey, and Louie. McQuarrie had seen that film's square, angular robots, so he'd made R2 round.

↑ A McQuarrie drawing showed how R2's arms might connect to his shell (with a kind of antenna on top).

FRONT ELEVATION ROBOT ARTOO

SET	ROBOT R2
DETAIL	FRONT ASSEMBLY (FOR 3"8 MAN)
DRG. NO.	67 (A)
DATE	JANUARY 20 1976
DRAWN BY	PETER J. CHILDS

← Peter Childs executed at least four blueprints of R2, one of which was reissued on January 23, with "top section of leg modified." "I had never worked on a science-fiction film before, but in my mind the concept really was *Flash Gordon* and these sort of gleaming white sets and pristine sorts of stuff, but *Star Wars* had a whole new dimension," said Reynolds. "It's something that George suggested, to have these muddy sets and beat-up reality. I remember the first impact of that was when we had Artoo made by an outside company. He was made in aluminum and to our designs, obviously, and he arrived white and with some blue patches on it. And the first thing George said was, 'We've got to make it all dirty.' And I thought for a moment, *This is terrible*, but we dirtied it all up and did a few dents and beat it up a bit, and George said, 'Well, that's better.' Well, that had a lasting effect on me, I have to say." (Reynolds also notes that one of the R2 units was manufactured from parts that would be used on the Death Star sets.)

SET	ROBOT R2
DETAIL	STARBOARD ELEVATION (FOR 3"8 MAN)
DRG. NO.	67 (B)
DATE	JANUARY 20 1976
DRAWN BY	PETER J. CHILDS

"I arrived, and I think there were a couple of people around, but they hadn't had the green light, you know, to actually spend money," said Reynolds. "So I remember John had got in Kenny Baker. They mocked up a little drum for Kenny to get into to establish the size of Artoo."

"We got Kenny and saw what he could do physically," Barry said. "There was a lot of finding out: Where it was going to hurt him, and all the techniques around the boots. We found it very critical that the boot should be a very positive fixture to his legs, that they lace tightly up and hold the robot's boot firmly to his leg so that it moves as one.

"But of course, this was all going on at the same time that we were trying to get the location stuff off. We had to get truckloads of stuff sent off pre-made to Tunisia, so they could start building sets there. And it was all going on at exactly the same time we were finishing off Kenny and Artoo. That was a really bad patch for us—the two robots were a nightmare to build."

A HARD FIRST DAY

Set dresser Roger Christian tells the story of a particular shot needed on the first day of principal photography on the Salt Flats of Nefta, Tunisia, Monday, March 22, 1976; in this shot, the top of a red droid was supposed to blow off, just after the Lars family purchases it. "John sent Les Dilley and I to Tunisia to look after the shoot," Christian said. "We were the only two crew from the art department there. Les would be stuck with the shooting unit the whole time. I was in and out of the shooting unit, while getting the sets ready in advance.

"The first day, the tensions were pretty unbearable. Director of photography Gil Taylor got uppity from the word go and didn't understand why George would want to look through a camera or set shots up. He just said, 'That's my job as the DP.' And that's not the way George worked or any of us worked.

"Moreover, a few weeks before we went out, John Barry had come to Les and I and said, 'You know, I don't think these radio-controlled robots are ever going to work… George is going to be in trouble. So I want you to build and take with you a secret Artoo-Detoo we can pull around.' So we built one that no one knew about it. We took it to Tunisia; it was on the truck.

"The special effects man, John Stears, was wonderful, very bumptious and very grand, always saying, 'I'm going to do this and do that,' but a lot of things never worked. Sure enough, on virtually the first shot, Stears' robot just malfunctioned completely and fell over. And John Stears was really funny. He had a standard excuse that obviously worked in London. He went in front of the whole crew and George, and said, 'It must be these bloody taxis. They're upsetting my radio.' But we were 50 minutes from the nearest little sleepy town, where the taxis were far and few between!

"I think he justified it later in some comment, saying, 'Oh, it was all the graphite and silicone under the sand.' So Les and I looked at George and the producer Gary Kurtz and we said, 'Look, we've got one. We'll get it ready and I think we should use fishing wire and pull it.' And George said, 'Do it.' So we quickly repainted Artoo, because it was going to be this little red one. And that's how a lot of the film was done: the prop boys pulling things with fishing wire."

"Gary Kurtz said, 'Les, go and get some monofilament,'" said Dilley. "Well, I had never heard that word before. I had absolutely no idea what he was talking about. So I went running off, sprinted around the back of the set to find another American. I found one who told me, but in the UK, we'd say, 'Go and get some fishing line.'"

→ Other droids were needed for scenes such as the ones in the Jawa sandcrawler. Because time and money were short, this technical drawing notes that its new "robot head" should fit on an R2 body and be dressed with purchased lenses. It was a one-off—that is, only one would be made—to be cast in fiberglass.

ABOVE TOP In March 1976, an advance group constructed the bottom half of the Jawa sandcrawler in Tunisia, per the technical drawings.

ABOVE Jawa traders inspect droids.

→ Ambrose's blueprint demonstrates how only the bottom portion of the Jawa sandcrawler would be built on location in Tunisia, with a horizontal line indicating where set construction should stop. It also details the "bogie wheels" (to keep the tread in place, usually used on railroad cars, they are non-driving wheels.) For stationary shots, ILM would provide a matte painting to complete the vehicle's upper half; for shots of a moving sandcrawler, ILM would build and shoot a miniature vehicle. Les Dilley also did many drawings for the sandcrawler.

"I think with this one we had to match the treads," said model maker Lorne Peterson. "We were free to do the other part of it. You can see that our profile is much different from what it shows here. This is much more squat and we didn't do it that way. I think even our treads are a little bit lower and a little bit wider."

"A lot of the things we did were quite original," said Barry. "Making the sets that went out on location, I designed them so that they nested one inside the other so that we would get a lot on the trucks. I made the track units of the sandcrawler in three sections, so that we could get them all out of this vacuum-forming. But you can do that in a surrealist design situation—you make your own rules."

SET	SANDCRAWLER
DETAIL	PLAN & ELEVATIONS
DRG. NO.	10
DATE	DECEMBER 10 1975
DRAWN BY	TED AMBROSE

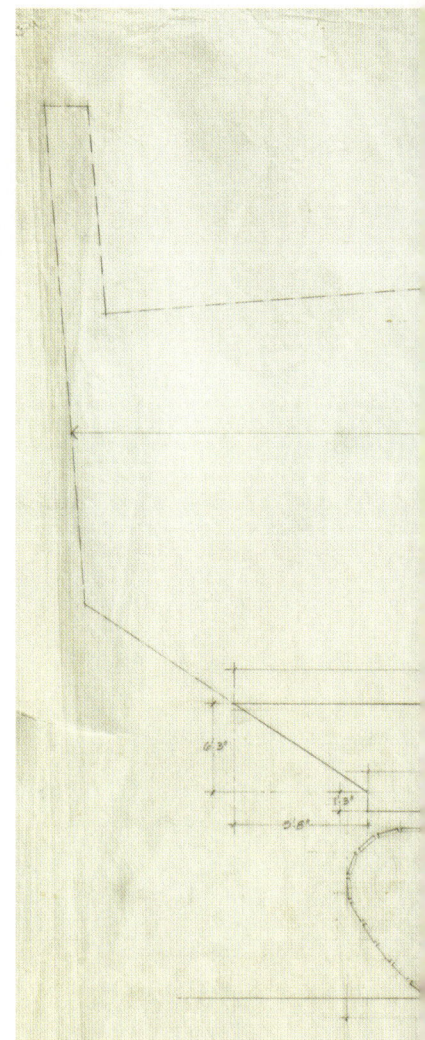

SET	OTHER ROBOTS
DETAIL	HEAD
DRG. NO.	120
DATE	FEBRUARY 6 1976
DRAWN BY	NORMAN REYNOLDS/PETER SHIELDS

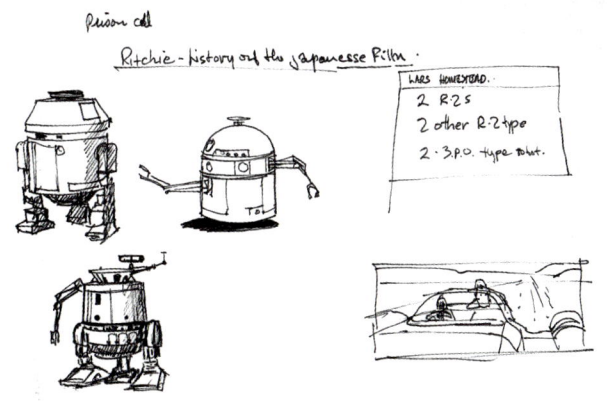

PURCHASED LENSES. etc.

LIGHTED PANELS.

"B"

ELEVATION FULL SIZE

Prison cell

Richie - history of the Japanese Film.

LARS HOMESTEAD.
2 R2s
2 other R-2 type
2 · 3.P.O. type robot.

↑ A John Barry sketch notes how many droids production would need on the Lars' homestead location, and how R2-D2 might fit into the back of the landspeeder (another note refers to Donald Richie, an author of numerous books on Japanese cinema.)

PAINTED MATTE.

'GONDOLA' & DOOR DET.1

TELESCOPIC TUBE. DET. 2

NOTE — ALL OPENINGS TO BE BOXED-IN.

EXTENT OF BUILD — EVERYTHING ABOVE THIS LINE WILL BE A PAINTED MATTE.

DET. 5

VOIDS.

VOIDS.

BOGIE WHEELS.

BOGIE WHEELS.

2' REVEALS TO ALL OPENINGS

LIGHTS DET.4.

ELEV'N "A-A"

HOMESTEAD GARAGE

The homestead where Luke Skywalker lives was made of perhaps the most complex combination of photography, with shots from two locations edited together with sets built on Elstree soundstages. Exteriors of the "igloo," the doorway to Luke's garage, were filmed on the salt flats of Nefta, while the core of the homestead was a dressed location in a bizarre hole in the ground that was actually a real hotel, the Sidi Driss, in Matmata. Luke's garage interior, on the other hand, was a set. But even the dressings on location had to be constructed first in England, then shipped out to Tunisia on trucks, then a train, then a boat, and then on more trucks.

"We had a stage at Elstree that was actually full up with stuff that was going out to Tunisia," said Reynolds. "Buildings for Mos Eisley and stuff for the salt flats. I didn't stay for too long in Tunisia because we were trying to get the sets ready back in the studio, but I remember Threepio was a real photo finish, as it were; he had been put together completely as one entity only once or twice, so the prop guys didn't know quite how to put him all together. So I stayed there. I remember staying up almost all of one night to finish the wiring of the hands, thinking, *What on earth am I doing here?* The following morning out on the salt flats of Nefta, I was putting him together with the prop guys, and there was some finishing off of the sandcrawler, I remember."

After his experience working there on Stanley Donen's *The Little Prince* (1972), with Norman Reynolds, Barry had returned to Tunisia and found locales for Lucas' space fantasy. "George came out [for the location scout] and we had this very jaunt run in Tunisia, which was a long way from USC," said Barry of Lucas' alma mater, the University of Southern California. "So it was all a bit of a new experience, but we settled on things like the hole in Matmata. The outside of the hole of the homestead, of course, is not the outside of the inside part. We dug another hole for the outside, not a very deep one, but just so you could have a look down and it could be cut together very sensibly with the other location. You get the feeling that when Luke looks over the edge that it's the same location, but you cut to over his shoulder and you are in fact down the hole, which was really a couple of hundred miles from the above-the-ground section.

"I mean, that's film: you find the situation and work out of it, and George was sensible enough to see that. It's incredible, that place we shot in is a hotel. We fixed it up and gave it that technological look, because the moisture farm has to look as though it does something, as though it really is some sort of enterprise that means something to the people in the movie."

Back in England, Luke's garage was made from various materials, including a selection of pipes and stock pieces to make the T-16 starhopper's underbelly and sides; other garage builds had a steel or satin alloy finish, and a turntable was constructed for the landspeeder. Both the landspeeder and T-16 skyhopper were full-sized props used only for the background.

Alan Roderick-Jones was hired as a draftsperson and drew several blueprints of the garage; Roderick-Jones also performed the duties of an art director, overseeing some set dressing while Christian was on location.

"The T-16 was really dressing for that set," said Reynolds. "It's like having your car in the garage." The full-sized prop was based on a miniature built by concept modeler Colin Cantwell.

→ The homestead roof and walls were built in 16 segments, so they could be shipped out to Tunisia, where, once constructed, they would have a 20-foot diameter. The rock dressing was to be culled from the location itself. This particular set piece was actually lost after filming, when a freak storm hit the location during the night of Saturday, March 27, 1976. "The top had gone off the homestead and that was already halfway to Algeria somewhere," said Robert Watts, production supervisor. "It was blown away," Barry said. "It blew three miles in the night, it just rolled and rolled and rolled."

SET	HOMESTEAD GARAGE
DETAIL	PLAN & ELEVATIONS
DRG. NO.	107
DATE	APRIL 21 1976
DRAWN BY	ALAN RODERICK-JONES

DETAIL ②
TOP STOREY

ROCK ETC
DRESSING
ON LOCATION

SUPPORT 1'-8" ABOVE GROUND LEVEL

GROUND LEVEL

40'-6" RAD.

40'-6" RAD.

ELEVATION 1"EQUALS 1'-0"

MAKE FULL CIRCLE

20'-0" DIAM

3'-0" RAD.

DETAIL ①

F.S OF TYPICAL BAY

ROOF & WALLS IN 16 SEGMENTS

3'-0"

PLAN 1"EQUALS 1'-0"

1'-0"   9'-0"

20TH CENTURY FOX
PRODUCTION: "THE STAR WARS"
SET: EXT. HOMESTEAD
DETAIL: ROOF OF GARAGE

SET	HOMESTEAD
DETAIL	ROOF OF GARAGE
DRG. NO.	24
DATE	DECEMBER 23 1975
DRAWN BY	PETER SHIELDS

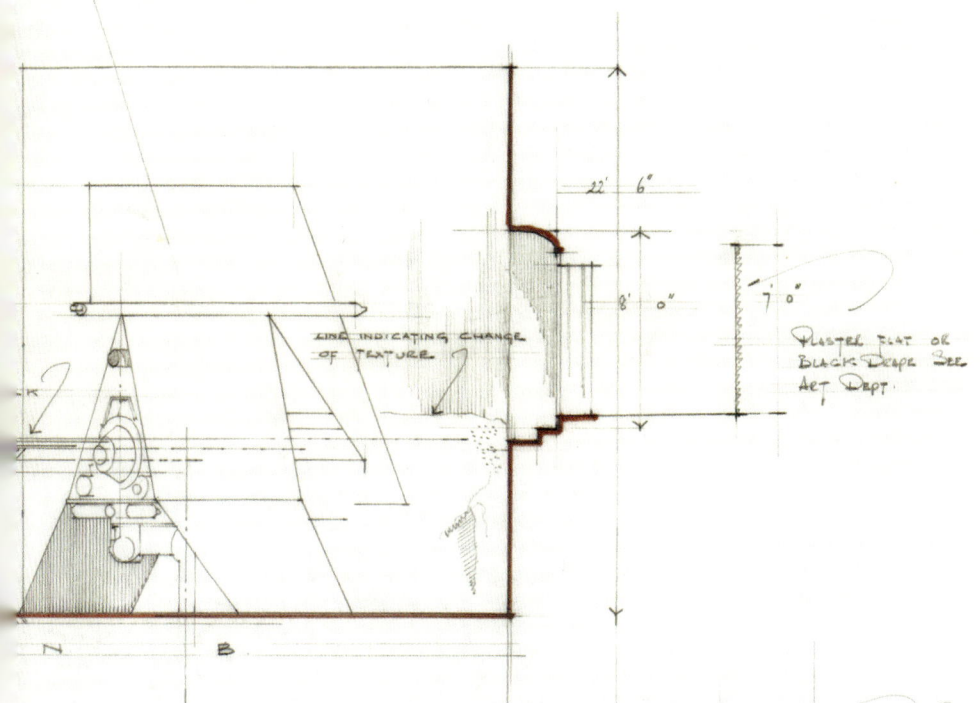

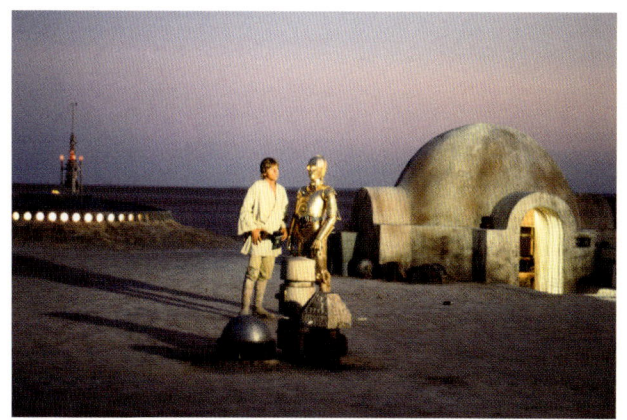

DET 1
STAR
HOPPER
DR N° 106

22' 6"

8' 0"

7'.0"

LINE INDICATING CHANGE OF TEXTURE

PLASTER FLAT OR BLACK DRAPE SEE ART DEPT.

↑ On location in Tunisia, Luke and C-3PO (Anthony Daniels) stand outside the "igloo" and the roof of the underground garage designed by Barry. Its exterior lights would correspond to those interior ones built into the garage set on stage at Elstree Studios.

SET	DESERT WASTELAND
DETAIL	OIL RIG CHRISTMAS TREE
DRG. NO.	01
DATE	NOVEMBER 26 1975
DRAWN BY	PETER CHILDS

→ The very first technical drawing for *Star Wars* was a design for a moisture vaporator prototype to be duplicated four times. Drawn by Peter Childs, it was known as the "Oil Rig Christmas Tree" because of its practical lights and because Lucas had described the moisture farmers as something equivalent to people out in the middle of nowhere mining oil. It was to be made mostly of plastic and plywood, with fiberglass collars and featured in a scene ultimately cut from the film in which Luke watches a space battle from his farm.

"The gritty quality that George wanted, I think we've got," said Barry. "That helped enormously, because it does make things look very real. The moisture collectors we made out of aeroplane junk, but somehow they look believable and you just accept them as something out on an infinite salt flat. They were designed to come apart in pieces so that we could reassemble them in all sorts of ways and so they could fit on the trucks. They're not rivetingly interesting, but they do sort of fit."

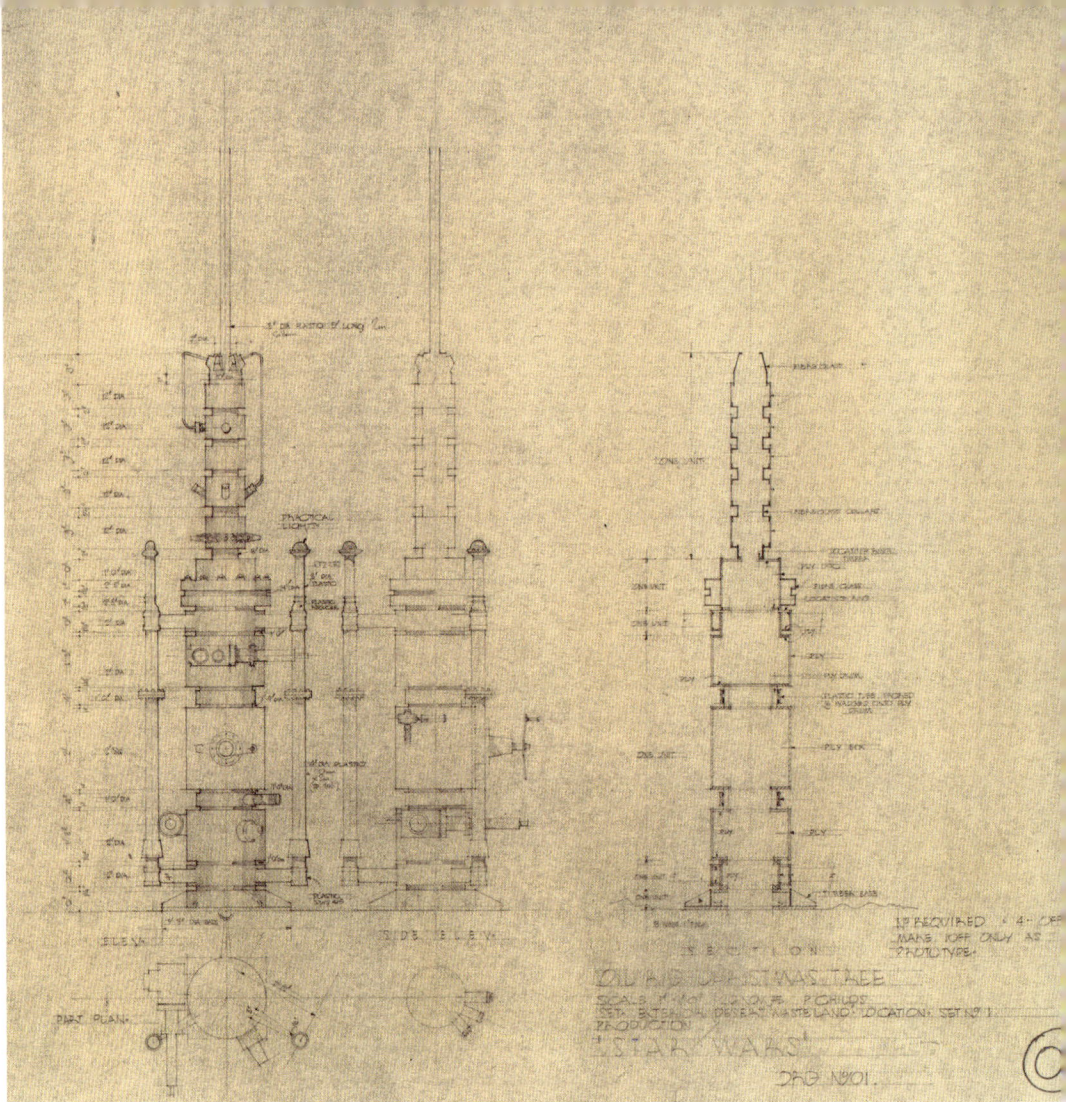

PETER CHILDS – FIRST DRAFTSPERSON

The first technical drawing completed for *Star Wars*, the "Oil Rig Christmas Tree," was executed by Peter Childs on November 25, 1975. Childs began his own film career not long after Christmas 1946. Thanks to his father who was a scenic painter at Gainsborough Studios, Childs was employed as a junior draftsperson at London Films (later, Denham Studio), the studio founded by British producer and director Alexander Korda.

Childs' first film was *Night Beat* (1947), starring Ronald Howard, son of actor Leslie Howard, and Maxwell Reed, a nephew of director Sir Carol Reed. Childs worked for the latter as a junior draftsperson in Vincent Korda's art department on *The Third Man* (1949). His next film was *State Secret* (1950; released as *The Great Manhunt* in the United States), starring Douglas Fairbanks, Jr.

As part of the "Class of 2001," Childs also labored on Kubrick's spaceship models. Though he was told he would work "hand-in-hand" with the director, it soon became apparent that Kubrick would not allow any second unit work. At Shepperton Studios, Childs did see some action on the moon set in the scene where the monolith is discovered for a second time.

While working as a draftsperson on several films at Elstree Studios (known at the time as the ABPC, Associated British Pictures Corporation), Childs became friends with Les Dilley, who was a charge hand in the plasterers' shop. According to Childs, Dilley was the youngest charge hand ever; however, Dilley wanted to move over to the art department, which meant changing unions. Childs sponsored him.

Years later, Dilley returned the favor, calling on Childs as the nascent *Star Wars* art department was getting up to speed at Lee Studios. "I couldn't come to terms with the film," said Childs. "These funny names and animals, and that Western bar with all those strange creatures."

In the art department, Childs met several old acquaintances, including Reg Bream. "Reg was one of our favorites," he said. "We called him Uncle Reg. He worked virtually seven days a week. He held the record of something like thirty-six weeks without a day off."

As the first draftsperson on the film, Childs was assigned to R2-D2. Childs remembers that while the droid was still in its very initial design, Kenny Baker quit. "We had quite a struggle on that one," Childs said. "Kenny Baker was going to be the one inside it, so Artoo was designed around him. But it was a difficult thing to move and after a while Kenny said he didn't want to do the picture."

Of course, Baker eventually relented and returned to the production, while Childs went on to draw many sets, including several on the Death Star. Childs also worked out how the "bottomless pit" matte paintings would fit into the power trench shots.

Childs's career would ultimately span over thirty films. Among his last were *The Abyss* (1989), a "tough" picture, and *Mission: Impossible* (1996), for which he drew the top-secret room in CIA headquarters—into which Tom Cruise is famously lowered. The star reportedly told the production designer of that film, who happened to be Norman Reynolds, that "it was the best set of the film."

Childs retired in 2000 at age 69. "I really do miss the drawing part of it," he said, "being on the drawing board, creating something."

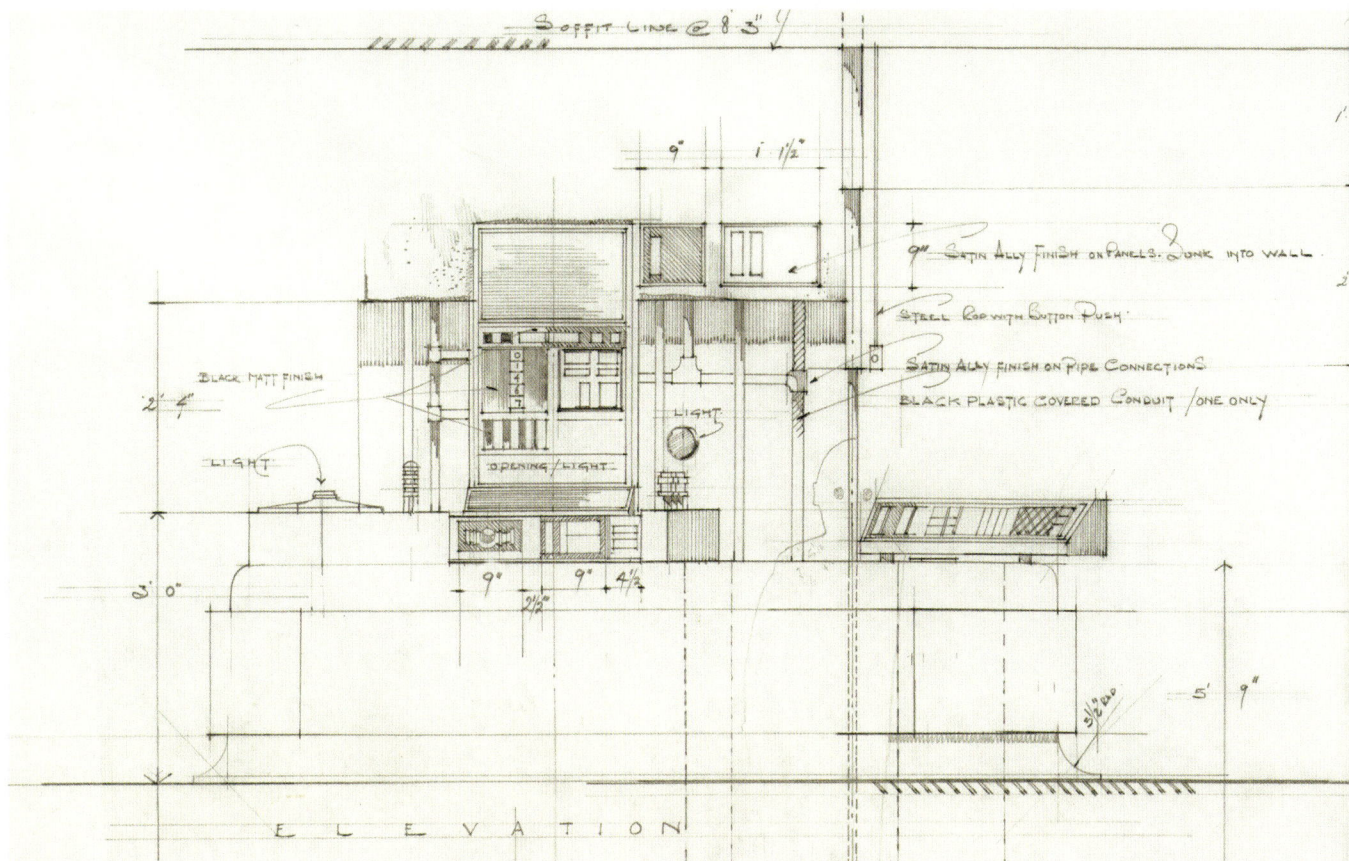

↑ In a deleted scene, Luke and a droid stand near the Oil Rig Christmas Tree prop in Tunisia.

→ In the scene where Luke is cleaning the droids, C-3PO takes an oil bath in a "practical," i.e., "real-world" tank, with a floor grill designed to take the weight of actor Anthony Daniels in the C-3PO costume. The fittings of the workbench, which was cast in fiberglass, were to be selected from stock metal airplane parts purchased by Christian. All surrounding panels were to have a satin alloy finish, while the light in one of the wall panels was to synchronize with a "lift" (elevator) engineered in the oil bath, as "rigged by special effects above set."

SET	HOMESTEAD GARAGE
DETAIL	WORKBENCH
DRG. NO.	108
DATE	APRIL 2 1976
DRAWN BY	ALAN RODERICK-JONES

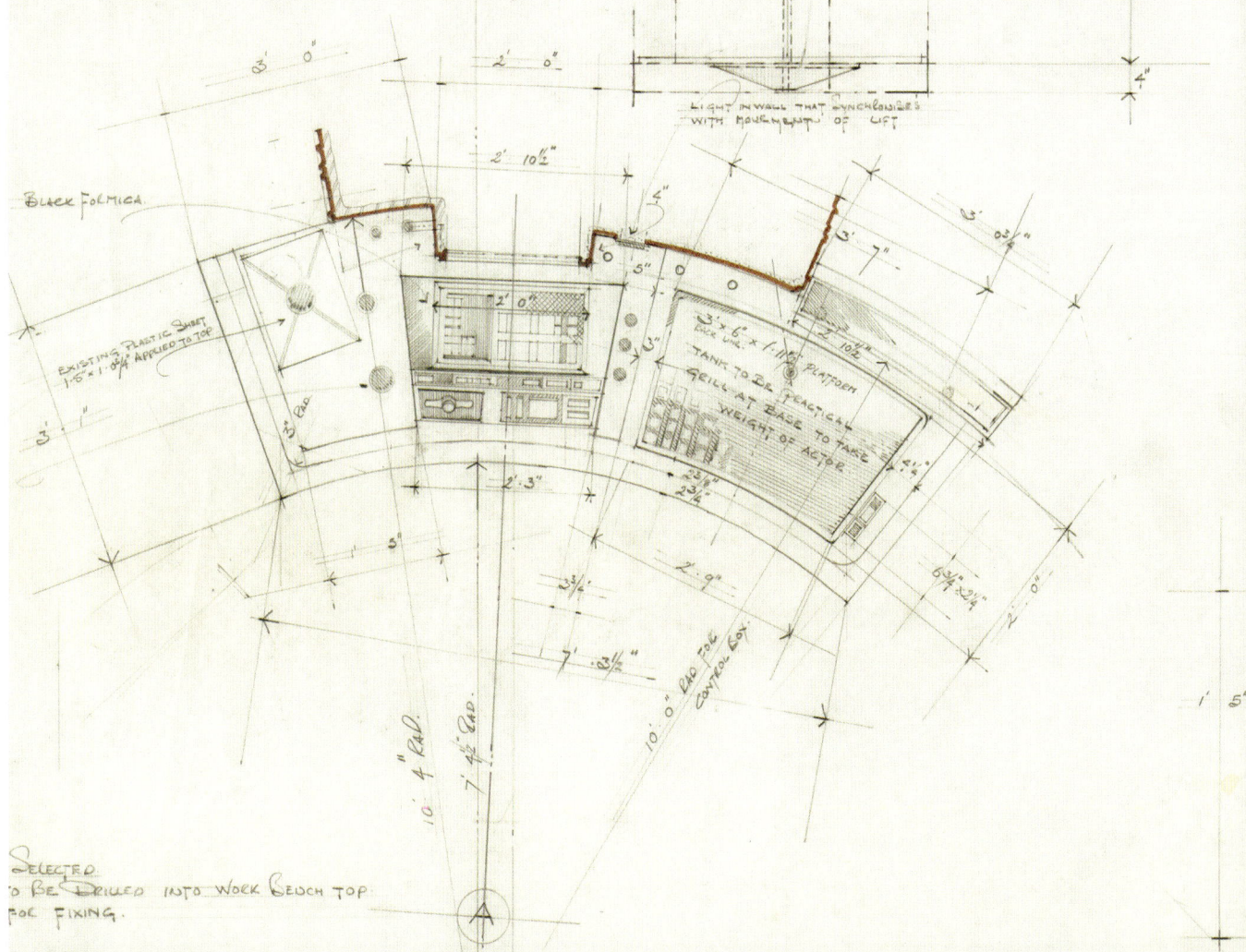

BEN'S HUT

"Cave Dwelling" was production's name for the home of Obi-Wan ("Old Ben") Kenobi, played by the incredible Alec Guinness. This is where the Jedi Knight introduces Luke to the philosophy of the Force and gives him his father's lightsaber.

Although Fox had green-lighted the picture, they also demanded budget cuts at the end of 1975. Obi-Wan's dwelling was therefore redesigned in January 1976. At one point, as this blueprint indicates, Obi-Wan's dwelling was going to be larger than the actual set built, as evidenced by the balcony. Lucas says that even earlier it was going to be three stories high, but budget cuts diminished its size.

"I remember John designing that set," said Reynolds. "He was influenced by the Swiss architect Corbusier, for the deep windows."

"The laser sword that Ben takes out of the chest was made from a flash gun," said Barry of the scene set in the Cave Dwelling. "And the reason the scene works is not because of [the set], it's because you're enjoying the movie. It's representative of something; you're thinking about the relationships. But it was nicely lit."

"I remember the day when Alec Guinness actually arrived on the set, when he walked on the stage, and I haven't experienced anything like that since or before," said Reynolds. "The entire stage went absolutely quiet. There was no noise—totally, totally quiet. And when he said his lines, it was absolutely perfect. I don't know whether there was a second take or not, but the quiet was—I've never seen anything like it. I was so impressed. Casting him was a stroke of genius, wasn't it? He gave the film another dimension, and the fact that this serious British actor was on the film had to be something special.

↑ A photograph of Obi-Wan's "home" reveals the edge between story and reality, with the end of the carpet marking that border. In addition to providing a look at the myriad props used to make the "Cave Dwelling" look lived in, the photograph exposes the carpentry underpinning the set.

→ An important element of production design and art direction is making sure that multiple sets on the same soundstage will actually fit. In the Lucasfilm Archives, many sketches, and sometimes quite elaborate drawings, indicate how sets will exist side-by-side. This particular stage layout reveals three sets, including the "Anchorhead power station," where Luke meets three of his friends—a scene that ended up on the cutting room floor.

"There was another set, too, that was never in the film because I think the scene was just a little bit too long," said Reynolds. "That's the thing that George can do quite ruthlessly. And what I mean by that is he'll shoot all the stuff and then quite ruthlessly only include and incorporate the stuff that is absolutely essential to make the film move along."

"INT CAVE DWELLING" SET N° 230

ALL "MUD" FINISH
TO SET AS PHOTO
REFERENCE.
NOTE/
OBSCURE WINDOWS
SEE ART DIRECTOR, PAPER
NO BACKINGS

SET	CAVE DWELLING
DETAIL	PLAN & ELEVATIONS
DRG. NO.	105
DATE	JANUARY 30 1976
DRAWN BY	REG BREAM

RELAXED THESPIANS

On some unlucky films, a set can become an albatross around a production designer's neck. For example, a director may not know if they've finished with a particular set—they may want to think about a scene—but the designer needs to get rid of that set so construction can start on the next.

Actors can also cause difficulties regarding sets. "Large stars can dig up these terrible problems," said Barry. "They suddenly disappear because they want to attend a premiere of their previous movie in the middle of the one you're making—so the set you've got ready is now no longer wanted and the director wants to do something else. Particularly very expensive stars, [they] never ever want to lose a minute of their time. So you do have to jump through hoops in those sorts of situations to keep it all running. But we've not had any of those problems on *Star Wars*."

"I remember being introduced to Mark Hamill, who was really so youthful, it's just amazing, and he was absolutely charming," said Reynolds. "And I remember being also introduced to Harrison, who had, I think, a bag on his shoulder with a six-pack in it. And they were all laid-back and very easygoing people."

↑ Bream's drawing suggests "tracing paper" to "obscure" the windows: that is, no painted backings would be used. Instead a white light would penetrate Old Ben's home, giving the scene an ethereal quality. These kinds of choices would be made in the planning stages, but other decisions might be made as the set was being constructed. "George has been very helpful, always ready to come and look at the sets after the rushes," Barry said during filming. "We're always walking around the sets at eight o'clock at night talking about them before we film on them. So, you know, nothing's a horrid surprise when George gets there. In general, this is not a good idea, to walk around as they are being built, very dangerous. You can get quite a wrong feeling about size and things when it's half up, but George, I felt, was interested enough and bright enough to play it fairly cool and discuss things like the colors and so on. Because you can't walk onto a set that fills the whole stage from end to end and say, 'Christ, you didn't tell me this, that, and the other. Well, do it again!'"

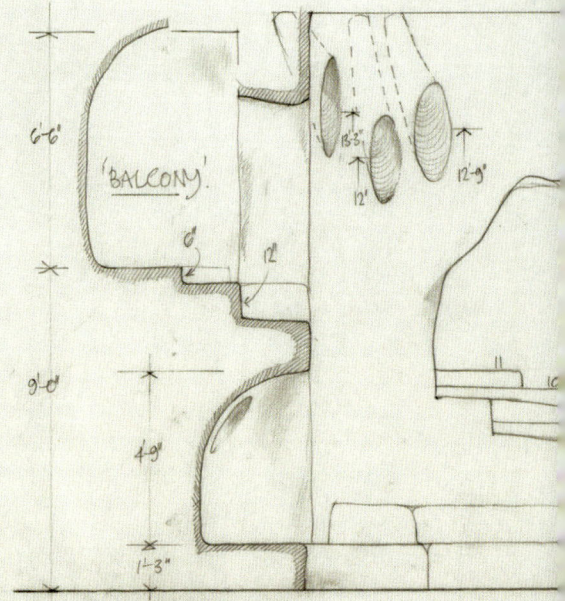

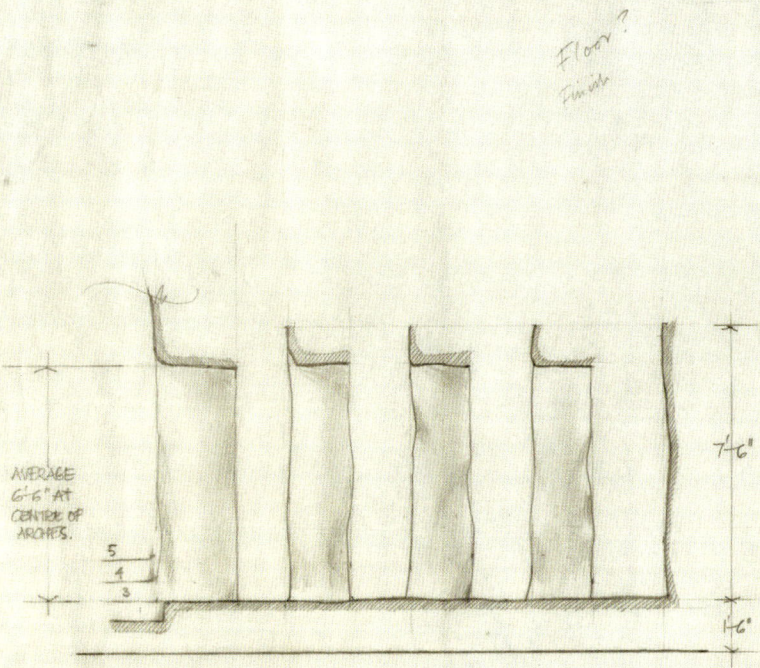

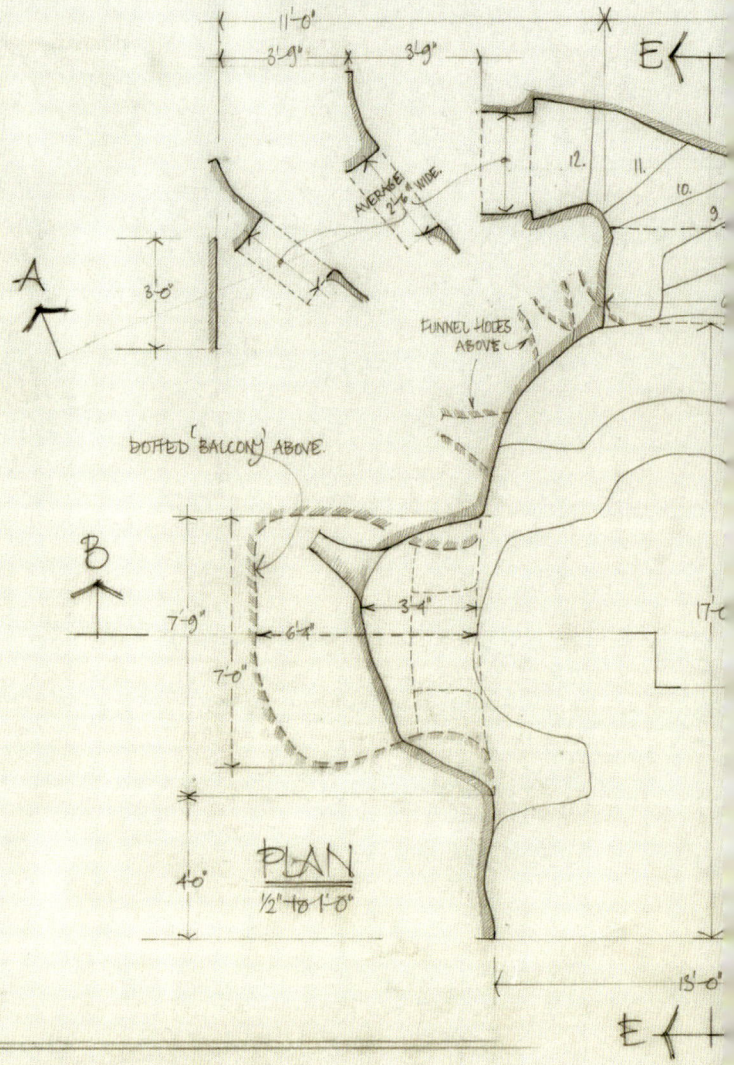

ELEVATION AA

STAGE FLOOR

LEDGE

ELEVATION BB

'BALCONY'

ELEVATION DD

AVERAGE
6'6" AT
CENTRE OF
ARCHES.

AVERAGE
2'6" WIDE

FUNNEL HOLES
ABOVE.

DOTTED 'BALCONY' ABOVE.

PLAN
½" to 1'-0"

Floor?
Finish

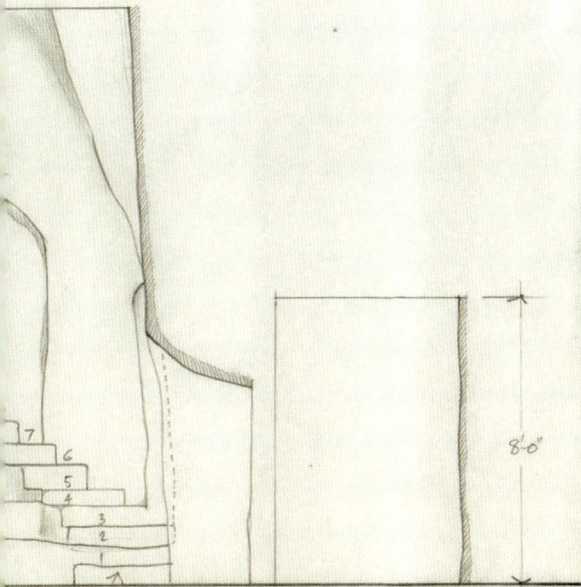

RISERS TO AVERAGE 6"

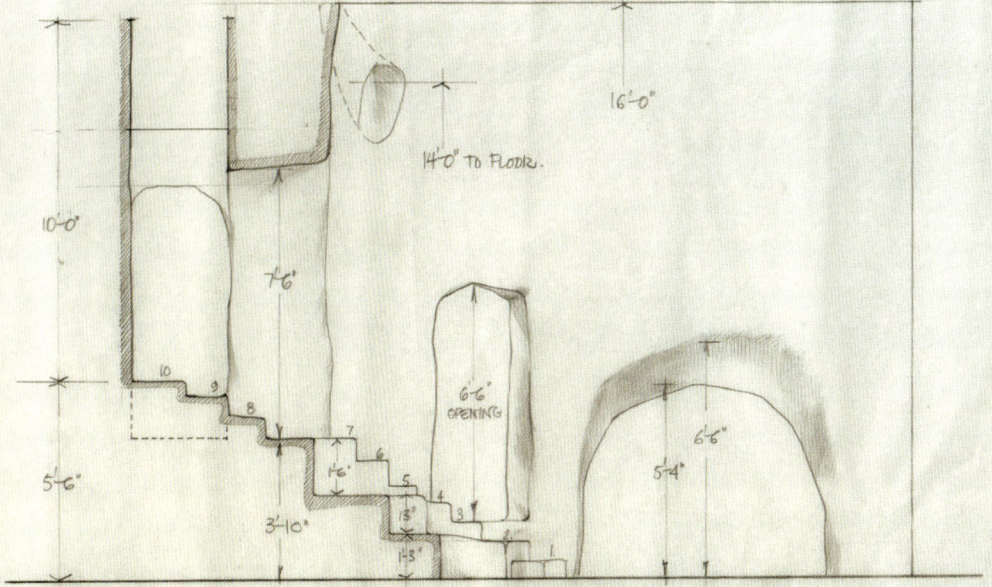

8'-0"

ELEVATION CC

16'-0"

14'-0" TO FLOOR.

10'-0"

7'-6"

6'-6" OPENING

6'-6"

5'-6"

5'-4"

3'-10"

1'-3"

FLOAT

7'-0"

7'-0"

5'-0"

AVERAGE 2'-0" WIDE LEDGE

AVERAGE 2'-9" WIDTH.

3'-0"

8'-0" FLOAT

FLOAT

3'-0"

7'-0"

ELEVATION EE

6'-0"

16'-0"

7'-6"

6'-1"

1'-3"

Producer

20ᵀᴴ CENTURY FOX

PRODUCTION:-
"THE STAR WARS"

SET:- INT. CAVE
DWELLING   30

DETAIL
PLAN & ELEVS.

SCALE
½" to 1'-0"   13-1-76   P.S.

SET   CAVE DWELLINGS
DETAIL   PLAN & ELEVATIONS
DRG. NO.   30
DATE   JANUARY 13 1976
DRAWN BY   PETER SHIELDS

CANTINA

When Luke, Obi-Wan, and the droids arrive in Mos Eisley, they go to a cantina in search of transport to Alderaan to deliver the plans hidden in R2-D2 to Princess Leia. The Cantina set was inspired by small town saloons from various Western films, but populated by alien creatures instead of cowboys and cowpokes. Makeup supervisor Stuart Freeborn was hard-pressed to finish the creatures in time when the Cantina scenes were moved up in the schedule—he was also ill—but the art department managed to create yet another iconic set, building on Lucas' direction and the fantastic talents of John Barry (only a very general atmospheric production painting was completed by McQuarrie).

"I think we felt perhaps not quite as much pressure as the makeup department, because they had a lot to do," said Reynolds. "They were struggling more than we were to come up with all their stuff in time. *Star Wars* has melded in my memory into one general sort of constant panic, but the Cantina doesn't leap out especially."

To populate the central bar, Barry used practical containers, two as polished, one chrome, three to be cased in fiberglass, and so on, as indicated on the drawing itself. A hard transparent plastic Perspex piece was to run the length of the bar and be lit from behind, with the top of the bar cast in fiberglass.

"I got in truckload after truckload of airplane scrap and taught the guys how to break it down and we made bins of different objects," said Christian. "They learned how to identify things that might look good on a set. We trained the draftsmen to walk down and identify pieces of interest. In the Cantina, there's some large kind of drink containers behind the bar that were all airplane scrap that the draftsmen had taken and drawn into the set."

"You can imagine the complexity of drawing that would have to go into making those very complex sculpted forms," said Barry. "But when you just take apart a jet engine, you get wonderful things. All the bar equipment in the Cantina, those are all the combustion chambers from jet engines, which we sprayed with a metallic gold process and put lights in and bubbles, and all the rest. But they have an interest, because somebody's worked over it and some intelligence has

gone into them, so they are far more interesting than anything you could have made from scratch in the time available."

The floor and the walls of the alien saloon were designed to simulate the stone building exteriors filmed on location on the island of Djerba, Tunisia. One blueprint (no. 89 on page 34) indicates that the structure and rough plaster finish would entail the services of two carpenters, one painter, and two plasterers. The studio floor would be covered in sand and the booth where Han Solo (Harrison Ford) and Chewbacca (Peter Mayhew) negotiate with Ben would be sparsely lit.

"George wanted those cubicles," said Barry. "There was the main part where the action was, but there was also a secret part where you could have a discussion. It's that sort of thing that came out of our talks over a long period of time, and those are the things that you want a set to do for you. It's got to work with the action. It's got to do what the director wants it to do. You had to have that maze quality where you could feel lost, so you wouldn't know what was around the next corner."

↓ The exterior of the Cantina was filmed on location in Djerba, Tunisia; this detail by Bream indicates that some of its "canopy" parts were recycled from "the wrecked spaceship," which is seen sticking out of "main street" when Luke and company enter Mos Eisley.

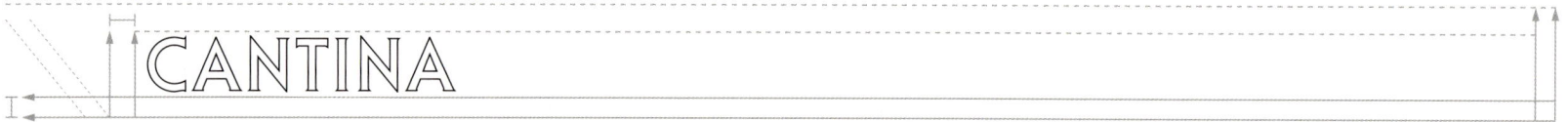

FRONT.

SECTION A-A.

SET	EXTERIOR CANTINA
DETAIL	CANOPY
DRG. NO.	N/A
DATE	JANUARY 5 1976
DRAWN BY	REG BREAM

SET	EXTERIOR CANTINA
DETAIL	GREEBLY, PANEL DETAIL
DRG. NO.	65
DATE	JANUARY 11 1976
DRAWN BY	NORMAN REYNOLDS

→ More details were created for the Cantina exterior, again with a dressed block-board mold for greebly units and vac-formed panels, along with fiberglass bezels made to fit purchased polypropylene (a thermoplastic polymer) pipes, and so on. This drawing is by Norman Reynolds, a superlative draftsperson (whose work was a benchmark long after he was promoted to art director).

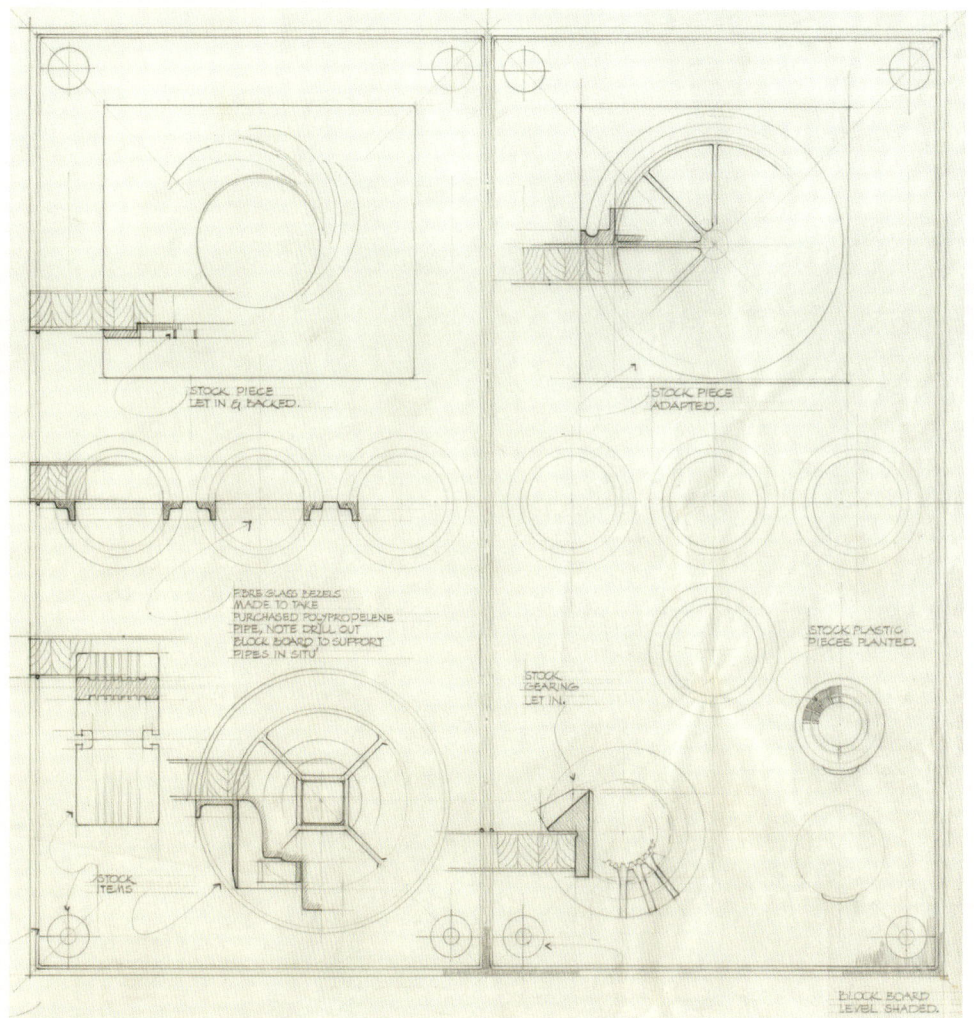

STOCK PIECE LET IN & BACKED.

STOCK PIECE ADAPTED.

FIBRE GLASS BEZELS MADE TO TAKE PURCHASED POLYPROPYLENE PIPE, NOTE DRILL OUT BLOCK BOARD TO SUPPORT PIPES IN SITU.

STOCK PLASTIC PIECES PLANTED.

STOCK GEARING LET IN.

STOCK ITEMS

BLOCK BOARD LEVEL SHADED.

PURCHASED DRESSING.

CUT OUT SLOTS.

PORTHOLES SEE F.S. DET.

DOMED PERSPEX WINDOW.

STOCK FIBRE/GLASS SPHERE.

MARK OUT AS PANELS.

RIB AT CEN' OF SPHERE TO BE ADD'

REPEAT.

APPLIED RIBBING.

5½"

10½"

2½"

ADD PLY SKIRT DIA. THAT OF OF OPENING IN EXISTING SPHERE. CUT HOLES—SEE F.S

ELEVATION

SET	TUNISIA LOCATION
DETAIL	FOURTH SPEEDER
DRG. NO.	UNKNOWN
DATE	DECEMBER 5 1975
DRAWN BY	TED AMBROSE

← Outside the Cantina is a space module that is a homage to the space-pod EVA from Stanley Kubrick's 1968 film, *2001: A Space Odyssey* (perhaps Mos Eisley is where astronaut Dave Bowman wound up?). Back then it was harder to find reference photos, so Lucas' craft is not identical to Kubrick's, but the technical drawings show what it was intended to be made of: plastic pipe collars; tubular legs as support; ribs around the circumference of the sphere; a domed Perspex window; and that the top of the pod was to be purchased dressing on top of a stock fiberglass sphere as the base. (In the early edition of blueprints published by Ballantine in 1977, this drawing was captioned "Ubrickian Landspeeder 9000 Z001," which reads a lot like "Kubrick 2001.")

→ A photograph of the Cantina bar shows to advantage the space fantasy decanters, one of which would be recycled as the head of a bounty hunter droid (IG-88) in the sequel to *Star Wars*, *The Empire Strikes Back*.

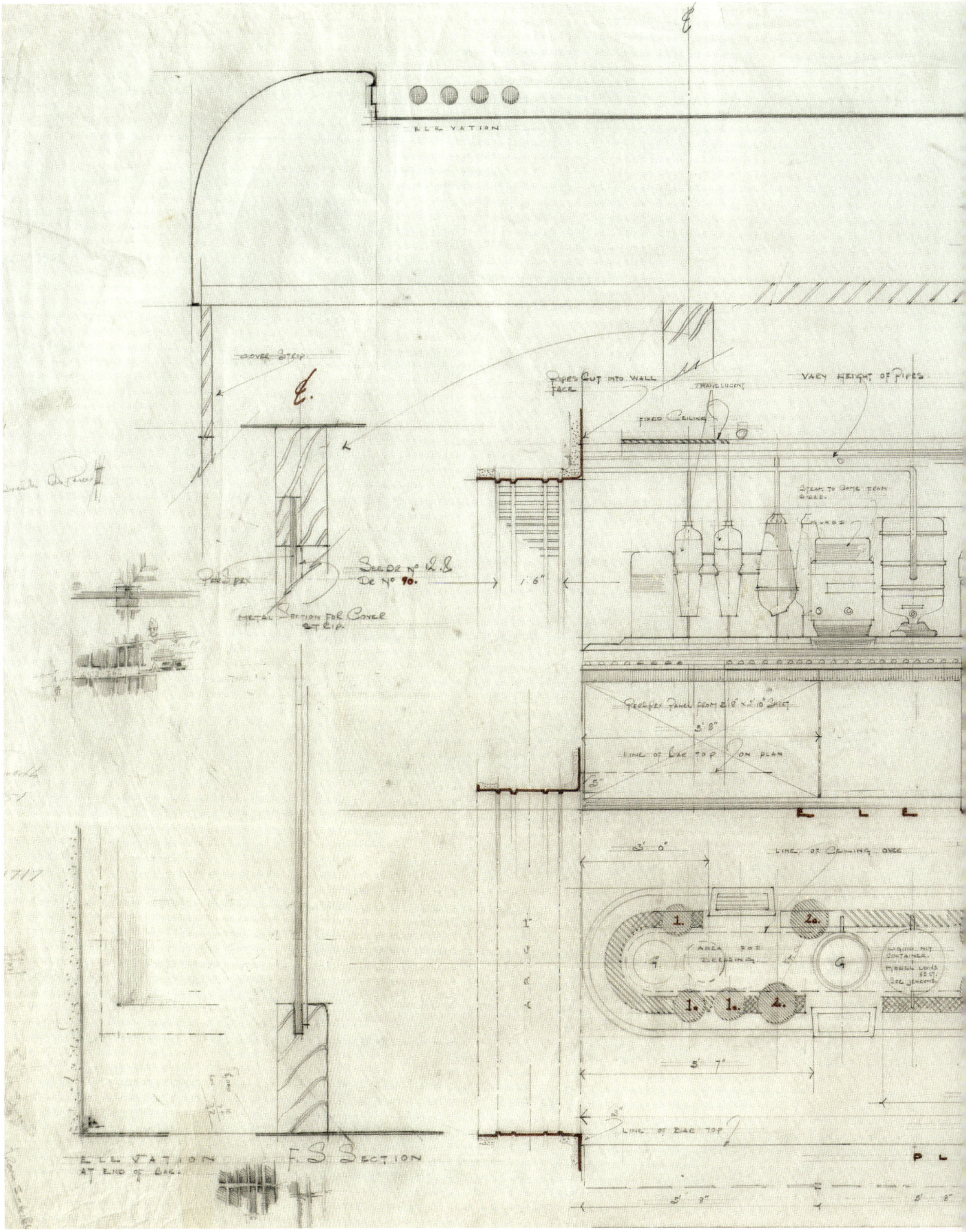

ELEVATION

COVER STRIP

PERSPEX

METAL SECTION FOR COVER STRIP.

SEE DR N° 28
DR N° 90.

1' 6"

PIPES CUT INTO WALL FACE

TRANSLUCENT

VARY HEIGHT OF PIPES

FIXED CEILING

PERSPEX PANEL FROM 3/8" x 2'10" SHEET

3' 8"

LINE OF BAR TOP ON PLAN

LINE OF CEILING OVER

1.   2a.

AREA FOR BLENDING

1.   1.   2.

5' 7"

ELEVATION
AT END OF BAR.

F.S. SECTION

LINE OF BAR TOP

PL

SET	CANTINA	DATE	JANUARY 24 1976
DETAIL	NO. 2	DRAWN BY	ALAN RODERICK-JONES
DRG. NO.	89		

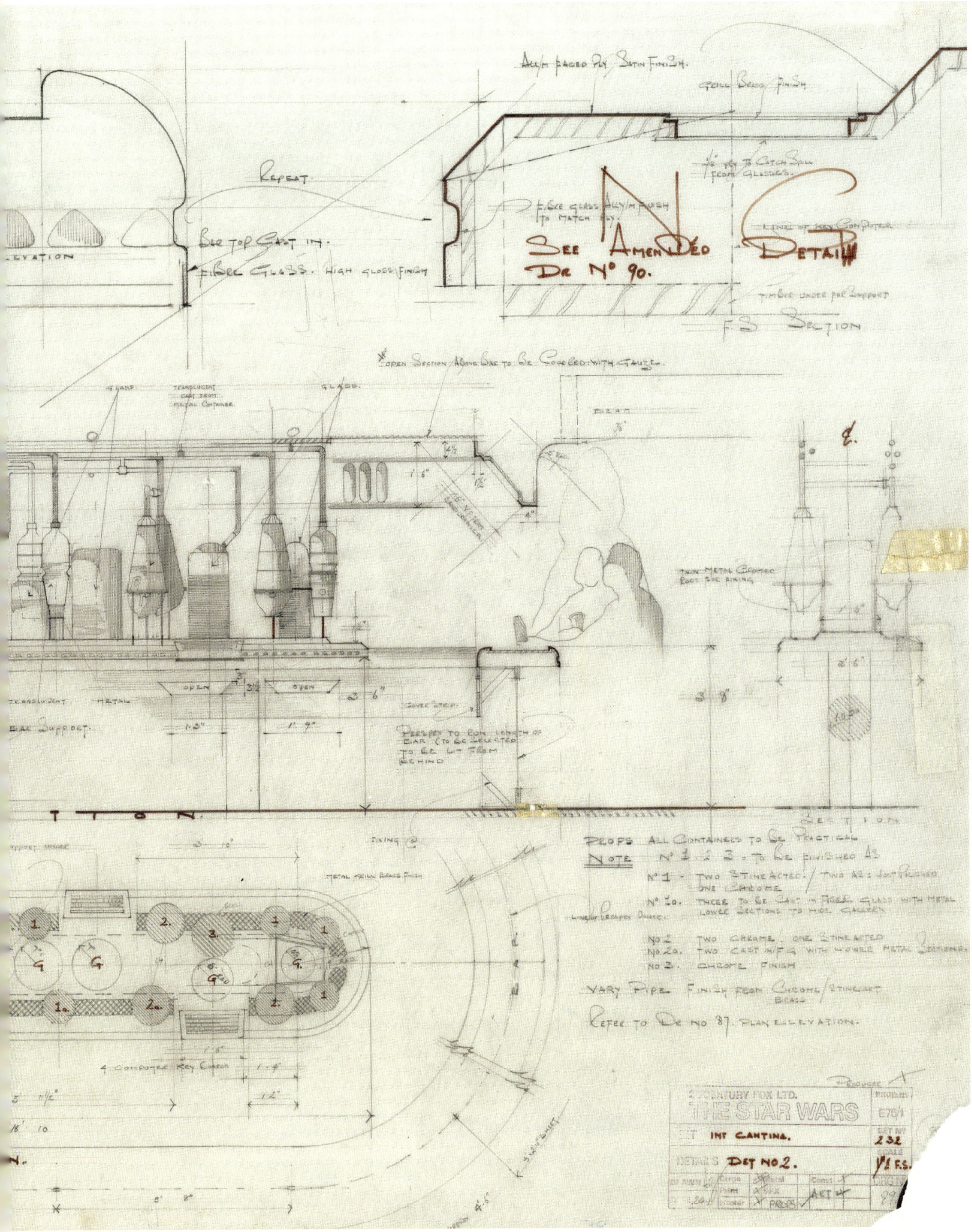

ALU/m FACED PLY SATIN FINISH.

GRILL BRASS FINISH

REPEAT.

1/8 PLY TO CATCH SPILL FROM GLASSES.

FIBRE GLASS ALU/m FINISH TO MATCH PLY.

LINE OF KEY COMPUTER

SEE TOP CAST IN.

N G
SEE AMENDED DETAIL
DR N° 90.

EVATION

FIBRE GLASS. HIGH GLOSS FINISH

TIMBER UNDER FOR SUPPORT

F.S. SECTION

OPEN SECTION ABOVE BAR TO BE COVERED WITH GAUZE.

GLASS.
TRANSLUCENT CAST FROM METAL CONTAINER.
GLASS.

BEAM

THIN METAL CHROMED ROOT PIPE FIXING

TRANSLUCENT. METAL
BAR SUPPORT.

OPEN 3½ OPEN
1'3" 1'9"

3'6"

COVER STRIP.

PERSPEX TO RUN LENGTH OF BAR (TO BE SELECTED) TO BE LIT FROM BEHIND

TTON.

SECTION

PROPS ALL CONTAINERS TO BE PRACTICAL
NOTE N° 1. 2. 3. TO BE FINISHED AS

N° 1 - TWO 3-TINE ACTED / TWO AS FOOT POLISHED. ONE CHROME

METAL GRILL BRASS FINISH

LINE OF DRAPES UNDER.

N° 1a. THREE TO BE CAST IN FIBRE GLASS WITH METAL LOWER SECTIONS TO HIDE GALLERY

N° 2. TWO CHROME. ONE 3-TINE ACTED
N° 2a. TWO CAST IN F.G. WITH LOWER METAL SECTIONS
N° 3. CHROME FINISH

VARY PIPE FINISH FROM CHROME / 3-TINE ACT BRASS

REFER TO DR N° 87. PLAN ELEVATION.

4 COMPUTER KEY BOARDS 1:4

20 CENTURY FOX LTD. PROD/No. E76/1
THE STAR WARS
SET INT CANTINA. SET N° 232
DETAILS DET N° 2. SCALE 1½" F.S.

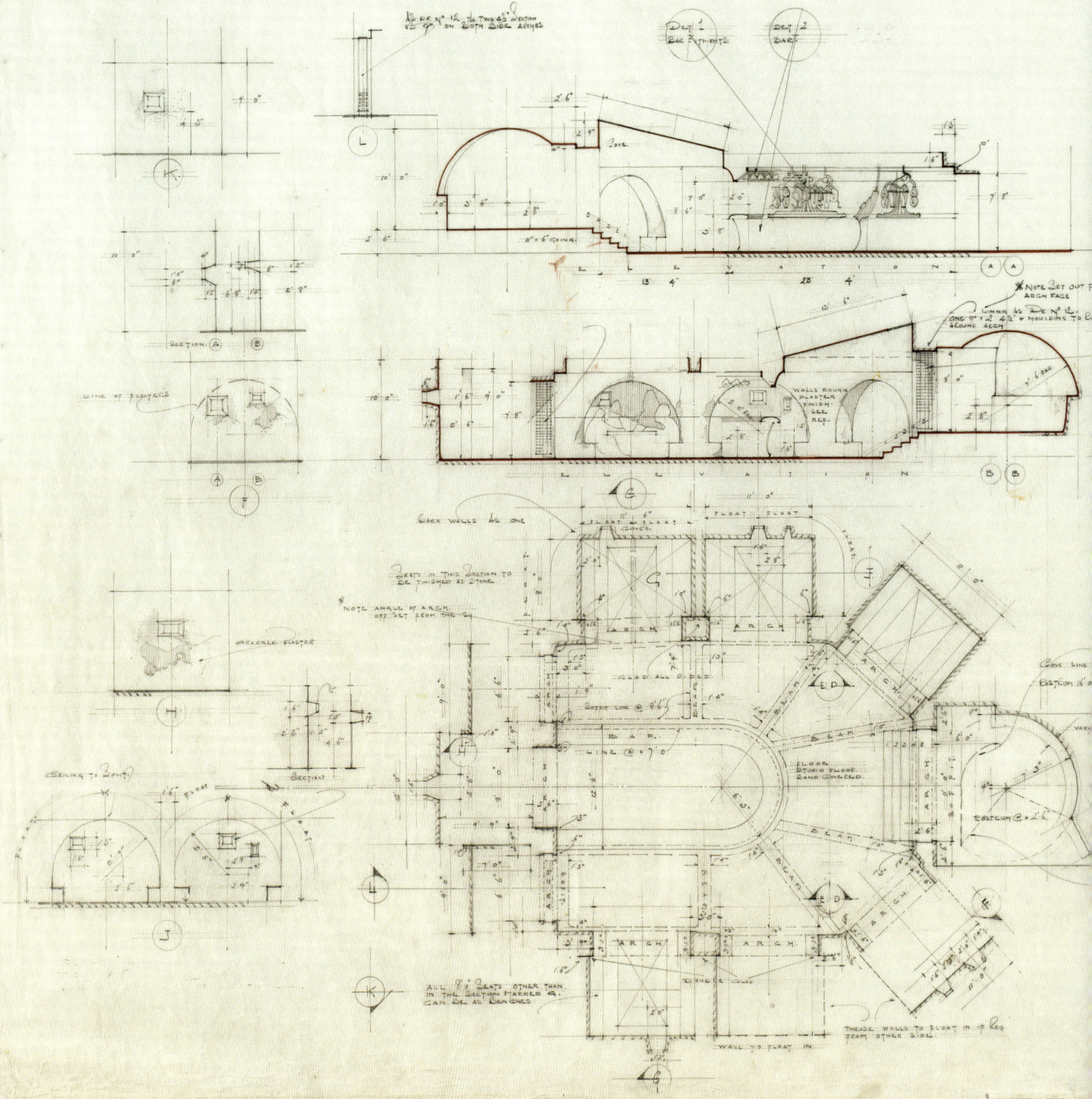

(87)

SET	CANTINA
DETAIL	PLAN & ELEVATIONS
DRG. NO.	87
DATE	JANUARY 1976
DRAWN BY	UNKNOWN

MOS EISLEY

Most people who see *Star Wars*, even experts, would not suspect that several scenes in Mos Eisley alleyways—for example, Luke and Ben hurrying to meet Han Solo while being tailed by an Imperial spy—were in fact filmed on Stage 8 at Elstree Studios. By applying mud textures, a sky-backing cyclorama, and forced perspective, the Elstree art department created a maze of streets that very conveniently doubled for Tunisian exteriors. (Forced perspective is a very old theater technique whereby architectural or other elements are, through mathematical equations and technical tricks, artificially diminished to make, for example, a 2-foot-long background alleyway seem like a 20-foot-long alleyway.)

"We had some very good scenic artists in those days, and a guy that's worth his salt really pays off," said Reynolds. "So we certainly used those backings quite a bit."

Of course, the nonstop activity of creating these complex sets did take a toll on its production designer. "I was complaining to someone the other day, saying it's driving me potty, because it's so absolutely time-consuming," said Barry during filming. "You work seven days a week, but you still can't do everything. Gloria and Willard [Huyck, who polished the final draft of *Star Wars*] asked, 'Why can't you delegate it to somebody else?' I said, 'Because you can't. It comes out another way.' You cannot phone in a piece of sculpture, you know, 'cause it doesn't come out the way you meant it. That's the problem."

↑ Luke and Obi-Wan hurry through a Mos Eisley alley built on Elstree's Stage 8 and shot mid-April 1976.

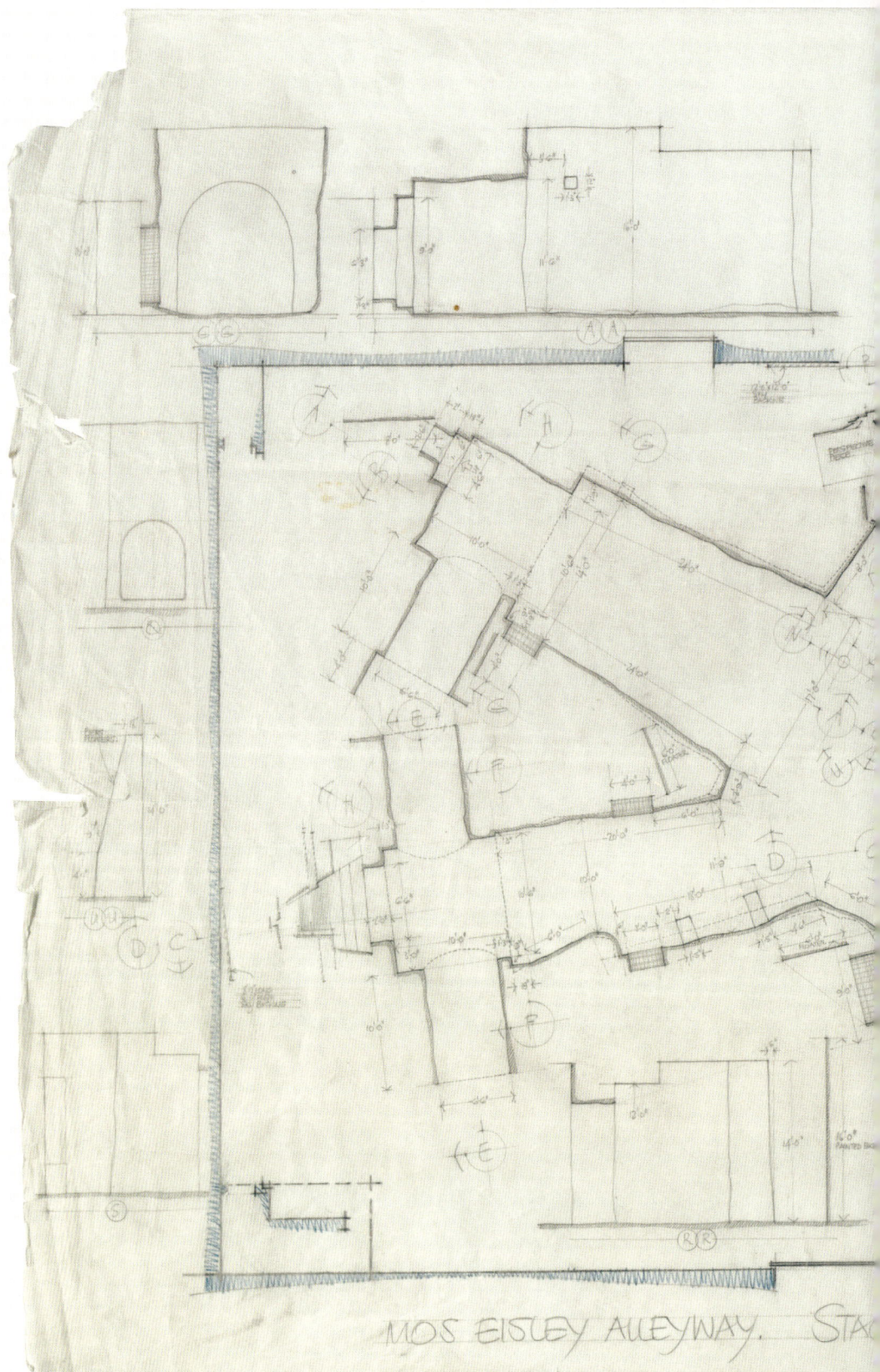

SET	MOS EISLEY ALLEYWAY
DETAIL	PLAN & ELEVATIONS
DRG. NO.	112
DATE	FEBRUARY 3 1976
DRAWN BY	REG BREAM

MOS EISLEY ALLEYWAY.   STAG

← Shots of scenes in Mos Eisley show the interior set with forced-perspective alleys and painted backgrounds for skies.

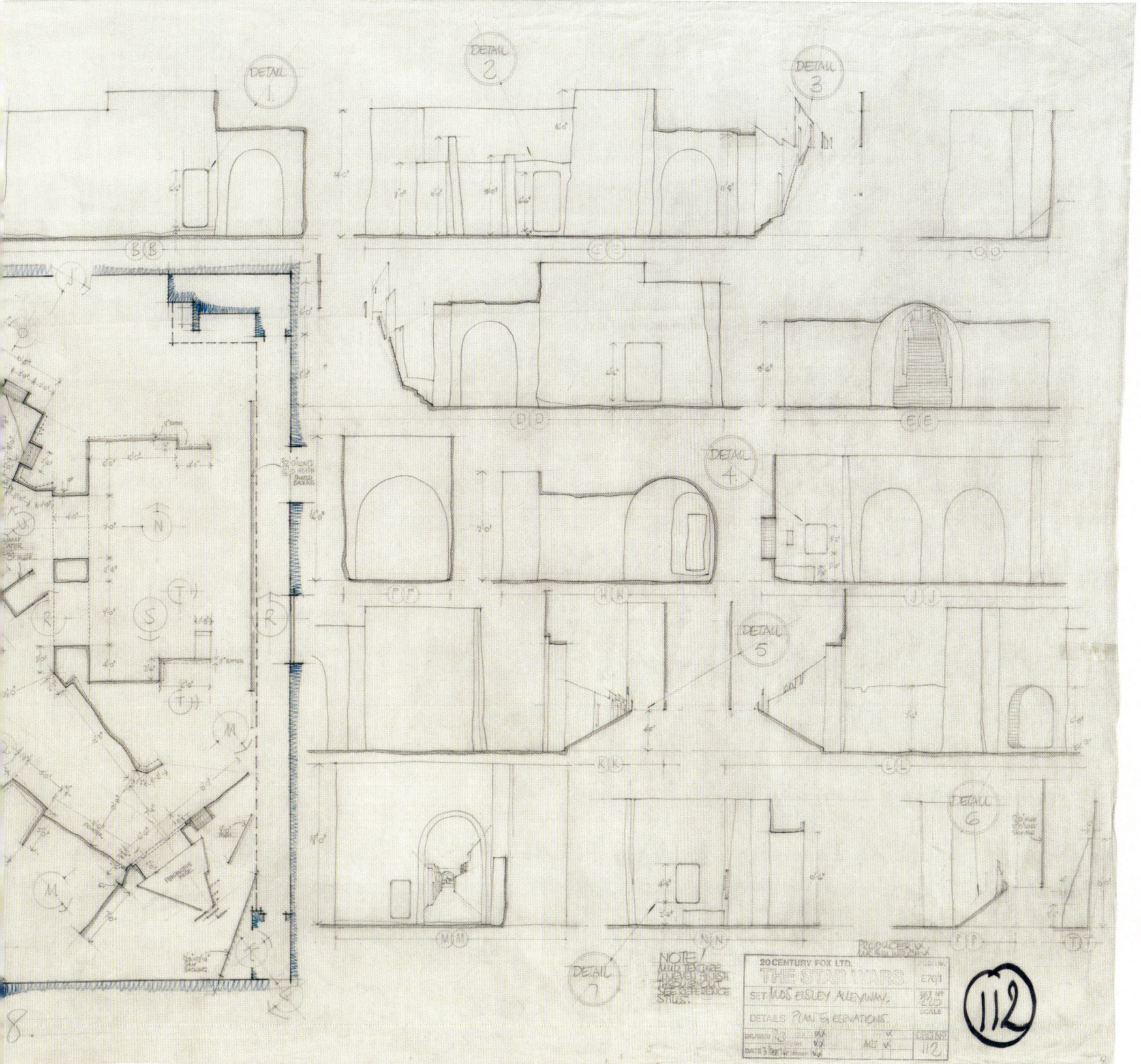

MILLENNIUM FALCON

The interiors of the *Falcon* were broken down into three main sets: the hold, cockpit, and gun port, which doubled for a second gun port in Han and Luke's dogfight with TIE fighters. Its floor was to be dressed with instruments and the ladder leading to the port was taken from another set. Joe Johnston had conceptualized some *Falcon* interiors, but again it was up to Barry to finish the job.

"We had to get the big things out of the way, like the Death Star and *Falcon* and its interiors," said Reynolds. "John had to come up with that pretty quickly."

"The interior of the pirate starship had to appear to fit the exterior, so it had to have an apparently curved design, a circular corridor," said Barry. "George wanted it to look like a spaceship from *2001* that was two hundred years old already. Then the hold had the whole sequence where Luke is fighting the remote with the lightsaber, so we had to have a wide area, so that gave us

→ Following the release of *Star Wars*, additional drawings of the *Falcon* were needed—not necessarily for the sequel, but for other projects, often linked to the licensing of the film. By that time, ILM had disbanded, its personnel having been hired for only the one film. Eventually Lucas rehired Joe Johnston, who delegated work to a new hire, Nilo Rodis-Jamero. Rodis-Jamero proceeded to do several drawings of the *Falcon* that linked up scenes and sets whose geography were not fully realized before.

For these three drawings, Rodis-Jamero probably traced the outline shape from reference photographs and then worked out, roughly, and with Johnston's supervision, the relationship of the ship's various interiors, including the sleeping quarters, engine bay, gun-port tunnel, main corridor, and main cabin elevations.

"I think the most complicated set that I had to do, that took the longest, was the *Falcon*, where the chess game is," said Christian. "They literally built the walls and then I just went in and clustered it. It took weeks and weeks, putting in all the scrap and pipe work to get that completely encrusted look—that and the cockpit. Because I needed switch panels so, again, we would use airplane parts to make all the levers and things. I would isolate those and a draftsman would draw them in."

The *Falcon* cockpit received all of Harry Lange's attention, who, according to Reynolds, made a "huge contribution. He did so much that he was the unsung hero of many of the cockpits in *Star Wars*," he said. Lange worked directly with the prop crew and created many technical drawings for the *Falcon*, among others.

SET	MILLENNIUM FALCON
DETAIL	INTERIOR LAYOUTS (ALL RIGHT)
DRG. NO.	15, ETC.
DATE	SEPTEMBER 1 1978
DRAWN BY	NILO RODIS-JAMERO

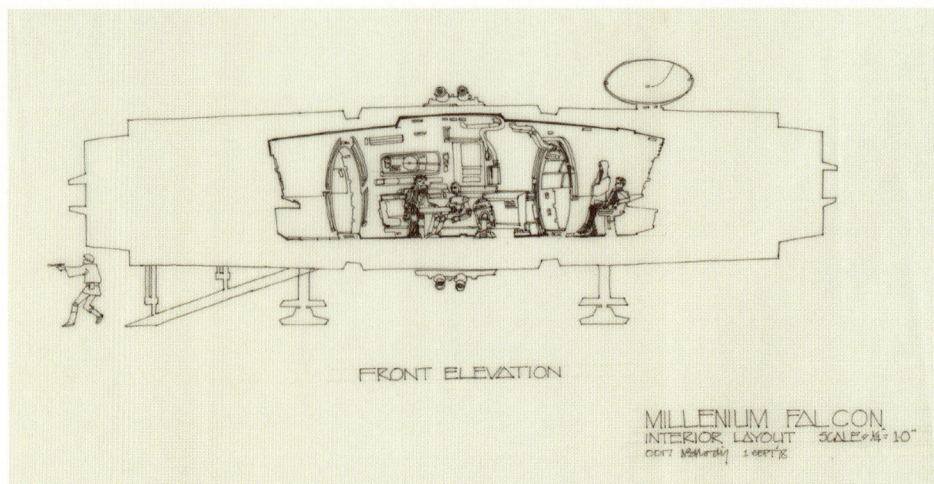

FRONT ELEVATION

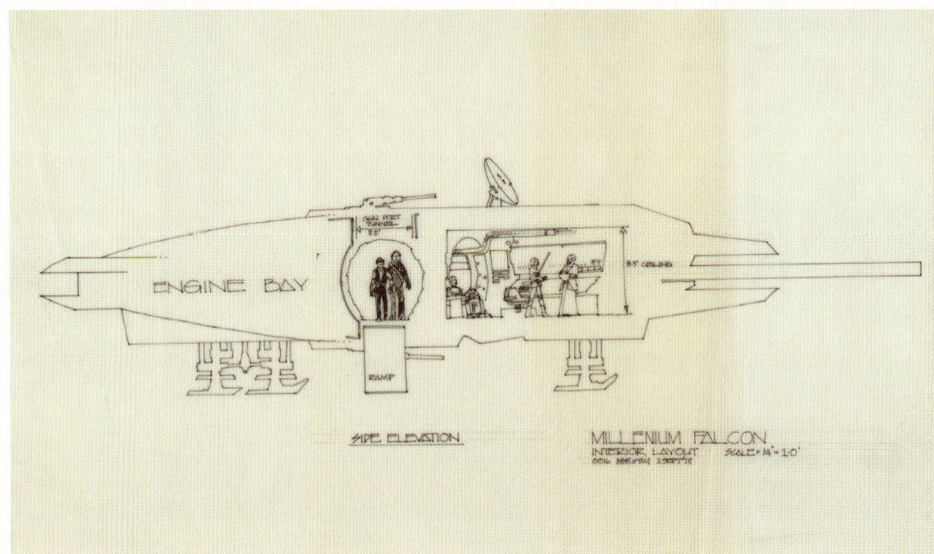

SIDE ELEVATION

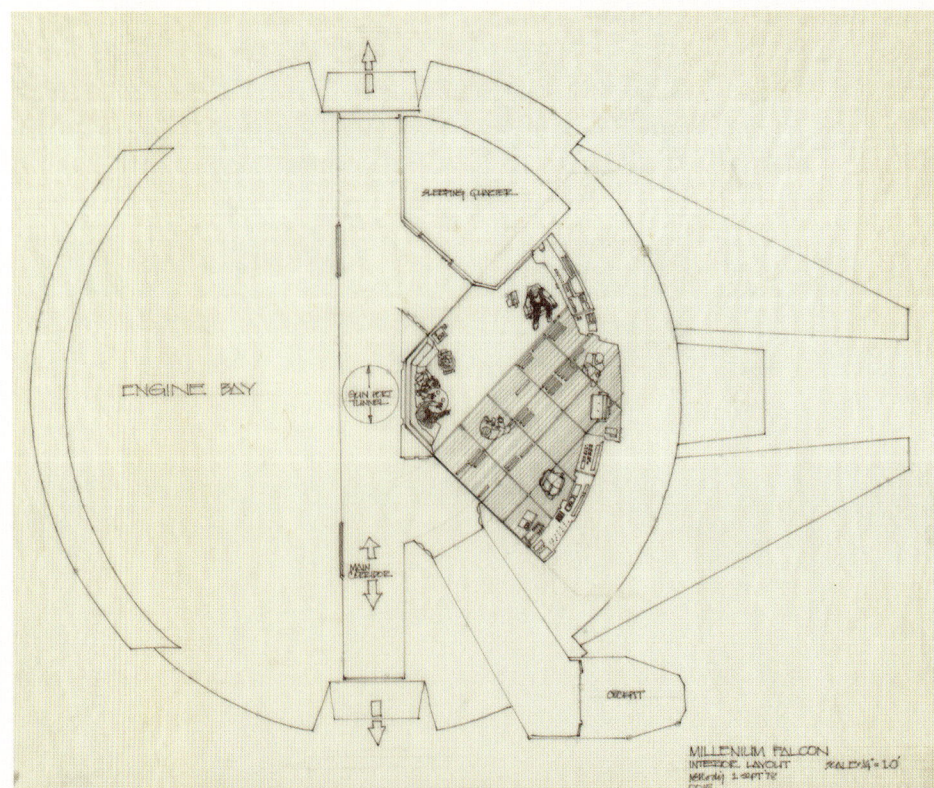

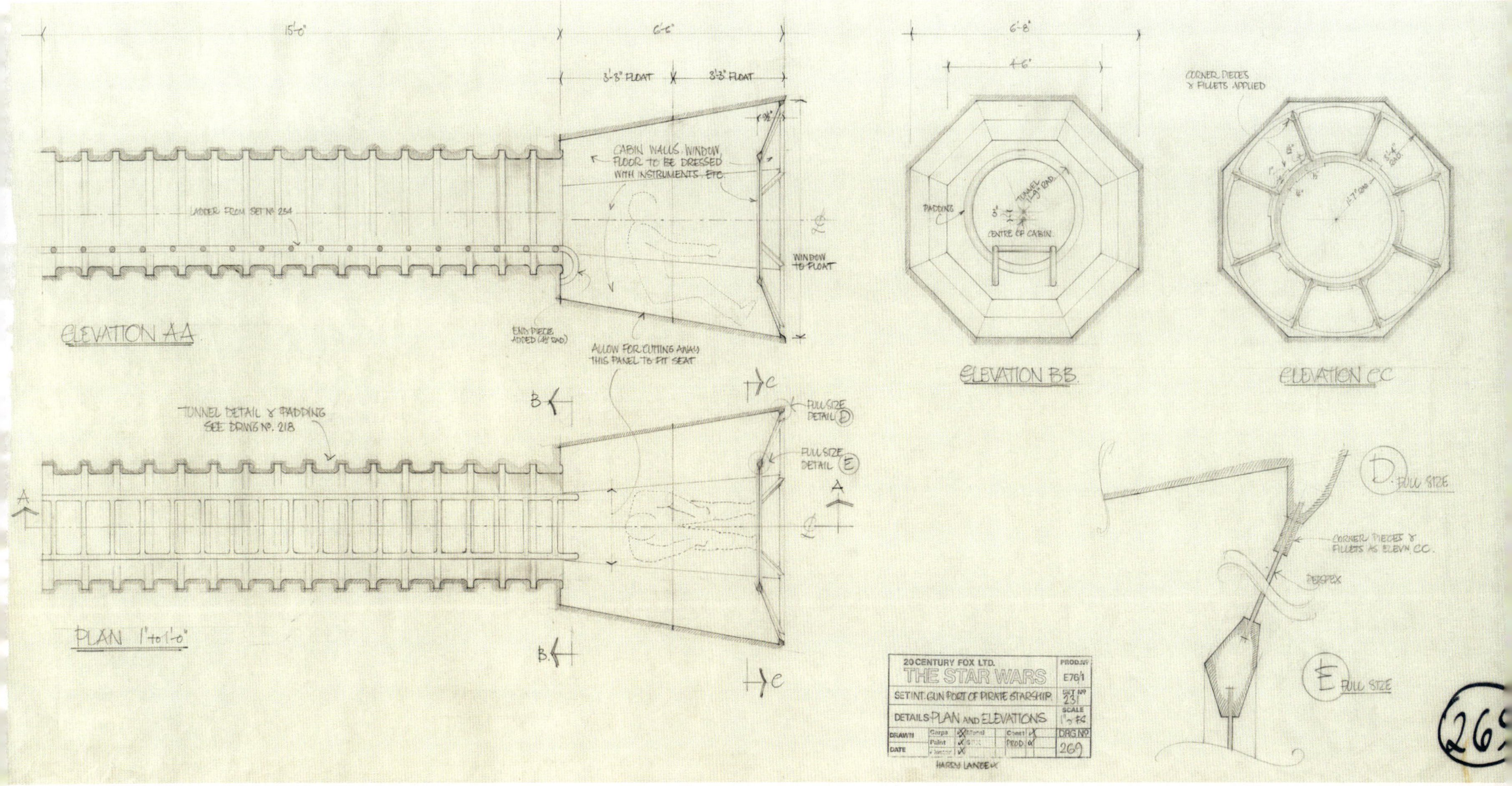

ELEVATION AA

PLAN 1'·to·1'·0"

ELEVATION BB

ELEVATION CC

SET	GUN PORT OF A PIRATE SHIP
DETAIL	PLAN & ELEVATIONS
DRG. NO.	269
DATE	UNKNOWN
DRAWN BY	UNKNOWN

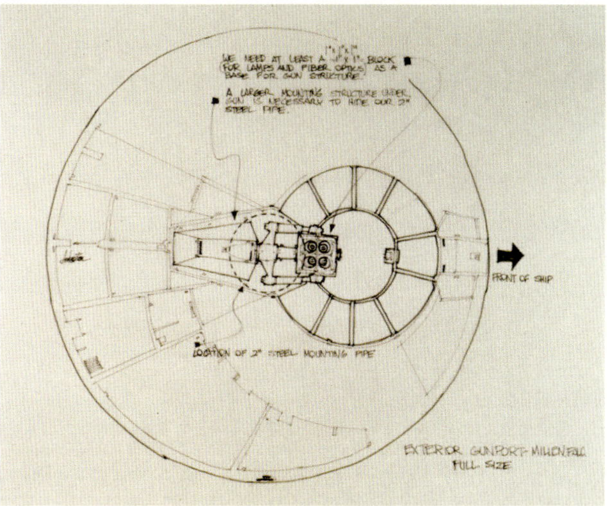

the foreground part. Then all the panels had to come off so that John Stears could get in the controls to the remote robot. Then the curved corridor had to be in panels, so we could take them off and get the lighting in. The ramp had to match exactly the exterior ship, which we'd already built.

"So gradually a design evolves out of all those problems. There are certain areas where you can choose, but they're very limited, in fact. And the constraints make it more interesting, too—because the more you've got to work into it, the more real it starts to look."

When it came to actually building the *Falcon*, construction manager Bill Welch found interpreting the blueprints of the *Falcon* to be particularly challenging due to its complicated shape and weight distribution. Yet he and his team found solutions, and both the interior and exterior of the pirate craft have since become classic designs.

RIGHT The completed gunport is on Stage 4 with elaborately detailed set dressing.

FAR RIGHT The gunport concept drawing was done by Johnston, circa winter 1975–1976.

THIS PART OF PIRATE SHIP BUILT FULL SIZE

HATCH DOOR AND RAMP WILL BE UNDERNEATH HERE. DRAWINGS AND DETAILS TO FOLLOW

COCKPIT

DUAL REAR LANDING GEAR LOCATION

NEW SHIP LOCATION — GEORGE SAYS

FORWARD GEAR LOCATION

OLD SHIP LOCATION

AREA WITHIN THIS LINE WILL BE BUILT FULL SIZE ON STAGE

SET	NEW PIRATE SHIP — STAGE SIZE
DETAIL	SIZE COMPARISONS
DRG. NO.	507
DATE	DECEMBER 11 1975
DRAWN BY	STEVE GAWLEY

← Ralph McQuarrie updated his production painting from the old to the new pirate ship (in Docking Bay 94) on January 13, 1976.

↑ Led by construction manager Bill Welch, carpenters and craftsmen constructed the half *Falcon* on Stage 3 at Elstree Studios, circa March 1976.

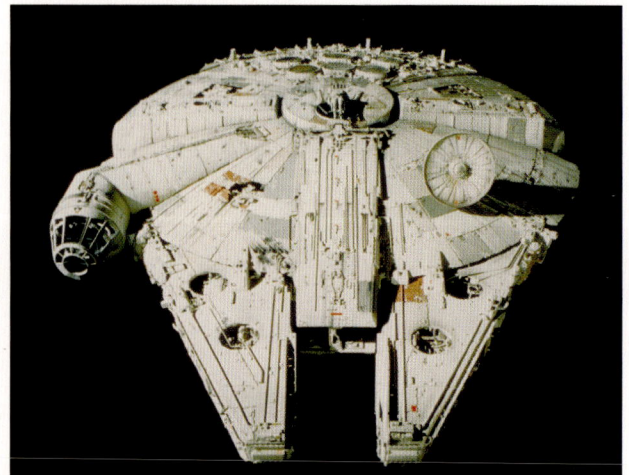

↑ The elaborate model of the *Falcon* was built at ILM; the Elstree art department had to match it.

INTERIOR PIRATE STARSHIP. –

↑ John Barry drew a concept of the first pirate ship's hold in November 1975, which featured a long hallway leading off it in keeping with the approved concept model.

← Clever editing of the shoot-out disguised the fact that very little space separated Han Solo from the stormtroopers; Stage 3 was small and the new pirate ship left the actors very little room in which to maneuver.

↑ A behind-the-scenes shot reveals the cramped quarters on Stage 3, where the hangar set was constructed.

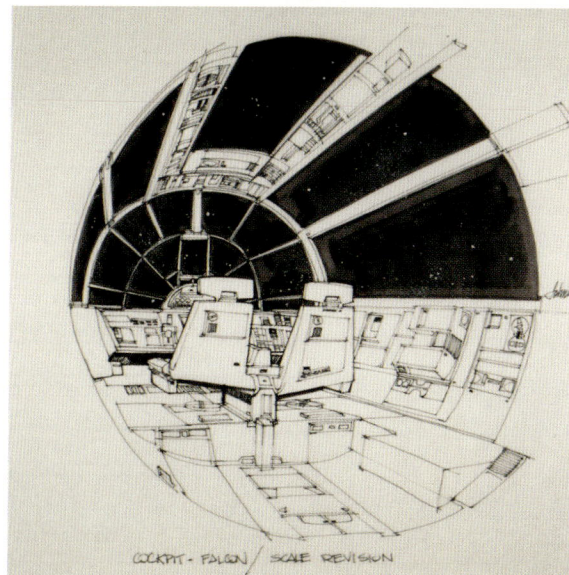

↓ An on-set photograph shows Chewbacca, Luke, Obi-Wan, and Han Solo in the full-size *Falcon* cockpit.

COCKPIT - FALCON / SCALE REVISION

↑ A Joe Johnston concept drawing is of the *Falcon* cockpit.

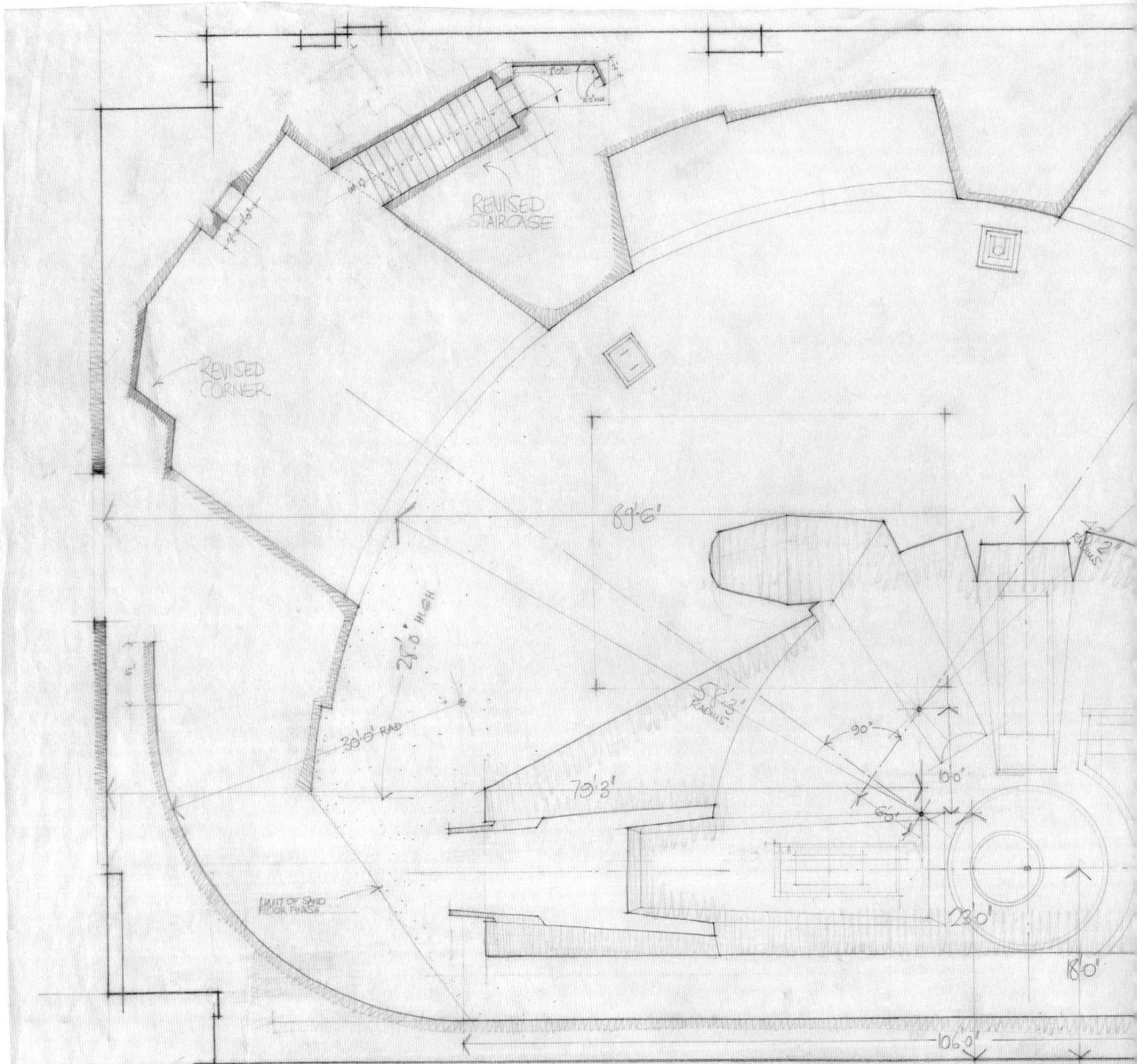

REVISED
STAIRCASE

REVISED
CORNER

89'6"

21'0" HIGH

30'0" RAD

LIMIT OF SAND
FLOOR FINISH

79'3"

90°

10'0"

60°

13'0"

18'0"

106'0"

STAGE LAYOUT - MOS EISLEY SPACEPORT.
SET N° 233

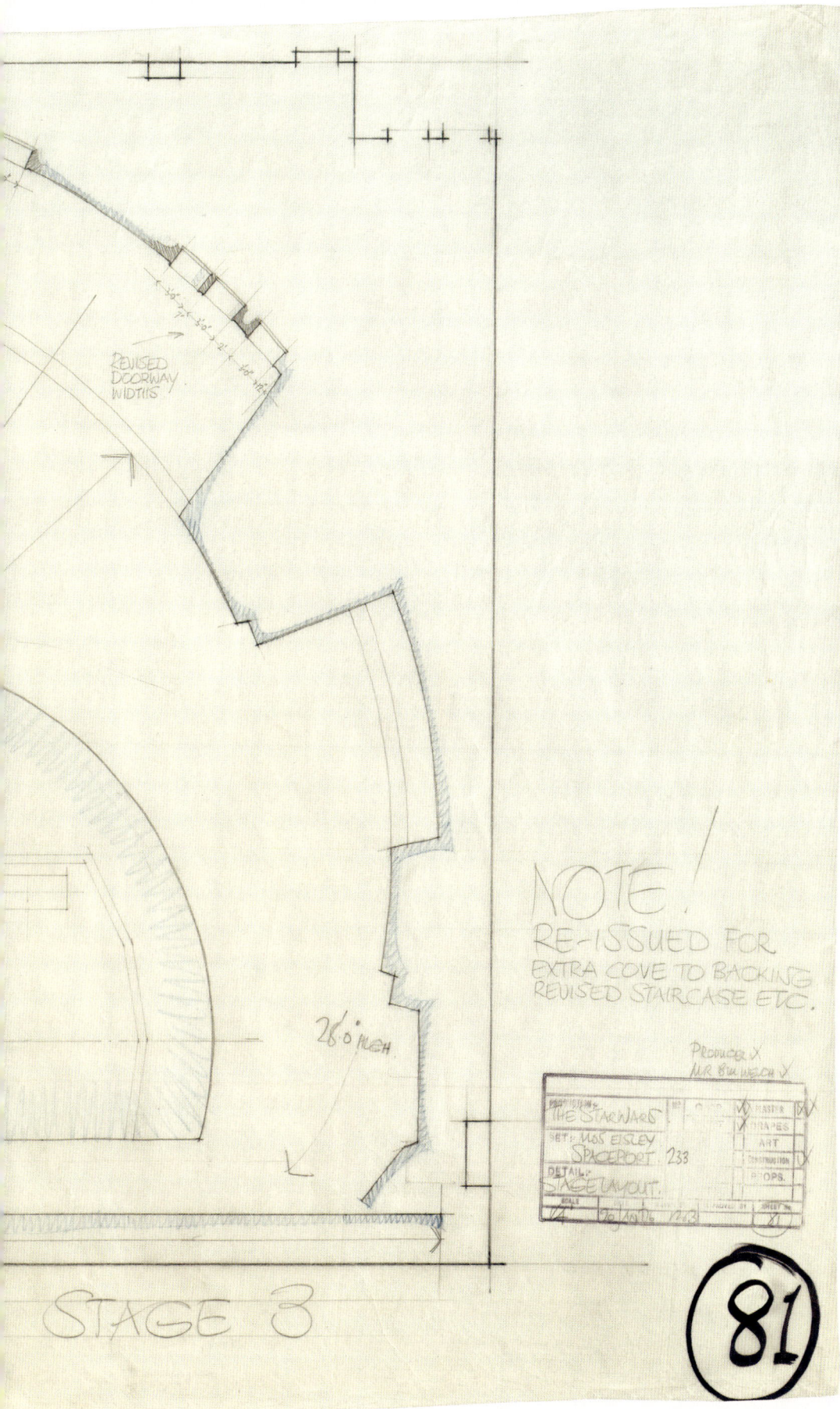

NOTE!
RE-ISSUED FOR
EXTRA COVE TO BACKING
REVISED STAIRCASE ETC.

28.0 HIGH

STAGE 3

(81)

SET	MOS EISLEY SPACEPORT
DETAIL	STAGE LAYOUT
DRG. NO.	81
DATE	JANUARY 20 1976
DRAWN BY	REG BREAM

← Another painted backing—160 feet long, 30 feet high, and divided into 48 sections—was used for the spaceport set, where the *Millennium Falcon* was parked. A reissued technical drawing (no. 81) detailed a revised staircase, the limit of the sand-floor finish, revised doorway widths—and showed clearly that only half the *Falcon* would fit. At one point, while scouting, Lucas and Barry had considered a location in Tunisia that would've placed Mos Eisley on a hill, but the *Falcon* also had to be parked in the Death Star—each set would be built around the stationary spaceship on Stage 3—which meant a very flat locale.

"The hill location would have been a bit hard to reach in terms of hotels and things," said Barry later. "It also depends on how you think of the locations as sets. When you've decided to do a thing like take the Tatooine set with the *Millennium Falcon* and utilize that same set with a perspective and then change it into the Death Star, I had to take chances that I would rather have not done, I must say. We ended up with two sides of the set that are just absolutely painted. We shouldn't have done that, but we had no choice because they were perspective-ized."

"George always complained about that set," said Dennis Muren, ILM visual effects photographer. "He had the *Falcon* taking up most of the stage, and then these stormtroopers had to run in and have a shoot-out with Han—and yet the space from one to another was really minimal. So George had to really pull the camera back from each angle to make each group look farther apart. But in fact the battle would have been over in a flash, because they were practically right next to each other. Pure cinema."

DEATH STAR HANGAR

In the early approved script, Luke, Obi-Wan, Han, Chewbacca, and the droids were to travel to the planet Alderaan to rescue Princess Leia. Budget constraints, however, once again necessitated changes, such as the transfer of all that action to the Death Star, as sets and scenes were combined or eliminated. It was then up to Barry and Lucas to find a way of building sets in as little space and using as few dollars as possible for maximum screen effect.

"For the Death Star, I spent some time, three or four weeks, with George and we were both sitting on the same stool in front of the drawing board," said Barry of their design sessions. "George has quite a good grasp of plans and things, and a lot of people don't—they can't talk about a plan and know what they are going to get. But George, he's a mechanically minded sort of person. So we talked about that for quite some time in November [1975]. The actual pages of scribbles that we did are very interesting—they look a little bit like a fly crawling across the paper. They are little endless scribbles, but we were both of us drawing at the same time, with George saying, 'Well, I don't need that. I will need that corridor; I will need this and I will need that.'

"It was at that stage that the concept of the Death Star came out," Barry continued. "Not the sphere, but the inside corridors which we had to build concentrically one inside the other to get them all on the stage [drawing no. 229, on pages 50 and 51]. Then Ralph did some more drawings, which were the navy blue Death Star based on this concentric concept of the corridors running around and round. I figured that although the Death Star is enormous, you have to always build it on a curve to remind yourself that you are in a curved thing."

Blueprints of the Death Star's largest space—the hangar—indicate one spot as being a key point, "action on this panel," which may be the wall panel where R2 plugs in to communicate with the battle station's computer. A large piece of black velvet was used behind the hangar entrance, where ILM would later add stars and the *Falcon* model, with white muslin lit from behind framing the shot.

"I suppose one shot that I always will remember is the *Falcon* when it comes into the Death Star hangar," said Ambrose. "Now, obviously, the first shot is done with a model and process stuff, and then when you see the actual *Millennium* in that huge hangar, it was done for real with the real mockup. The only bit that wasn't for real was the top bit, which was matted in at a later date from a high angle."

"All the time we are designing sets, George is talking about what he wants to do with the movie, ideas that really have an immense influence on the look of the picture," Barry said. "Like, say, he wanted it to look as though it had been shot on location in your everyday sort of Death Star or Cantina; he wanted it to feel like, 'Well, everybody knows about this.' We just happened to be shooting. Do you know what I mean? Rather than look at this wonderful place that we built—the usual, 'Here is your big, wide establishing shot,' and that sort of filming—instead, bang!, now we'll go into the close-up. He has a tendency to use bits and pieces, so you build up the image in your mind over the length of the scene."

← R2 plugs into the computer terminal socket as designated in drawing no. 243; the set was completed with dressings supervised by Harry Lange.

↓ A storyboard designated "Disney" meant that Harrison Ellenshaw, who was at ILM on leave from the Disney studio, would complete the shot with a matte painting.

SHOT #	BACKGROUND:	P.P. #	PAGE #
872-14			
OPTICAL:			FRAME COUNT: BOARD #

DISNEY

DESCRIPTION: POV OF STARSHIP IN HANGAR DECK - TROOPS ENTER
DIALOGUE: ROTO:

ELEVATION (DOORS SHOWN OPEN.)

↑ A detail of the control room "closet" in which the droids hide featured dummy switches, small practical lights, and a note telling builders to refer to sketch artist Harry Lange in the art department if they have questions. Much of the control room was recycled from other sets.

SET	CONTROL ROOM DEATH STAR (REVAMP)
DETAIL	LOCKER DETAIL
DRG. NO.	281
DATE	MAY 10 1976
DRAWN BY	PETER J. CHILDS

↑ C-3PO is discovered by stormtroopers as he and R2 hide in the control room "locker."

← In postproduction, ILM filmed the arrival of the miniature *Falcon* in the Death Star hangar; a giant black velvet curtain had masked the entryway on set at Elstree so that later the miniature and the set might be composited together.

DRAFTING FOR DUMMIES

"Ideally, the best people have acquired some knowledge about the orders of architecture: i.e., Corinthian, Doric, Ionic, etc., and have a basic grasp of building construction," said Norman Reynolds on what makes a good draftsperson. Indeed, he recalled a book very much in vogue during his early days of set construction, *A History of Architecture* by Banister Fletcher. Also popular was the *Handbook of Ornament* by Franz Sales Meyer, apparently essential for mastering basic architectural details. Another—still essential—part of the draftsperson's kit is the *American Cinematographer Manual*, which provides a wealth of information in terms of camera angles.

But Reynolds believed the broader the base of one's knowledge, the more helpful it is for different types of films. "In terms of actual drawing, a fluid architectural style fits the bill, where the change in density of line can bring a drawing to life and make sections and other elements so easily discernable."

Reynolds also counseled neatness and an eye for good proportion. "I almost forgot that patience is a great asset for a draftsman to have—this will enable him or her to deal with a fussy production designer."

"British drawings are just different from American drawings," said Lorne Peterson. "They put in the shading and made it a little bit more three-dimensional than Americans. Twenty or thirty years ago, you could put an American drawing next to a British drawing and you could tell the British one because it had a different look—an alternating thicker and thinner line, which really brought it to life."

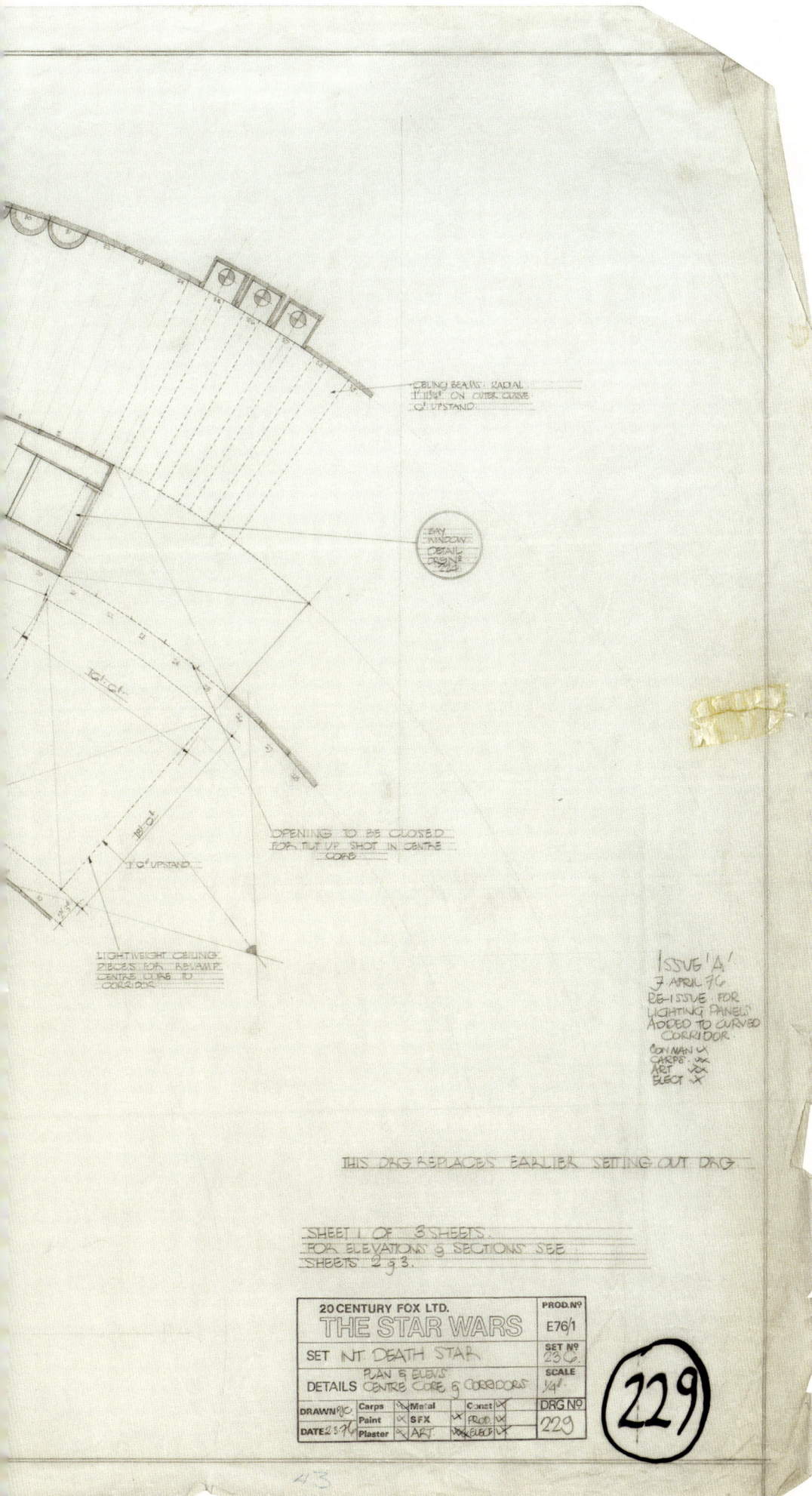

CEILING BEAMS RADIAL 1'11½" ON OUTER CURVE 9" UPSTAND

BAY WINDOWS DETAIL DRG N°

OPENING TO BE CLOSED FOR TILT UP SHOT IN CENTRE CORE

1' 0" UPSTAND

LIGHTWEIGHT CEILING PIECES FOR REVAMP CENTRE CORE TO CORRIDOR

ISSUE 'A'
7 APRIL 76
RE-ISSUE FOR
LIGHTING PANELS
ADDED TO CURVED
CORRIDOR.
CON MAN ✗
CARPS ✗✗
ART ✗✗
ELECT ✗

THIS DRG REPLACES EARLIER SETTING OUT DRG

SHEET 1 OF 3 SHEETS.
FOR ELEVATIONS & SECTIONS SEE
SHEETS 2 & 3.

20 CENTURY FOX LTD.		PROD.N°
THE STAR WARS		E76/1
SET INT DEATH STAR		SET N° 23 C
DETAILS PLAN & ELEVS CENTRE CORE & CORRIDORS		SCALE ¼"

DRAWN	Carps	Metal	✗	Const ✗	DRG N°
	Paint ✗	SFX	✗	PROD ✗	229
DATE 2.5.76	Plaster ✗	ART	✗	ELECT ✗	

(229)

← The fairly large composite set of the Death Star integrated a main corridor and a center core, thanks to the talents of two carpenters, a painter, two plasterers, four electricians, and others.

SET	DEATH STAR
DETAIL	ELEVATION INNER WALL, CENTER CORE, & SECT.
DRG. NO.	229
DATE	APRIL 6 1976
DRAWN BY	PETER J. CHILDS

PRISON CELL

Once again using forced perspective, Barry designed a corridor for the "Alderaan prison" that was relocated to inside the Death Star. This set also made use of simple but effective building elements for the walls and floor. "Those plastic palettes they used for the floor seem foreign to us because we didn't have plastic palettes at the time in the US," said Peterson. "Whereas in England they might have thought, *No big deal*."

Barry recounted that the corridor walls on the Death Star were created out of plastic panels that were built by an outside company. "They're all designed in multi-sizes and dimensions, so that they can fit together in a lot of different ways like a great big construction kit," said Barry. "In fact, we have used panels on a lot of other sets as well, because it helps us with speed. They've been quite a big help, although they are quite expensive, but it was the only way to get it done in time."

Because of various factors, the original forced perspective corridor would be replaced with a digital one in the Special Edition (1997). "It didn't follow the perspective lines," said ILM visual effects supervisor John Knoll. "The camera was in various places in the corridor. And so the vanishing point of the actual foreground corridor sometimes didn't match the vanishing point of the forced-perspective corridor. Because the latter corridor only works from one point in space; it only works from the exact center of the corridor. As soon as you got off axis, all the perspective lines had a kink at the joint. And that was pretty visible in the final film."

Dilley remembers that John Stears somewhat overestimated how much explosive power he needed during the prison shoot-out scenes. "It all crashed down, the set just came crashing down," Dilley said. "John said, 'Oh, it's these weak sets.' But what he'd done, technically, was blow the set to bits. He was supposed to be just making a hole in the elevator door!"

SET	PRISON CELL
DETAIL	DOOR & CELL (BELOW AND BOTTOM)
DRG. NO.	UNKNOWN
DATE	APRIL 1976
DRAWN BY	MICHAEL LAMONT

← The set of the prison corridor used forced perspective to give the illusion of a much longer hallway.

→ Princess Leia (played by Carrie Fisher) is in her cell, built on Stage 4 as part of the prison set where filming took place in late May 1976.

↑ In this detail, the draftsperson, who of course had not read the script, places a male instead of Leia in the cell. He also notes that the ceiling panels are floating (meaning they were removable), that the walls should have a spray paint finish, and that the cell door would slide up.

SET	ALDERAAN GARBAGE ROOM
DETAIL	REVISED PLAN, ETC.
DRG. NO.	240
DATE	APRIL 8 1976
DRAWN BY	REG BREAM

← Sometimes major script changes would take a while to wind their way through production—and news of some changes would never make it to everyone. Although the garbage room had been transferred to the Death Star months before, two technical drawings still place it in Alderaan even as late as April 1976. Shields' drawing also indicates that the walls were to close until only 2 feet apart on center (no. 153). An additional blueprint drawn by Reg Bream notes that the water level would be 5 feet high in an 8-foot tank and that much of the garbage floating in the water was painted blocks of Styrofoam. "It was just the effects guys literally pushing the walls on tracks," said Reynolds. "They actually squeezed them together with enough people. It's a very simple method and very effective." On the day of filming, production avoided placing Peter Mayhew (Chewbacca) into the water, given his knitted mohair and yak-hair Wookiee suit; instead he was placed on a ledge throughout the scene. Nevertheless, his costume retained an unpleasant odor from the dampness for the rest of the shoot. The other actors wore rubber suits beneath their costumes.

↑ Leia, Luke, and Han Solo are caught in the garbage masher. Note Chewbacca perched out of water's reach on the ledge.

↑ The garbage masher room was probably photographed after filming wrapped on that set (note the dianoga tentacle lying on the floor), on Stage 4, mid June.

SET	ALDERAAN GARBAGE ROOM
DETAIL	PLAN & ELEVATIONS
DRG. NO.	153
DATE	FEBRUARY 23 1976
DRAWN BY	PETER SHIELDS

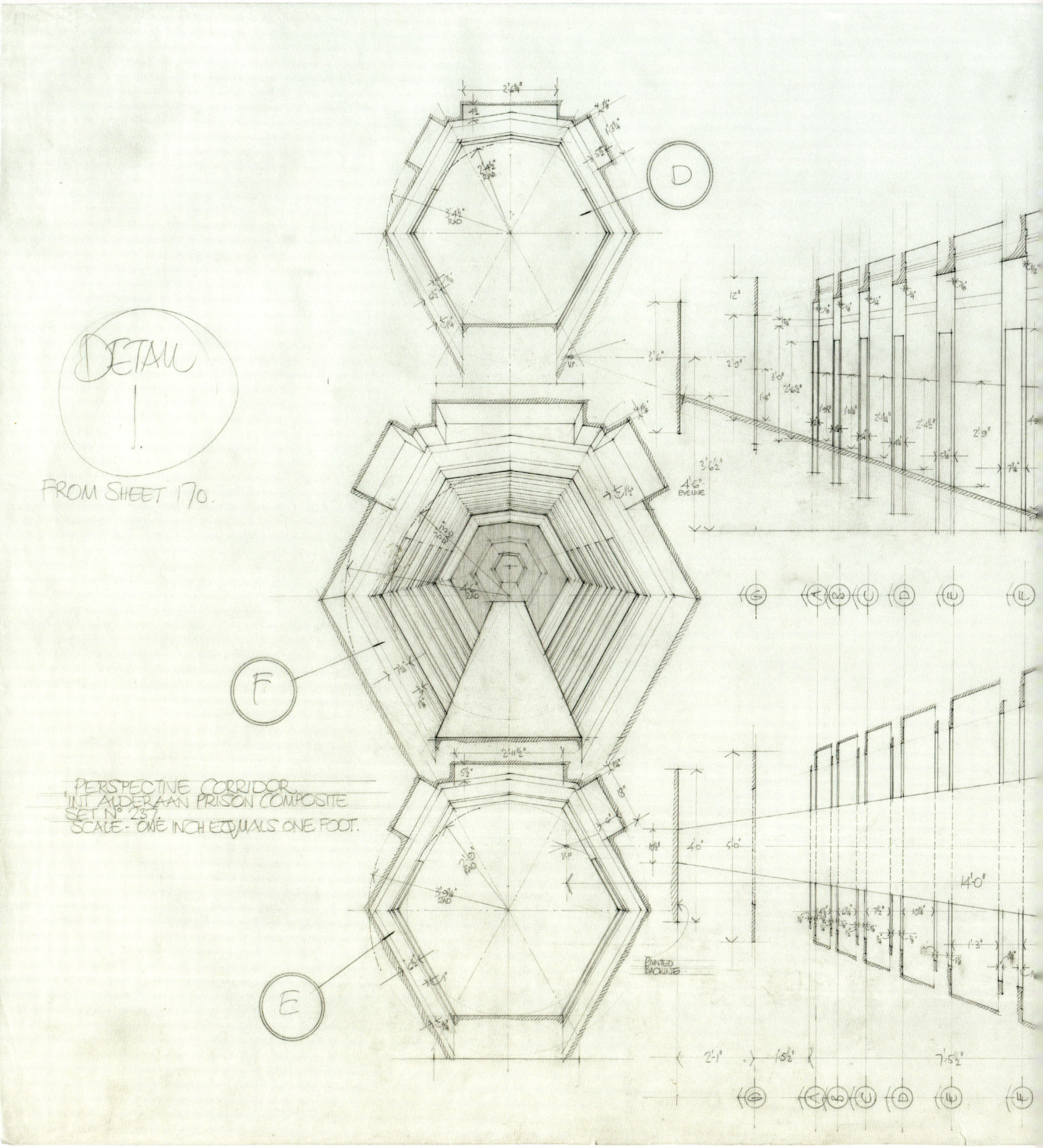

DETAIL
1

FROM SHEET 170.

D

F

E

PERSPECTIVE CORRIDOR.
'INT ALDERAAN PRISON COMPOSITE
SET N° 237'
SCALE · ONE INCH EQUALS ONE FOOT.

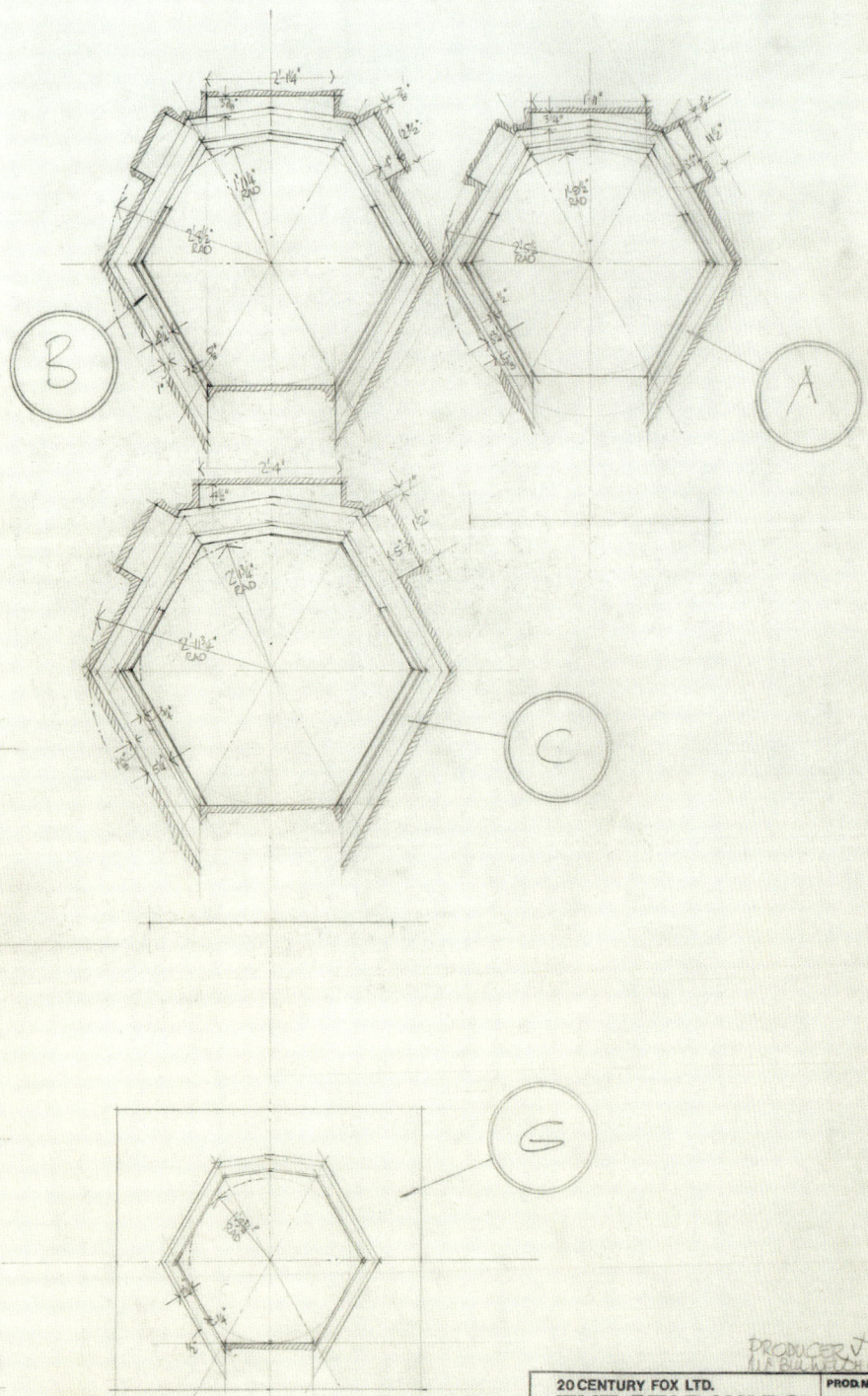

SET   PRISON COMPOSITE
DETAIL   PERSPECTIVE PIECE
DRG. NO.   169
DATE   MARCH 1 1976
DRAWN BY   REG BREAM

POWER TRENCH

The power trench set was used for two short but key scenes on the Death Star: Ben switching off the tractor beam, along with Luke and Leia's swing across the chasm. In both cases, the chasm floor was in reality only a few feet below the actors, hence a note on one of the blueprints to prepare for a "high camera tilt down for matte shot lift sequence." ILM would add the matte painting of the chasm in postproduction.

The seemingly massive center "cores" that hang over the trench when Luke and Leia make their swing were revamped as the central core around which Obi-Wan sneaks to find the tractor-beam controls. The dressing for the practical control panel on the central core also had to be suited for the action of Obi-Wan throwing switches.

"You would build the set and then when they finished shooting, utilize part of that same set into another set, which would be changed and painted and seen from a different angle," Reynolds said. "One could be made into another very economically."

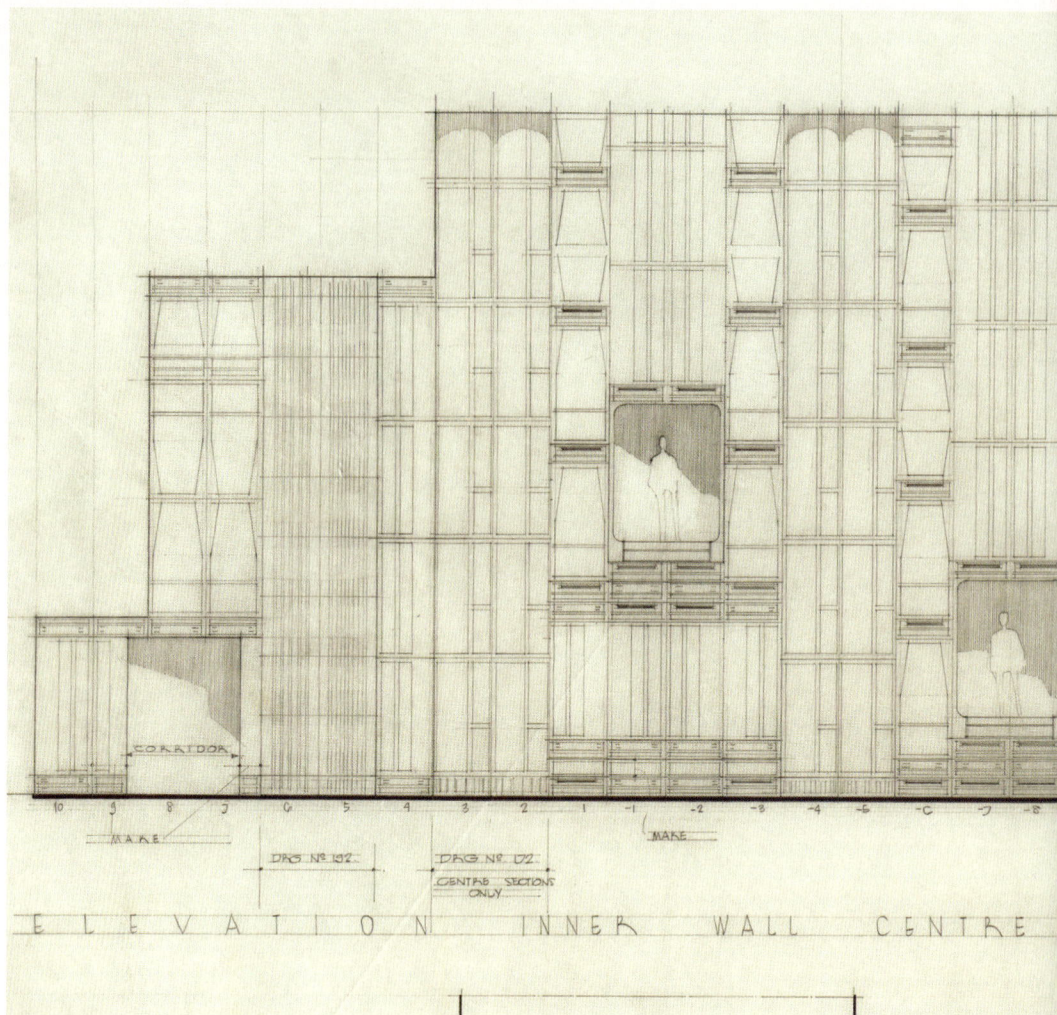

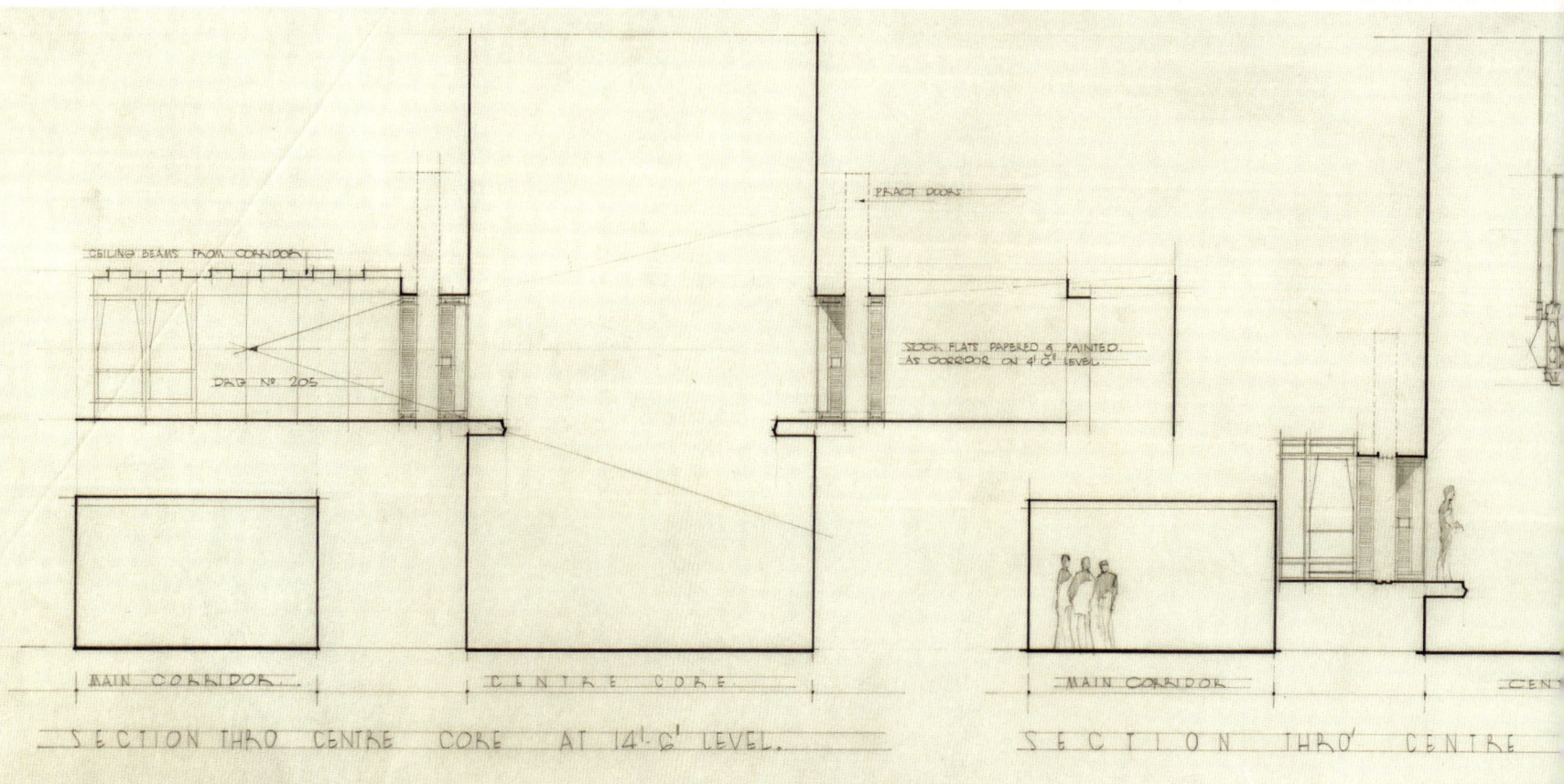

← The Death Star set is prepared for filming.

↑ A single Death Star set was built on Stage 2. It was first used for Luke and Leia's swing and then redressed for Obi-Wan's scene in which he turns off the tractor beam.

↑ Luke and Leia make their dramatic swing to safety with the hanging cores (no. 229) in plain view. Much of the Death Star set was constructed with pieces created by an outside fabricator found by Reynolds, who injected a mixture of fiberglass and resin into concrete molds. This technique allowed the sets to be completed on time.

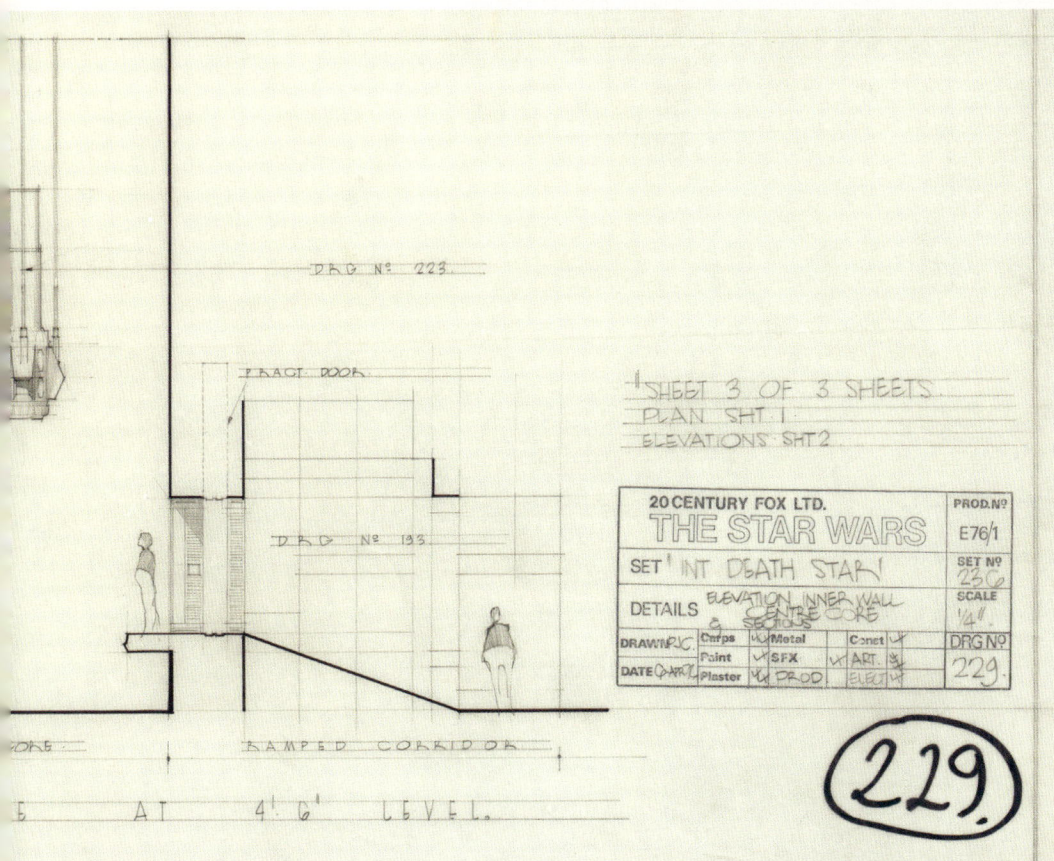

SET	DEATH STAR
DETAIL	PLAN & ELEVATIONS, CENTER CORE & CORRIDOR (ABOVE LEFT AND LEFT)
DRG. NO.	229
DATE	MARCH 2 1976
DRAWN BY	PETER J. CHILDS

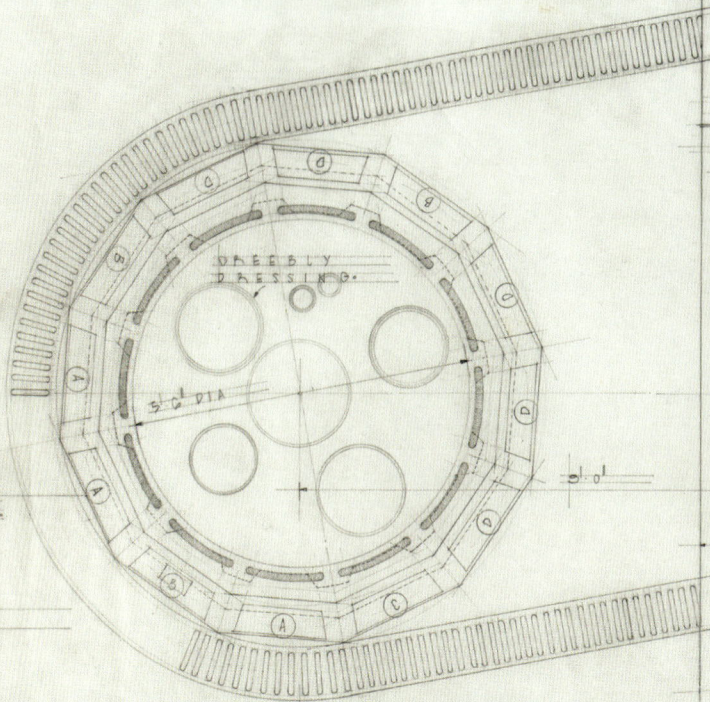

WEEBLY
DRESSING·

PANEL TYPES
SEE SECTIONS·

P L A N ·

5' WIDE
BRIDGE

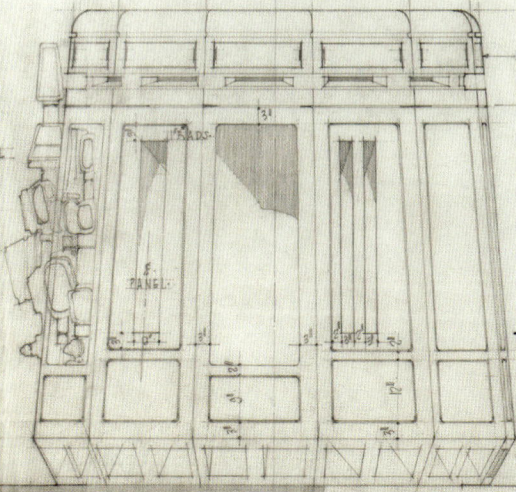

NOTE:
DETAILS OF VERTICAL
OVERHEAD HANGING
GENERATORS TO
FOLLOW·

SEE P⁵ DETAIL

DIM⁵ SHOWN ARE TRUE
FACE DIM⁵

LOWER GENERATOR

SEE P⁵
DETAIL·

BRIDGE
AT 4' 6" LEVEL·

MAKE FROM
EXTRACTOR UNITS
DOUBLE MODULE
(DRG N° 173)

E L E V A T I O N

SET	POWER TRENCH (REVAMP CENTER CORE)
DETAIL	LOWER GENERATOR
DRG. NO.	255
DATE	APRIL 23 1976
DRAWN BY	PETER J. CHILDS

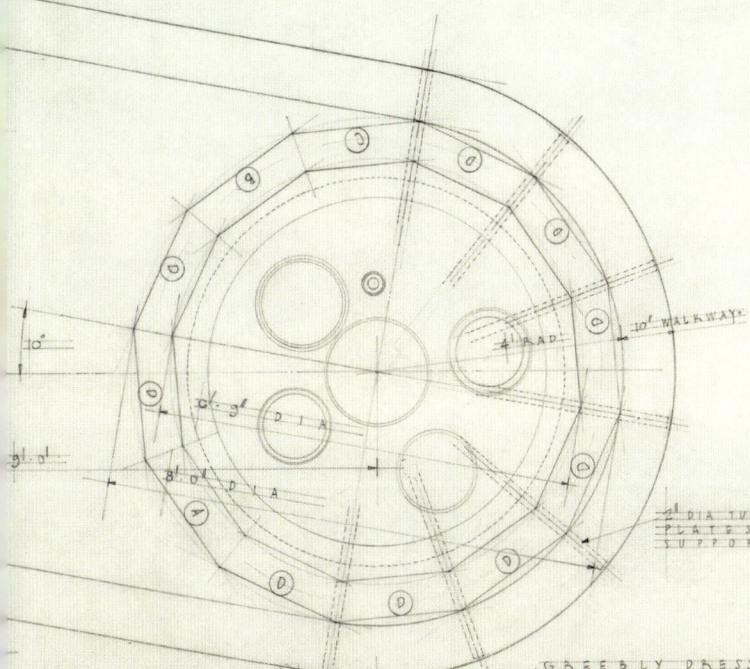

4" DIA TUBES WITH WELDED
PLATES. WALKWAY
SUPPORTS TO DETAIL.

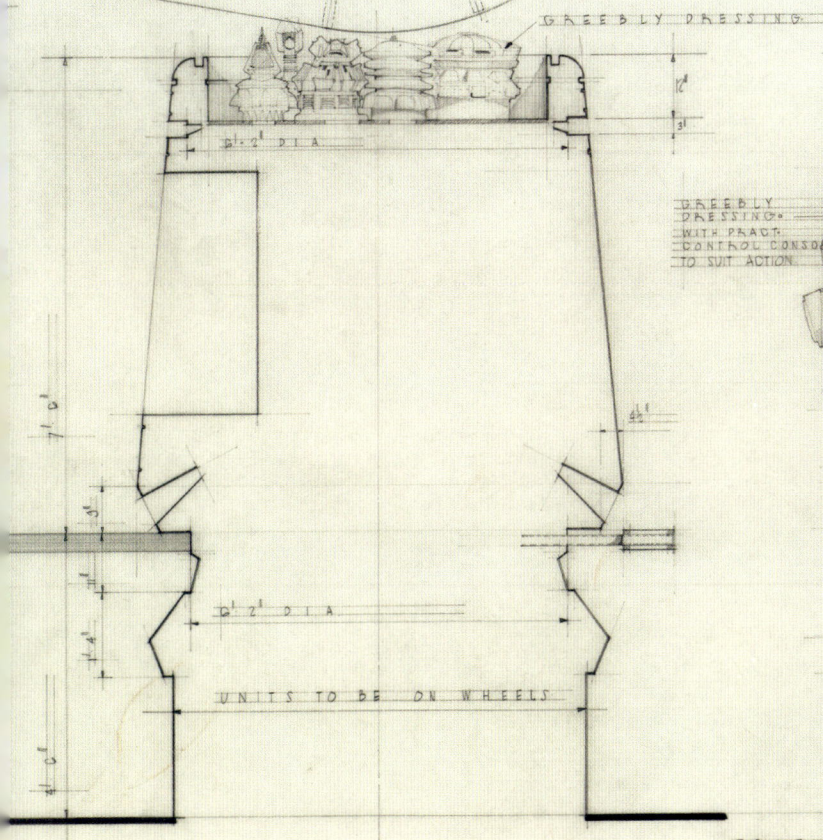

10' WALKWAY.

GREEBLY DRESSING.

GREEBLY
DRESSING.
WITH PRACT.
CONTROL CONSOLE
TO SUIT ACTION.

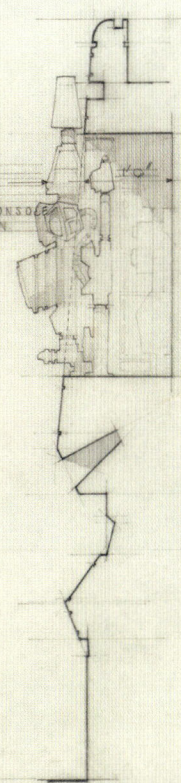

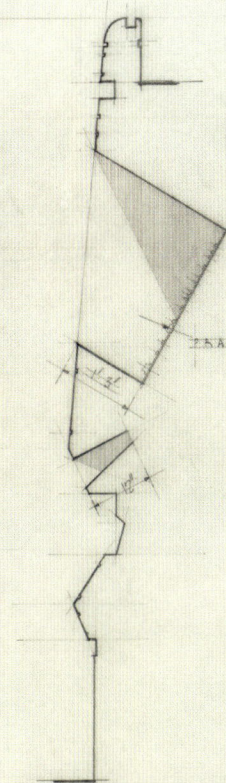

PRACT. LIGHTS.

UNITS TO BE ON WHEELS.

SECTION THRO
PANEL TYPE 'A'

SECTION THRO
PANEL TYPE 'B'
SECTION THRO PANEL
TYPE 'C' SIMILAR
PANEL TYPE 'D' AS
B&C. BUT PLAIN PANELS
ONLY.

20 CENTURY FOX LTD.			PROD. N°
THE STAR WARS			E76/1
SET INT POWER TRENCH (Revamp Centre Core)			SET N° 251
DETAILS LOWER GENERATOR DETAIL			SCALE 1"
DRAWN PJO	Corps	Metal	DRG N°
	Paint	SPX	AAS
DATE 23.4.76	Plaster		255

255

X-WING FIGHTER

At ILM, the early method was for Joe Johnston to do conceptual artwork of the vehicles. Then once Lucas had approved all the aspects of a particular spaceship, such as the X-wing, it would be handed over to Steve Gawley for orthographic drawings. Then the ILM model shop—headed by Grant McCune—would tackle its three dimensions. Finally, one of the resultant models and all of its corresponding orthographic drawings would be sent to the Elstree art department, which would generate its own technical drawings.

Then the process would reverse in postproduction, with the UK sending ILM photo reference of the actual sets (because of this back-and-forth and because they were reused on subsequent films and either modified or lost in the shuffle, blueprints of some key ships for Episode IV are missing from the Archives).

A core group of ILM had graduated from Cal State Long Beach (which Steven Spielberg also attended): Steve Gawley, Joe Johnston, and Lorne Peterson. "Steve and Joe were classmates and I was not," said Peterson. "I was like four or three years ahead of them. So when Joe got the job at ILM, a month later he brought Steve in. Joe was better at the concept drawings and Steve was better at the drafting, so he did those things."

Gawley's very early drawings show several views of the X-wing and its "pod for electric wing motor"; the R2 "bump location"; landing gear; and the electric wing motor location. At this point, it was envisioned that the model, and possibly the practical set, would have a motor to open and close the starfighter's S-foils into and out of attack position. Later, it was decided to build the life-sized cockpit with the S-foils permanently in the open position (which has created some continuity problems in the film—the S-foils are open before the order is given to open them).

Once in the UK, the starfighters took on additional life, as cockpits and exteriors—as much set as Lucas would need to sell his vision to the audience—were planned, built, and dressed. The art department's practical X-wing and Y-wing were dressed not at Elstree Studios, but at Shepperton Studios, whose huge H Stage was necessary to house the rebel's secret hangar and the Throne Room. Elstree lacked the space. Only one X-wing was actually built; the rest were either painted backdrops or a matte painting completed later at ILM. A cockpit for close-ups was constructed on Stage 8.

"Other people did the actual full-sized mockup of the X-fighter, but I was involved with the cockpit part of that," said Ambrose. "We dressed it up, me and Harry Lange. We worked overnight at Shepperton Studios on the big silent stage there, the huge Stage H, working right through the morning. I had a caravan there with a drawing board, just so we could get it ready for the next day's shoot. I'll never forget that."

"Harry Lange's tremendous advantage is that he doesn't bother to draw things or get somebody to do it, he does it all much quicker," said Barry in 1976. "Harry did all the cockpits with all the lights and panels and things. When we started the movie, we didn't know what any of us were quite going to do, but gradually people took up areas where they were happy and the picture developed."

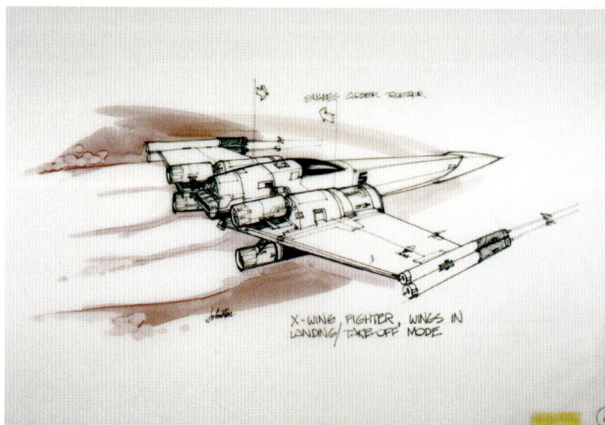

FORWARD VISUAL
COMPUM

X-WING FIGHTER, WINGS IN
LANDING/TAKE-OFF MODE

↑ Concept sketches of the X-wing by Johnston, along with the miniature, served as guides to the production art department in making the full-sized X-wing craft.

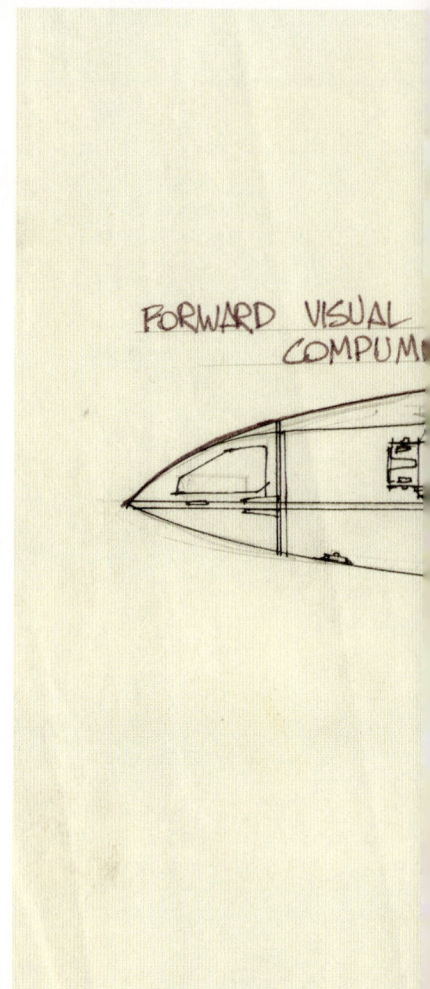

← Hamill sits in the full-sized X-wing cockpit, as drawn by Ted Ambrose and dressed by Lange, housed on Stage H at Shepperton Studios, where production moved from June 9 to 14, 1976.

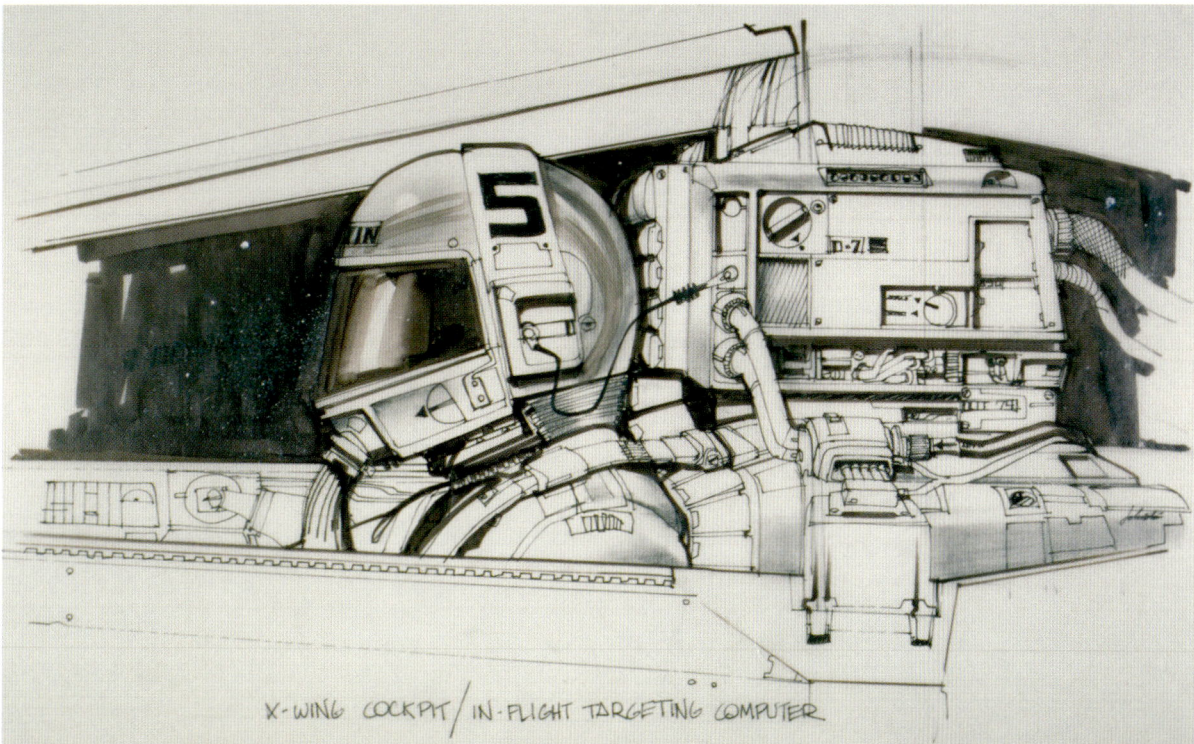

← A concept sketch by Johnston of the X-wing cockpit and targeting computer.

X-WING COCKPIT/IN-FLIGHT TARGETING COMPUTER

→ The dressed X-wing cockpit was constructed for filming close-ups of the various pilots, on Stage 8 back at Elstree Studios, late June and early July 1976.

▌ APPROXIMATE PILOT SIZE & POSITION

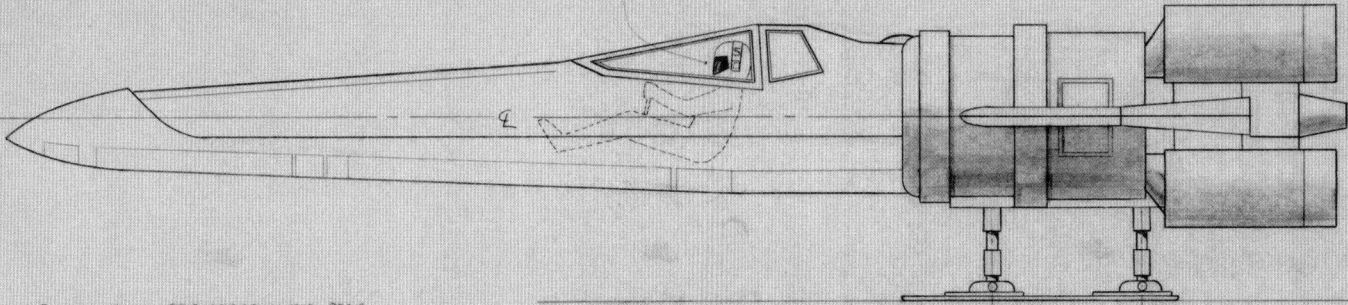

▌ X-WING — LESS LASER WING PODS

▌ APPROXIMATE 6' PILOT

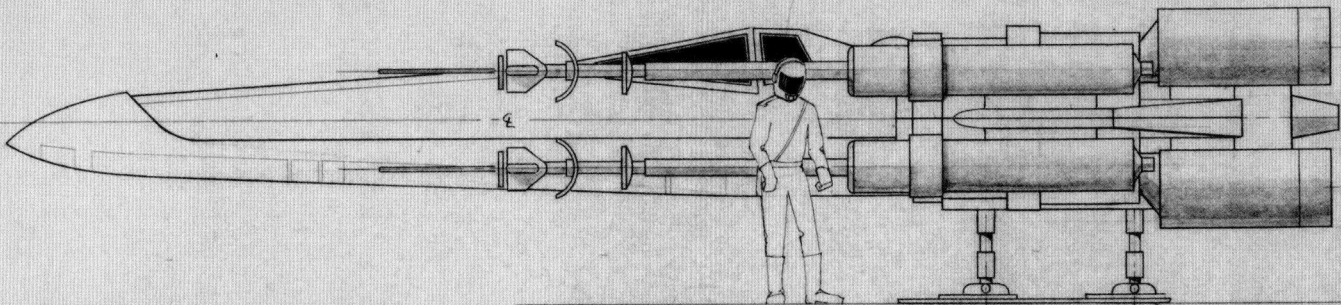

▌ X-WING — WITH LASER WING PODS

▌ APPROXIMATE LANDING GEAR LOCATION

▌ R-2 D-2 "BUMP" LOCATION

▌ X-WING — LESS ENGINES & LASER WING PODS

▌ POD FOR ELECTRIC WING MOTOR
SEE SHEET 2 FOR FRONT VIEW

X-WING

PROFILES

SET	X-WING FIGHTER
DETAIL	PROFILES
DRG. NO.	504
DATE	SEPTEMBER 3 1975,
	REVISED OCTOBER 2 1975
DRAWN BY	STEVE GAWLEY

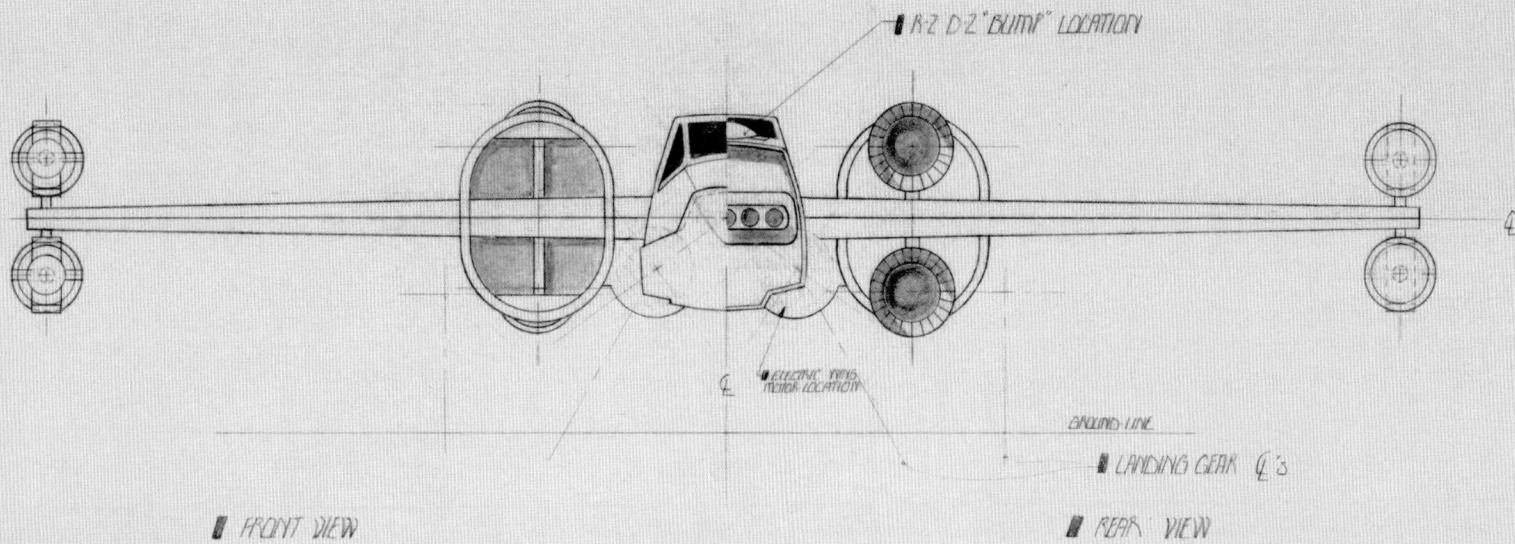

15° — 15°

FRONT VIEW   WING "EXTENDED"   REAR VIEW

R-2 D-2 "BUMP" LOCATION

ELECTRIC WING
MOTOR LOCATION

GROUND LINE

LANDING GEAR ℄'s

FRONT VIEW   REAR VIEW

SET	X-WING FIGHTER
DETAIL	RETRACTING WING — FRONT & REAR
DRG. NO.	504
DATE	SEPTEMBER 4 1975,
	REVISED OCTOBER 3 1975
DRAWN BY	STEVE GAWLEY

↓ Gawley's early Y-wing orthographic blueprint reveals a torpedo tube underneath the cockpit, as well as an aluminum central support tube used in its center engine pod. While Gawley's drawings are important records of the design process, they were not always precisely followed at ILM or overseas.

"At one time, before I got there—and this was what they originally thought had to happen—Joe would do the drawings and Steve would do these blueprints and drafting and then we would make them in the model shop," said Peterson. "Well, by the time the film got bigger and bigger, with more people, we abandoned that kind of thing and Steve didn't do the drawings much anymore. We went directly from Joe's sketches. We became a group that knew each other really well and knew everybody's talents, so we

were able to just take Joe's drawings and interpret them and not have to go through this other stage. We could make them faster this way.

"Quite frankly, I thought it was a little bit constricting to go off of the drawings," Peterson added. "It was nice to know how long it was, how high it was, and all that stuff, but these drawings aren't incredibly elaborate—not really like the English ones where they were building off the blueprints they were drawing. Eventually Steve became a model maker like the rest of us and didn't really do as much drafting upstairs."

In the UK, though they had the complete reference model, they built only about half of the practical Y-wing, leaving off one of its wings.

∎ APPROXIMATE PILOT SIZE & POSITION

∎ R2-D2 LOCATION

∎ ALUMINUM USED IN

∎ LASERS

∎ APPROXIMATE 6' PILOT

∎ TORPEDO TUBE

∎ WING LOCATION

∎ Y-WING—LESS LEFT ENGINE

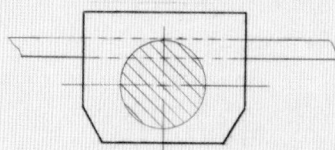

∎ SECTION A-A   ∎ SECTION B-B

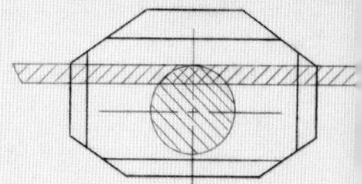

∎ SECTION C-C

ABOVE AND TOP Concept sketches of the Y-wing by Johnston paved the way for the miniature and the full-scale vehicle built at Elstree Studios.

SET	Y-WING FIGHTER
DETAIL	PROFILES
DRG. NO.	501
DATE	SEPTEMBER 8 1975
DRAWN BY	STEVE GAWLEY

ABOVE CENTER The partially complete full-sized Y-wing at Shepperton Studios.

ABOVE The model of the Y-wing built by ILM arrived at Elstree (EMI Studios) in a specially padded box (the *Star Wars* Corporation was a subsidiary of Lucasfilm).

TIE FIGHTER

Gawley's TIE fighter drawing notes that the front, top, and rear of the sphere should come off for access to the support-rod holders, but in fact the actual model became even more intricate. "The detail of the TIE fighter wing became much more delicate than this drawing is, partly because of materials that we had," said Peterson. "They came out better than any drawing."

For several reasons, despite their intimacy with the vehicle models, nobody at ILM ever flew over to England to interface with the art department. "I know George didn't want any effects people over there," said Dennis Muren. "Because they would have told George what he could and couldn't do. And he didn't think that was necessarily true, that we were all too rigid in our old ways of working. George wanted to be free to imagine

the way the movie would be in his mind, not whether somebody said yes or no.

"And it's true," Muren added "Some of my friends were traditional Hollywood effects people and they had all these rules: Lock the camera down; if you have to duplicate the film, it'll look terrible; always try to use an original negative; and others. These were the rules and George didn't buy those. Not that he didn't believe that there would be an artifact of some sort if you broke those rules, but he was more interested in the energy of the shot. He felt it'd be okay if there was a little technical blemish here or there—if it had the right energy."

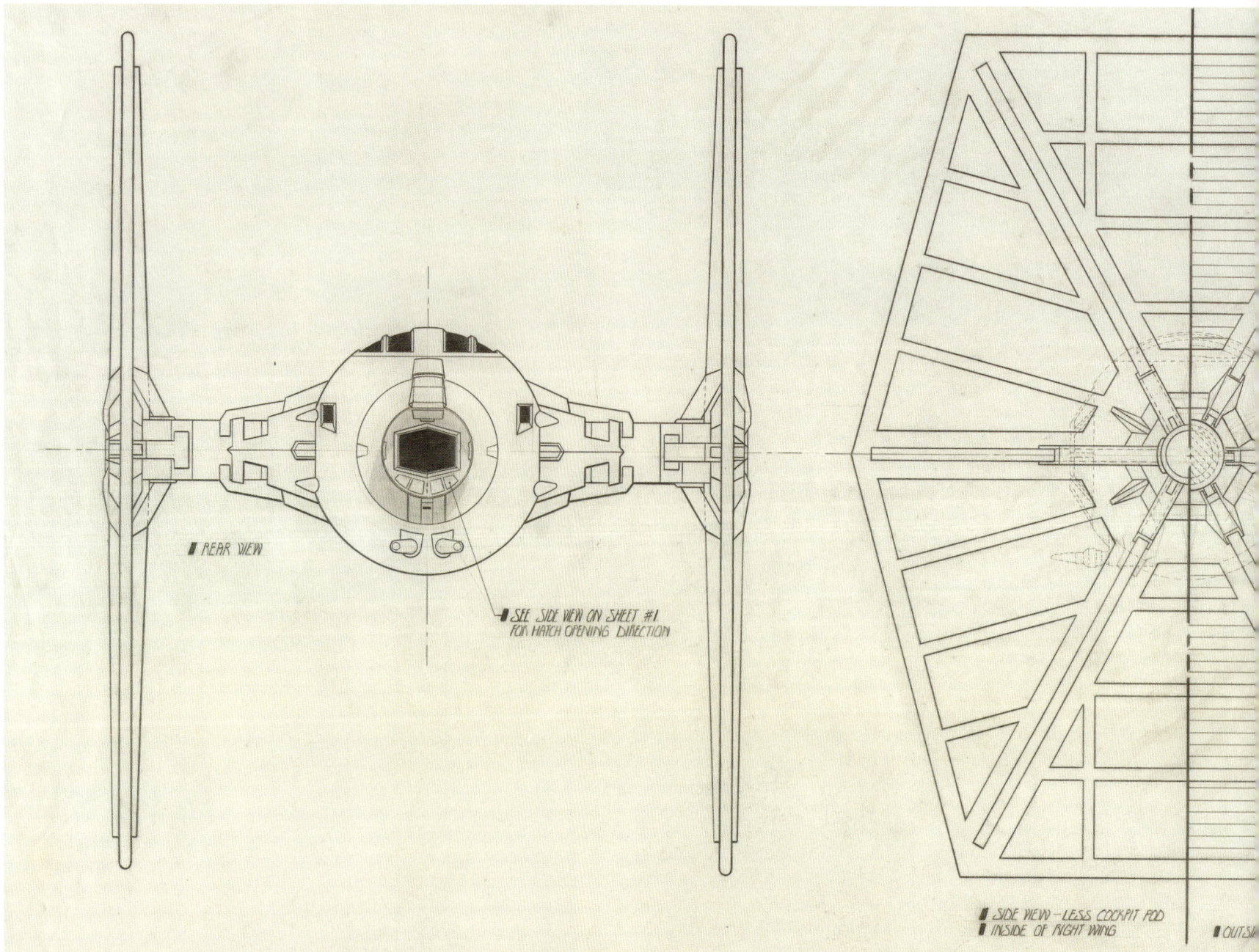

REAR VIEW

SEE SIDE VIEW ON SHEET #1.
FOR HATCH OPENING DIRECTION

SIDE VIEW—LESS COCKPIT POD
INSIDE OF RIGHT WING   OUTSI

ELEVATION EE

ELEVATION FF

↑ One of the few blueprints of starfighters to survive from the first *Star Wars* is Shields' TIE cockpit exterior. Following Gawley's drawing for the model, based on Cantwell's concept, its window has a spoke in the noon position—ironically, the one element that would change. Once on set, the spoke was rotated slightly by Lucas so he could film the pilot's face.

SET	IMPERIAL TIE FIGHTER
DETAIL	PLAN & ELEVATIONS
DRG. NO.	256
DATE	APRIL 23 1976
DRAWN BY	PETER SHIELDS

↑ Although Vader was filmed in the same cockpit as the other TIE fighter pilots, in post, Lucas made the decision to give the Sith Lord an enhanced vehicle with curved wings, as seen in this final frame along with the more uniform TIE.

↑ At Elstree, the front window of the TIE fighter is seen with the strut, alas, at the noon position. That strut would be rotated, come filming, so that Lucas could film the pilots.

SET	TIE FIGHTER
DETAIL	REAR & SIDE
DRG. NO.	502
DATE	SEPTEMBER 19 1975
DRAWN BY	STEVE GAWLEY

↑ Darth Vader (David Prowse) is in the TIE fighter cockpit at Elstree on Stage 8 (with dressing courtesy of Lange).

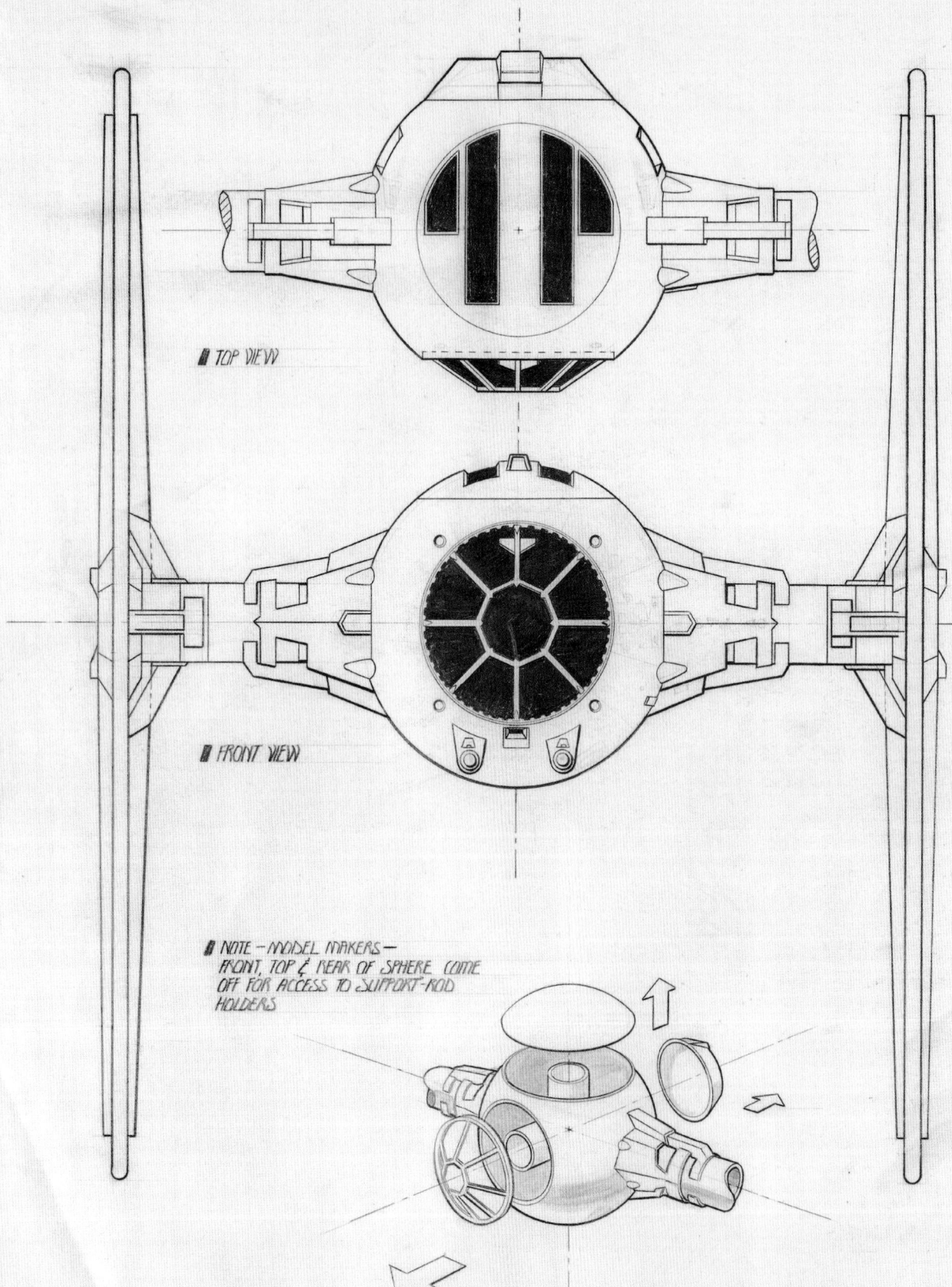

▮ *TOP VIEW*

▮ *FRONT VIEW*

▮ *APPROXIMATE PILOT SEATING LOCATION*

▮ *NOTE — MODEL MAKERS — FRONT, TOP & REAR OF SPHERE COME OFF FOR ACCESS TO SUPPORT-ROD HOLDERS*

▮ *SOLAR PANEL LOCATIONS*

ONE PIECE REAR
HATCH COVER

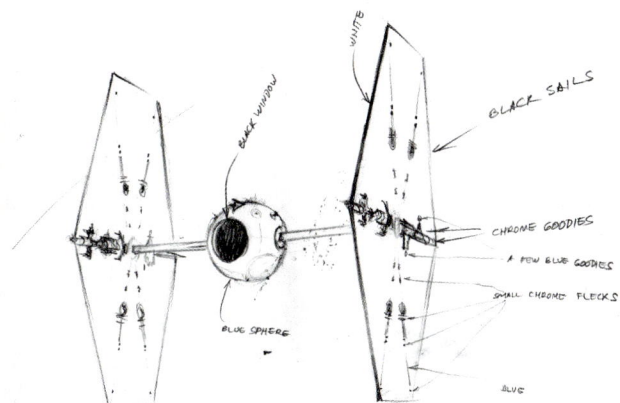

BLACK WINDOW

WHITE

BLACK SAILS

CHROME GOODIES

A FEW BLUE GOODIES

SMALL CHROME FLECKS

BLUE SPHERE

BLUE

THIS IS THE ONLY PREDOMINANTLY BLACK SPACEC
IT WILL BE STAGED AGAINST LIGHT BACKGROU

DRAWING BY COLIN CANTWELL - R·M·O/75

↑ Concept model builder Colin Cantwell sketched out the
first details of the TIE fighter in early 1975.

E VIEW—LESS LEFT WING

T.I.E. FIGHTER

SCALE: APPROVED BY: DRAWN BY GAWLEY
DATE: 18 SEP '75 REVISED

FRONT ¢ SIDE ¢ TOP

SHEET 1 OF 2 SHEETS DRAWING NUMBER 502

SET   TIE FIGHTER
DETAIL   FRONT, SIDE, & TOP
DRG. NO.   502
DATE   SEPTEMBER 18 1975
DRAWN BY   STEVE GAWLEY

THRONE ROOM

After blowing up the Death Star, Luke and Han receive medals from the Rebel Alliance, which are draped around their necks by a smiling Princess Leia. The 152-foot-long set on which this occurs was called the Throne Room and was built on H Stage at Shepperton after the hangar set was struck. The drawing indicates that "ageing" should appear on the stone surfaces, with "various corner sections to be broken away; thickness to vary from one- to three-inches." The columns were made from polystyrene sheets, while the staircase—the center of which was also to be worn from age—was cement with a stone finish.

"I had a session with George on the Throne Room, particularly, and George went back to the States and described it to Ralph, who then did the painting from the concept we knew we could handle," said Barry of the set. "Because we were building such an enormous set in such a short time, it had to be something that had those wing effects that keep disappearing, so you don't have to keep building the part round the corner, otherwise you'd just go on forever and forever building things. We changed the hangar into the palace where they get that medal in, maybe, three or four days; they were both enormous sets, but they were all on huge wheeled units, about forty feet tall, so we had trucks and sort of lugged them into place."

"The Throne Room was a very filmic set," said Reynolds. "Each column masked the area in front of it, so you never see the stage walls. As sets go, it was really simple. We then locked off the camera and moved groups of people around for one shot and then locked the camera off and moved them again to fill up the seating, to make a much bigger audience out of the handful of extras that they had. The transporting of the large set pieces wasn't a huge deal. There were some outside companies that handle that very well."

↑ For this shot, the extras were placed toward the rear; the forward crowd would be a matte painting created at ILM.

← The heroes are on the podium in a key-set photo.

← A McQuarrie illustration painted on December 5, 1975, based in part on John Barry's ideas for the set, conceptualized the final scene for the art department at Elstree.

THE JOINS SHOULD BE GIVEN APPROX 1½" IN WIDTH. THE AGEING
TO APPEAR ON THE STONEL SURFACES. VARIOUS STONEL SECTIONS
TO BE BROKEN AWAY (SEE ART DEPT).
THICKNESS TO VARY FROM 1' TOO 3'

EPILOGUE FOR A DESIGNER

At the completion of principal photography, Lucas still had around 365 visual effects shots to complete at ILM in less than a year's time; he was tired and demoralized by what had been a very, very difficult shoot. He felt he had compromised his film—and was counting on work at ILM to come through. But when he got back to the US in the summer of 1976, he discovered to his horror that they had completed only one or two shots and did not have a postproduction pipeline in place. At that time, Lucasfilm's vice president of marketing and merchandising, Charles Lippincott, interviewed Lucas on his state of mind; not long afterward, he conveyed some of Lucas' thoughts to John Barry.

"I think George has gone through these trials and tribulations for a long time," Lippincott said to Barry in their unpublished interview from 1977. "I remember when we were working in the fall [of 1975], he was very concerned about the production design because he had never worked with you. That was what he was most worried about of all the things—but when he came back, the thing that he was happiest with was the production design. We talked about it because I wanted to find out what areas he felt the happiest with and how he felt—and he said, on a rating scale, 'I would rate the production design department the highest of the whole movie.'"

SET	THRONE ROOM
DETAIL	STONE DETAIL
DRG. NO.	182
DATE	SPRING 1976
DRAWN BY	UNKNOWN

ICE CORRIDORS & CAVE

Ted Ambrose's technical drawing of the ice corridors contains several notes for scenes that were either not shot or which didn't make the final cut. In the shooting script, not only do the rebels have to deal with the Empire's attack on their secret base, they are also attacked by wampa ice monsters. On the blueprint, the wampas are called "Yuzzem," which were in fact different creatures (which didn't make it into the film). Sometimes the names of exotic beasts were inadvertently mixed up.

Ambrose noted on the technical drawing, "Hand of Yuzzem breaks through wall of this section of corridor…Yuzzem to break through dotted area." In the ensuing battle, wampas were to damage the *Falcon*, hence its engine problems throughout the story. But when it came to actual filming, the wampa costume was so unwieldy that the actor inside, Des Webb, could barely extend his arms. Breaking down walls was pretty much out of the question.

"The major problem was the snow creature being nine or ten feet tall," said Brian Johnson, visual effects supervisor. "The operative's arms are only half the length of the snow creature's, so, in effect, he's trying to propel force from the elbows; he couldn't actually push the wall himself. In the end, we pulled the bottom of the wall out, but you're just at the mercy of how the wall breaks up."

The corridor was to be dressed by Michael Ford with practical lights, pipes, and cable dressing. Detail three consists of a forced perspective ramp.

SET	ICE CORRIDORS & CAVE
DETAIL	ELEVATIONS
DRG. NO.	137
DATE	DECEMBER 5 1978
DRAWN BY	TED AMBROSE

→ Inside the wampa costume, Des Webb takes a break on location in Norway.

↑ Production designer Norman Reynolds's concept drawing of the ice corridor from September 1978.

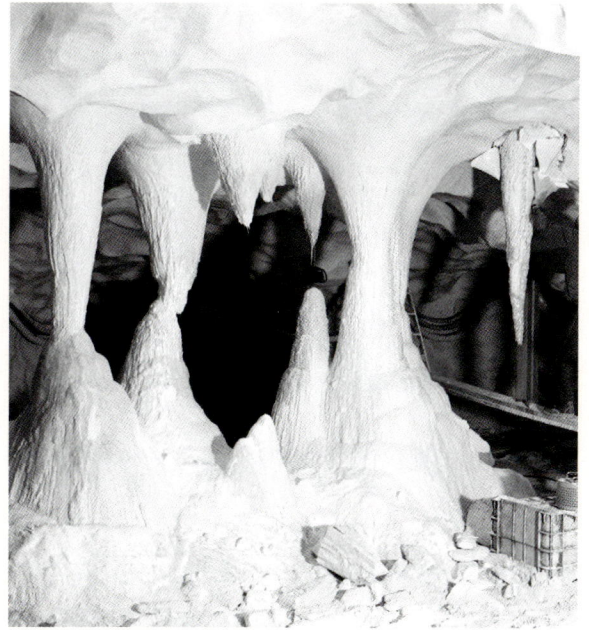

TOP AND ABOVE The ice corridor technical drawings instructed construction to create a stalactite alcove off the ice corridor set on Stage 1, where a tauntaun wounded by attacking wampas would be examined. These scenes were abridged in the final film.

↑ Detail of an ice corridor corner illustrates the minute workmanship that went into the sets of The Empire Strikes Back.

→ Lit and unlit, the forced perspective ice corridor was built on Stage 1 at Elstree Studios and shot in late March 1979. The dressing of the corridor—the cables and wire that snake along the walls—may have been inspired by photographs of the Maginot Line: the underground complex built by the French along their border with Germany after World War I.

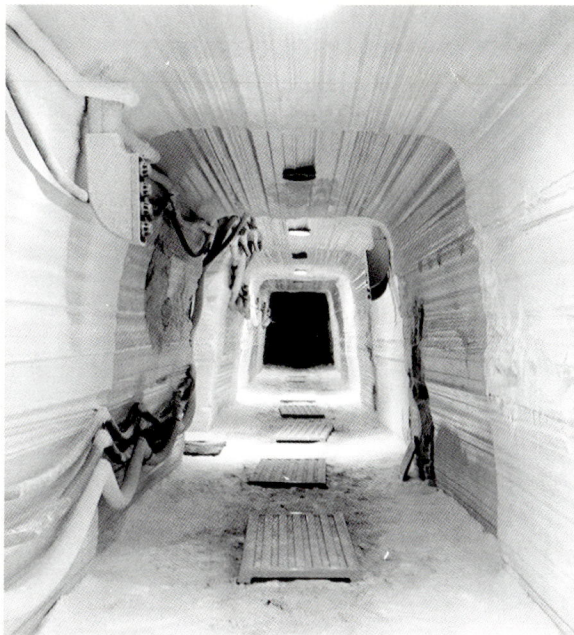

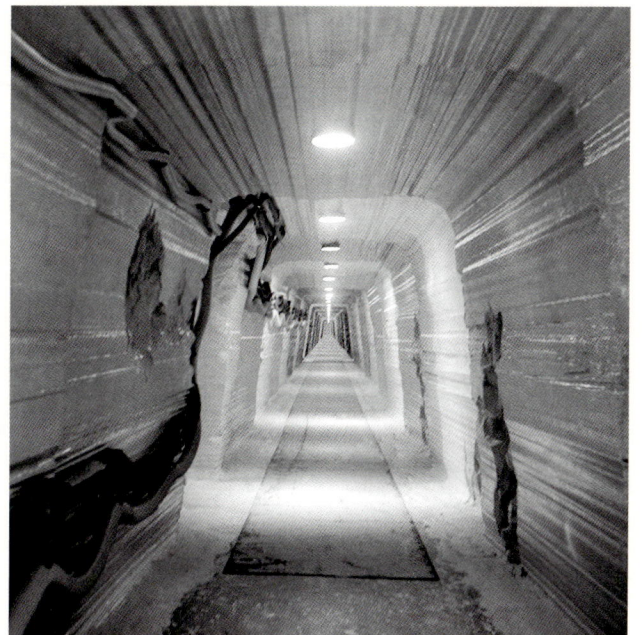

REBEL BASE

A truly fantastic technical drawing (no. 36 on page 82) of the rebel base's main hangar deck is a large central section flanked on all four sides by details. The bottom portion indicates the ice cave entrance, with areas of laser-cut ice face broken away; a purpose-made gantry with working lights; and another laser-cut ice corridor leading to the medical and control centers. The top portion is devoted mostly to cutout X-wings (*Empire* had three full-scale fighters).

The main drawing shows a "random shaped aperture" at 38 feet above the stage floor. Cave access conveniently coincided with stage doors, so crew could enter and exit without smashing through walls. To accent the set's forced perspective, second unit director Barry actually dressed up children in flight gear and placed them in key positions. When the camera was rolling, they would appear as adults in an artificially enlarged space.

"I thought we would never finish that hangar, actually," said Reynolds. "I remember how daunting it was, really, to arrive at that stage thinking, *Not only do we have to build these walls and make a set of it, but we also have to fill it up with material.* And the amount of material that we put in there was just a huge, huge undertaking—and it was all done while other things were being made ready on other sets. It doesn't look it in this drawing, but there was so much in there, so many speeders and so much dressing and stuff on the floor, apart from the *Falcon* and the X-wings and all that. Even now I have a bit of a sinking feeling when I look at it. But at the time I felt a little bit reassured because John Barry was doing the second unit. So I felt like there was this kindred spirit there who wouldn't bring anything too nasty on me."

In fact, before filming began in the hangar, as the set was being dressed—and despite being housed in the newly completed, immense *Star Wars* Stage—it became painfully self-evident that production still didn't have

enough room. The *Falcon* was taking up more space than anyone had anticipated. The solution was to tack on additional walls to provide approximately 60 more feet in length.

"It was a 'carry on' moment, really, because it became apparent that we needed something more," said Reynolds. "We'd used up all the space inside the stage. It was just ridiculous. So we actually kept the doors open, built some backing pieces, and enclosed the opening beyond the stage doors, sort of like a lean-to, in order to put the scenic backing in there."

When filming did begin on the hangar, production was even more behind schedule. This time the solution became to shoot in one area while construction continued in another area, the noise of which made Carrie Fisher quite uneasy when she was trying to perform. Moreover, given the time crunch, two units were almost always working simultaneously on the same set, which was big enough to accommodate two crews simultaneously.

"So it was just a nightmare, in the nicest possible way," Reynolds concluded. "I say 'nice' because when it's all over and it's all in the can, then it's wonderful. I suppose that's the motivation that makes you do the job in the first place: at the end of the day, there is a reward for all your labor."

↓ Crew work feverishly on the rebel base, right down to the hanging of fake icicles, as production slipped behind schedule.

↓ McQuarrie conceptualized the walls and atmosphere of the massive rebel base in several paintings during preproduction and production.

SET	MAIN HANGAR DECK
DETAIL	SECTIONS CC & DD
DRG. NO.	93
DATE	NOVEMBER 9 1978
DRAWN BY	MICHAEL LAMONT

← Reference photography of the rebel base maquette.

↓ A unique panorama reveals the fantastic set as it was built by the art and construction departments.

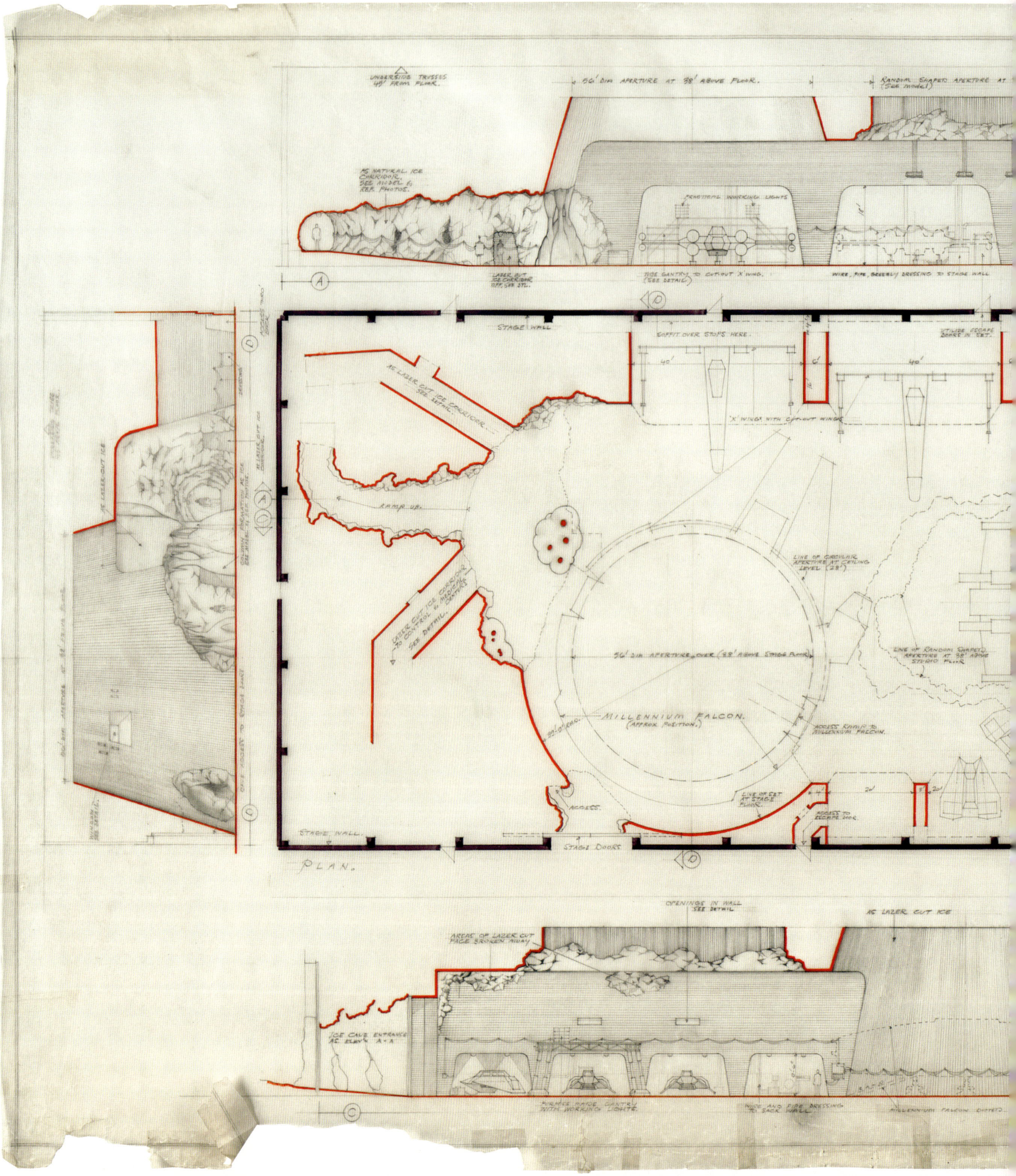

UNDERSIDE TRUSSES 49' FROM FLOOR.

56' DIA APERTURE AT 38' ABOVE FLOOR.

RANDOM SHAPED APERTURE AT (SEE MODEL)

AS NATURAL ICE CORRIDOR. SEE MODEL & SEE PHOTOS.

PERIMETAL WORKING LIGHTS

LASER CUT ICE CORRIDOR 10FT. SEE DTL.

ICE GANTRY TO CUTOUT X WING. (SEE DETAIL)

WIRE, PIPE, GENERAL DRESSING TO STAGE WALL

STAGE WALL

SOFFIT OVER STOPS HERE.

STAGE ESCAPE DOORS IN SET.

AS LASER CUT ICE CORRIDOR SEE DETAIL.

40'

40'

X WINGS WITH CUTOUT WINGS

RAMP UP.

LINE OF CIRCULAR APERTURE AT CEILING LEVEL (28')

AREAS CUT TO CORRIDOR TO CONTROL & MEDICAL CENTRE.

56' DIA APERTURE OVER (28' ABOVE STAGE FLOOR)

LINE OF RANDOM SHAPED APERTURE AT 38' ABOVE STUDIO FLOOR

MILLENNIUM FALCON. (APPROX. POSITION.)

ACCESS RAMP TO MILLENNIUM FALCON.

LINE OF CUT AT STAGE FLOOR.

ACCESS.

20'

20'

ACCESS TO ESCAPE DOOR.

STAGE WALL

STAGE DOORS

PLAN.

OPENINGS IN WALL SEE DETAIL.

AS LAZER CUT ICE

AREAS OF LAZER CUT FACE BROKEN AWAY.

ICE CAVE ENTRANCE AS ELEVN. A-A.

PERMICE RANGE CONTROL WITH WORKING LIGHTS

WIRE AND PIPE DRESSING TO BACK WALL.

MILLENNIUM FALCON OUTLINE

STAR WARS 'EPISODE II' THE EMPIRE STRIKES BACK

SET	MAIN HANGAR DECK
DETAIL	PLANS & ELEVATIONS
DRG. NO.	36
DATE	SEPTEMBER 22 1978
DRAWN BY	MICHAEL LAMONT

SET	MAIN HANGAR DECK
DETAIL	GANTRY DETAIL (DRESSING)
DRG. NO.	131
DATE	NOVEMBER 30 1978
DRAWN BY	MICHAEL LAMONT

SET	MAIN HANGAR DECK
DETAIL	X-WING
DRG. NO.	N/A
DATE	FALL 1978
DRAWN BY	MICHAEL LAMONT

↑ On the final set, the repair gantry faithfully mirrors the technical drawing, no. 131.

METAL ARMATURE FOR MODEL SNOW LIZZARD

← A very early drawing in the Archives was a one-off, meaning only one full-sized snow lizard, or tauntaun, would be built. The drawing diagrammed the front elevation of the creature's arms and legs. Based on stop-motion animator Phil Tippett's approved concept, the tauntaun had to be constructed early on and tested before being shipped out to Finse, Norway, for filming in the bitter cold.

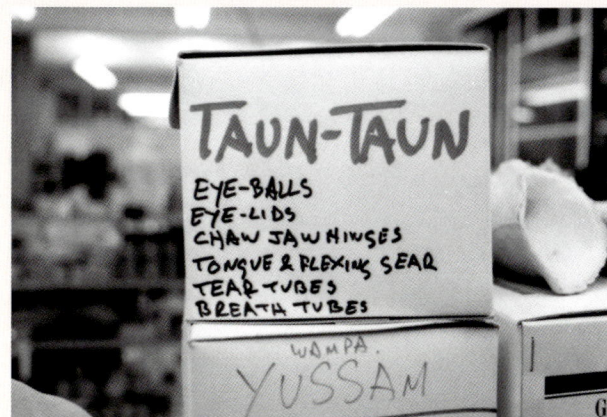

SET	MODEL SNOW LIZARD
DETAIL	METAL ARMATURE
DRG. NO.	03
DATE	JULY 20 1978
DRAWN BY	STEVE COOPER

TAUN-TAUN
EYE-BALLS
EYE-LIDS
CHAW JAW HINGES
TONGUE & FLEXING SEAR
TEAR TUBES
BREATH TUBES
WAMPA.
YUSSAM

↑ In the art department at Elstree, notes on a box list some key tauntaun parts. (The box underneath continues the confusion between "wampas" and "yussam.")

← On set, the full-sized tauntaun is filmed.

↑ An art department maquette of the rebel hangar is complete with cutouts for people, craft, and the tauntaun.

REMEMBERING JOHN BARRY

Les Dilley recalls several stories about the late John Barry, some of which are new and some of which lend yet another dimension to what's already been told. Early in Barry's career, during the location shoot for *Kelly's Heroes*, a young runner would often talk to the production designer.

"The future director John Landis was eighteen or nineteen years old, and he was a runner," said Dilley. "And he became very good friends with John and showed him a script and asked John if he would do it. John said, 'Well, I don't think I'll do it. But if you get your film financed and you come to England to make it, call Norman and ask him or Les Dilley to do it.'

"And that's exactly what happened. John Landis did come to England with it some ten years later and asked Norman. Norman was working, but I was finishing on a job, so he said, 'Can I meet you?' And I said, 'Certainly.'" The film turned out to be *An American Werewolf in London* (1981).

Norman Reynolds recalled that Barry was dumbfounded one day while working with Stanley Kubrick on *A Clockwork Orange*. They were on an apartment set and, although the fridge would remain closed throughout the scene, Kubrick insisted that Barry fill it with food props that the character would've stocked. "They had a bit of a falling out as a result of that," Reynolds said.

Dilley also recalled that one of Barry's problems on *Saturn 3* was the different direction that Kirk Douglas wanted for the film. "Kirk Douglas was a superstar and he was trying to turn the script into something that John didn't like," Dilley said. "On the other hand, it probably was Kirk Douglas' name that got the film made in the first place. But that's where the falling out came and Kirk Douglas had the power to have John removed."

What Dilley remembered the most about Barry is his intelligence and humor. "John was a brilliant man. He was articulate, he spoke two or three languages fluently, and he had a disarming way with words," said Dilley. "Even Gary Kurtz, at John's funeral, said that about John. He could just strip apart any subject you were talking about."

MEDICAL CENTER

After being attacked and mauled by a hungry wampa, Luke escapes from the ice creature's cave. With the help of Han Solo, he returns to the rebel base, where he is placed in a bacta tank to heal his wounds. "Up until that time I'd been sort of a trainee, if you like," said draftsperson Michael Boone. "And so I wasn't allowed to draw a set. So I think the Medical Center is probably one of the first full sets that I was responsible for."

Built on Stage 1, the Medical Center set had sliding glass doors, a bunk, and a floating wall for camera placement. Its centerpiece was a tank containing 400 gallons of chlorinated water, which British Aerospace, a company experienced in the manufacturing of Perspex cockpits for pressurized aircraft, had helped design; at 7 feet, 6 inches high and 3 feet, 8 inches in diameter, the tank was the largest of its kind ever made. (In 1960, Vickers-Armstrong's Limited merged with The Bristol Aeroplane Company, English Electric, and Hunting Aircraft to form the British Aircraft Corporation, or British Aerospace.)

"Oh, that tube, there's a story there," Boone remembered. "I actually persuaded Vickers, the aircraft company at Weybridge, to make that for us. I visited them and told them what we wanted, and they formed that tube in two halves over a cylinder and welded it together. I don't know how, but they did it per our specs and it was a great success."

Boone was eventually able to visit the set during filming and saw Hamill submerged. But he didn't see the more dangerous moment. "We had a large transparent tube in one of our sets, with a liquid inside it, within which Luke Skywalker was to be suspended," said Peter Suschitzky, director of photography. "My idea was that the tube should be the major source of illumination and the rest of the set should be lit very low-key. Problem: How to get a lot of light into a small tube with liquid in it? I solved this by using an army searchlight on the studio floor with a mirror suspended above the set. This all worked very well, photographically, for a few days until, for some inexplicable reason, the heat from the searchlight shattered the mirror above the set—not once, but twice!"

Huge slivers of glass sliced into the water—had Hamill been in the tank at the time, it might have been the end for him.

STARWARS
"THE EMPIRE STRIKES BACK"

INT. MEDICAL CENTER
SCALE ¼" = 1'-0"

SET	MEDICAL CENTER
DETAIL	LAYOUT
DRG. NO.	N/A
DATE	WINTER 1978
DRAWN BY	STEVE COOPER

INT MEDICAL CENTER.

→ A Reynolds concept sketch of the Medical Center interior from August 1978.

SW/E 13

SWEC 91348

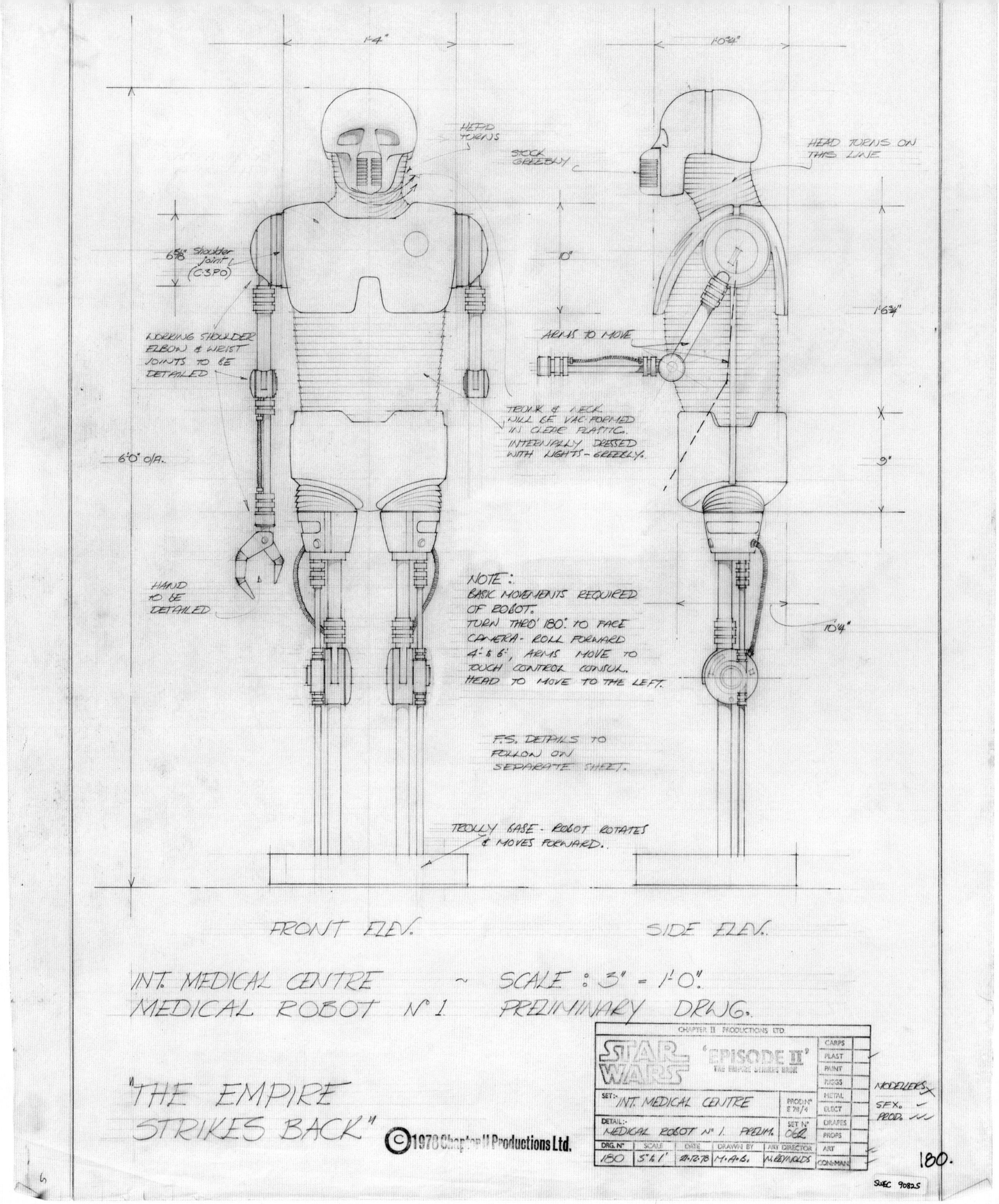

FRONT ELEV.   SIDE ELEV.

INT. MEDICAL CENTRE   ~   SCALE : 3" = 1'0".
MEDICAL ROBOT Nº 1   PRELIMINARY DRWG.

"THE EMPIRE
STRIKES BACK"   © 1978 Chapter II Productions Ltd.

Labels on drawing:
- HEAD TURNS
- STOCK GREEBLY
- HEAD TURNS ON THIS LINE
- 6⅝" Shoulder joint L (C3PO)
- WORKING SHOULDER ELBOW & WRIST JOINTS TO BE DETAILED
- 6'0" O/A.
- HAND TO BE DETAILED
- ARMS TO MOVE
- TRUNK & NECK WILL BE VAC-FORMED IN CLEAR PLASTIC. INTERNALLY DRESSED WITH LIGHTS-GREEBLY.
- NOTE: BASIC MOVEMENTS REQUIRED OF ROBOT. TURN THRO' 180°: TO FACE CAMERA - ROLL FORWARD 4'-6', ARMS MOVE TO TOUCH CONTROL CONSUL. HEAD TO MOVE TO THE LEFT.
- F.S. DETAILS TO FOLLOW ON SEPARATE SHEET.
- TROLLY BASE - ROBOT ROTATES & MOVES FORWARD.

SET	MEDICAL CENTER
DETAIL	MEDICAL ROBOT, NO. 1, PRELIMINARY
DRG. NO.	180
DATE	DECEMBER 21 1978
DRAWN BY	MICHAEL BOONE

↑ The notes on Boone's blueprint of the medical droid were essential to the modelers: "Basic movements required of robot: turn through 180 degrees to face camera; [able to] roll forward 4 to 6 feet; arms move to touch control console; head to move to the left; on trolley base, robot rotates and moves forward; mouth is stock greebly; working shoulder, elbow, and wrist joints to be detailed [in additional blueprints]; trunk and neck will be vac-formed in clear plastic; dressed with lights," and so on.

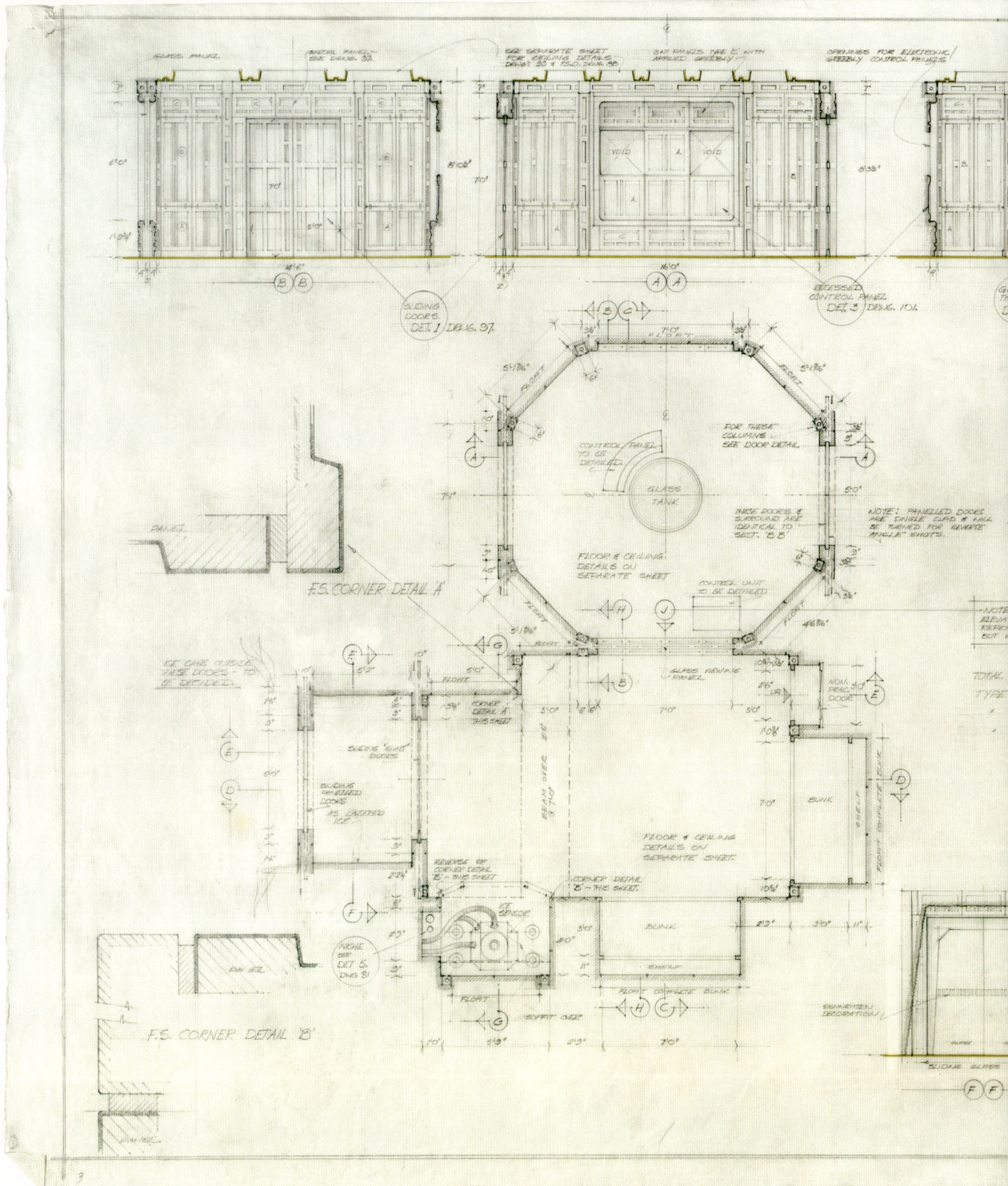

SET	MEDICAL CENTER	DATE	NOVEMBER 3 1978
DETAIL	PLANS & ELEVATIONS	DRAWN BY	MICHAEL BOONE
DRG. NO.	96		

"THE EMPIRE STRIKES BACK"
INT. MEDICAL CENTRE
1/2" SCALE PLAN & ELEVATIONS

GLASS VIEWING PANEL TO PIVOT

PANELLED 'CUPBOARDS' SEE BUNK DETAIL

POSTS & WALL PLATE DET. 2

FRONT FACE OF SHELF SEPARATELY

6'8"

5'0"

2'5 5/8"

14'6"

11"

12'3"

C C

SINGLE DOOR SURROUND DET. 5 DRWG. 98.

BUNKS DET. 6 DRWG. 98.

2'6"

FOR SLOTTED POSTS & WALL PLATE - SEE DET. 2 DWG. 65

BUNK SOFFIT - USE TYPE C PANELS. SEE BUNK DETAIL.

BEAM

FLOAT

LAZERED ICE

7'0"

ICE CAVE IN THIS AREA TO BE DECIDED.

11"

3'0"

D D

ICE SENSOR DET. 7

BEAM DET. 8 DRWG. 99.

IS A MIRRORED REFLECTION 'AA' OR GLASS VIEWING PANEL

ASSORTED LIGHTS & GREEBLY DRESSING TO PANELLED REVEALS

LS REQUIRED :-
76.
8.
68.

7'0"

LAZERED ICE

SLIDING PANELLED DOORS AS DETAIL 1. DRWG 37. (SINGLE CLAD)

SINGLE DOOR REVEAL DET. 5 DRWG. 98.

6'6"

1'6"

E E

NICHE SEE DET. 5 DWG 81.

SLIDING GLASS DOORS DET. 10.

FOR SLOTTED POSTS & WALL PLATE SEE DET. 2. DWG Nº 65

TYPE C PANELS —

GLASS VIEWING PANEL DET. 9 DRWG. 102.

SLIP PANELS

SOFFIT LEVEL

BUNK SOFFIT OF TYPE C PANELS SEE BUNK DETAIL

REVERSE SIDE OF BEAM TO MATCH IN SLIP PANEL SEE DRWG Nº 99.

7'0"

7'0"

USE PART 4 PANELS SEE BEAM DETAIL DRWG Nº 99.

USE PART A PANELS

SLIDING GLASS DOORS

SLIP PANEL

G G

H H

96

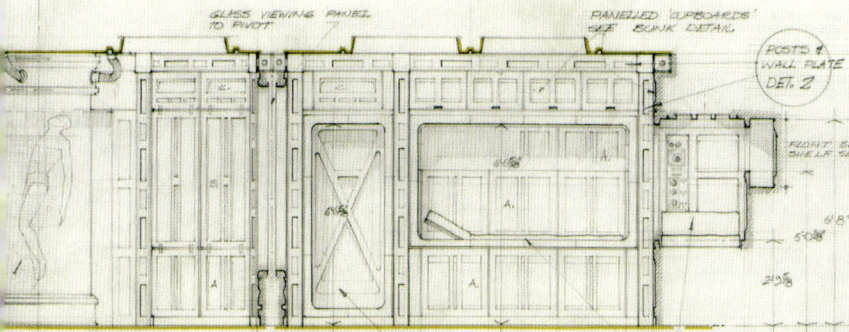

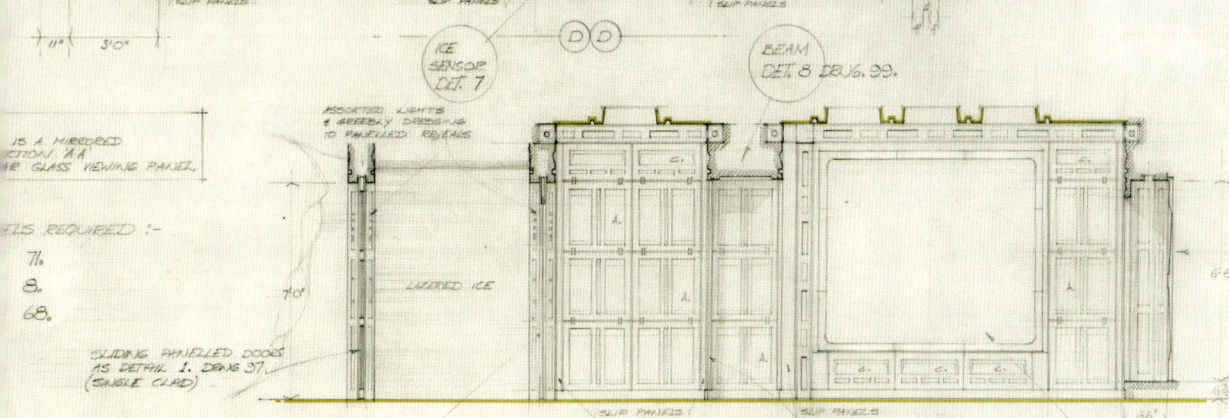

COMMAND CENTER

The rebel command center was another key room in their secret base on Hoth. According to the technical drawing, the set was to be dressed with a "weave of pipe and cable." Floating "power blocks" would allow camera placement, and the studio floor would be covered with an ice finish.

To gather information on what large amounts of ice look like in the real world, Reynolds took the train to Jungfraujoch, Switzerland. "I visited these ice caverns to see if I could get a feeling from them and I certainly did get the feeling," he said. "But to actually achieve what I saw was almost impossible. So when I got back, we experimented with Styrofoam and wax and melted fiberglass, all sorts of things; we were trying out salt and marble dust…Ultimately a combination of all those things was used to achieve the results we needed.

"That was the first time any of the construction people, the plasterers, and any of us had been involved with snow and icy sets like that."

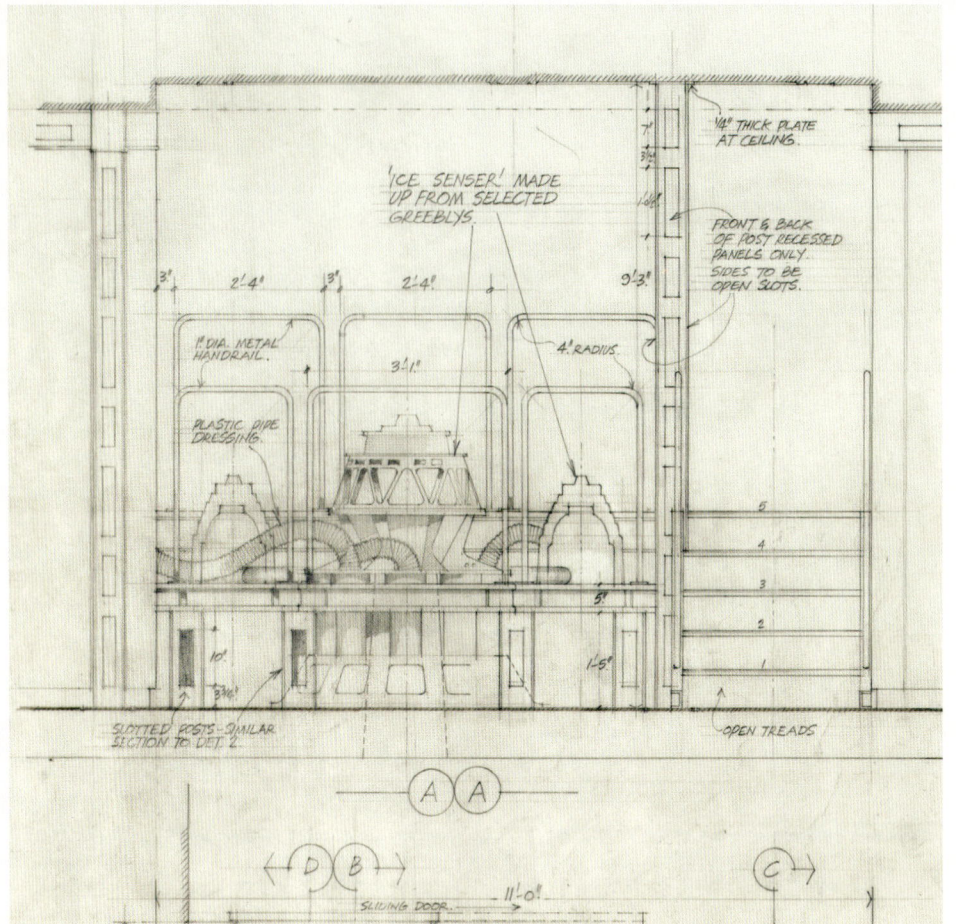

↑ A McQuarrie production illustration of the Command Center from May 1978.

↑ An on-set photograph reveals details of the set dressing of the Command Center, built on Stage 1 at Elstree, where scenes were shot in late March 1979.

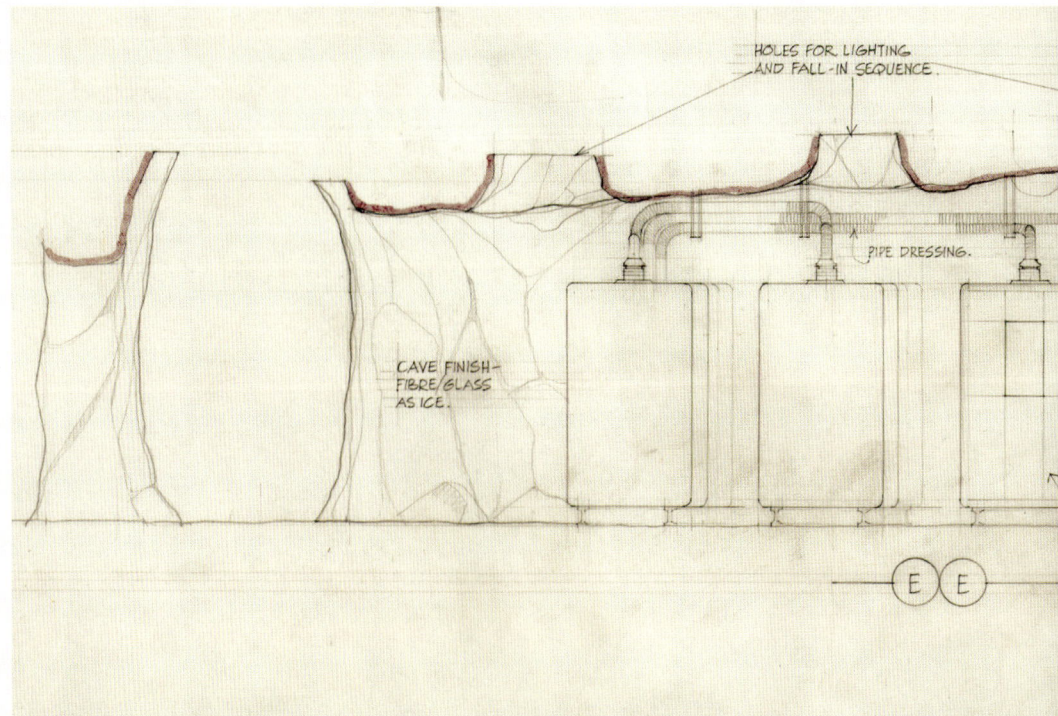

SET	COMMAND CENTER
DETAIL	ICE SENSOR, STEPS, & LANDING
DRG. NO.	122
DATE	NOVEMBER 27 1978
DRAWN BY	TED AMBROSE

INT. ICE CORRIDORS—COMMAND CENTRE—MEDICAL CENTRE COMPOSITE.

SET	ICE CAVE & CORRIDORS, LAYOUT
DETAIL	STAGE 1 PLAN
DRG. NO.	136
DATE	DECEMBER 1 1978
DRAWN BY	TED AMBROSE

↑ Another blueprint of the rebel base indicates where the wampas were to attack, revealing the relation of the Medical and Command Centers to an "island" of stalactites and stalagmites. The latter location is where Solo finds a dead tauntaun being tended to in the final film, the victim of a wampa attack.

SET	COMMAND CENTER
DETAIL	ELEVATIONS
DRG. NO.	64
DATE	NOVEMBER 1 1978
DRAWN BY	TED AMBROSE

MILLENNIUM FALCON

Very early in preproduction, Marcon Fabrications Ltd. contacted the *Empire* production office and pointed out that its facility—with hangar doors that were 160 feet wide and with 60-odd feet clearance to the eaves—was big enough for the recreation of the *Millennium Falcon*. For this film, Solo's pirate ship was to be constructed full-sized, but the metal armature job was so enormous that it had to be farmed out.

Consequently, a year after work had begun, Norman Reynolds, Bill Welch, and Alan Tomkins, "boarded a tiny Cherokee plane at the Elstree airfield to fly to Pembrokeshire to see the *Falcon* being constructed." According to unit publicist Alan Arnold, who joined them, "it was a bitterly cold morning." Marcon was a firm of maritime engineers in Wales, 260 miles west of London. Upon arriving at Pembroke Docks, the *Empire* crew examined the 23-ton prop. Talk in the town pub was that Marcon was building a genuine spaceship, perhaps because the company, about a decade before, had made the iconic centrifuge for *2001*.

"I did fly down once, but the overriding thought in my mind was actually coming back in this small plane, because I thought we wouldn't make it there to begin with," remembered Reynolds. "I really thought the game was up, because we were losing height and being buffeted around in that little plane. I remember thinking, *Well, I'm not going to finish* Empire *after all*."

The *Falcon* had to be reconstructed and redrawn in part based on little clips of 35mm film. Because no one had anticipated the success of *Star Wars*, the previous ship had not been properly photographed and catalogued, and the actual set had been left out in the rain for months until it had wasted away to almost nothing. Indeed, Dawking's blueprint (no. 166A on page 94) instructs other departments to recreate the craft's battle damage using photo reference; he also asks for greeblies in the recesses, while shaded areas generally indicated basic cladding beneath applied paneling.

"We had little pieces of film for some parts," Tomkins said. "It was virtually trying to see the way the top of the set worked and how all the buttons and panels joined together into the angle, things like that."

↑ The metal infrastructure for the full-sized *Falcon* exterior was constructed by Marcon Fabrications Ltd.

↑ The exterior hull and dressing are added to the *Falcon* by the construction and art departments.

→ The ramp was typical *Star Wars* construction, making use of greeblies, a recycled practical telescopic tube, applied rubber strips, false hinges, and so on. On *Empire*, the *Falcon* and its ramp would remain stationary while several sets would go up and be torn down around it: the rebel hangar, the space worm "stomach," and the Cloud City landing platform.

SET	*MILLENNIUM FALCON*
DETAIL	RAMP & DOCKING BAY
DRG. NO.	156
DATE	DECEMBER 13 1978
DRAWN BY	RICHARD J. DAWKING

SECTION AA : THRO

PLAN - BOTTOM CHORD E-E SCALE:- 1:20
TIMBER SUPPORT BRACKET DETAILS SIMILAR TO TOP CHORD,
BUT HANDED ABOUT ₵ SPACESHIP.

ONE-OFF FRAME AS DRAWN — MARKED FR 16 FOR ERECTION

↑ This early blueprint was generated by the art department for Marcon's welded construction of the spaceship's internal metal frame. Of course, this was a "one-off frame as drawn for full-scale *Falcon*."

SET	MILLENNIUM FALCON
DETAIL	DETAILS FRAME, FR. 16
DRG. NO.	UNKNOWN
DATE	SEPTEMBER 20 1978
DRAWN BY	RHH/GED

SIDE ELEVATION : RAMP CLOSED :

SIDE ELEVATION : RAMP OPEN :

PART ELEVATION : CLOSED POSITION :

DOCKING BAY ELEVATION :

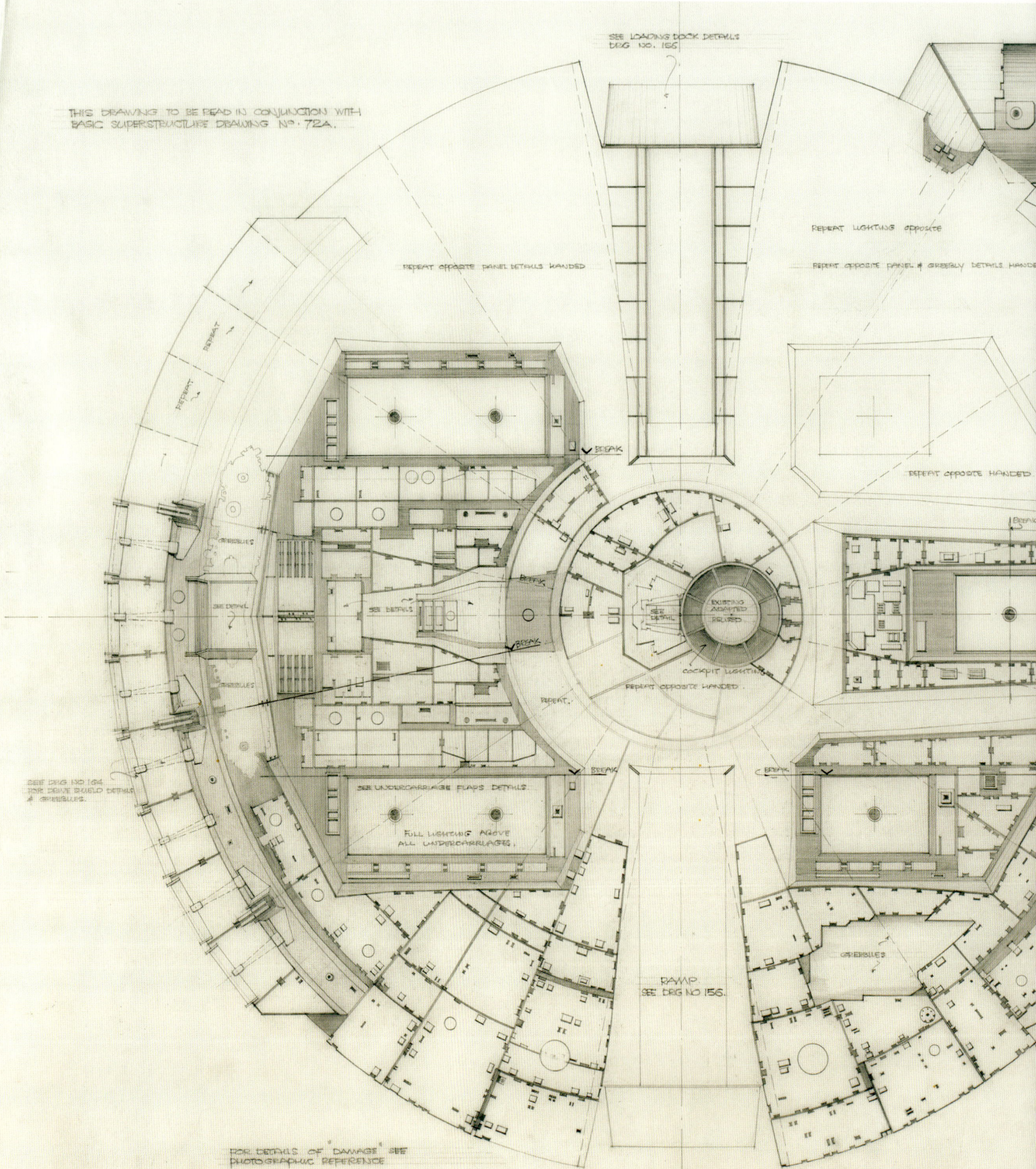

SEE LOADING DOCK DETAILS
DRG NO. 156

THIS DRAWING TO BE READ IN CONJUNCTION WITH
BASIC SUPERSTRUCTURE DRAWING Nº 72A

REPEAT LIGHTING OPPOSITE

REPEAT OPPOSITE PANEL DETAILS HANDED

REPEAT OPPOSITE PANEL & GREEBLY DETAILS HANDED

REPEAT OPPOSITE HANDED

REPEAT

REPEAT

GREEBLIES

SEE DETAIL

SEE DETAILS

BREAK

BREAK

BREAK

EXISTING
ADAPTED
REUSED

SEE
DETAIL

COCKPIT LIGHTING

REPEAT OPPOSITE HANDED

GREEBLIES

REPEAT

BREAK

BREAK

BREAK

SEE DRG NO 164
FOR DEEIL RELD DETAILS
& GREEBLIES.

SEE UNDERCARRIAGE FLAPS DETAILS

FULL LIGHTING ABOVE
ALL UNDERCARRIAGES.

GREEBLIES

RAMP.
SEE DRG NO 156.

FOR DETAILS OF DAMAGE SEE
PHOTOGRAPHIC REFERENCE

LIGHTING INSIDE COCKPIT.

SEE COCKPIT DETAILS.

SHADED AREAS GENERALLY INDICATE
BASIC CLADDING BENEATH APPLIED PANELLING.

©1978 Chapter II Productions Ltd.

FOR DETAILS OF GREEBLIES REFER TO
RELEVANT PHOTOGRAPHIC REFERENCE

REPEAT OPPOSITE MANDIBLE OUTRIGGER

SEE PANEL & GREEBLY DETAILS
WITHIN PROW SECTIONS

LIGHTING INSIDE PROW

LIGHTING TO BE AGREED.

SEE DETAILS OF ADDITIONAL DRESSING

LIGHTING TO BE AGREED.

GREEBLIES IN BOXES

GREEBLIES IN PROPS

GREEBLIES IN PROPS

LIGHTING : USE COLOURED PRINT

USE 1000 WATT QUARTZ FLOODS.

ALL LIGHTING POSITIONS TO BE SEPARATELY
WIRED & TO HAVE DIMMERS FITTED

○ SINGLE UNIT

○ 4 LAMP UNIT.

LAMPS SET IN 6" FROM CLAD FACE
& HOUSED IN ASBESTOS PIPES.

UNDERSIDE PANELLING :
PLAN LOOKING UP :

REVISION A. LIGHTING POSITIONS ADDED. 30.3.79. RJD.

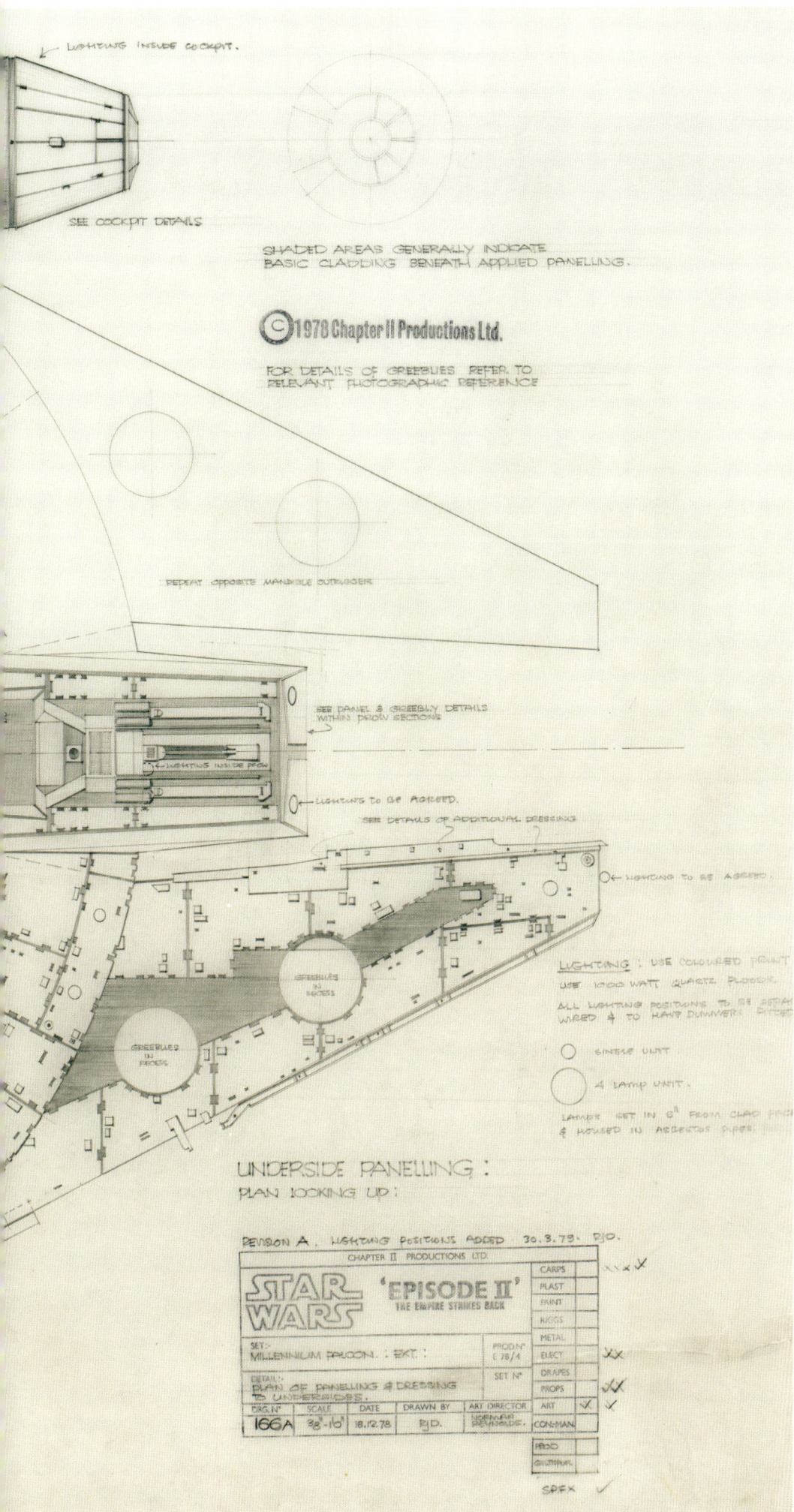

↑ The Elstree art department had to match the detailed underside of the ILM *Falcon* model when preparing the technical drawings.

SET	*MILLENNIUM FALCON*
DETAIL	PLAN OF PANELING & DRESSING TO UNDERSIDES
DRG. NO.	166A
DATE	DECEMBER 18 1978
DRAWN BY	RICHARD J. DAWKING

INT. MILLENIUM FALCON HOLD.

REVISED SEAT UNIT. READ WITH DRWG'S 16 & 17.

CHAPTER II PRODUCTIONS LTD.

STAR WARS 'EPISODE II' THE EMPIRE STRIKES BACK

CARPS	
PLAST	
PAINT	
RIGGS	
METAL	
ELECT	
DRAPES	
PROPS	
ART	
CONST MAN	

SET: INT. MILLENIUM FALCON HOLD.   PROD Nº E.78/4
DETAIL: REVISED SEAT LAYOUT.   SET Nº
DRG. Nº 24   SCALE 1"-1'0"   DATE 5 SEPT.   DRAWN BY AL.T.   ART DIRECTOR N. REYNOLDS

© 1978 Chapter II Productions Ltd.

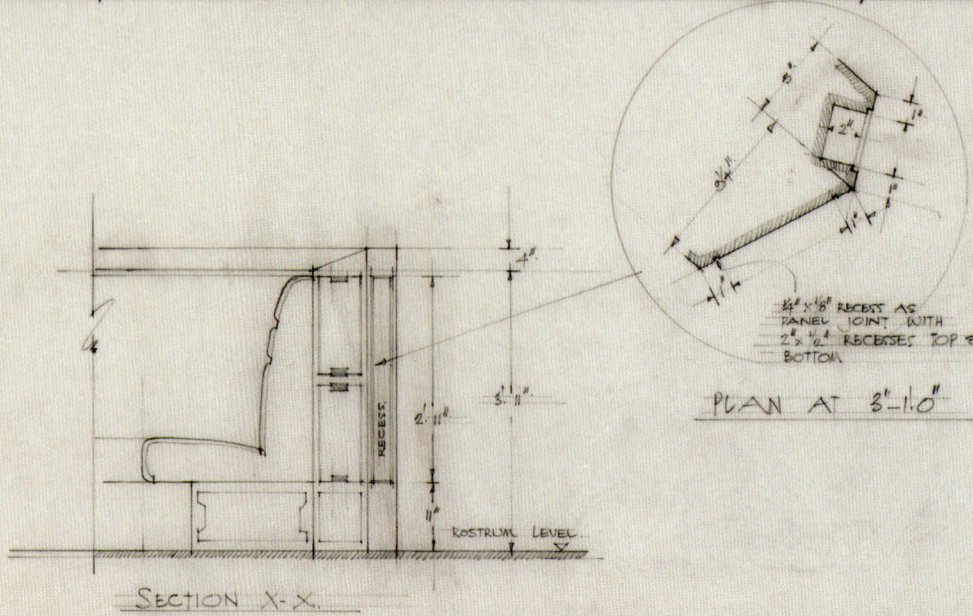

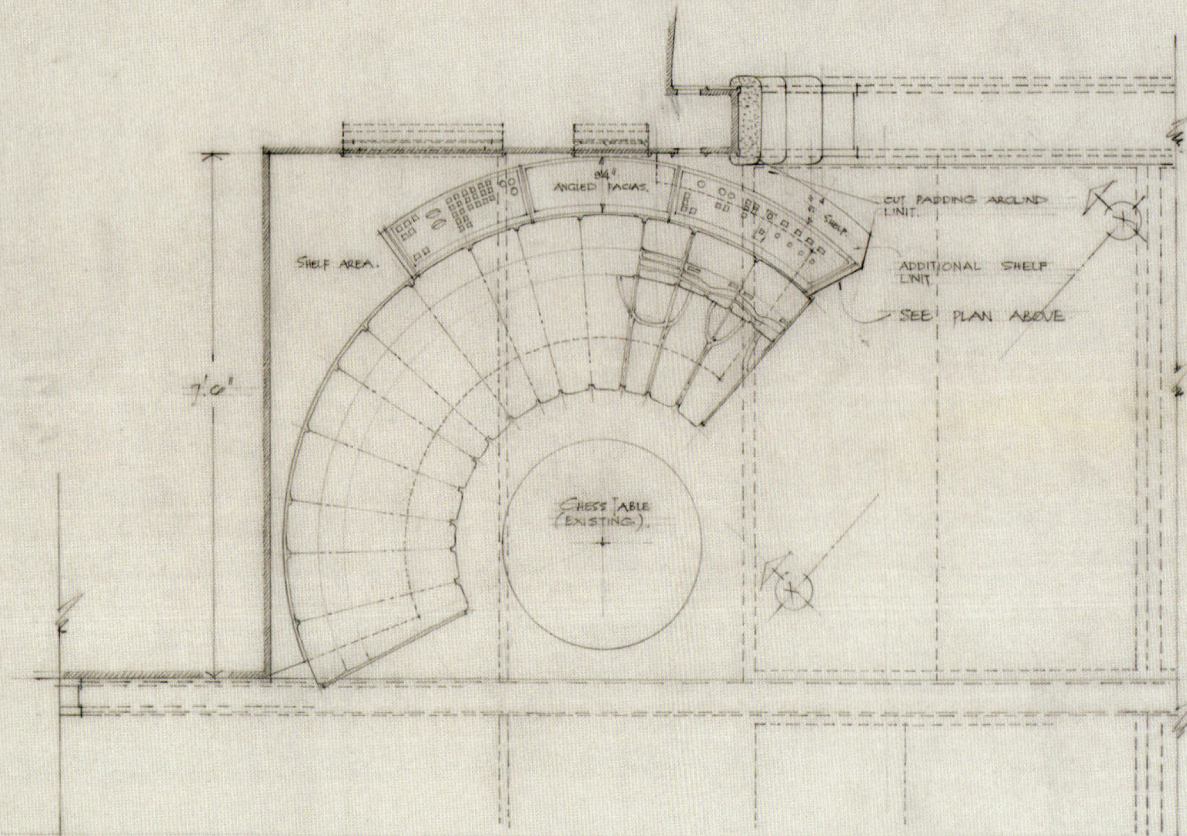

½" x 6" RECESS AS PANEL JOINT WITH 2" x ½" RECESSES TOP & BOTTOM

PLAN AT 3'-1.0"

SECTION X-X.

SHELF AREA.

ANGLED FACIAS.

CUT PADDING AROUND UNIT.

ADDITIONAL SHELF UNIT.

SEE PLAN ABOVE

CHESS TABLE (EXISTING.)

7'.0"

REVISED PART PLAN.

SET	*MILLENNIUM FALCON* HOLD
DETAIL	REVISED SEAT LAYOUT
DRG. NO.	24
DATE	SEPTEMBER 5 1978
DRAWN BY	ALAN TOMKINS

↑ The reconstructed hold also contained a rebuilt chess set, though no one is seen playing with it in *Empire*.

LEFT AND BELOW LEFT
Both photographs reveal
details of the complex
set dressing and build
of the *Falcon*'s main hold.

↓ This drawing is a reissue of "Int. Pirate Ship Compo,
Sitting and Bunk Area," originally drawn for *Star Wars*
by Bream on March 28, 1976, with a note indicating that
"Basic re-dressing only shown on this sheet, more pipes
and gear required (see photos)." Bream's artwork was
reused for "Episode II," noted as "the original copy, not
to be disposed." This kind of recycling also illustrates
why certain original drawings or their original blueprint
copies went missing: they served for multiple films and
sometimes the forces of organization couldn't keep up
with the forces of chaos inherent in moviemaking.

SET	*MILLENNIUM FALCON*, HOLD AREA
DETAIL	SEATING & CONTROL CONSOLE AREA
DRG. NO.	17
DATE	SEPTEMBER 4 1978
DRAWN BY	REG BREAM

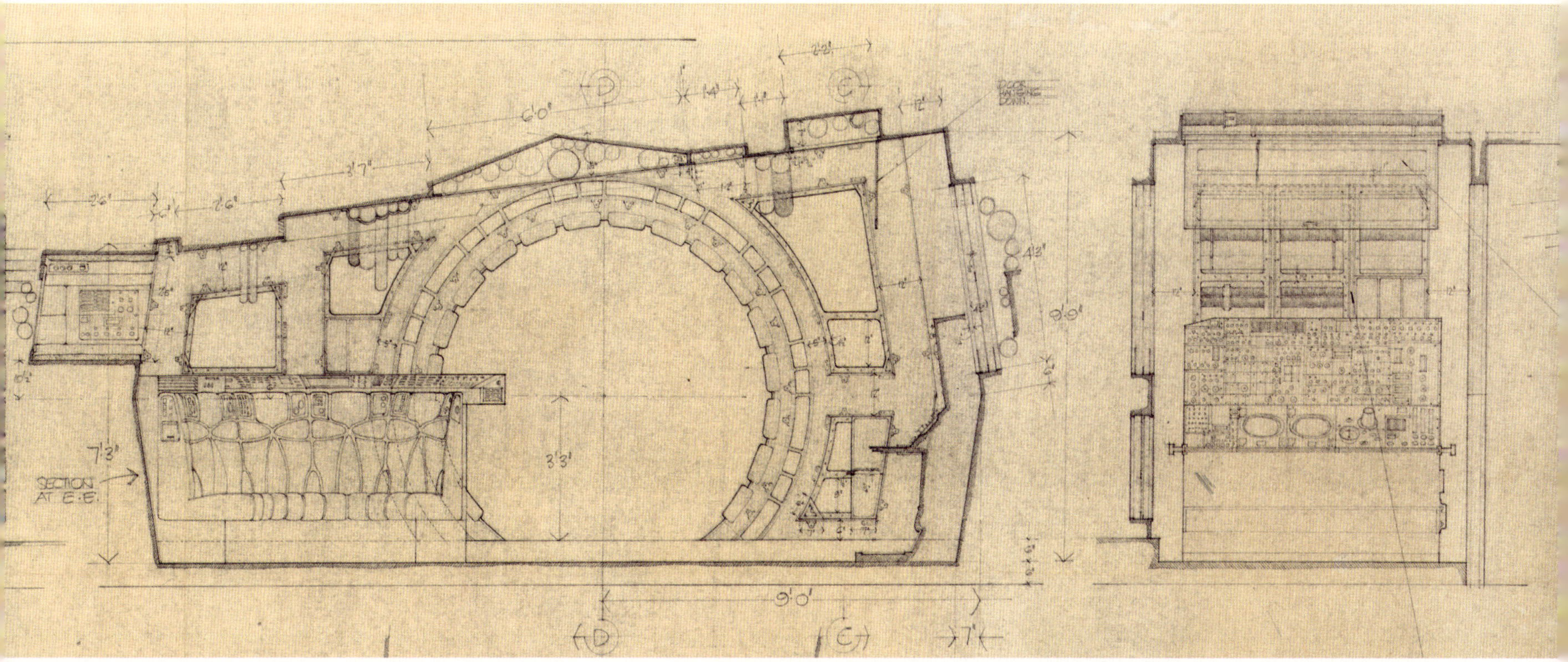

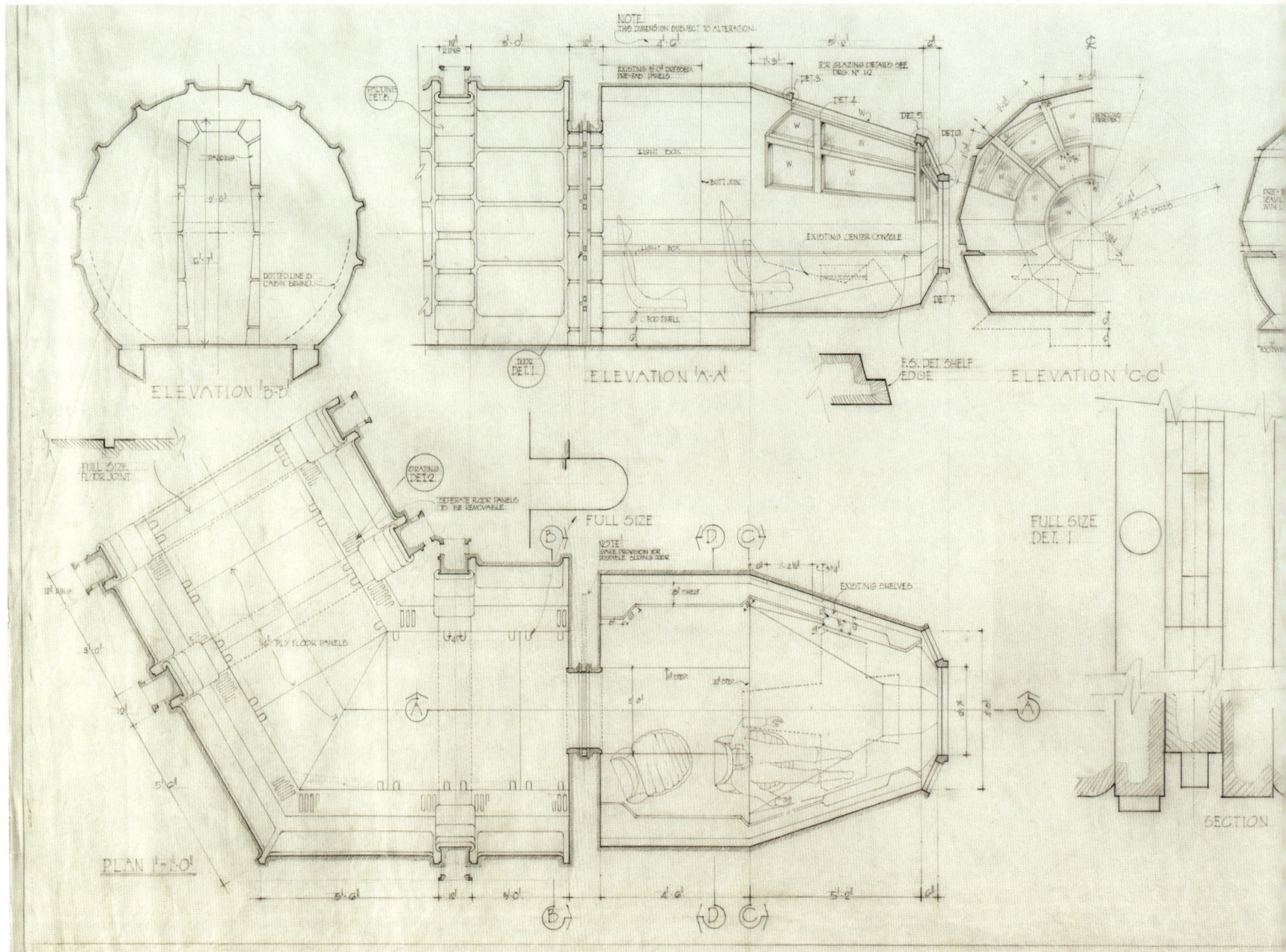

LEFT AND FAR LEFT
The *Falcon* cockpit set construction and dressing is seen from front and behind. Visible on the dashboard are three pistons (spares) from C-3PO's legs that Lange grabbed for the cockpit.

INT COCKPIT 'MILLENNIUM FALCON'
SCALE 1" = 1'-0"

READ IN CONJUNCTION WITH
DRG. NO. 10
SET TO MATCH ORIGINAL – CHECK FOR
EXISTING PARTS STILL LEFT, IE:- CENTER
CONSOLE

SET TO BE MOUNTED ON ROSTRUM –
SECTION ALONG F-F TO FLOAT AT 48.
MOUNTED ON ROCKING ROSTRUM – TO BE
DISCUSSED.

© 1978 Chapter II Productions Ltd.

SET	MILLENNIUM FALCON, COCKPIT
DETAIL	MAIN PLAN & ELEVATIONS
DRG. NO.	11
DATE	AUGUST 23 1978
DRAWN BY	STEVE COOPER

← While the blueprint indicates that the cockpit set was to match the original—and to check for existing parts still left, such as the center console—producer Gary Kurtz requested that the set be made larger to give the actors more room. (Only certain props and dressings could be conserved, as storage space was limited and costly; it was usually cheaper to rebuild something rather than save it for years.) Kurtz did not consult Lucas, however, and the latter was not pleased when he saw the set, given that the first cockpit had been designed to be crowded, duplicating the claustrophobic conditions of most jet fighters and command modules. But it was too late to change, so the cockpit seems to grow slightly between films.

The cockpit was mounted on a rostrum (a raised platform), so that it could be rocked by stagehands. The pre-fab panels (over the doorway) were to be heavily dressed with lights and switches.

↑ The ILM model's radar antenna, or rectenna, served as the basis for the art department's technical drawings.

SET	MILLENNIUM FALCON
DETAIL	RADAR ANTENNA
DRG. NO.	121
DATE	NOVEMBER 27 1978
DRAWN BY	RICHARD J. DAWKING

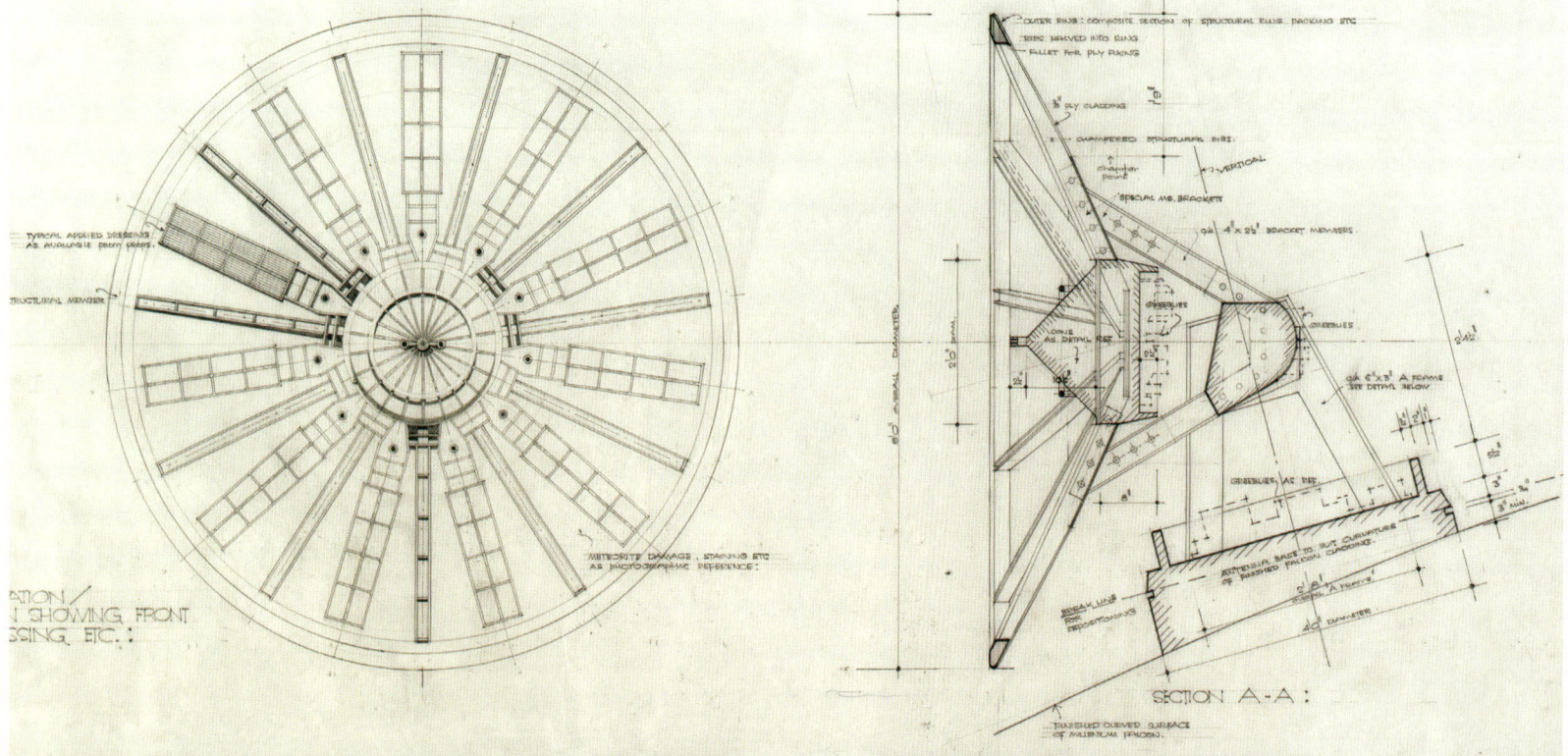

SECTION A-A:

STAR DESTROYER

In one of the only drawings of its kind in the Lucasfilm Archives, an artist drew a view of an alcove off the main bridge of the Star Destroyer. The bridge itself had been conceptualized by McQuarrie with wraparound windows and almost a galley feel, with Imperial underlings toiling on a lower level, while Vader, ever the taskmaster, paces above. (The Elstree artwork is actually two sheets, with the color placed on the sheet below, but seen through the nearly transparent top sheet.)

The bridge of the Star Destroyer was constructed on Stage 5 and would actually be only half built; the other half would be the same set, flipped photographically, with actors repositioned; the two mirrored halves would then be composited together with a matte painting of the ceiling by ILM. This set would also serve as the bridge of two different Imperial ships: Vader's *Executor* and Captain Needa's *Avenger*. The alcove, adjoining corridor, and control rooms could be rejiggered, relit, and redressed for all the necessary interior scenes—in many of which Vader would be dealing with less-than-satisfactory help by using the Force to throttle them.

↑ On Stage 5, construction progresses on the alcove near the Star Destroyer bridge.

← A 1978 McQuarrie production painting conceptualized the look of the Star Destroyer bridge; the design element of the large tubes embedded in the ceiling was carried over to the alcove design.

→ The technical drawing of the composite set indicates a floating window wall, stock doors, stock consoles, Darth Vader's meditation pod (with screen on wall), and hologram pod.

SET	STAR DESTROYER COMPOSITE
DETAIL	SECTIONS & ELEVATIONS (STAGE 5)
DRG. NO.	255
DATE	FEBRUARY 12 1979
DRAWN BY	RICHARD J. DAWKING

SECTION ON LINE BB:

↑ On-set photography shows the partial bridge set, including the one practical window.

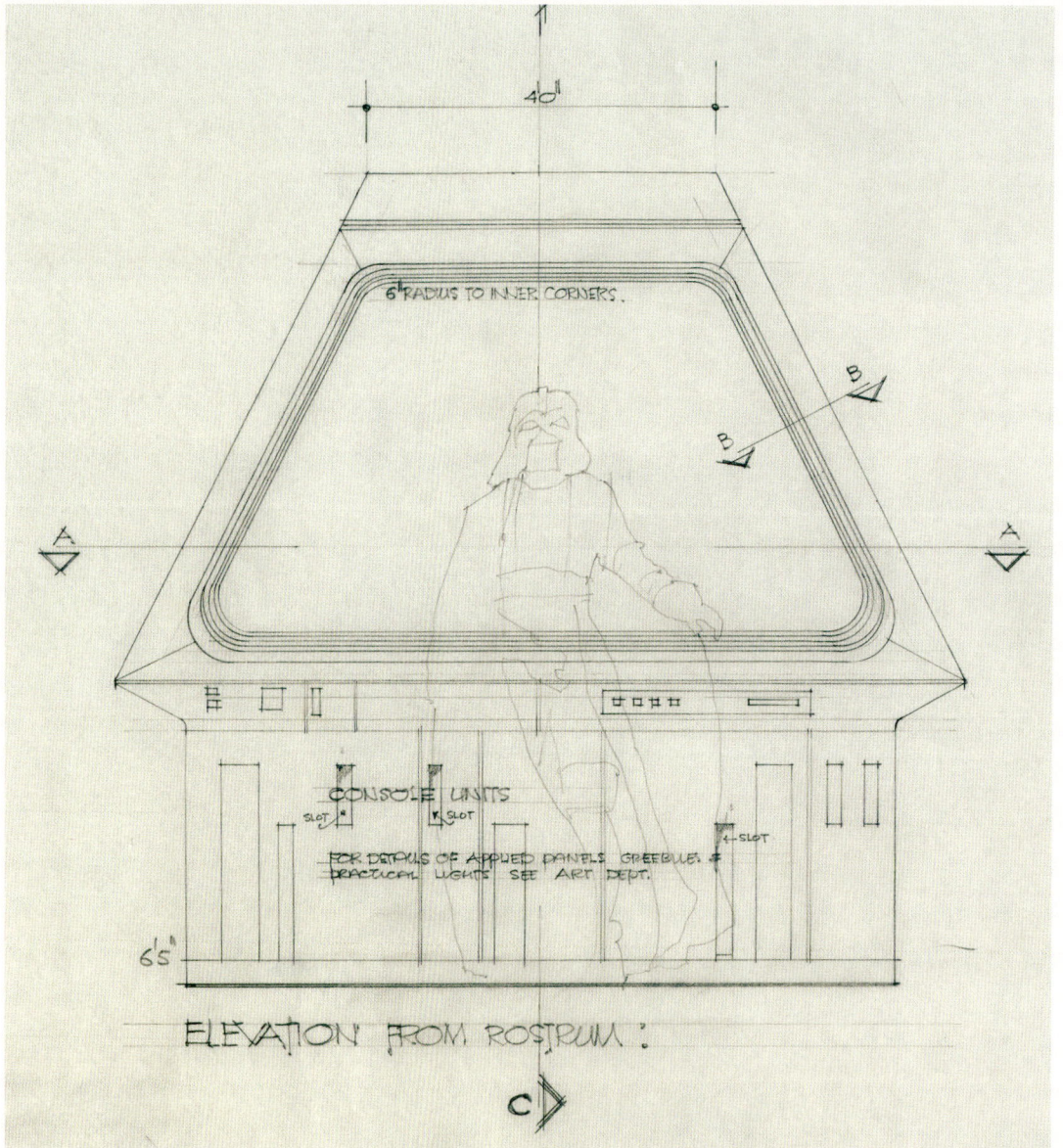

→ A detail of the 7-foot- and 7-inch-high fore window specifies a masonite finish.

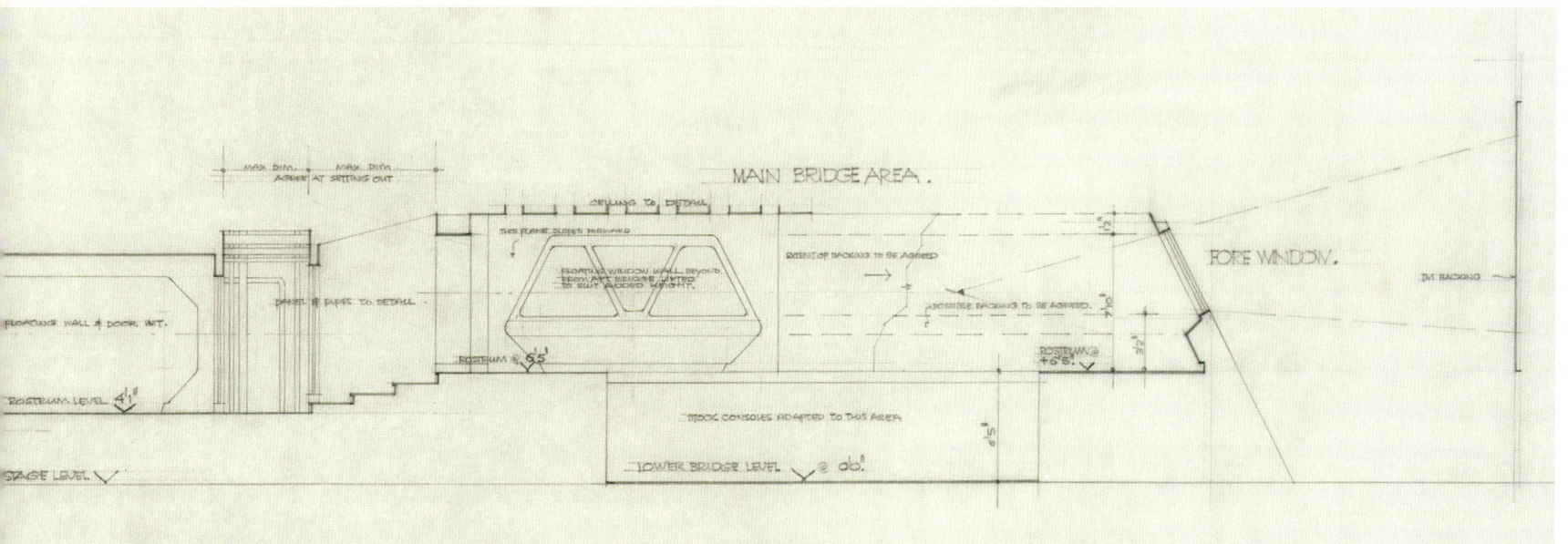

SET	STAR DESTROYER
DETAIL	FORE WINDOW, MAIN BRIDGE AREA
DRG. NO.	267
DATE	FEBRUARY 23 1979
DRAWN BY	RICHARD J. DAWKING

ELEVATION FROM ROSTRUM.

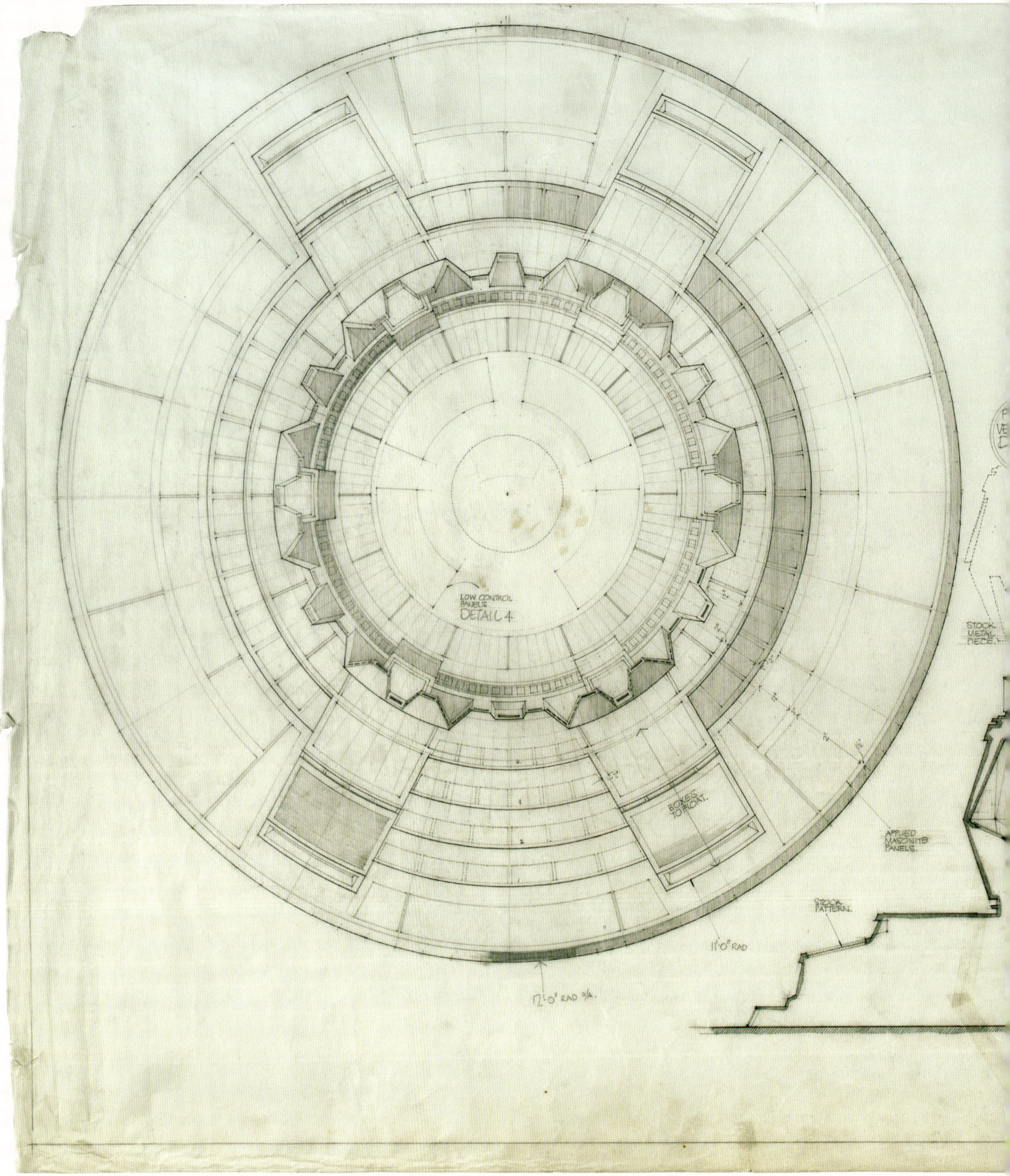

LOW CONTROL
PANELS
DETAIL 4

BOXES
TO FRONT.

STOCK
METAL
PIECE.

APPLIED
MASONITE
PANELS.

STOCK
PATTERN.

11'0" RAD

17'0" RAD O/A.

SET	STAR DESTROYER	DATE	FEBRUARY 16 1979
DETAIL	VADER'S MEDITATION POD	DRAWN BY	REG BREAM
DRG. NO.	276		

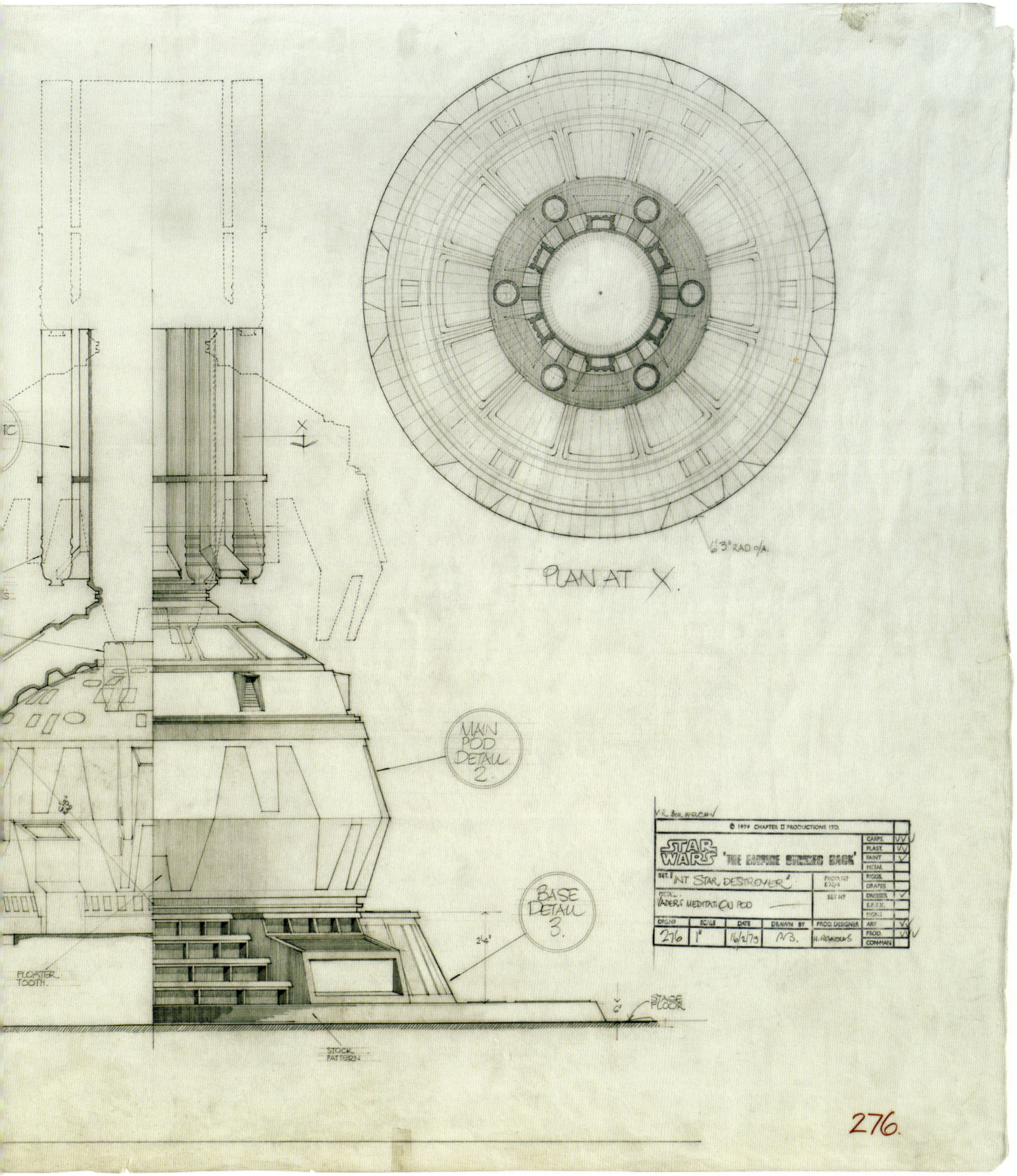

6'3" RAD O/A.

PLAN AT X.

MAIN
POD
DETAIL
2.

BASE
DETAIL
3.

FLOATER
TOOTH.

STOCK
PATTERN

2'4"

STAGE
FLOOR

© 1979 CHAPTER II PRODUCTIONS LTD.

STAR WARS	'THE EMPIRE STRIKES BACK'		CARP.	✓✓
			PLAST.	✓✓
SET: INT STAR DESTROYER	PRODN. N°		PAINT	✓
	E704		METAL	
DETAIL: VADER'S MEDITATION POD	SET N°		RIGG.	
			DRAPES	
			DRESSER	✓
			S.F.T.X.	
			SIGNS	
DRG N°	SCALE	DATE	DRAWN BY	PROD DESIGNER	ART	✓✓
276	1"	16/2/79	N.B.	N. REYNOLDS	PROD.	✓✓
					CON-MAN	

276.

MEDITATION CHAMBER

Within Vader's flagship Star Destroyer is his meditation pod, also referred to as his "chamber," where the dark side equivalent to Jedi meditation takes place. The set design was by Reynolds and its teeth-like pod halves contain a "floater tooth," for camera or lighting access.

The script had described the chamber as follows: "a dark cubicle is illuminated by a single shaft of light from above. The brooding Dark Lord sits on a raised meditation cube." It was up to the production designer to flesh it out.

"I was at a loss at quite what to do for that," said Reynolds. "But certain things take a certain amount of time to prepare: drawing takes two or three weeks, depending, so the making of it would be, say, six weeks, and then installing it in the set is more time needed. The greatest spur to coming up with a design is to know that the date is coming fast upon you. Yet I had reached a point of still not knowing quite what to do. I was literally sitting in the kitchen at home, wondering what on earth I was going to *do* for this.

"Well, I thought, *This guy suffers from asthma and has alopecia*, so maybe he just goes into a chamber, and it's filled with purified air and other materials that

→ A set concept drawing by Reynolds of Vader's meditation pod, October 1978.

→ The exterior of Vader's meditation chamber as it was being constructed on Stage 5, where scenes were shot in April 1979.

→ An art department maquette of the meditation pod.

SET	STAR DESTROYER COMPOSITE
DETAIL	SECTIONS & ELEVATIONS (STAGE 5)
DRG. NO.	255
DATE	FEBRUARY 12 1979
DRAWN BY	RICHARD J. DAWKING

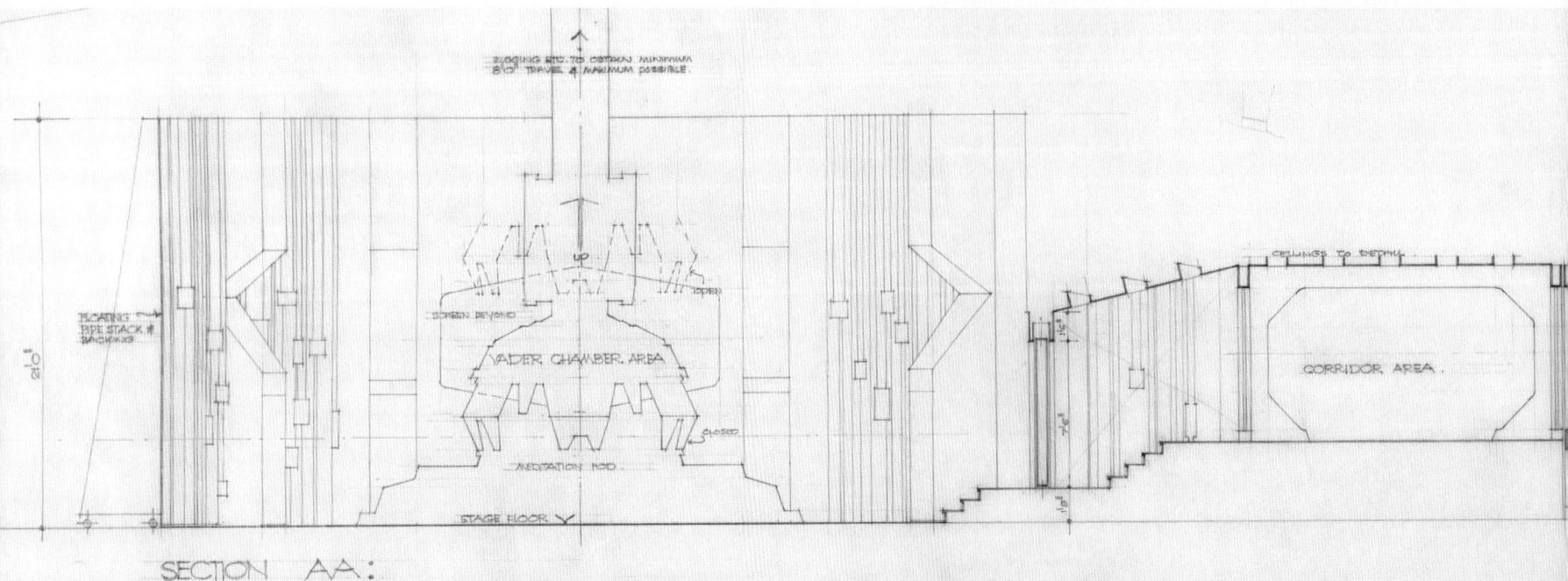

SECTION AA:

SET   VADER'S STAR DESTROYER
DETAIL HOLOGRAM POD
DRG. NO. 281
DATE   FEBRUARY 18 1979
DRAWN BY STEVEN COOPER

regenerate him. Then I came up with that idea of this claw-like thing that seals him in. I thought that might fit the bill. I drew that while sitting at the kitchen table that night, just scribbling, and then it later became a reality."

Armed with this concept, Reynolds worked up the blueprints in conjunction with Reg Bream. "Reg was so fast," said Tomkins. "We all aspired to the level of his drawings. There's a marvelous one of Darth Vader's pod with these big teeth coming down. Reg was the top draftsman who never wanted to do anything but draw and who was an absolute master with a pencil."

Reynolds added that actually building the pod was another matter. "Bill Welch did a first-class job," said Reynolds. "It was a very tricky thing to evolve, develop, and actually make.

← In *Empire*, the Emperor makes his first appearance, albeit only as a hologram. To initiate their trans-galactic conversation, Vader kneels on his hologram pod, the base and top of which was to be lit through Perspex panels. To help his department visualize what would only be completed in post, Reynolds drew several conceptual sketches that showed the relative sizes of the Emperor and Vader: to visually convey his dominance, the former was to be larger, 12 or 13 feet to Vader's 6 foot, 6 inches.

During principal photography and until fairly late in postproduction, the idea was that the Emperor would enter through a kind of inter-dimensional door. Ultimately, Lucas decided to show only the Emperor's head as a giant hologram.

← The Emperor makes his holographic appearance in *The Empire Strikes Back*.

BATTLE OF HOTH

The Imperial walker, or AT-AT, was a concept designed by Joe Johnston. Jon Berg then engineered the first working prototype, consulting with his fellow stop-motion animator Phil Tippett in the summer of 1978. At the same time, at Elstree, Kershner was working with Ivor Beddoes on storyboards of the Hoth battle. Although the visual effects would be done by ILM in post, the production crew in the UK had to have an idea of what was going to happen at every stage of the battle in order to film its live-action and background plates—even though they wouldn't see the AT-ATs in motion until long after principal photography had wrapped.

"I was asked to work out the proportion of the snowspeeder to the walker," said Tomkins of his size comparison layout. "I was told that the snowspeeder wants to go through the legs of the walker in the action. So I put the legs on the outside of the body to give it more stability, and, if you look, you can see that it does look a lot more stable than what Joe Johnston came up with, with the legs right underneath, very narrow. The whole thing looks like it's going to fall over before the wire goes around."

But the fact that Johnston's designs made for unstable machines was part of Lucas' idea—the Imperials were like the Americans in Vietnam:

using the wrong sort of technology to attack. Who wants to be in a giant machine walking on ice?

Beddoes' storyboard also showed additional aspects that were never filmed at ILM: for example, "pairs of tow-line" snowspeeders, hoping to trip the AT-ATs.

Although Beddoes only storyboarded in the art department, he was multitalented. He'd started professional life in the theater. He was a ballet dancer in his youth, and then went on to become a choreographer, a designer, and an artist, doing his first film work as an actor/dancer in a short, *Windmill Revels* (1937). One of his major contributions to the cinematic art was as special painter for the Michael Powell/Emeric Pressburger masterpiece, *The Red Shoes* (1948).

"Ivor was one of those amazing people," said Tomkins. "I suppose you're taught it as a dancer, but he could throw himself down a flight of steps like a stuntman, get up, say, 'Sorry about that,' and dust

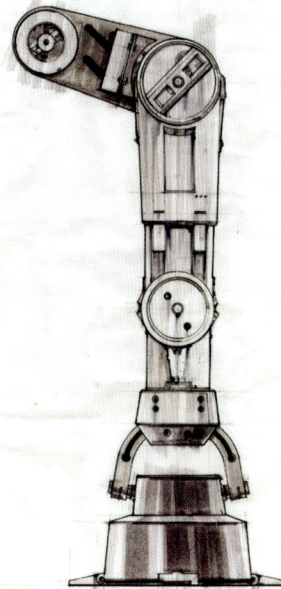

SET	BATTLE OF HOTH
DETAIL	SIZE COMPARISON LAYOUT
DRG. NO.	N/A
DATE	WINTER 1978
DRAWN BY	ALAN TOMKINS

→ At ILM, a high-speed camera was used to record the walker foot crushing the model snowspeeder.

↓ An aerial view of the rebel base shows the ice plain to the east, where walkers are attacking. It also discloses perimeter markers; the rebels' "big gun," the west hangar with transport ships, the main hangar with the *Falcon* inset, the south hangar with more X-wings, the medical center, control center, and the power generator, which the AT-ATs are trying to destroy.

Like storyboards, layout drawings were intended to give all the departments a larger sense of the story and a sense of the geography of the action.

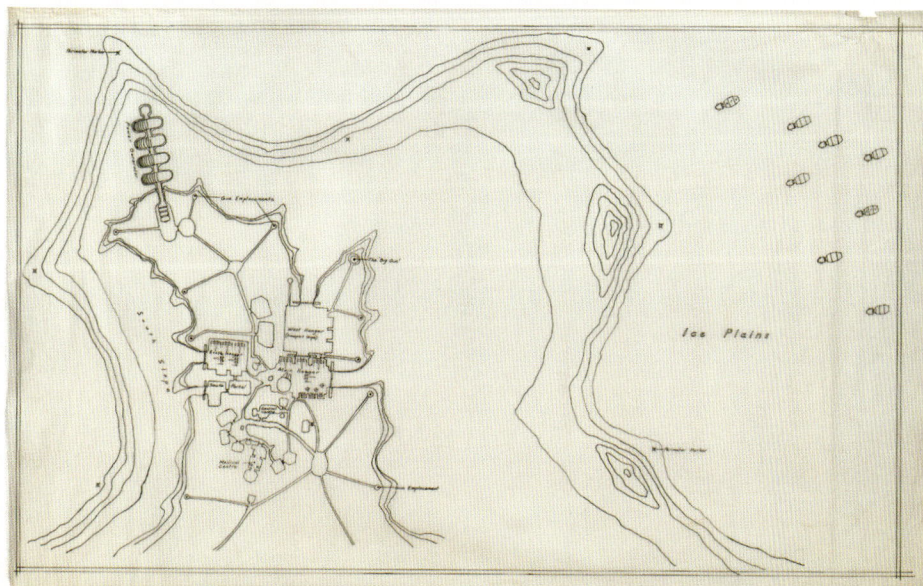

SET	AERIAL VIEW OF BATTLE
DETAIL	LAYOUT
DRG. NO.	N/A
DATE	WINTER 1978
DRAWN BY	UNKNOWN

SET	BATTLE OF HOTH
DETAIL	SIZE COMPARISON LAYOUT
DRG. NO.	N/A
DATE	WINTER 1978
DRAWN BY	ALAN TOMKINS

SET	BATTLE OF HOTH
DETAIL	SNOW WALKER LEG
DRG. NO.	341
DATE	WINTER 1978
DRAWN BY	MICHAEL BOONE

himself off. We'd think he was almost dead! But he used to do it so often. And he had an enormous voice, so in the commissary at MGM, he'd suddenly shout out something—and the whole place would stop and look around. But he would just be eating. He was a bit of a comedian, a really nice guy."

Back at ILM, Beddoes' storyboards circulated but were passed over in favor of designs more conducive to Lucas' vision and the facility's needs. "When I first saw this, I said, 'God, the legs are way too wide,'" said Muren. "I just don't think it looks nice. It looks bowlegged. But where did that come from? It came from, obviously, flying between the legs. I think that was the request and they just said, 'We'll make it this wide.' But when we got it back to ILM, we said, 'It doesn't matter, we can cheat it.' We made them narrower because it looked better and the hands could grab them better. We wanted the walkers to be hand-animated, so we made them a size that was comfortable for Jon Berg and Phil Tippett."

← One piece of action slated for studio shooting was a walker foot crushing Luke's snowspeeder. Several blueprints and drawings were executed, including Boone's (no. 341), which indicates that the AT-AT's "toe" was "to move as shown and return to lower position… Bottom and leg to compress on impact."

As shooting became bogged down in Elstree, however, this shot was farmed out to ILM, which accomplished the scene with miniatures that were comped into a live-action plate of Hamill jumping away from his doomed snowspeeder.

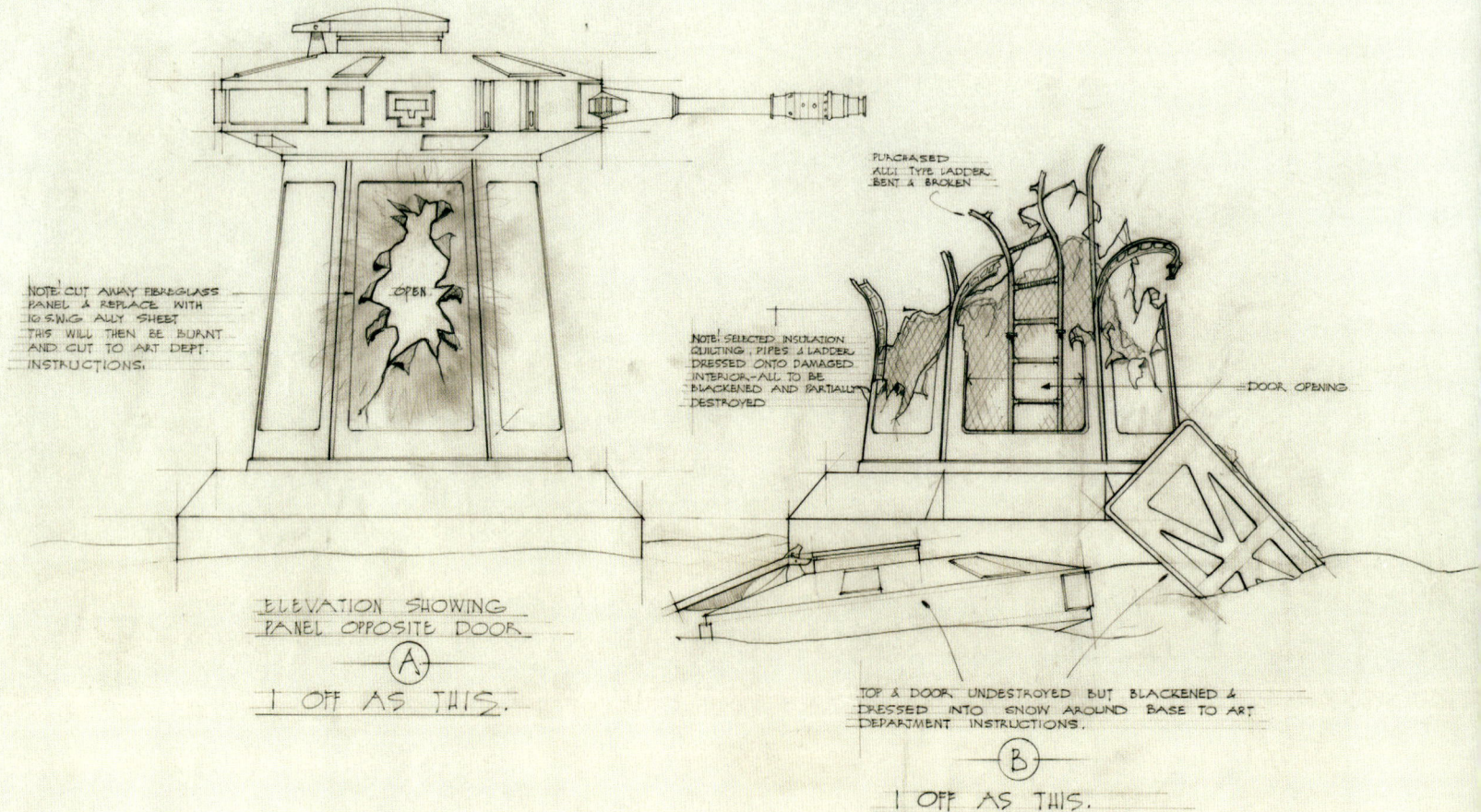

"THE EMPIRE STRIKES BACK"
GUN EMPLACEMENTS FOR NORWEGIAN LOCATIO[N]

NOTE: CUT AWAY FIBREGLASS
PANEL & REPLACE WITH
16 S.W.G. ALLY SHEET
THIS WILL THEN BE BURNT
AND CUT TO ART DEPT.
INSTRUCTIONS.

OPEN

ELEVATION SHOWING
PANEL OPPOSITE DOOR
Ⓐ
I OFF AS THIS.

PURCHASED
ALLI TYPE LADDER
BENT & BROKEN

NOTE: SELECTED INSULATION
QUILTING, PIPES & LADDER
DRESSED ONTO DAMAGED
INTERIOR—ALL TO BE
BLACKENED AND PARTIALLY
DESTROYED

DOOR OPENING

TOP & DOOR UNDESTROYED BUT BLACKENED &
DRESSED INTO SNOW AROUND BASE TO ART
DEPARTMENT INSTRUCTIONS.
Ⓑ
I OFF AS THIS.

NORWAY REQUIREMENTS.
ONE OFF COMPLETELY INTACT
ONE OFF ⅔ RDS FULL SIZE (DRWG Nº 108) INTACT
THREE CUT-OUTS ⅔ RDS FULL SIZE
ONE AS Ⓐ CAN BE TURNED TO DOUBLE AS COMPLETE GUN
ONE AS Ⓑ
ONE AS Ⓒ

© 1978 Chapter II Productions Ltd.

↑ "I remember when the train first pulled up outside the station in Finse, Norway," said Reynolds. "I saw the hotel wall that was maybe ten yards away from the station, quite close, with these huge, huge icicles hanging from it. I thought, *What on earth is this*?"

The frightful reception continued for Reynolds and the rest of the crew with blizzards that cut them off from the outside world. Filming commenced, however. First unit would work with the actors for about a week, then second unit would record battle footage with extras for several more weeks. Trenches were dug and props erected to simulate the rebels' preparations and defense of their base using small arms and large guns, which were designed and made at Elstree and then shipped to Finse.

The gun turret was to turn 360 degrees and be able to tilt up and down. Greebly dressing included what looks like a mini-satellite dish along with access doors. "There was no piece of action designed for those doors," said Reynolds. "Kersh never asked for a specific thing to happen. It was just something that seemed like the logical thing to do." And one never knew: a design element might inspire a new bit of action.

Although explosives were used in second unit filming, the gun emplacements were actually designed for a post-explosion shot in a drawing by Tomkins (no. 181): "Note! Selected insulation quilting, pipes, and ladder dressed

SET	EXTERIOR NORWAY LOCATION
DETAIL	GUN EMPLACEMENT REQUIREMENTS
DRG. NO.	181
DATE	DECEMBER 28 1978
DRAWN BY	ALAN TOMKINS

onto damaged interior—all to be blackened and partially destroyed. Top and door undestroyed, but blackened and dressed into snow around base to art department instructions. Part of revolving turret very badly damaged dressed into snow. Remainder of turret left hanging."

"It was a fantastic location," Reynolds added. "It worked really, really well because the hotel was right there, which made filming convenient, but it was also twenty degrees below. It was really, really freezing… if we wanted a piece of wall, the thing to do was to just screw up some chicken wire over a frame and then spray it with water—and it would freeze almost instantly. The weather had its advantages: instant wall."

↑ In late March 1979, second unit filmed much of the live-action Hoth battle in Finse, Norway. The gun emplacement was placed just behind the trench; explosions went off behind it, but for the shot of a smoldering gun, an artfully designed "destroyed" prop was used (top).

SNOWSPEEDER

In early storyboards, the rebels were trying to bring down the walkers using tanks with tow cables; not long afterward, their weaponry was upgraded to snowspeeders, as designed by McQuarrie and Johnston. Drawings and a model were sent to the UK, where technical drawings were soon generated, showing basic fuselage sections (no. 09 on page 112).

Production had two ideas for the snowspeeder that weren't brought to fruition: one was to film the model as a remote-controlled miniature in Finse (thus preempting some of the postproduction work); the second was to place the full-sized set on a gimbal (pivoted support), so it could bank and rock while being filmed against blue screen or, possibly, front or rear projection. "We used to make some rocking devices for the shooting of people in cars and things, but, invariably, we used manual labor," said Reynolds. "Terribly old-fashioned, I suppose, in some ways, but very effective. You can go faster, slower, rougher, smoother, and so on."

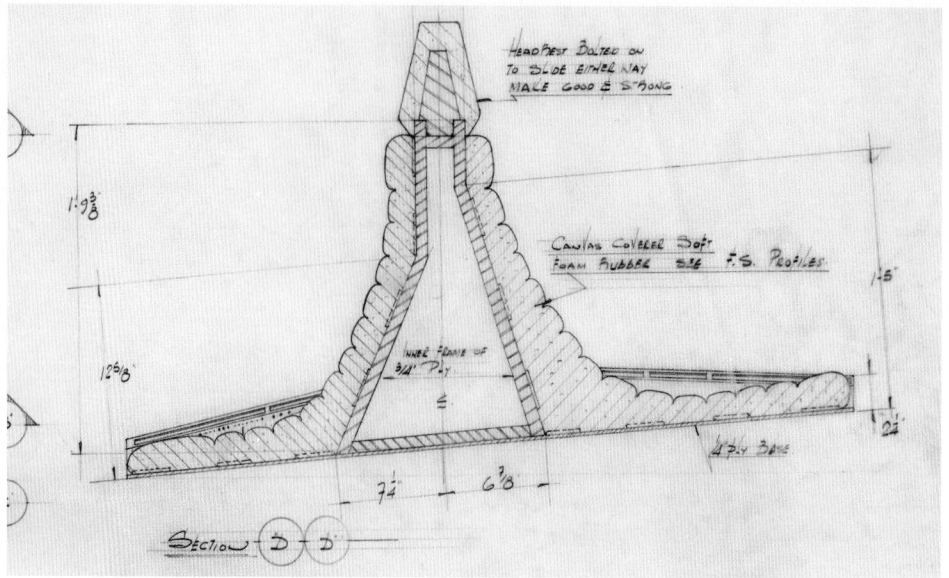

↑ According to the technical drawing, the snowspeeder's seat was to be canvas covered with soft foam rubber, and its headrest bolted on.

SET	SNOWSPEEDER
DETAIL	SEAT
DRG. NO.	148
DATE	DECEMBER 8 1978
DRAWN BY	FRED HOLE

↑ Concept art is by Radis-Jamero.

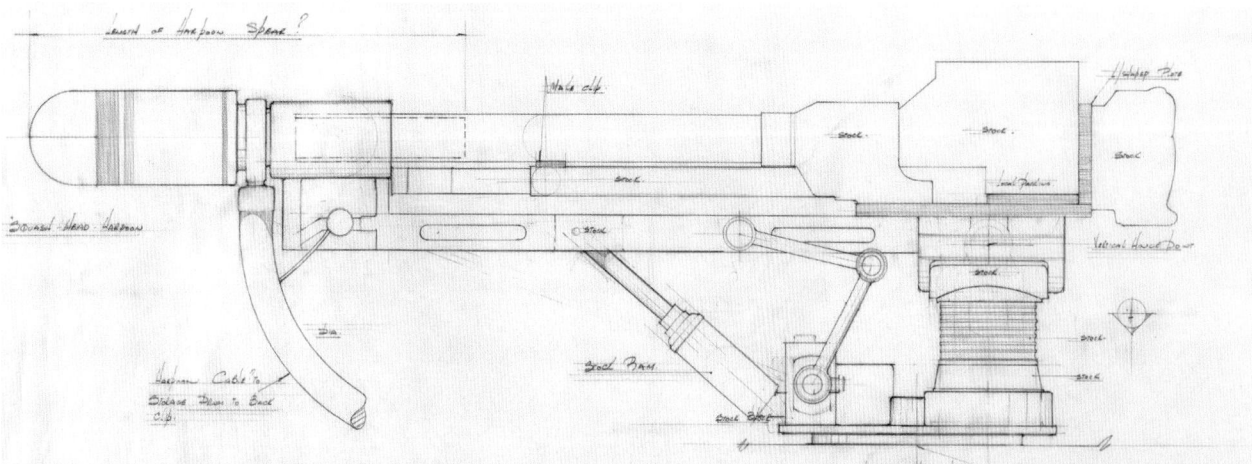

SET	EXT. SNOWSPEEDER
DETAIL	REAR HARPOON GUN
DRG. NO.	77
DATE	NOVEMBER 2 1978
DRAWN BY	FRED HOLE

↑ The snowspeeder's back-to-back seats were photographed on the backlot at Elstree before being placed in the full-sized craft.

← The blueprint instructs that the snowspeeder's rear harpoon gun was "to maneuver in shot."

SPEEDER TO BE ATTACHED
TO EXISTING GIMBLE
SEE CONSTRUCTION MANAGER
FOR FIXING DETAILS.

45°

2'0"?

6'0"?
SIZES TO BE DECIDED
BY CONSTRUCTION MANAGER

The same proved true for the snowspeeder, whose cockpit would ultimately be rocked by hand on Stage 8. A full-sized prop was also shipped to Finse for shots in the snow. "My first job was to redraw the snowspeeder, which had previously been drawn by Alan Tomkins," said Fred Hole. "But the design had changed slightly."

Hole's blueprint was then sent out-of-house for fabrication at Ogle Design Limited, famous for its car creations, such as the Reliant *Scimitar*. "With *Empire*, with the amount of work we had, we just couldn't cope," said Welch. "So we contacted them to see if they would do the snowspeeder, which they did. They also made the gun turrets for us."

SET	SNOWSPEEDER
DETAIL	GIMBAL & BASE FOR SPEEDER
DRG. NO.	343
DATE	MARCH 19 1979
DRAWN BY	STEVE COOPER

NOTE! DIMENSIONAL CHANGES
FROM ORIGINAL DRAWING.

BRAKE FLAP DRAWN
ON DOWN POSITION.

END ELEVATION.
SNOW SPEEDER DESIGN "A"

↑ Shown are details of the full-sized prop that was built by the art and construction departments at Elstree.

↑ Details of the snowspeeder were finalized at ILM in drawings by Nilo Rodis-Jamero, August 1978.

→ The snowspeeder mockup was also photographed against a real background. At one point, the art department toyed with the idea of building a remote-control model snowspeeder that would somehow fly and thus avoid having to shoot a model against blue screen back at ILM.

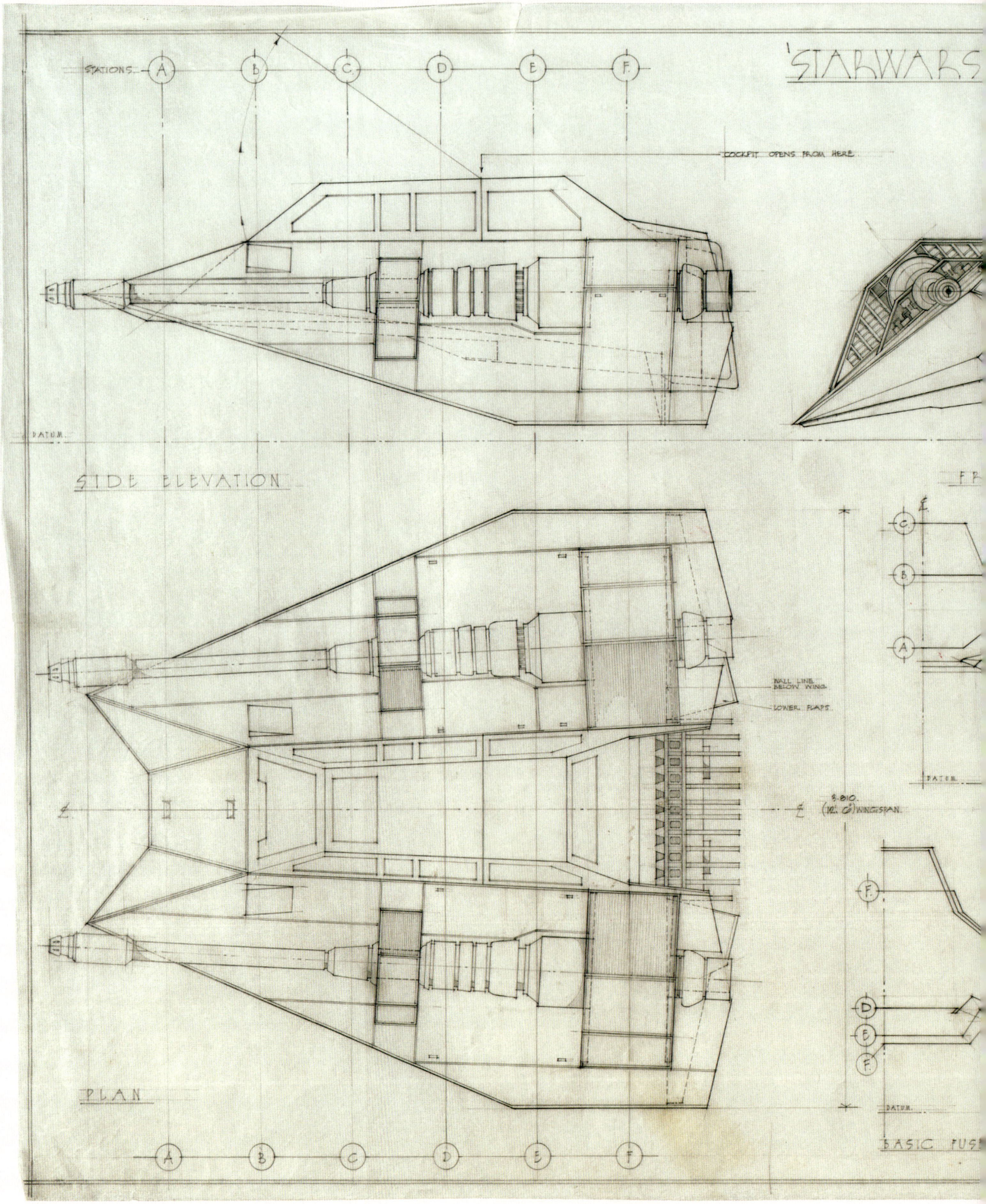

STATIONS — (A)   (B)   (C)   (D)   (E)   (F)

'STARWARS

COCKPIT OPENS FROM HERE

DATUM

SIDE ELEVATION

WALL LINE BELOW WING

LOWER FLAPS

8·810
(10' 0") WINGSPAN

PLAN

(A)   (B)   (C)   (D)   (E)   (F)

BASIC FUS

SET	EXTERIOR PLAINS OF HOTH	DRG. NO.	09
DETAIL	PRELIMINARY LAYOUT	DATE	AUGUST 18 1978
	SNOWSPEEDER SHEET	DRAWN BY	ALAN TOMKINS

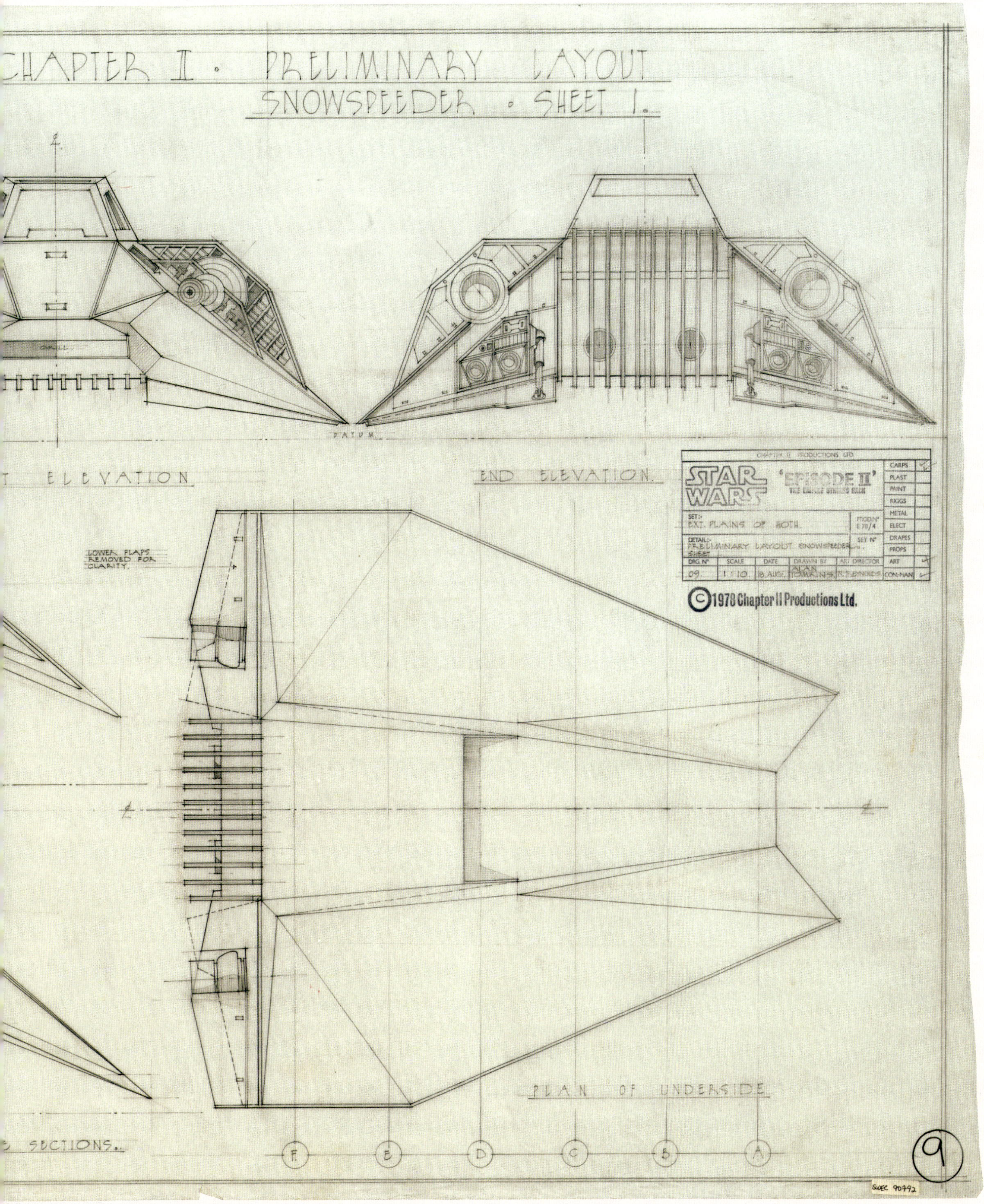

CHAPTER II · PRELIMINARY LAYOUT
SNOWSPEEDER · SHEET I.

ELEVATION

END ELEVATION.

DATUM

LOWER FLAPS
REMOVED FOR
CLARITY.

PLAN OF UNDERSIDE

SECTIONS.

F   E   D   C   B   A

STAR WARS	'EPISODE II' THE EMPIRE STRIKES BACK	CARPS	
		PLAST	
SET:- EXT. PLAINS OF HOTH.	PROD N° E 70/4	PAINT	
		RIGGS	
		METAL	
DETAIL:- PRELIMINARY LAYOUT SNOWSPEEDER SHEET	SET N°	ELECT	
		DRAPES	
DRG N° 09.	SCALE 1:10	DATE 18 AUG	DRAWN BY ALAN TOMKINS	ART DIRECTOR N.REYNOLDS	PROPS	
					ART	
					CON-MAN	

© 1978 Chapter II Productions Ltd.

CHAPTER II PRODUCTIONS LTD.

⑨

SWEC 90792

X-WING FIGHTER

Although X-wing blueprints for the first film are scant in the Lucasfilm Archives, a few more survived from *Empire*. In addition to the one full-sized X-wing prop preserved from *Star Wars*, two more were built for the sequel's hangar scenes, along with a cockpit for close-ups.

Ted Ambrose's drawing (no. 400) notes the 35mm camera positions for filming R2 in the starfighter, and that the engine and lasers were "to be adjustable to suit camera." Cooper's drawing (no. 106) indicates that a "sign writer" would be employed to create markings, following art department designs, on the fuel intake panel, missile port, undercarriage of bay doors, engine covers, and so on. Like the markings on Darth Vader's breastplate, the letters sometimes seem inspired by the Hebrew alphabet.

When filming process shots, however, the droid's panels were repainted black; R2's normally blue parts would have been transparent when filmed against the blue screen. Until the release of the Special Edition of *Empire* in 1997, therefore, R2 would change colors from blue to black, when in space.

↑ In 1980, *The Empire Strikes Back* was released with a "black" version of R2 for shots of the droid against the backdrop of space. Filmed against blue screen, the original blue droid would have been transparent. The Special Edition, released in 1997, corrected his color back to blue.

SET	X-FIGHTER COCKPIT
DETAIL	GENERAL COCKPIT
DRG. NO.	400
DATE	APRIL 27 1979
DRAWN BY	TED AMBROSE

→ On-set photography captured the full-sized X-wing prop.

SET	X-WING FIGHTER
DETAIL	STENCIL MARKINGS
DRG. NO.	106
DATE	NOVEMBER 17 1978
DRAWN BY	STEVE COOPER

STAR WARS 'THE EMPIRE STRIKES BACK'

STENCILS FOR 'X' WING FIGHTERS
REFER TO PHOTOGRAPHS AND ART DEPT. REFERENCE

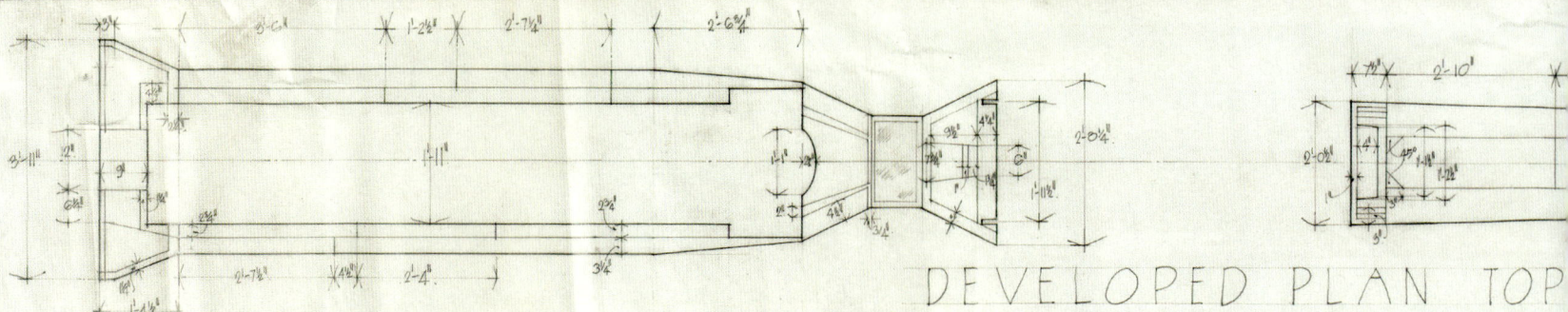

DEVELOPED PLAN TOP

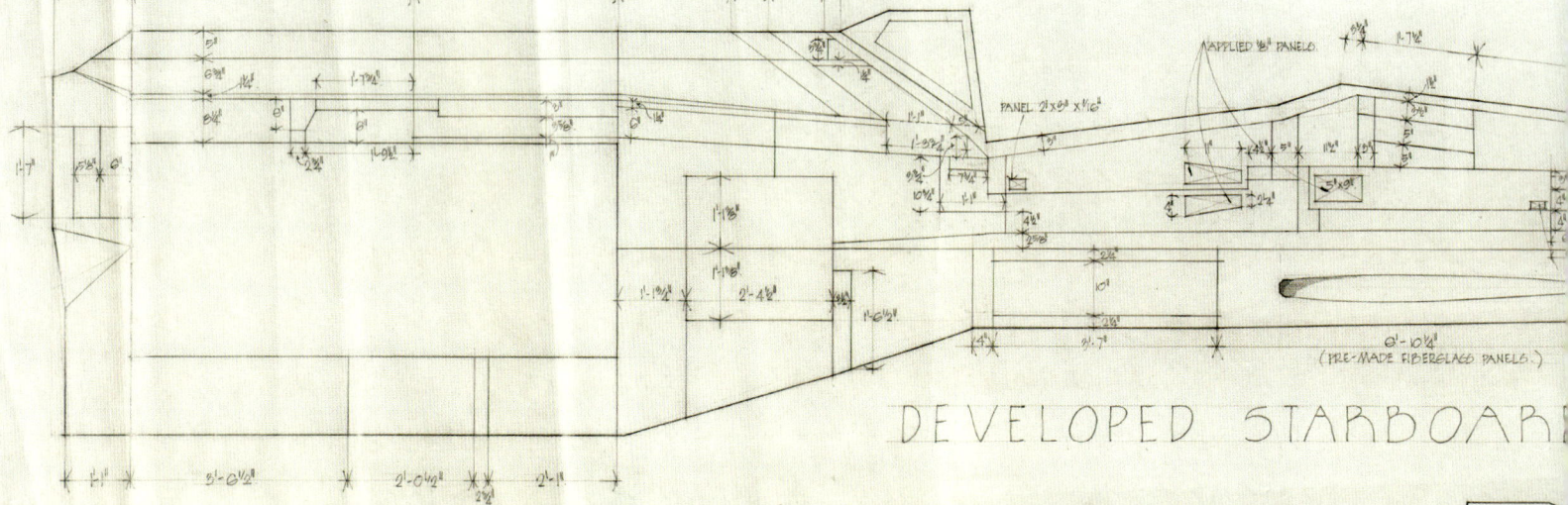

DEVELOPED STARBOAR

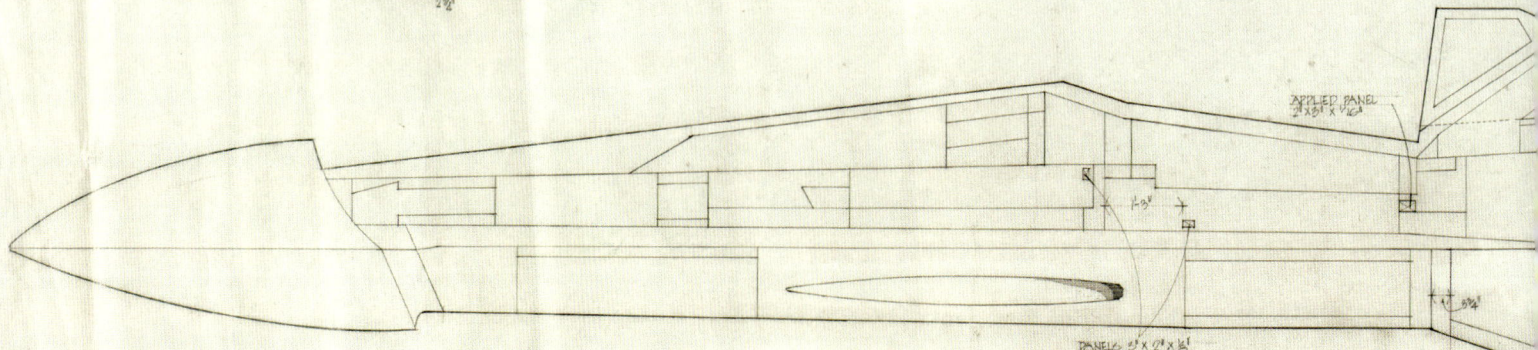

(PRE-MADE FIBERGLASS PANELS.)

APPLIED 'B' PANELS.

PANEL 2"x 8½" x ½6"

APPLIED PANEL
2"x 3½" x ½6"

DEVELOPED PORT ELEVATION.

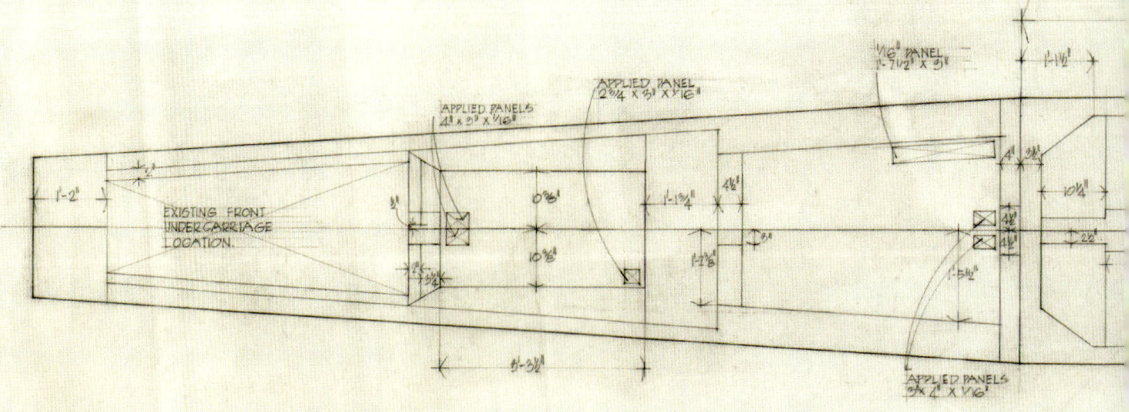

PANELS 5" x 2" x ⅛"

APPLIED
⅝" BACK
⅛" THIC

APPLIED PANEL
2¾" x 3½" x ½6"

APPLIED PANELS
4½ x 2½ x ½6"

EXISTING FRONT
UNDERCARRIAGE
LOCATION.

½6" PANEL
1-7½" x 3½"

APPLIED PANELS
3" x 2" x ½6"

DEVELOPED PLAN UNDERSI

STAR WARS

CHAPTER II PRODUCTIONS LTD.

'EPISODE II'
THE EMPIRE STRIKES BACK

			CARPS	✓
SET:-	X-WING FIGHTER	PROD N° E.70/4	PLAST	
			PAINT	
			RIGGS	
DETAIL:-	DET APPLIED PANELS	SET N°	METAL	
			ELECT	
DRG.N°	SCALE	DATE	DRAWN BY	ART DIRECTOR	DRAPES	
					PROPS	
02	1" = 1'-0"	80.10.13	S COOPER	N REYNOLDS	CON·MAN	
				PROD	3	ART	✓

"THE EMPIRE STRIKES BACK"
DET. APPLIED PANELS ON FUSELARGE
OF X-WING FIGHTER

NOTE!
ALL ELEVATIONS DEVELOPED —
READ WITH REFERENCE STILLS

ALL DIMENSIONS GIVEN APPLY TO ACTUAL
PANEL SIZE — LEAVE ⅛" GAPS BETWEEN PANELS

D E.

ELEVATION.

62

SET	X-WING FIGHTER
DETAIL	APPLIED PANELS
DRG. NO.	62
DATE	OCTOBER 30 1978
DRAWN BY	STEVE COOPER

BOBA FETT

As many *Empire* aficionados know, bounty hunter Boba Fett started out as an all-white supertrooper. The origins of his evolution began in February/March 1978 when Johnston did several concept drawings of the next-generation stormtrooper's armor and secret weaponry. In April, Lucas' second draft introduced Fett, a bounty hunter, though in May the costume was still designated as a "stormtrooper II" in Reynolds' very early backpack drawing (no. 02). In June, a film test in the US, using a prototype based on Reynolds' series, still featured an all-white costume, presumably that of the supertrooper. But in September a fully clothed and painted Fett marched through Marin County in his final incarnation during a local fair. In November, Fett appeared to the rest of the United States as an animated character in the *Star Wars Holiday Special* on television.

The exact day or month that Fett and the supertrooper costume combined is subject to speculation. Clearly for the *Holiday Special* to be aired in November, plans had to have been finalized at least a couple of months earlier—possibly around the time Lucas was writing his second draft in March or, at the latest, June 1978, when a concept drawing by Johnston was clearly labeled "Boba Fett."

"As I recall, just before I started full-time on *Empire*, Robert Watts received a sketch from ILM depicting what was described as a super stormtrooper," said Reynolds. "He asked me if I would develop the character and produce an outfit for George to consider, so I enlisted the aid of a sculptor, Jan Stevens, and model maker, Brian Archer [who previously had helped me with Threepio's costume], and produced the outfit complete with backpack and helmet range finder. When George finally received the outfit, he decided to change the concept from stormtrooper to bounty hunter."

That would also pinpoint the change in May/June. Eventually, Watts' half-brother, Jeremy Bulloch, was cast to play Fett—partially because he fit in the costume—and an iconic character was born, despite his relatively brief screen time.

↑ The all-white supertrooper costume, like C-3PO's, came with a "poster" to aid assembly, as shown here at Elstree.

SET	SUPERTROOPER II (PROTOTYPE MOCKUP)
DETAIL	HELMET
DRG. NO.	N/A
DATE	MAY 1978
DRAWN BY	NORMAN REYNOLDS

SET	STORMTROOPER II BACKPACKER
DETAIL	FULL-SIZED
DRG. NO.	02
DATE	MAY 2 1978
DRAWN BY	NORMAN REYNOLDS

← The Boba Fett backpack prop is shown painted.

→ A Reynolds drawing of the jetpack is now labeled as being for "Boba Fett."

SET	BOBA FETT'S COCKPIT
DETAIL	PLAN & ELEVATIONS
DRG. NO.	466
DATE	AUGUST 14 1979
DRAWN BY	TED AMBROSE

↓ Fett's starship existed as a matte painting, a painted model, and a constructed cockpit—the only element built on a soundstage. Part of the cockpit was stock control panels recycled from the Star Destroyer set "turned upside down and redressed with switches."

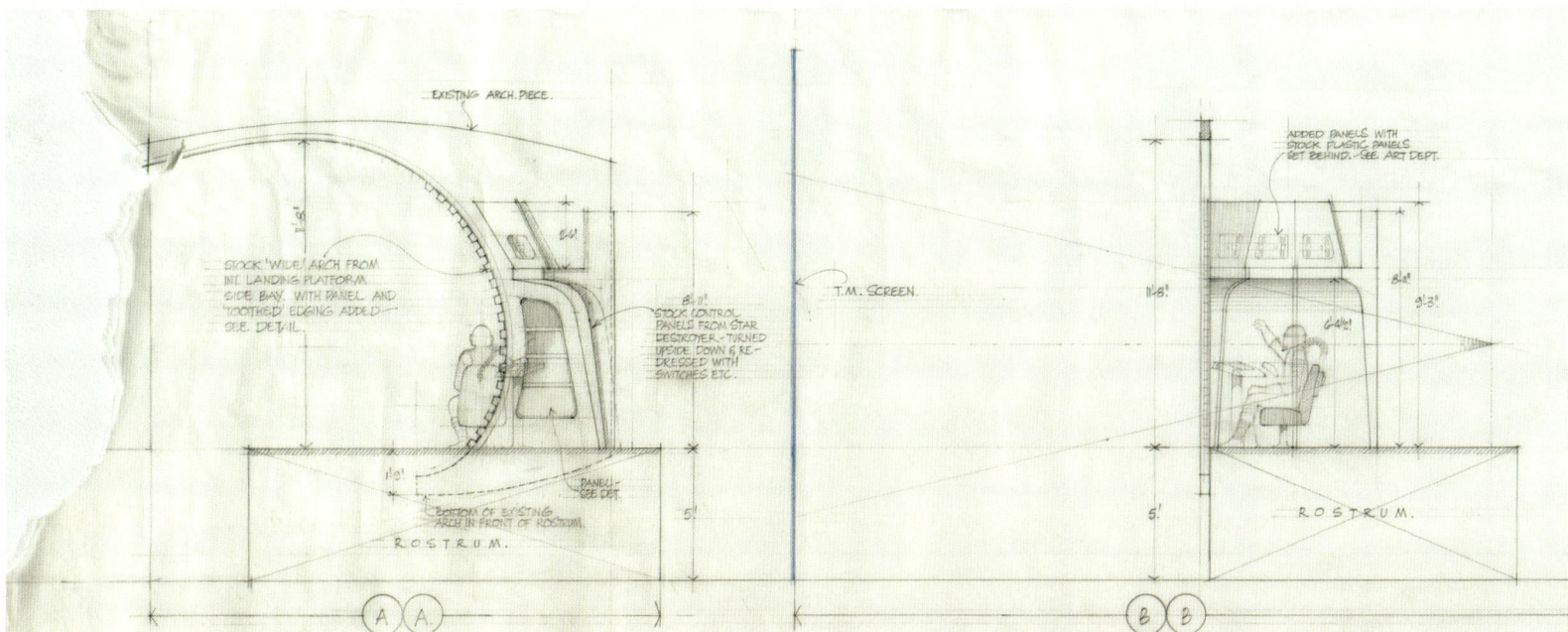

YODA'S HOUSE

The philosophical core of *Empire* rests on the shoulders of Yoda, a puppet operated and voiced by Frank Oz, who had been trained as a Muppeteer by Jim Henson. The creation of Yoda's animatronic puppet took place in England, through a collaboration between Henson and three of his group—Oz, Wendy Midener, and Kathy Mullen—and makeup artist supervisor Stuart Freeborn, who was sculpting Yoda's face based on McQuarrie's and Johnston's earlier concepts. Simultaneously, Yoda's humble home was being planned down the hall in the art department (Freeborn's office was located at the back of the front office building, while the art department was situated some distance away from the main gate, above the drapes department and carpenter's shop.) Oddly enough, the interior of the Jedi Master's abode was designed before the outside look of the house was established; McQuarrie and Reynolds continued their concepts of the exterior well into August 1978.

Michael Boone's notes on the interior (no. 372 on page 122) read, "Areas of floor not permanently fixed, are to float in sections of convenient size—details to be decided. Areas of ceiling to float." An aerial view shows the location of the hut's practical fire and where R2 would be placed outside of the window through which he peeks. The set would be built on Stage 9, while the exterior was part of the much larger Dagobah swamp set that was housed on the *Star Wars* Stage after the hangar and *Falcon* were moved out, which may explain its longer design schedule.

"I think I started off with little models of the trees, art department models, made out of wire and plasticine, basically, just to get the scale of the thing," said Ambrose of the swamp set. "Then we did stage plans. Michael oversaw that when they were actually building the set, and he was there all the time with the dressing of it and everything."

"Yoda's house was an interesting set," said Reynolds. "I never had done that before, actually, build a set off the ground, so that Frank Oz and the Muppeteers could get their arms up through the floor and operate Yoda.

"The moment he actually came to life, it was quite... I had never experienced anything like that either," Reynolds added, still with wonder in his voice. "It was really quite startling that this lump of cloth and rubber, and sort of a plastic face, suddenly assumed a character all its own. I was absolutely knocked out by that."

↓ Hamill is in the finished and dressed set of the interior of Yoda's house.

→ The interior details of Yoda's house were explored by Reynolds in this September 1978 drawing.

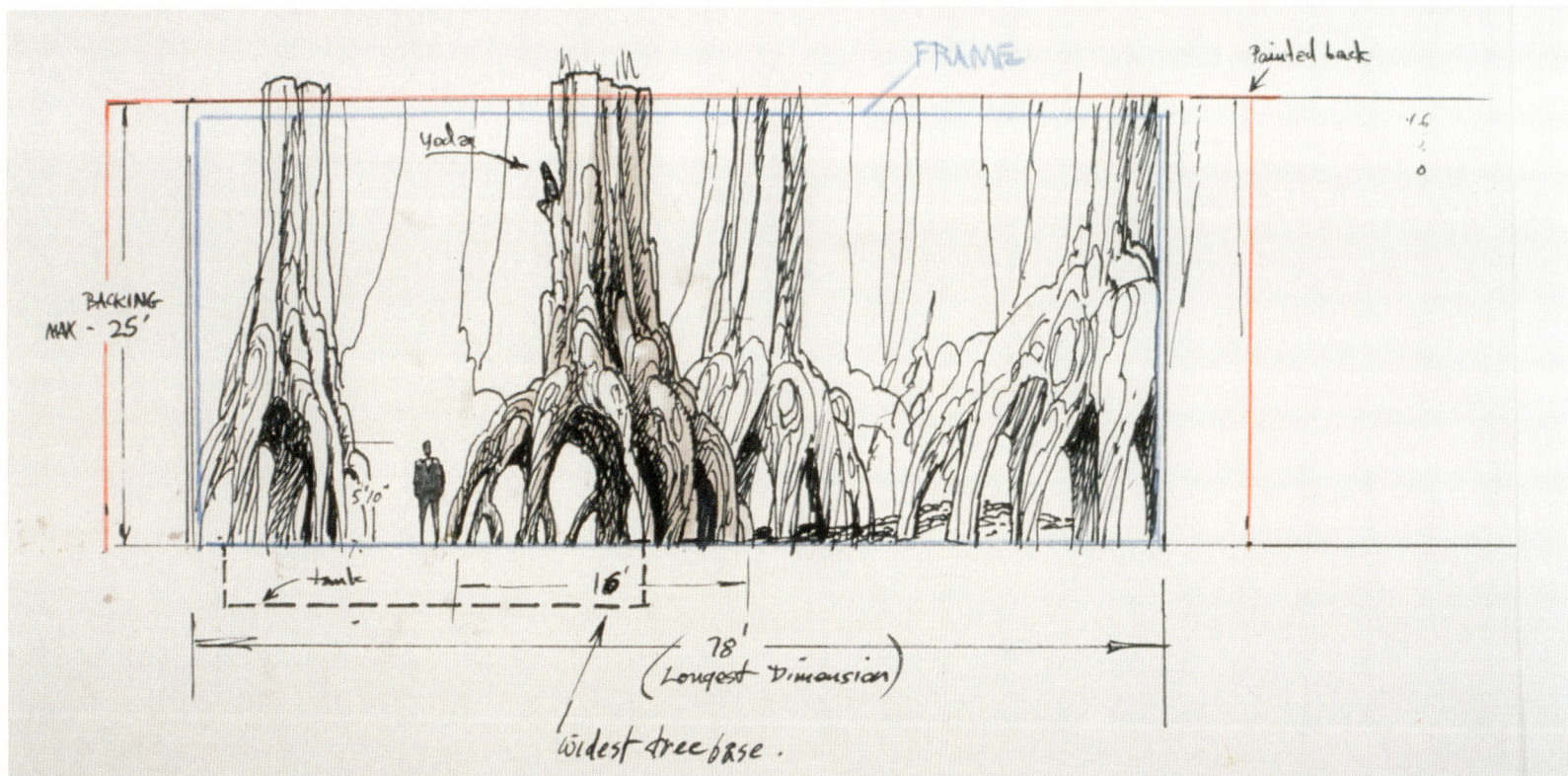

↑ A production sketch is of the trees and backing for the swamp set.

↑ An aerial view shows the Dagobah set on the *Star Wars* Stage as the trees were placed.

↑ Another McQuarrie production painting shows the trees of the Dagobah swamp, July 1978.

→ The exterior of Yoda's house is in its final dressed state.

FLOAT CEILING.

3'0"

1'0" 1'5"

3'

DATUM

1'7"

2'3"

R2 00

SECTION A·A

3'1"

1'8"

4"

2'6"

SECTION B·B

D

4'7"

3'8"

3'4"

4'0"

E

C

SECTION C·C

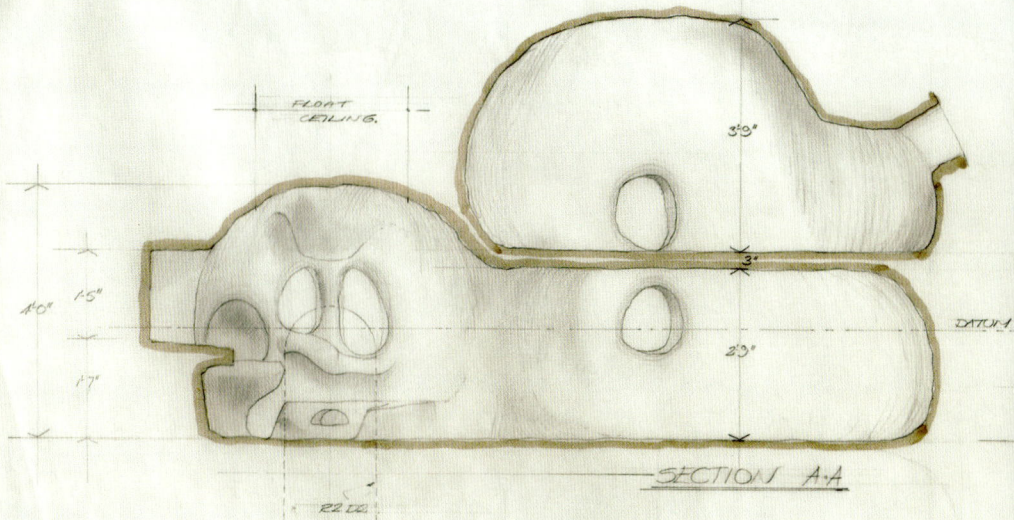

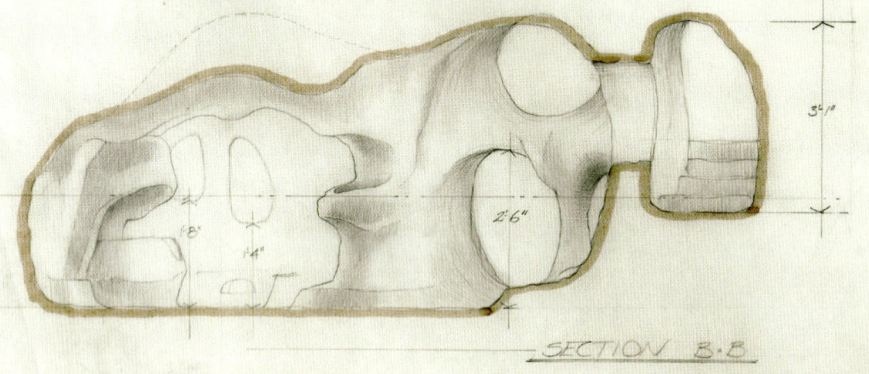

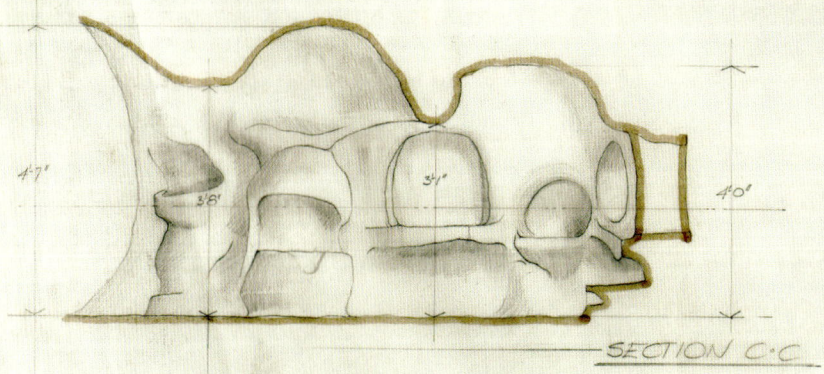

HEIGHT OF SET FLOOR TO
STUDIO FLOOR IS TO
BE DECIDED.

STUDIO FLOOR

SET	YODA'S HOUSE
DETAIL	PLANS & ELEVATIONS
DRG. NO.	372
DATE	APRIL 2 1978
DRAWN BY	MICHAEL BOONE

SECTION D·D — FLOAT.

SECTION E·E

FLOAT CEILING.

4'7"   5'8"

3'6"

4'0"

2'9"

2'9"

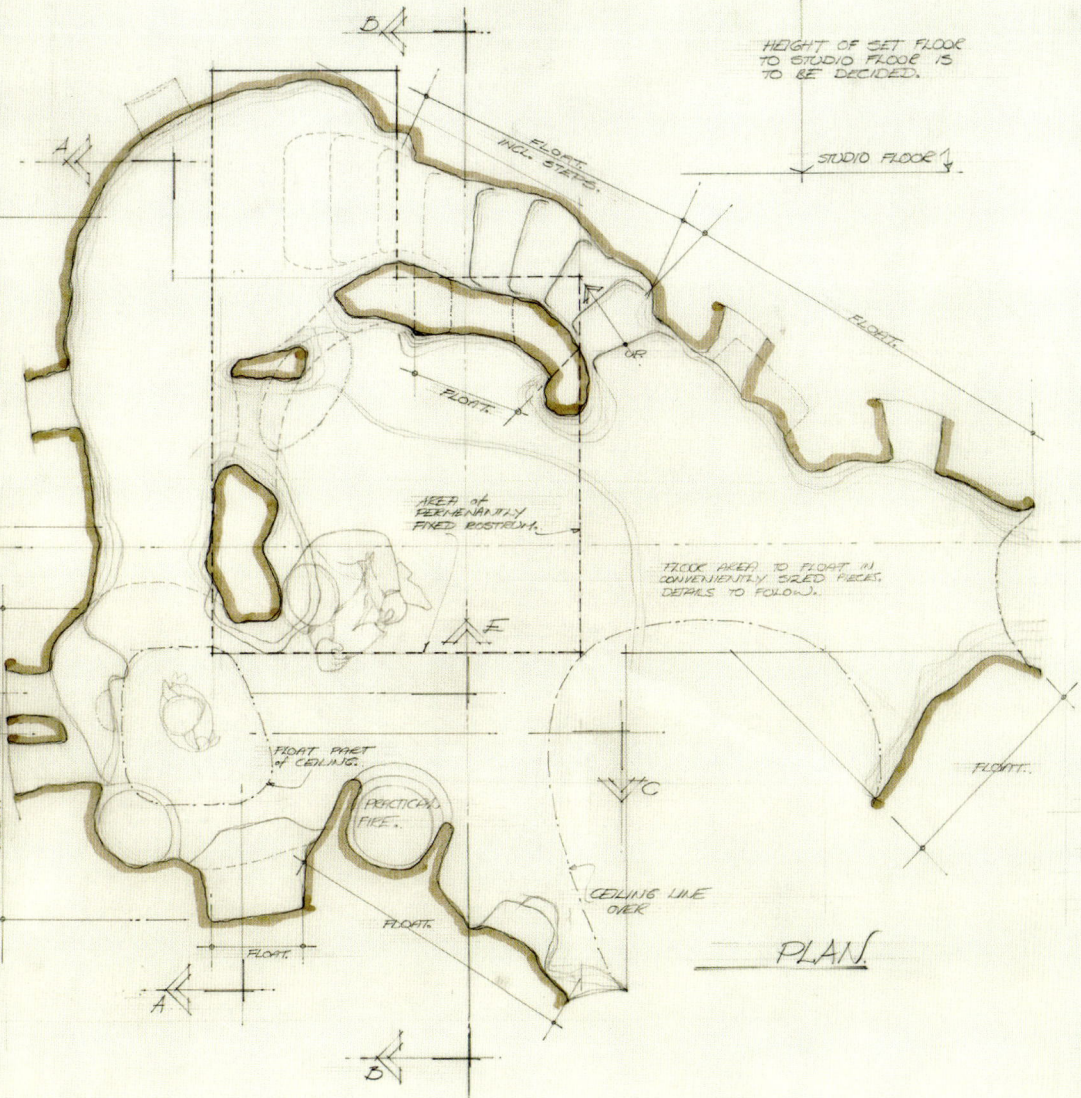

HEIGHT OF SET FLOOR
TO STUDIO FLOOR IS
TO BE DECIDED.

STUDIO FLOOR

NOTE
AREAS OF FLOOR NOT PERMENANTLY FIXED
ARE TO FLOAT IN SECTIONS OF
CONVENIENT SIZE ~ DETAILS TO BE
DECIDED.

AREAS OF CEILING TO FLOAT · SEE ART DEPT.

THIS DRAWING TO BE READ IN CONJUNCTION
WITH 1/2" & 1'0" SCALE MODEL ~ SEE ART DEPT.

FLOAT INCL. STEPS.

FLOAT.

AREA OF
PERMENANTLY
FIXED ROSTRUM.

FLOOR AREA TO FLOAT IN
CONVENIENTLY SIZED PIECES.
DETAILS TO FOLLOW.

FLOAT PART
OF CEILING.

PRACTICAL
FIRE.

CEILING LINE
OVER

FLOAT.

FLOAT.

FLOAT.

SCALE : 1" to 1'-0"

INT. YODA'S HOUSE
PLAN & SECTIONS.

PLAN.

STAR WARS 'THE EMPIRE STRIKES BACK'	© 1979 CHAPTER III PRODUCTIONS LTD.		
		CARPS.	
		PLAST.	
		PAINT	
		METAL	
SET. INT. YODA'S HOUSE	PROD. No. E9124	RIGGS.	
		DRAPES	
DETAIL PLAN & SECTIONS	DET No. 078	CHARGEH.	
		E.F.FX.	
		SIGNS	
DRG No. 372	SCALE 1"=1'0"	DATE 2·4·79	DRAWN BY M·A·B.	PROD. DESIGNER N.Reynolds	ART	
					PROD.	
					CON·MAN	

372

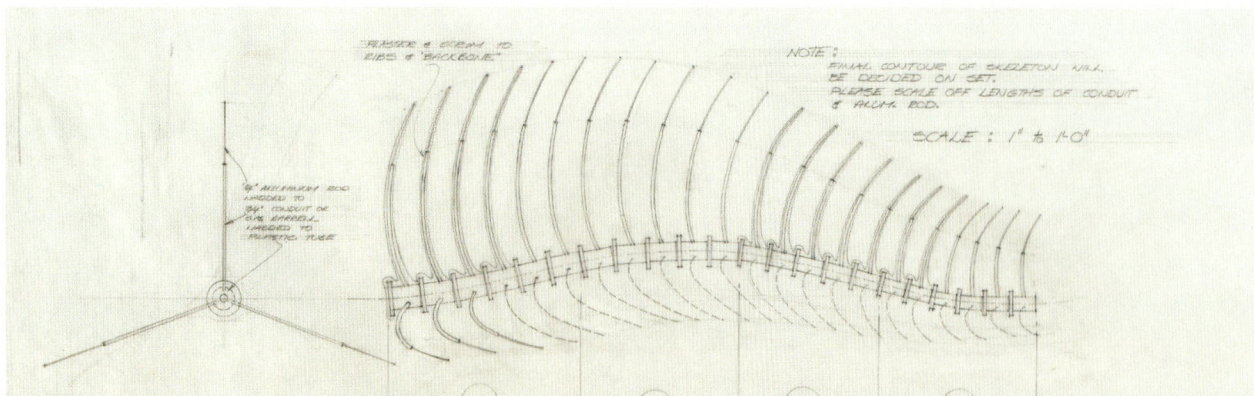

← Part of the dressing
for Dagobah included the
skeleton of some long-
deceased and devoured
creature—made from plaster—
the final contour of which
was to be decided on set.

SET	BOG SWAMP
DETAIL	ARMATURE FOR LARGE SKELETON
DRG. NO.	447
DATE	JULY 6 1979
DRAWN BY	MICHAEL BOONE

RIGHT AND BELOW The most complex sequence filmed on the bog
planet was Yoda's levitation of Luke's X-wing from the very
realistic swamp set. It took more than an entire day to
shoot less than a minute of screen time. Tomkins' drawings,
executed in conjunction with Kershner and Reynolds, note the
camera lens, degree of tilt, and placement heights, because
everything had to be planned in advance. While the X-fighter
was in the water, sitting on a ramped track, the existing
tank depth of 4 feet necessitated the removal of its
undercarriage and "possibly nose section." "Well, you don't
want to have too much water in the swamp, just enough to
make the X-wing look like it's sunk," said Tomkins. "And
then you had to build up the sides of the tank, because the
deeper it is, the more pressure builds up, exponentially.
But Bill Welch was a very, very capable man. He was another
MGM-trained construction guy who had worked with us on *2001*;
I knew him as a friend as well as a construction manager."

"I remember when we did that, actually, the water was very
mucky, and as we went on shooting in that set, it became
more and more slippery, and the pool really became almost a
health hazard," said Reynolds. "The *Star Wars* Stage was so
big that you would sometimes hear a splash coming from the
other end and say, 'Oh, another one fell into the pool.'"

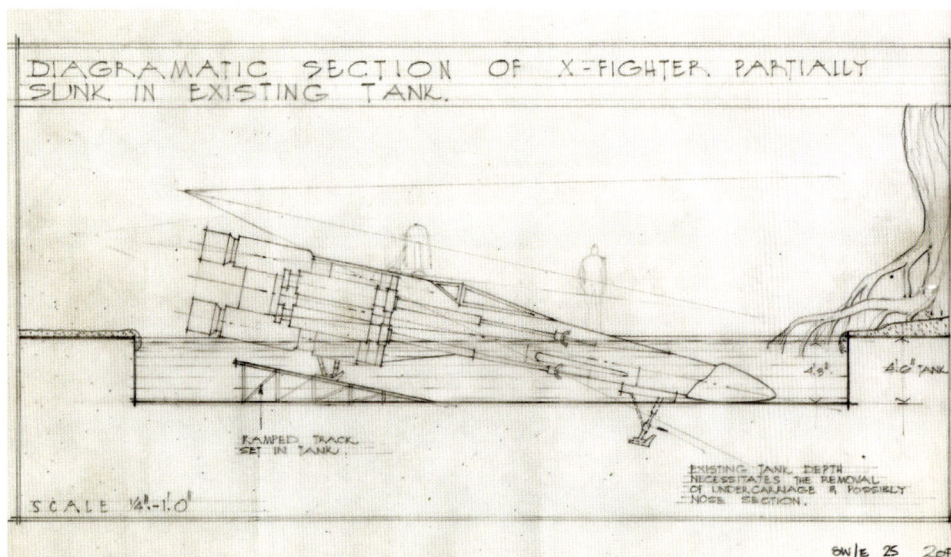

SET	DAGOBAH
DETAIL	DIAGRAMMATIC SECT OF X-FIGHTER IN TANK (ABOVE AND LEFT)
DRG. NO.	N/A
DATE	SUMMER 1979
DRAWN BY	ALAN TOMKINS

→ Luke attempts to raise
his X-wing from the bog.

SET	R2-D2
DETAIL	PRACTICAL HAND
DRG. NO.	02
DATE	MAY 30 1979
DRAWN BY	FRED HOLE

↓ R2-D2 reaches out with his specially designed "claw," as designed in the technical drawing, and engages in a tug-of-war with Yoda.

↑ Fred Hole, master of the mechanical, drew R2's "hand," which was to struggle with the Yoda puppet over Luke's flashlight. His blueprint illustrates the droid claw's open and closed position, a concealed spring arm that was to extend up to 18 inches from R2's body ("make like a watch"), and an outer telescope tube built on a central control rod.

SET	DAGOBAH
DETAIL	INSIDE TREE (LEFT AND BELOW)
DRG. NO.	N/A
DATE	SUMMER 1979
DRAWN BY	MICHAEL LAMONT

← Additional sketches were prepared to help Kershner plan out the dark side tree sequence, again with camera views noted, in which Luke faces off against himself as Vader.

CLOUD CITY

Given the economic and logistical limitations of making *Empire*, production had to reuse the same few hallways and circular area built for Cloud City several times for many scenes—or as Bream's blueprint (no. 401 on page 128) notes, "revamps for circular portion." By the time Kershner, cast, and crew arrived on Elstree's Stage 2 in May 1979, they were over budget and behind schedule. No new corridors could be built and scenes had to be shot as quickly as possible. So, for example, on the same walk Han Solo would go past the same window twice and a stairway would appear in two shots, filmed from a different angle, for the different scenes. In one shot, Lando Calrissian (Billy Dee Williams) would lead Leia and friends down a corridor that Luke would later sneak through, now in a blue light to denote a new corridor.

"Although we had quite a few corridors for Cloud City, one often wants to make a set look bigger than it really is," said director of photography Peter Suschitzky. "In one particular shot, I wanted to make the return into the same corridor look like a different one. So whilst the camera was round the corner, I worked out a series of light changes to be done rapidly during the shot, so that by the time we got back into our old territory, it looked like a new and differently lit corridor."

↓ From left to right, the blueprint layout shows the disposition on the soundstage of the observation room with painted backing, the living quarters, and so on.

SET	CLOUD CITY COMPOSITE, STAGE 2
DETAIL	FLOOR LAYOUT, ROSTRUMS
DRG. NO.	90
DATE	NOVEMBER 9 1978
DRAWN BY	RICHARD J. DAWKING

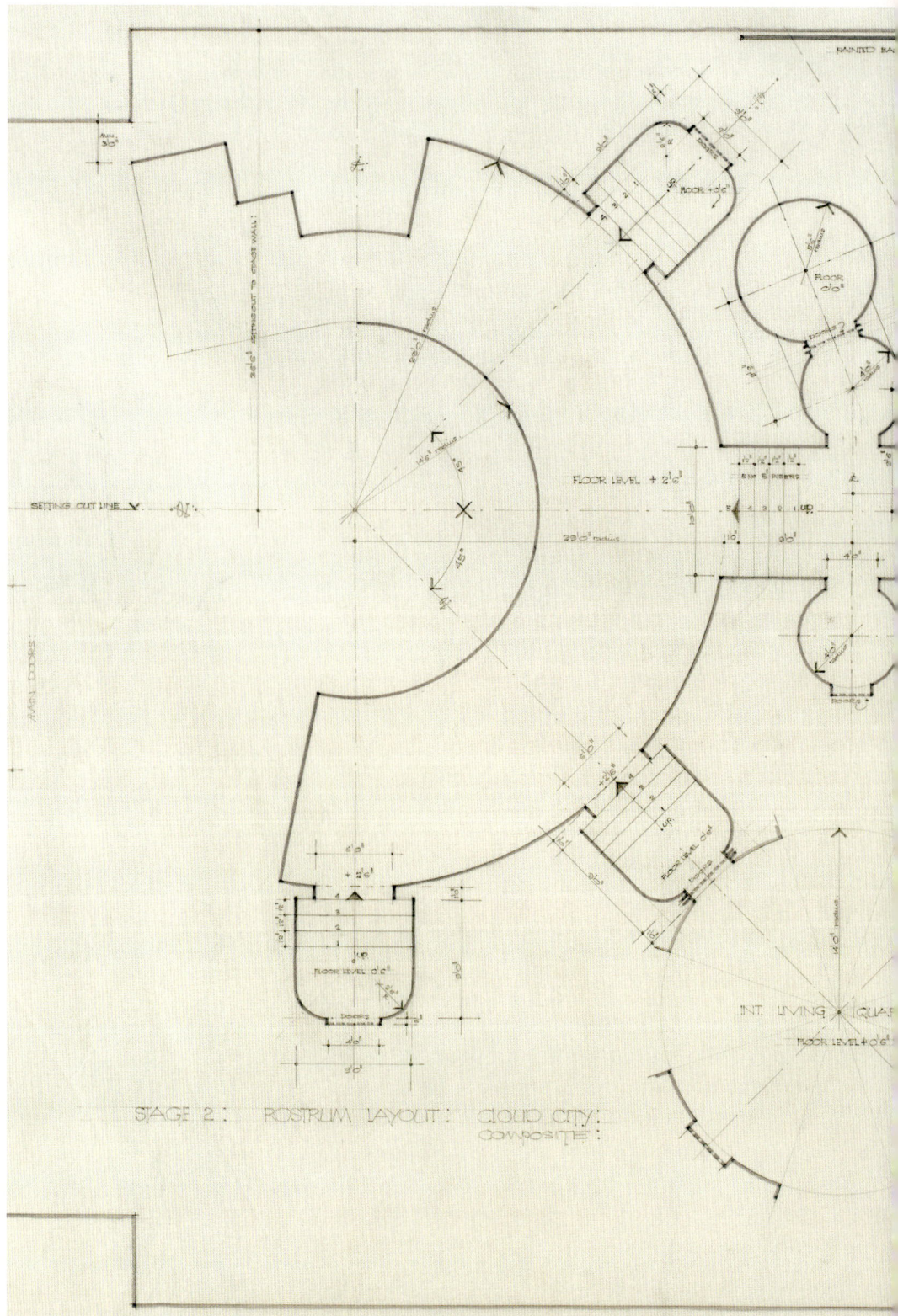

SET	CLOUD CITY BUILDINGS
DETAIL	SCENIC BACKINGS
DRG. NO.	N/A
DATE	1979
DRAWN BY	UNKNOWN

↑ Each *Star Wars* film kept its scenic painters busy with jobs like the above: Cloud City buildings that would appear outside of select on-set windows.

← A Reynolds concept drawing of Cloud City, June 1979.

↓ Preliminary maquette shows a Cloud City environment, with a cutout of Leia.

↑ A maquette of the Cloud City set design is seen from above, with dining room, living room, and hallways.

↑ Shooting on the Cloud City interiors took place in mid-April 1979. Many of the shots were of characters running through the hallways.

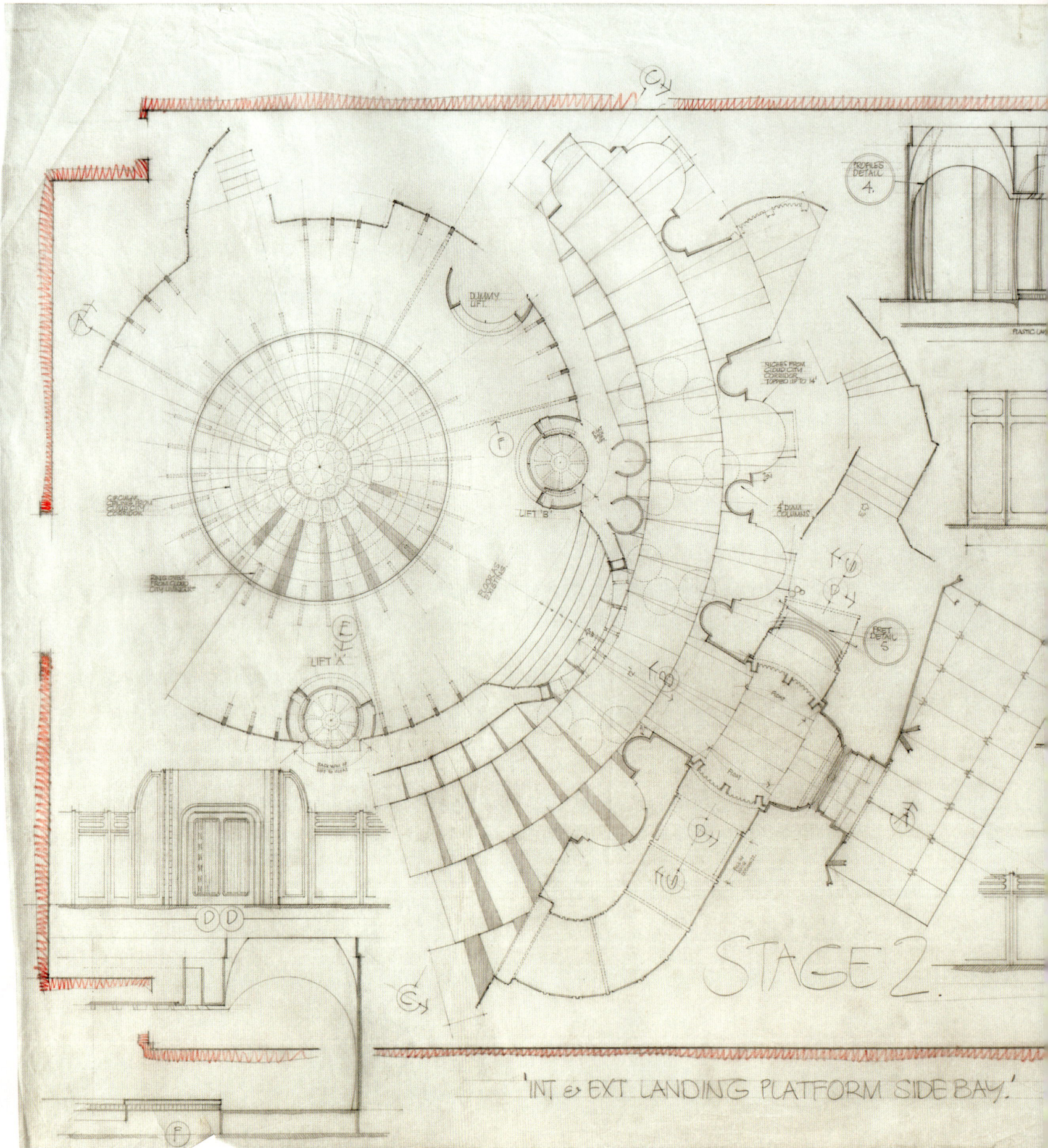

STAGE 2.

'INT & EXT LANDING PLATFORM SIDE BAY.'

Plans and elevations of Landing Platform Side Bay.

SET   LANDING PLATFORM SIDE BAY,   DRG. NO.   401
         CLOUD CITY   DATE   APRIL 28 1979
DETAIL   PLANS & ELEVATIONS   DRAWN BY   REG BREAM

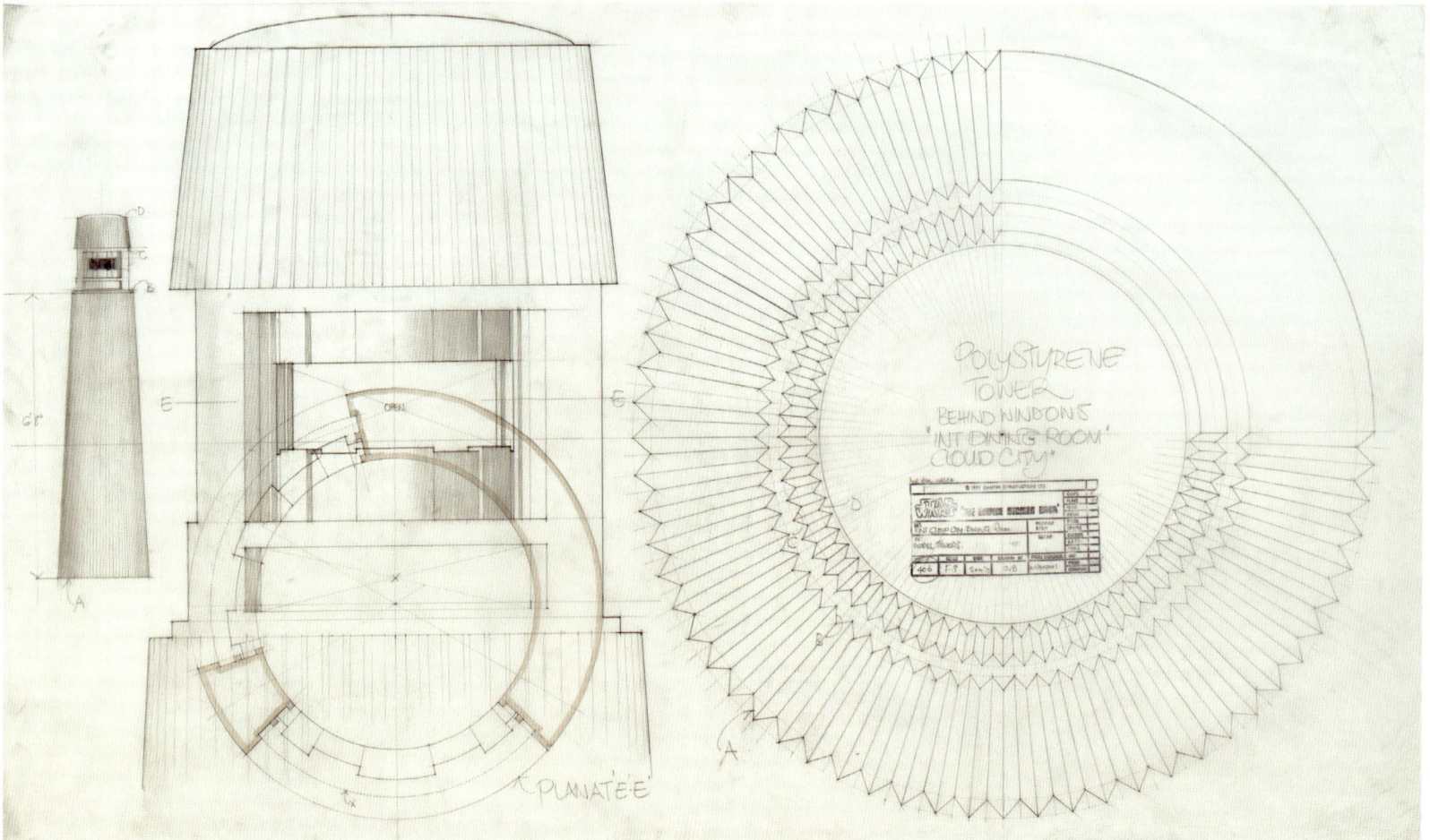

POLYSTYRENE
TOWER
BEHIND WINDOWS
"INT DINING ROOM"
CLOUD CITY"

SET	CLOUD CITY DINING ROOM
DETAIL	MODEL TOWERS
DRG. NO.	406
DATE	MAY 2 1979
DRAWN BY	REG BREAM

↓ The Cloud City fountain in situ on the finished set.

↑ Several drawings have survived of the dining room interior, where Darth Vader ambushes Solo, Leia, and Chewbacca. "I remember the chairs for Darth in the dining room, those very high-backed chairs," said Reynolds. "I was a little bit influenced by the Scottish architect Charles Rennie Mackintosh. For Leia's living quarters, I was influenced by the Bauhaus architects, for the entrenched sculptural forms."

CLOUD CITY : FOUNTAINS : 2 OFF :

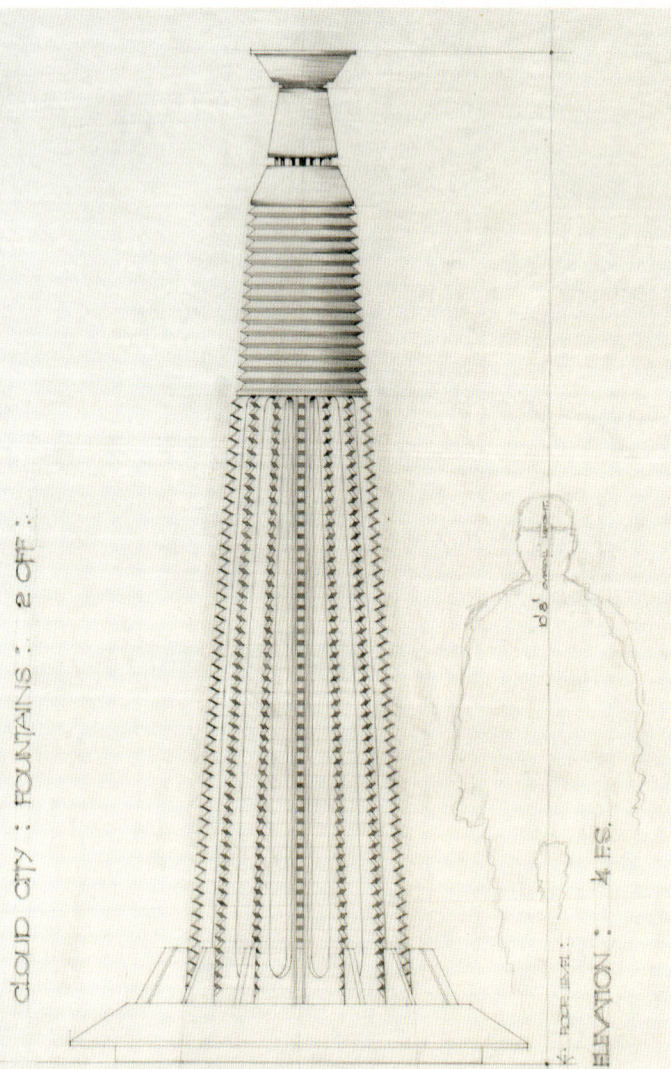

ELEVATION : ¼ F.S.

← This technical drawing notes that two fountain ornaments were to be 10-foot, 8-inches in height, with a "steinhard" high-gloss finish.

SET	CLOUD CITY INTERIORS
DETAIL	FOUNTAIN, PLAN & ELEVATION
DRG. NO.	218
DATE	JANUARY 15 1979
DRAWN BY	RICHARD J. DAWKING

→ 14 chairs were made from the approved drawing (no. 236), two of another model (perhaps the two placed at the head and foot of the table in no. 283). Behind Vader is a window; behind that was a polystyrene tower built and painted as a scenic backdrop.

NEN FACING OF FIBREGLASS PANELLING
FINISH TO BE DECIDED.

NEN PLY 'ARCHITRAVE'
TO MATTER ENDS OF
FIBREGLASS. SEE F.S.D.

SECTION @ D·D

F.S.
ARCHIT

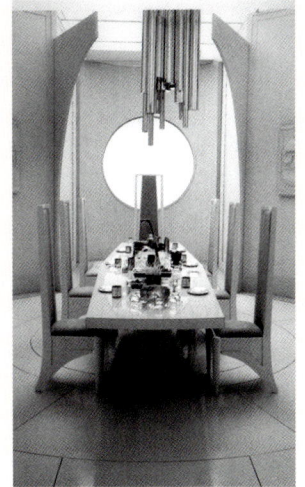

↑ The dining room set is seen before filming.

SET	DINING ROOM, CLOUD CITY
DETAIL	PLANS & ELEVATIONS
DRG. NO.	283
DATE	FEBRUARY 20 1979
DRAWN BY	MICHAEL BOONE

↑ From October 16 to 18, 1978, McQuarrie painted the dining room scene on Cloud City (with a mistakenly all-white Boba Fett present; Johnston had already painted his costume, but information was sometimes slow in being disseminated).

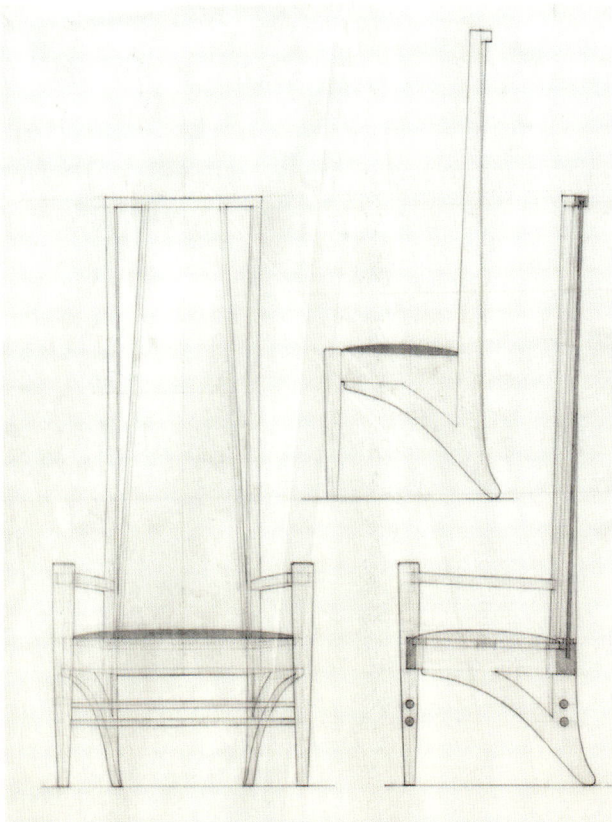

SET	DINING ROOM, CLOUD CITY
DETAIL	FURNITURE
DRG. NO.	236
DATE	JANUARY 29 1979
DRAWN BY	REG BREAM

→ An early concept drawing by Reynolds of "Darth's Banquet Room", circa November 1978.

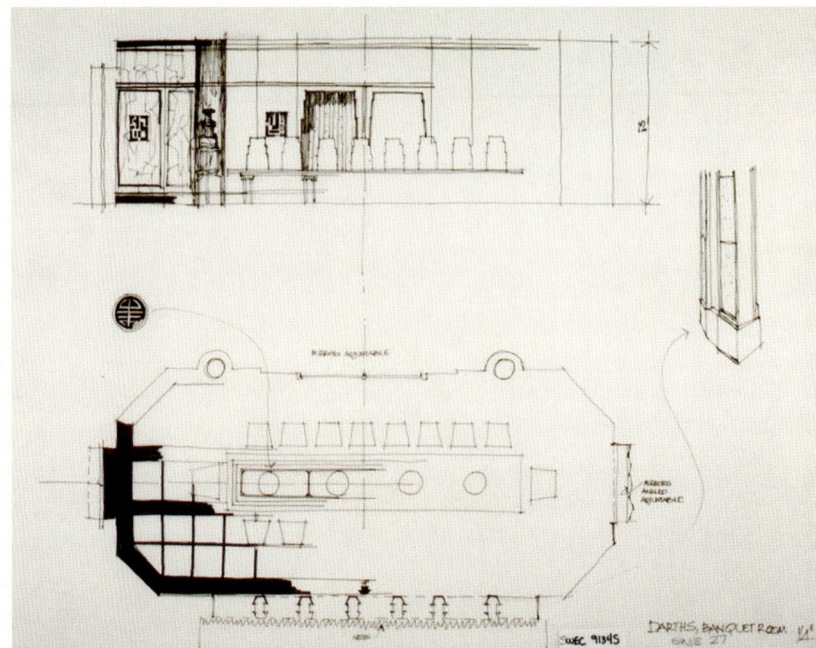

CARBON FREEZING CHAMBER

One of *Empire*'s most iconic sets—the Carbon Freezing Chamber—didn't take final form until shortly before principal photography began. Following Lucas' directives, McQuarrie had imagined it as an industrial space, filled with rectangular shapes. But Reynolds had other ideas.

"I didn't know quite what to do with that one," he said "I really labored on that. I mean, *What does a carbon freezing chamber look like, for heaven's sake?* And in fact, I had no idea until I actually dreamt it! I woke up one night knowing what it would look like. So I did a very simple little drawing, a little scribble, and I worked with Reg Bream and came up with this idea as it appears in the film, with that central circular set, the various appendages hanging down, and the illuminated risers of the stairs."

As originally imagined, Reynolds' set design was even more enigmatic, as can be seen in his early drawings and McQuarrie's subsequent painting based on those concepts. "It never materialized, but the idea was that there would be two enormous sort of pipe-like things in limbo with one or two other ones in this vast area of darkness. I thought there might be three or four of these chambers, doing similar functions. So I envisioned one in the foreground with one or two other ones in the distance behind, illuminating part of the darkness beyond it, just to give it some regression, really, to take your eye farther and farther away."

Even in its compromised form, the set was non-traditional: built about 12 feet off the ground, it lacked walls—something that ILM members noted with admiration when they saw it later on. Because it was so unusual, Reynolds showed Kershner the set every week as it progressed.

"Finally we reached the point where we had dressed the set, however, and I showed Kershner," said Reynolds. "He walked around and then he said, 'Well, I can't shoot this.' And I said, 'Why not, Kersh?' And he said, 'Well, it's just…I can't. How would you shoot it?' Well, when you design something, you have to have an idea of how it's going to be shot, so I just ran it by Kersh—in desperation. And he said, 'I'll see you on Monday.'

"So it was a weekend of purgatory, because there was nothing I could do. He'd said, 'I can't shoot it.' A miserable, miserable time. I went home wondering if I should bite on the pill, leave the country, or just go into hiding. My wife thought I was a bit subdued. Those are the moments when you think, *Perhaps I shouldn't have agreed to design this job.*

"When I saw Kersh Monday morning, I was expecting to be burnt at the stake. I said to him, 'I've had the worst weekend of my life.' And he said, 'Well, why is that?' I said, 'Well, you said you couldn't shoot it, and here we are, everyone's arriving, the camera crew and everyone's here.' And he said, 'I just felt a little bit nervous at the time. It's going to be fine. In fact, I think it's going to be great.' And he ended up really loving it."

Although the director was placated, it did prove to be an extremely difficult scene to work out, with a massive claw, a carbon block, huge clouds of steam, dozens of lights—and one of the film's most complex emotional moments. But the DP Peter Suschitzky lit it in wonderful ways and everyone played at the top of their game. There was one person still a bit surprised by the set, however. "I did say to George later on, 'What did you think?'" Reynolds recalled "And he said, 'Well, it's okay, but I prefer sets with walls.'"

↑ A McQuarrie painting of the Carbon Freezing Chamber from August 1978.

↑ McQuarrie's revised Carbon Freezing Chamber painting provides a glimpse of what Reynolds had in mind—with enormous floating pipe-like structures receding in the distance.

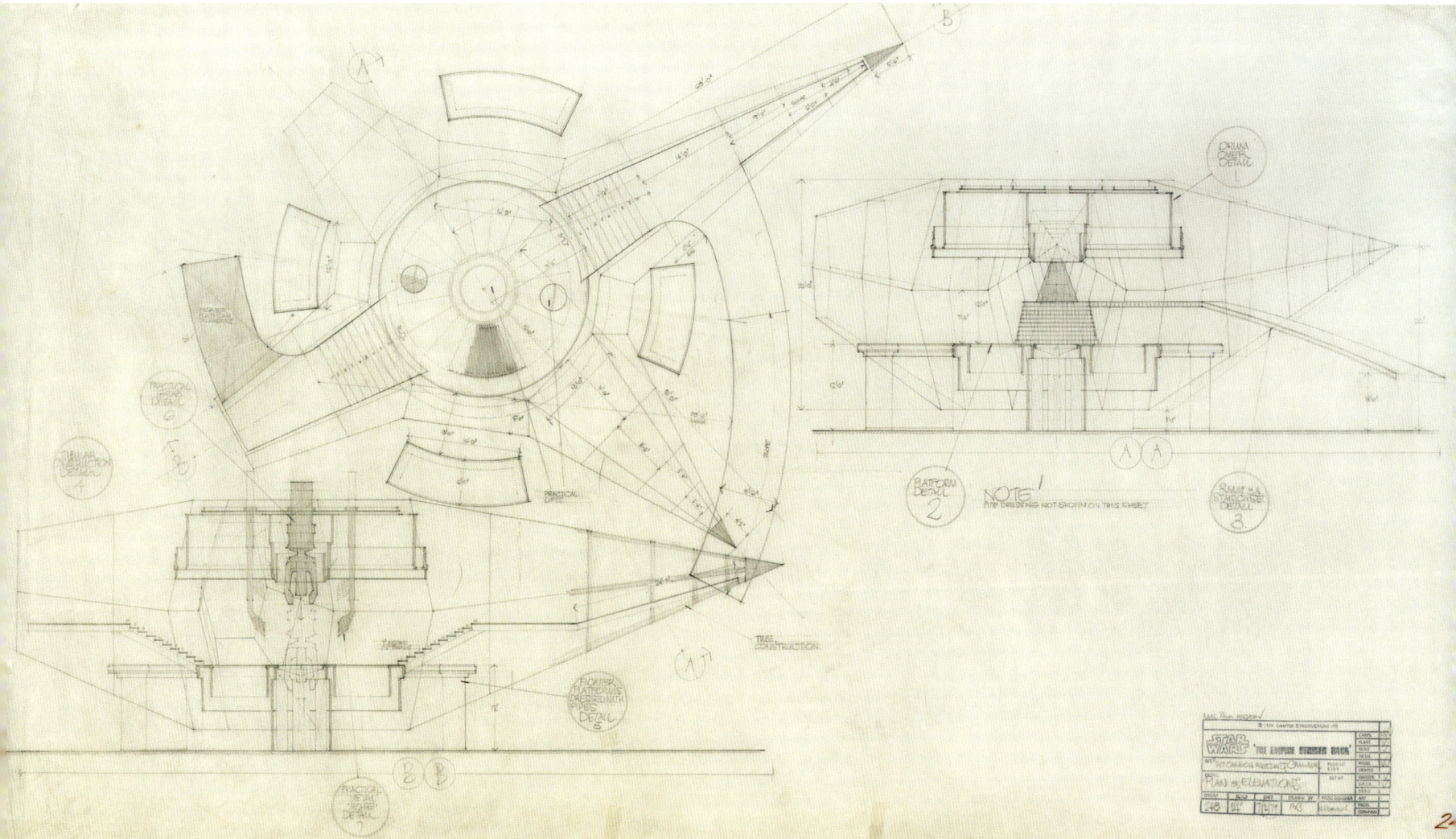

← This maquette is based on the early McQuarrie concept of the Carbon Freezing Chamber.

SET	CARBON FREEZING CHAMBER
DETAIL	PLANS & ELEVATIONS
DRG. NO.	248
DATE	FEBRUARY 7 1979
DRAWN BY	REG BREAM

PRELIM CARB FREEZING.

→ Reynolds redesigned the Carbon Freezing Chamber in December 1978.

SET	CARBON FREEZING CHAMBER
DETAIL	PLATFORM
DRG. NO.	245
DATE	FEBRUARY 5 1979
DRAWN BY	REG BREAM

← Bream's drawing of the Carbon Freezing Chamber shows the platform and the claw that would be able to do a "practical grab" of the carbon block; the claw could also be lowered and raised, and pivoted. A later scene when Luke arrives as if on an elevator necessitated a grating in the floor that would slide open in two sections.

"The big claw was simply a logical way of pulling up the block," said Reynolds. "It wasn't hugely elaborate, just a straightforward, manually operated thing. I'm a great believer in manually operated props, because a minimum amount of things can go wrong when you have adopted that sort of approach. If you need a little bit more beef, then you get more people; and you can stop things instantly. Sometimes with electrically or digitally operated machines, things can just go slightly astray and it's not always easy to stop the thing instantly."

→ A McQuarrie concept drawing of the machinery housed in the ceiling of the Carbon Freezing Chamber.

← The final carbon cell block was created with Solo's arms up as though to ward off his entombment.

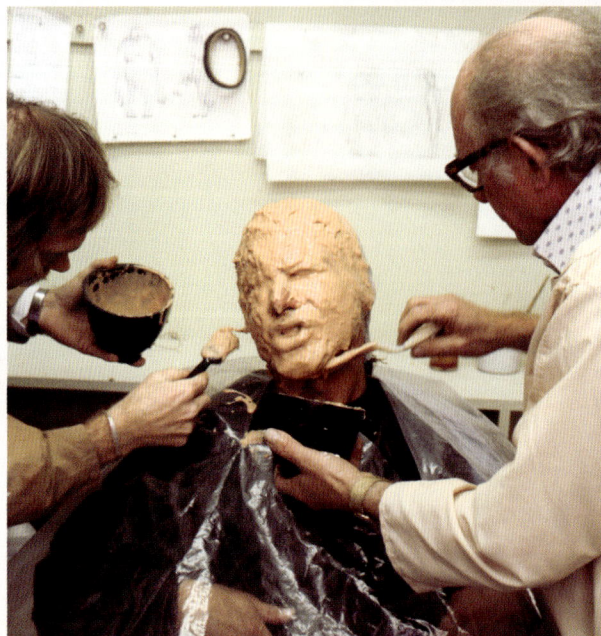

↑ In Act I of their duel, Luke and Vader face off in the Carbon Freezing Chamber set on Stage 4, early July 1979.

← Makeup supervisor Stuart Freeborn applies the plaster to Harrison Ford for his portrait in the carbon block.

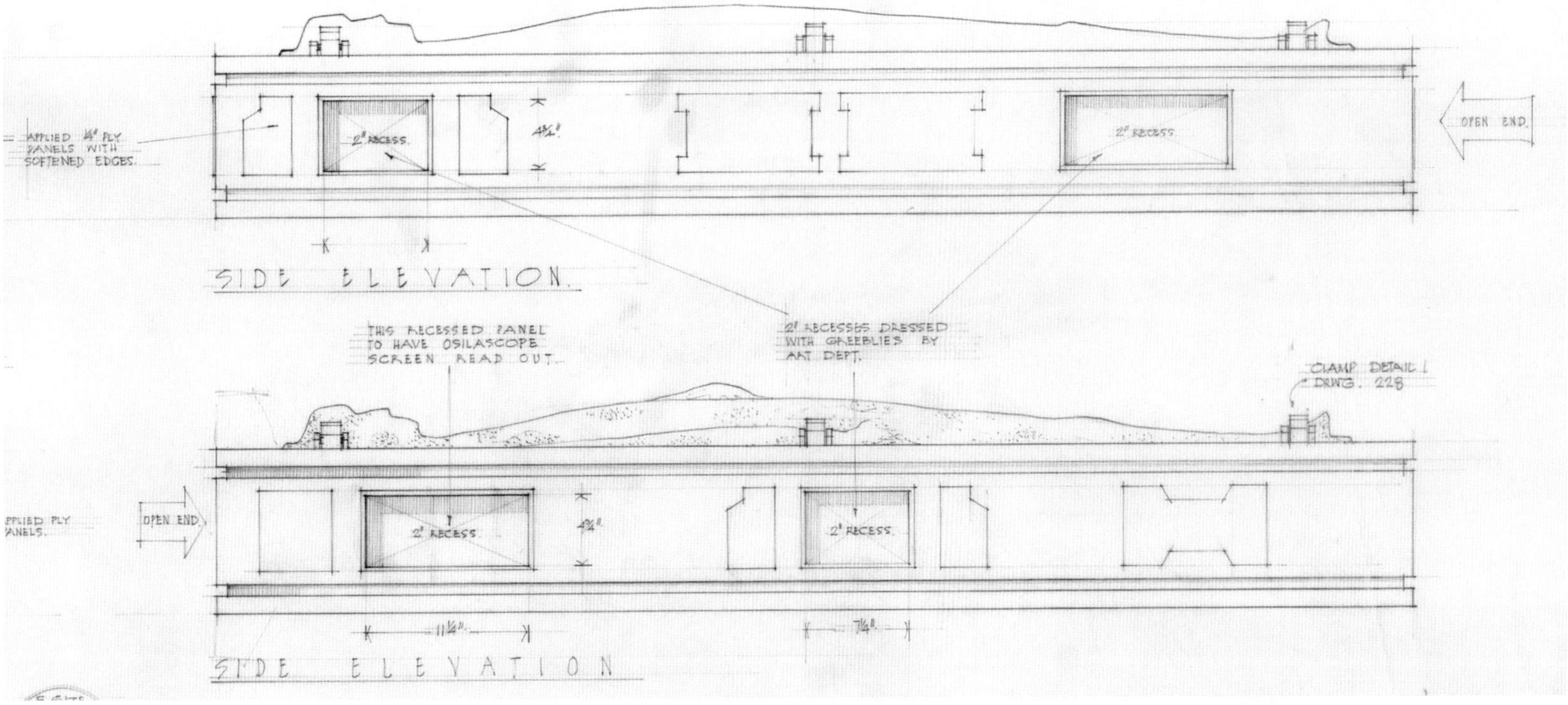

SIDE ELEVATION.

APPLIED ¼" PLY PANELS WITH SOFTENED EDGES.

2" RECESS

4½"

OPEN END.

THIS RECESSED PANEL TO HAVE OSILASCOPE SCREEN READ OUT.

2" RECESSES DRESSED WITH GREEBLIES BY ART DEPT.

CLAMP DETAIL DWG. 228

APPLIED PLY PANELS.

OPEN END

2" RECESS

4½"

2" RECESS

SIDE ELEVATION

SET	CARBON FREEZING CHAMBER, CLOUD CITY
DETAIL	CARBON CELL BLOCK
DRG. NO.	227
DATE	JANUARY 21 1979
DRAWN BY	ALAN TOMKINS

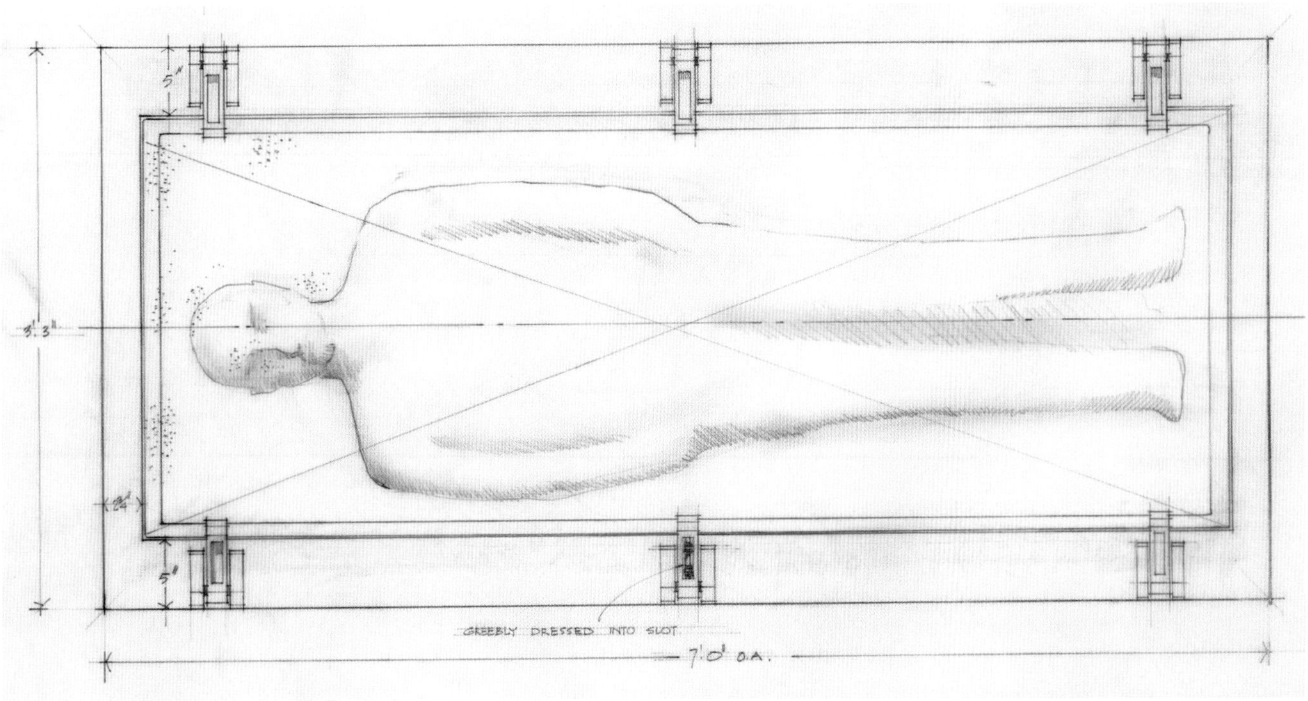

GREEBLY DRESSED INTO SLOT.

7'-0" O.A.

SET	CARBON FREEZING CHAMBER
DETAIL	CARBON CELL BLOCK
DRG. NO.	228
DATE	JANUARY 21 1979
DRAWN BY	ALAN TOMKINS

↑ With a recessed panel for an oscilloscope readout and other greeblies, the actual carbon block in which Han Solo is encased was made from three individuals: Harrison Ford, of course, for the face; another person for the body, and yet a third individual for the hands. The third person was needed because in the first block, as these drawings show, Solo's hands were to the sides. Kershner would later have them redone with Solo's hands pushing out, raised in protest, feeling that it would be more realistic emotionally, and more dramatic.

 "The guy that set the carbon block in my plaster shop was Sid Whitlock," said Clarke. "We made it all up in plaster, in an architectural way, with the body parts of the beings. The only part of Harrison Ford was his face, because it was very, very rare you could get him offstage anyway."

REACTOR CONTROL ROOM

After Han Solo is frozen in carbonite, Luke Skywalker arrives to try and save his friends—but of course it is all a well-laid trap by Vader. Luke and the Sith Lord first face off on the Carbon Freezing Chamber. The second act of their duel takes place in the Reactor Control Room, where, for the first time in the saga, a big round window appears to dramatic effect (in an early script, both characters risked being chopped to pieces by a blade-like mechanism).

"The breakaway window was a concern but more so for the stunt department than the art department," said Reynolds. Indeed, stuntman Colin Skeaping would double for Luke, executing a running forward flip, turning in midair, and then crashing backward through the already broken window.

Another feature of the set was yet another corridor built in forced perspective, which can be seen behind Luke when he ignites his lightsaber to confront Vader. "Some of the corridors leading up to the gantry, linking up with my set, were drawn by a wonderful draftsman called Reg Bream," said Ambrose. "We all admired him because he did such wonderful drawings, you know, and so fast."

→ The circular window is being built on Stage 1 at Elstree Studios with Reynolds's modified design.

→ A great number of blueprints in the Archives are actually full-scale drawings of important parts of sets, created for the shops that had to execute thousands of unique objects: for example, Boone's grating segment. Holes in the rostrum had been drilled for steam effects in the Reactor Control Room, which meant that a basic grating had to be designed, drawn, and then duplicates fabricated, placed on set, and perhaps dressed—for a part of the film that most in the audience would never ever notice.

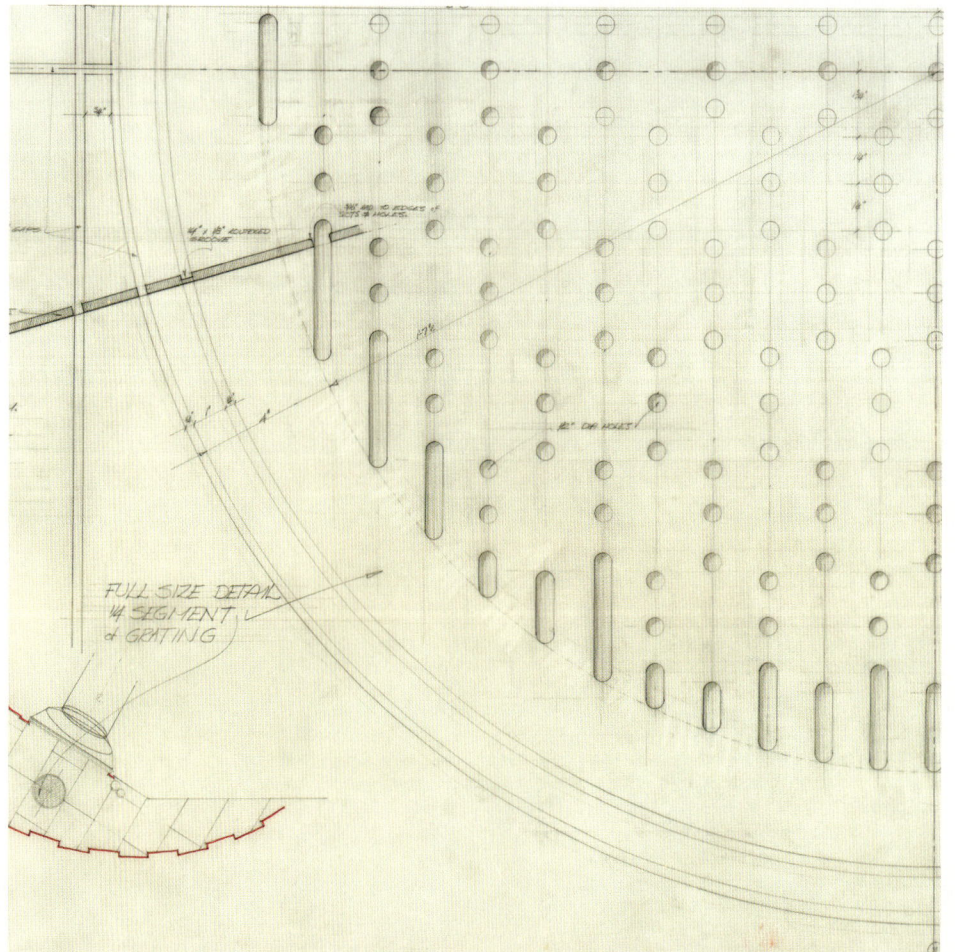

SET	REACTOR CONTROL ROOM
DETAIL	STEAM EFFECT GRATINGS
DRG. NO.	419
DATE	MAY 17 1979
DRAWN BY	MICHAEL BOONE

SET	REACTOR CONTROL ROOM
DETAIL	TUBE & SLIDING GRILL
DRG. NO.	311
DATE	MARCH 9 1979
DRAWN BY	REG BREAM

↑ Bream's drawing of the sliding grill, which closes behind Luke, is a superb example of the kind of throwaway, yet fantastic, design that permeates the *Star Wars* films.

↓ Stuntman Colin Skeaping hurls himself through the already broken window.

↑ A McQuarrie color study for his production painting of the Reactor Control Room set shows the prominent round window, August 1978.

↑ A Reynolds concept drawing of the Reactor Control Room set, February 1979 (note the sliding grill).

SET	REACTOR CONTROL ROOM	DATE	MARCH 5 1979
DETAIL	PLANS & ELEVATIONS	DRAWN BY	REG BREAM
DRG. NO.	305		

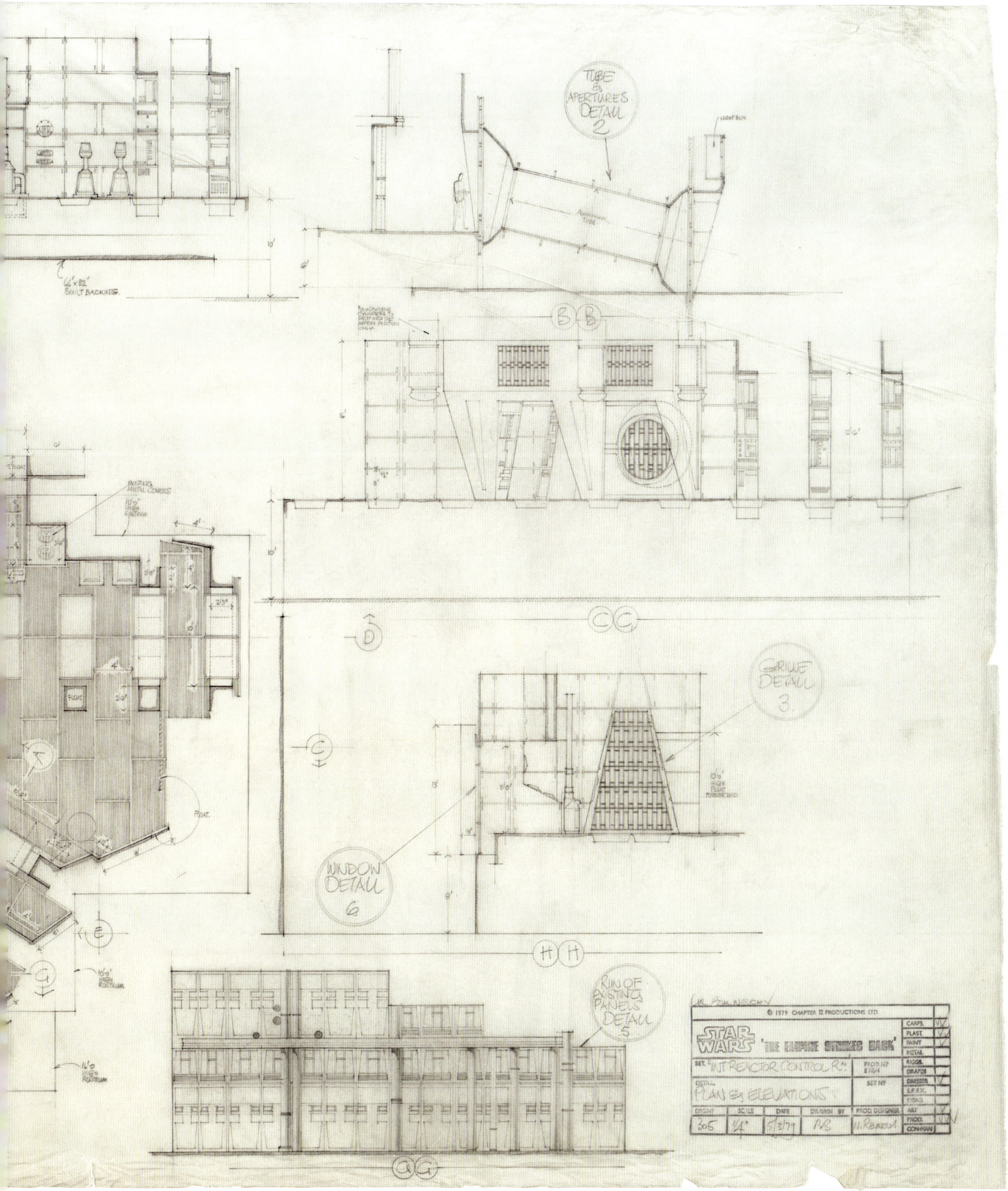

TUBE
&
APERTURES.
DETAIL
2

Light Box

B B

C C

D

C

GRILLE
DETAIL
3.

WINDOW
DETAIL
6

H H

RUN OF
EXISTING
PANELS
DETAIL
5

© 1979 CHAPTER II PRODUCTIONS LTD.

STAR WARS "THE EMPIRE STRIKES BACK"

SET: INT REACTOR CONTROL Rm

DETAIL PLAN & ELEVATIONS

			CARPS.	
			PLAST.	
			PAINT	
			METAL	
	PROD. No 27314		RIGGS	
	SET No		DRAPES	
			DRESSER	
			S.F.FX.	
			SIGNS	
DRAWN	SCALE	DATE	DRAWN BY	PROD DESIGNER	ART
305	¼"	5/3/79	NS	H Reynolds	PROD
					CON MAN

G G

GANTRY

In late July 1979, after one hundred days of shooting, Kershner and his crew finally made it to the gantry, which, in the film, is perched over a very deep reactor shaft; on set, of course, the height was closer to 30 feet, but still dangerous for the actors and crew. The third act of the Vader vs. Luke duel takes place here—and it is during this climactic scene that Vader reveals that he is Luke's father.

Ted Ambrose drew nearly all of the blueprints connected with this set, while the director had worked out the camera angles with Reynolds in advance. Because it was the last in a long line of constructs, created by hundreds of craftsmen working almost nonstop, the Plan and Elevation blueprint reveals that parts of the gantry were recycled from previous sets: an "existing walkway piece" and pieces taken from the Reactor Control Room, along with a "purchased aluminum angle as door trim" and a tubular tower on one end. "I got Ogle Designs involved in the rocket unit at the end of the pinnacle, the gantry control," said Welch.

But the key to selling the fantastic locale to the audience was perhaps the most complex scenic background (no. 316 on page 144) ever created for a *Star Wars* film. Two backings were made: one for straight-ahead shots and another for tilting shots up or down, with camera angles worked out in advance to achieve a proper flattened, cylindrical perspective. Parts of the backing were painted, while others were three-dimensional, an extremely effective combination.

"That was actually drawn in the art department and mixed with little pieces of plywood made up and planted on to form the structure of the panels and holes cut for illuminating from behind," said Reynolds. "It was really a prebuilt perspective piece that was painted almost like a straightforward set, as opposed to a purely scenic backing.

SET	GANTRY OUTSIDE CONTROL ROOM
DETAIL	PLAN & ELEVATIONS
DRG. NO.	366
DATE	MARCH 27 1979
DRAWN BY	TED AMRBOSE

↓ Another of Ambrose's technical drawings reveals "breakaway pieces for duel." In addition, part of the walkway would be floating, the floor would be made of rubber, and replacement breakaway railing should be provided for "laser sword fight sequence."

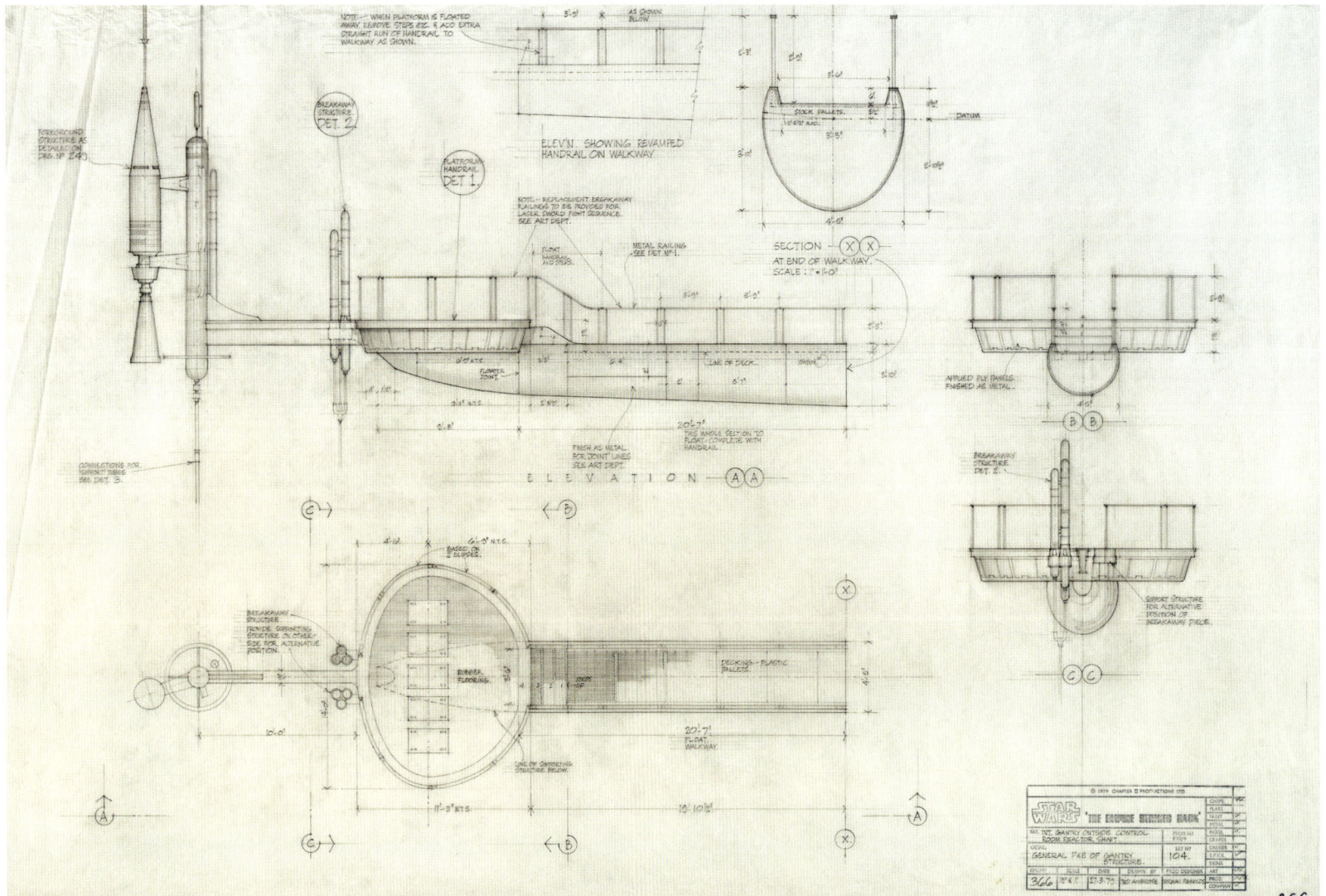

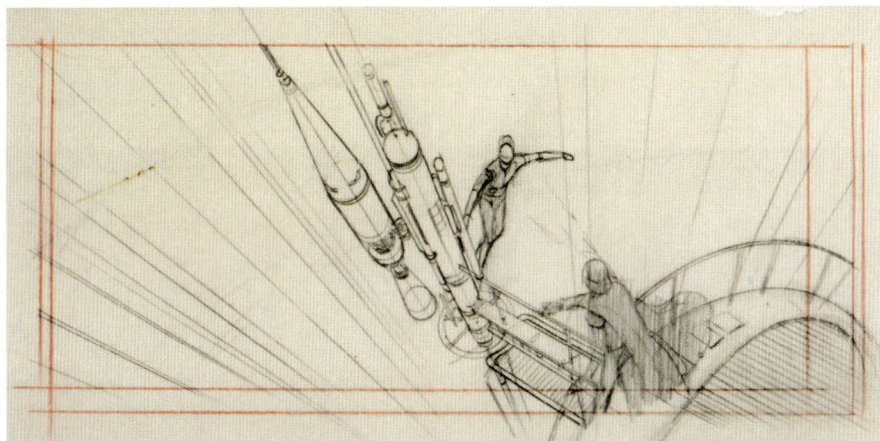

→ The gantry set on Stage 1 was about 30 feet off the ground, so mattresses and boxes were piled high for Hamill's plunge off the rocket unit.

← McQuarrie's preparatory pencil sketch from August 1978 shows Luke letting himself fall into the reactor shaft.

← The gantry set included the built backing for straight-ahead shots.

→ The tilt-up and tilt-down shots would use the same built backing, repositioned for each set-up.

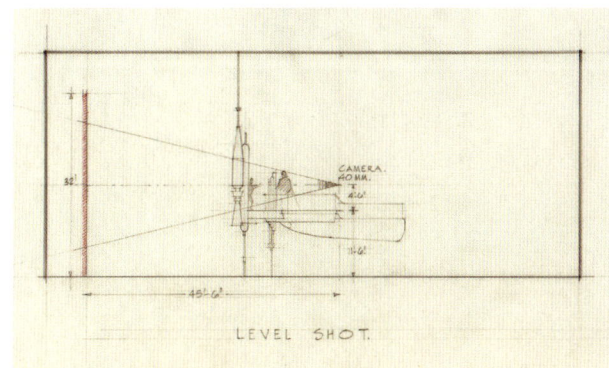

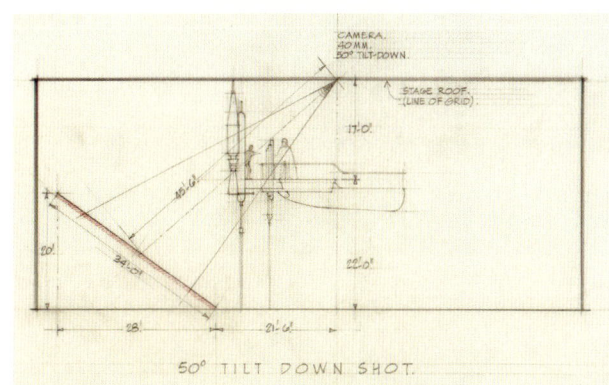

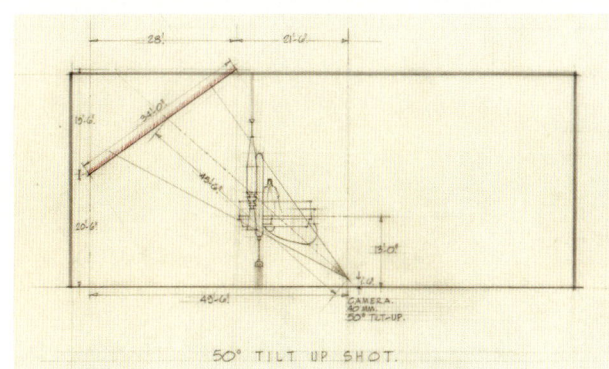

LEVEL SHOT.

50° TILT DOWN SHOT.

50° TILT UP SHOT.

SET	GANTRY END OF POD REACTOR SHAFT
DETAIL	MAIN SETUPS (ALL ABOVE)
DRG. NO.	379
DATE	APRIL 5 1979
DRAWN BY	TED AMBROSE

It was actually a geometrical perspective built to give the impression of a circular shaft."

"The gantry is something I was really, really proud of, because you don't know if it's going to work or not, but it did," said Ambrose. "We had fantastic sketches from Ralph, and obviously we were under Norman Reynolds' guidance. But it was quite difficult because it was a sort of drum-shaped set, and was supposed to be like five miles deep and a half-mile wide or something. It was this huge thing, so I had to work out all the perspectives."

"I think it really looked good in the film and, in point of fact, it saved a lot of money," said Reynolds. "It would have been very hard to do what we did without that built backing. The only other way would have been blue screen shots. People would tend to probably do that today, because there aren't too many people around with the knowledge of how to do what we did. But it actually saved the company a lot of process work, and so, a lot of money."

While ILM would create a matte painting for the establishing shot of the reactor core, the area behind Luke and Vader during closer shots of their climactic confrontation was nearly always a "set," which meant that it looks more realistic. Replacing a blue screen with process shots or mattes would have created noticeable artifacts during the swirling lightsaber action that would have taken audiences away from the immediacy of the scene.

PLAN — TAKEN AS SECTION THRO. DATUM LINE – 10'-0" LEVEL.

SET	GANTRY OUTSIDE	DRG. NO.	424
	REACTOR SHAFT	DATE	MAY 31 1979
DETAIL	PLAN & ELEVATIONS	DRAWN BY	TED AMBROSE

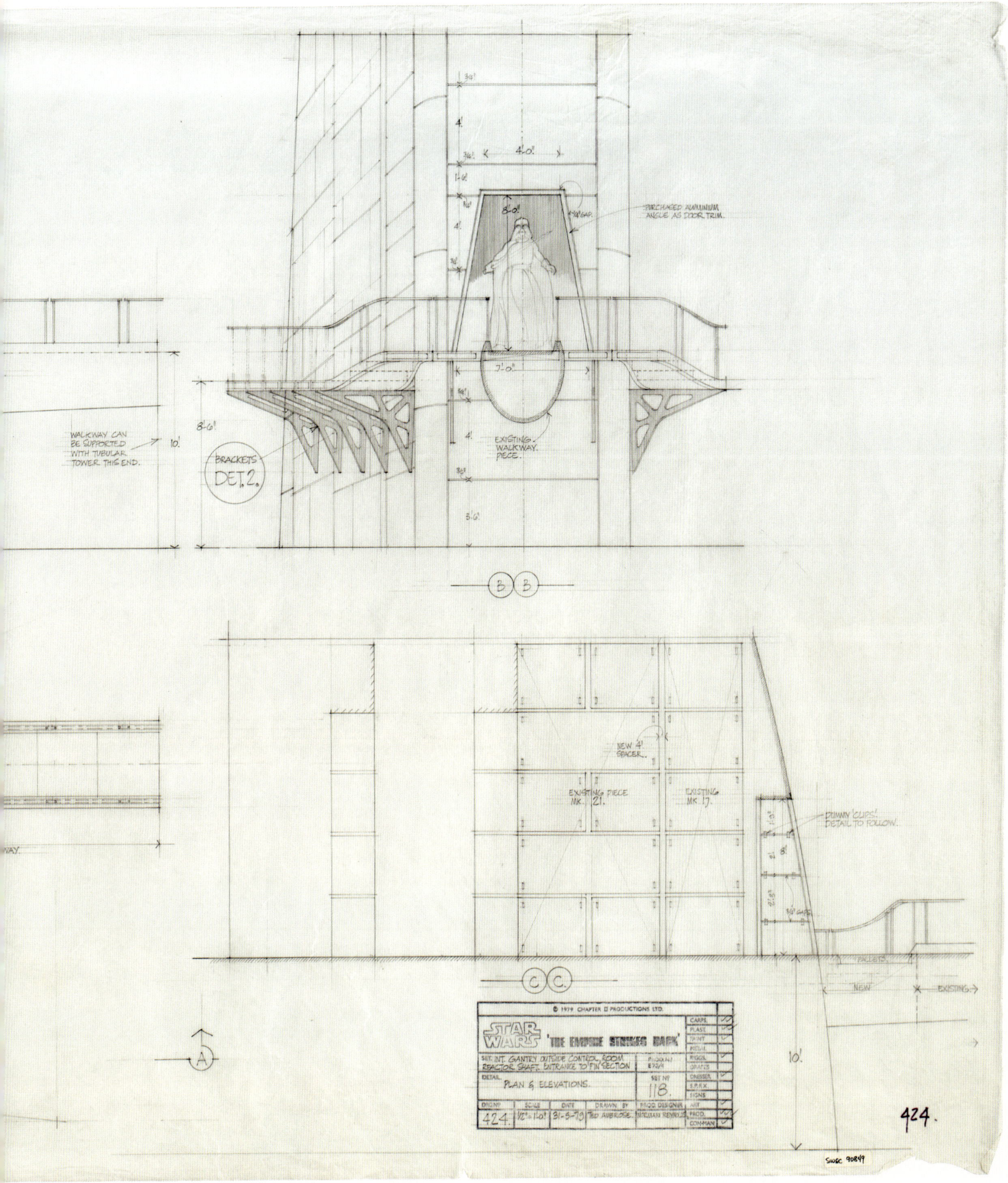

PURCHASED ALUMINIUM
ANGLE AS DOOR TRIM.

4'-0"

8'-0"

¼" GAP.

7'-0"

WALKWAY CAN
BE SUPPORTED
WITH TUBULAR
TOWER THIS END.

10'

8'-6"

BRACKETS
DET. 2.

EXISTING
WALKWAY
PIECE.

8'-6"

B B

NEW 4'
SPACER.

EXISTING PIECE
MK. 21.

EXISTING
MK. 17.

DUMMY 'CLIPS'
DETAIL TO FOLLOW.

¼" GAP.

PALLETS

NEW   EXISTING

C C

A

10'

© 1979 CHAPTER II PRODUCTIONS LTD.

STAR WARS 'THE EMPIRE STRIKES BACK'

SET: INT. GANTRY OUTSIDE CONTROL ROOM
REACTOR SHAFT, ENTRANCE TO FIN SECTION

DETAIL: PLAN & ELEVATIONS.

SET N° 118.

DRG N°	SCALE	DATE	DRAWN BY	PROD DESIGNER		
424	½"=1'-0"	31-5-79	TED AMBROSE	NORMAN REYNOLDS		

CARP.		
PLAST.		
PAINT		
METAL		
RIGG.		
GRAPH.		
CHARGE		
S.F.X.		
SIGNS		
ART		
PROD.		
CONSTR.		

424.

SET	GANTRY OUTSIDE CONTROL ROOM
	REACTOR SHAFT
DETAIL	BUILT BACKING FOR TILT-DOWN & TILT
	UP SHOTS
DRG. NO.	316
DATE	MARCH 13 1979
DRAWN BY	TED AMBROSE

→ The giant backing built and painted for the tilt-up and tilt-down shots during the gantry sequence was 66 feet wide and 34 feet high, with a vanishing point on the center line. Ambrose noted on the technical drawing: "All four panels with holes in them [are] to be removable and replaced with alternative ones for tilting up shot; holes cut for light effects."

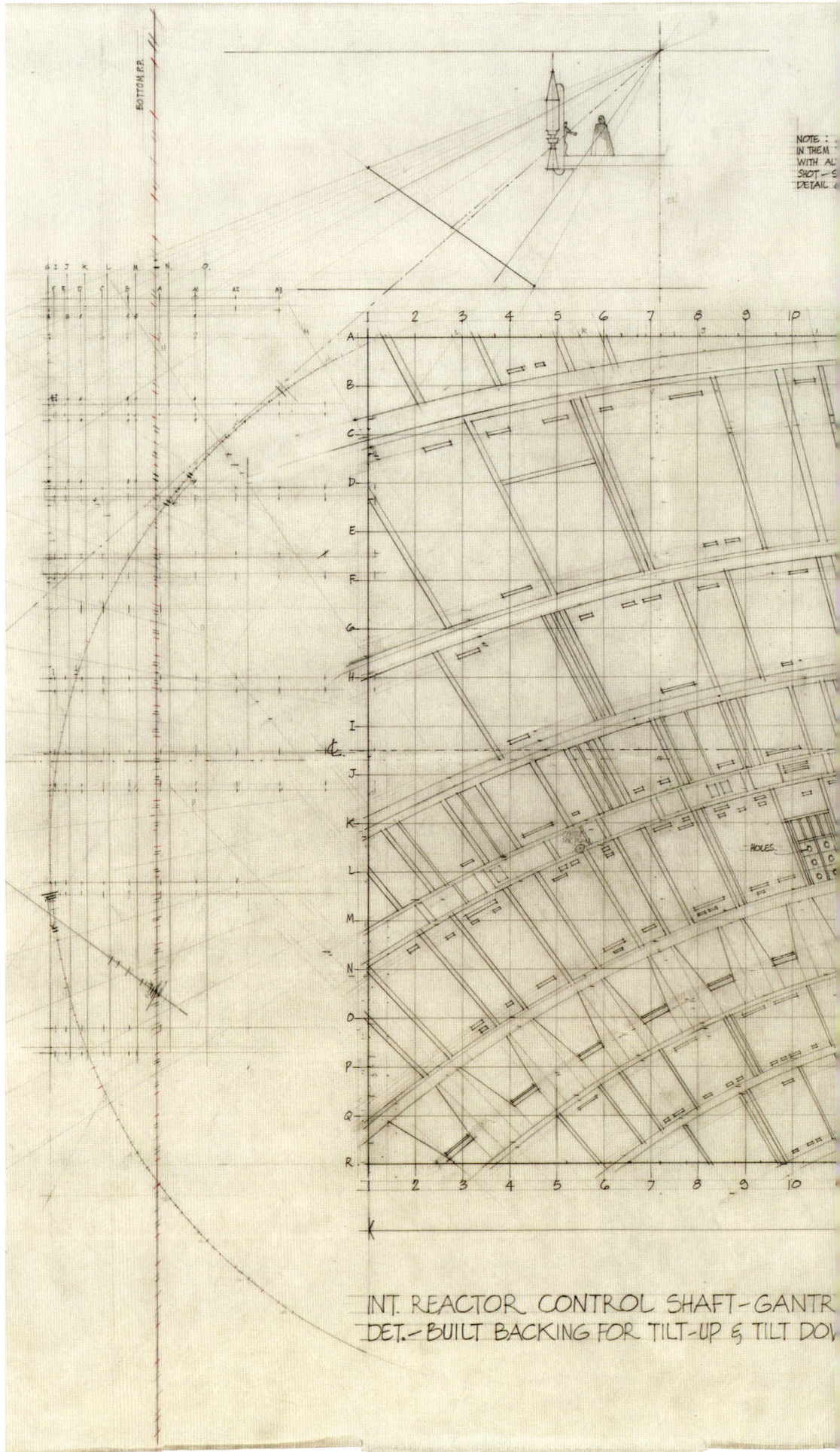

↑ A matte painting by McQuarrie in postproduction; the black area is where the live-action, with the on-set backing, would be placed; the two parts would then be composited into a final frame.

INT. REACTOR CONTROL SHAFT – GANTR
DET.– BUILT BACKING FOR TILT-UP & TILT DOW

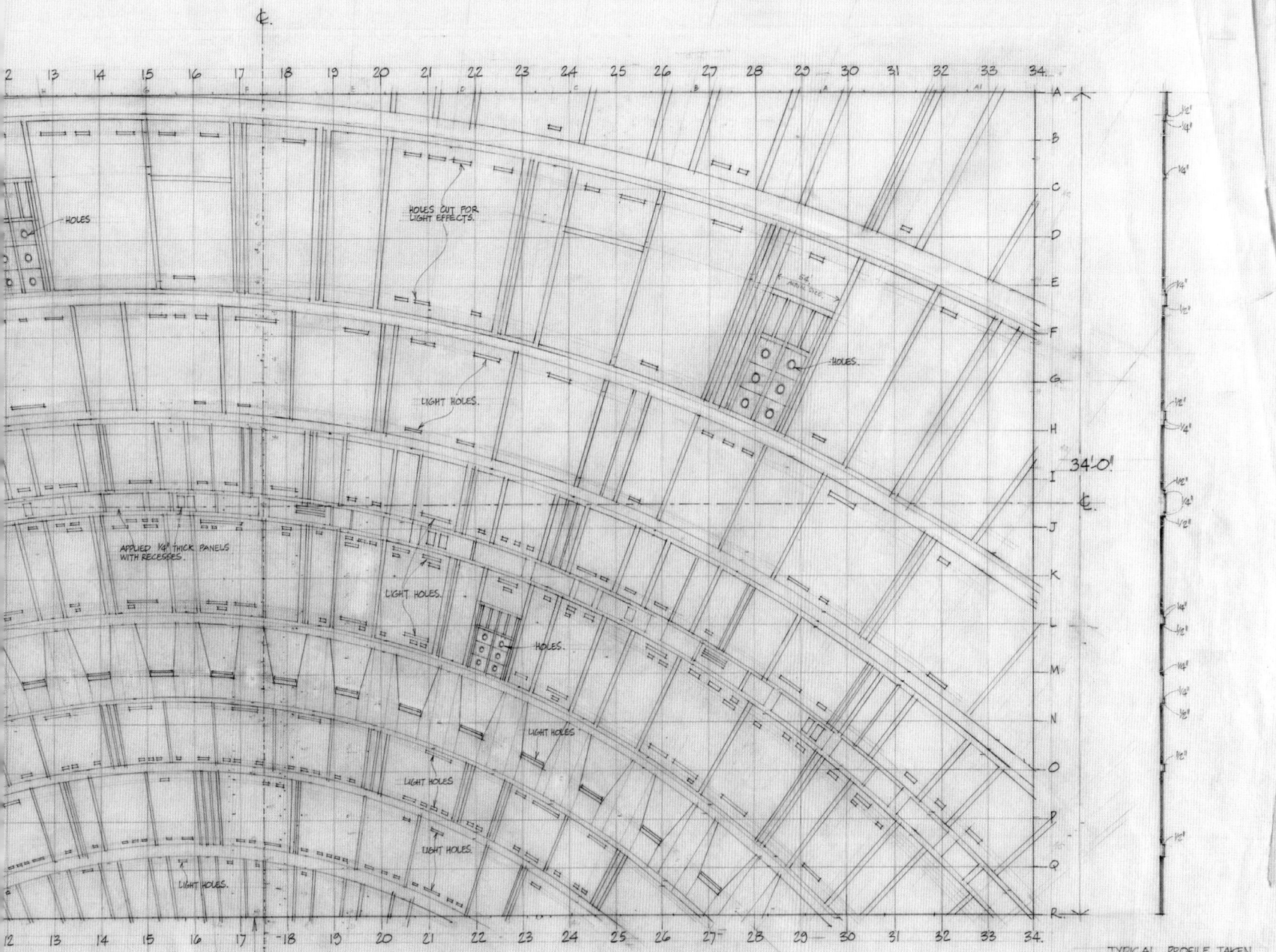

PANELS WITH HOLES
OVABLE & REPLACED
ONES FOR TILTING UP
ATE DRAWING FOR.

STATIONS SHOWN AT EVERY 2'-0".

—HOLES.

HOLES CUT FOR
LIGHT EFFECTS.

—HOLES.

LIGHT HOLES.

34'-0"

APPLIED 1/8" THICK PANELS
WITH RECESSES.

LIGHT HOLES.

HOLES.

LIGHT HOLES.

LIGHT HOLES.

LIGHT HOLES.

LIGHT HOLES.

66'-0"

VANISHING POINT
26'-2" ON CENTRE LINE.

TYPICAL PROFILE TAKEN
AT CENTRE LINE SHOWING
PLY THICKNESSES.

SHOTS.

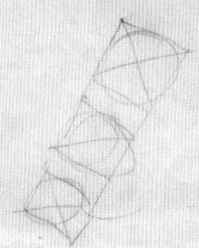

© 1979 CHAPTER II PRODUCTIONS LTD.

STAR WARS 'THE EMPIRE STRIKES BACK'

CARP.	
PLAST.	✓
PAINT.	✓
METAL	✓
RIGGER	✓
DRAPES	
DRESSER	
S.P.F.X.	
SIGNS	
ART	✓
PROD.	✓
CON-MAN	✓

SET. INT. GANTRY OUTSIDE CONTROL
ROOM REACTOR SHAFT.

PROD.No R.72/4

DETAIL
BUILT BACKING FOR BOTH TILT-
DOWN & TILT-UP SHOT.

SET No 104.

DRG.No	SCALE	DATE	DRAWN BY	PROD. DESIGNER
316.	1/2"=1-0"	13-3-79	TED AMBROSE	NORMAN REYNOLDS

SHEC 90838

REACTOR SHAFT

Rather than submit to Vader, Luke throws himself into the reactor shaft, where he is sucked into a tube that was, in fact, a repurposed element from an existing piece of the Reactor Control Room. Light panels on either side of the tube entrance were to have equal spacing (no. 460 on page 148), with stock greeblies applied to the circular opening. Boxes and mattresses were to be placed beneath the tube, as Hamill was to be perched, again, about 25 feet off the studio floor.

Luke is ejected from the tube and barely manages to grab onto an antenna beneath Cloud City. He tries to climb up, but the exhaust pipe doors close automatically. More greeblies were to adorn those doors, which the blueprint indicated would have concealed hinges and be powered by "stock practical hydraulic rams, sleeved with plastic tubes to give a heavier appearance."

Of course, Luke is handicapped in his efforts because his father has cut off one of his hands. This dismemberment follows the destruction of C-3PO earlier in the film; indeed, the droid then spends about a quarter of the movie as only a torso and a head.

"One time Anthony Daniels and I were on a stage together in front of an audience, and Anthony was being very coy about what was going to happen to See-Threepio in the next movie," said Lorne Peterson. "I said, 'Anthony, what is all this dismemberment? George has this obsession with dismemberment.'

And of course the audience laughed and he laughed, and then he was like, 'Oh yeah, okay, bad things happen to See-Threepio *again*…'"

Fortunately for Luke, bionic limb replacements are easy to come by in the *Star Wars* galaxy. For the last sequence in the film, after a cast had been taken of his real limb, Hamill acted with a practical prop of his lower arm designed by Fred Hole (no. 461), with milled slots with holes; holes for telescoping rods; and what seems to be a dental drill part.

↓ Reynolds' storyboard of Luke's trip from the reactor shaft tunnel to the antenna below Cloud City is undated, circa February 1979.

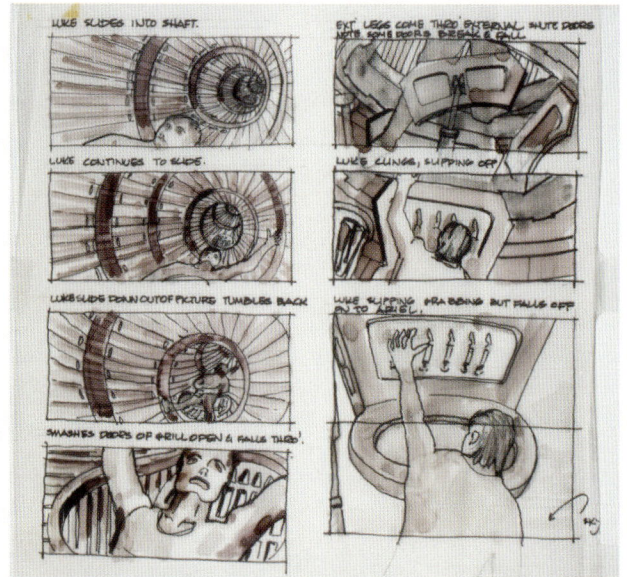

↑ Luke beneath Cloud City, hanging onto an antenna, late May 1979.

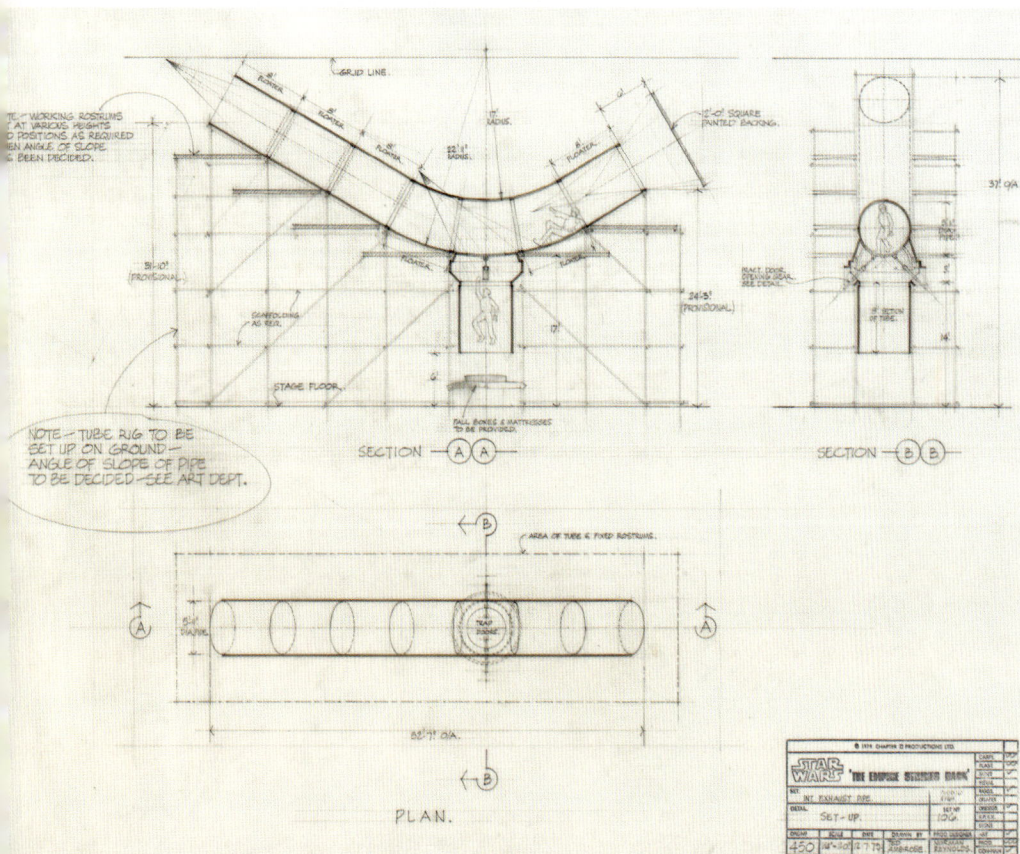

SET	EXHAUST PIPE
DETAIL	SETUP
DRG. NO.	450
DATE	JULY 12 1979
DRAWN BY	TED AMBROSE

NOTE— EXTENT OF
SURROUNDING WALL
TO BE DECIDED.

ON SURROUND.

SECTION.

EXTERNAL ELEVATION.

INTERNAL ELEV'N OF DOORS.

DET. 1 — F.S. DOOR
PANEL SECTION.

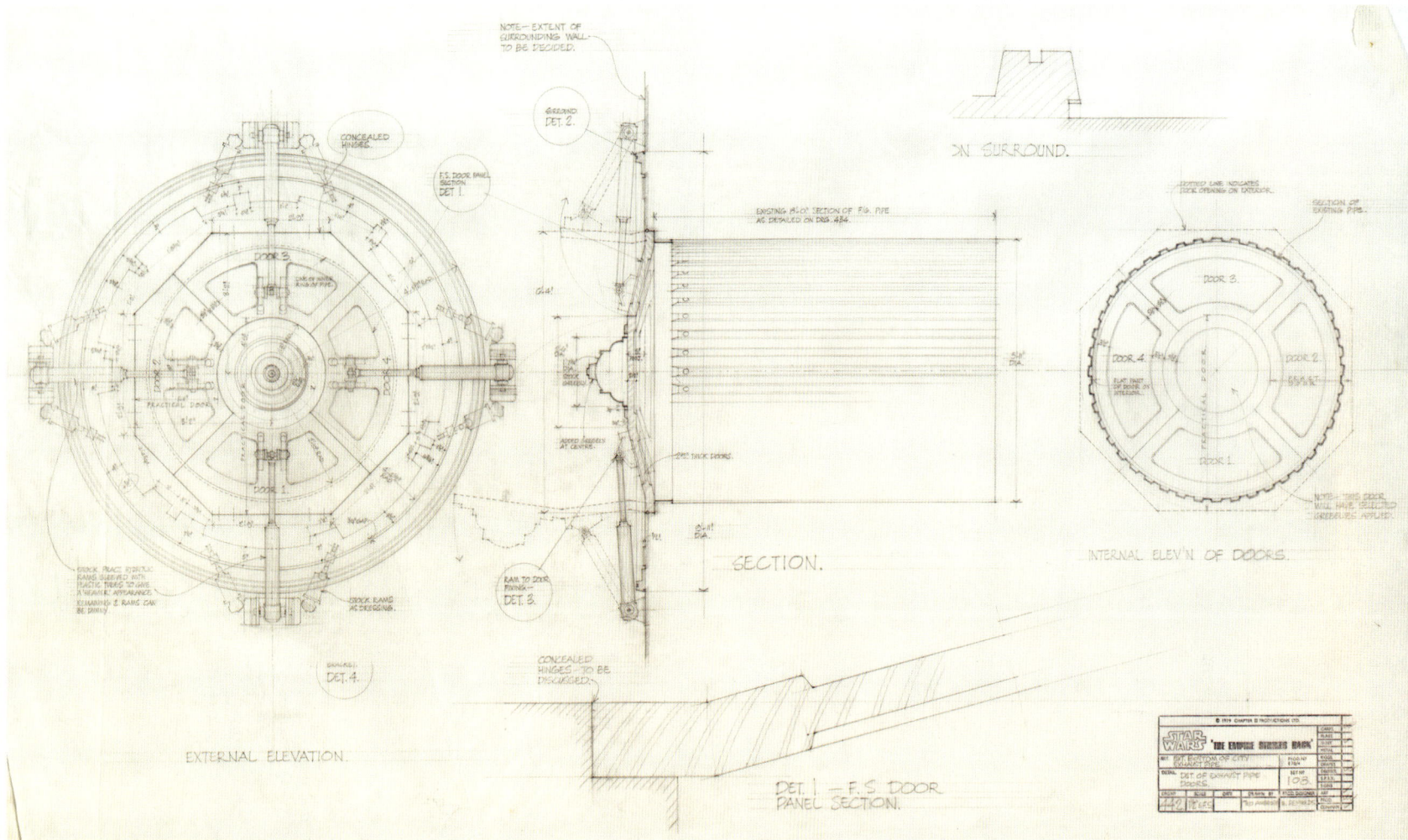

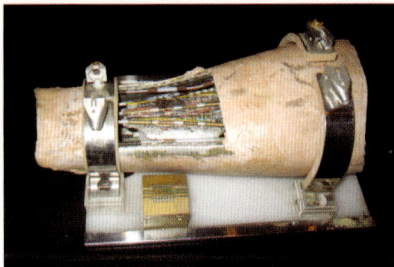

← For the scene in which the medical droid
repairs Luke's hand and lower arm, a fake section
of his limb was created at Elstree with movable
parts, as based on Fred Hole's technical drawing.
The fake arm was then used on Stage 8 for the
scene with Hamill, shot mid-July 1979.

SET	EXHAUST PIPE, BENEATH CLOUD CITY
DETAIL	EXHAUST PIPE DOORS
DRG. NO.	442
DATE	SUMMER 1979
DRAWN BY	TED AMBROSE

→ Luke slides
through the reactor
shaft tunnel.

SET	MEDICAL FRIGATE
DETAIL	BIONIC HAND BASIS
DRG. NO.	461
DATE	AUGUST 1 1979
DRAWN BY	FRED HOLE

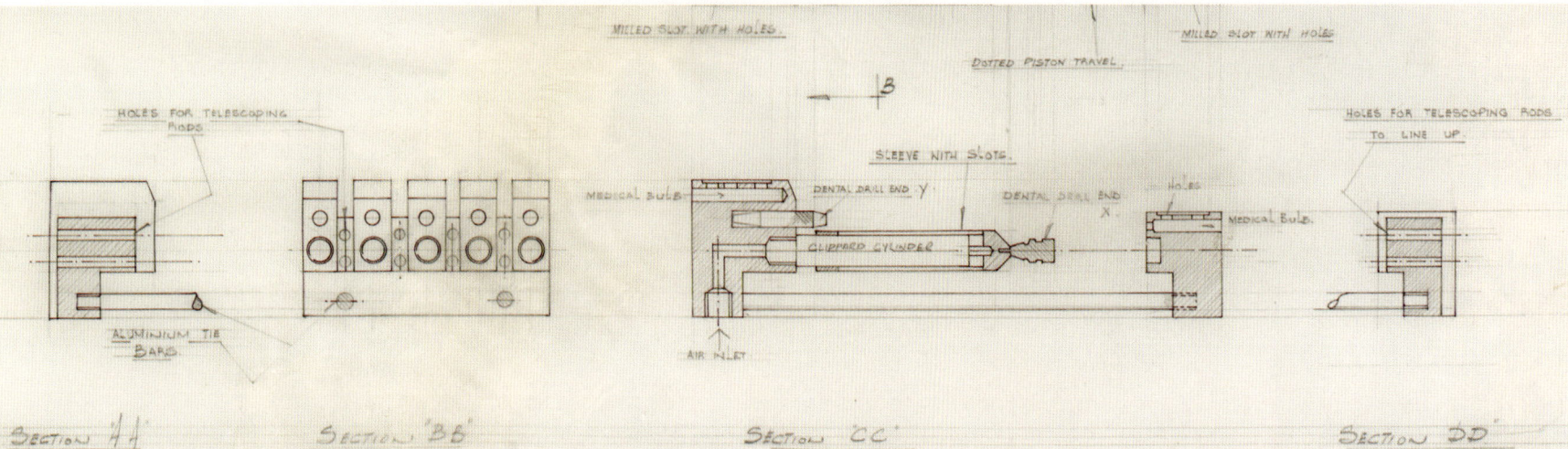

MILLED SLOT WITH HOLES.

MILLED SLOT WITH HOLES

DOTTED PISTON TRAVEL.

HOLES FOR TELESCOPING
RODS

HOLES FOR TELESCOPING RODS
TO LINE UP.

MEDICAL BULB

SLEEVE WITH SLOTS.

DENTAL DRILL END Y

DENTAL DRILL END
X

HOLES

MEDICAL BULB.

KNURLED CYLINDER

ALUMINIUM TIE
BARS.

AIR INLET

SECTION "AA"

SECTION "BB"

SECTION "CC"

SECTION "DD"

STOCK F/G.
GREEBLIES
APPLIED.

1/4" THICK PANELS
APPLIED.

6'-5" (CHECK)
LIGHT PANELS TO BE OF
EQUAL SPACING.

2" RADIUS
CORNERS.

LIGHT
PANELS.

EXISTING
PIECE.

STOCK F/G.
GREEBLIES
APPLIED.

42'-3"

E L E V A T I O N.

SET	REACTOR SHAFT — EXHAUST INLET
DETAIL	GENERAL DETAIL
DRG. NO.	460
DATE	AUGUST 1 1979
DRAWN BY	TED AMBROSE

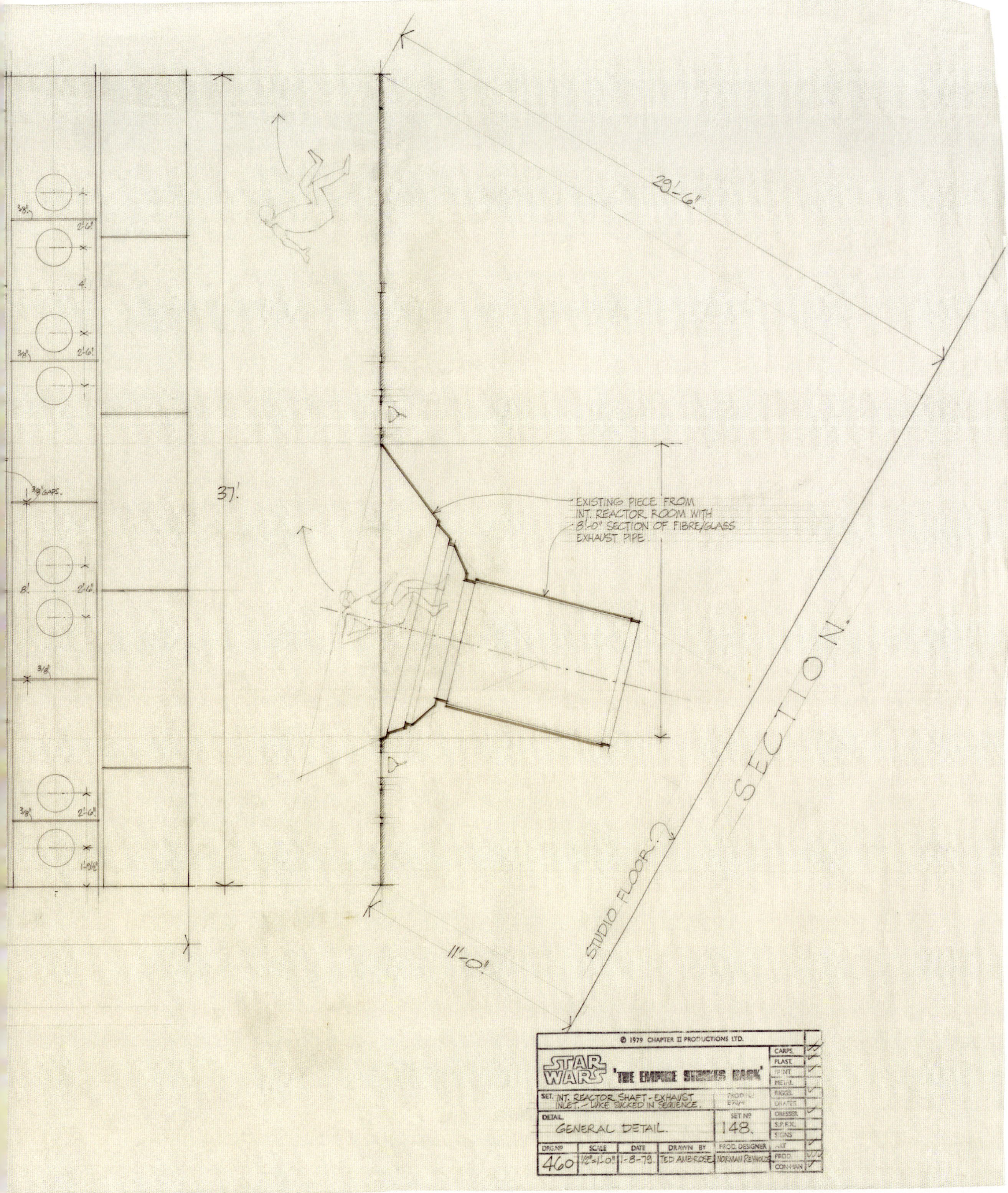

EXISTING PIECE FROM
INT. REACTOR ROOM WITH
8'-0" SECTION OF FIBRE/GLASS
EXHAUST PIPE.

29'-6"

37'

SECTION.

STUDIO FLOOR.?

11'-0"

3/8"

2'-6"

4'

3/8"

2'-6"

3/8" GAPS.

8'

2'-6"

3/8"

3/8"

2'-6"

1'-0"

© 1979 CHAPTER II PRODUCTIONS LTD.

STAR WARS 'THE EMPIRE STRIKES BACK'

CARPS.		
PLAST.		
PAINT		
METAL		

SET. INT. REACTOR SHAFT - EXHAUST
INLET. - LUKE SUCKED IN SEQUENCE.

RIGGS.		
GRATER		
DRESSER		
S.P.FX.		
SIGNS		

PROD. N°
E.P.74

DETAIL
GENERAL DETAIL.

SET N°
148.

DRG.N°	SCALE	DATE	DRAWN BY	PROD. DESIGNER	ART	
460	1/2"=1'-0"	1-8-78	TED AMBROSE	NORMAN REYNOLDS	PROD.	
					CON-MAN	

EXTERIOR, JABBA'S PALACE

Return of the Jedi, as *Star Wars* did before it, begins by following the adventures of the two droids, C-3PO and R2-D2, who have been given a mission. As the third film opens, they are already on Tatooine and need to gain access to Jabba the Hutt's Palace. Their first obstacle is a sentry right out of *The Wizard of Oz*; but instead of a human they come up against a mechanical "eye," as drawn in Fred Hole's blueprint after being dreamed up, according to Reynolds, in the art department.

Hole's early drawing (no. 30) contains more complex machinery than seen in the final film; it also indicates that the preliminary challenge would be the mechanical eye's movement, as "eye drops down to inspect R2-D2." However, by the time of the filming, the mechanics seem to have been reduced to someone on the other side of the door holding a kind of dressed-up fishing pole. Hole's detail of the eye (no. 166) stipulates a "simulated muscular trunk clapping mechanism; a defused light source [in eye]; a concealed spring and/or flexible tube core to give required action." This early idea, also not fully realized in the film, was that the eye would pop out of the door and its "petals open."

In Lamont's technical drawing (no. 85), he shows the position of the eye in the immense door, specifies that the area of sand would be determined on stage, and indicates that the wall's finish should be rough plaster, well-weathered, with adobe blocks showing in places. In addition, the door finish should be "as copper with verdigris" (i.e., simulation of the color that copper attains after being exposed to the elements for a number of years).

As shot, the final scene would place the eye higher up in the door in order to accentuate visually its position of power over the droids. It must have been an odd sight when filming, because this relatively small set, consisting of the door and inner palace corridor, was built on the gigantic *Star Wars* Stage in the empty space between two walls of the Death Star docking bay.

↑ At Jabba's Palace, C-3PO speaks with the "eye" and then the door opens, Elstree Studios, the *Star Wars* Stage, mid-January 1982.

SET	EXTERIOR JABBA'S PALACE
DETAIL	EYE
DRG. NO.	30
DATE	FALL 1981
DRAWN BY	FRED HOLE

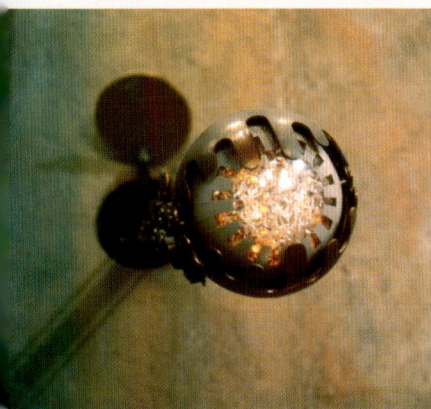

↑ A still depicts the detail the art department put into creating the eye.

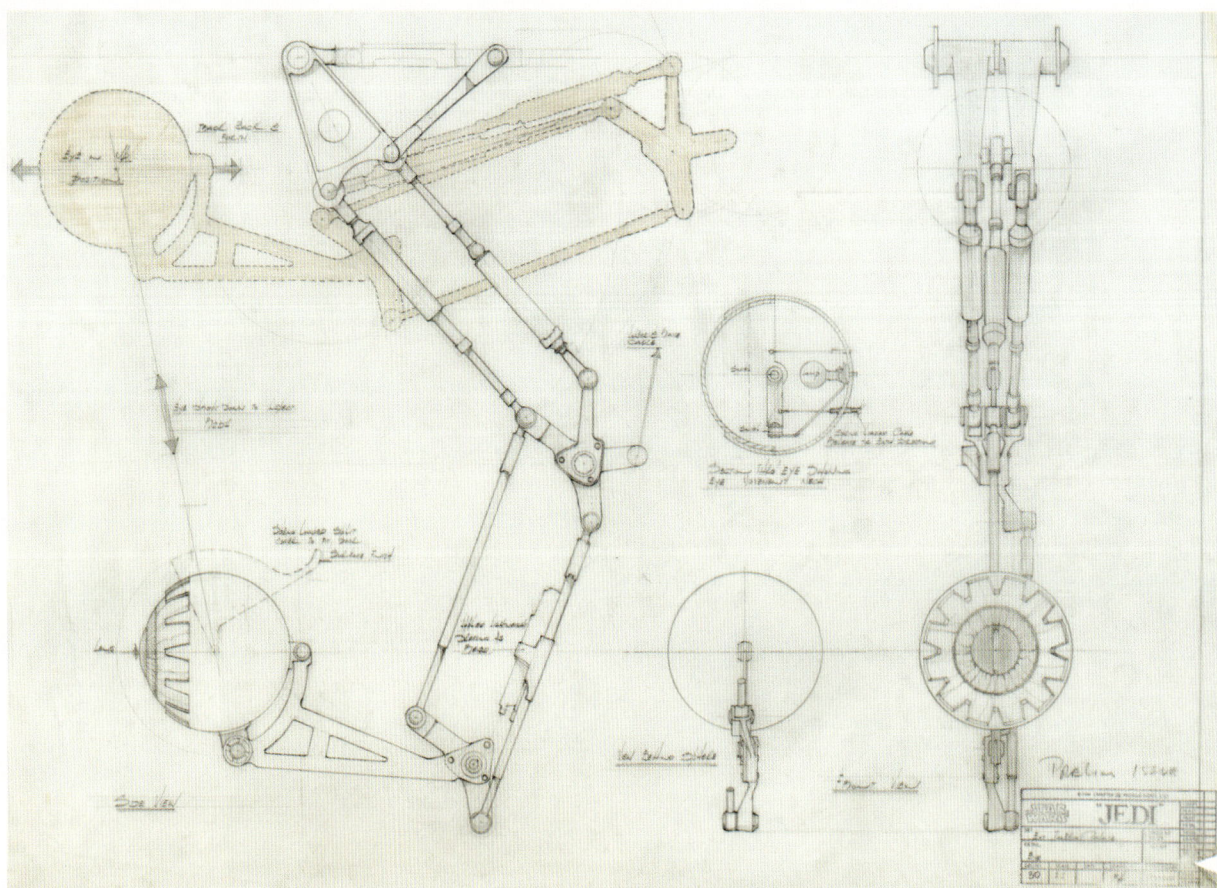

'SECURITY EYE'
DETAIL TO FOLLOW.

AS SHEET METAL CLADDING
SEE ART DEPT.

WALL FINISH.
ROUGH PLASTER, WELL
WEATHERED WITH 'ADOBE'
BLOCKS SHOWING IN PLACES
SEE PRODUCTION DESIGNER
FOR COLOUR

SEE F.S.D. 1
TOOTHED LOCKING DEVISE
DRWG. N° 86

RECESSES TO RECEIVE TOOTHED LOCKING DEVICE

EXT. ELEVATION ~ JABBAS PALACE.

SET	EXTERIOR, JABBA'S PALACE
DETAIL	PLAN & ELEVATIONS, ENTRANCE DOOR
DRG. NO.	85
DATE	OCTOBER 6 1981
DRAWN BY	MICHAEL LAMONT

DOOR TO RISE

BOSS ~ DOOR OPENS & EYE POPS OUT
PETALS OPEN, EYE DROPS DOWN
TO SURVEY R2D2

RESOLVE OPERATING ROOM

NOTE PROVISION S
THAT OUTER PETALS
CAN SNAP WIDE OPEN
IF NEED.

JABBAS ENTRANCE DOOR.

TO SCALE

SET	EXTERIOR, JABBA'S PALACE
DETAIL	EYE THROUGH DOOR (RIGHT AND BELOW)
DRG. NO.	166
DATE	NOVEMBER 8 1981
DRAWN BY	FRED HOLE

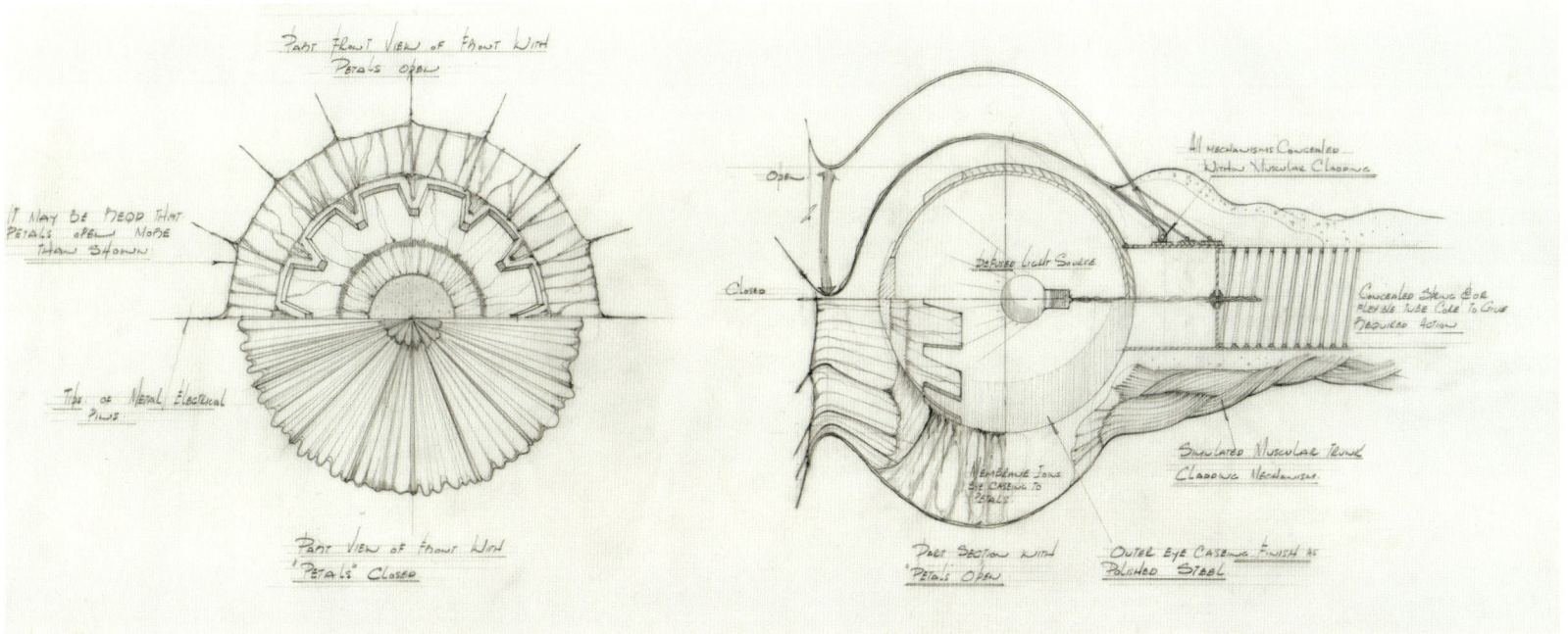

PART FRONT VIEW OF FRONT WITH
PETALS OPEN

IT MAY BE NEED THAT
PETALS OPEN MORE
THAN SHOWN

TIPS OF METAL ELECTRICAL
PINS

PART VIEW OF FRONT WITH
'PETALS' CLOSED

OPEN

CLOSED

ALL MECHANISMS CONCEALED
WITHIN MUSCULAR CLADDING

DIFFUSED LIGHT SOURCE

CONCEALED SLEEVE DOOR
REUSABLE TUBE CAN TO GIVE
REQUIRED ACTION

WEATHERED ZONE
SEE CASING TO PETALS

SIMULATED MUSCULAR TRUNK
CLADDING MECHANISM

PART SECTION WITH
'PETALS' OPEN

OUTER EYE CASING FINISH AS
POLISHED STEEL

JABBA'S THRONE ROOM

The two droids succeed in entering Jabba's Palace and are escorted to his Throne Room, a complex set. On the actual throne sits Jabba, an enormous animatronic puppet operated by several people. Because Jabba would have only limited movement, much of the action for the first quarter of the film would be staged around him in successive audiences with a series of visitors: first the droids, then a disguised Leia and Chewbacca, and finally Luke Skywalker. Their mission of course is to save Han Solo, who is still a prisoner encased in carbon.

The Throne Room would take up all of Stage 8, and its preparation was witnessed by John Phillip Peecher as recounted in his book, *The Making of Star Wars: Return of the Jedi*: "The Throne Room is being built about six feet off the floor because many of the puppeteers and operators will be concealed under the floor [of the set]. These are great scenes in the screenplay, but because of the sheer number of people involved, they are going to be difficult, time-consuming scenes to shoot."

"The range of creatures in Jabba's Palace did compound my problems," said Reynolds. "The entire area of the floor had to be removable panels—sort of like trapdoors—and that became very expensive. The other problem was the sheer number of people involved: makeup, puppeteers, video engineers, wardrobe. I remember once going in there when we were trying to finish the set and screaming at everyone, 'Get off! Get off!' It was like Piccadilly Circus."

Brought in to mitigate his immobility, dancers moving to the rhythms of the house band often upstaged Jabba. The musical creatures were designed in the ILM shop in conjunction with the art department, which was responsible for their instruments. The most complex of the instruments was a kind of organ designed for the character Max Rebo by George Djurkovic. Djurkovic's notes on the blueprint indicate that the organ would consist of a 30-by-22.25-inch elliptical cushion with an opening for the puppet operator in the middle; the organ's claxons were to drop open when the keys were depressed and soft knobs would "squeltch" when pressed. There were lamps behind the keys.

"I remember George Djurkovic drawing the organ for me and what fun we had working it out," said Reynolds.

RIGHT AND RIGHT ABOVE
The interior of Jabba's
Throne Room is seen in
maquette form.

↑ Concept art of the Throne Room by McQuarrie, 1981.

→ Jabba the Hutt,
a dancer, and Salacious
B. Crumb are on the slab
within the finished set.

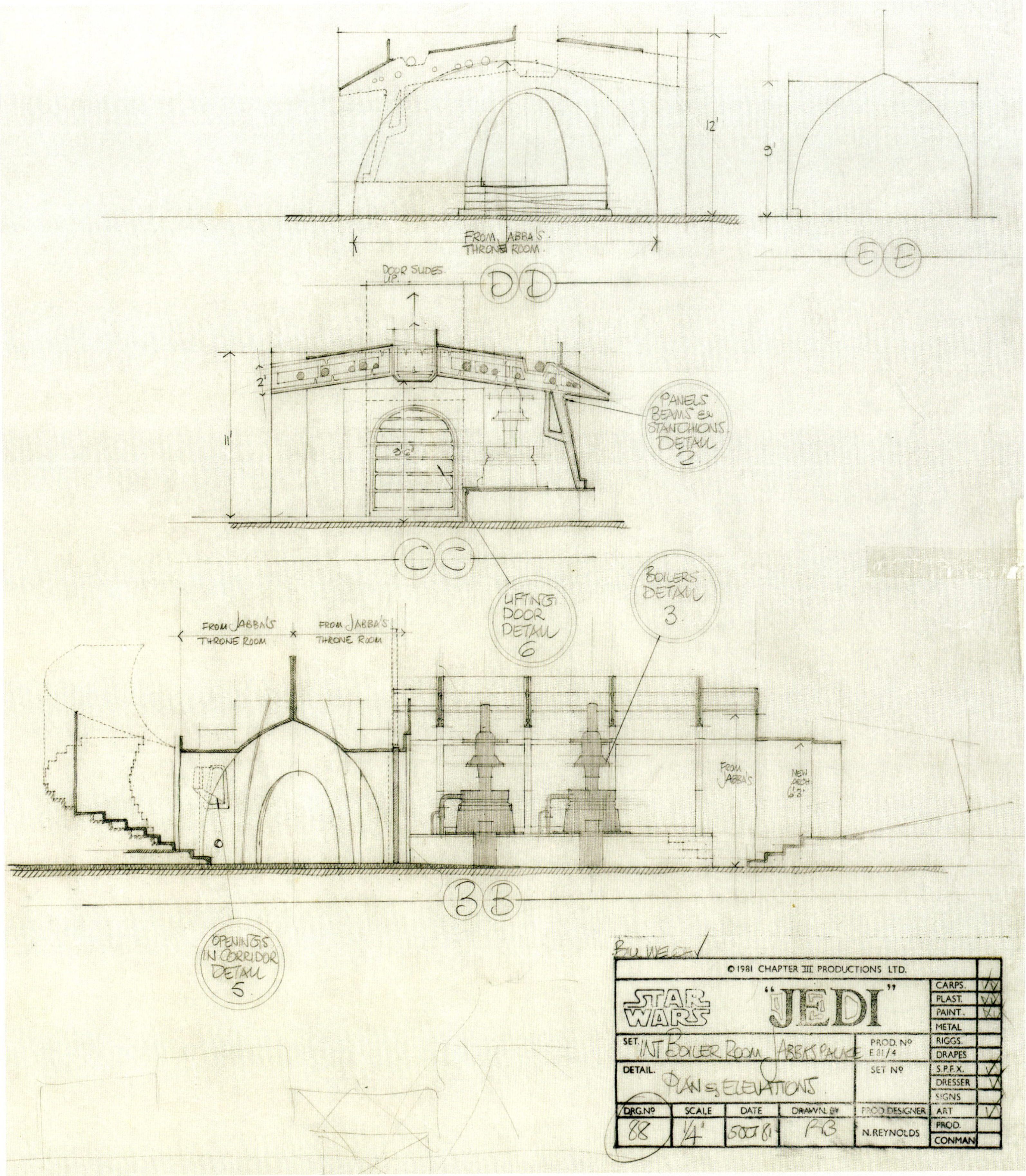

FROM JABBA'S THRONE ROOM

12'

E E

9'

D D

DOOR SLIDES UP.

2'

11'

3'6"

PANELS BEAMS & STANCHIONS DETAIL 2

C C

LIFTING DOOR DETAIL 6

BOILERS DETAIL 3

FROM JABBA'S THRONE ROOM   FROM JABBA'S THRONE ROOM

FROM JABBA'S

NEW ARCH 6'3"

B B

OPENINGS IN CORRIDOR DETAIL 5

BILL WELCH

© 1981 CHAPTER III PRODUCTIONS LTD.

STAR WARS "JEDI"

SET. INT BOILER ROOM JABBA'S PALACE   PROD. No E.81/4

DETAIL. PLAN & ELEVATIONS   SET No

CARPS.	√
PLAST.	√√
PAINT.	√
METAL	
RIGGS.	
DRAPES	
S.P.F.X.	√
DRESSER	√
SIGNS	
ART	√
PROD.	
CONMAN	

DRG.No	SCALE	DATE	DRAWN BY	PROD DESIGNER
88	¼'	5 OCT 81	RB	N. REYNOLDS

↑ Part of the Throne Room set would be reused in the boiler room, or droid torture chamber, which also contained a "gulley to take running water." The torture rack would be a floating prop.

SET	BOILER ROOM, JABBA'S PALACE
DETAIL	PLAN & ELEVATIONS
DRG. NO.	88
DATE	OCTOBER 5 1981
DRAWN BY	REG BREAM

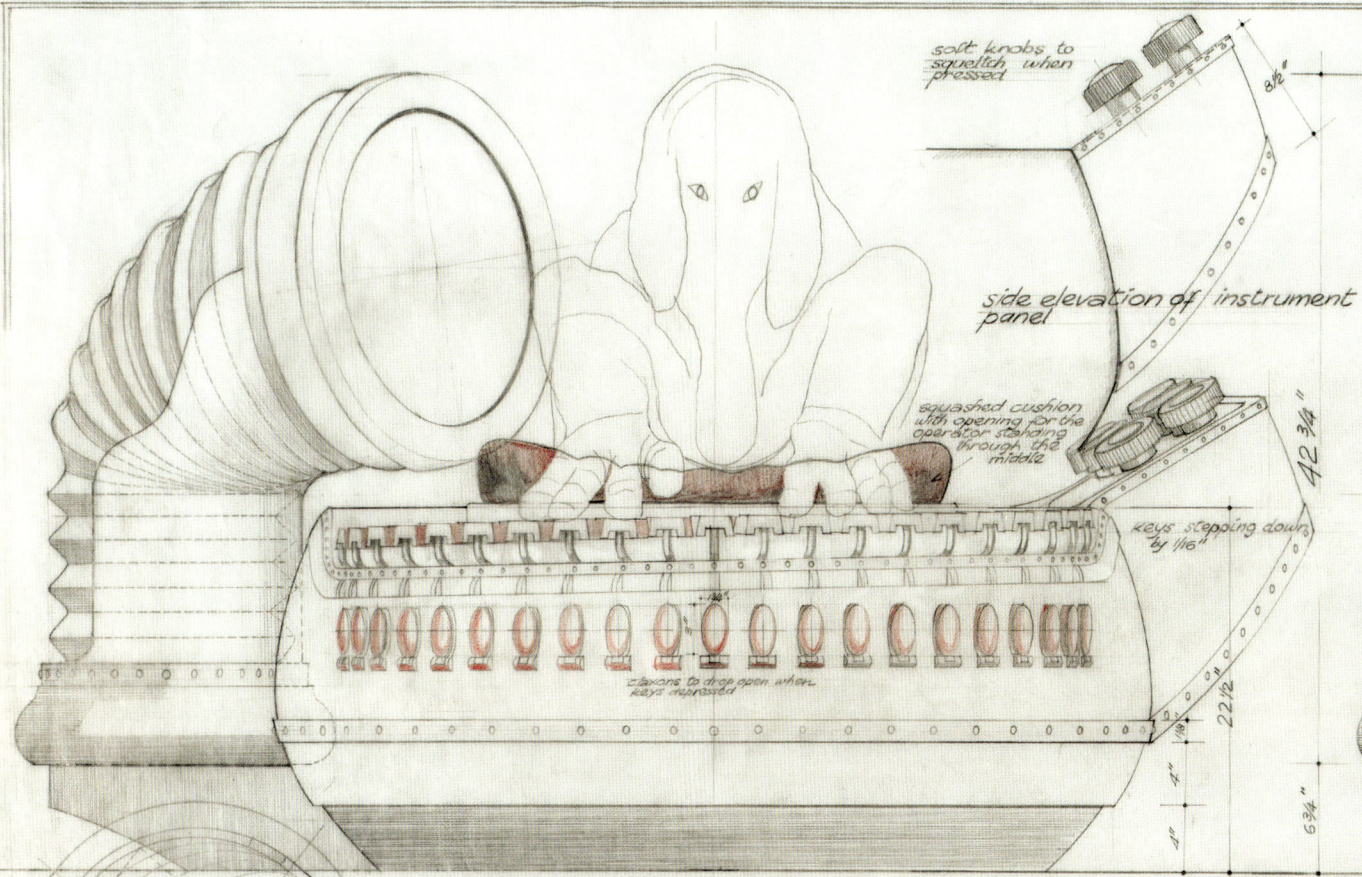

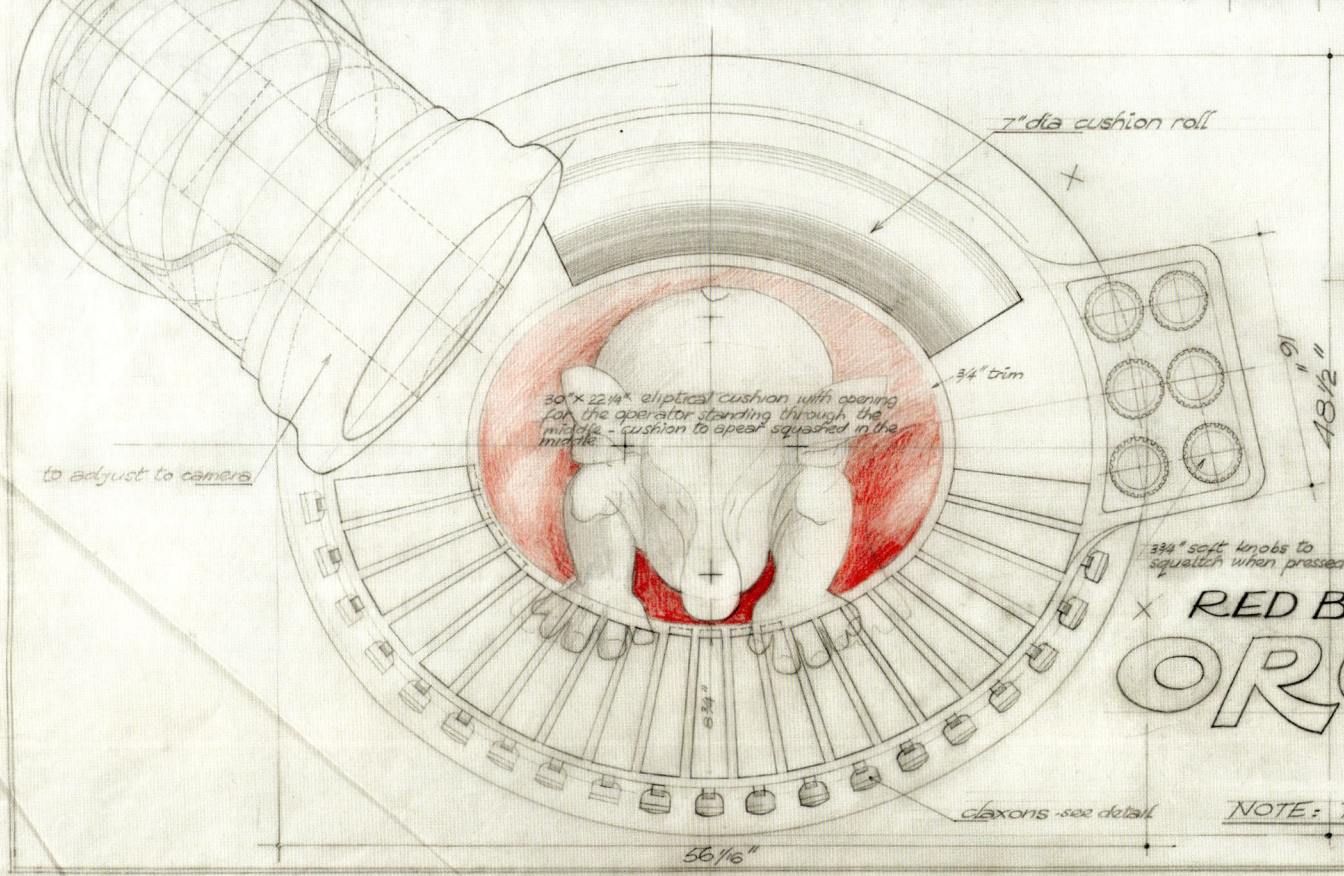

soft knobs to
squelch when
pressed

8 1/2"

side elevation of instrument
panel

squashed cushion
with opening for the
operator standing
through the middle

42 3/4"

keys stepping down
by 1/16"

22 1/2"

claxons to drop open when
keys impressed

6 3/4"

1"   4"

7" dia cushion roll

30" x 22 1/4" eliptical cushion with opening
for the operator standing through the
middle - cushion to apear squashed in the
middle

3/4" trim

9"

18 1/2"

to adjust to camera

3 3/4" soft knobs to
squelch when pressed

PLAN   1/4"=

RED BALL JETT

ORGAN

56 1/16"

claxons - see detail

NOTE: Tretment to be discuss

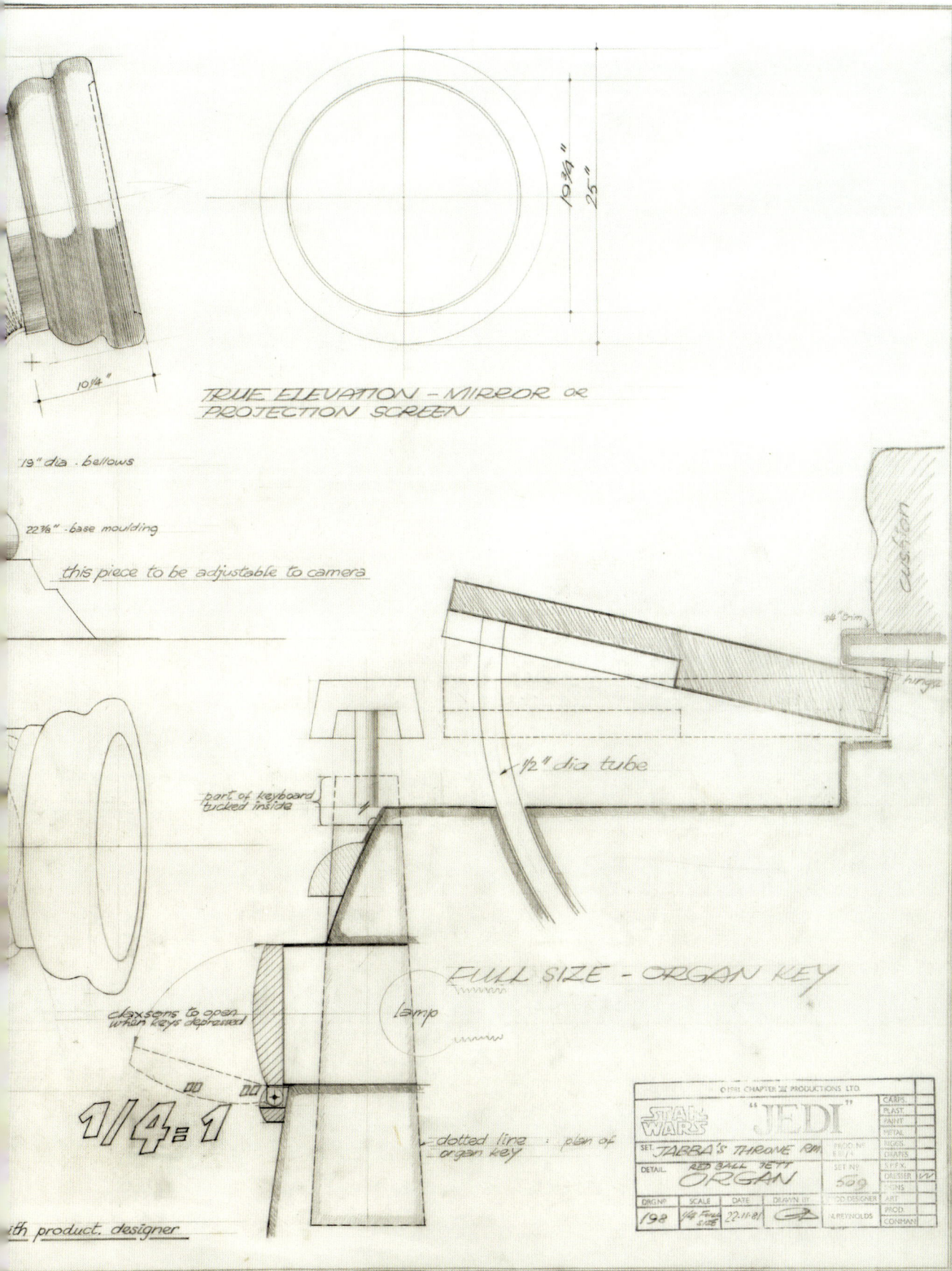

TRUE ELEVATION – MIRROR or
PROJECTION SCREEN

10¾"
25"

10¼"

19" dia . bellows

22⅞" base moulding

this piece to be adjustable to camera

cushion

¾" trim

hinge

½" dia tube

part of keyboard
tucked inside

FULL SIZE – ORGAN KEY

lamp

claxsons to open
when keys depressed

1/4 = 1

dotted line : plan of
organ key

...ith product. designer

© 1981 CHAPTER III PRODUCTIONS LTD.

STAR WARS	"JEDI"		CARPS.
			PLAST.
			PAINT
			METAL
SET JABBA'S THRONE RM	PROD Nº E9/4		RIGGS
			DRAPES
DETAIL RED BALL JETT ORGAN	SET Nº 509		S.F.FX.
			DRESSER W/M
			CONS.
DRG Nº 198	SCALE ¼ Full Size	DATE 22·11·81	DRAWN BY	PROD. DESIGNER N. REYNOLDS	ART.
					PROD.
					CONMAN

SET   JABBA'S THRONE ROOM   DATE   NOVEMBER 22 1981
DETAIL   RED BALL JETT ORGAN   DRAWN BY   GEORGE DJURKOVIC
DRG. NO.   198

STAGE 8

SET	JABBA'S THRONE ROOM
DETAIL	STAGE 8 LAYOUT
DRG. NO.	58
DATE	SEPTEMBER 18 1981
DRAWN BY	MICHAEL LAMONT

↑ Lamont's layout schematic of Stage 8 was colored in red to indicate the position of Jabba's trap door and the grill over the rancor pit.

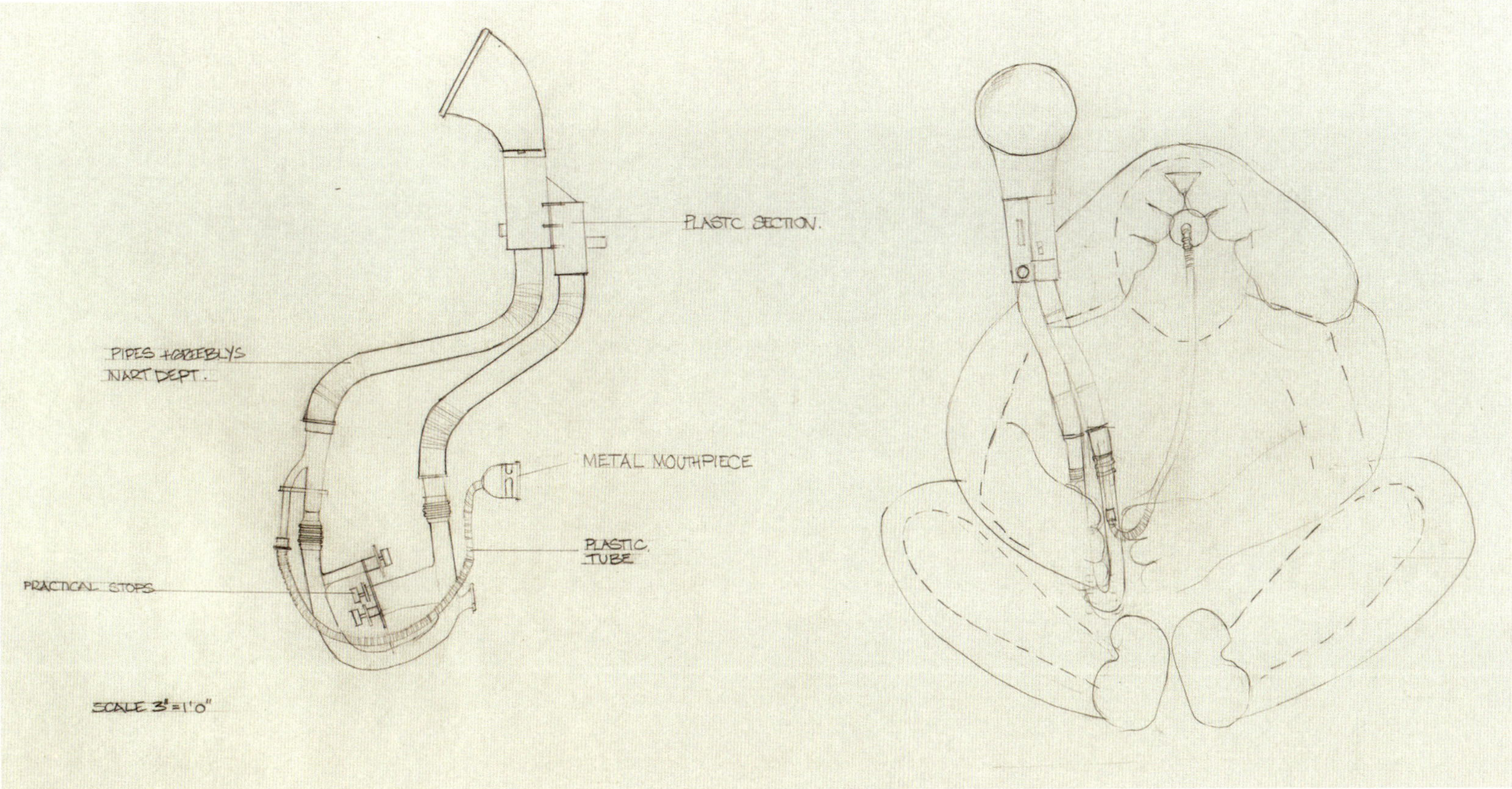

PLASTIC SECTION.

PIPES +GREEBLYS
N ART DEPT.

METAL MOUTHPIECE

PLASTIC.
TUBE

PRACTICAL STOPS

SCALE 3"=1'0"

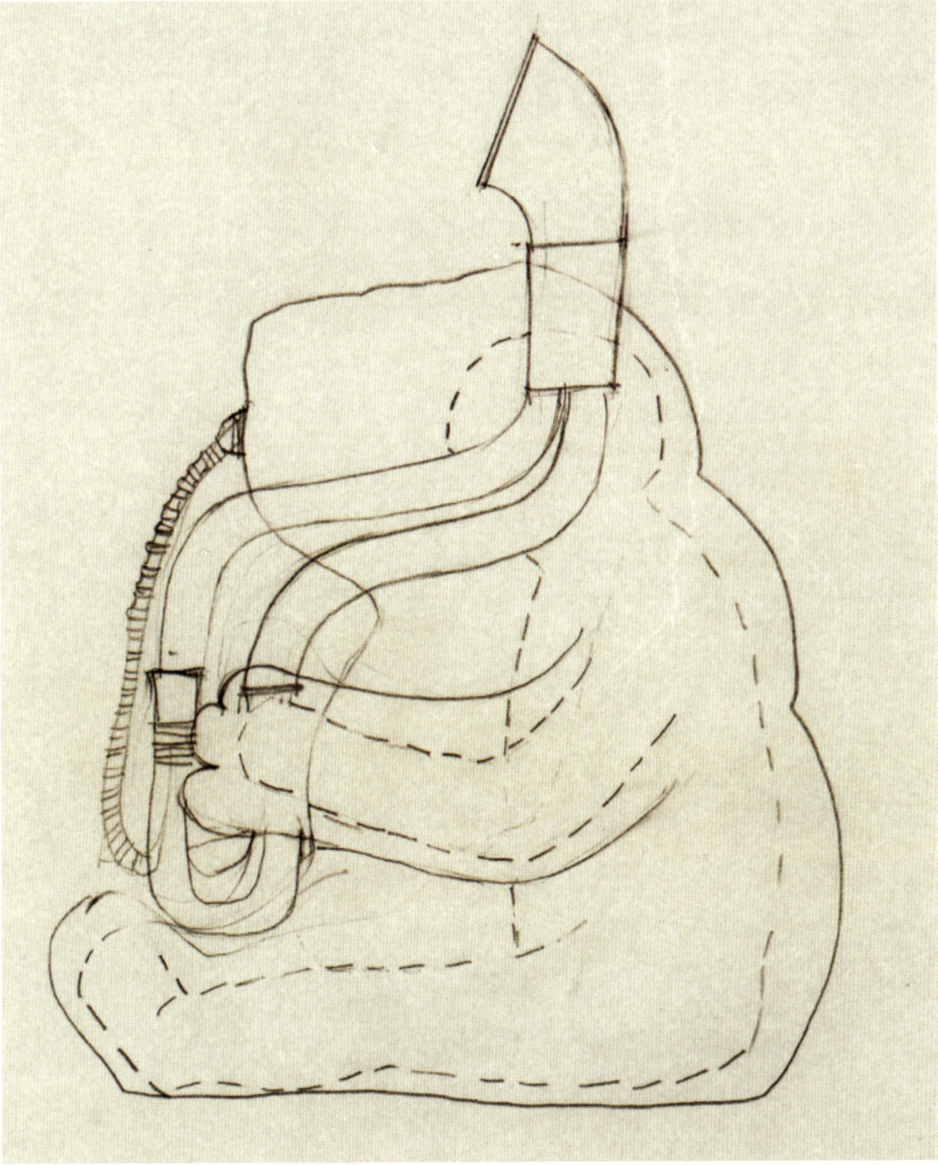

SET   JABBA'S BARGE & THRONE ROOM
DETAIL   MUSICAL INSTRUMENT (LEFT AND ABOVE)
DRG. NO.   180
DATE   NOVEMBER 17 1981
DRAWN BY   STEVE COOPER

LEFT AND ABOVE Droopy McCool was designated as an alien saxophonist and was to appear in the Throne Room and Jabba's barge. Cooper designed McCool's instrument to be "made mostly of plastic with greeblies" and equipped with a metal mouthpiece, with practical stops—all to fit the approximate size of the creature costume with the puppeteer inside.

↓ Max Rebo plays the organ prop, while Droopy McCool wails on his musical instrument.

JABBA'S DROIDS

A series of fantastic technical drawings by master draftsperson Fred Hole sets forth, in full-scale, the robot population of Jabba's droid torture chamber. Although it's sometimes debated whether droids have feelings, this scene makes it pretty clear that they do, as the audience witnesses their sufferings. One droid has their "feet" seared, while another hapless robot is quartered by a medieval-style torture rack.

The two Tourquemadas of torture were drawn by Hole, who planned to use dressings from stock parts already used on the large sets (no. 9). The full-scale drawing shows the as-yet-unnamed droid that would operate the feet-burning machine, whose anthropomorphic features make them slightly chilling.

The supervising droid, robot U8-D8 (no. 11), would have a speaking part, voiced by director Richard Marquand, though ultimately only one of their arms was made to move. While the more organic aliens were designed at the new creature department at ILM, supervised by Phil Tippett, the hard-surface droids were manufactured in the UK.

An early hard-surface droid, helpless on the rack, resembles another Oz denizen, the Tin Man (no. 140 on page 160). Not surprisingly, their look was revised in other Hole drawings of droids (no. 192 on page 161), for which he noted many details, some of which did not make it to the final film: the droid's legs, arms, and neck would be built by Hargreave & Co.; sparking and smoke would occur as the leg and shoulder joints left the torso; and, two aspects that may have been deemed excessive for such a short shot, a "transparent vac-formed cover with internal organs showing through (shiny)" along with "a lower jaw that moves and trembles." The victim's eyes were to be Perspex opal white with red center inserts pulsing and flashing, and their head made to jerk back and forth.

↓ C-3PO and R2-D2 are in the boiler room/torture chamber on the completed and dressed set.

↓ The torture droid (later given the "name" UD8) at work is searing the feet of an unfortunate droid.

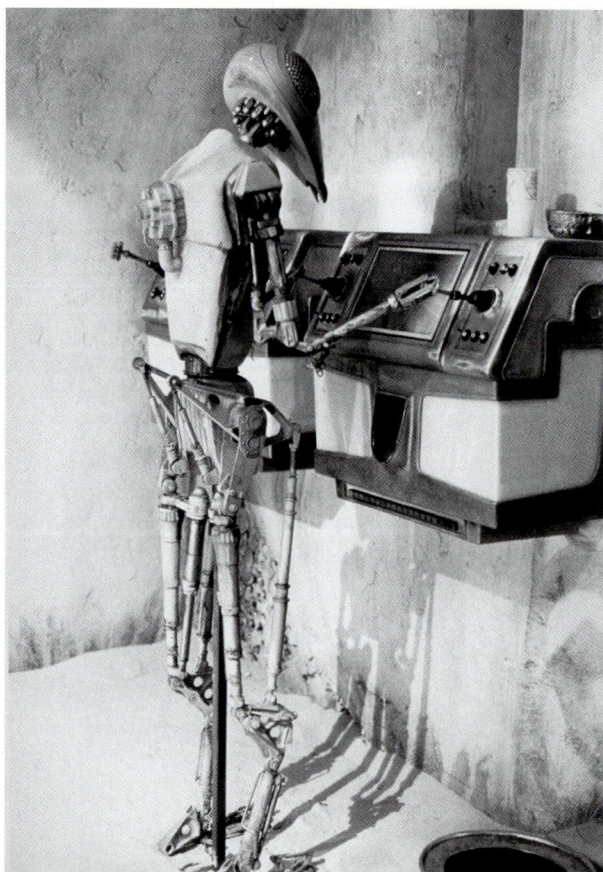

→ A photo of a similarly built gambling droid operating a slot machine in Jabba's throne room.

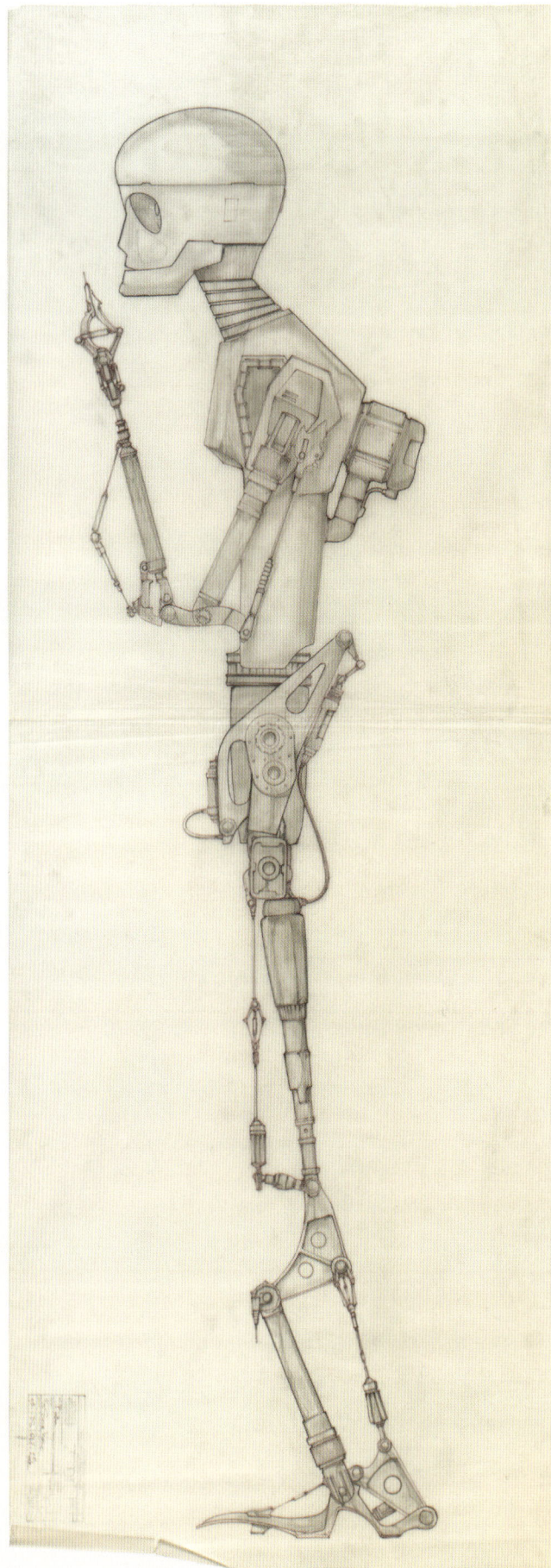

SET	ROBOT U8-D8
DETAIL	LAYOUT
DRG. NO.	11
DATE	JUNE 18 1981
DRAWN BY	FRED HOLE

SET	ROBOT
DETAIL	SIDE VIEW
DRG. NO.	09
DATE	JUNE 18 1981
DRAWN BY	FRED HOLE

SET	ROBOT TORTURE RACK
DETAIL	REVISION
DRG. NO.	189
DATE	NOVEMBER 19 1981
DRAWN BY	FRED HOLE

↑ A maquette depicts the torture chamber set.

SET	BOILER ROOM
DETAIL	TORTURE RACK
DRG. NO.	140
DATE	OCTOBER 27 1981
DRAWN BY	FRED HOLE

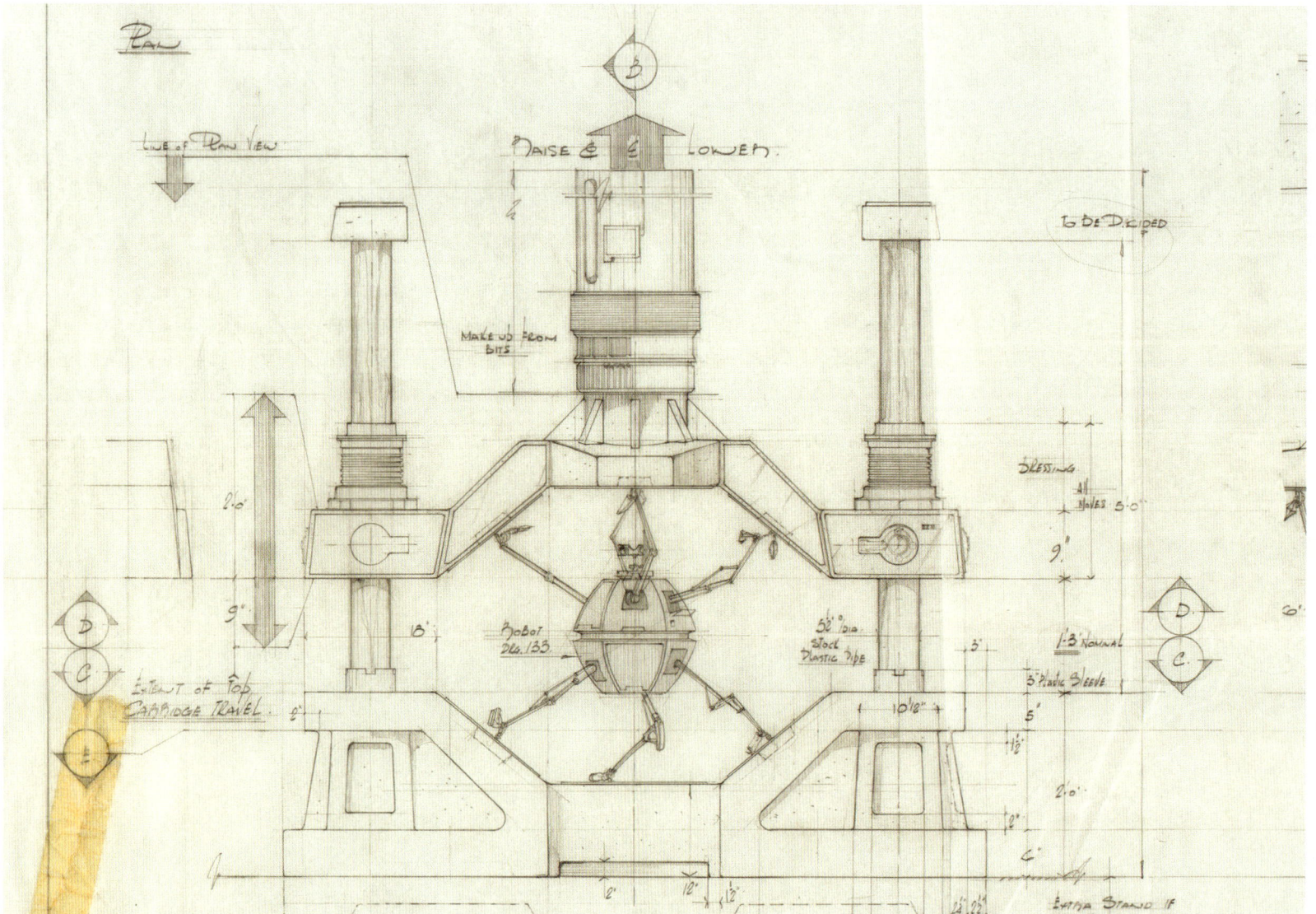

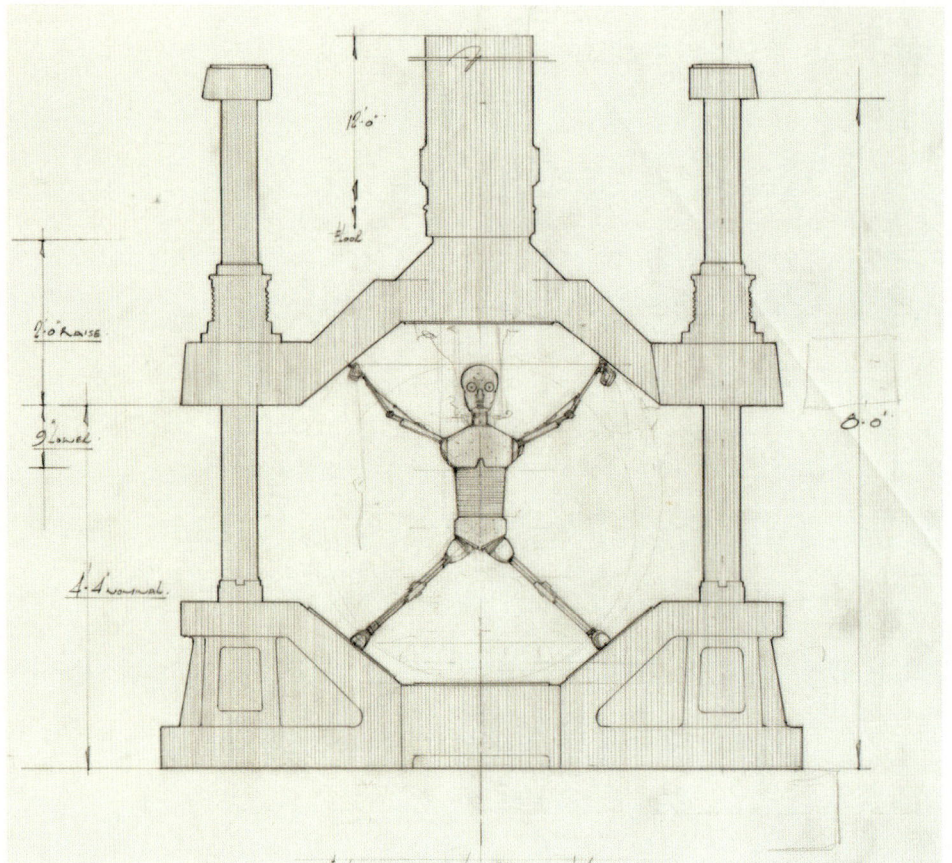

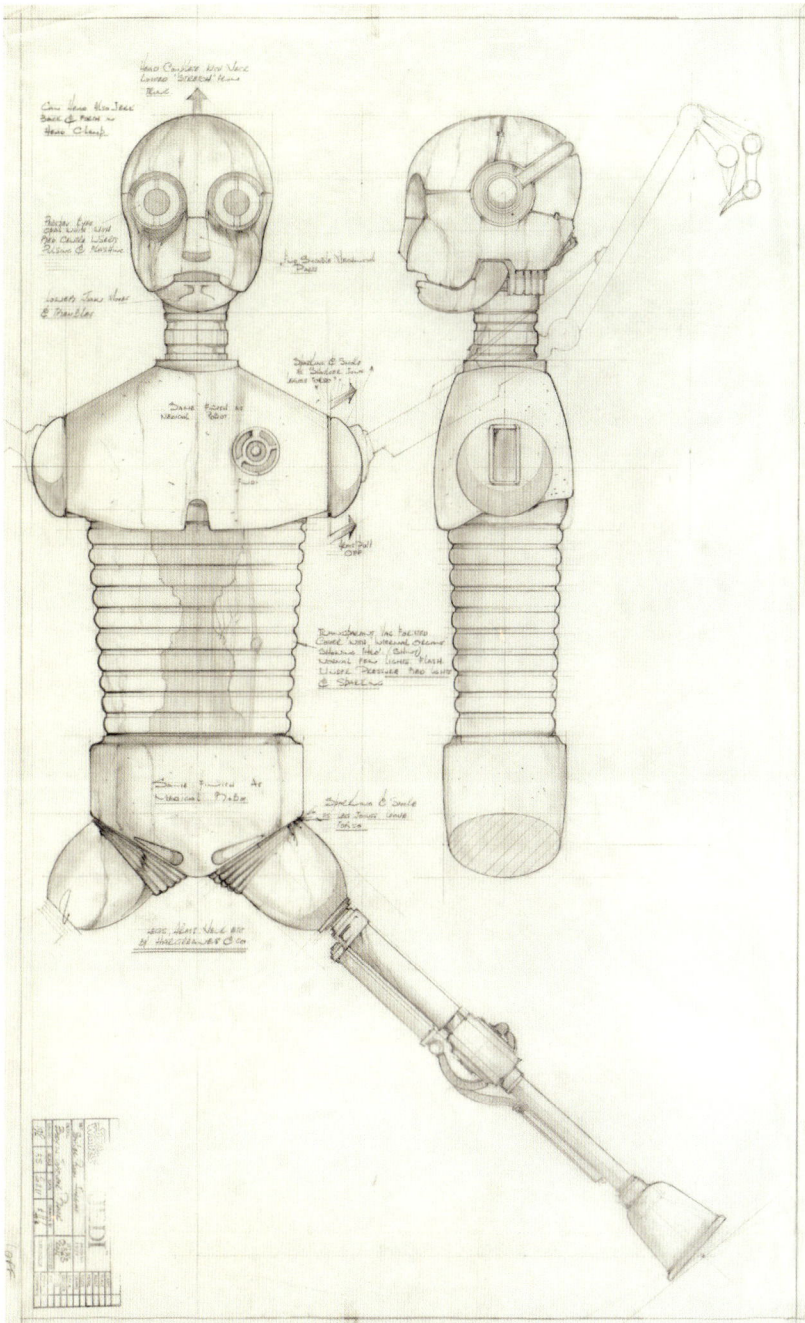

SET	BOILER ROOM, JABBA'S PALACE
DETAIL	BODY IN TORTURE RACK
DRG. NO.	192
DATE	NOVEMBER 20 1981
DRAWN BY	FRED HOLE

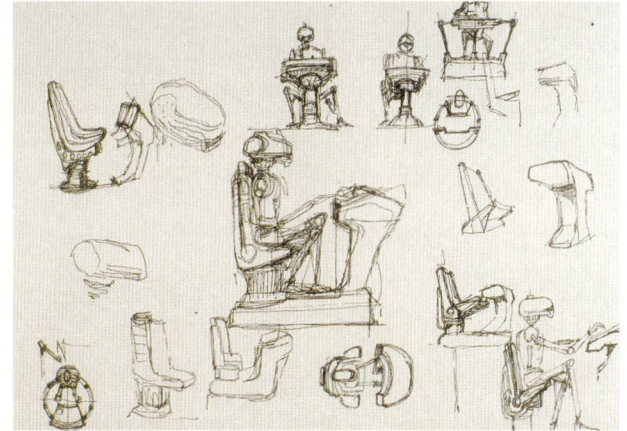

↑ This concept drawing would eventually become robot EV-9D9.

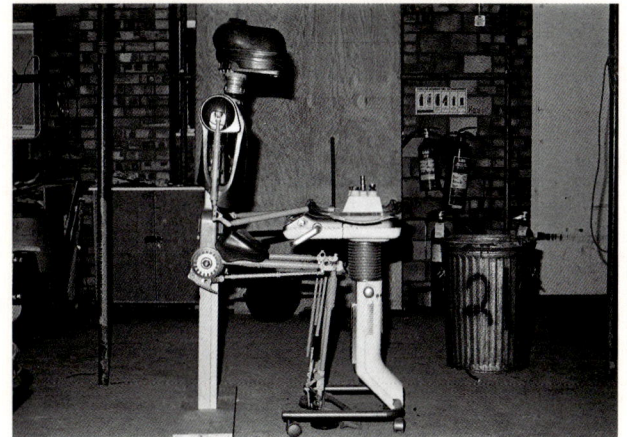

↑ A reference photo shows robot EV-9D9 sitting down.

→ A reference photo taken for *Jedi* of a bounty hunter (Zuckuss in *Empire*), whose head was perhaps going to be recycled into another creature as conceptualized in Fred Hole's technical drawing of an insect head.

↓ This lizard-like droid was to have a flexible neck in a latex sheath; a head based on a preexisting "flat" head; while its neck joint provisions required consultation with Bill Hargreaves and Co.

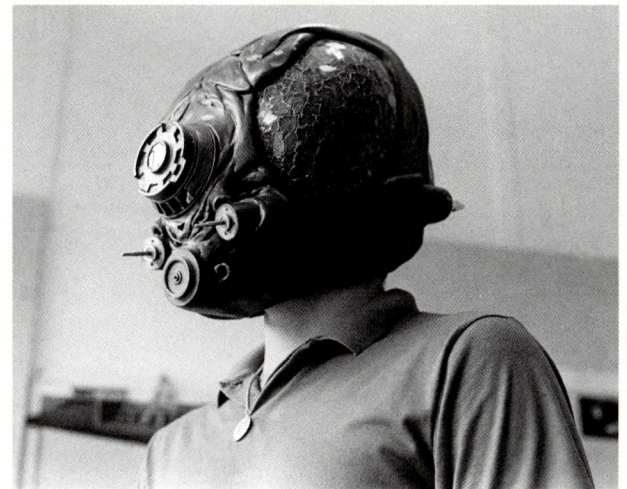

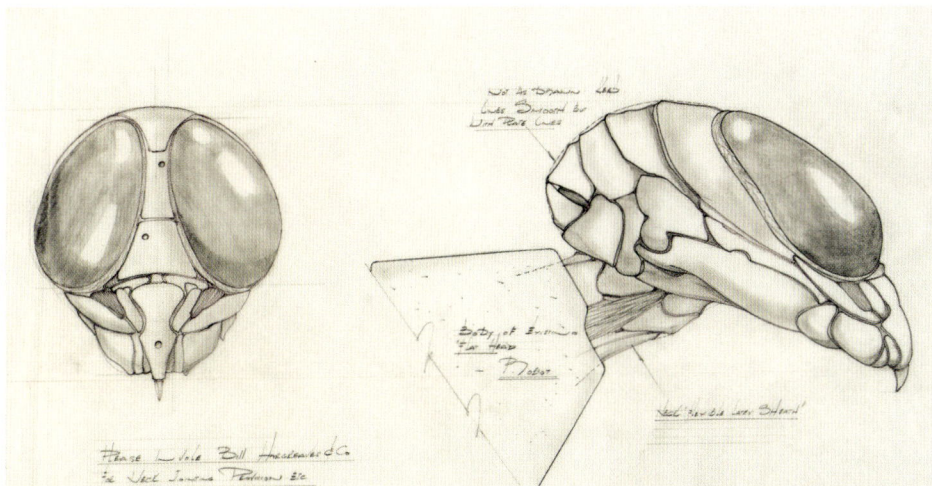

SET	ROBOTS
DETAIL	INSECT HEAD
DRG. NO.	196
DATE	NOVEMBER 22 1978
DRAWN BY	FRED HOLE

RANCOR PIT

Luke's discussion with Jabba doesn't go well, and the Jedi is unceremoniously dropped through a trapdoor into a rancor pit. Jabba and his minions then gather round above to watch the rancor—a huge, slobbering monster—eat Luke. The rancor and its pit were accomplished via three separate sets: a full-sized rancor pit built on Stage 1 for the live-action shoot of Hamill and the Gamorrean guard; a stop-motion rancor on a miniature set back at ILM; and, slated for shooting on March 18 and 19, 1982, a smaller set on Stage 9 for a man in a rancor suit with a toy model of Luke for certain key shots. The blueprint for the smaller set (no. 56) notes camera angles, the position of floater rocks, and the dimensions of the rostrum.

    Lamont's drawing of the chute and gate leading to the pit (no. 379), probably built in conjunction with the larger set on Stage 1, includes notes: The gate was "to slide up (quickly) to a position completely clear of chute shaft"; a stunt double would be used in the chute; and the texture of the chute itself should be well worn, "smooth as stone" (no doubt because Jabba had sent hundreds down before).

→ A Johnston concept sketch of the rancor is from 1981.

SET	RANCOR PIT
DETAIL	BLUE BACKING, SETUPS
DRG. NO.	56
DATE	MARCH 11 1982
DRAWN BY	JOHN FENNER

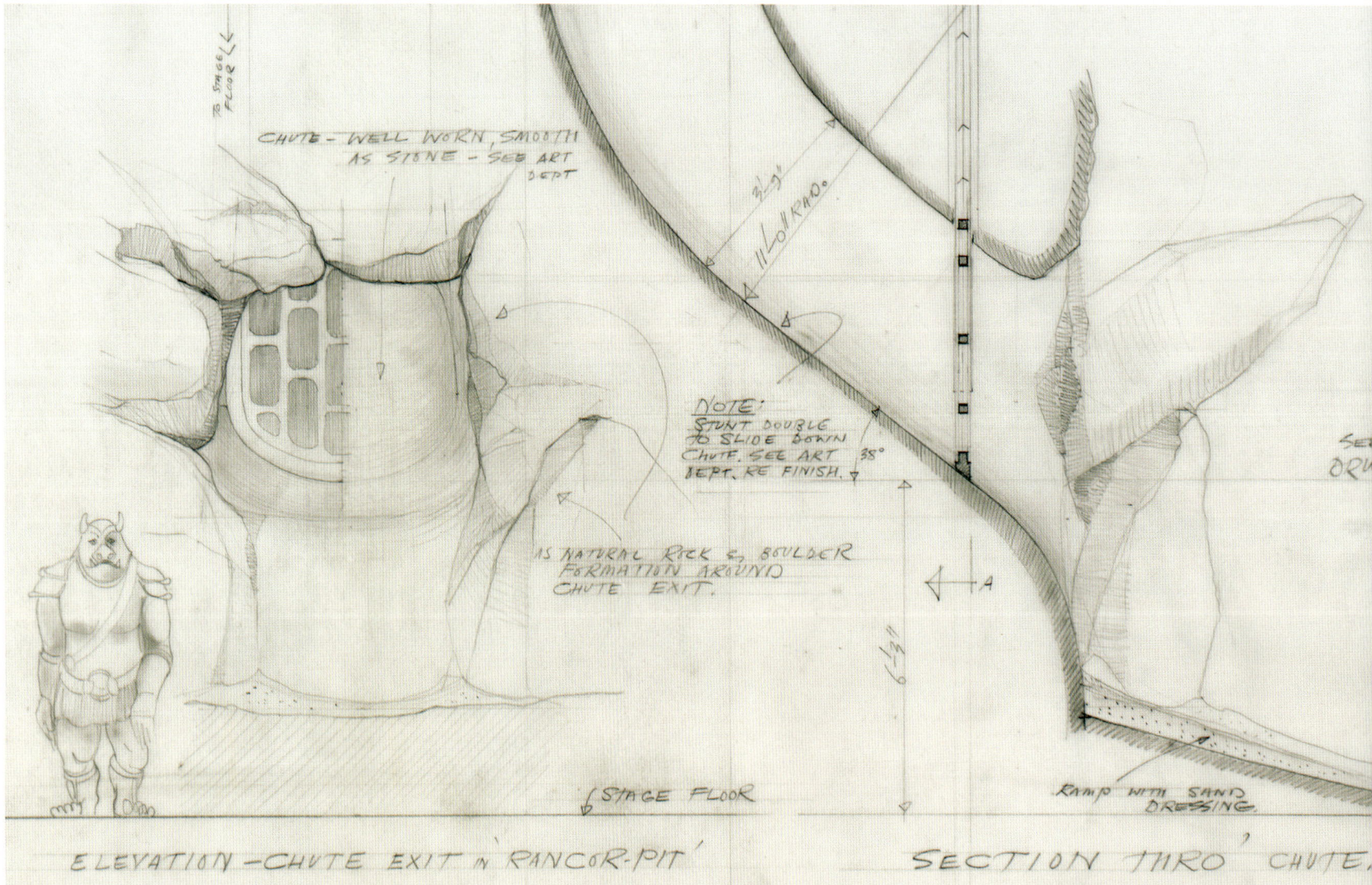

ELEVATION - CHUTE EXIT N 'RANCOR-PIT'   SECTION THRO' CHUTE

SET	RANCOR PIT
DETAIL	CHUTE EXIT & GATE
DRG. NO.	379
DATE	JANUARY 26 1982
DRAWN BY	MICHAEL LAMONT

↑ The stop-motion rancor is seen with mini-Luke at ILM.

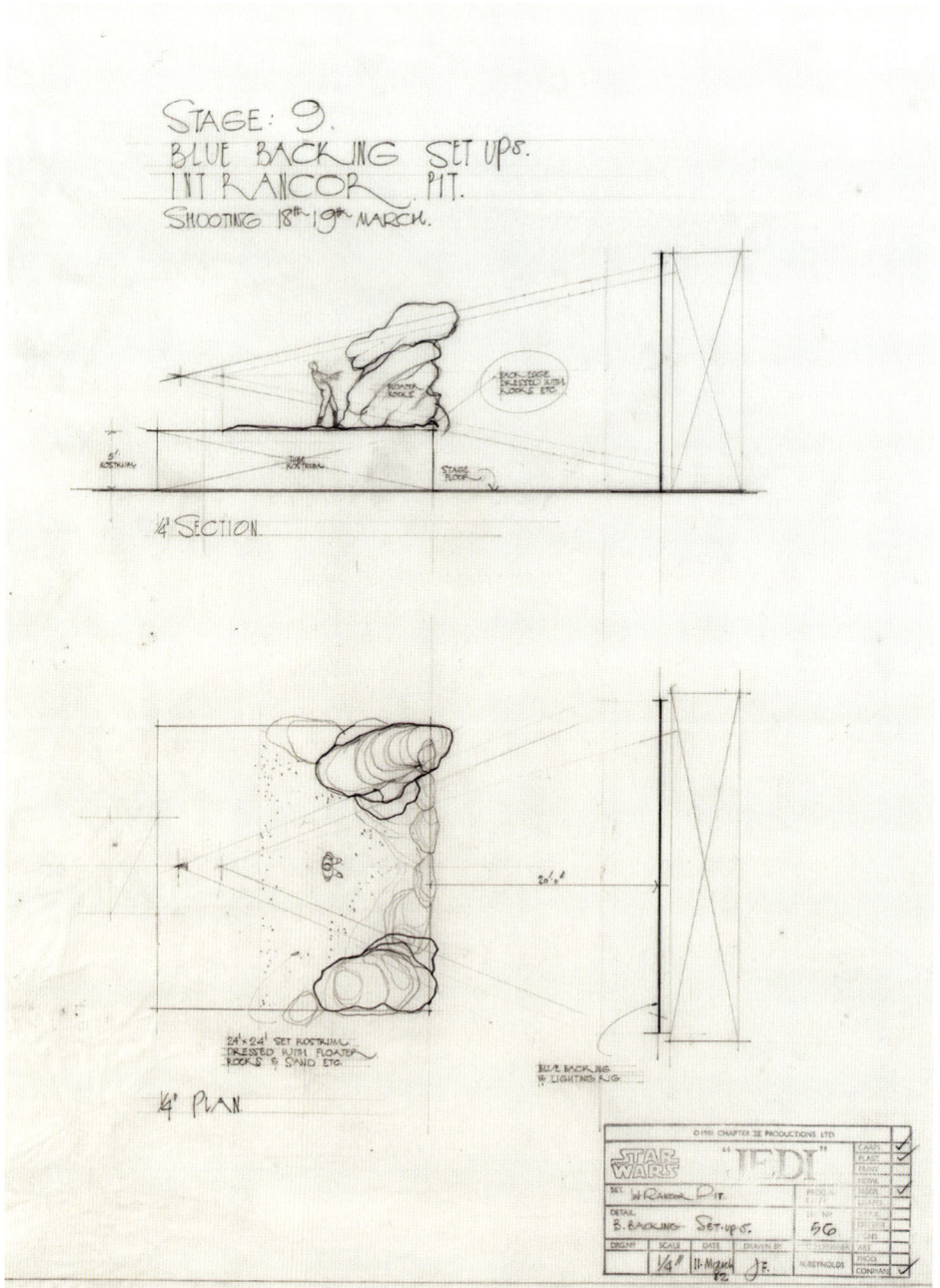

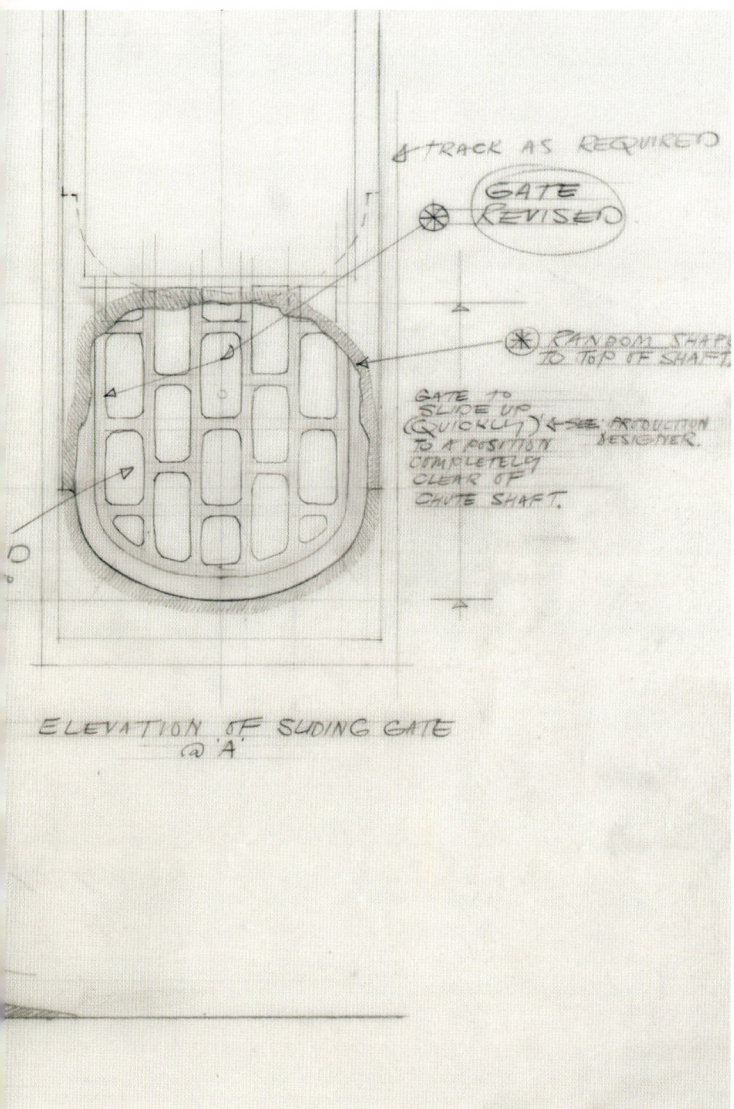

STAGE: 9.
BLUE BACKING SET UPS.
INT RANCOR PIT.
SHOOTING 18th-19th MARCH.

¼" SECTION

¼" PLAN

ELEVATION OF SLIDING GATE
@ 'A'

↑ The final rancor beast as seen in the final film.

JABBA'S BARGE

As the script developed, so did Jabba's barge, into the biggest *Star Wars* set built on location (in Buttercup Valley, Yuma, Arizona, which had prettier and more accessible sand dunes than those in Tunisia). With a stern elevation of about 40 feet, a width of 42.6 feet, and a length of 135 feet (per blueprint no. 40), topped by 60-foot masts, the barge engendered a reaction in Reynolds' art department of disbelief: "Building what? Building where?"

Assistant art director Chris Campbell said, "You see streets and whole towns that are really huge, but, for a single set, this is probably it."

Reynolds was given a million dollar budget to clear the desert of all vegetation over a 4-acre area, and to construct a chain-link fence around the whole locale. There was concern that the set would be literally carried off piece by piece by fans, so guards were posted 24 hours a day. Timber and labor were shipped in, the latter from Los Angeles, but the blueprints were once again drawn in the UK. A worry of producer Jim Bloom and Reynolds was the sails themselves, which went through several designs.

"We were building away up there on this elevated platform, fifteen or sixteen feet up, and it was like a forest of these great twelve-foot-by-twleve-foot timbers," said Reynolds. "In the afternoons, I noticed that there would be this wind coming up, so it occurred to me that if it got very windy and the sails were up, then it would actually tear them all off! So I found quite a well-known

yachtsman and he devised a rig for lowering it all very, very quickly, which could have saved our bacon. It never actually transpired. It was never really windy enough, but at least my mind was at rest."

While the yachtsperson, "Commodore" Warwick Tompkins, helped with the sails and rigging, issuing orders to his 12-person crew, Bill Welch's construction team built the barge in 38 days, a job that normally would have taken four months. In the end, the total set would cost $2.5 million for only a few minutes of screen time during which Jabba's barge, the heroes on the skiff, and more villains on a second skiff engage in a do-or-die battle. A miniature of the barge would be blown to bits at ILM for the scene's climax.

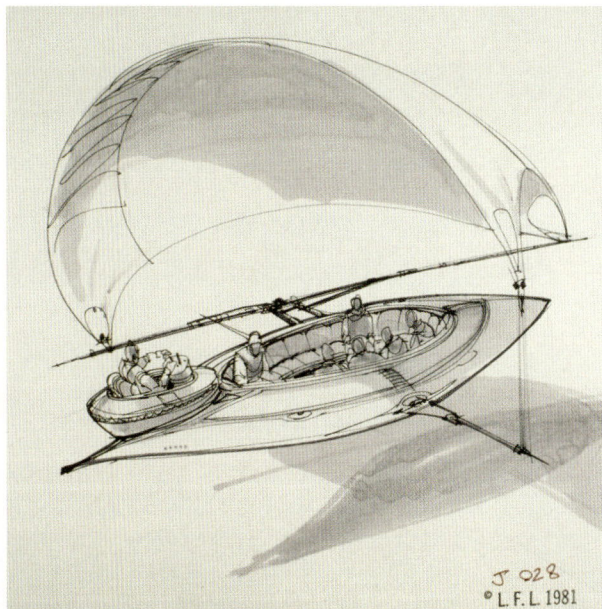

→ Concept art is for the desert skiff, by Johnston, 1981.

↑ A maquette of the desert skiff.

SET	JABBA'S BARGE
DETAIL	PLAN & ELEVATIONS
DRG. NO.	40
DATE	AUGUST 21 1981
DRAWN BY	REG BREAM

↑ The underlying steel struts supporting the skiff are visible in this photograph taken on location in the Arizona desert.

← A full-size practical prop was created of the skiff.

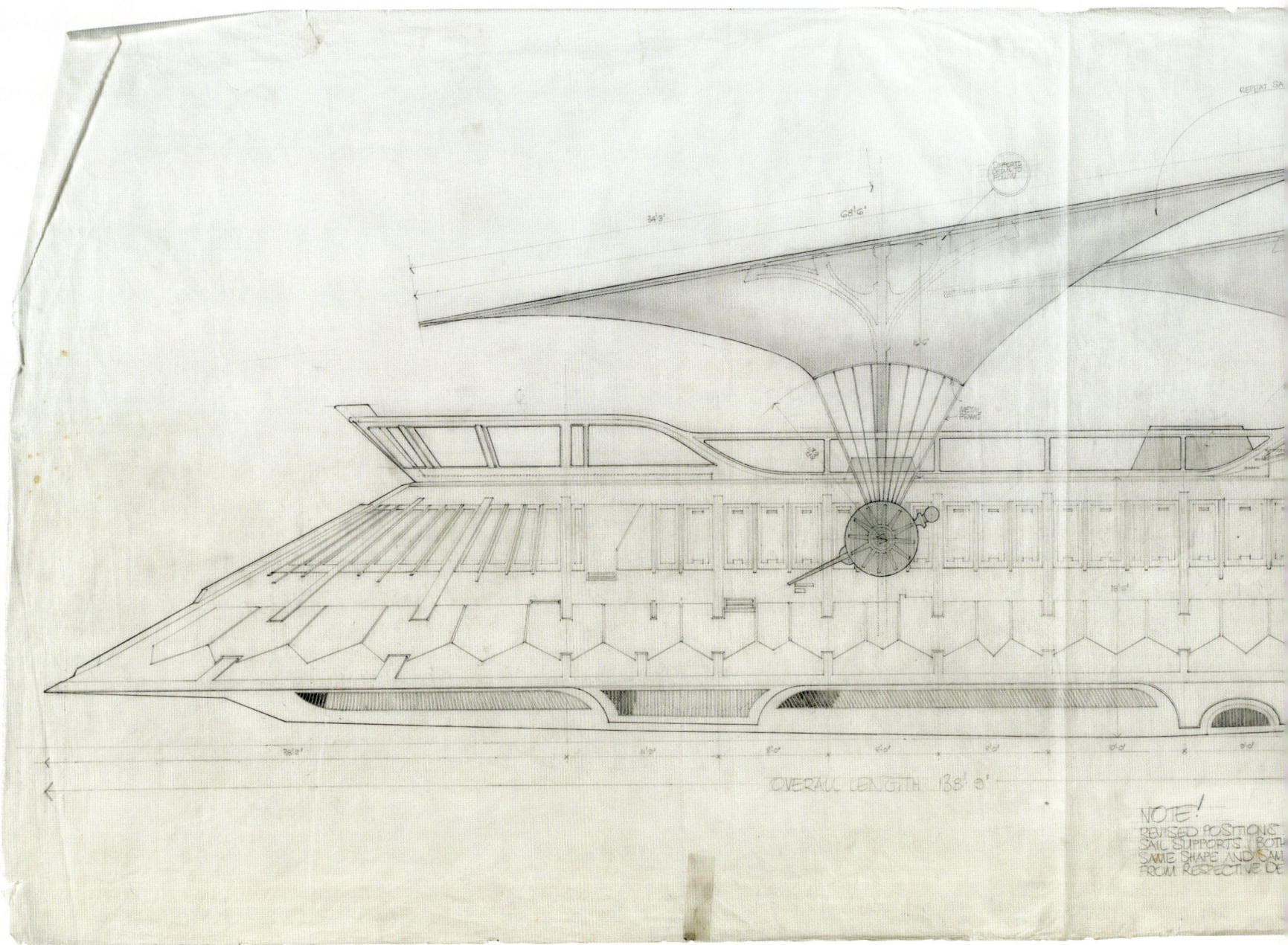

OVERALL LENGTH 138' 3"

NOTE!
REVISED POSITIONS
SAIL SUPPORTS (BOTH
SAME SHAPE AND SAIL
FROM RESPECTIVE DE

↑ The barge and "pit" shown on location in Buttercup Valley, Yuma, Arizona, April 1982.

↑ Underneath the barge set, several production buildings were located among the scaffolding.

SET	JABBA'S BARGE
DETAIL	REVISED ELEVATION
DRG. NO.	387
DATE	JANUARY 27 1982
DRAWN BY	REG BREAM

← Bream's revised elevation drawing bears *Jedi*'s code title, designed to put reporters and fans off the scent: "Blue Harvest." In his blueprint, the barge's overall length is given at 138 feet, 9 inches.

↑ Jabba's barge on location in Yuma, Arizona.

SET	JABBA'S BARGE
DETAIL	FANCIFUL ILLUSTRATION
DRG. NO.	N/A
DATE	1981
DRAWN BY	M.B.

→ Given the initials "M.B.," it's probable that this colorful drawing was produced in the ILM art department by set draftsperson Mark Billerman. His illustration makes plain the pirate element inherent in the barge/skiff sequence, during which Luke is made to "walk the plank."

EXT. JABBA'S BARGE : LOCATION

SAIL PLAN TO SEPARATE DETAILS.

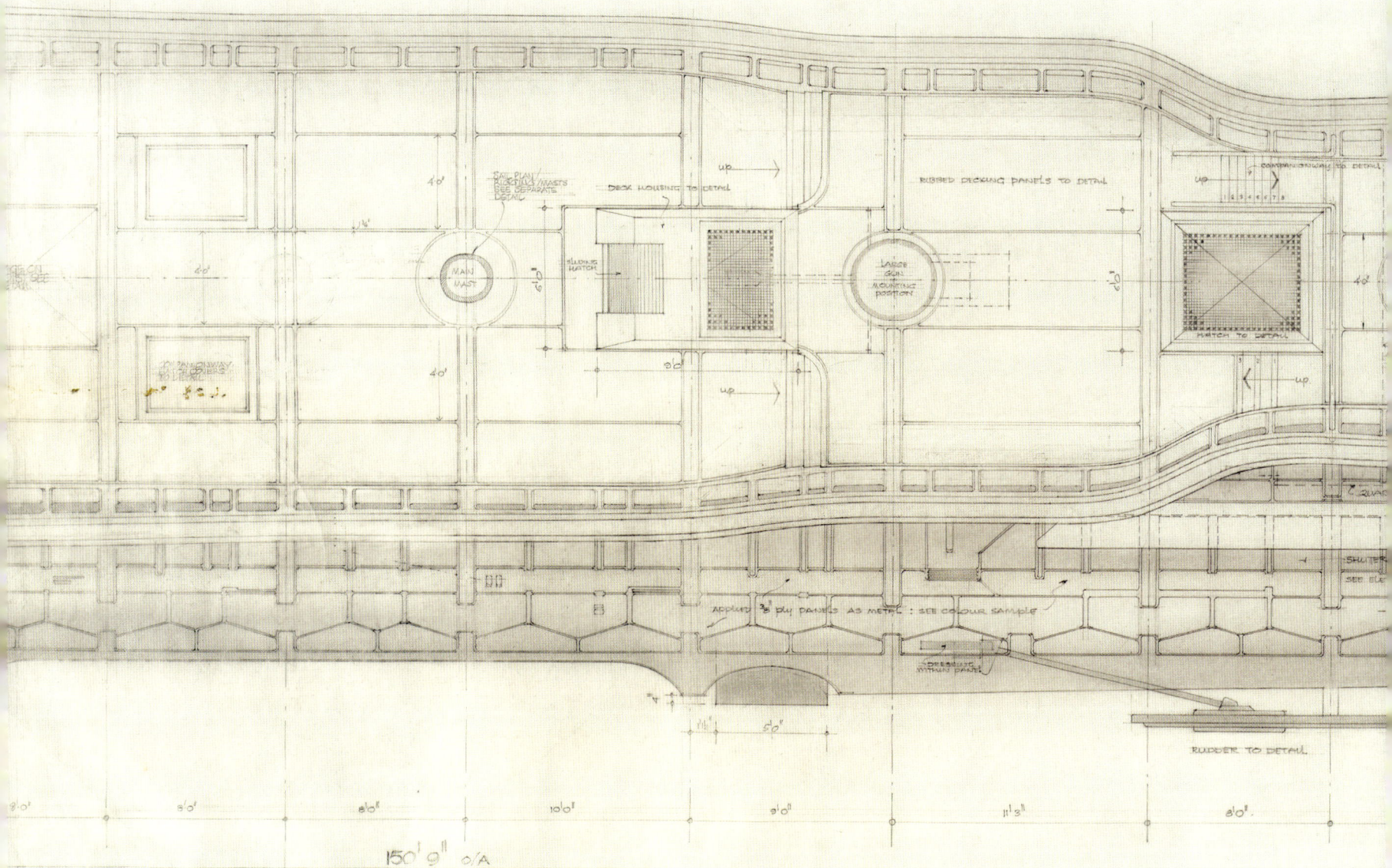

← Jabba's barge and the skiffs are seen in the final film.

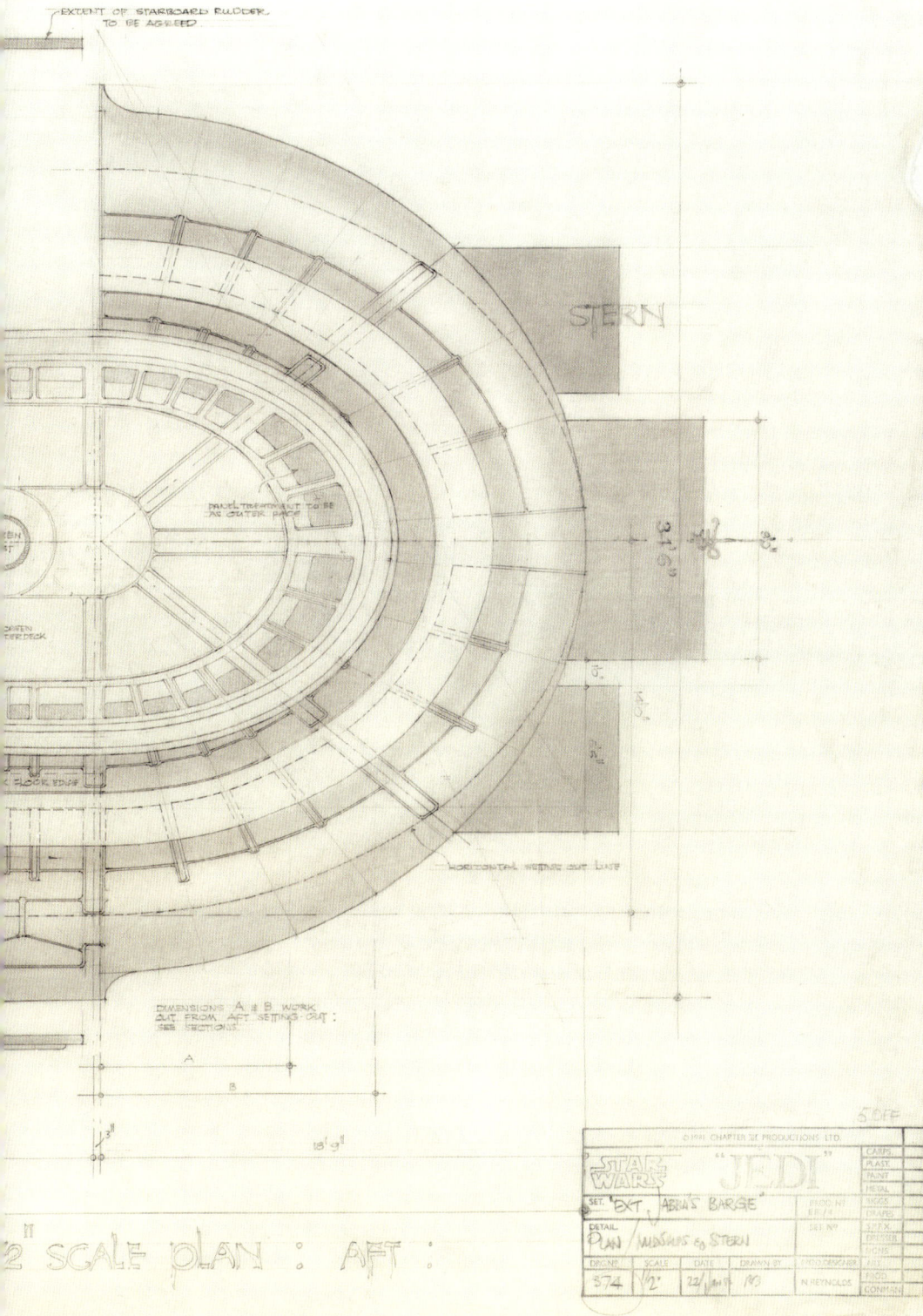

SET	JABBA'S BARGE
DETAIL	PLAN, MIDSHIPS & STERN
DRG. NO.	374
DATE	JANUARY 22 1982
DRAWN BY	REG BREAM

← Bream's expert drawing shows the position of the large gun and mizzen mast, and that the barge would be constructed partially of metal panels.

↑ At ILM, Jabba's barge is detonated in miniature.

SET	JABBA'S BARGE
DETAIL	LARGE DECK GUN
DRG. NO.	430
DATE	MARCH 9 1982
DRAWN BY	GAVIN R. BOCQUET

→ In Bocquet's technical drawing of the gun, the main barrel assembly was to be made from assorted tubing, the barrel stiffened with an insert when assembled on site ("suggest scaffolding tube?" notes the blueprint), its main support recess to be dressed with greeblies, and its gun seat and control to be obtained on location.

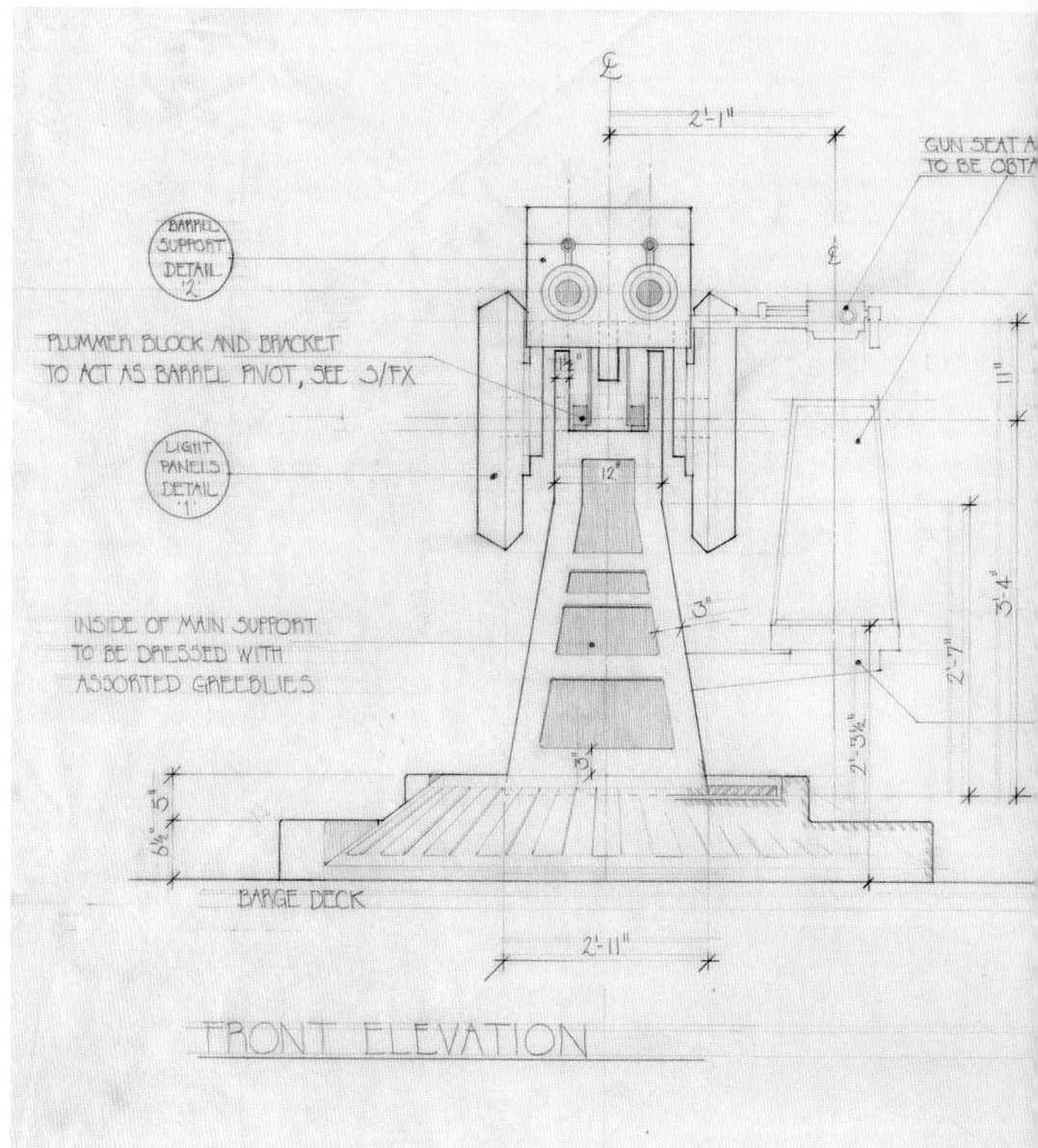

FRONT ELEVATION

SET	JABBA'S BARGE
DETAIL	REVISED LONGITUDINAL SECTION
DRG. NO.	369
DATE	JANUARY 22 1982
DRAWN BY	REG BREAM

↓ The barge's quarterdeck and observation deck are detailed, along with its companion way and handrails to main deck.

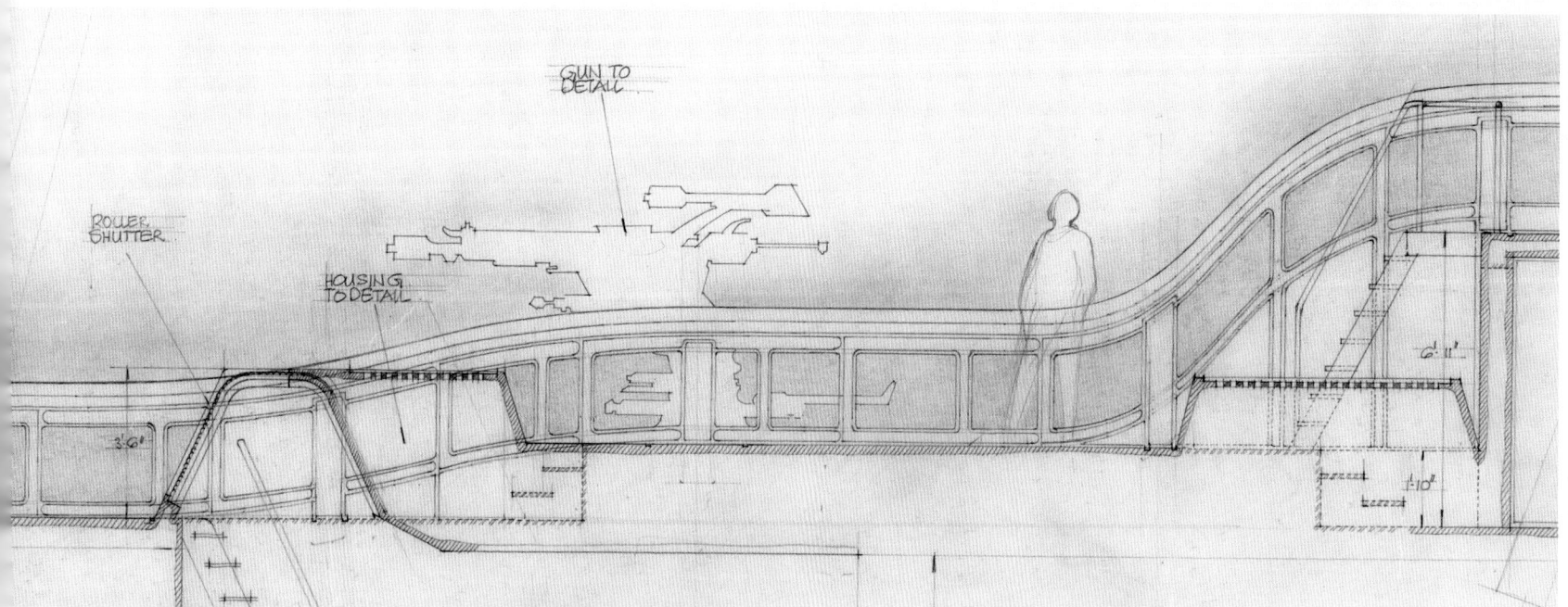

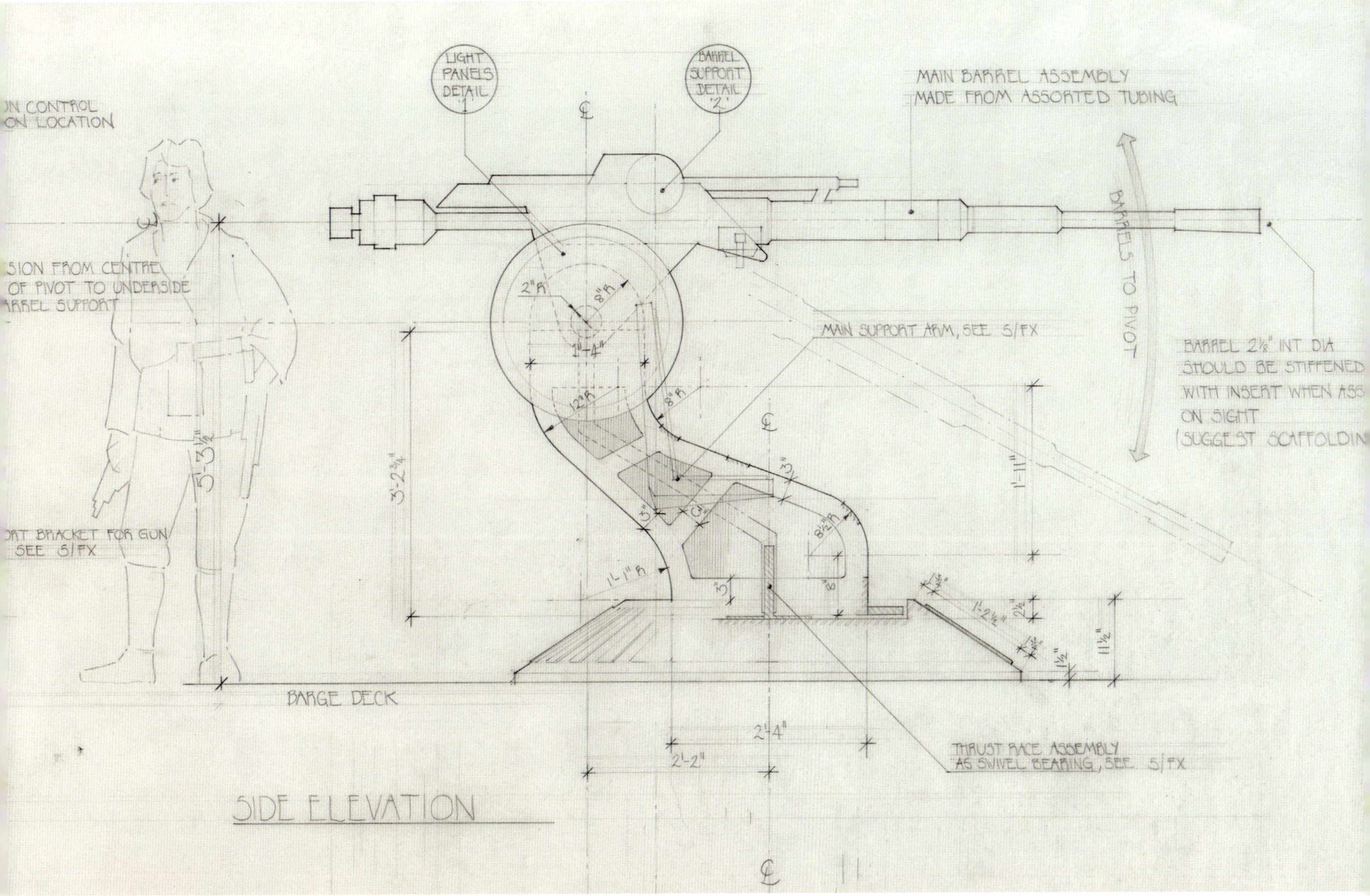

LIGHT
PANELS
DETAIL
'1'

BARREL
SUPPORT
DETAIL
'2'

MAIN BARREL ASSEMBLY
MADE FROM ASSORTED TUBING

ON CONTROL
ON LOCATION

BARRELS TO PIVOT

SION FROM CENTRE
OF PIVOT TO UNDERSIDE
ARREL SUPPORT

MAIN SUPPORT ARM, SEE S/FX

BARREL 2½" INT DIA
SHOULD BE STIFFENED
WITH INSERT WHEN ASS
ON SIGHT
(SUGGEST SCAFFOLDIN

2" R

8" R

1"-4"

8" R

AT BRACKET FOR GUN
SEE S/FX

3'-2¾"

5'-3½"

12" R

3"

1"-11"

3"

8½"

BARGE DECK

3"

11"R

8"

1'-2½"

11½"

2'-4"

2'-2"

THRUST RACE ASSEMBLY
AS SWIVEL BEARING, SEE S/FX

SIDE ELEVATION

← The final full-sized prop
of the deck gun can be seen
behind the Gamorrean guard.

→ The gun is in situ in
another view of the deck.

SET	R2-D2
DETAIL	ACCESSORIES
DRG. NO.	69
DATE	WINTER 1981
DRAWN BY	FRED HOLE

↑ One of the most intriguing blueprints in the Archives is Fred Hole's blue-sky compendium of R2 appendages and uses: nozzles from his "head" for dispensing drinks, a vacuum attachment, a tool for cutting through Ewok nets, a two-pronged arm, a pointer arm to gesture toward a "strange post with meat on it," a new chain cutter, and so on. He also suggests R2-D2 pushing a broom, helping Luke "operate" on a deadly weapon, and projecting a laser sword to Luke, "like a rocket."

  As Hole matter-of-factly explained: "I was also involved with various attachments for Artoo-Detoo. Some were used, others discounted."

→ R2-D2 with the drink-server attachment props that were detailed in the technical drawing (no. 252).

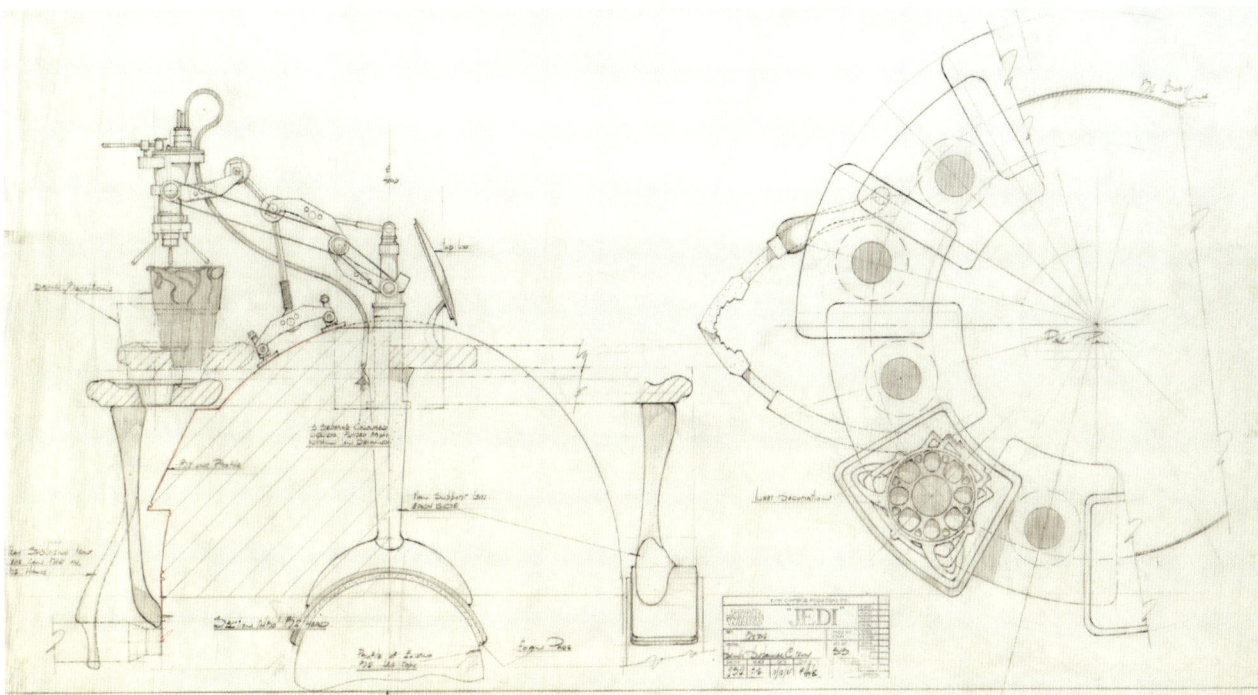

← In his detail drawing, Hole reveals "foam pads on [R2's] legs for mechanics to sit on and three separate colored liquids pumped from within on demand"—all to manufacture a very odd-looking concoction.

SET	R2-D2
DETAIL	DRINK DISPENSER & TRAY
DRG. NO.	252
DATE	DECEMBER 10 1981
DRAWN BY	FRED HOLE

SET	C-3PO
DETAIL	TECHNICAL DUMMY
DRG. NO.	293
DATE	DECEMBER 24 1981
DRAWN BY	FRED HOLE

↑ As filming progressed, one puppet emerged as a star: Salacious B. Crumb. Laughing at Jabba's every evil deed, a kind of Muppet Ed McMahon, Crumb's final act of defiance toward our heroes is to chew out one of C-3PO's eyes. Hole's blueprint shows that, at one point, production considered having the droid eye popped out by a human finger or by a screwdriver-like tool pushed from behind.

→ C-3PO contends with an injured eye in this shot from the final film.

SARLACC PIT

Marquand had made three preproduction scouting trips to Yuma, Arizona: "And I had this horrific experience the second time of finding that all the sand dunes had moved," he said. "Once we made the third trip down and decided precisely where the Sarlacc pit was going to be built, and where the dunes were going to be built, and, therefore, where the barge was going to be situated—then, really, it became a huge logistical problem for the art department and the construction people as to whether they could get the set built in time. That was a colossal job."

Production had chosen a flat area of the desert where Welch and his department threw everything into constructing a 25-foot-high platform, with a sand-covered 20-square-foot, 13-foot-deep cone built into it—a pit within a false mountain—home to the hungry Sarlacc. Indeed, the space under the barge and around the pit was so large that it housed offices, storage areas, an ILM workshop, and a 150-seat commissary—all scattered between the 27-foot-high posts that were holding up the barge and the platform. Production, medical, and carpentry rooms were outside the hill, but disguised as sand dunes.

Reynolds' crew was also hard put to finish in time, as, Sisyphus-like, they would sometimes spend all day carrying sand to the top of the fake hill, only to have the night winds blow it off and expose anew the bare boards by next morning. And then, when everything was more or less under control, Lucas decided that the heretofore invisible Sarlacc monster was going to make an appearance in the film.

"That whole thing, the barge and the Sarlacc pit was like filming a whole picture unto itself," said Reynolds. "And I was really a bit behind there with the pit, when the lovely Phil Tippett came to my rescue and helped with the monster. He got us out of trouble. Because we weren't going to actually see anything, but then the tentacles became something that George actually wanted to see, so it was another photo finish."

After one grain of sand fouled up the Sarlacc's intricate hydraulics system during filming, mechanical effect supervisor Kit West and special effects supervisor Roy Arborgast decided to operate the tentacles using poles and wires controlled by six men.

↑ Another concept sketch shows how production planned to build up the platform perched on a forest of timbers.

SET	SARLACC PIT
DETAIL	PROVISIONAL SKETCH
DRG. NO.	N/A
DATE	1981
DRAWN BY	MARK BILLERMAN

← A crew member fixes the Sarlacc tentacles in preparation for filming.

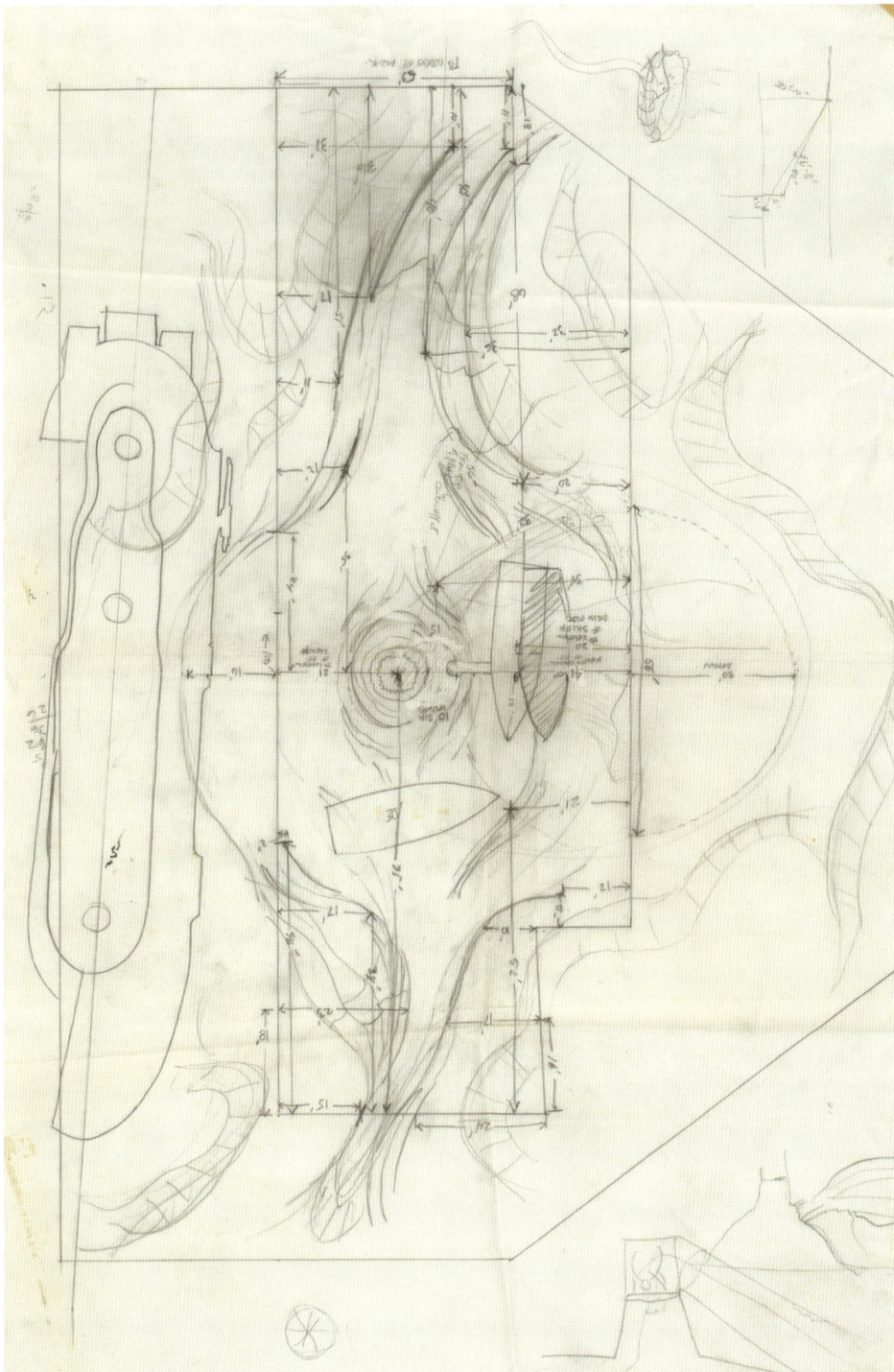

SET	SARLACC PIT
DETAIL	EARLY CONCEPT SKETCH
DRG. NO.	N/A
DATE	1981
DRAWN BY	MARK BILLERMAN

← The Sarlacc pit was built in the Arizona desert.

THE ARTWORK OF HARRY

Academy Award®–nominated film designer Hans-Kurt (Harry) Lange was born in Eisenach, Germany, in 1930; he passed away on May 22, 2008. According to his obituary, Lange intended to be an archaeologist. During the Second World War, teenage Lange was in Hamburg during the Allies' three-day bombing of the city. After the war, Eisenach became part of the Russian occupied zone of Germany, so Lange fled across the border into the west under cover of night.

Next in his picaresque life, after making his way to the United States, was a stint working with the Army Ballistic Missile Agency in Huntsville, Alabama, as an illustrator of space vehicles and missions to other planets. Later, under NASA, he become section head of the future projects staff, collaborating with a group of selected illustrators on interplanetary, intersolar, and deep space projects in close coordination with the Werner von Braun team. (Von Braun was the controversial engineer behind Nazi Germany's V-2 rocket and the United States' Saturn V rocket, which carried the Apollo Mission to the moon.)

In 1965, author Arthur C. Clarke, who was working with Stanley Kubrick on the project that would become 2001, invited Lange to meet the demanding director. According to Lange's website, Kubrick "perused Lange's technical illustrations, looked him in the eye and announced that he could get illustrators to do better work for 'peanuts— they're a dime a dozen.' As Lange scooped up his drawings and made for the door, Kubrick added, 'But they don't have your NASA background'—and hired Lange on the spot."

Working in earnest on the film, Lange's designs were so accurate that production, reportedly, had to submit them for security clearance. "They had to be designed as if they could travel to the edge of the solar system and beyond," said Lange. "I got along with Kubrick very well. He was an absolute stickler for detail and a good taskmaster. That was fine with me, because I was new to filmmaking."

Following 2001, Lange worked on the original *Star Wars* trilogy and on Jim Henson's movies *The Great Muppet Caper* (1981) and *The Dark Crystal* (1982). He was aeronautics consultant on *Superman 2* (1980) and, as production designer, fit in with the Monty Pythons on *The Meaning of Life* (1983).

"A piece of board with blue squares stuck on it may do for TV, but not when you want to do something on a Cinerama screen," Lange said. "It had to be absolutely perfect. It doesn't cost that much more to do something properly and accurately."

For the *Star Wars* original trilogy, Lange's work ethic and aesthetics were particularly evident in the cockpits, where he successfully melded his real-world experience with space fantasy.

SHUTTLE

Despite the unprecedented success of the first two *Star Wars* films, production was never profligate. A good case in point was the Imperial shuttlecraft, which was used three times as three different ships: for Darth Vader, the Emperor, and the rebels. Based on concept art by Johnston, McQuarrie, and Rodis-Jamero, its design elements harkened back to the skyhopper and TIE fighter. But like the *Falcon*, the shuttle never strayed from the *Star Wars* Stage, where it was moved around the Death Star docking bay and the rebel hangar as needed, while successive sets cycled through. Although photos exist of the ship in the rebel hangar appropriately dressed as a more banged-up, dirty craft, it always appears as a pristine ship in the film.

"It started as a little sketch by Ralph," said Lorne Peterson. "Because I think Joe Johnston wouldn't have drawn up something quite like this. It's a very stubby-nosed hull, not an incredibly graceful ship like an X-wing or a TIE fighter. As I remember, there was a small painting of the shuttle in the background somewhere by Ralph. That was the inspiration for it. But it worked well on a live-action set because it was stubby and they could put it on a ramp."

On October 26, 1981, the always speedy Bream executed two blueprints, beautifully done, of the shuttle. His notes indicate that the height of the wings, which were to be built in relation to the matte painting that would complete the illusion of the immense hangar, was not yet determined.

↑ In this photograph, the full-sized shuttle set is being built on Stage 4 at Elstree.

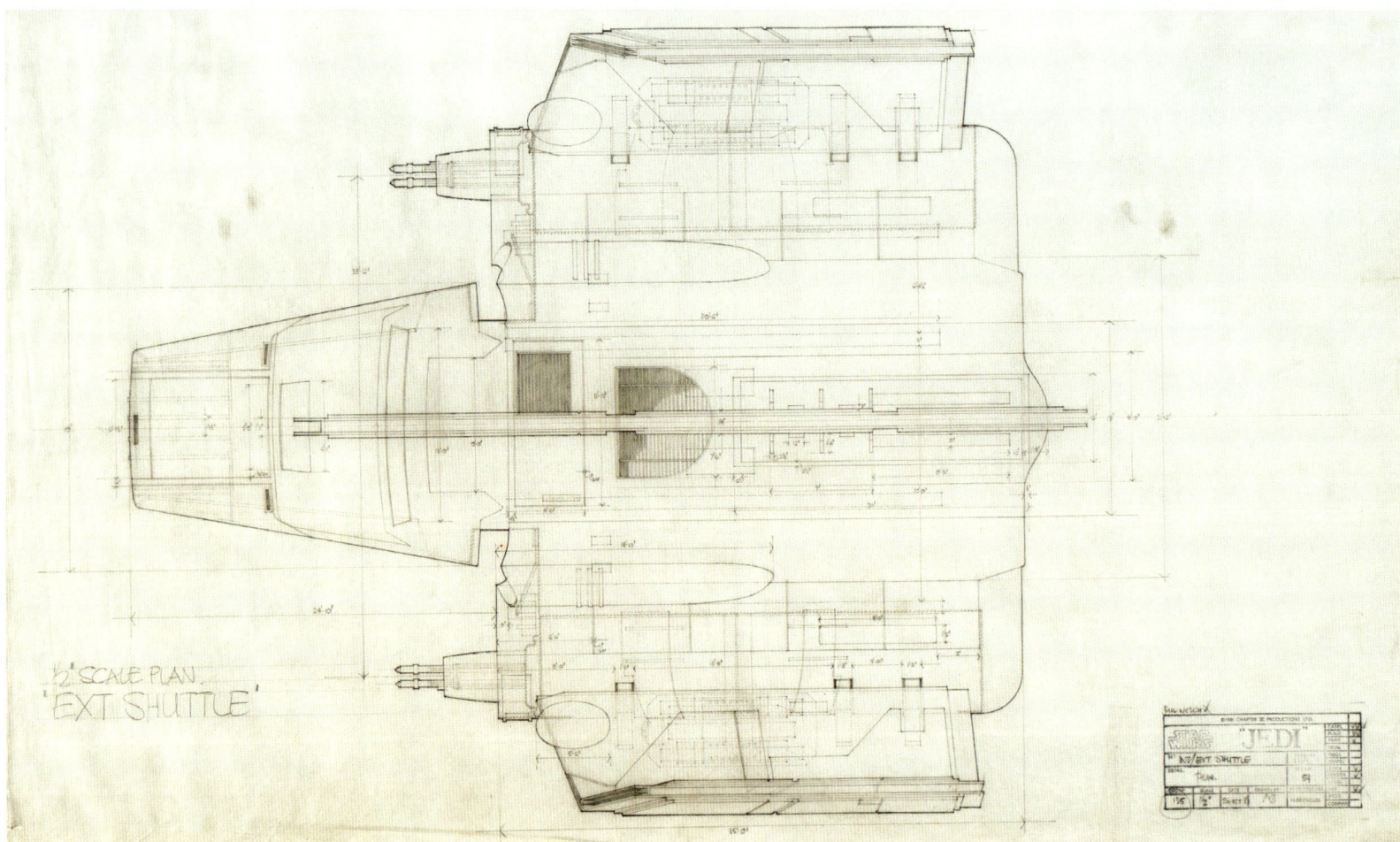

½" SCALE PLAN.
'EXT SHUTTLE'

SET	SHUTTLE
DETAIL	PLAN
DRG. NO.	135
DATE	OCTOBER 26 1981
DRAWN BY	REG BREAM

'DEATH STAR DOCKING BAY'

SET	DEATH STAR DOCKING BAY
DETAIL	BUILT/MATTE CONCEPT
DRG. NO.	N/A
DATE	1981
DRAWN BY	NORMAN REYNOLDS

← One of the few surviving Reynolds conceptual drawings for *Jedi* is an early idea for the Death Star docking bay, which also illustrated the extent of the physical set that they were going to build on the stage. "I drew a little figure of Darth in the middle ground to show its relative size," Reynolds said. "But, really, I preferred spending time with the draftsmen on the drawing board rather than doing lots of sketches, because it's so very time-consuming. Concept drawings were simply a starting point. George would have the casting vote."

SET	DEATH STAR DOCKING BAY
DETAIL	AERIAL AND SIDE VIEW
DRG. NO.	N/A
DATE	1981
DRAWN BY	UNKNOWN

↑ An all-digital incarnation of the Imperial shuttle arrives in a Star Destroyer hangar in a newly created moment for the 1997 special edition release of *The Empire Strikes Back*.

↓ The Death Star hangar is being built on Stage 4.

→ A one-of-a-kind drawing in the Archives combines two views to show how the practical set (in green) would connect to a matte painting and where the Throne Room was. The Death Star docking bay would ultimately cost about $800,000 to build.

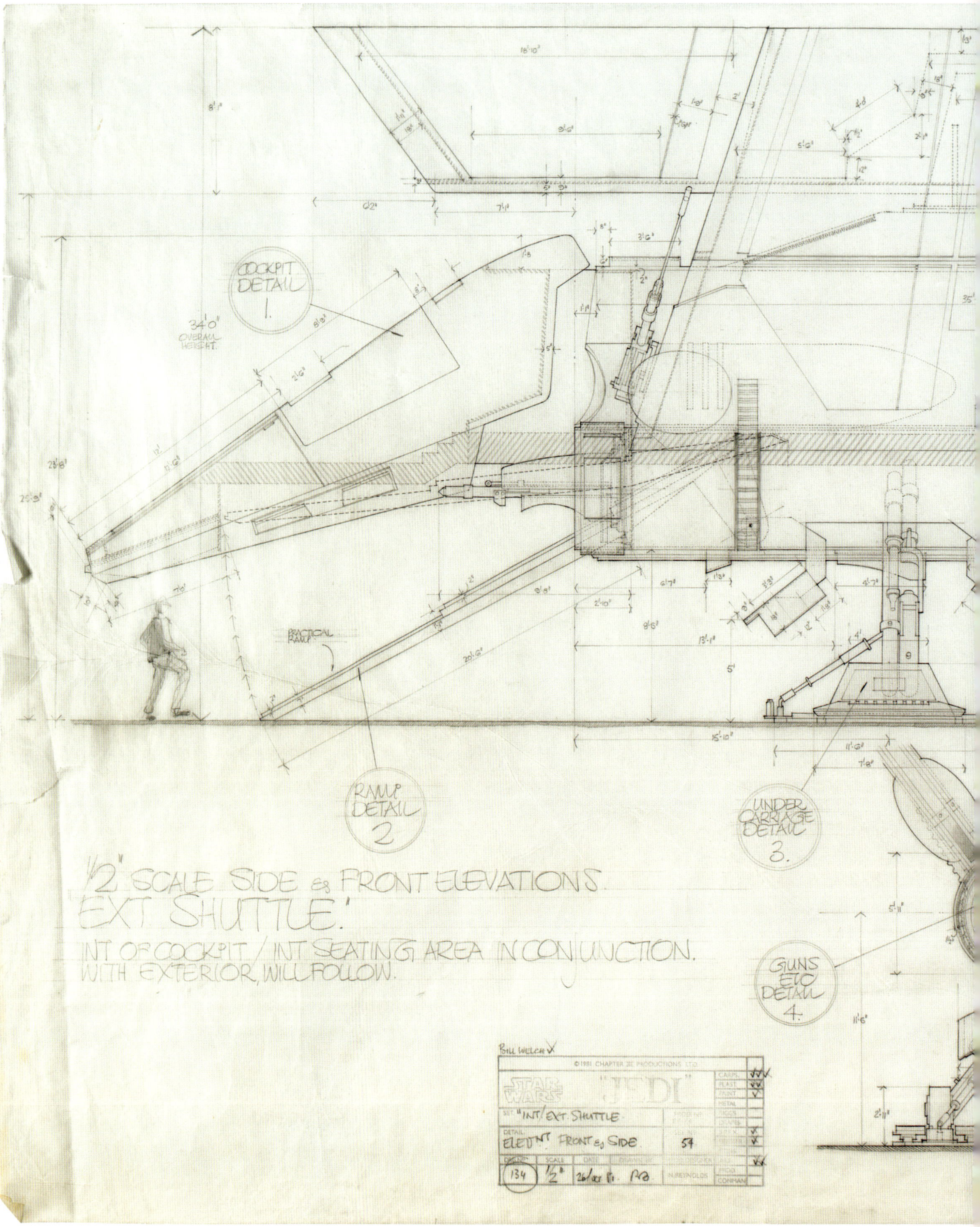

COCKPIT
DETAIL
1.

34'0"
OVERALL
HEIGHT

PRACTICAL
RAMP

RAMP
DETAIL
2

UNDER
CARRIAGE
DETAIL
3.

½" SCALE SIDE & FRONT ELEVATIONS
'EXT. SHUTTLE.'
INT OF COCKPIT / INT SEATING AREA IN CONJUNCTION.
WITH EXTERIOR, WILL FOLLOW.

GUNS
ETC
DETAIL
4.

BILL WELCH

©1981 CHAPTER III PRODUCTIONS LTD.

STAR WARS JEDI

SET "INT / EXT. SHUTTLE

DETAIL ELEM'T. FRONT & SIDE   57

134   ½"   26/10 81   RB

SET	SHUTTLE	DATE	OCTOBER 26 1981
DETAIL	ELEMENTS, FRONT & SIDE	DRAWN BY	REG BREAM
DRG. NO.	134		

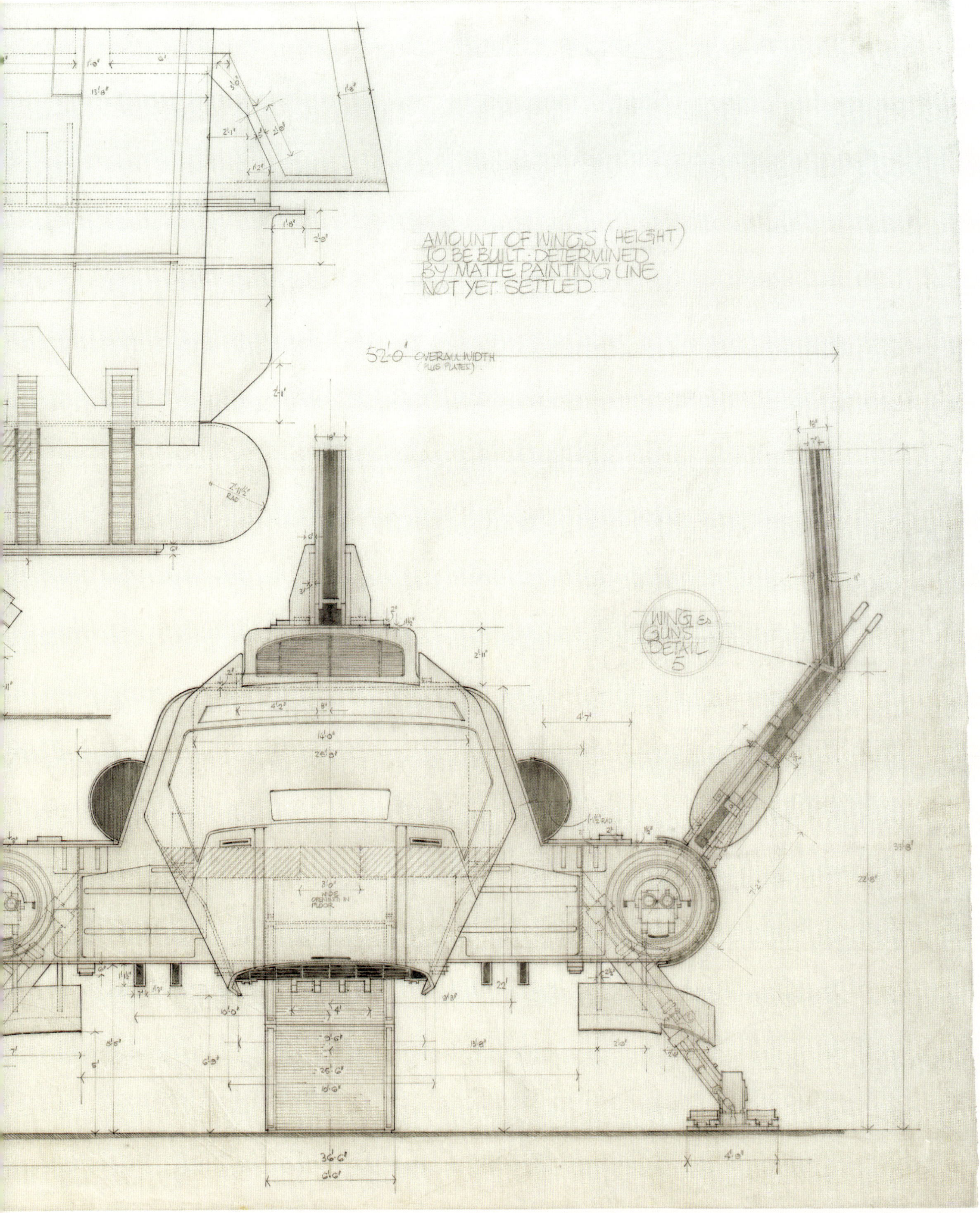

AMOUNT OF WINGS (HEIGHT)
TO BE BUILT. DETERMINED
BY MATTE PAINTING LINE
NOT YET SETTLED.

52'-0" OVERALL WIDTH
(PLUS PLATES)

WING &
GUNS
DETAIL
5

INSIDE THE PLASTERERS' SHOP

By 1981, master plasterer Kenny Clarke had worked for Stanley Kubrick, Steven Spielberg, and George Lucas. He would later work for James Cameron, Jim Henson, Terry Gilliam, Ridley Scott, Robert Zemeckis, and many others.

"The construction department worked mainly with straight timber, would stand it up and there's your film set…" said Clarke. "And then one would come in with all the architectural stuff. We were the department that actually bent a straight line; anything that was curved had to be molded and cast from models made in plaster."

Clarke's department would "segregate" all of its jobs by numbers, sometimes hiring specialists. The nerve center of his department was the workshop, within which resided the shop supervisor, who always stayed put. Clarke's "walking supervisor" would oversee work on all the stages in conjunction with Clarke, who would delegate the rest of the job details among about 20 "charge hands," who would then supervise the other 100 members of the shop.

During the period leading up to and including the original *Star Wars* trilogy, the plasterers' shop began working with fiberglass, which was relatively new, and, of course, vacuum-forming. "Then I started to look at carbon fiber and Kevlar," said Clarke. "When we got into Ewoks, with the animatronics, we had to mold bodies."

Clarke believed that while the starcraft in *Star Wars* and *Alien* were never meant to be taken seriously from an engineering point of view, their aesthetic inspired a generation of industrial designers. "For me, the lines that were taken on the craft, whether it be the X-wing or the Y-fighters or the *Millennium Falcon* or the *Nostromo*, these lines have to be brought on paper and designed—and if it looks good, it can fly. These designers knew nothing about actually flying these things, let's be honest; it's films. But when you actually get to the point, the lines that have been taken from that era are in the lines of everything we take for granted: the *Concorde*, the spaceships. These beautiful lines make these things fly. I strongly and absolutely believe that the *Star Wars* era was the blueprint for today and, I might add, the future."

← Reference photography taken at ILM shows the miniature shuttle.

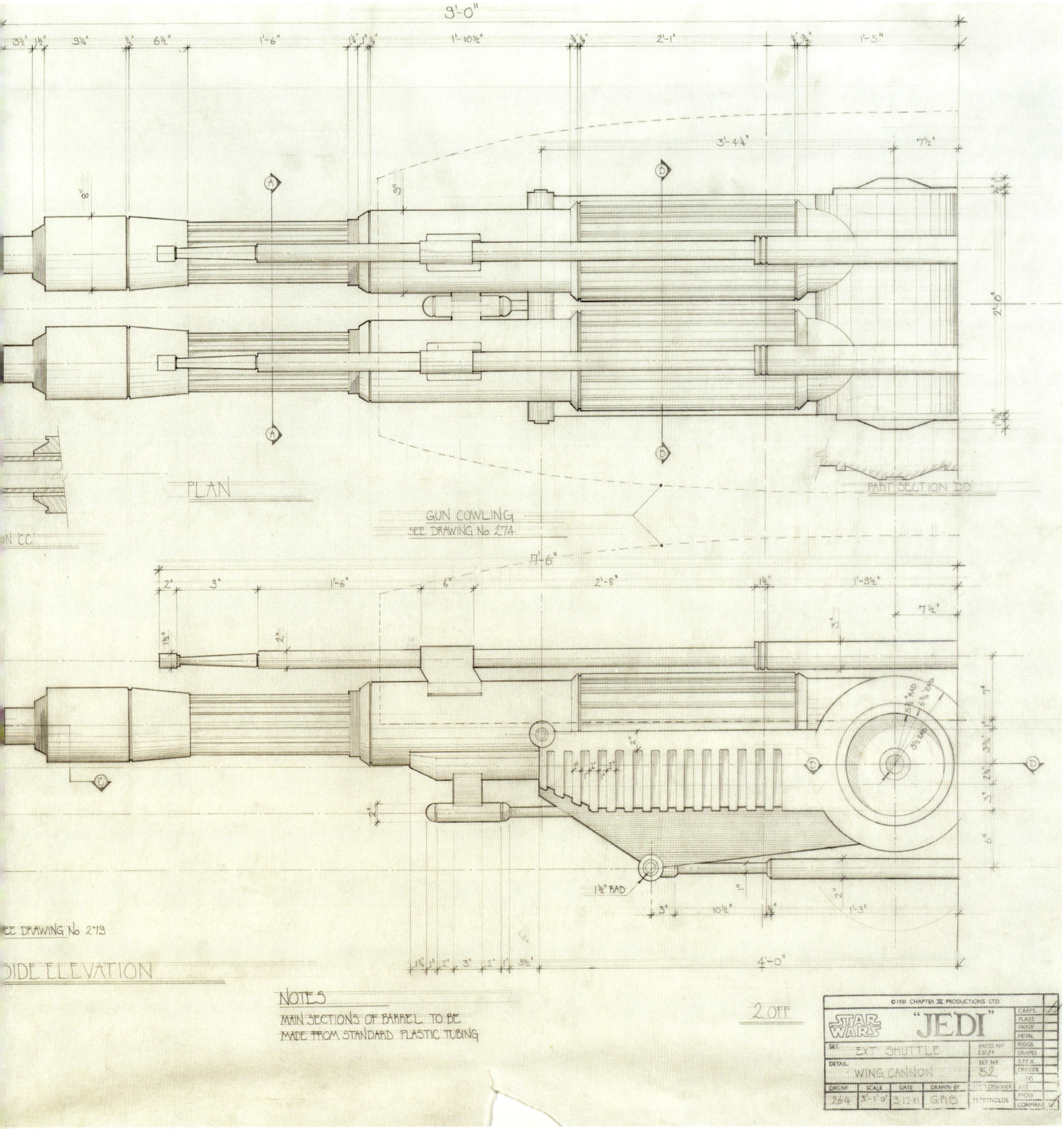

9'-0"

3½" 1½" 9¾" ½" 6½" 1'-6" 1'-10½" 2'-1" 1'-5"

3'-4¼" 7½"

A

B

2'-0"

PLAN

A

D

PART SECTION DD

GUN COWLING
SEE DRAWING No 27A

7'-6"

2" 9" 1'-6" 6" 2'-8" 1'-9½"

7½"

1½" RAD

C

D

D

SEE DRAWING No 279

SIDE ELEVATION

1½" RAD

3" 10½"

1'-9"

4'-0"

NOTES

MAIN SECTIONS OF BARREL TO BE
MADE FROM STANDARD PLASTIC TUBING

2 OFF

© 1981 CHAPTER III PRODUCTIONS LTD.

		CARPS.
STAR WARS	"JEDI"	PLASE. PAINT
SET	EXT SHUTTLE	PROD Nº EII/4	METAL RIGGS.
DETAIL	WING CANNON	SET Nº 52	DRAPES S.F.F.X. DRESSER
DRG Nº 264	SCALE 3"=1'-0"	DATE 3.12.81	DRAWN BY G.R.B.	ART DESIGNER T. REYNOLDS	PROD COMPANY

SET	SHUTTLE
DETAIL	WING CANNON
DRG. NO.	264
DATE	DECEMBER 9 1981
DRAWN BY	GAVIN R. BOCQUET

↑ In Bocquet's sketch of the shuttle's
wing cannon, he notes that the main
sections of the barrel were to be made
from standard plastic tubing.

DAGOBAH

The Dagobah set from *Empire* was made mostly of elements that could not be saved for the third film, with the exception of the cutout trees, which were used in the background. Most of these were preserved because they were flat and could be easily stored (the larger three-dimensional trees were so heavy that they had to be chainsawed out of position).

For *Jedi*, the art department redesigned—and the construction department built— three new "hero" trees at a height of 32 feet and a basic trunk diameter of 7 feet. On Stage 2, they then reconstructed the entire Dagobah set on a slightly smaller scale than its predecessor, dressing it and "flooding" the swamp. Even Yoda was rebuilt by Stuart Freeborn, who only finished it the night before his scenes. On the actual morning of shooting, Yoda was deemed too green and fresh looking so the makeup department aged him (his house had been stored from the previous film).

The blueprint (no. 289) notes: the mist and general atmosphere were to match *Empire*'s, the number and disposition of the cutout trees were to be determined by the art department representative on stage, the X-fighter was to bridge the stream, and the marsh water lake was not to exceed a maximum of 3 feet deep.

SET	DAGOBAH
DETAIL	STAGE LAYOUT/PLAN
DRG. NO.	289
DATE	DECEMBER 22 1981
DRAWN BY	KEVIN M. PHIPPS

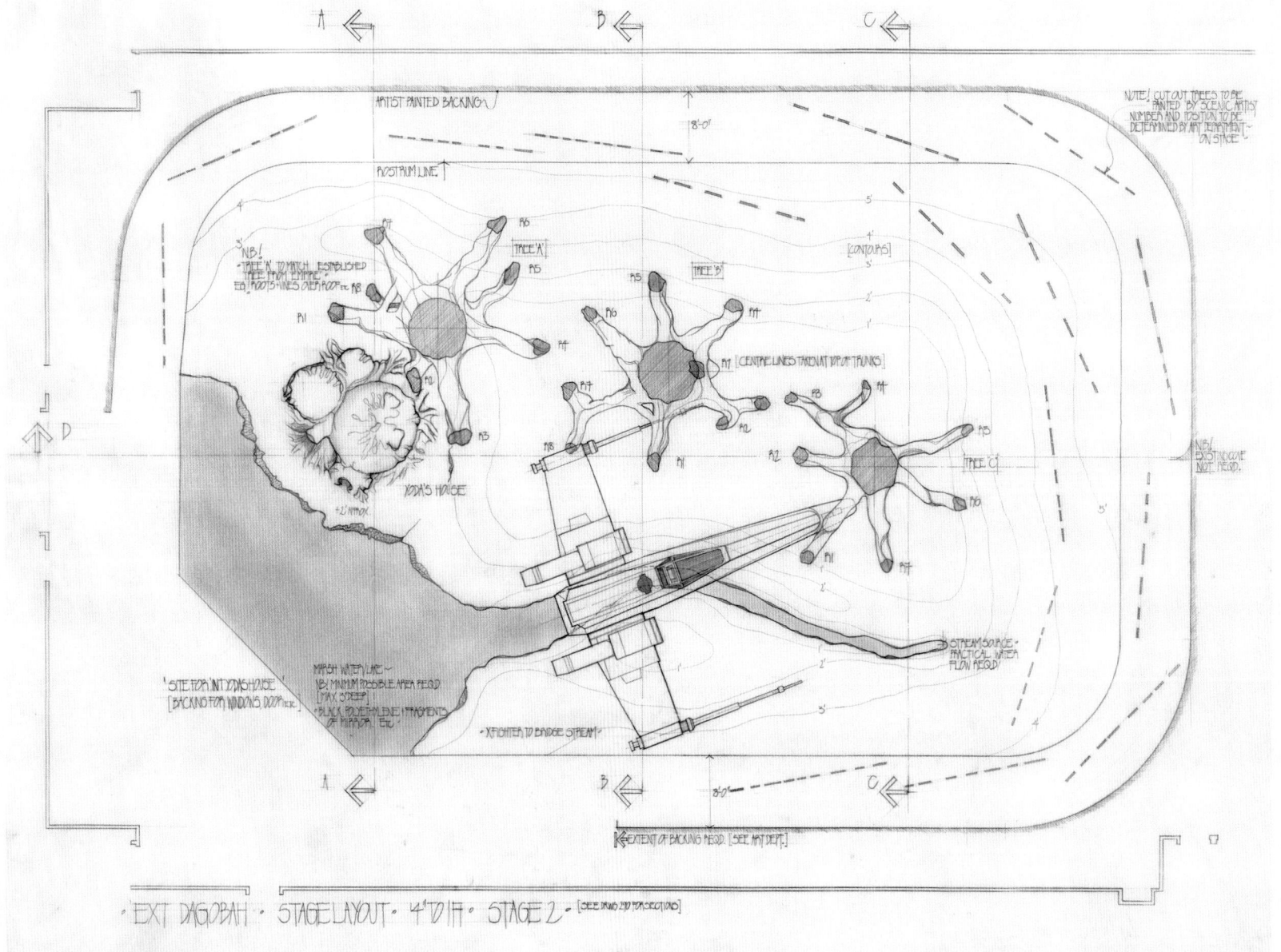

TREE 'B' 2' SECTION A-A [ROOTS 1,2 +3 OMITTED]

HEIGHT- 32'-0"

SECTION B-B

PLAN

BASIC TRUNK DIA OF 4'0" ±

TREE 'B'

SECTION C-C

SET	DAGOBAH
DETAIL	TREE "B" — ROOT PROFILES
DRG. NO.	284
DATE	DECEMBER 20 1981
DRAWN BY	KEVIN M. PHIPPS

→ Yoda's house exterior and the X-wing are on the recreated Dagobah set, complete and dressed, on Elstree's Stage 2.

SPEEDER BIKE

The scooter, or speeder bike as it was later named, was not a set but an essential vehicle prop, and therefore the subject of several Fred Hole drawings. Based on designs by ILM artist and costume designer Nilo Rodis-Jamero, Hole's early scooter was camouflaged, while another had a more bulbous front. The final scooter would be filmed in front of blue screen.

The key drawing (no. 62 on page 186) contains Hole's notes, as worked out with Reynolds and the rest of production. Six scooters were to be built, though only two were required for operation in front of blue screen; those two were to be equipped with different "plugs" for different shots, their front fins were to turn with the movement of front control handles, and the rear flaps would elevate when the motor was switched on.

The four remaining scooters were to be equipped with side, rear, and bottom suspension points and would have removable engine covers. All six would be equipped with adjustable stands and measure approximately 8 feet, 8.5 inches long with suitable hanging points (one plan may have been to hang the bikes by wires).

For the stunts, Hole executed yet another blueprint (no. 66 on page 187) on which he wrote: "With the use of four springs of suitable strength and stiffness, the scooter driver, by shifting his body weight, should be able to simulate the attitudes of climb, dive, and banking… Han Solo [sic] has to transfer from his damaged scooter to the back of Princess Leia's scooter."

↓ Reference photography is of the completed full-scale scooter bike prop.

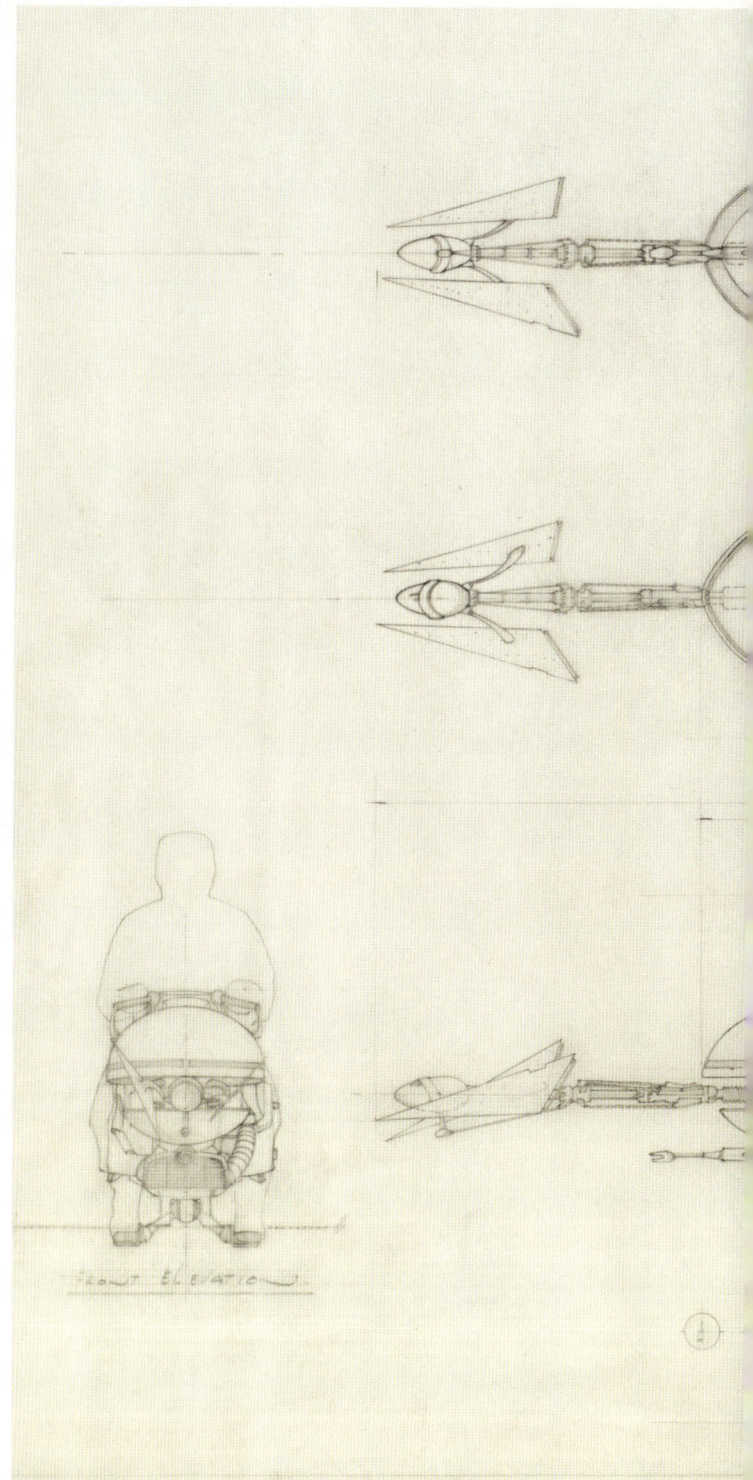

FRONT ELEVATION

SET	SCOOTER
DETAIL	VIEWS
DRG. NO.	37
DATE	MID-SEPTEMBER 1981
DRAWN BY	FRED HOLE

Plan of U/side

Section T–T   Section B–B

Plan

Side Elevation

Side Elevation

Rear View   Section C–C

→ These scooter bike concept drawings were created by Johnston in 1981.

SET	SCOOTER
DETAIL	STANDS & BREAKDOWN
DRG. NO.	62
DATE	SEPTEMBER 24 1981
DRAWN BY	FRED HOLE

SET	SCOOTER
DETAIL	VIEWS
DRG. NO.	N/A
DATE	FALL 1981
DRAWN BY	FRED HOLE

SET	SCOOTER
DETAIL	MEASUREMENTS
DRG. NO.	UNKNOWN
DATE	CIRCA JUNE 1981
DRAWN BY	ILM ARTIST

SET	SCOOTER
DETAIL	MODEL PREPARATORY SKETCH
DRG. NO.	UNKNOWN
DATE	CIRCA 1981
DRAWN BY	ILM ARTIST

↑ In a thickly inked sketch in the Archives, a rider is placed on the speeder bike prop. "This looks like somebody took an opaque projector, put the drawing on it, shot it up on the wall, and traced it," said Peterson. "Usually you do something like that to show somebody how really big it will be or to make a foam core mockup to say, 'Okay, this is what you'll get on the stage.'"

SET	SCOOTER
DETAIL	FRONT MATTE SETUP
DRG. NO.	66
DATE	SEPTEMBER 25 1981
DRAWN BY	FRED HOLE

→ The speeder bike is filmed against a blue screen at ILM.

← Two speeder bikes are seen in a final frame.

EWOK VILLAGE

The Ewok village was another elevated set, but built even higher than usual—20 feet off the studio floor. Actors and crew would get to the set via a forklift. Housed in Stage 3, which had been reconstructed following *The Shining* fire (the first set to occupy the rebuilt stage had been *Raiders*' Well of Souls), each Ewok hut was made up of composite vertical struts, with door and window openings assembled around composite small branch hoops, and finished with a mud spread over their basket frames. All of this was supported by tubes inserted into the giant fake trees at the base and top of each tree house.

The huts and trees were surrounded by a scenic cyclorama painted to match the location shoot that would take place in a redwood forest in Northern California (near Crescent City). Most of the scenes on set would be filmed in simulated night or twilight, which would match the lighting of the location exteriors. The smaller trees on set were live ones, which provided realism to the décor. Many of the Ewok forest elements would be recycled for the next set to occupy Stage 3, the Imperial landing platform.

↓ The Ewok village takes form on Stage 3.

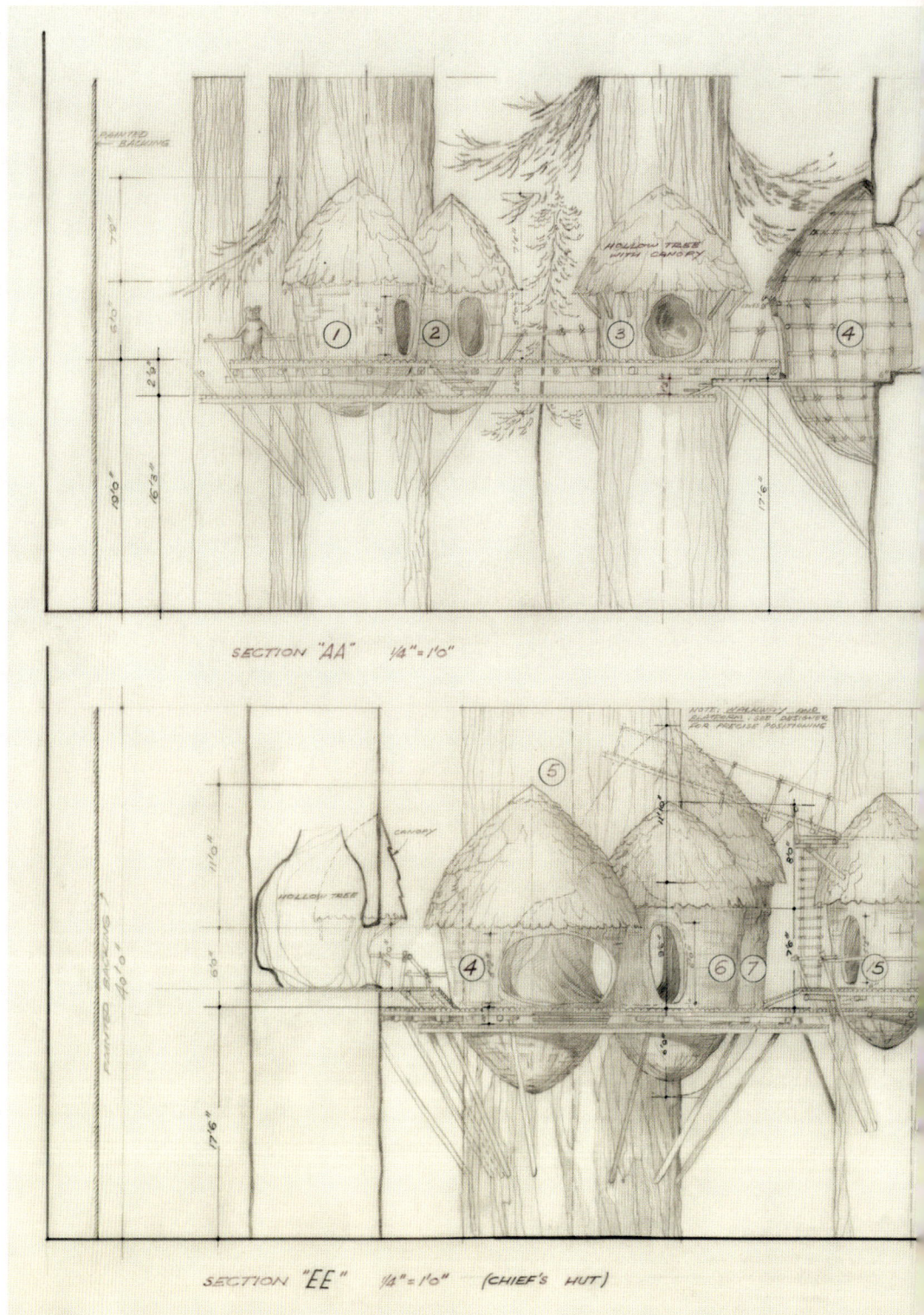

SECTION "AA"   ¼"=1'0"

SECTION "EE"   ¼"=1'0"   (CHIEF'S HUT)

↑ Concept artwork of the Ewok village from 1981 was sketched by Johnston.

"The Ewok village plan was very interesting and was a fun thing to build, to provide the maximum vertical angle," said Reynolds. "I determined the level of the set floor to be exactly halfway between the stage floor and the stage ceiling. I had never done that before. Everyone was very nervous to begin with, but we did have protective handrails and that sort of stuff, so it did all work out."

The Ewoks were portrayed by little people wearing five-piece suits with full head masks, elements of which had been cast in the plasterers' shop. "I was second unit director for six weeks, and they put me on the Ewok village, which I started during the end party," said Christian. "And George fell in love with these things, the Ewoks. And the more I shot what he wanted, the more he kept saying, 'Oh, have the babies dancing, and do this and do that.' We spent ten days shooting the Ewoks dancing and falling and doing acrobatics for the whole ending sequence."

"I did a series of drawings of Ewoks for fun," said Peterson. "You know, after a while you got pretty tired of Ewoks. So I drew friendly Ewoks stepping out to meet new people in the woods, but they turn out to be stormtroopers—and the stormtroopers would blast away and you'd have Ewok eyeballs and guts flying."

Djurkovic's drawings show the 2-inch diameter handrails, a necessary safety precaution for the elevated set. In drawing no. 100 (see page 190), he notes that the floor was to be made possibly of stripped bark, and that the chief's hut would be constructed within a hollow tree and house a practical fire. The fire would be used for a scene in which C-3PO tells the Ewoks of the heroes' adventures.

SET   EWOK VILLAGE
DETAIL   SECTIONS AA, EE, & PARTIAL SECTION HH
DRG. NO. 82
DATE   OCTOBER 1981
DRAWN BY GEORGE DJURKOVIC

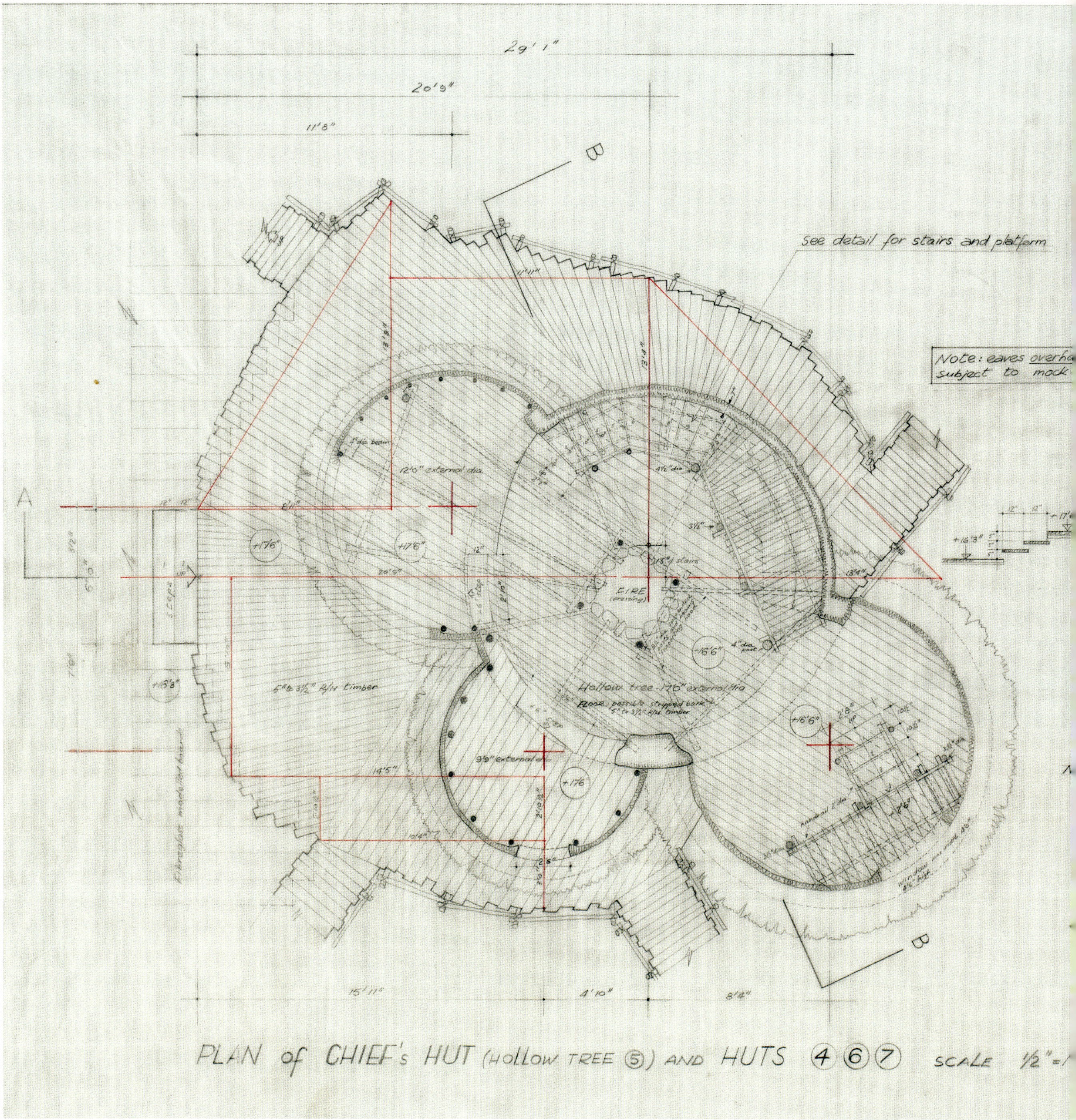

29'1"

20'9"

11'8"

See detail for stairs and platform

Note: eaves overha
subject to mock

A

12" 12"

+1'6"

+1'6"

12'0" external dia.

20'9"

FIRE
(brazing)

+1'6"

5" to 3½" R/H timber

Hollow tree -1'6" external dia
FLOOR: possible stripped bark
15" to 3½" R/H timber

9½" external di

+1'6"

+1'6"

14'5"

+16'3"

15'4"

+16'6"

Fibreglass moulded boards

15'11"

1'10"

8'4"

PLAN of CHIEF's HUT (HOLLOW TREE ⑤) AND HUTS ④ ⑥ ⑦   SCALE ½"=1

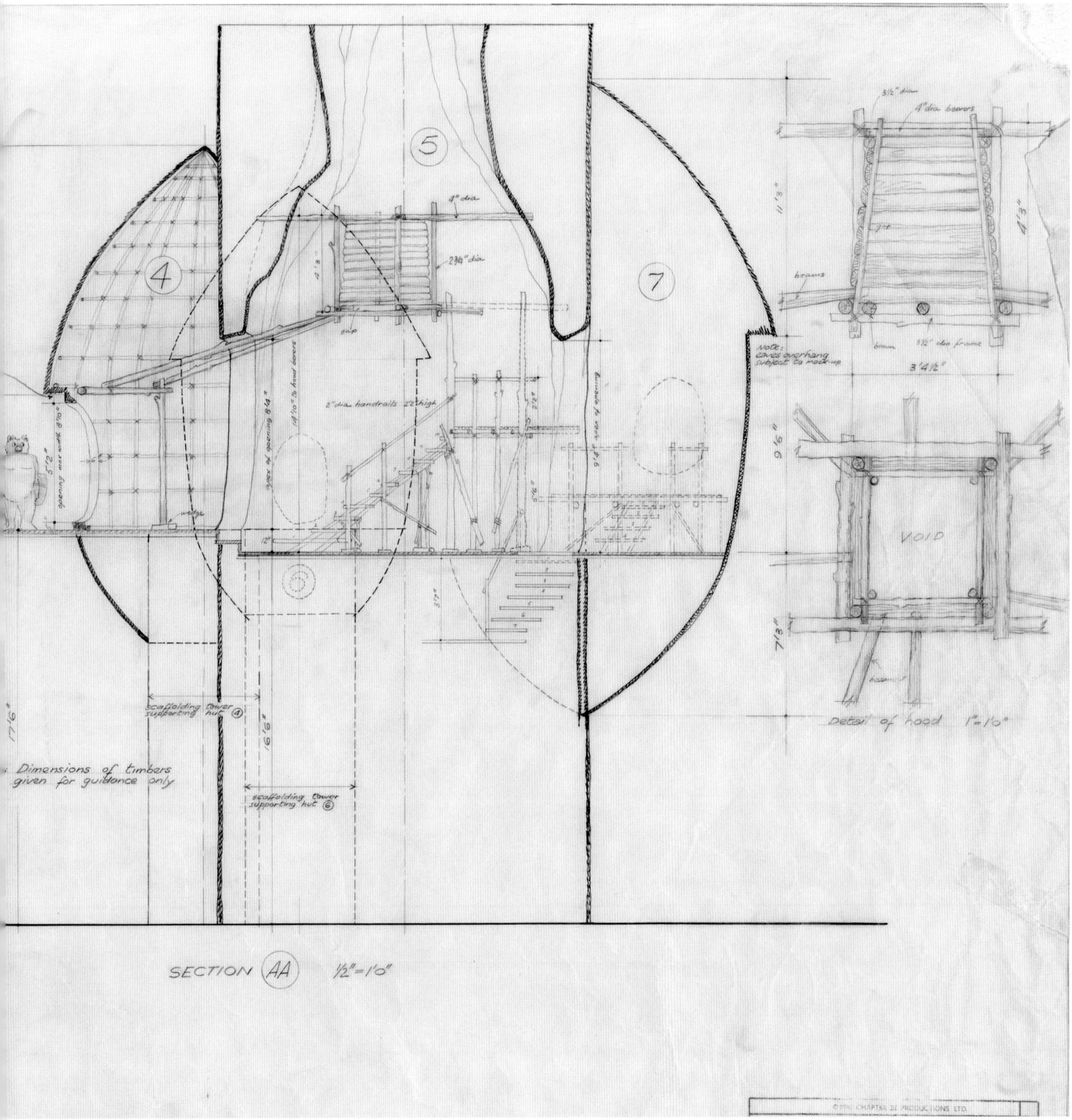

⑤

④

⑦

4" dia

2¾" dia

Note:
eaves overhang
subject to mock-up

2" dia handrails 22" high

gap

scaffolding tower
supporting hut ④

scaffolding tower
supporting hut ⑥

Dimensions of timbers
given for guidance only

SECTION (AA) ½"=1'0"

3½" dia

4" dia beavers

beams

3½" dia frame

3' 4½"

VOID

Detail of hood 1"=1'0"

SET	EWOK VILLAGE
DETAIL	CHIEF'S HUT AND HUTS, PLANS AND SECTIONS
DRG. NO.	100
DATE	OCTOBER 14 1981
DRAWN BY	GEORGE DJURKOVIC

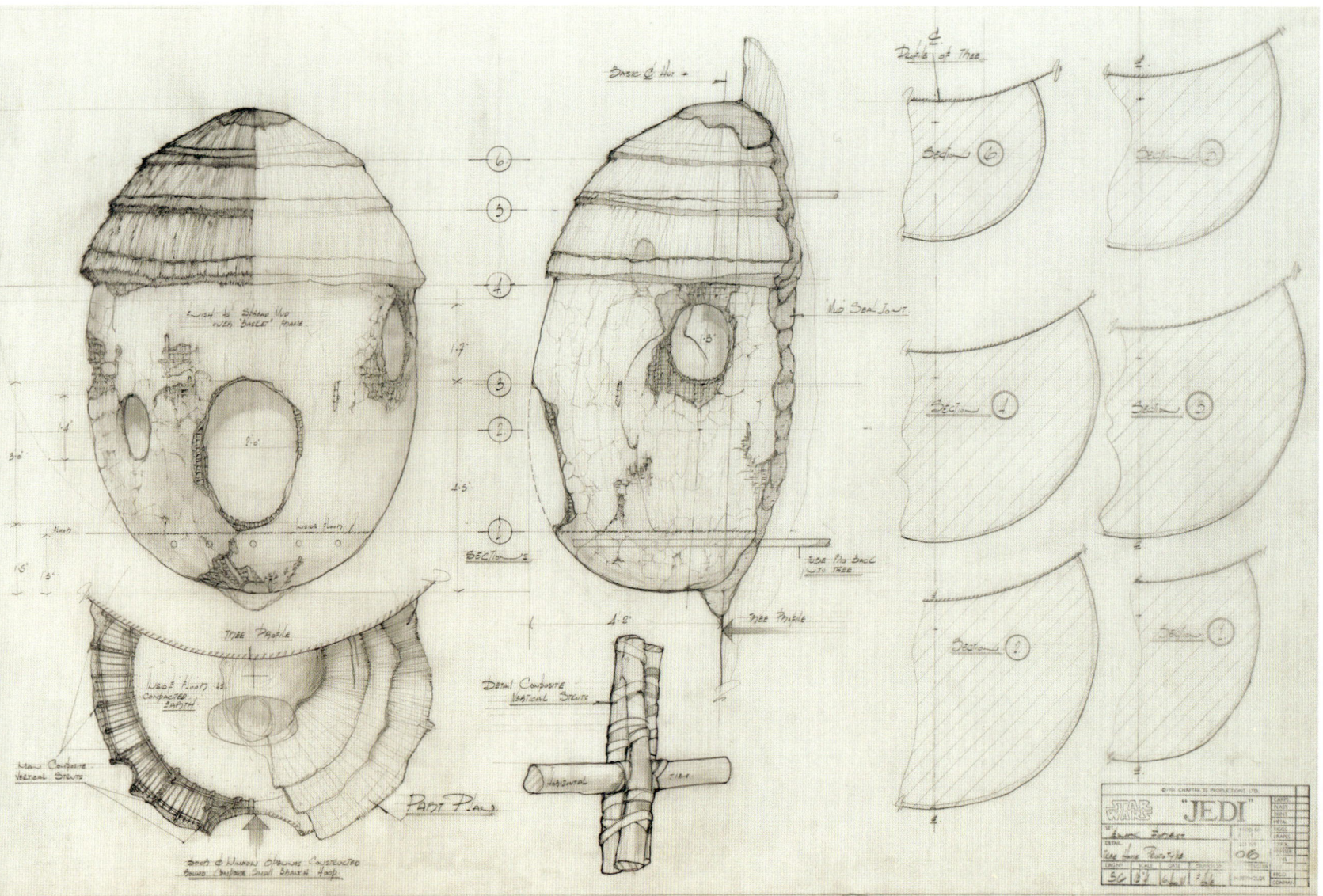

← Reynolds' sketch
works out the Ewok
hut measurements.

SET	EWOK FOREST
DETAIL	TREE HOUSE PROTOTYPE
DRG. NO.	36
DATE	AUGUST 6 1981
DRAWN BY	FRED HOLE

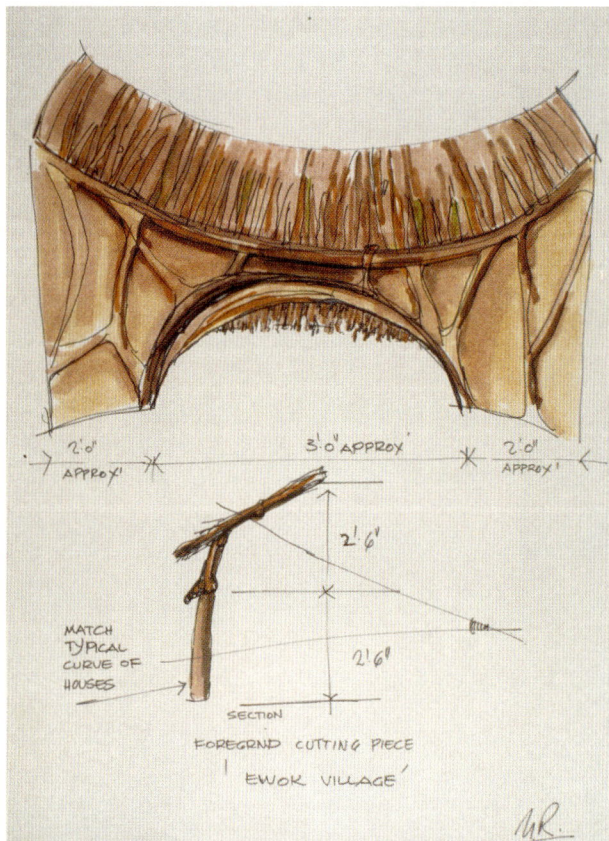

↓ On-stage photography is of an Ewok hut prototype.

beams sloping

SET	EWOK VILLAGE
DETAIL	INTERIOR HUT STRUCTURE (WITH EWOK)
DRG. NO.	N/A
DATE	OCTOBER 1981
DRAWN BY	GEORGE DJURKOVIC

↓ A final frame from the film combines live-action shot on stage with a matte painting.

→ The Ewok huts are more elaborate in this production illustration by Michael Angelo Pangrazio.

sedan chair for C-3PO built by EWOKS

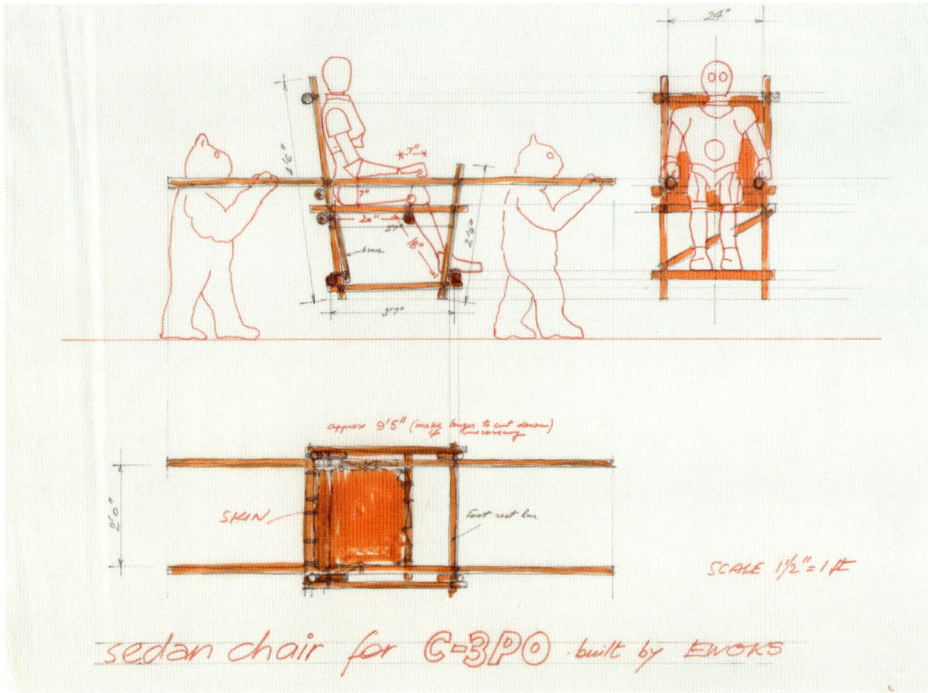

→ Building on Hole's earlier plan, Djurkovic's blueprint notes that 12 huts of one type would be made, with four of another type.

↓ C-3PO is borne on the Ewok sedan chair.

SET	EWOK VILLAGE
DETAIL	SEDAN CHAIR FOR C-3PO, BUILT BY EWOKS
DRG. NO.	N/A
DATE	OCTOBER 20 1981
DRAWN BY	GEORGE DJURKOVIC

↑ The technical drawing for C-3PO's sedan chair notes that the seat would be made of animal skin and have a footrest bar; support poles would measure approximately 9 feet, 5 inches.

SET	EWOK VILLAGE
DETAIL	DRESSING
DRG. NO.	228
DATE	NOVEMBER 30 1981
DRAWN BY	FRED HOLE

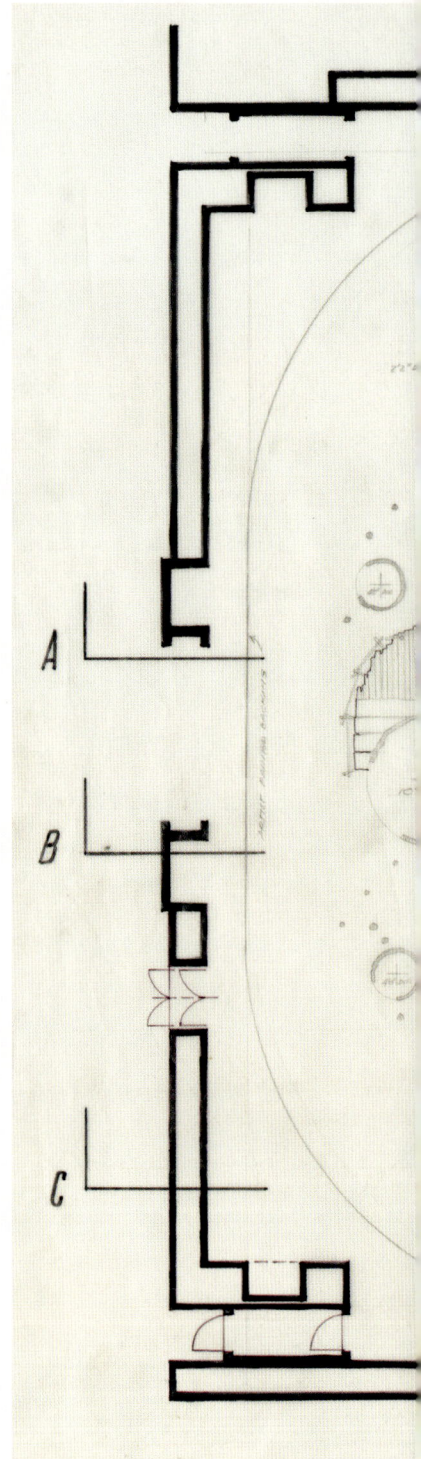

LEFT AND FAR LEFT After the Ewoks capture the rebel heroes, the surprisingly ferocious forest denizens contemplate roasting and eating Han Solo. Hole's drawing conceptualizes several positions of the pirate suspended over a fire.

SET	EWOK VILLAGE
DETAIL	REISSUE OF FULL STAGE PLAN
DRG. NO.	81
DATE	OCTOBER 5 1981
DRAWN BY	GEORGE DJURKOVIC

← A reference photo shows the C-3PO "sedan chair" built by the Ewoks (and the prop department).

← An Ewok baby pops up out of a basket.

IMPERIAL BUNKER

A beautiful concept drawing of an exterior along with a blueprint of an interior captures the two aspects of the Imperial bunker: the former was filmed in Northern California on location, and the latter on a stage at Elstree Studios. The two were then joined during postproduction editing.

Notable aspects of the Elstree interior build (no. 395 on page 198) were a stairway banister taken from the Emperor's Throne Room set, reliable stock pallets for the floor (that were lit from below recalling those of the Death Star), and section "E" with a painted perspective backing.

The exterior recalls the classic James Bond sets of production designer Ken Adam, perhaps an homage to the master with whom many in the art department had worked. It was eventually unloaded on a private 40-acre property belonging to a lumber company, a more or less flat area that was prepped for filming by widening old trails, clearing new roads, and dressing the landscape with new ferns and manufactured giant trees. Particular attention was paid by preproduction crews to removing what lumberjacks call "widow makers," huge dead branches precariously balanced in the forest canopy that could fall at any moment to kill or injure someone below. Vines from the UK were also shipped across the sea as dressing. Known as "old man's beard," the same type of vines had been used for Dagobah and in the ancient temple of *Raiders'* opening sequences. The location had to be a private property where trees already were slated for clear-cutting, because no state or national park would have permitted the demolition that production had in mind for its big battle scenes.

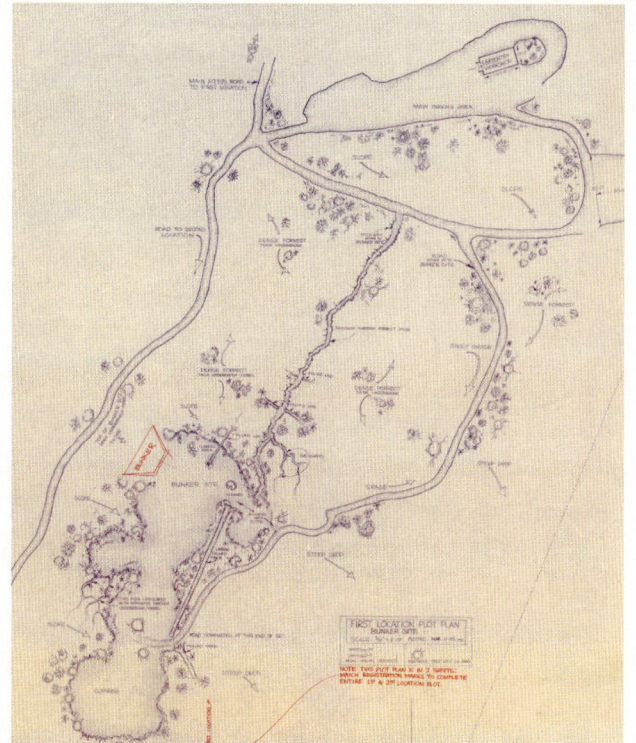

SET	BUNKER SITE
DETAIL	PLAN
DRG. NO.	N/A
DATE	MARCH 1982
DRAWN BY	MARK BILLERMAN

SET	IMPERIAL BUNKER
DETAIL	BUNKER BASIC STRUCTURE
DRG. NO.	N/A
DATE	1981
DRAWN BY	UNKNOWN

BUNKER BASIC STRUCTURE.

← An art department
maquette is of the
bunker exterior.

```
SET          FIRST LOCATION PLOT PLAN
DETAIL       BUNKER SITE
DRG. NO.     N/A
DATE         MARCH 11 1982
DRAWN BY     MARK BILLERMAN
```

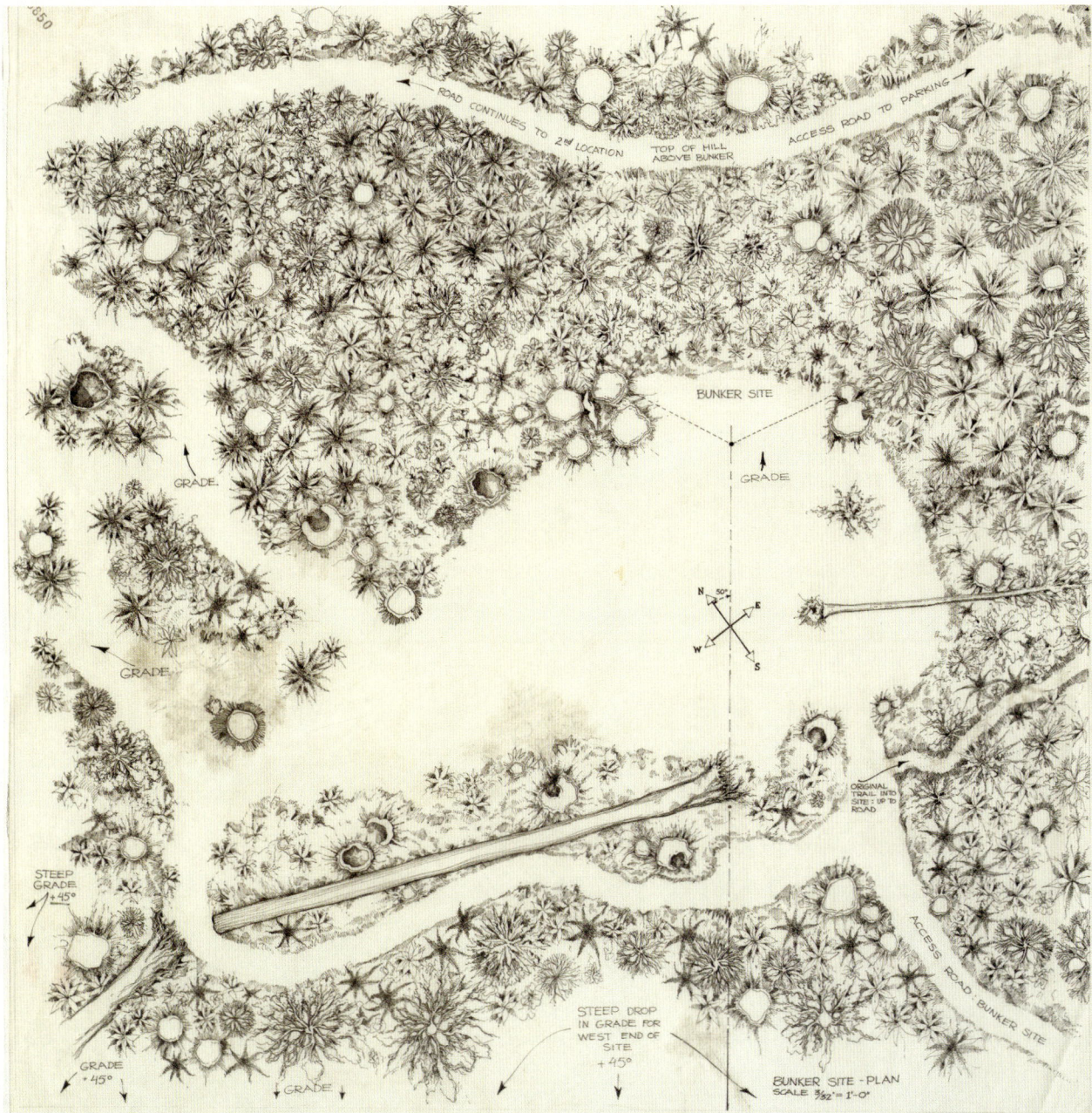

While the site was being prepared, set construction, based on technical drawings done in the UK, took place at a warehouse 4 miles away. The artificial tree trunks and logs were created there, along with a full-sized AT-ST. Once transported onto location, the Imperial vehicle was firmly planted in front of the Imperial bunker.

Two elaborate drawings by ILM draftsperson Mark Billerman note felled trees, steep drops, and the location of the carpentry workshop, the main parking area, the main access road, and the bunker site in the middle of all this.

"Just the terrain was difficult," said Marquand. "We were always going up and down hills and we were very spread out. It's not easy to keep a hold on an open location. If you've got sequences in woods or fields or hills, everything flows off the edges of the camera range, so you're always asking people to come back together, to move back to the center."

ROAD CONTINUES TO 2ND LOCATION   TOP OF HILL ABOVE BUNKER   ACCESS ROAD TO PARKING

BUNKER SITE

GRADE

GRADE.

GRADE

N 50°
E
W
S

ORIGINAL TRAIL INTO SITE: UP TO READ

STEEP GRADE +45°

ACCESS ROAD BUNKER SITE

STEEP DROP IN GRADE FOR WEST END OF SITE +45°

GRADE +45°

GRADE

BUNKER SITE - PLAN
SCALE 3/32" = 1'-0"

INT BUNKER CONTROL ROOM
& CORRIDOR   SET N° 32.
1/4" PLAN   1/2" ELEVATIONS.
1/4" STAGE LAYOUT TO FOLLOW.

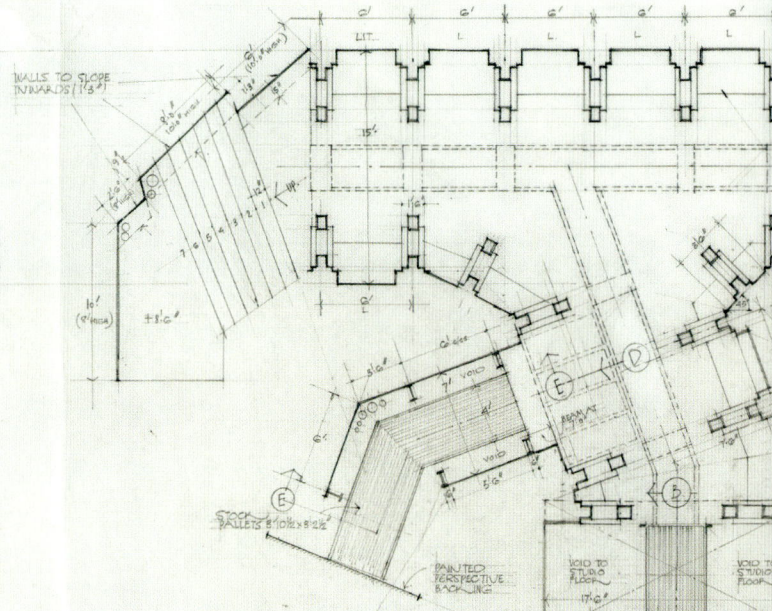

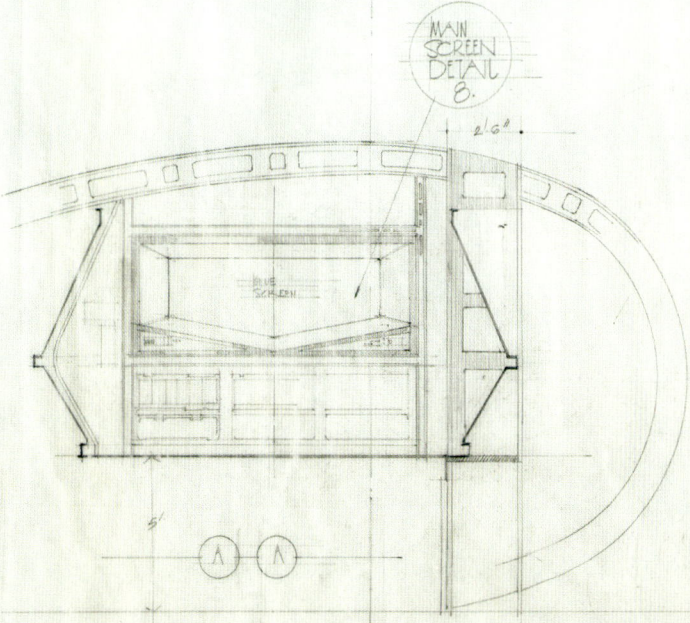

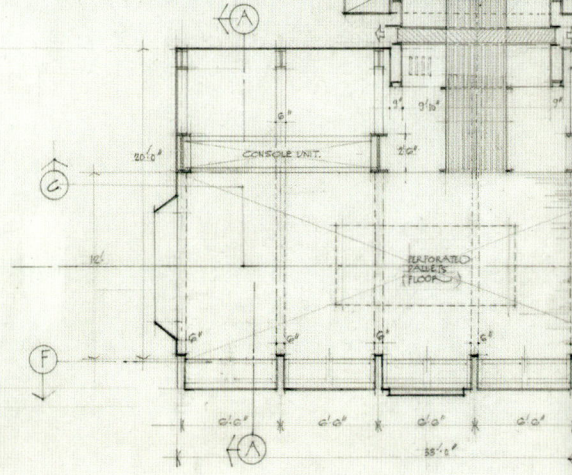

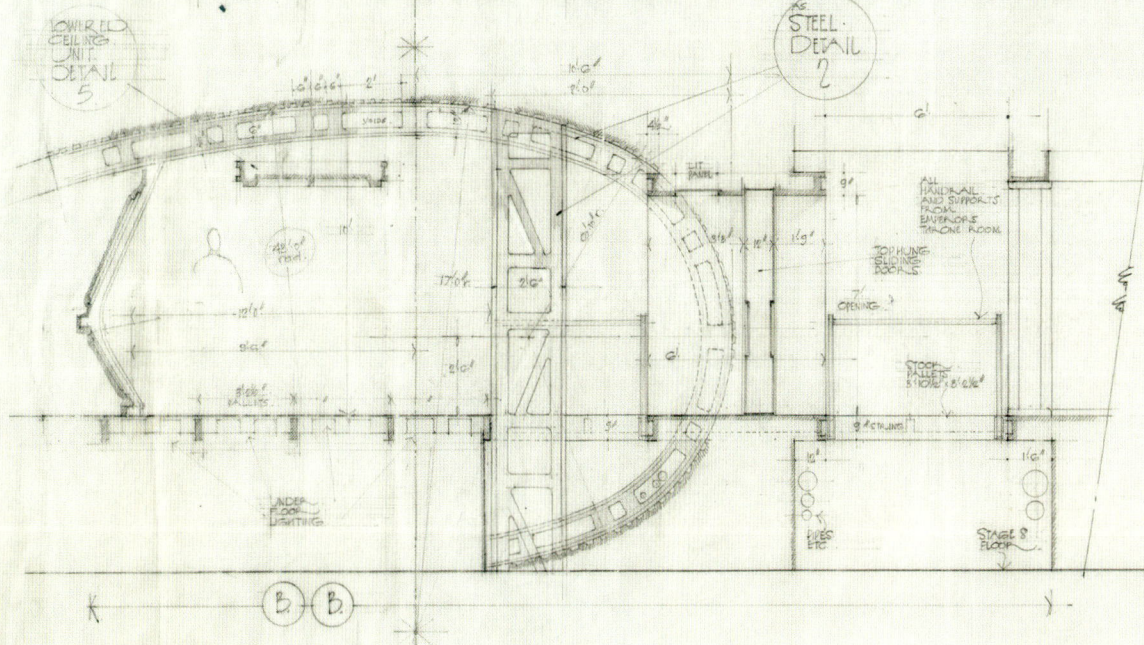

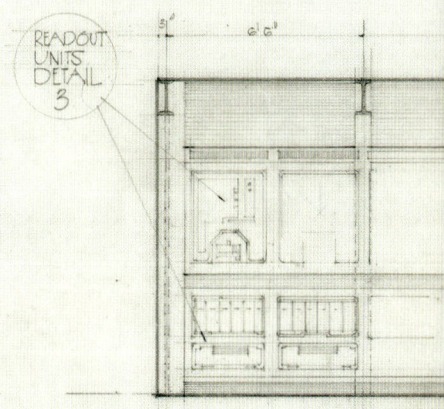

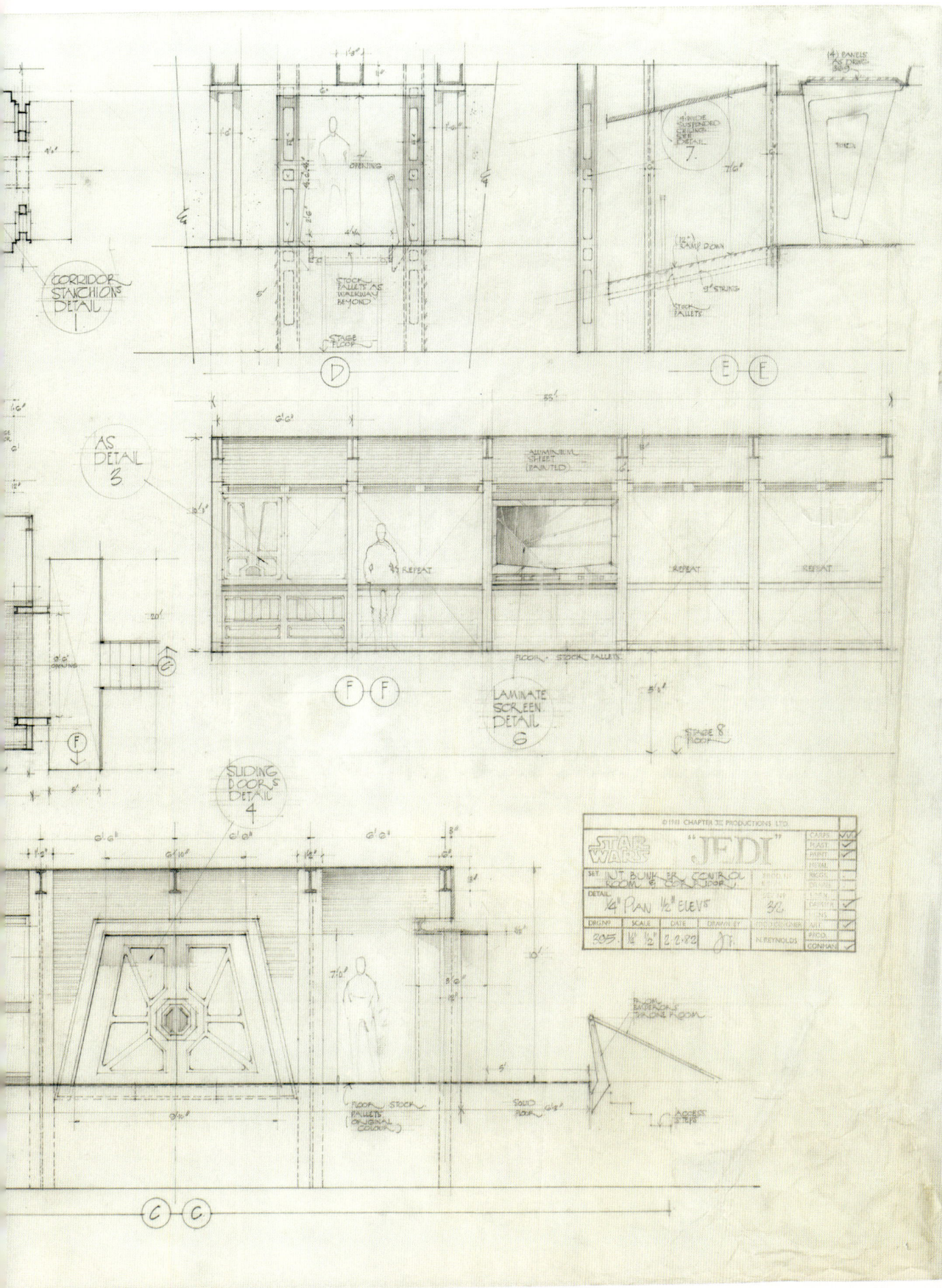

CORRIDOR
STANCHIONS
DETAIL
1

OPENING

STOCK
PALLETS AS
WALKWAYS
BEYOND

STAGE
FLOOR

D

9" WIDE
SUSPENDED
CEILING PANEL
DETAIL
7

RAMP DOWN

9" STRING

STOCK
PALLETS

E E

AS
DETAIL
3

ALUMINIUM
SHEET
(PAINTED)

REPEAT

REPEAT

REPEAT

FLOOR - STOCK PALLETS

F F

LAMINATE
SCREEN
DETAIL
6

STAGE 8
FLOOR

F

SLIDING
DOORS
DETAIL
4

FLOOR - STOCK
PALLETS
(ORIGINAL
COLOUR)

SOLID
FLOOR

ACCESS
STEP

C C

STAR WARS	"JEDI"		
SET	INT. BUNKER CONTROL ROOM & CORRIDOR		
DETAIL	1/4" PLAN 1/2" ELEVS	3/2	
DRG.Nº	SCALE	DATE	DRAWN BY
395	1/4" 1/2"	2.2.82	J.F. N. REYNOLDS

© 1981 CHAPTER II PRODUCTIONS LTD.

SET	BUNKER CONTROL ROOM AND CORRIDOR	DATE	FEBRUARY 2 1982
DETAIL	PLAN & ELEVATIONS	DRAWN BY	JOHN FENNER
DRG. NO.	395		

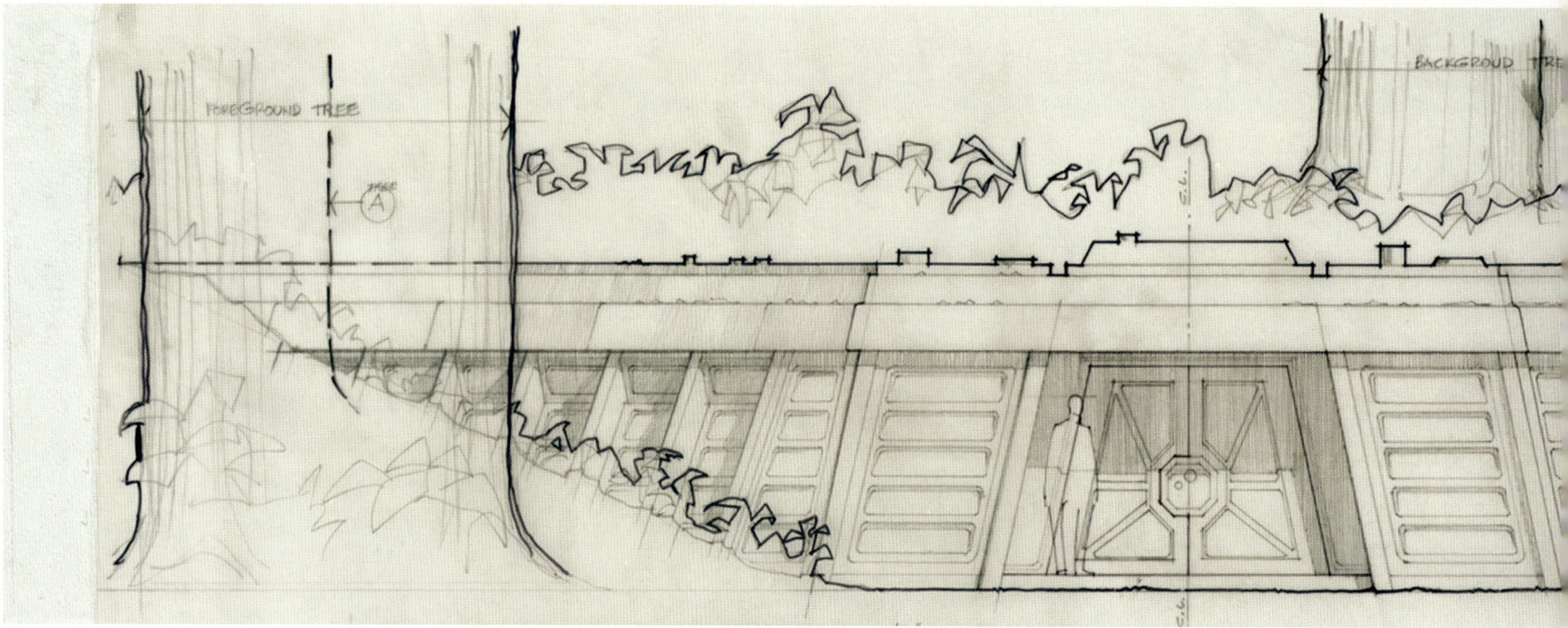

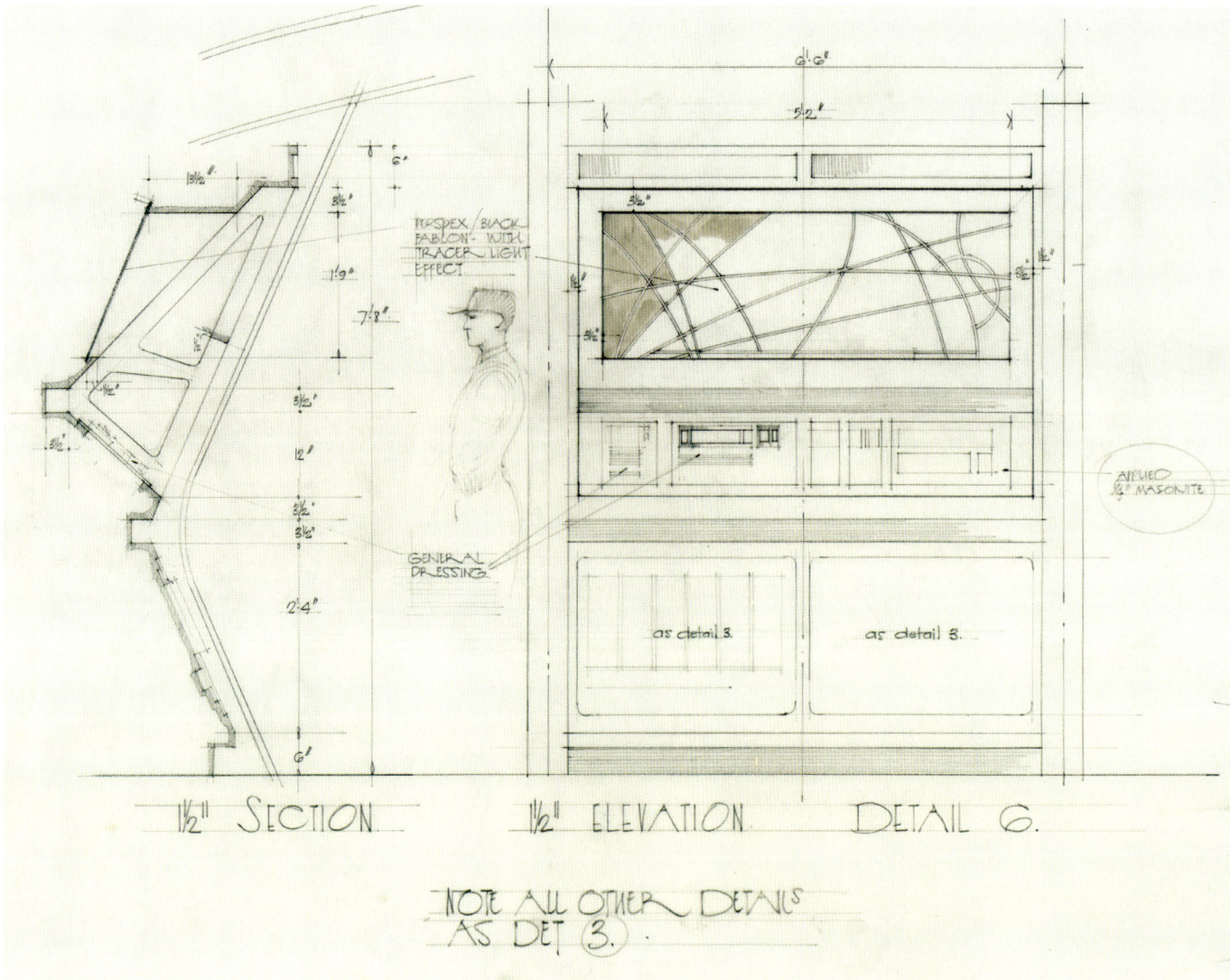

1½" SECTION   1½" ELEVATION   DETAIL 6.

NOTE ALL OTHER DETAILS
AS DET 3.

SET	BUNKER CONTROL ROOM
DETAIL	DETAIL 06
DRG. NO.	412
DATE	FEBRUARY 10 1982
DRAWN BY	JOHN FENNER

SET	BUNKER
DETAIL	SKETCH ELEV. SITE PLAN & SECTION
	(TOP, RIGHT, AND BELOW RIGHT)
DRG. NO.	309
DATE	DECEMBER 31 1981
DRAWN BY	CHRIS CAMPBELL

→ Blueprint no. 309 notes that the site's naturally thick underbrush was to be retained and the bunker set to be built accordingly.

↑ On-set photography is of the complete and dressed set.

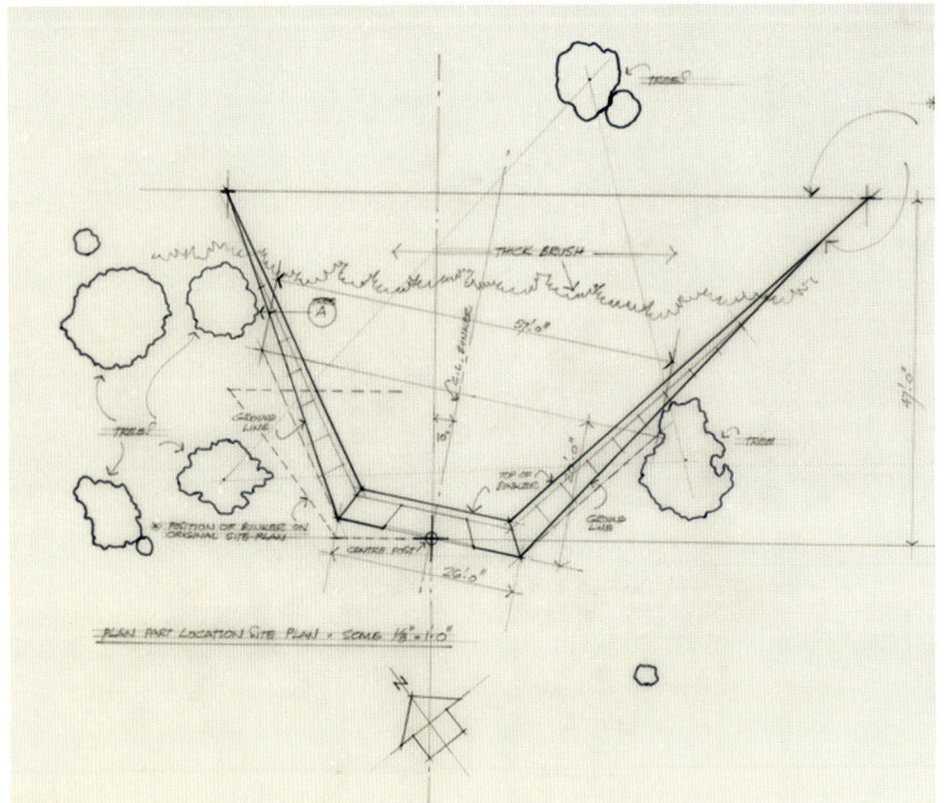

↑ More photo reference of the interior set built at Elstree.

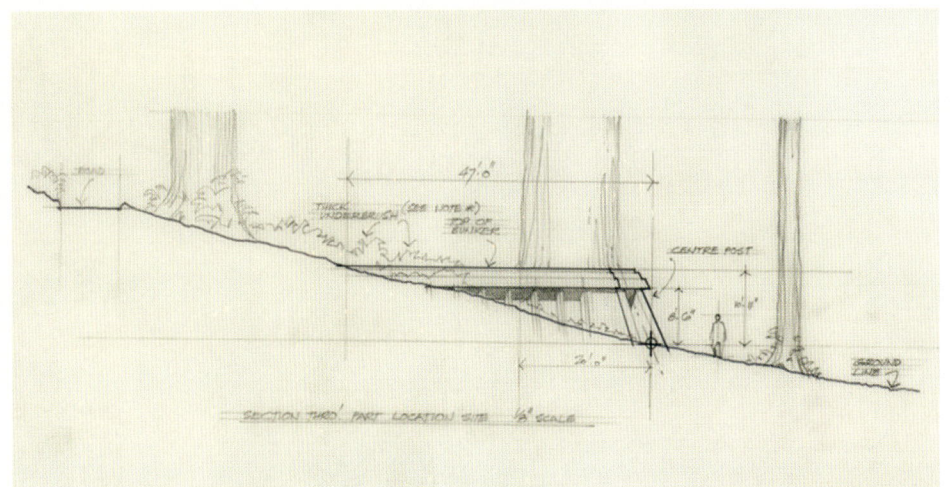

REBEL CRUISER BRIDGE

Built on Stage 5, the bridge was actually a split-level set, the bottom of which was used for the rebel briefing scene; the upper level was used as Admiral Ackbar's control center, from where he directs the rebel fleet during the film's climactic space battle.

Fenner's blueprint (no. 268) suggests that upper level's pilot consoles be built on small castors (under dais) for better maneuverability.

During actual filming, because Stage 5 was mostly used as a storage area, its walls and ceiling were covered with tin and not soundproofed, so it was very noisy. Particularly because it happened to be raining outside, all the dialogue ended up having to be re-looped in postproduction. A family of pigeons living in the rafters also made life difficult.

SET	BRIEFING ROOM
DETAIL	CENTRAL CONSOLE
DRG. NO.	170
DATE	NOVEMBER 10 1981
DRAWN BY	JOHN FENNER

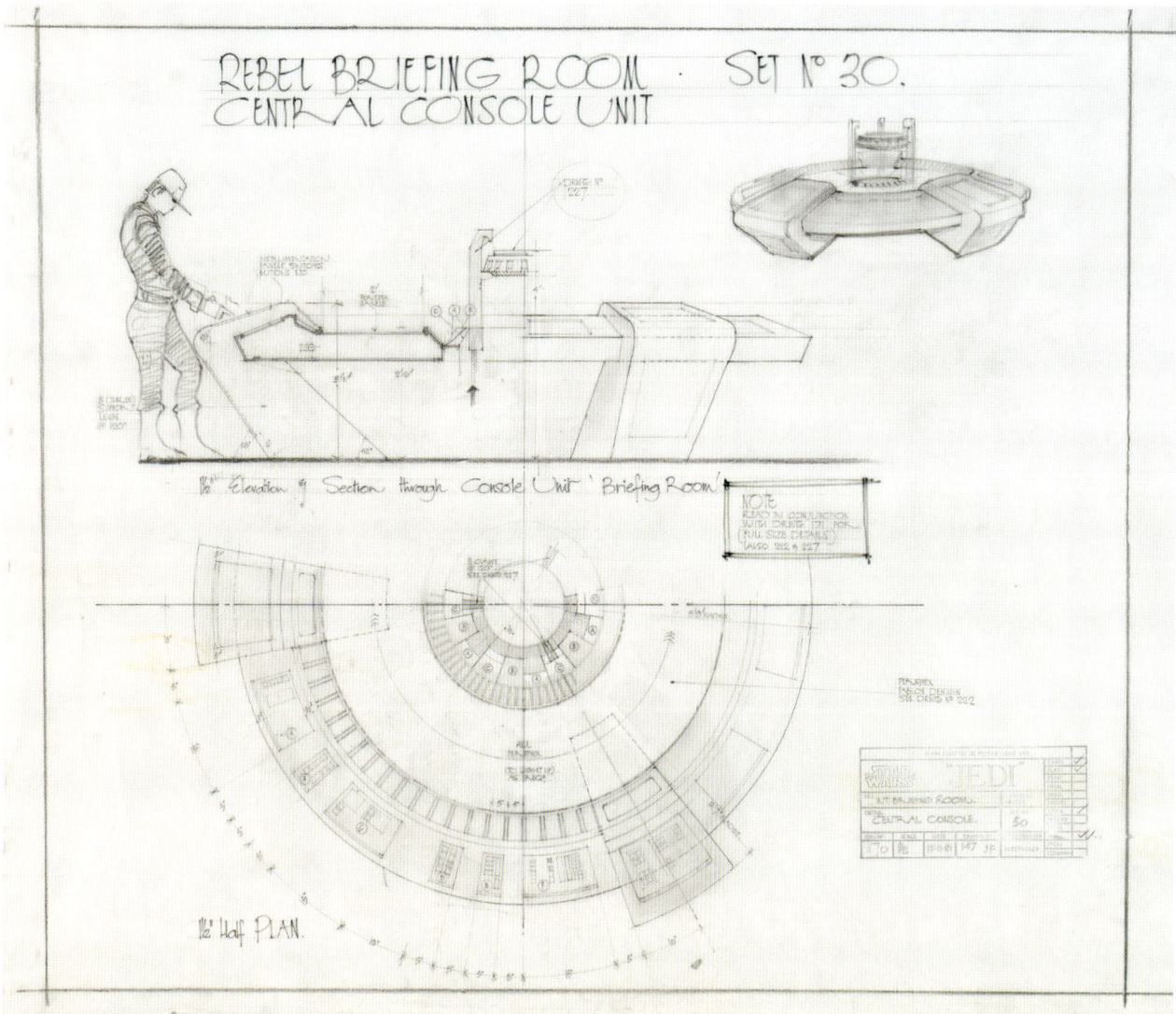

↑ Reference photography is of the rebel cruiser briefing room/bridge, with sliding doors, on Stage 5.

REBEL BRIEFING ROOM · SET Nº 30.
CENTRAL CONSOLE UNIT

1½" Elevation & Section through Console Unit 'Briefing Room'

1½" Half PLAN.

← For the instrumentation panels on the 11.5-foot central console, from where the hologram would be projected during the debriefing scene, Fenner notes that the Perspex buttons were to light up as required.

INT BRIDGE
PORT & STAR'BD: CONTROL UNITS.

SET	BRIDGE
DETAIL	CONTROL/PILOT CONSOLES
DRG. NO.	268
DATE	DECEMBER 9 1981
DRAWN BY	JOHN FENNER

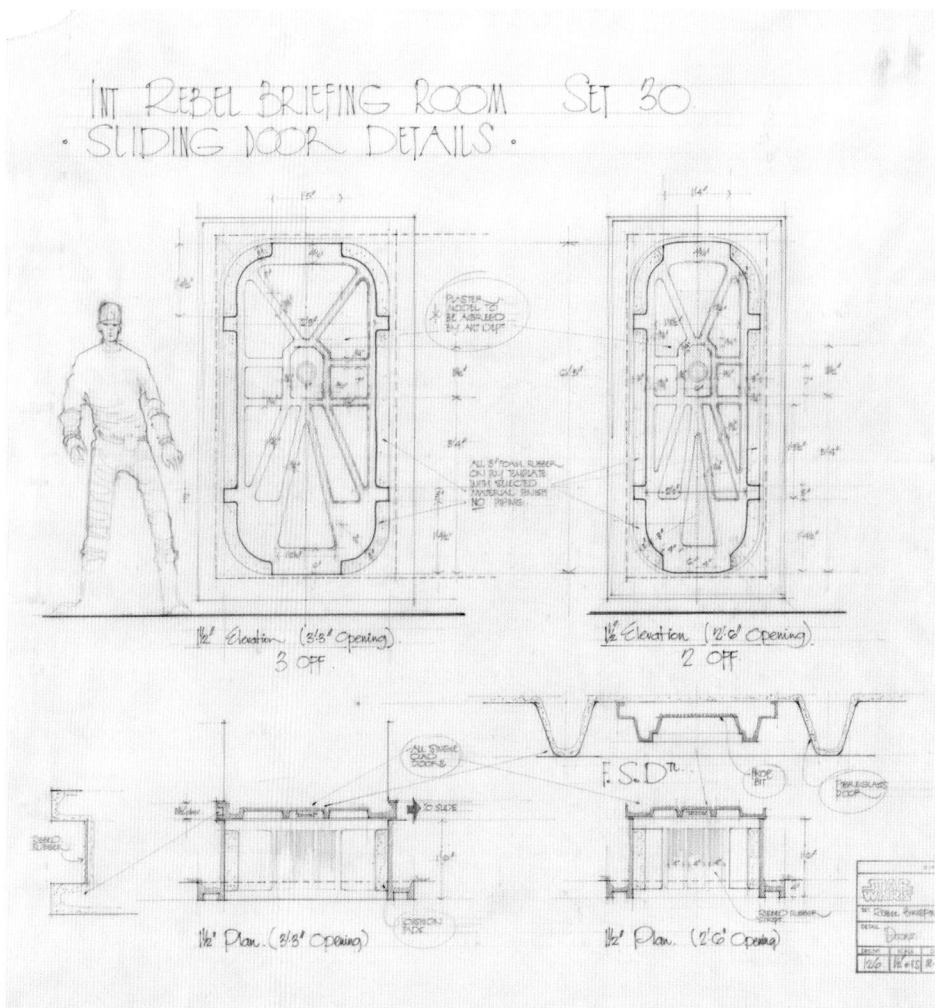

INT REBEL BRIEFING ROOM   SET 30.
· SLIDING DOOR DETAILS ·

→ Details on the bridge doors included 3-inch foam rubber
on a plywood template with selected material finish, as
determined by the art department crew, and no piping; the
fiberglass door itself was 6 foot, 3 inches high.

SET	REBEL BRIEFING ROOM
DETAIL	SLIDING DOORS
DRG. NO.	126
DATE	OCTOBER 18 1981
DRAWN BY	JOHN FENNER

TIE FIGHTER

For the finale's aerial battle, Lucas envisioned a much bigger dogfight than the end battle of the first *Star Wars*. New craft were created, such as the A-wing and B-wing, as a huge number of Imperial and rebel craft face off. The B-wings existed only as miniatures, with no cockpit scenes. The Elstree art department did construct a cockpit for the A-wing, and Kevin M. Phipps' blueprint (no. 375) notes that an "existing navigation chair" should be revamped from the Imperial shuttle's interior, "cut down to fit."

Hole's recreation of the Imperial TIE (no. 92) notes that raised vac-formed dressing pieces were to be applied "as on existing pieces" from the previous sets, that panels were to be cut out and back lit, and that construction should use a preexisting control column. This time the TIE fighter spokes are in the right position for filming. (Although Hole has placed Darth Vader at the controls, this was for scale and position only.)

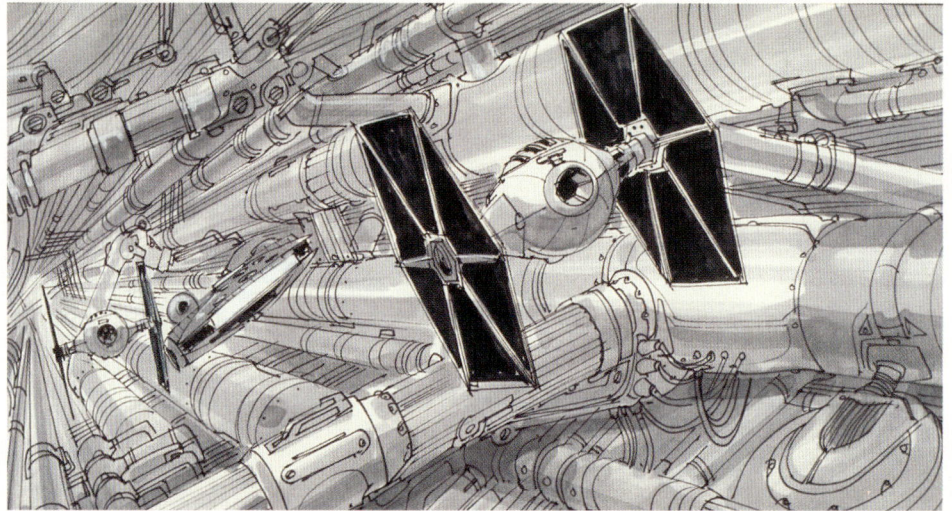

↑ ILM concept art shows spacecraft zipping through the innards of the second Death Star.

SET	TIE FIGHTER
DETAIL	COCKPIT
DRG. NO.	92
DATE	OCTOBER 8 1981
DRAWN BY	FRED HOLE

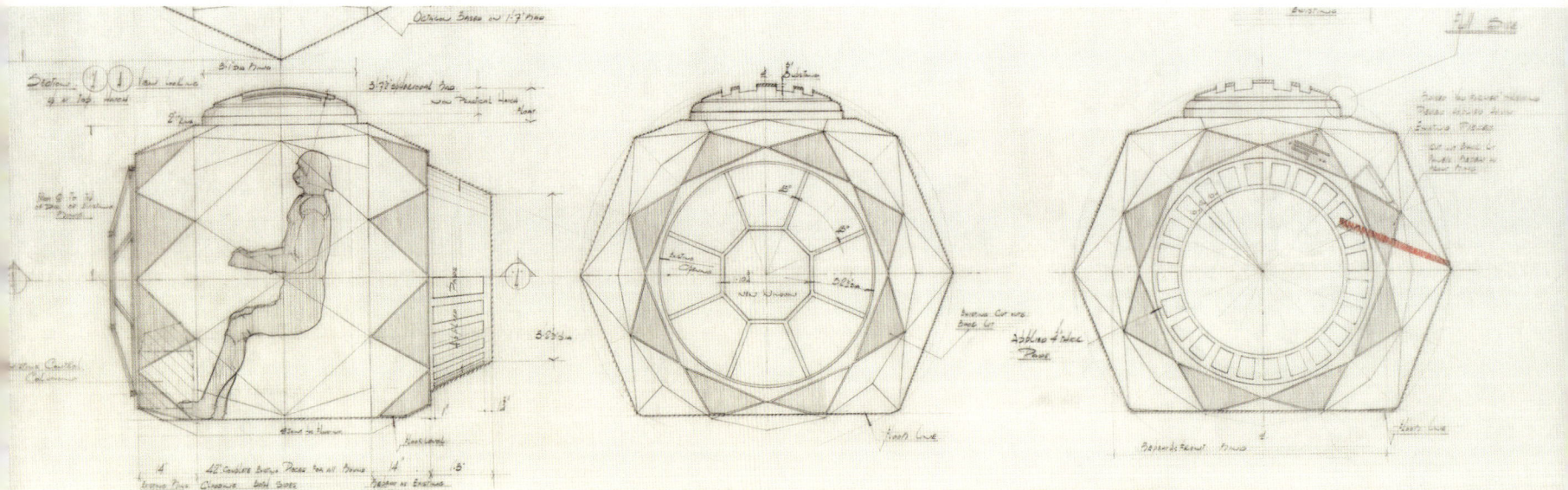

← ILM concept art shows A-wings attacking the second Death Star.

FRONT

11"

GUN DETAIL ~ DRESSING AS PER ART DEPT

DETAIL (EXISTING)

DETAIL ~ SIDE PANNELS

DETAIL ~ UNDERSIDE

DETAIL ~ UNDER CARRIAGE

ENGINE~ BLOCK DETAIL ~ APPLIED DRESSING TO MATCH

SIDE

SET	Y-FIGHTER
DETAIL	GENERAL LAYOUT
DRG. NO.	216
DATE	NOVEMBER 25 1981
DRAWN BY	KEVIN M. PHIPPS

↓ ILM model maker Wesley Seeds works on an A-wing—and the completed ILM A-wing model.

'A' WING FIGHTER

SET	A-WING COCKPIT
DETAIL	SECTIONS
DRG. NO.	375
DATE	JANUARY 26 1982
DRAWN BY	KEVIN M. PHIPPS

EMPEROR'S THRONE ROOM

While working out the general plan and look of *Jedi*'s most crucial set, Reynolds turned to stellar draftsperson Reg Bream. Early script drafts had the Emperor's lair located deep below a palace on the capital world, overlooking a lake of lava, so the first conceptual blueprints drawn up by Bream (nos. 16 and 17) made use of a 4-foot, 6-inch-deep tank to be constructed on Stage 5, with 24-feet maximum head room, steps into the lair, and so on. Presumably the tank would have been filled with a material resembling molten lava.

Other early concepts had the Emperor's Throne Room either as a contained sphere held away from the second Death Star by two bracketing arms, suspended by a thick cylindrical arm, or on a central elevated platform connected by a bewildering array of curving catwalks.

The final locale of the Emperor's Throne Room was atop a spire towering over the second Death Star, the set of which was built on Stage 4. It would be here that the *Star Wars* saga would come to its metaphysical close, with a climactic duel between father, son, and Emperor. So important were the scenes, and so hectic the shooting schedule, that Lucas filmed a few of them himself when Marquand was busy elsewhere.

The final set construct recycled to great effect the concept of a circular window first used in *Empire*'s Reactor Control Room. Beyond the 20-feet-by-36-feet window was a curtain of black felt that ILM would replace with spectacular shots of the immense aerial battle between the rebel and Imperial fleets. The backdrop of a large-scale military action juxtaposed with the intense personal conflicts of the foreground make the cinematic climax of *Jedi* one of the most memorable.

"I tried to keep this set as simple as possible by utilizing some of the elements that had been established and were familiar to the audience," said Reynolds, "always remembering the evil that should pervade the place."

On this more or less three-level set (no. 193 on page 212), stairs led up the dais, while two-story tulip-shaped consoles (no. 266 on page 211)—based on those seen on the first Death Star—frame the action. Blueprint no. 347 (on page 208) reveals light sources and notes that greeblies were to be added as per Harry Lange.

↑ An art department maquette is of the Emperor's revised Throne Room set.

↑ The final Throne Room set was constructed on Stage 4.

SET	EMPEROR'S THRONE ROOM
DETAIL	SECTION
DRG. NO.	17
DATE	JUNE 16 1981
DRAWN BY	REG BREAM

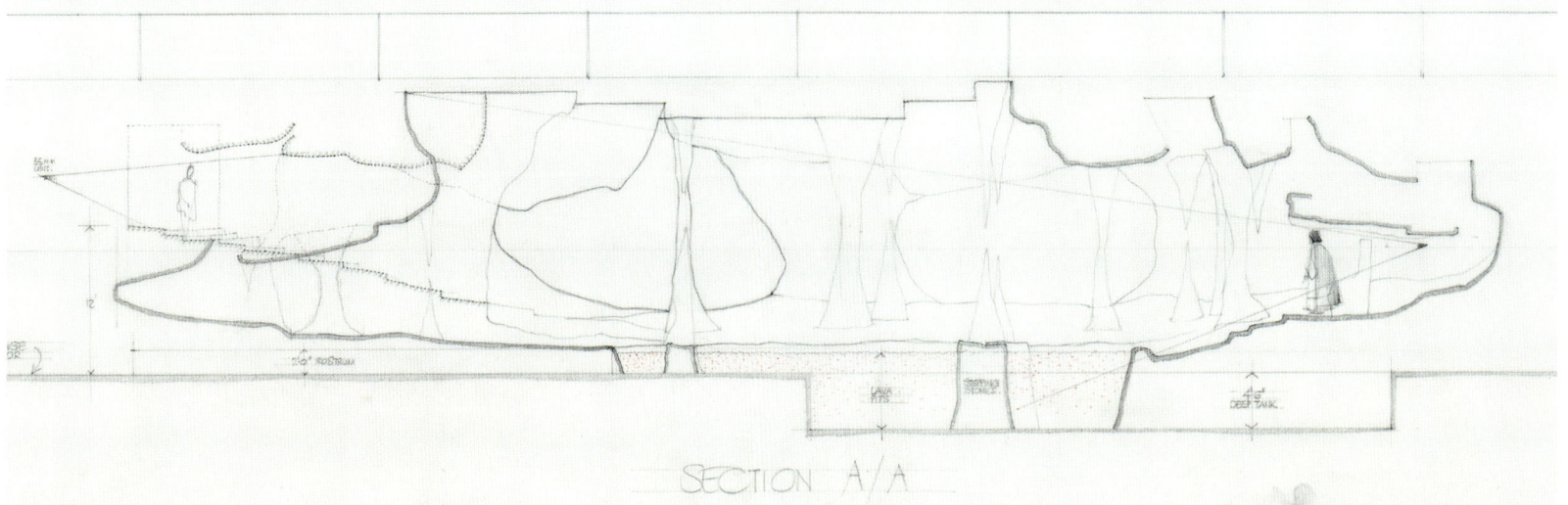

SECTION A/A

SET	EMPEROR'S THRONE ROOM
DETAIL	PLAN
DRG. NO.	16
DATE	JUNE 16 1981
DRAWN BY	REG BREAM

Once the scenes were shot and principal photography wrapped, the Throne Room, like all sets, was demolished to make room for the next movie. "I actually always looked forward to the set being struck because it meant the job was done," said Reynolds. "I could move on to the next phase, knowing that the whole thing had been captured on film—or at least I hoped it had. To a certain extent that last part always depended on the director or, in some cases, the cameraman.

"I once worked for a director who told me after I had joined the movie 'not to worry about the sets,' because he was more interested in the actors' faces; while a cameraman once told me I should be happy just to see a small part of the set in the final film!"

← Concept art of Darth Vader in the Emperor's cave is by Norman Reynolds.

¼ SCALE ELEVATIONS OF 'INT EMPERORS THRONE ROOM'.

PERISCOPES
DETAILS TO FOLLOW

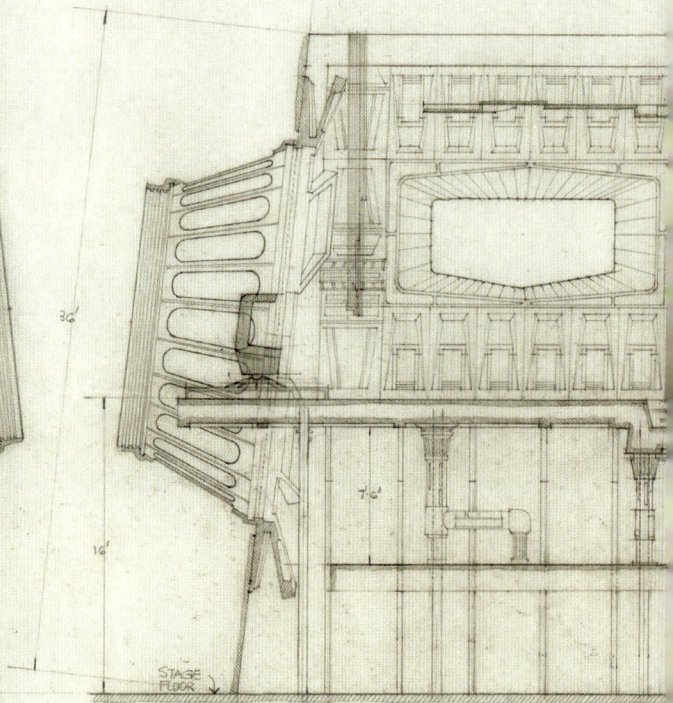

STAGE
FLOOR

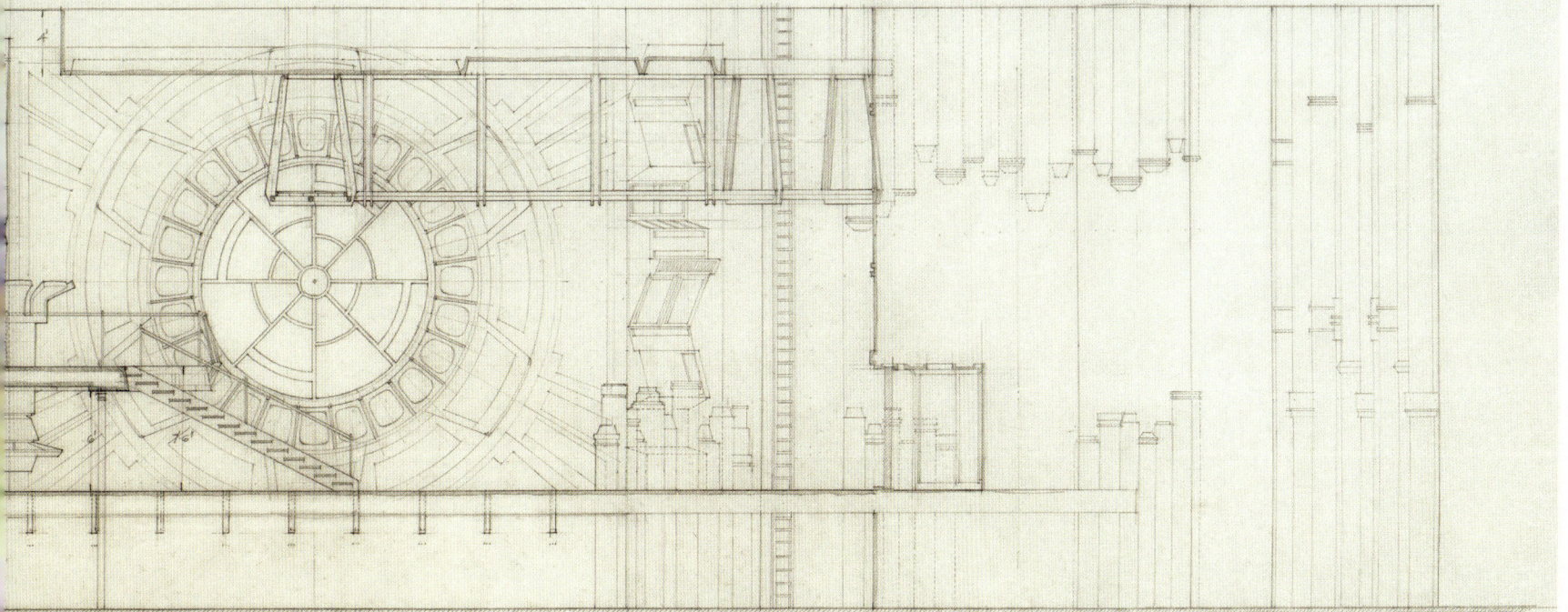

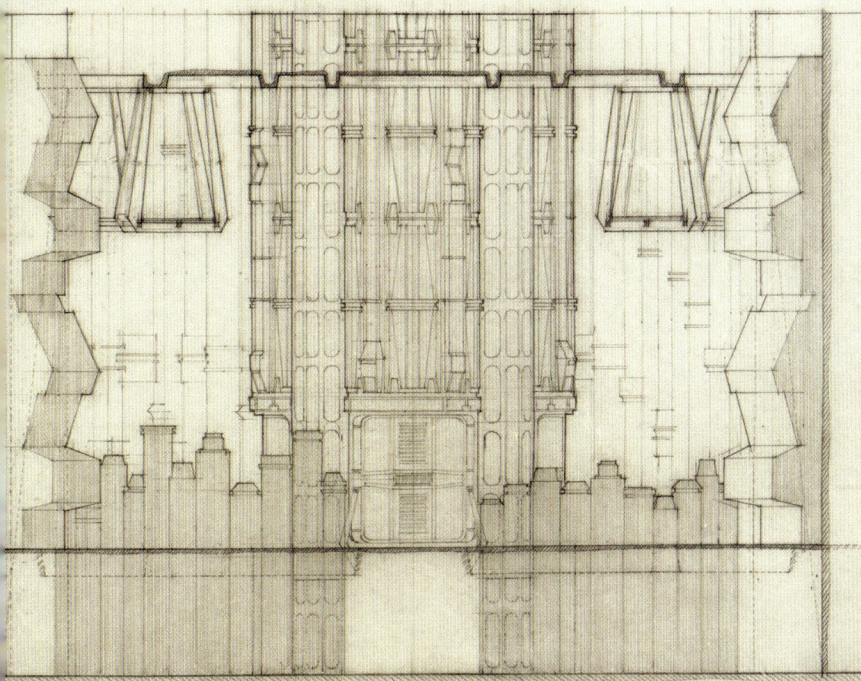

Title block on drawing:

© 1981 CHAPTER III PRODUCTIONS LTD.

STAR WARS "JEDI"

SET: INT EMPEROR'S THRONE R.
DETAIL: 1/4" SCALE ELEVATIONS

CARPS.	VV
PLAST.	VV
PAINT	V
METAL	
RIGGS.	
DRAPES	
S.P.F.X.	V
DRESSER	
SIGNS	
ART	V
PROD.	
CONMAN	

PROD. N° E81/4
SET N° 20

DRG. 347 · SCALE 1/4" · DATE 10 JAN 82 · DRAWN BY R.B. · PROD. DESIGNER N. REYNOLDS

SET	EMPEROR'S THRONE ROOM
DETAIL	ELEVATIONS
DRG. NO.	347
DATE	JANUARY 10 1982
DRAWN BY	REG BREAM

↑ Ian McDiarmid as the Emperor films a scene in late February/early March 1982.

↑ Vader and Luke battle before the Emperor, framed by the giant circular window.

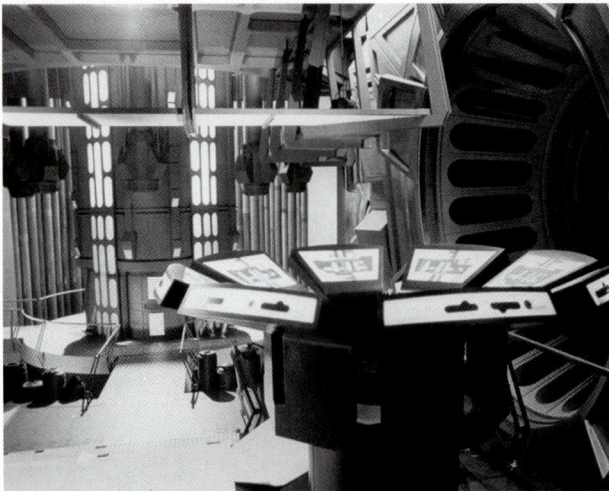

↑ On-set reference photography reveals the details of the "tulip" consoles built into the Emperor's Throne Room set.

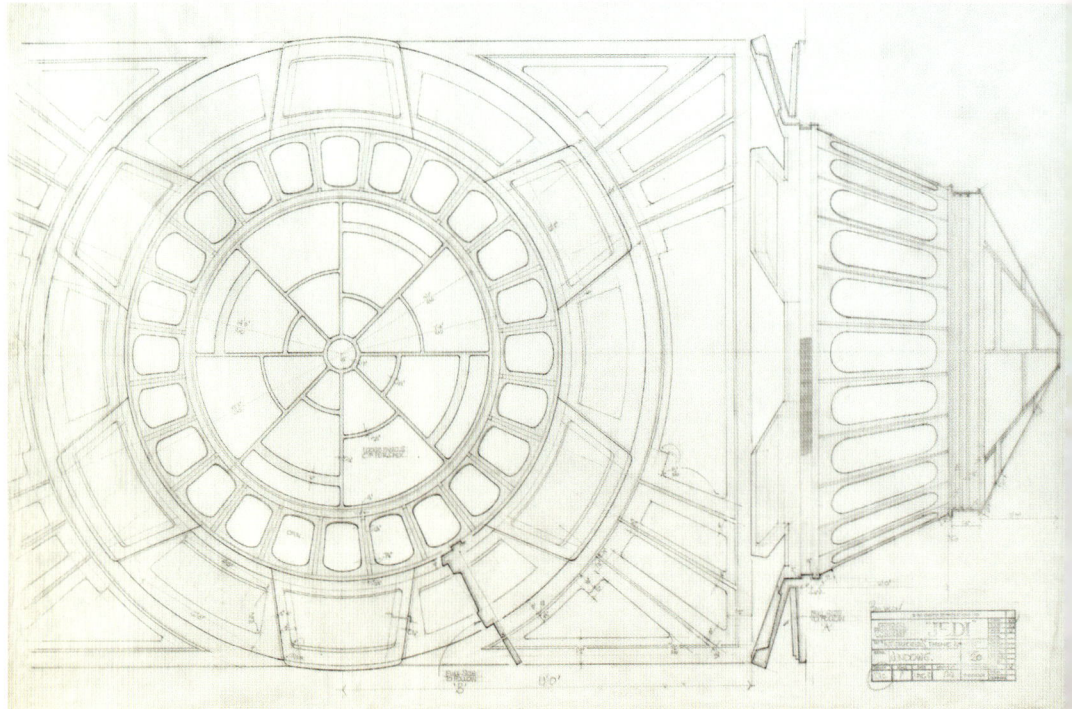

SET	EMPEROR'S THRONE ROOM
DETAIL	WINDOWS
DRG. NO.	232
DATE	DECEMBER 1 1981
DRAWN BY	REG BREAM

SET	EMPEROR'S THRONE ROOM
DETAIL	PROJECTION WINDOW CUT OUT
DRG. NO.	364
DATE	JANUARY 20 1981
DRAWN BY	GEORGE DJURKOVIC

→ The tulip-like consoles had opal Perspex lit panels and tracing paper diffusers on the bottom parts of the columns; some panels were removable, while some were dressed with flashing lights, switches, buttons, and greeblies.

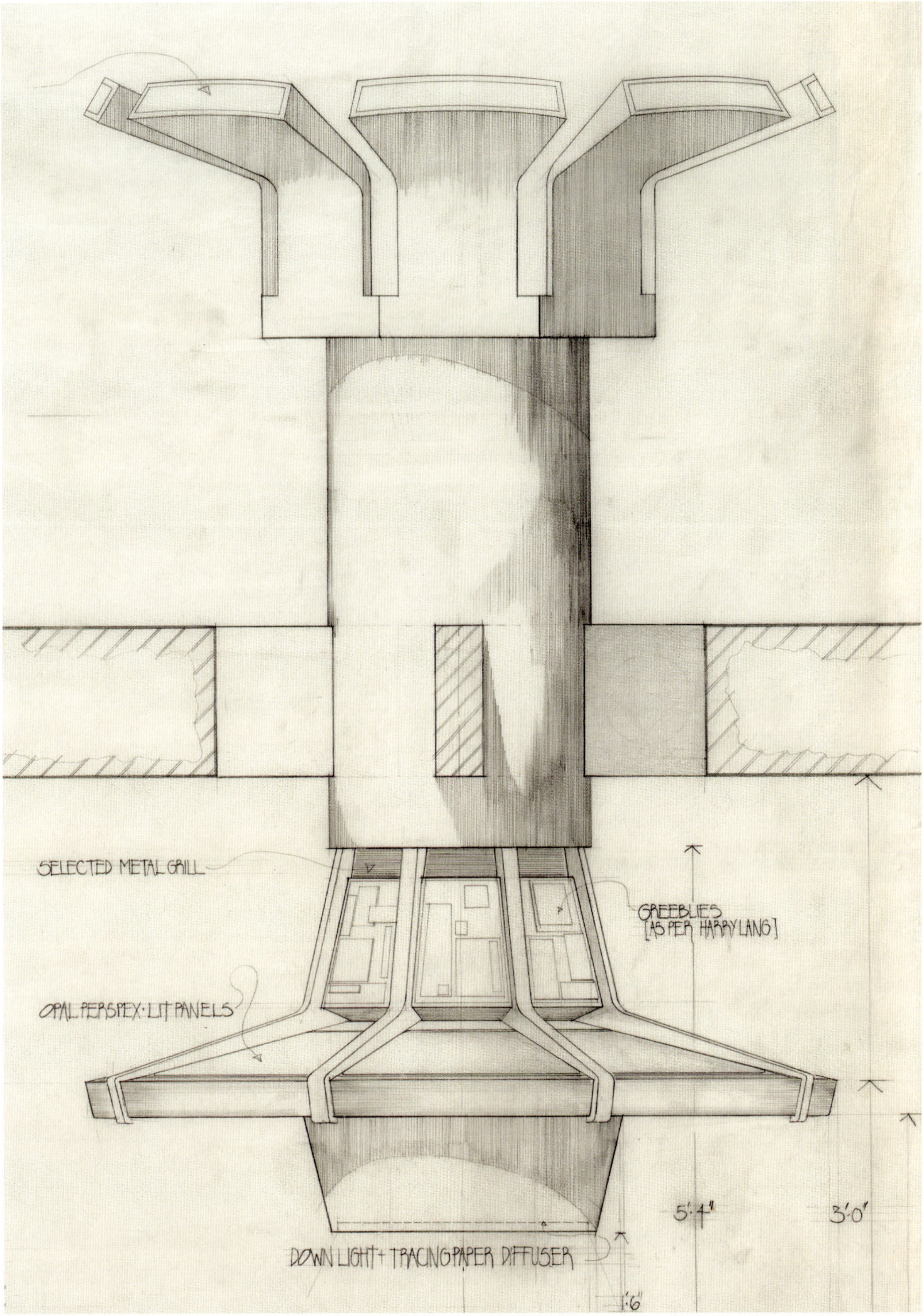

SELECTED METAL GRILL

GREEBLIES
[AS PER HARRY LANG]

OPAL PERSPEX · LIT PANELS

DOWN LIGHT + TRACING PAPER DIFFUSER

5'·4"

3'·0"

1'·6"

SET	EMPEROR'S THRONE ROOM
DETAIL	CONSOLE COLUMN
DRG. NO.	266
DATE	DECEMBER 9 1981
DRAWN BY	KEVIN M. PHIPPS

SET	EMPEROR'S THRONE ROOM
DETAIL	TRUE ELEVATION OF SIDE WALL
DRG. NO.	193
DATE	NOVEMBER 20 1981
DRAWN BY	KEVIN M. PHIPPS

↑ Guarding the throne room, and seen flanking the Imperial shuttle, are the Emperor's Red Guards. Their staves had lights fixed on their tops with holes drilled through the centers to fit tubes for batteries. The six staves made for the film were built from fiberglass and fishing rods, with existing metal pieces from the prop department.

SET	SHUTTLE (PROPS)
DETAIL	STAVE FOR SHUTTLE GUARD
DRG. NO.	215
DATE	1981
DRAWN BY	STEVE COOPER

SET	VADER'S MASK
DETAIL	HINGE
DRG. NO.	393
DATE	JANUARY 30 1982
DRAWN BY	FRED HOLE

↑ A late decision to show Darth Vader's face as he lies dying meant making a removable mask (and casting actor Sebastian Shaw as his human half). "This was done in a great hurry to show to George Lucas and the director," said Hole. "When approved, the actual death scene mask had to be constructed by an excellent prop maker, Brian Archer."

The destination for the mask was Stage 6 and the blueprint is appropriately marked, "Urgent!" Hole also notes that the hinge would be made out of aluminum and that it would have a hidden hinge pin.

→ Concept art is of the Throne Room elevator, artist unknown.

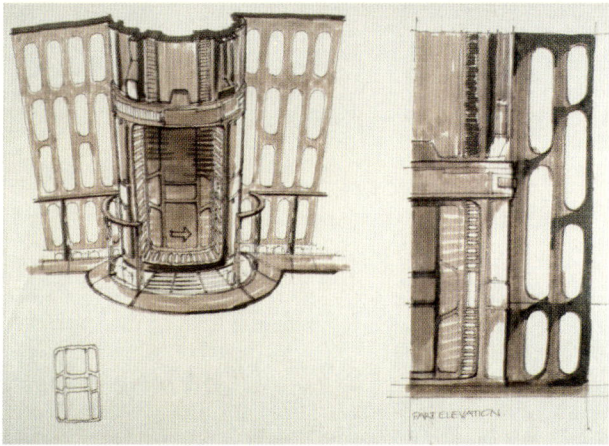

INTRODUCTION
EPISODES I, II, III: THE PREQUEL TRILOGY

After the release of *Jedi*, *Star Wars* became a thing of the past for most of the movie-going audience. Fans continued with the franchise by reading comic books and novels, purchasing action figures, and playing early video games. But eventually the stores no longer carried the toys in any great quantity, the Marvel comic-book series was canceled, and licensing generally flatlined. Lucas was busy with other projects, helping friends and fellow directors produce their films.

The individuals of the Elstree art department separated and reunited depending on their respective projects, as some junior draftsmen became senior draftsmen, assistant art directors, and then art directors themselves, slowly mastering their trade. "I was learning a lot from Norman Reynolds, but I often worked very closely with Fred Hole," said Gavin Bocquet. "We did *Empire of the Sun* where Fred was the art director in Shanghai and I was his number two and we had four months working together out there, and then onto Spain. In terms of the nuts and bolts of the art department, I probably learned more from Fred than I did from Norman. But from Norman, I was learning about how you run and control a large-scale art department."

Seven years after the release of the last *Star Wars* film, in early 1990, Lucas let it be known that he was planning a television series, *The Young Indiana Jones Chronicles*, which would once again feature a largely British crew. Even its American producer, Rick McCallum, had worked almost entirely in the United Kingdom.

"I had heard about *Young Indy* starting up around Pinewood, and I had just designed a very small TV show [*Yellowthread Street*, 1990]," said Bocquet. "After mainly working in the feature film world as an art director, and having just designed a TV show, I thought I might be a suitable candidate."

Just before attempting to contact McCallum, Bocquet production designed Steven Soderbergh's film *Kafka* (1991). "I came back from Prague and heard again that they were looking for a designer," he said. "And I found out that Rick lived on the street next to me in London, so I just put a letter through his door introducing myself and hoped for the best." Bocquet interviewed with McCallum the following January and was hired for a show that literally traveled the world, shooting in exotic locations from Europe to Africa to China.

"As a learning designer, to have thirty-five

↑ A *Star Wars* production returns to the Tunisian desert, near Nefta, to film the homestead scenes. Production designer Gavin Bocquet (on left) inspects the garage roof on location for Episode II, September 2000.

← During principal photography Lucas is visited by Indiana Jones producers Frank Marshall and Kathleen Kennedy, who chat with Episode I second unit director Roger Christian.

episodes with a different director each time was a brilliant education on being a production designer," he said. "Working with different directors in different countries, all with different personalities and their own way of working, was a great education. You may not have got on with all of them in the same way, but there was always something to be learned from each one of them.

"You've got to be a very gregarious sort of person," he added. "You've got to really love meeting lots of different people, from the guy who sweeps up the stage to the producer who comes in by helicopter. And to a certain extent you need to enjoy the politics that come with a large production. That is part of the production designer's world.

"But I think the main thing for me is about communication. It's about always listening to people and always reacting and keeping everybody informed and having a good spirit about you, really. I think Norman always had that. You always felt that there was a good spirit in the art department."

WAY BACK TO THE FUTURE

The electric shock needed to jolt the *Star Wars* prequel trilogy into life occurred in 1993 with the release of Spielberg's *Jurassic Park*. ILM's photo-realistic dinosaurs proved that digital visual effects, which Lucas had helped bankroll, were now mature enough to fulfill his grander vision. Two additional boosts were the release of Timothy Zahn's *Heir to*

the Empire novel, which spent many months as number one on the *New York Times* bestseller list in 1991, and the surprising success of the Special Edition of the *Star Wars* trilogy six years later, both of which proved that audiences were as insanely eager as ever to re-embrace their beloved galaxy from long ago and far away.

As Lucas had planned, his embryonic production crew on *Young Indy* proved themselves many times over as quick, efficient, and immensely talented and were able to segue into the next *Star Wars* trilogy. "I was talking with Rick McCallum and the DP, David Tattersall, and Rick just dropped into the conversation, 'When we all do *Star Wars…*'" said Bocquet. "That was Rick's way. He never told you outright, he would just include you in the conversation, so you would think, *Well, does that mean I might be doing that?* "George was probably looking for a new group of people as well, maybe younger and, in a way, less experienced, that might bring fresh ideas to the prequels. That is said with no disrespect to Norman Reynolds and John Barry. If it wasn't for Norman, I wouldn't have been doing the prequels. And if George was to ever do another group of three *Star Wars* films, he would quite rightly look for yet another group. It would be quite the right thing to do."

For the prequels, Lucas would also employ a new set of what were known by this time as "concept artists." McQuarrie had retired and Joe

Johnston had become a director of such films as *The Rocketeer* (1991) and *Jumanji* (1995), and would continue with *Hidalgo* (2004), and *Captain America: The First Avenger* (2011). Replacing them were concept design supervisors Doug Chiang, Erik Tiemens, and Ryan Church, along with as many as 10 additional artists all producing an enormous output. Nevertheless, their set designs were always big-picture concepts. When it came down to the nuts and bolts, the details and greeblies, it was up to the production art departments to build the sets and dress them as always.

Bocquet and his lieutenant, supervising art director Peter Russell, worked with many of the same people on one or more of the Episodes, including art directors Ian Gracie and Phil Harvey, draftsperson Jacinta Leong, and others. Only one member of the original art department crew was employed on the prequels: Fred Hole, who worked on Episodes I and II (along with second unit director Roger Christian and master plasterer Ken Clarke, who both worked on Episode I). At least one second-generation draftsperson signed on: Gary Tomkins, son of Alan.

While the art department had lots of experience working with prequel producer McCallum, Lucas had been a remote figure during *Young Indy*. But now he would be returning to the director's chair for the first time since 1976, which caused some degree of anxiety for the crew at Leavesden, the studio in England where they would make Episode I, and considerable worries for Lucas himself.

"He talked a lot about returning to directing," said Christian. "*Star Wars* was a very deep, psychologically difficult film for him because of the incredible pressures on it and I think that remained with him. So this was the first time that he was going back in the saddle. When I went up to Leavesden, the organization was exactly the same. Rick was running it the same way as the original trilogy. The budgets were bigger than what we'd had, but they were still a lot below what it would have been, say, if a Hollywood movie had been done that way."

"There were a lot of things going on," said Bocquet. "In the early days of concepting with Doug Chiang, while the script was being developed, we revisited some of the old drawings. Some of the old set designs in Tunisia and those sort of places were going to be used again in a different way and some of the technical drawings that were coming out were mine and George loved that sort of continuity."

Christian recounted visiting Lucas and McCallum and being told that Bocquet wanted to see him. "So I went to see Gavin, who said, 'How do I talk to George?' And I said, 'George is quite shy, but it's very simple: If George doesn't say anything, it's approved. He will tell you what he doesn't like or what to change, but otherwise you've just got to get on with it. You're doing fine. You've just got to carry on like that.' I know George missed John Barry terribly, but Gavin was doing a great job."

After his conversation with Bocquet ended, Christian was told that the set decorator wanted to see him. "I had the same conversation for an hour with Peter Walpole. He said, 'What do I do? George doesn't say anything to me.' So I explained it to him, too: 'That's a good thing. That's the way you work. Just get on with it. Do it. Show him. He'll approve or not.'

"I had given the DP David Tattersall his first job, a big commercial to do in Rome, so he was an old mate, and he said, 'Why aren't you doing second unit on this?' And I said, 'Well, I hadn't thought about it.' And he said, 'We need you.' So I went in to Rick and I asked, 'What are you doing about second unit?' And he said, 'Oh, we don't really need much. Ben Burtt is going to do about a week, that's all.' But I kind of looked at the schedule, and there were twelve weeks to shoot, and I thought, *This is a monster.* I said, 'You know what, Rick? Put my name down, and then if you need any help, I'll come and help.' And that was it. I didn't think more about it."

A few weeks later, Christian got the call. Dropping everything, he drove back up to Leavesden. "I went and sat with George, and he said, 'Are you serious about second unit?' And I said, 'Yeah, I was serious, of course. I'll do anything. You know that.' And he said, 'How do you work second unit?' So I explained how I did my second units. And George said, 'That's exactly what we need. Low-tech. It doesn't cost anything.' And Rick said, 'Come with me.' I walked two doors down. He said, 'Here's your office. Here's your assistant.' Everything was ready in a minute and a half."

Indeed, anyone who has ever visited a well-run production during principal photography of a sizeable film knows that the immense operation is run quickly and efficiently; directors and producers often equate it with waging a small war, given the logistics of moving people, feeding the crew, managing the finances and the emotions, purchasing the tons of materials, the layers of organization, and so on.

"Basically, the global control of all of the art department is down to Gavin," said Peter Russell. "Directly below Gavin is the main art department, set decoration, and props. Gavin takes concepts and works them up into viable set proposals, which are then handed down through myself or the other art directors to our eight draftsmen—and they're the backbone of the department; they're the guys who

actually do the mileage. Up until then, it's all sketches. From then on, it can be measured, priced, budgeted, and painted. Next, you do an overall assembly drawing and up to twenty subsequent drawings for detail."

Of course, the director is consulted at each stage. "I guess I've been accused of being a micromanager," Lucas said in a 2004 interview. "But as far as I'm concerned that's what making a movie is all about. I'm really responsible for every single detail on the picture. I work with a lot of very talented and creative people, but I have to make sure that it's exactly what I want it to be, because it's so critical that it look natural and fit into the environment. So I have to spend a lot of my time answering questions and making decisions about every little thing. And it goes on for three years solid, for each of the films, nearly every day of the week, hundreds of questions every single day. It never lets up. A friend of mine once said in every shot of a movie, there are 1,000 ideas—and that's true actually."

TUNISIAN GRAFFITI

Production traveled to Tunisia for both Episodes I and II, where some of the same locations used for *Star Wars* were revisited. Duplicating an event of the first stay in 1976, a storm blew through the Episode I set in 1997, leaving a swath of destruction. Both Episodes also had location shooting in Italy.

↑ Producer Rick McCallum, set decorator Peter Walpole, director George Lucas, and production designer Gavin Bocquet meet during Episode I preproduction.

Said Bocquet: "When you are working abroad on location, you have to enjoy adapting to local social structures and working methods, and not always presume that the way you do things is the only way to do things."

Although Episode I was shot on film, Lucas took the revolutionary jump to digital tape on Episode II, also moving his production company to Fox Studios in Sydney, Australia. Concurrently, small digital inroads were made into the art department, with new software programs for drafting, though most aspects of their trade remained the same. Of course, the move Down Under meant that for Episodes II and III the art department would use more local talent.

For Bocquet and his art department, the prequel trilogy represented a major challenge: tackling set design and construction for three truly huge productions. Though the new trilogy sets would make greater use of blue and green screen than the original trilogy, the majority of the virtual sets occurred during the pickups that followed principal photography. After each film wrapped, Lucas would do a rough cut and then determine what new scenes he needed. Those scenes, shot during pickups, often had a reduced budget and timetable, so production would resort to blue screen sets supplemented by digital work. But, contrary to popular belief, dozens of complex practical sets would cycle through the studios at a breakneck speed during principal photography, 60 for Episode I alone, from the Theed hangar, podracers, and the Jedi Council chamber to Watto's shop, Queen Amidala's space cruiser, and Anakin's hovel.

As they had for the original trilogy, production would take over an entire film studio, creating a nerve center within the art department and its tributary sections: props (constructing electrical boards as well as lightsabers), construction (with a carpentry shop as large as a football field), paint (with whole walls full of colored liquids), plaster, and so on.

"In the digital world, the palate is much broader than it was in the old days, but you're still designing your concept and then breaking it down into foreground, background, middle ground, live action, and enhancement," said Bocquet. "The visual technology these days is much more sophisticated now compared to the days of matte paintings and models. But I don't think the design process has changed a great deal; the principles are still the same. Star Wars was always at the forefront of digital technology, but a lot of the discussions we would have on a daily basis would simply be about

how much set to build for real and how much to do digitally. And people like John Knoll, the visual effects supervisor, would always be saying, 'Build as much as you can.'"

Indeed, in his book about the interrelation of visual effects and practical sets, Creating the Worlds of Star Wars, Knoll insists that the mixture of "old" and digital effects is the most effective way of minimizing budgets and tricking the human eye into thinking that what it is seeing is real. "There are no hard and fast rules," Knoll writes in his introduction. "Our goal at ILM is always the same: to do the visual effects correctly, so the audience won't know how the environments were created. They won't know which was a set, a miniature, a digital or practical matte painting or if the set was entirely computer generated (CG). They will be transported to other worlds and believe all the more fully in the fantastic story being told on the screen."

"I think a lot of what we do is not rocket science," Bocquet said. "You just have to break down the visual requirements, the budgetary requirements, the schedule requirements, and many other requirements in a clever and sensible way. For example, we know how much our sets cost to build: the nails, wood, number of carpenters, etc. But the cost of visual effects depends on a different set of factors, which all have to be balanced out with the art department's [costs]. If you have a long scene in one small environment, you are probably going to try and construct that as a full set as you don't want to be digitally enhancing every shot in that scene. But if you have a short scene in a huge environment, then it will probably be better visually, and better for the budget, to produce that set as a digital environment.

"But often, at the early planning stages, John Knoll and his team were still fully engaged on other projects at ILM and would not come onto the prequels on a full-time basis until maybe four months before shooting. But we had such a good understanding between our departments after Episode I that we would could often make pretty good judgments about what to build and what not to build before John and his team joined the production full time."

ANOTHER DAY

At ILM, model shop crews had similar feelings to those of the art department, but even more so: Would they be replaced entirely by digital technology? But, in fact, the Episode III model department probably built more than what was created for the first two films combined, notably the

volcano planet Mustafar, whose belching craters and lava flows were manufactured as a fantastic miniature labored on and shot for months.

Similarly, even the last significant pickups, shot at Shepperton Studios, contained at least one substantial set: the cockpit of the Alderaan ship that would become the rebel blockade runner that opens Star Wars (the very last shot would be a blue screen one at Elstree Studios in 2005).

The last film of the prequel trilogy was accepted enthusiastically by crowds around the world, as the Star Wars saga came to a close on May 19, 2005. Although it signaled an end, for those in the art department it was simply a milestone in careers that continued with many other films. Before retiring, Fred Hole would work on Die Another Day (2002). He passed away in February 2011. Peter Russell would reunite with Gavin Bocquet on Stardust (2007) and Jack the Giant Killer (2011); draftsperson Jacinta Leong would work as an assistant art director with now supervising art director Ian Gracie on The Chronicles of Narnia: Voyage of the Dawn Treader (2010); assistant art director Damien Drew would graduate to art director on Superman Returns (2006) and the mini-series The Pacific (2010); Phil Harvey would work as art director on Joe Johnston's The Wolfman (2010) and on John Carter of Mars (2012).

Each in turn would learn from those with more experience and mentor those with less. "Nobody ever comes into the art department knowing what the job fully entails," said Bocquet. "If they have been to film school or design school, it's great that they come in with a basic understanding of filmmaking, but you can only really become an art director or assistant art director by experiencing the way the film business works firsthand. And it's always the experience that someone has that matters when you are putting an art department together.

"I was part of the generation of designers slightly after people like Norman Reynolds and John Barry, and likewise, they were the generation of designers after people like Elliot Scott and Terry Marsh. And now there are a number of designers following my generation, so it just continues. And, hopefully, even though technology changes, the skills and knowledge we all learn are passed on from generation to generation."

THEED PLAZA

Lucas chose to film *Star Wars*: Episode I *The Phantom Menace* at Leavesden Film Studios, a converted Rolls Royce factory (not of cars but of aircraft) in Hertfordshire, about 18 miles northwest of London. The first motion picture to shoot there had been *GoldenEye* in 1995; the *Star Wars* team moved in during August of 1996 and, as usual, they eventually took over the entire facility (which McCallum booked for about two years), converting a large part of its backlot into the central plaza of Theed, capital city on the planet Naboo.

The Lucasfilm Archives have over 50 plans of buildings designed for this luxurious locale, as Lucas' vision of the Republic era was of a rich society not unlike Renaissance Italy. Thanks to advances in visual effects, a combination of practical set building coupled with digital set extensions (the dotted line on the blueprints mark the limits of the real-world builds) meant the creation of a cityscape that, in turn, combined classical architecture with a high-tech space fantasy world.

"Whether it's the Naboo Palace, going up to Norway for Hoth, or the forest for Endor, or Tunisia for Tatooine, George will always, if possible, try to find a location to base his other worlds on, because there's an integrity and detail in that design," said Bocquet. "It's different when you've got a water planet or a fire planet to find those locations, but, generally, he would always try to find locations for other worlds. So a lot of our set design for Naboo came from what we found on location, bouncing off of the Villa Balbianello, Caserta Palace, and Lake Como in Italy. You have to get out there and find the locations, and then that's your inspiration."

Part of the necessity, of course, is drawn from the fact that the production art department, unlike the concept art department, had to create so much detail, from stone finishes to door handles, which requires knowledge of the tangible. The conceptual artists, though given reams of photo reference, generally dealt with landscapes of the imagination.

"The work we did for the Theed Plaza epitomizes a lot of what we did on *Star Wars*," said supervising art director Peter Russell. "Although we only built to maybe a height of twenty or twenty-five feet, we did a lot of drawings to express what these buildings would look like as computer-generated extensions: that is, Gavin designed them in toto. We drew any number of completed beautiful, very fanciful, romantic, Romanesque-looking buildings."

↑ A detail is from an ILM Theed model.

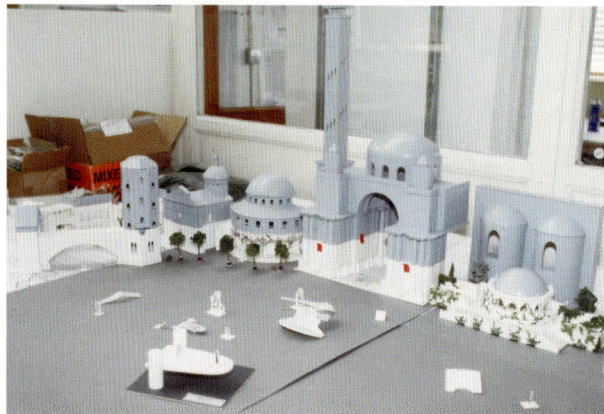

↑ On this maquette of Theed Plaza the bluish portions would all be digital extensions of the white/built portions.

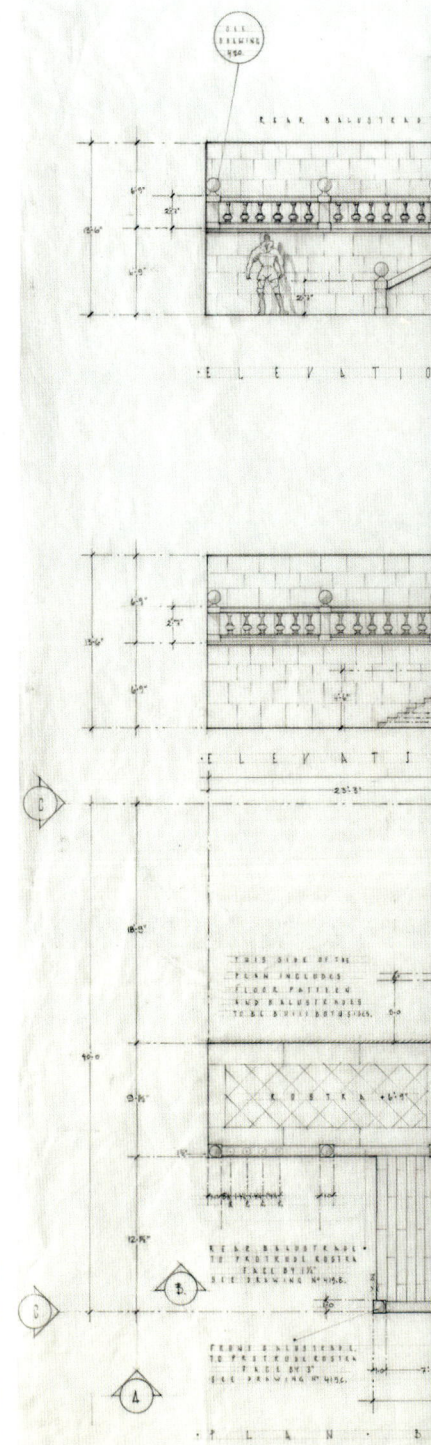

↑ Miniatures of Theed Plaza and the estuary at ILM.

SET	THEED PLAZA
DETAIL	BUILDING NO. 3, MAIN PLAN & ELEVATION
DRG. NO.	416
DATE	JUNE 18 1997
DRAWN BY	PAUL CROSS

← In the final film, Theed Plaza is seen complete with digital extensions.

NABOO ROYAL STARSHIP

The royal spacecraft of Naboo harkened back to the 1940s aesthetic of vehicle designs in *Flash Gordon* and *Buck Rogers*. "The queen's spaceship always looked more like an art piece than a piece of real engineering," said visual effects supervisor John Knoll.

The interior layout divided the ship into several sections: queen's chamber, rear gangway, droid hold, and so on. The blueprint of the engine component (no. 462), later referred to as the "hyperdrive," was to have set dressing on its face and top, along with "light veins" circulating throughout and fluorescent tubes inserted into certain areas.

John King did nearly all of the drawings of the queen's spaceship. He would later be supervising art director on a number of films, including *Troy* (2004), *Robin Hood* (2010), and *X-Men: First Class* (2011). One of his more elaborate technical drawings, designed in conjunction with Bocquet, was for the airlock door opening system (no. 435), which was to use counterweights with pulley cables.

"John did the droid hold for the Naboo ship, and it's a lovely old design," said Peter Russell. "It's like a rather elegant yacht hold." (Christian would shoot second unit of the droid hold set seen in drawing no. 572 on page 222, which originally had a scene of Jar Jar Binks, played by Ahmed Best, being tossed around as the ship rolled in space.

SET	NABOO QUEEN'S SPACESHIP
DETAIL	MAIN AREA, ENGINE COMPONENT
DRG. NO.	462
DATE	JUNE 18 1997
DRAWN BY	JOHN KING

→ The engine component was built as part of the Naboo spaceship set on the FS2 Stage, August 1997. This is reference photography of the hydraulic pump in "Flight Shed 2 Stage," in Leavesden.

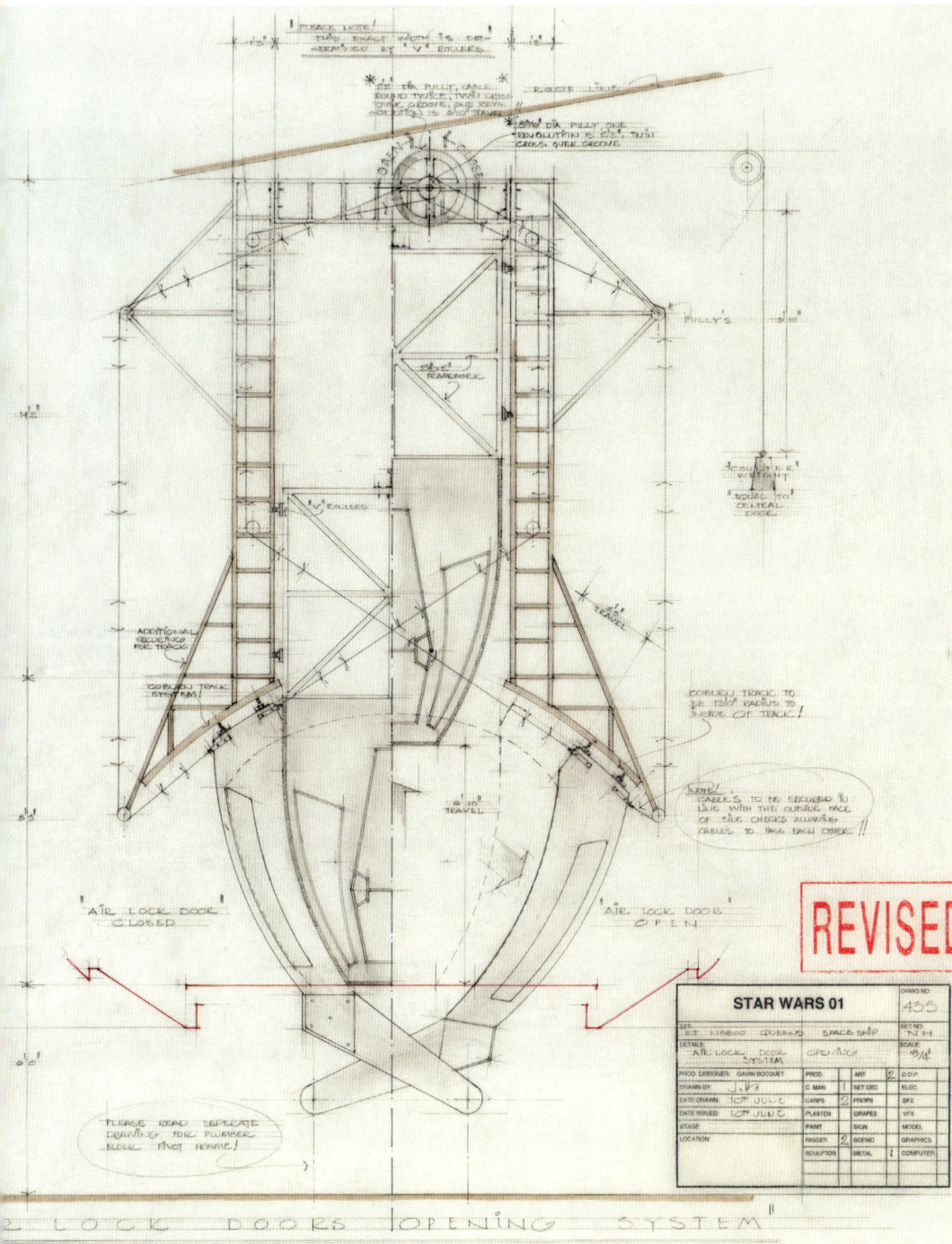

↑ The interior hallway and complex door mechanism are being constructed out of wood on FS2 Stage, per the technical drawing no. 435 and others. The wood has now been painted to appear to be exotic materials from a galaxy far, far away (bottom). Filming took place on Leavesden's FS2 Stage in mid-August 1997.

SET	QUEEN'S SPACESHIP
DETAIL	AIRLOCK DOOR OPENING SYSTEM
DRG. NO.	435
DATE	JUNE 10 1997
DRAWN BY	JOHN KING

SET	QUEEN'S SPACESHIP
DETAIL	QUEEN'S CHAMBER
DRG. NO.	17
DATE	SUMMER 1997
DRAWN BY	PETER RUSSELL

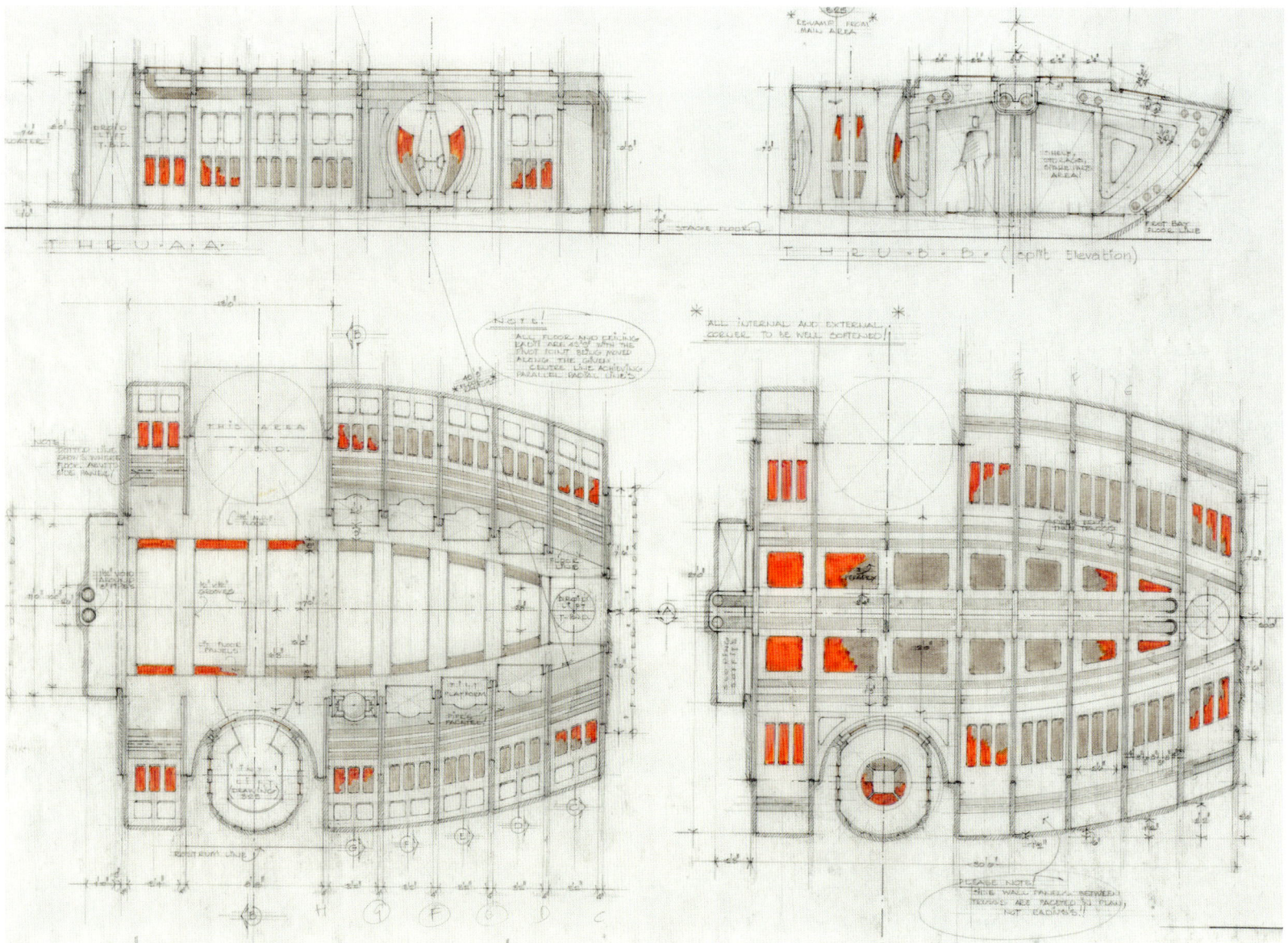

SET	QUEEN'S SPACESHIP, DROID HOLD
DETAIL	SET PLAN & ELEVATIONS
DRG. NO.	572
DATE	JULY 4 1997
DRAWN BY	JOHN KING

← The exterior of the Naboo spaceship was a model built at ILM, seen here in a final frame.

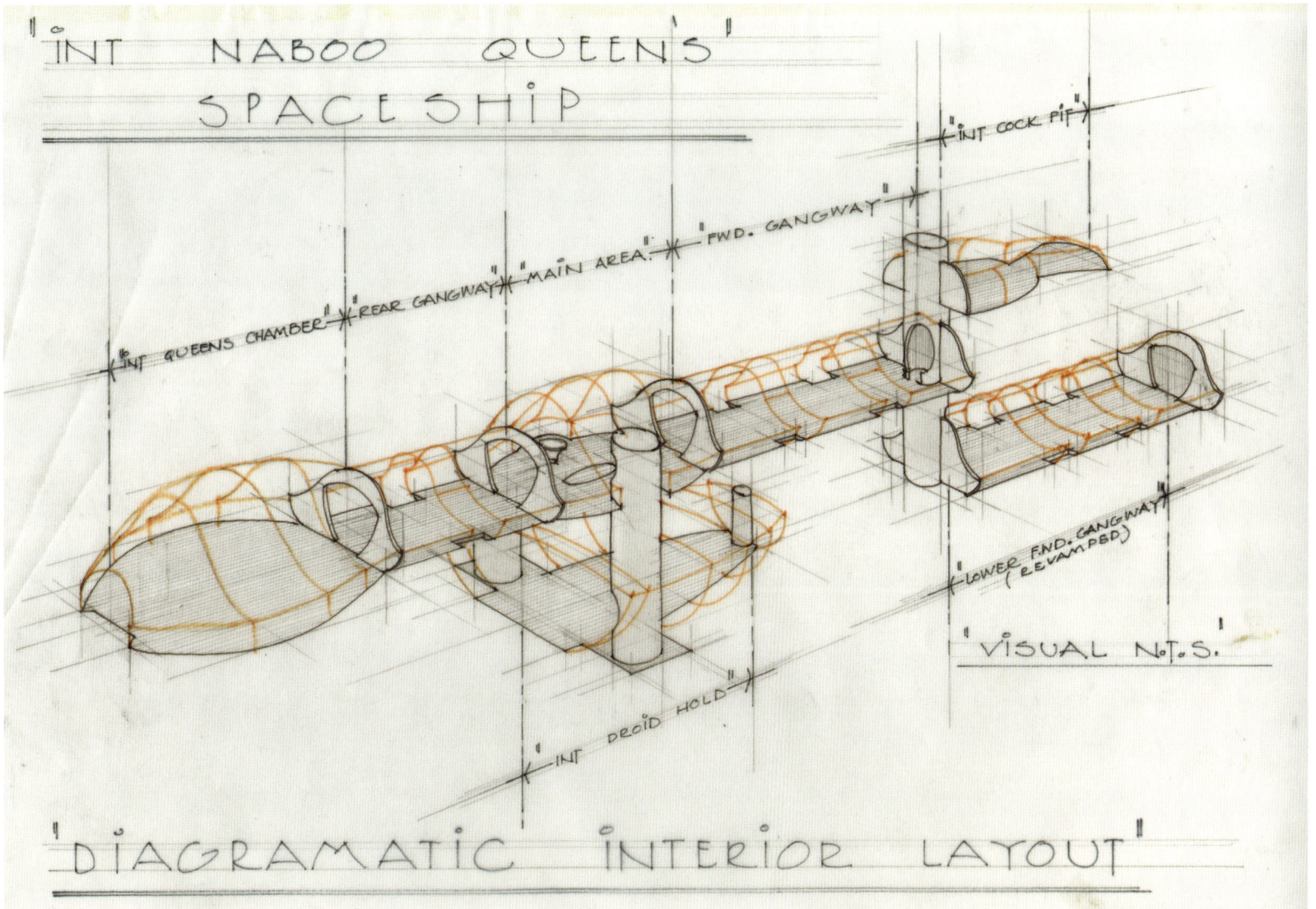

"INT NABOO QUEEN'S SPACESHIP"

"INT COCK PIF"

"INT QUEENS CHAMBER" — "REAR GANGWAY" — "MAIN AREA." — "FWD. GANGWAY"

"LOWER F.ND. GANGWAY"
(REVAMPED.)

VISUAL N.T.S.

"INT DROID HOLD"

"DIAGRAMATIC INTERIOR LAYOUT"

SET	NABOO QUEEN'S SPACESHIP
DETAIL	DIAGRAMMATIC INTERIOR LAYOUT
DRG. NO.	N/A
DATE	SUMMER 1997
DRAWN BY	UNKNOWN

→ A wooden maquette depicts the infrastructure of the queen's spacecraft.

↑ The interior hallway was constructed out of wood on FS2 Stage, per the technical drawing no. 435 (on page 221) and others, and then skillfully painted.

MOS ESPA

When Jedi Knights Qui-Gon Jinn (Liam Neeson) and
Obi-Wan Kenobi (Ewan McGregor), along with Queen
Amidala (Natalie Portman) and her retinue, make an
emergency landing on Tatooine, audiences were treated
to another town on that planet: Mos Espa. While of
course studying what had been done for Mos Eisley on
Star Wars, Bocquet had his art department design many
buildings, from which Lucas chose a select few. Mos
Espa was then built on location in Chott el Gharsa,
Tunisia, as one large T-shaped street that stood in for
Watto's junk shop, Sebulba's café, the market, and so on.

Clever camera angles and lighting, editing, and
varied set dressings made locations that were right next
to each other in reality seem blocks apart on screen. One
of the many drawings (no. 176) executed for these scenes
indicates that sets were to be partially constructed and
were to use reference photos for creating aged, crumbling
plaster. "Each one of these main plans and elevation
sheets would lead into fifteen, twenty, or thirty more
detailed drawings," said Russell. The partial set build
would later be combined with miniatures and matte
paintings during post at ILM.

↑ Building 24, the
"fruit stand," was
partially built by the
art and construction
departments on the
Chott El Gharsa and
shot in July 1997.

SET	MOS ESPA STREET
DETAIL	BUILDINGS 9, 7, 11, & ARCH B
DRG. NO.	176
DATE	APRIL 17 1997
DRAWN BY	JULIE PHILPOTT

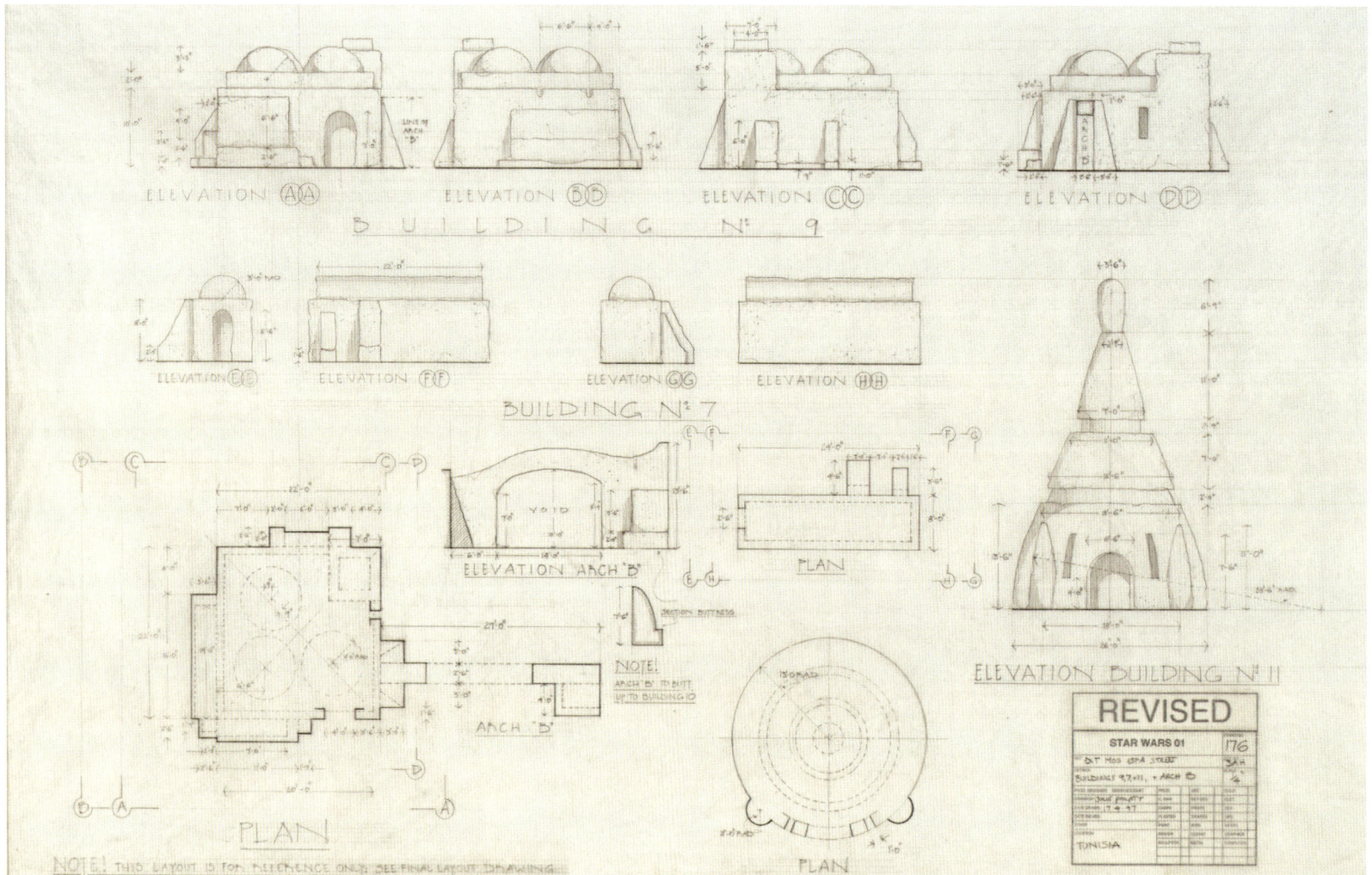

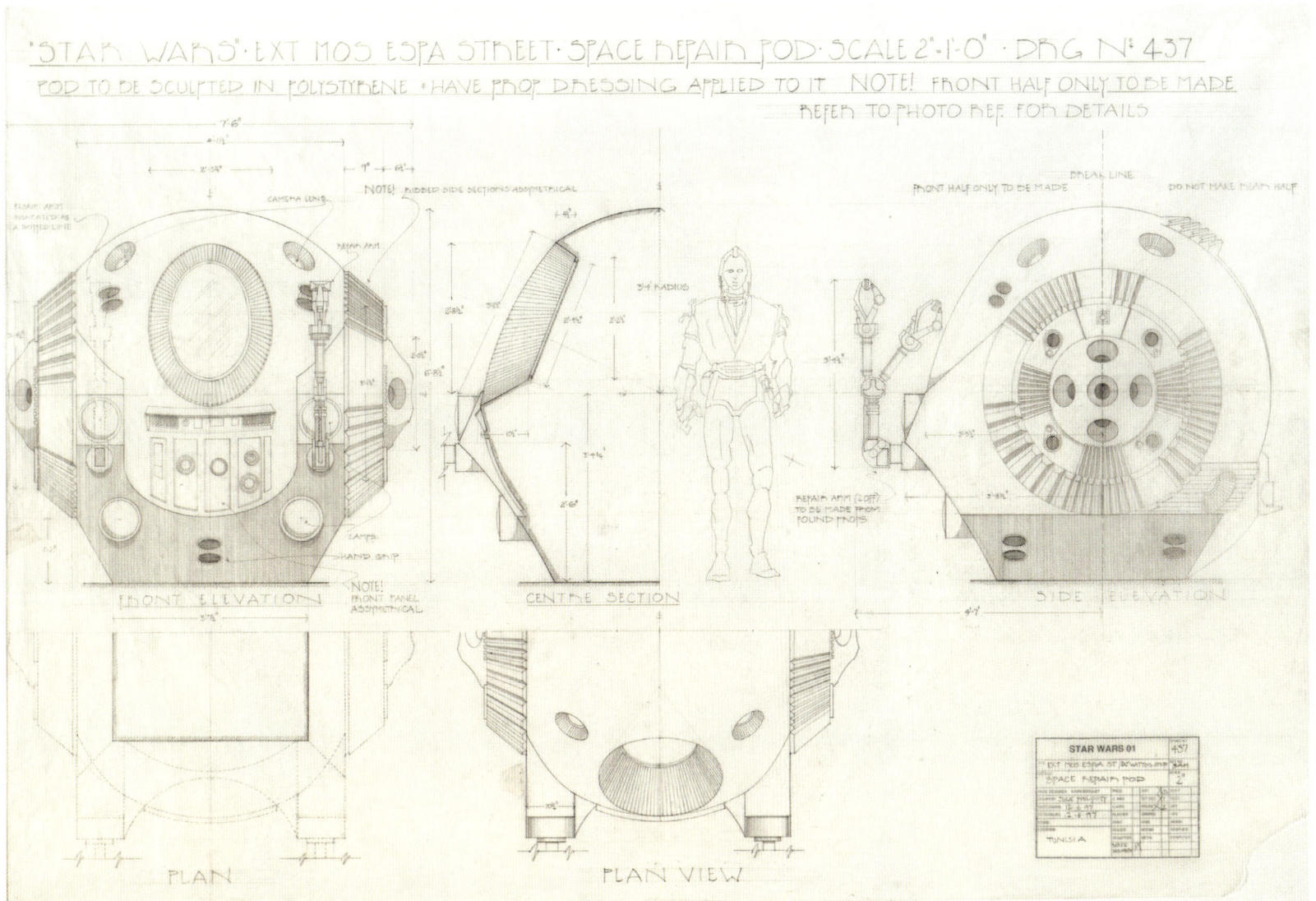

'STAR WARS' EXT MOS ESPA STREET · SPACE REPAIR POD · SCALE 2" · 1'·0" · DRG No 437

POD TO BE SCULPTED IN POLYSTYRENE · HAVE PROP DRESSING APPLIED TO IT   NOTE! FRONT HALF ONLY TO BE MADE

REFER TO PHOTO REF FOR DETAILS

FRONT ELEVATION CENTRE SECTION SIDE ELEVATION

PLAN PLAN VIEW

↓ The "space repair pod" in Watto's junkyard bears a resemblance to the EVA pod in *2001*—and the space pod outside the Cantina in Episode IV. Filming took place in "Watto's junk yard, behind shop," in Chott El Gharsa, Tunisia, early August 1997.

SET	MOS ESPA
DETAIL	SPACE REPAIR POD
DRG. NO.	437
DATE	JUNE 12 1997
DRAWN BY	JULIE PHILPOTT

Philpott's space repair pod drawing (no. 437) was not only a second salute to *2001*, but also a nod to the original film's homage—perhaps the same pod somehow migrated from the rear of Watto's junk shop in Mos Espa to the front of the Cantina in Mos Eisley. The blueprint notes that the pod was to be sculpted in polystyrene and have prop dressing applied, while only the front half needed to be made; the repair arm would be made from found props.

WATTO'S SHOP

Like the other dwellings constructed on location in Tunisia, the exterior of Watto's junk shop was only partially built (no. 167 on page 228). "There's a shot where Qui-Gon says, 'We'll go to one of the larger shops,'" said Knoll. "And on location we pan over and we see Watto's and you could see where the set ends. I did an extension for the top of it that kind of looked like this drawing. I think Doug Chiang did a sketch to indicate what he wanted it to look like."

The interior of the shop was filmed in Leavesden on Stage C, with a found engine unit, sand/dirt covering the new flooring, found elements dressed into the walls—and steps. In an important moment for the film, young Anakin Skywalker (Jake Lloyd) comes running down those steps into the junk shop, his introduction into the saga.

"Anakin comes running down the steps and I think it's a much better shot than coming in on a flat," said Bocquet. "That tends to give you a TV feel, because in the old days you had flat floors because they had their cameras on wheels and they had to roll around. But George has always had a humorous problem with having steps in sets. He thinks it just slows the shoot down. I was always arguing for having different levels because, you know, you only have a few things you can use to make a set interesting, from texture and color to shape, and levels is one of them. So there's quite a few steps in there, but I really had to argue for them, because George also had the problem that Artoo can't get down steps."

"Neil Morfitt's drawing [no. 02] was a very early one of Watto's shop, and that texture and that style of architecture was a one-off," said Russell. "We've never done anything the like before or since."

Preproduction actually had a luxury that was also a one-off: a certain amount of extended time before filming began, which led to some ironic negotiations between McCallum and the art department. The producer felt that the more time he gave them, the more time the art department would take and the more money it would cost; in the end, a reasonable period was agreed upon—several weeks—after which time Stage C was locked down and no more work could be done on Watto's shop.

SET	WATTO'S SHOP
DETAIL	PLAN, SECTIONS & ELEVATIONS
DRG. NO.	02
DATE	DECEMBER 4 1996
DRAWN BY	NEIL MORFITT

SET	WATTO'S SHOP
DETAIL	SHELVES
DRG. NO.	06
DATE	MARCH 6 1997
DRAWN BY	AMANDA BERNSTEIN

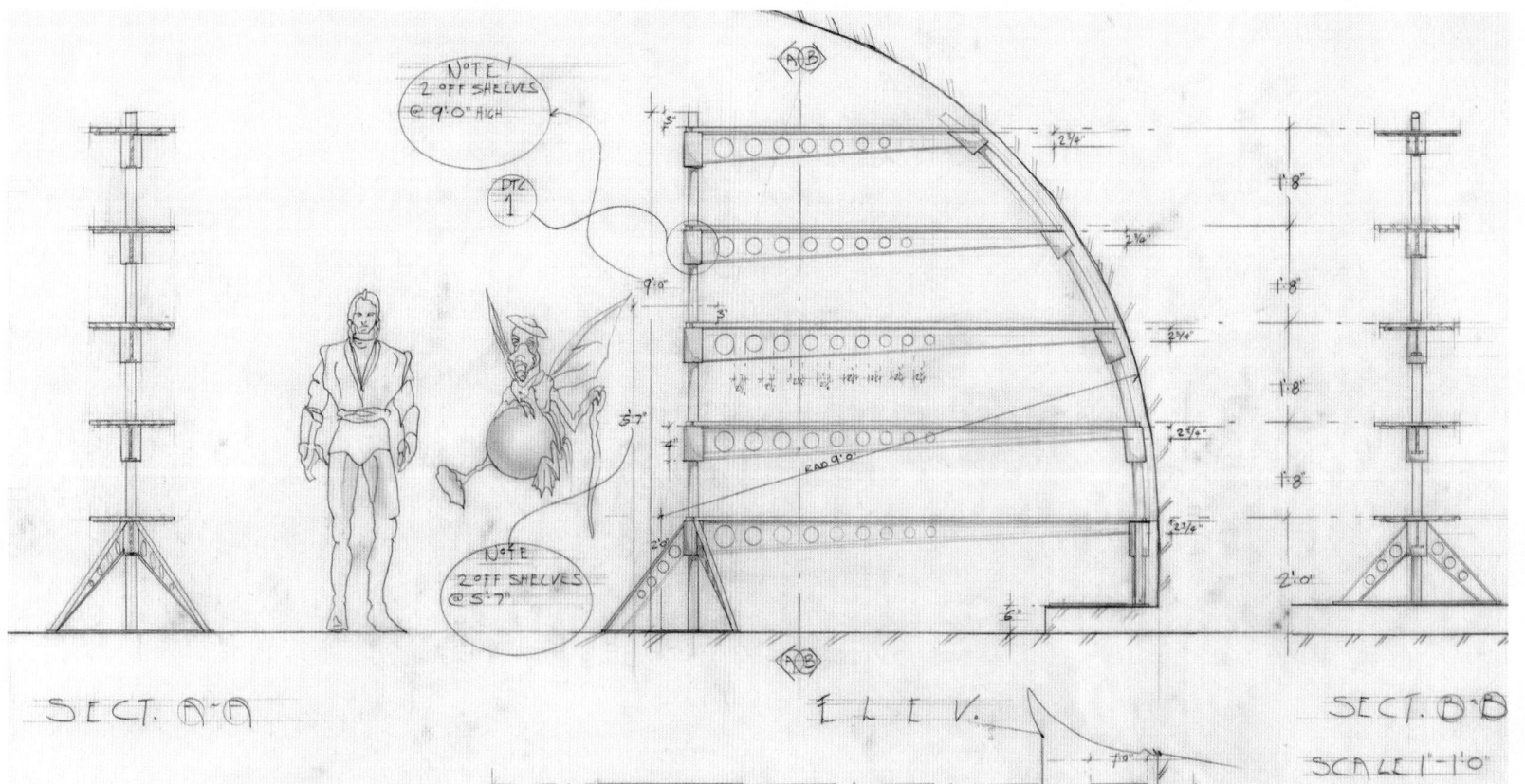

← The exterior of Watto's shop was built on location in Tunisia; its tower would be added in postproduction.

→ A final frame provides a glimpse of the digital extension added to Watto's shop exterior.

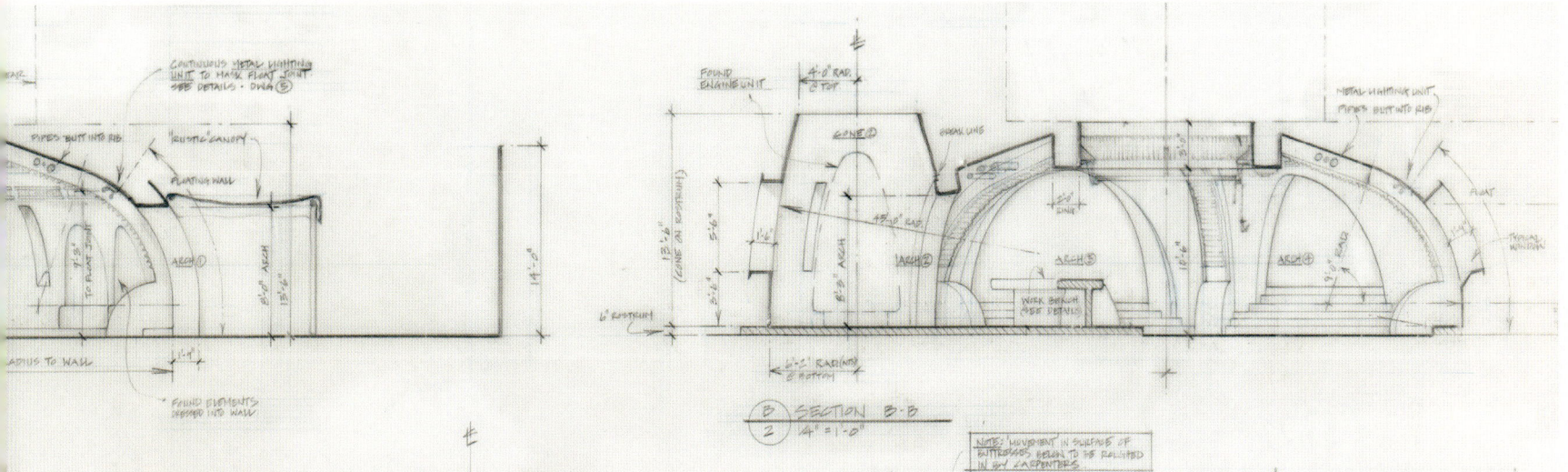

← The interior of Watto's shop is constructed on Stage C, Leavesden Studios.

SET	WATTO'S SHOP
DETAIL	EXTERIOR CONCEPTS
DRG. NO.	N/A
DATE	WINTER 1996
DRAWN BY	UNKNOWN

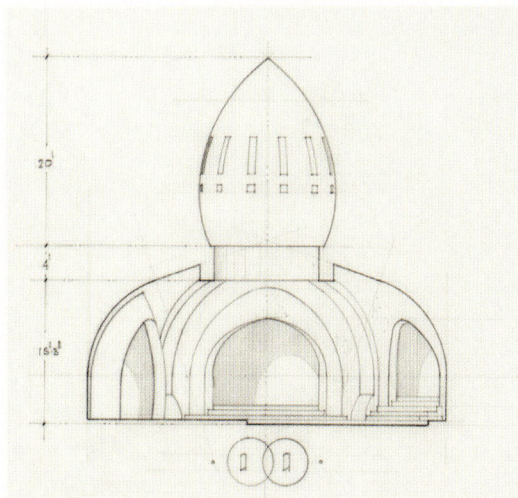

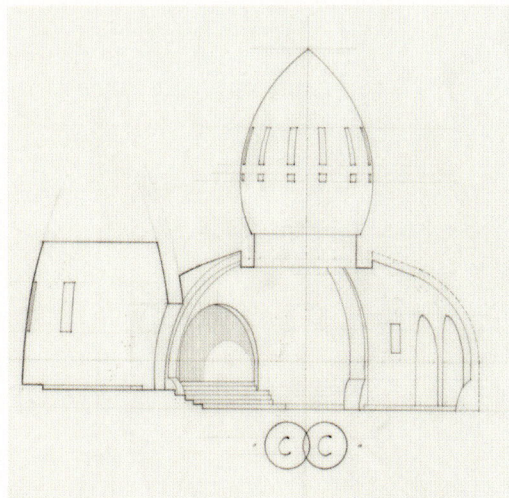

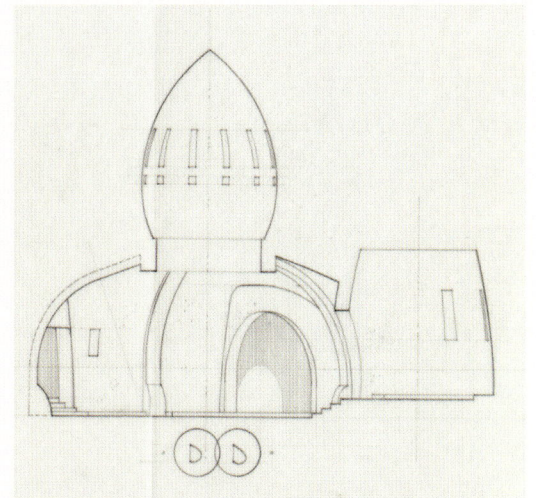

'STAR WARS' · EXT MOS ESPA · EXT WATTO'S SHOP (CONTINUIT

NOTE! SET TO BE PARTIALLY CONSTRUCTED ONLY

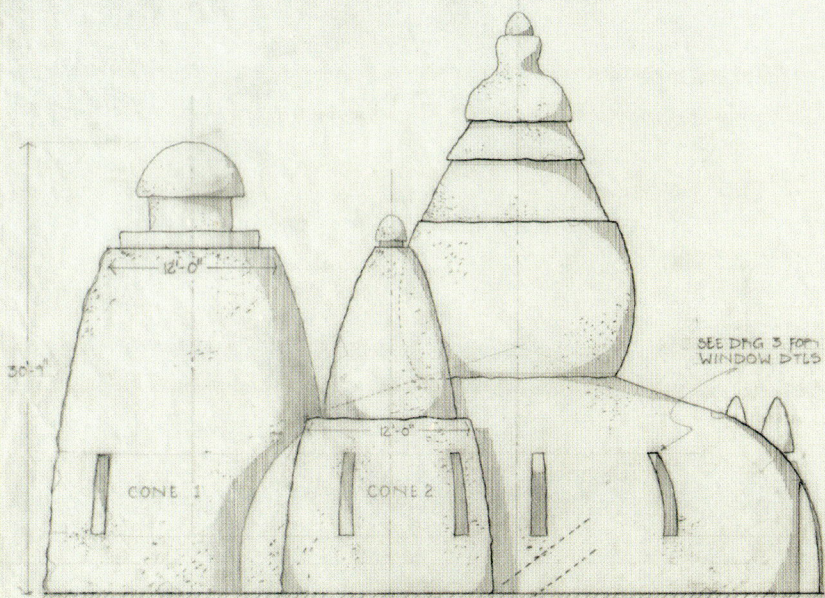

CONE 1   CONE 2

SEE DRG 3 FOR
WINDOW DTLS

Ⓐ Ⓐ ELEVATION

DOOR A   43'-6"

Ⓑ Ⓑ ELEVATION

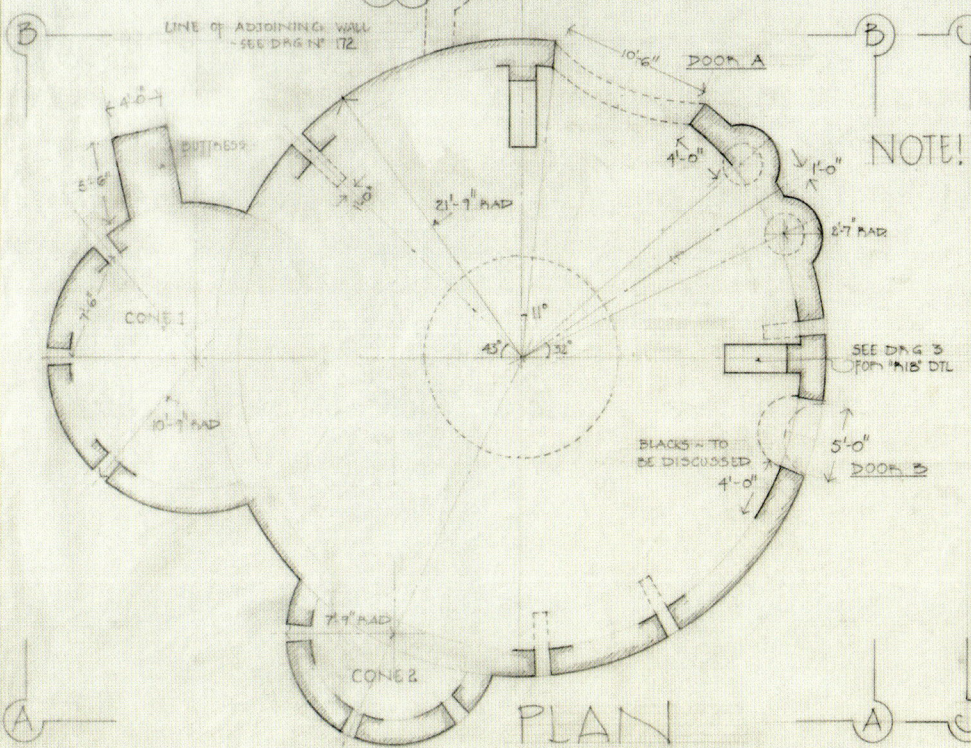

LINE OF ADJOINING WALL
— SEE DRG N° 172.

DOOR A

BUTTRESS

21'-9" RAD

CONE 1

SEE DRG 3
FOR 'RIB' DTL

BLACKS + TO
BE DISCUSSED

DOOR B

CONE 2

PLAN

SCALE ¼"-1'-0"

NOTE! FLOOR PLAN IS DIFFERENT TO INT. WATTOS SHO

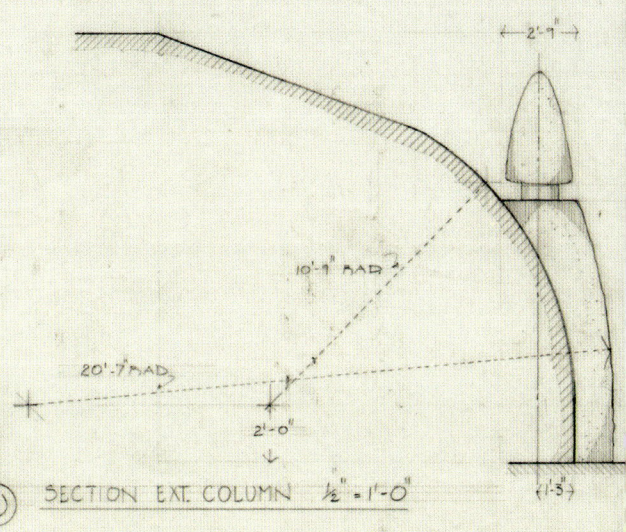

SECTION EXT COLUMN ½"-1'-0"

167

SET). SCALE ¼"·1'-0" DRG N° 167

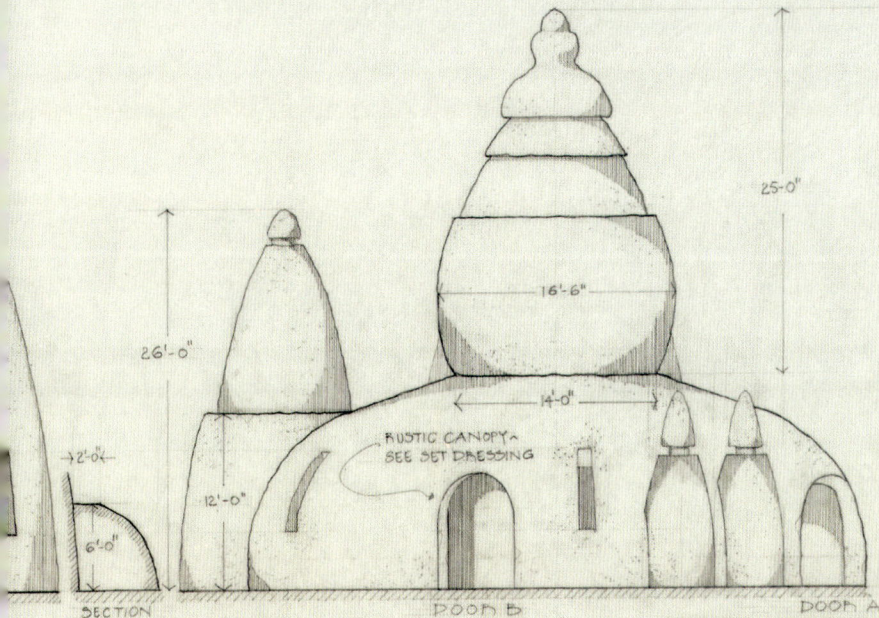

25'-0"

26'-0"

16'-6"

14'-0"

RUSTIC CANOPY~
SEE SET DRESSING

12'-0"

12'-0"

6'-0"

SECTION
BUTTRESS

DOOR B

DOOR A

C C ELEVATION

REVISED

STAR WARS 01		167	
SET EXT MOS ESPA			
DETAILS EXT. WATTOS SHOP BUILDING 1.		SCALE ¼"·½"	
PROD DESIGNER GAVIN BOUQUET	PROD.	ART	D.O.P.
DRAWN BY JULIE PHILPOTT	C. MAN	SET DEC.	ELEC.
DATE DRAWN 15·4·97	CHIPS	PROPS	SFX
DATE ISSUED	PLASTER	DRAPES	VFX
STAGE	PAINT	RIGGING	MODEL
LOCATION TUNISIA	SKELETON	SCENIC	GRAPHICS
	SCULPTOR	METAL	COMPUTERS

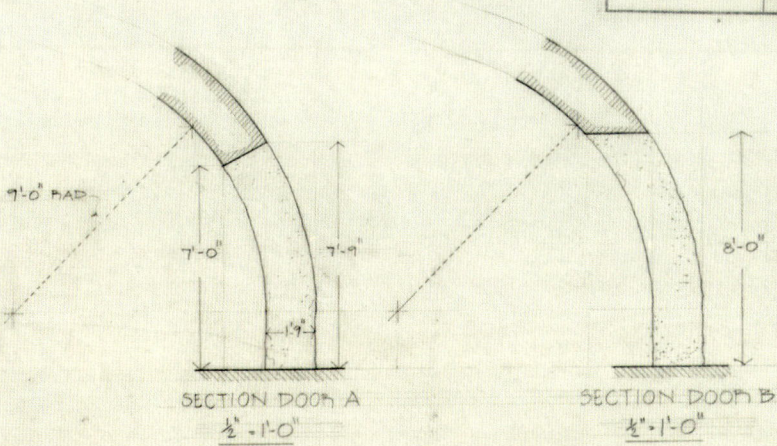

7'-0" RAD

7'-0"

7'-9"

8'-0"

1'-9"

SECTION DOOR A
½"·1'-0"

SECTION DOOR B
½"·1'-0"

SET	MOS ESPA
DETAIL	WATTO'S SHOP BUILDING
DRG. NO.	167
DATE	APRIL 15 1997
DRAWN BY	JULIE PHILPOTT

ANAKIN'S HOVEL

Like Watto's shop, Anakin's hovel was a combination of an exterior filmed on location
in the extreme heat (temperatures reached 128 degrees Fahrenheit) and an interior shot
at Leavesden. Lucas actually took advantage of John Barry's original scouting trips and
shot the slave quarters exterior outside what had been a grain storage warehouse in
Medenine, Tunisia, but which had been converted into a hotel in the interim. Barry
had visited the same premises in 1975 and at one time scenes for *Star Wars* had been
envisioned for the locale.

"Once we established that with George and suggested that idea to him, to dress
them up as a slave quarters, then the shape of those grain stores to me obviously
brought a shape and a size to the inside," said Bocquet.

The inside of Anakin's hovel was built on Stage D. The technical drawing indicates
that the set would have practical sliding doors, light openings in ceilings, a "very uneven
plaster" finish for the walls, a workbench and sleeping area, and a wardrobe and bed
with floating wall. It is one of the more extensively dressed interiors of the film.

Drawn on a grid by Russell so it could be easily transferred from blueprint to
backing, a scenic painting (no. 405) was used on set. Seen from the interior of the
hovel, it matched the grain storage exterior on location in Tunisia.

"For the interior set here, there was a door that opened to the 'outside,' when
Anakin and the others are coming in from the dust storm," said Knoll. "So we're
looking out into the street where you see that painted backing."

SET	ANAKIN'S HOVEL
DETAIL	PLAN, SECTIONS
DRG. NO.	438A
DATE	JUNE 12 1997
DRAWN BY	HELEN XENOPOULOS

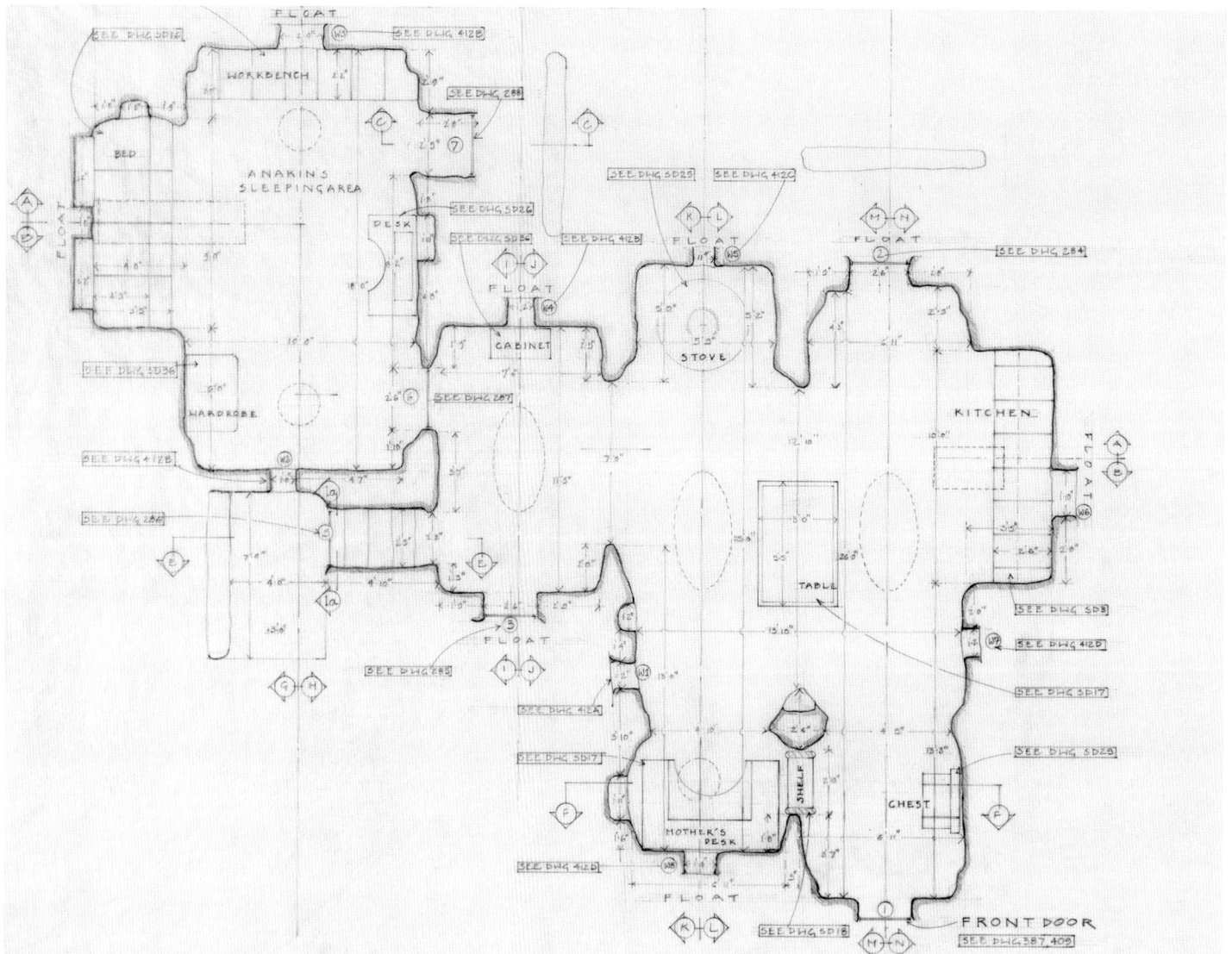

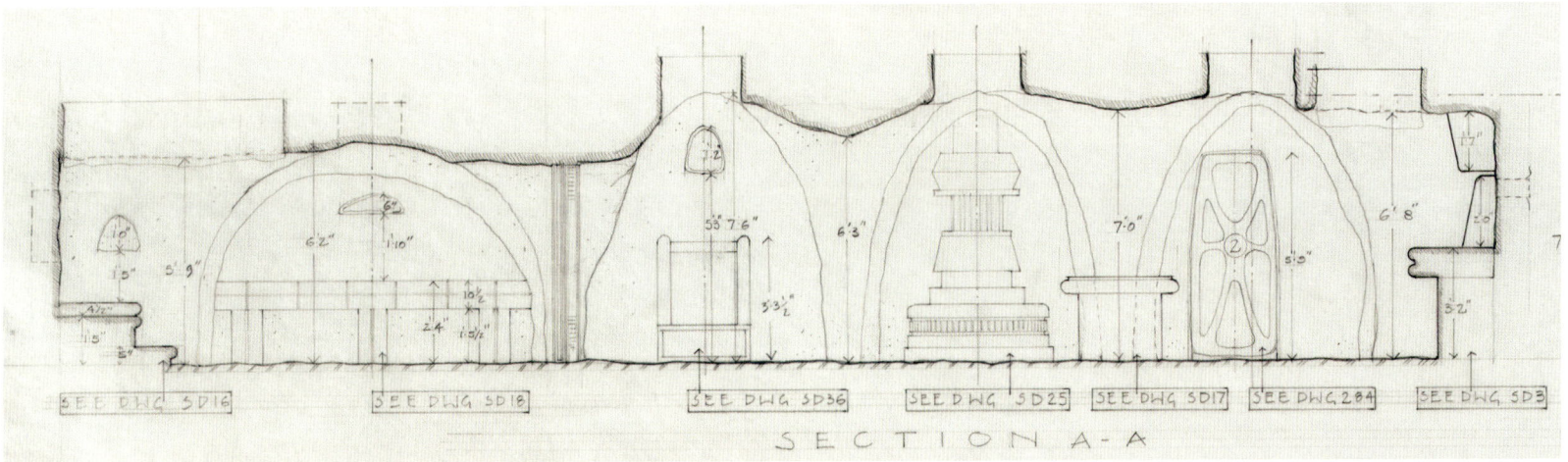

SECTION A·A

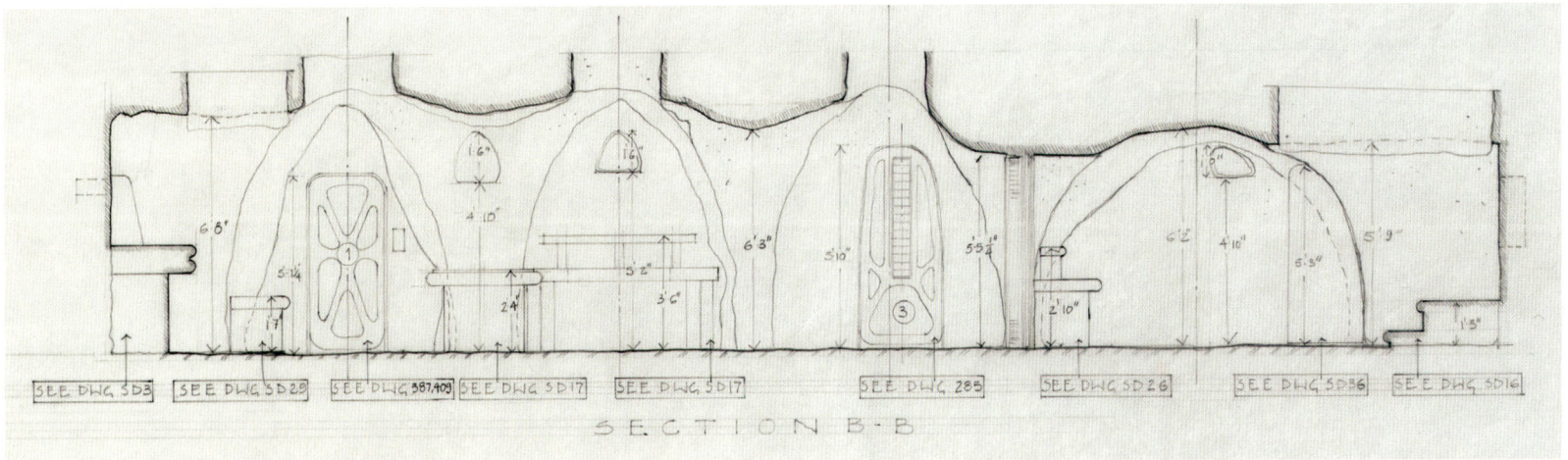

SECTION B·B

SET	ANAKIN'S HOVEL
DETAIL	BACKING DETAIL (TOP AND ABOVE)
DRG. NO.	405
DATE	JUNE 2 1997
DRAWN BY	PETER J. RUSSELL

EXT·ANAKINS·BACKING FOR FRONT DOOR·½" TO 1'0" SCALE

*RAMP NEEDED TO HIDE LACING

FOUME. TATAHOUINE. GHORFA. HOTEL. ①

LEFT AND ABOVE The backing (left), seen outside Anakin's front door, was modeled on the Tunisian location that John Barry sketched back in 1976 (above) as a possible locale for a shot in which the landspeeder goes through a Jawa village (Barry's note reads, "Foume. Tatahouine. Ghorfa. Hotel.").

↓ The interior of the hovel is now dressed and ready for filming, July 1997.

→ Anakin's hovel took form thanks in part to many carpenters on Stage D (a cutout of C-3PO stands before it).

PODRACE

Perhaps the greatest sequence in Episode I is the podrace. Much of the high-speed contest was created digitally, but nine full-sized podracers were constructed, along with many more cutouts, for scenes in the Mos Espa hangar, filmed at Leavesden, and the starting grid, filmed in Tunisia. Tozzi's technical drawing (no. 102), based on Doug Chiang's concept art, includes Anakin, at 4-foot, 6-inches tall, for scale. He also notes that for Anakin's podracer "smoke and heat will be required to emit from tail section—but no flame; space for possible power plant to operate fins to be discussed; turbine may be motorized."

"There were three or four podracers that were finessed to the nth degree," said Russell. "But, financially and spiritually, some of the other ones were much more generic shapes that we just dressed and found things for, in the old *Star Wars* way. It was a much more, 'Oh, that's a great bit, let's put it on,' rather than, 'This is a great idea, let's draw it and manufacture it.' So it was really kind of a cool last hurrah of using the backs of televisions and things like that."

Despite the intense security surrounding all aspects of Episode I, the podracers were shipped from Leavesden to the airport on open flatbed lorries for all to see, though essentially unrecognizable. "It was very funny to see them drive out and go around the M25," added Bocquet. "I think they were so bizarre that no one knew what to make of them. They didn't have '*Star Wars*' written on the side."

The vehicles were then flown on the largest cargo transport McCallum could find, a huge Russian craft, which sadly crashed into a mountain about six months after delivering the podracers to Tunisia. On location, Christian filmed second unit of the podracers for several setups of the starting grid. But only two days after the shoot had started, a powerful storm ripped through the sets. "The storm was over by morning, but when we arrived at the shooting location, we were appalled at the devastation," remembered Knoll. "The neatly laid out podrace starting grid looked like it was the victim of an angry child who had tossed the podracers in the air and then smashed them into the ground."

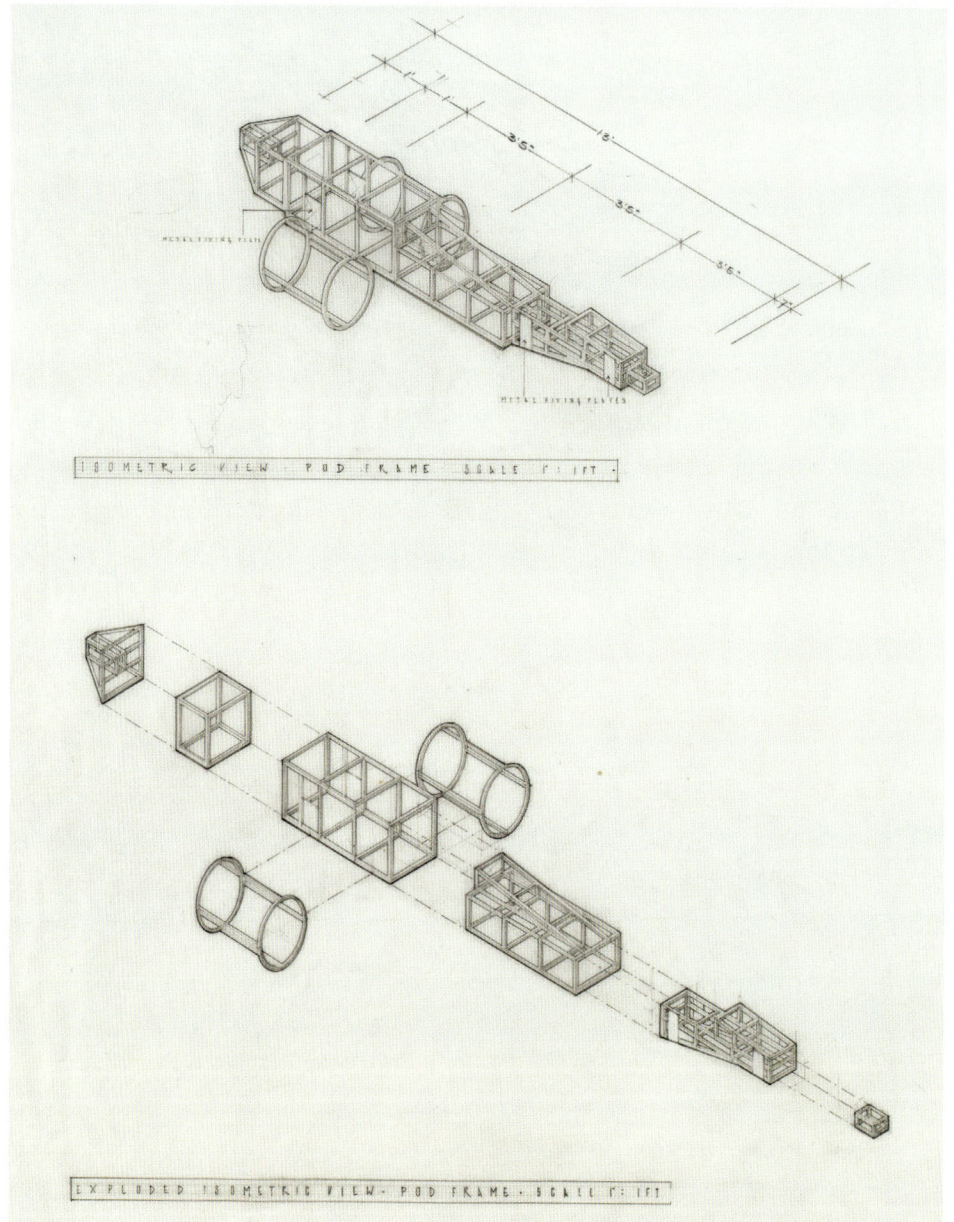

SET	PODRACER
DETAIL	EXPLODED ISOMETRIC VIEW, POD FRAME
DRG. NO.	N/A
DATE	1997
DRAWN BY	MIKE BISHOP

← On-set reference photography is of the cockpit of Anakin's full-sized podracer prop.

POD RACE FLAG DESIGNS   SHEET 2

SCALE : 1" TO 1'O"

RATTS TYERELL

TOY DAMPNER

TEEMTO PAGALIES

ARK "BUMPY" ROOSE

ALDO BEEBO

ELAN MAK

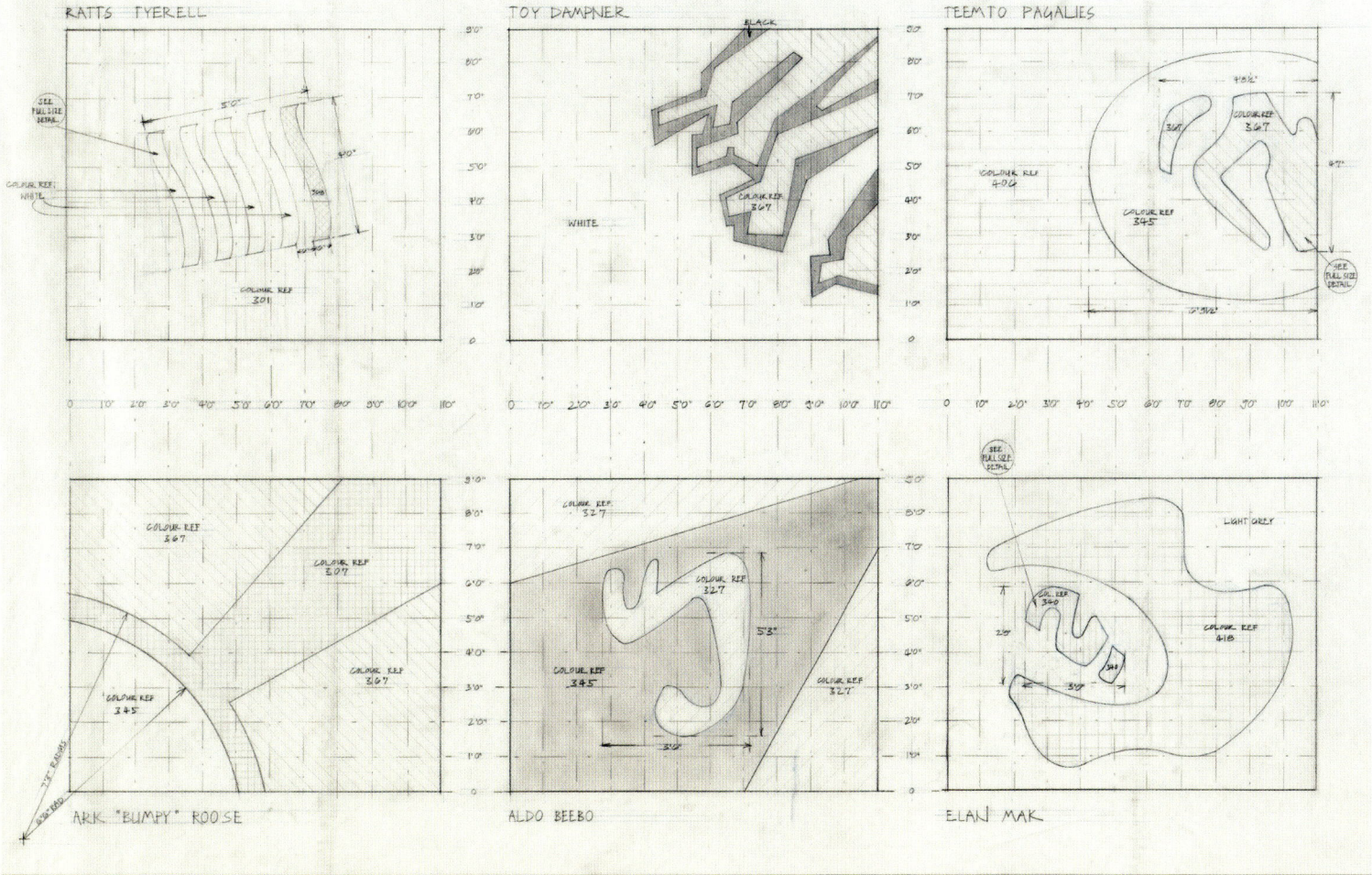

↑ An art department assistant, Emma Tauber, drew flag designs for podracers Rats Tyerell, Toy Dampner, Ark "Bumpy" Roose, Elan Mak, Teemto Pagalies, and Aldo Beedo.

SET	MOS ESPA ARENA
DETAIL	PODRACE FLAG DESIGNS
DRG. NO.	243
DATE	MAY 22 1997
DRAWN BY	EMMA TAUBER

→ Before the race, the podracer flags are exhibited, filmed on location, August 1997.

← The miniature podrace arena was built at ILM by the model shop (thousands of painted Q-tips stood in for the crowd).

↑ A final frame from the film shows the result of combining live-action footage shot in Tunisia with the miniature and elements shot at ILM.

→ A full-sized podracer sits in the Tunisian desert.

↑ Reference photography shows the starting gate lap-light cluster model.

← Concept art of the podrace start/finish line was sketched by Doug Chiang in July 1995.

↓ Podracer props are on location in Tunisia, August 1997.

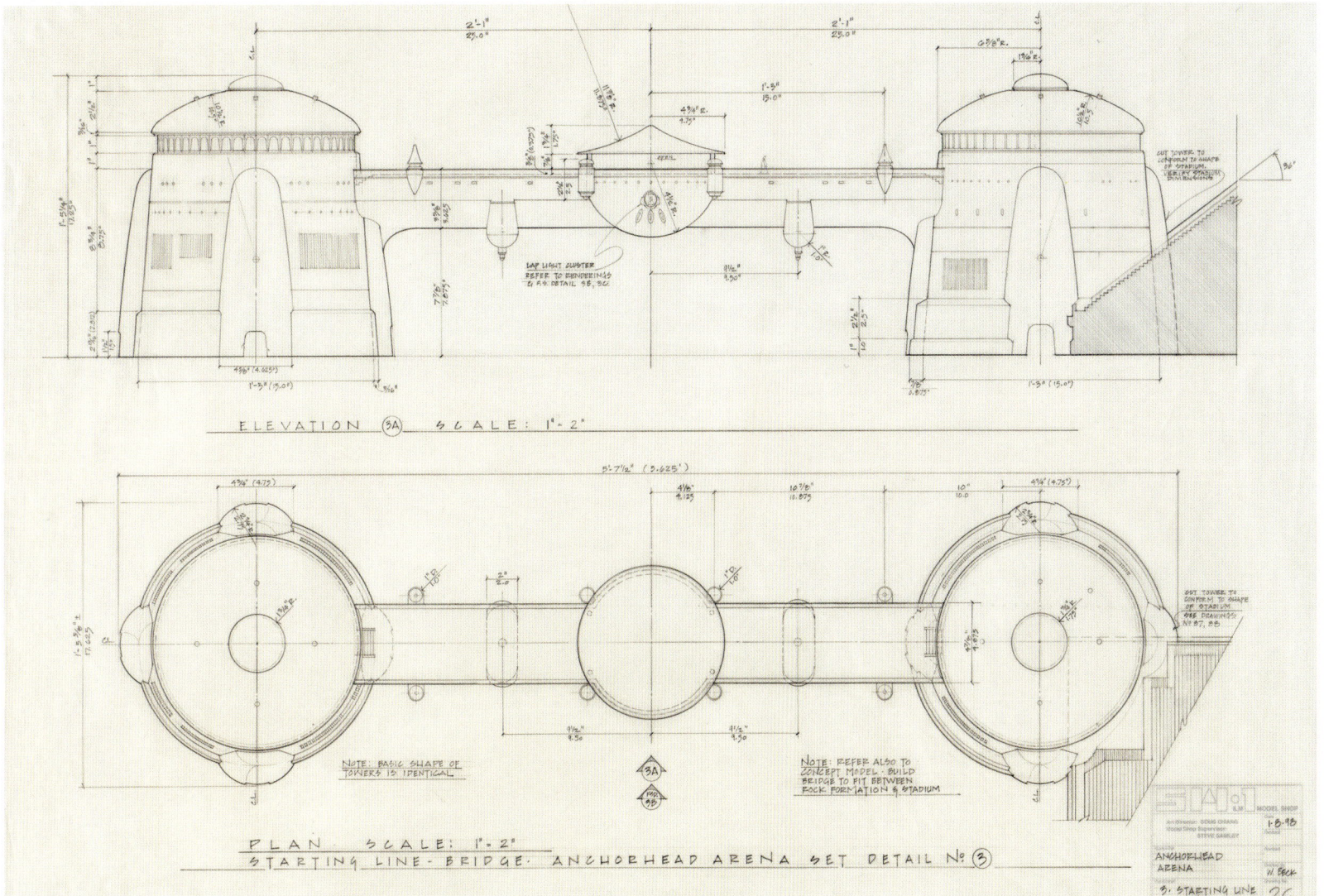

ELEVATION (3A)   SCALE: 1"=2"

PLAN   SCALE: 1"=2"
STARTING LINE-BRIDGE·ANCHORHEAD ARENA·SET DETAIL No (3)

↑ The full-sized podracers filmed on location were later combined with shots of several miniatures built by ILM's model shop, including a quarter-scale starting grid, which included a lap-light cluster that ticked off the number of circuits completed.

SET	ANCHOR HEAD ARENA
DETAIL	STARTING LINE BRIDGE
DRG. NO.	26
DATE	JANUARY 8 1998
DRAWN BY	WILLIAM BECK

JEDI TEMPLE

The Jedi High Council Chamber was built on a platform 6 feet above the studio floor to enable puppeteers to manipulate three of the council members: Yoda, Yaddle, and Yarael Poof, who was built directly into his chair so that an operator could work him from inside.

Thanks to the flexibility provided by digital visual effects, Lucas was able to modify the Jedi Council set in postproduction. "George later decided he didn't like the window design," said Knoll. "So we ended up removing the central pillar. And I think we actually lowered the window frame, too; some surgery went into the plates to give us a little better view. Then when this got built a second time for Episode II, we built it more like the modified version."

The first set had been too large to store (only the seats were saved), so the second build was not only updated, but also used for additional sets, including the Jedi Analysis Chamber (which was cut from the final film but shown on the DVD release), by repainting the floor, altering the windows, and inserting three consoles; the Jedi Youngling Training Room, by again repainting the floor and adding plants and several columns; and the first version of Jedi Master Mace Windu's office (later revised to be less bureaucratic looking and more Zen-like), by adding a desk and other office furniture.

"The Jedi Council Chamber got built three times," laughed Knoll. "It was built again for Episode III, but only as half a set, not the whole 360 degrees."

For each visit to the Chamber in the prequel trilogy, views through the Council windows looked onto blue screens that were later replaced by ILM with panoramic cityscapes and skylines above the city planet of Coruscant.

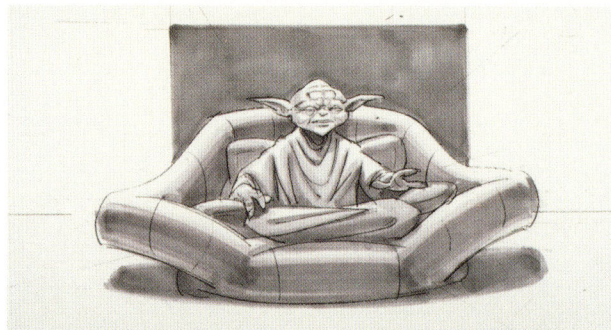

↑ Concept art by Ed Natividad is of Yoda's chair, 1997.

← Reference photography of the final chair is complete with the Yoda puppet. Filming took place on the MS2 Stage in early September 1997.

→ The floor was elaborately painted for the final Jedi Council set in Episode I (note the central window pillars that would be eliminated digitally in post).

SET	PALACE OF JEDI, COUNCIL CHAMBERS
DETAIL	YODA'S JEDI CHAIR
DRG. NO.	10
DATE	1997
DRAWN BY	AMANDA BERNSTEIN

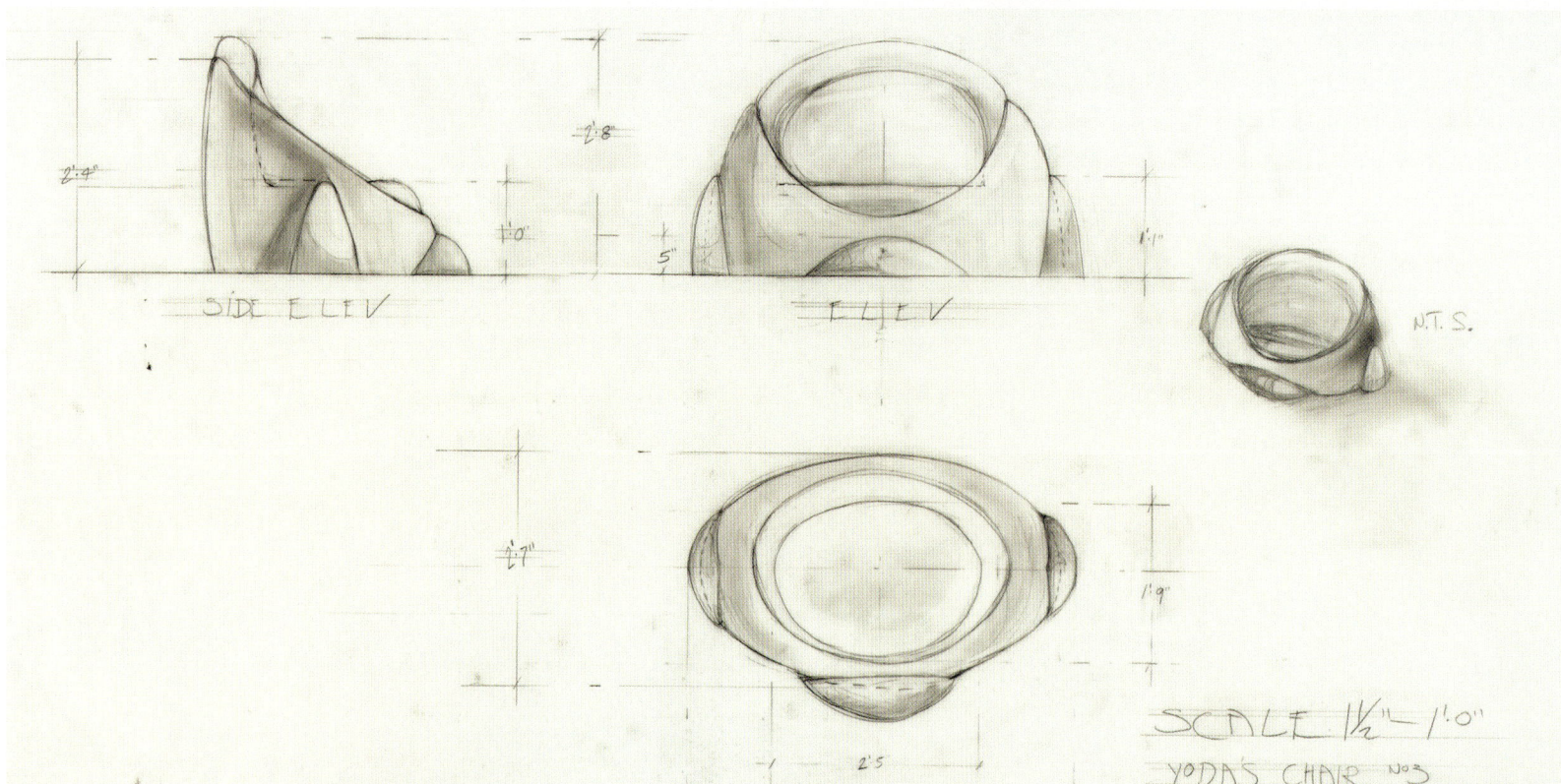

SIDE ELEV   ELEV   N.T.S.

SCALE 1½" - 1'.0"
YODA'S CHAIR Nº3

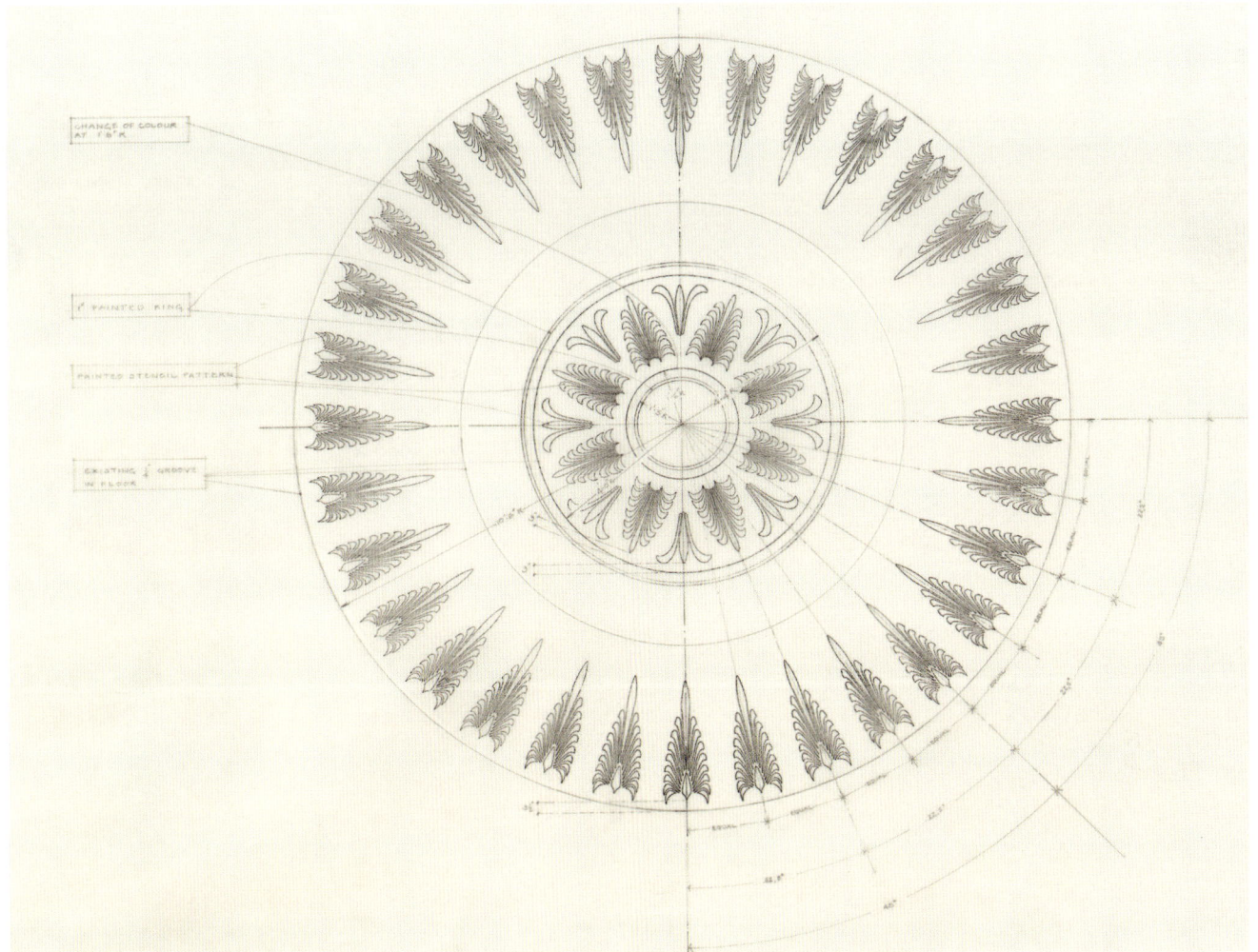

↓ An art department maquette of the Jedi Council set for Episode III, without central window pillars.

SET	COUNCIL CHAMBER, PALACE OF JEDI
DETAIL	MAIN AREA, FLOOR PATTERN
DRG. NO.	711
DATE	AUGUST 22 1997
DRAWN BY	HELEN XENOPOULOS & REMO TOZZI

↓ Concept art of the Jedi Council was drawn by Ed Natividad, 1997.

↓ The Jedi Council set was constructed at Leavesden.

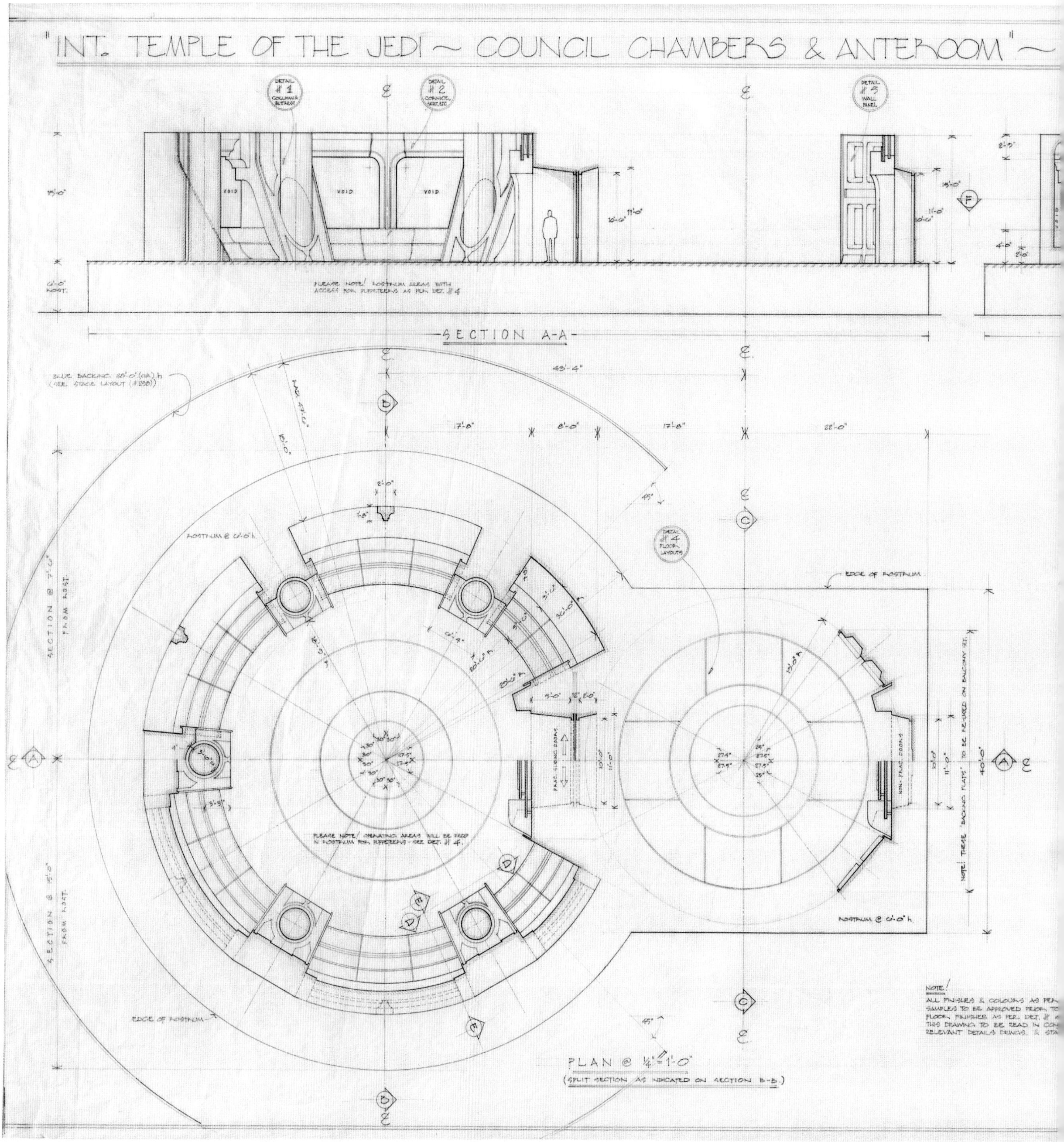

"INT. TEMPLE OF THE JEDI ~ COUNCIL CHAMBERS & ANTEROOM" ~

SECTION A-A

PLAN @ ¼"=1'-0"

(SPLIT SECTION AS INDICATED ON SECTION B-B.)

AN & ELEVATIONS ~ SCALE ¼"=1'-0"

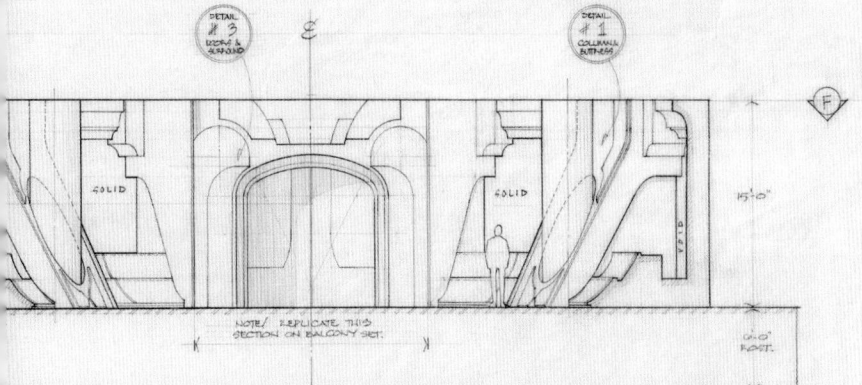

DETAIL #3 DOORS & SURROUND

DETAIL #1 COLUMNS & PLINTHS

SOLID

SOLID

15'-0"

NOTE/ REPLICATE THIS SECTION ON BALCONY SET.

— SECTION B-B —

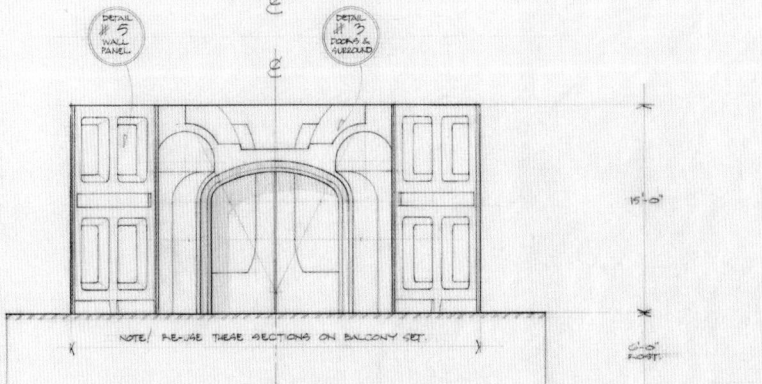

DETAIL #5 WALL PANEL

DETAIL #3 DOORS & SURROUND

15'-0"

NOTE/ RE-USE THESE SECTIONS ON BALCONY SET.

— SECTION C-C —

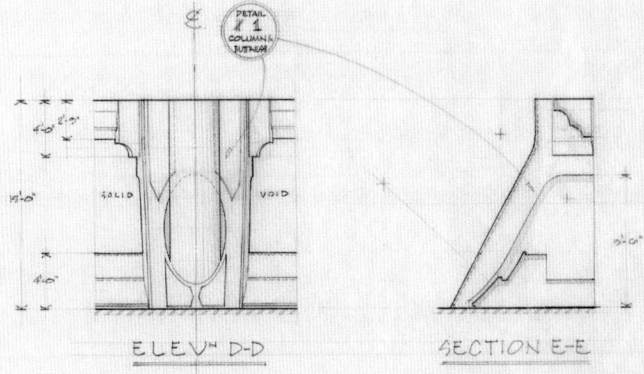

DETAIL #1 COLUMNS & PLINTHS

SOLID

VOID

ELEVⁿ D-D

SECTION E-E

STAR WARS 01	294
TEMPLE OF THE JEDI ~ COUNCIL CHAMBERS & ANTEROOM	JC/JA
PLAN & ELEVATIONS	¼"=1'-0"

SET	TEMPLE OF JEDI, COUNCIL CHAMBERS
DETAIL	PLAN & ELEVATIONS
DRG. NO.	294
DATE	MAY 12 1997
DRAWN BY	GARY TOMKINS

EPISODE I VEHICLES

Most of the vehicles and spaceships in Episode I are CG. Even Darth Maul's Sith speeder was a metal work and plywood shape covered in blue fabric (no. 316), later replaced with a detailed digital version, right down to the control console (although the practical version did have an adjustable headrest).

A "hero" droid tank, on the other hand, was built full-sized and placed in the Theed Plaza constructed on the Leavesden backlot. Working from a concept by Doug Chiang, original trilogy veteran Fred Hole drew up several blueprints in the art department. "Fred was great to have back; he had just a really nice hand," said Bocquet. "He loved the technology. He just loved the gadgets and the gizmos. He loved drawing that sort of semi-technical engineering work, but with a bit of flair."

Made primarily from polystyrene foam, the tank was placed on wheels so it could be repositioned wherever needed. "It was quite a stunning prop in the end, that droid tank," said Russell. "And one of the few objects that we actually made in toto. There's no CG add-ons. We had it on wheels because we were always pushing it around the back of the lot."

Also pushed around the backlot was the "Naboo Speeder One" (no. 59 on page 245). Built with an aerofoil on its back to support an unmanned gun in some scenes, the re-dressable speeder was to have engines and wings made by the plaster shop with a steel frame extending through the wings to support the engines.

"I find that documents like the speeder blueprint, which fits all of the plan elevations and parts on one sheet, always look very dramatic," said Russell. "The speeder was actually made in a garage in Hemel Hempstead [northwest of London] by Michael Kelm, a model maker, and his daughter. We were getting prices for this to be made by various people, and he said he would do it for a lot less than anyone was prepared to, so he hired a garage and built it there."

ABOVE AND TOP The full-sized prop of the tank is seen in Theed Plaza with visible wheels.

↑ A final frame shows the levitating tank with all the VFX added.

↓ Concept art by Doug Chiang depicts the Trade Federation tank, 1995.

SET	SITH SPEEDER
DETAIL	METAL WORK & PLYWOOD PROFILE
DRG. NO.	316
DATE	MAY 16 1997
DRAWN BY	NEIL MORFITT

↓ Concept art of Darth Maul's speeder is by Doug Chiang, 1997.

↓ On location, Ray Park (Darth Maul) acts with a prop in the shape of the speeder draped in blue so that ILM would be able to add the vehicle in postproduction.

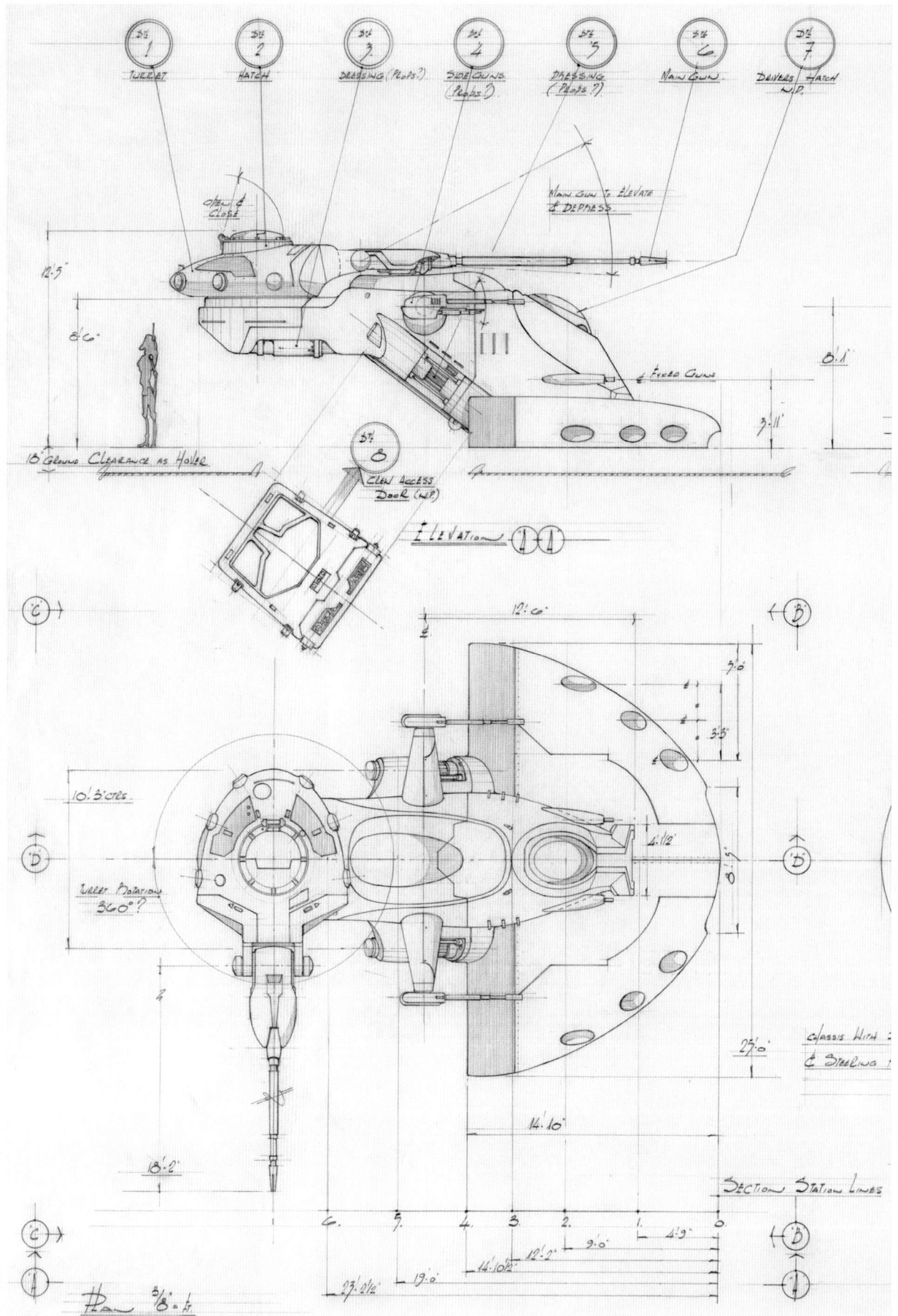

SET	DROID TANK
DETAIL	GENERAL ARRANGEMENT
DRG. NO.	223
DATE	APRIL 29 1997
DRAWN BY	FRED HOLE

Technical drawings of Naboo Speeder One showing Section X-X, Side Elevation, Plan, Front Elevation, Rear Elevation, and Plan Looking Up.

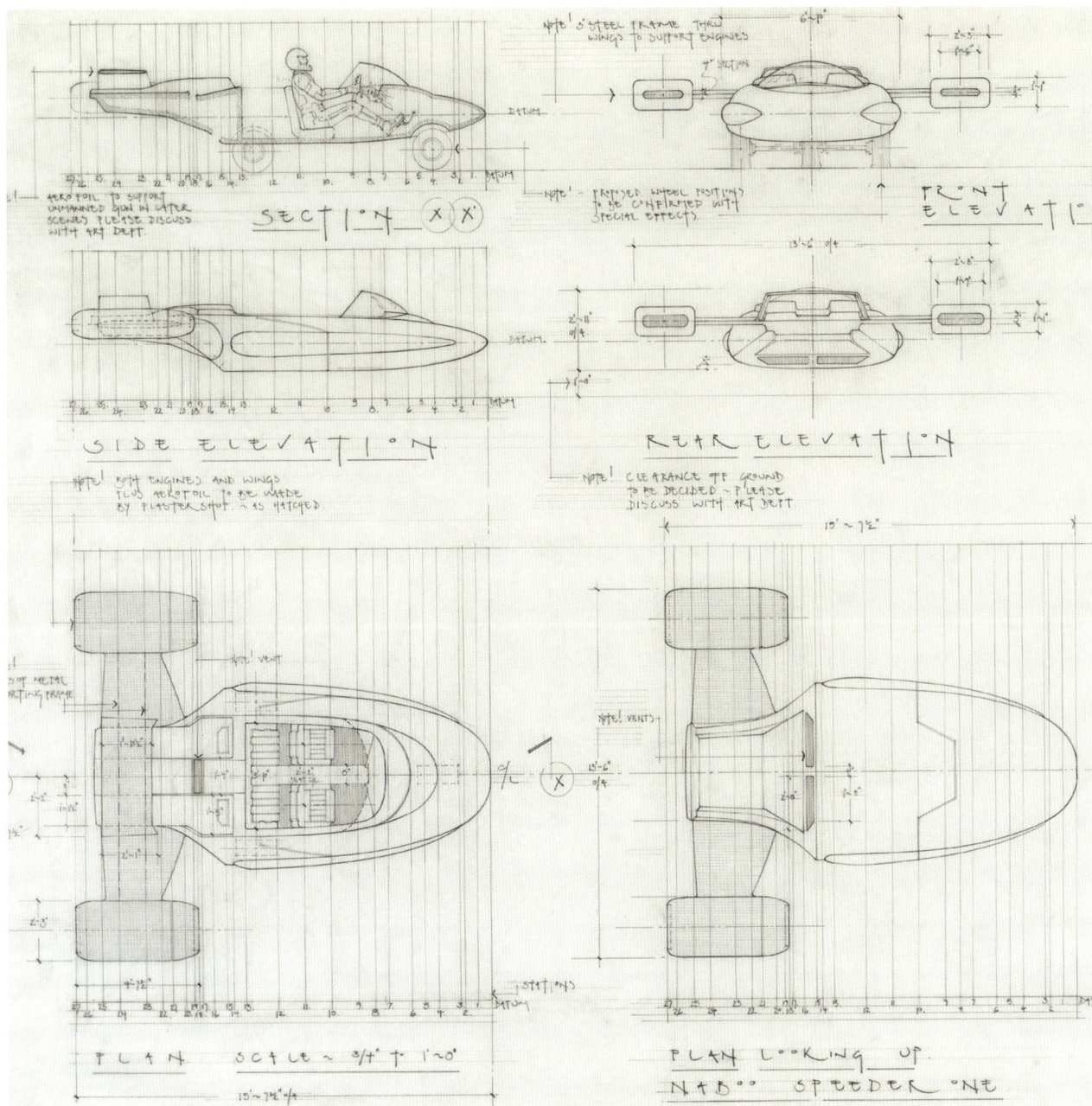

SET	NABOO SPEEDER ONE
DETAIL	ELEVATION & SECTIONS
DRG. NO.	59
DATE	MARCH 3 1997
DRAWN BY	ROD MCLEAN

↓ Chiang's illustration of the Naboo military speeder dates from the same day in December 1996.

↓ Preparatory concept sketches of the Naboo landspeeder are by Doug Chiang, December 1996.

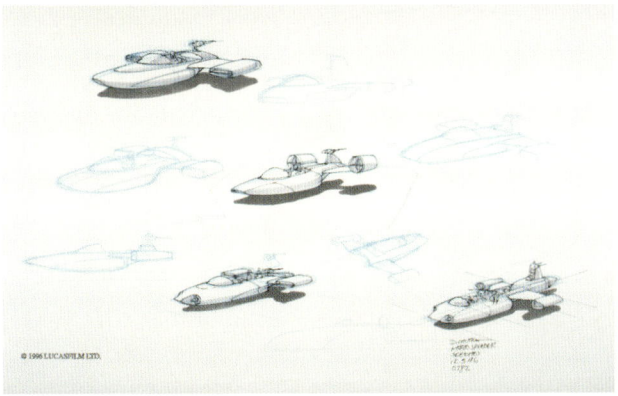

D. CHIANG
NABOO MILITARY SPEEDER
12.5.96
0783

THEED MAIN HANGAR

The Phantom Menace closes with a multipart climactic battle: Gungans fight droids in a massive land war; an aerial dogfight takes place in space between Naboo pilots and Trade Federation drones; two Jedi duel a single Sith in a hangar; and Queen Amidala leads a secret raid on Theed Royal Palace. The biggest set in all of this was the Theed hangar (no. 139).

Paul Cross' technical drawing outlines the whole, a quarter of which was actually built on Stage A at Leavesden, making it the largest interior set of Episode I (it was fitting that the studio's converted aerodrome factory temporarily housed a spaceship hangar, albeit a fictional one). One row of seven docking bays with fighters was constructed with an expansive faux marble floor and plaster walls made to resemble stone. Set decorator Peter Walpole and his team used lightweight plastics for details like piping.

"We only built a quarter of it," said Knoll. "It was meant to be symmetrical in both directions, but that's all that got built. Obviously this worked fine for shots in one direction, but then there were a whole bunch of shots looking from the other direction, so I tried to convince George that we should shoot them in a certain way and then mirror everything. But when we started

trying to figure out how to do that, everybody was getting confused about screen direction. No one could figure it out. George said, 'No, no, I'll just shoot this.' So for those reverse shots we ended up shooting characters in front of blue screen, even though we had a set that represented what it was meant to be."

An intriguing blueprint in the Archives (no. 527) reveals another plan that never came to fruition: a real-world helicopter meant to be redressed as a revamped spacecraft. To the practical bottom half, the art department planned to add radar, front struts, painted decals, and a fuel line. Its top half was to be extended by matte paintings. In some shots, the helicopter would be lifted up by cables. "I don't think they actually ever made it," said Knoll. "*GoldenEye* had shot at Leavesden right before Episode I, so the helicopter was probably left over from that shoot."

In post, ILM completed the hangar with many more ships and digital matte paintings that extended the set and the queen's ship. For those scenes with the latter, only its boarding ramp and landing gear existed as real props and sets in the hangar above the city planet of Coruscant.

↓ The giant hangar set was photographed as it was being constructed on Stage A at Leavesden.

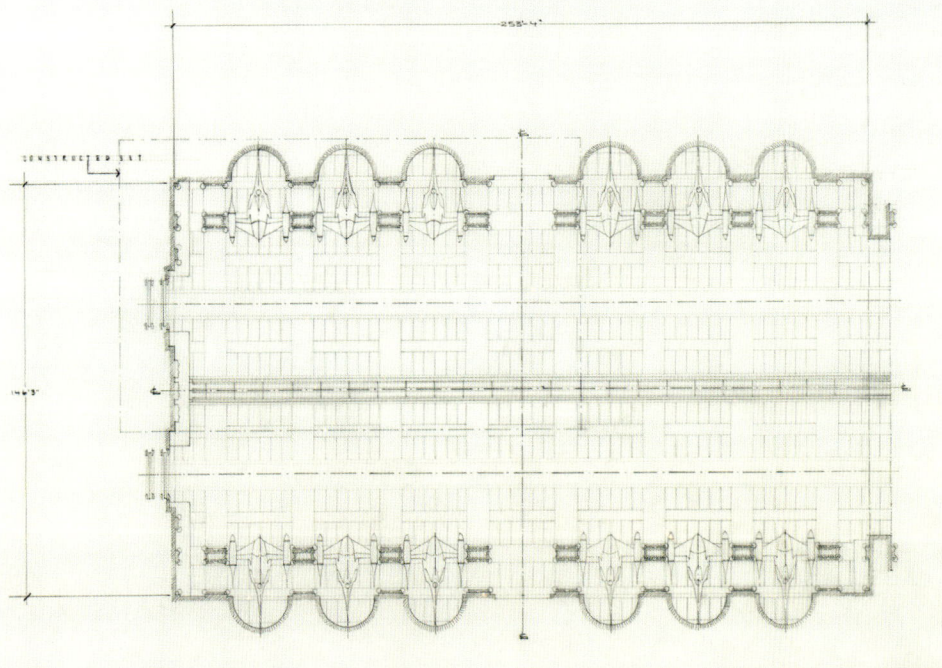

SET	THEED MAIN HANGAR
DETAIL	MAIN PLAN (INFORMATION ONLY)
DRG. NO.	139
DATE	APRIL 8 1997
DRAWN BY	PAUL CROSS

↑ On-set photography shows the hangar doors closed. Filming took place on Stage A at Leavesden, July 1997.

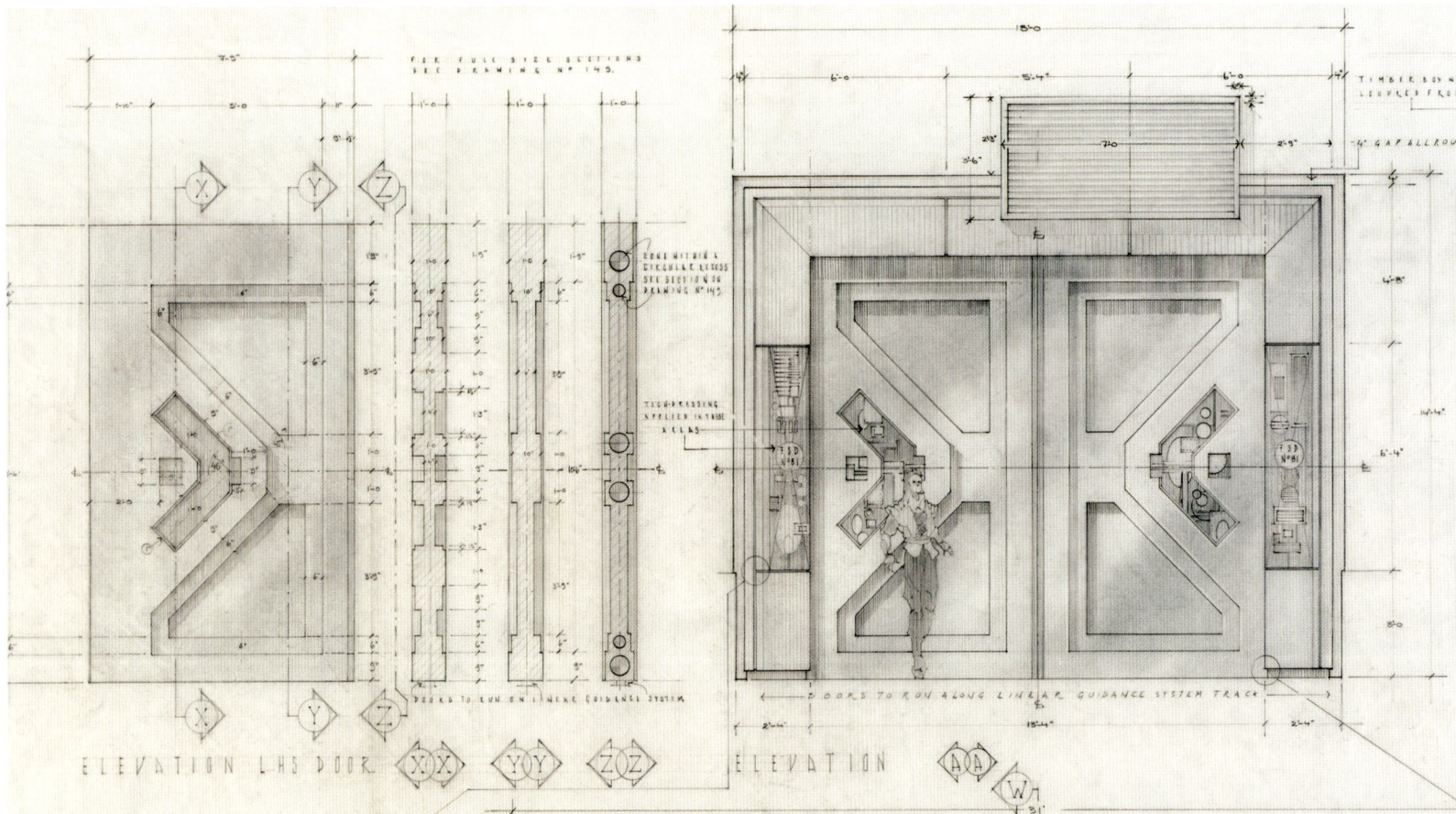

↑ Within the hangar set was a pair of giant doors that open to reveal Darth Maul. At 14 feet, 4 inches high, the doors were to run along a "linear guidance track" and to have tech dressing applied to certain cavities, such as mechanical parts recycled from aircraft scrap.

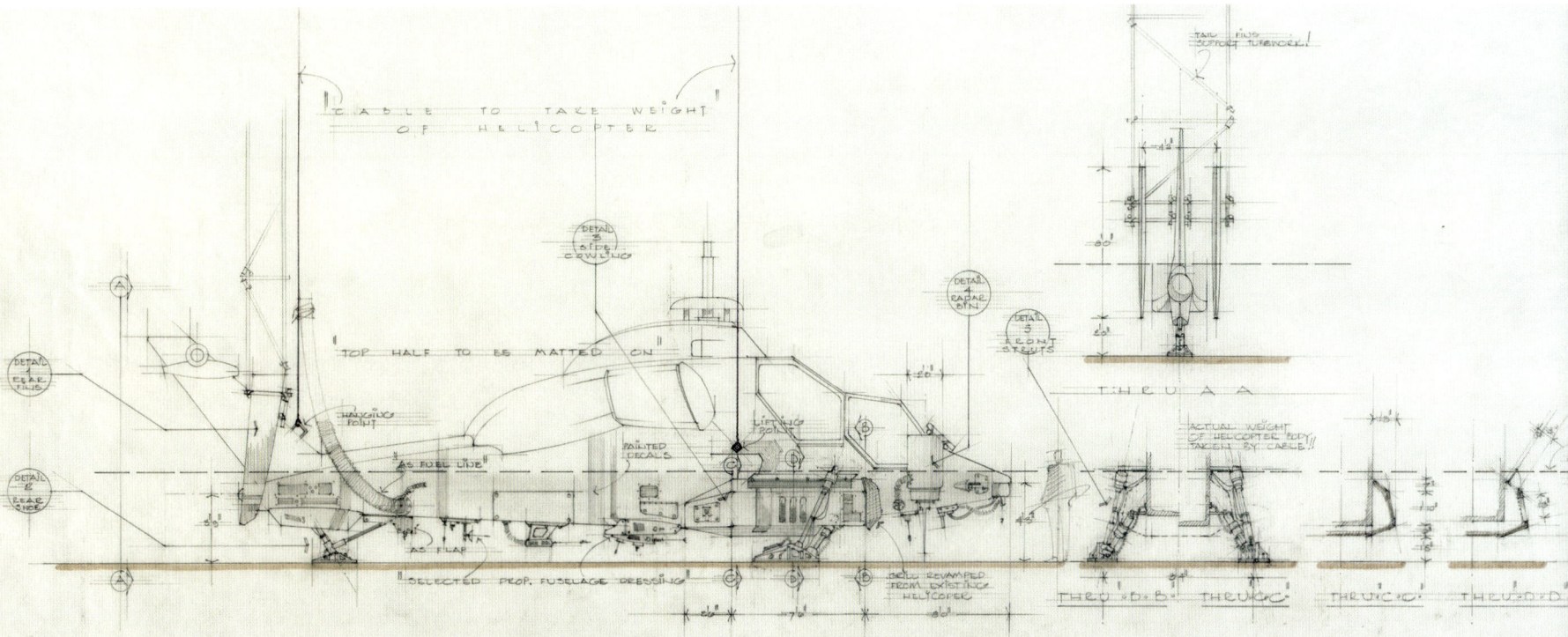

TUNISIA LOCATION

For *Star Wars*: Episode II *Attack of the Clones*, production designer Bocquet moved his art department from the UK to Australia, taking some of his staff, but also employing several local draftspeople and art directors at Fox Studios in Sydney.

In the second movie of the prequel trilogy, Anakin Skywalker (Hayden Christensen) returns to Tatooine. Searching for his mother, he first hires a rickshaw to take him and Padmé to visit his old master, Watto. Based on Marc Gabbana's concept art, the practical transport was built on a trolley frame with tires suitable for operation over soft sand, as Lucas once again took production to Tunisia. On the day of the shoot, a pickup truck would pull the rickshaw. Fred Hole's blueprint (no. 462 on page 250) also notes that parts of the rickshaw were to be painted blue, so that ILM could later make it look like it was floating above the ground being pulled by a droid.

"Another Fred Hole classic," said Russell. "Not quite such a complicated one as the droid tank, but he just has such a sweet hand. You know, he could make a toilet seat look good."

From Watto, Anakin learns that his mother has married a man named Cliegg Lars, so the Jedi Knight travels to the Lars' homestead, where audiences first met Luke Skywalker in the original film more than two decades before. "I think the biggest moment was when we all walked onto that location near Nefta, Tunisia," said Bocquet. "We had reproduced the homestead igloo out there, but it was only really Anthony Daniels, myself, and George who had ever been part of that world, and of course the only two people who had been there were George and Anthony. George never went to see the set before we shot it and I have to say, and Anthony said it, too, that George looked visibly moved when he walked out onto that completed and dressed location. It was a nice thing. I suppose for him that was a big moment of his life, remembering that whole environment and establishing *Star Wars*, because it's so iconic now. The rim of the crater [seen in] the shot with the two suns, it was still there. We had to replenish it a bit, but it was still there."

Indeed, once again, the homestead was a combination of two locations: the berm and surface "igloo" outside of Nefta and the Sidi Driss hotel pit in Matmata, though this time around, thanks to the advances made in effects, the surface and pit could be combined in one shot. "There's a bar in the hotel, and on the wall inside the bar, there's a bunch of pictures of the set being used in *Star Wars*," said Knoll. "I think there are some articles up about it, too."

Art director Phil Harvey's blueprint (no. 25) notes that the homestead layout plan was based on approximated survey measurements and that all measurements were to be rechecked on site. Boxes and crates were to be added as dressing, along with a vaporizer cluster (no. 02), with blue and red bulbs, which recalls the very first blueprint of the "Oil Rig Christmas Tree" (see pages 26 and 27) created for the first *Star Wars*. Said Russell: "I love the drawing of the old vaporizer, the homage to the original."

SET	HOMESTEAD LAYOUT
DETAIL	PLAN LAYOUT
DRG. NO.	25
DATE	DECEMBER 9 1999
DRAWN BY	PHIL D. HARVEY

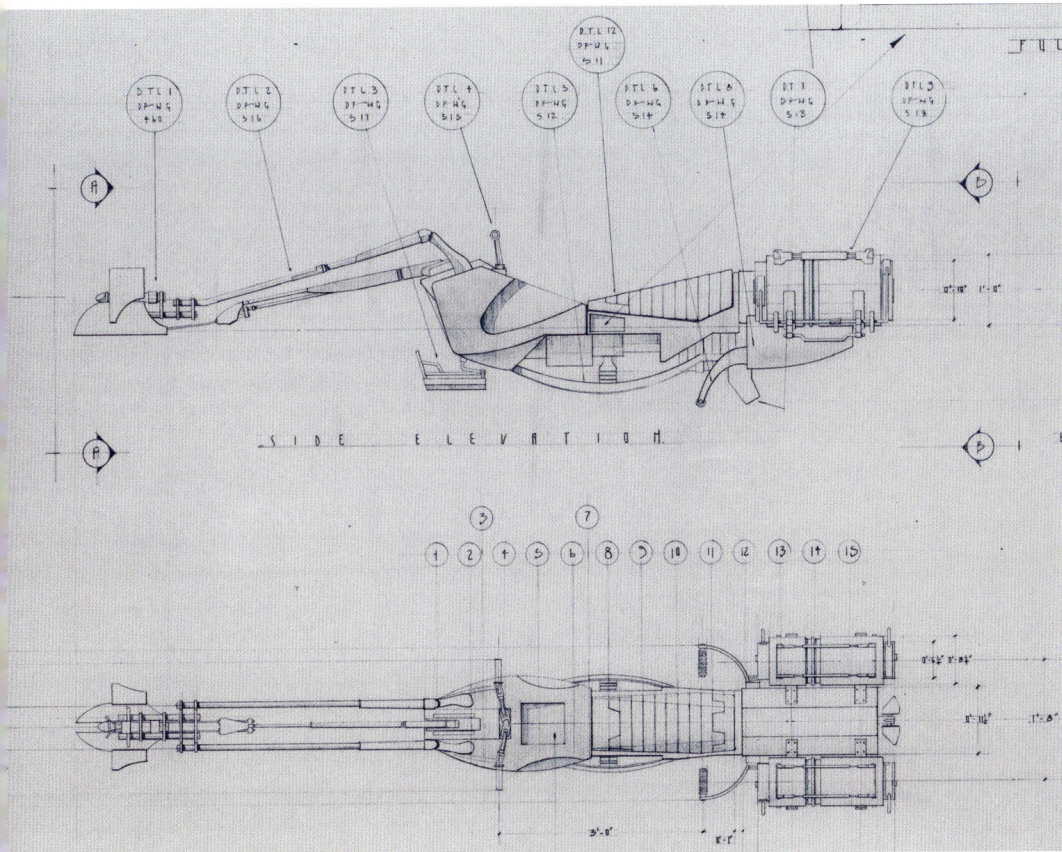

SET	SPEEDER BIKE
DETAIL	GENERAL ARRANGEMENTS
DRG. NO.	461
DATE	JUNE 15 2000
DRAWN BY	MARK BARTHOLOMEW

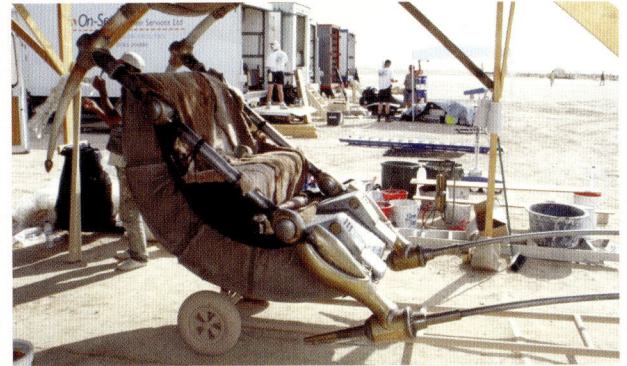

↑ The rickshaw prop had wheels that would be digitally painted out, as are seen in this reference photo taken on location in Tunisia, September 2000.

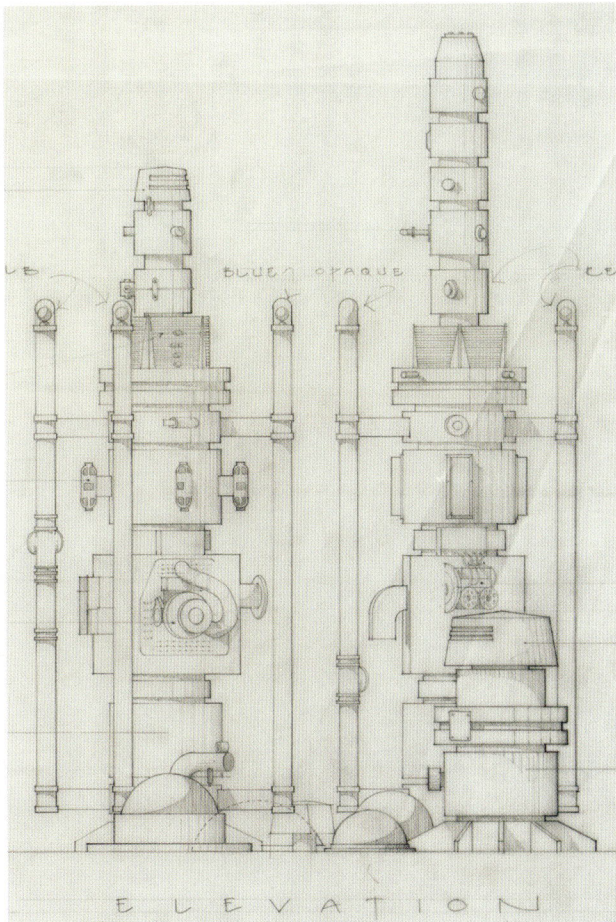

→ The full-sized speeder bike prop was placed before the "igloo" on location.

↓ The vaporizer cluster is seen on location at the Sidi Driss Hotel in Matmata, where production returned in September 2000 for the first time since the original *Star Wars*.

SET	LARS HOMESTEAD
DETAIL	VAPORIZER CLUSTER
DRG. NO.	02
DATE	DECEMBER 7 1999
DRAWN BY	B. SCOTT

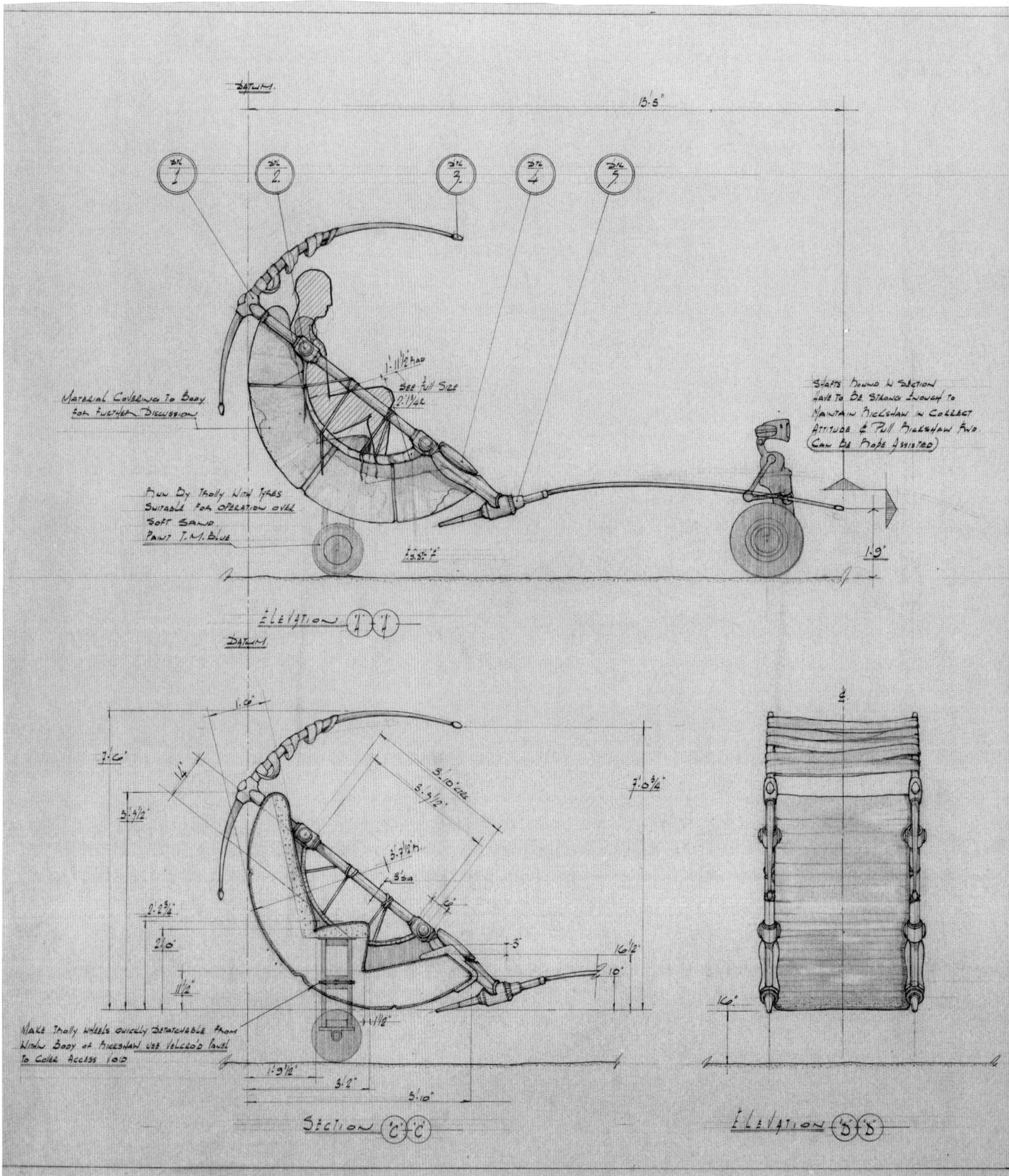

DATUM.

15·5"

1·11½ HAD
SEE FULL SIZE
2·13/42

MATERIAL COVERING TO BODY
FOR FURTHER DISCUSSION

RUN BY TROLLY WITH TYRES
SUITABLE FOR OPERATION OVER
SOFT SAND
PAINT T.M. BLUE

13·5½ 7"

SHAFTS BOUND IN SECTION
HAVE TO BE STRONG ENOUGH TO
MAINTAIN RICKSHAW IN CORRECT
ATTITUDE & PULL RICKSHAW FWD
(CAN BE PROBE ASSISTED)

1·9°

ELEVATION A A

DATUM

1·0°

7·6°

3·3½°

3·10° CRS

3·9½°

3·7½ h

3 DIA

7·0¾°

2·0¾°

2·0°

11½°

5

16½°

10°

MAKE TROLLY WHEELS QUICKLY DETATCHABLE FROM
WITHIN BODY OF RICKSHAW USE VELCRO'D PANEL
TO COVER ACCESS VOID

1·11½°

1·9½°

3·2°

5·10°

SECTION C C

16°

ELEVATION B B

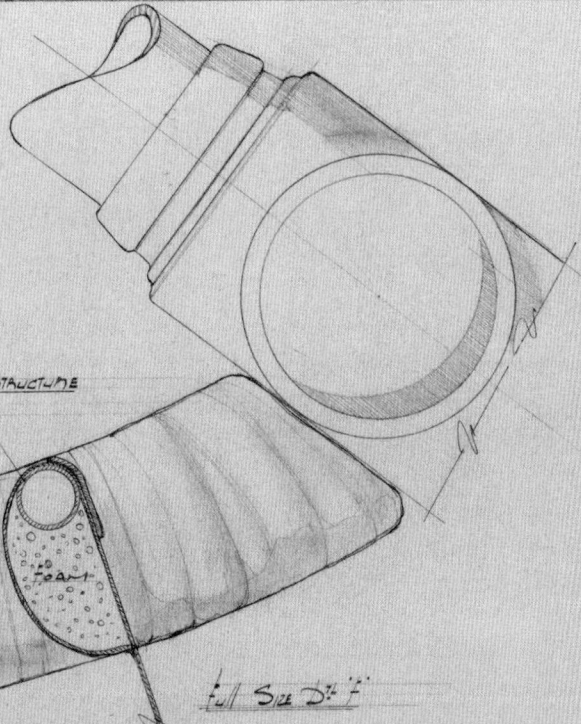

TUBE STRUCTURE

FOAM

Full Size Det F

Elevation ③ ⑧

Plan ⓒ

Set RICKSHAW +DROID
MARC GABBANA
05-25-2000
147

AVAILABLE SEATING
SPACE 3·60'

SEAT

PERFORATED ALUMINIUM FLOOR
FIND NEAREST STOCK SHEETING

OVERHEAD CLOTH OMITTED FOR CLARITY

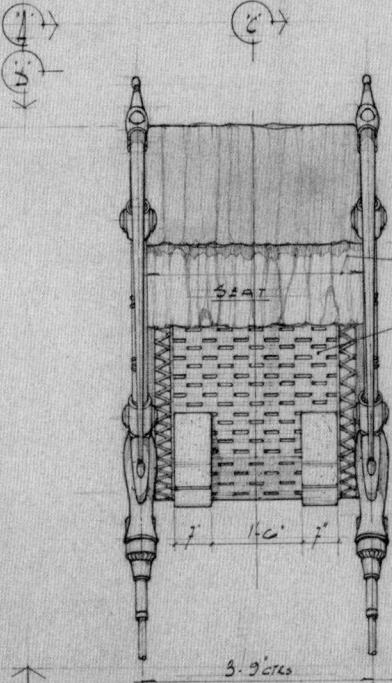

3·9'CTRS

NOTES

1/. RICKSHAW WILL HAVE TO PERFORM OVER SAND
IN THE TUNISIAN DESSERT IN EXTREME HEAT.

2/ RICKSHAW MIGHT BE PARTLY DISMANTLED FOR
SHIPPING. WILL INVESTIGATE.

3/ WEIGHT WILL BE A FACTOR FOR SUCCESSFUL OPERATION
USE LIGHTWEIGHT MATERIAL CONSISTANT WITH
STRENGTH

4/ RICKSHAW BODY CONSTRUCTED OVER STRONG LIGHT FRAME
CLAD WITH DENSE POLY. ALL COVERED WITH SELECTED
CLOTH MATERIAL

5/ PAINT TO SPECIFICATION. COLOURS TO BE ADVISED

6/ PROGRESS DELIVERY SCHEDULE TO FOLLOW

STAR WARS EPISODE II			DRWG NO. 462.
SET TUNISIA LOCATION			SET NO.
DETAILS RICKSHAW			SCALE 1 of 6 Fs
PRODUCTION DESIGNER GAVIN BOCQUET	PROD.	ART	D.O.P
DRAWN BY F. HOLE	C. MAN	SET DEC	ELEC.
DATE DRAWN 2 JUNE 2000	CARPS	PROPS	SFX
DATE ISSUED	PLASTER	DRAPES	VFX
STAGE	PAINT	SIGN	MODEL
LOCATION	RIGGER	SCENIC	GRAPHICS
	SCULPTOR	METAL	COMPUTER

SET	TUNISIA LOCATION	DATE	JUNE 2 2000
DETAIL	RICKSHAW	DRAWN BY	FRED HOLE
DRG. NO.	462		

EPISODE II VEHICLES

Notes on Anakin's Coruscant speeder (no. 86) indicate that the control unit was to pivot up to allow access to its seat and that its front would have a wraparound Perspex windscreen. The art department in Sydney built a beautiful section of the yellow airspeeder (an homage to the yellow hot-rod of Lucas' *American Graffiti*) on a rig. ILM then had to take that vehicle and make it fly through the sky lanes of Coruscant. To do so, Knoll's team had to digitally recreate exactly what had been built on the soundstage.

"The drama was that we very carefully photo-surveyed what got built as a set piece, with the idea that we were going to match it exactly with the CG model," said Knoll. "But the photo survey was only kind of loosely referred to. Despite all the assurances that our CG department had worked very precisely to match it, our digital model didn't match what actually got built. One surface was too high and one was too narrow and the curvature didn't match there and the windshield was the wrong shape. You know, like a million little things that just made all those shots really hard."

Within the Sydney art department, technical changes were also occurring. While making Episode II, it became clear that CAD and other software programs could be useful when solving certain kinds of problems. "The Jedi fighter that Obi-Wan used [no. 56] was one of the last space fighters we did as a pencil drawing, by hand," said Russell. "As clean and clinical as it looks, there was an awful lot of preparation to arrive at this document, in order to understand how a sphere is transcribed by the wing root or how jet pods are to be attached, and the like.

"Nowadays we would probably do this by not actually drawing it at all but by creating a digital model, because we'd then understand instantly how those shapes come together in a way to express a drawing; whereas before, you could draw for two weeks, just to get to a moment where you'd realize you'd made a serious error and have to start all over again."

↑ The full-sized prop for Anakin's airspeeder, or "Coruscant airspeeder II," is painted and dressed on Stage 2 for filming at Fox Studios, Sydney, July 2000.

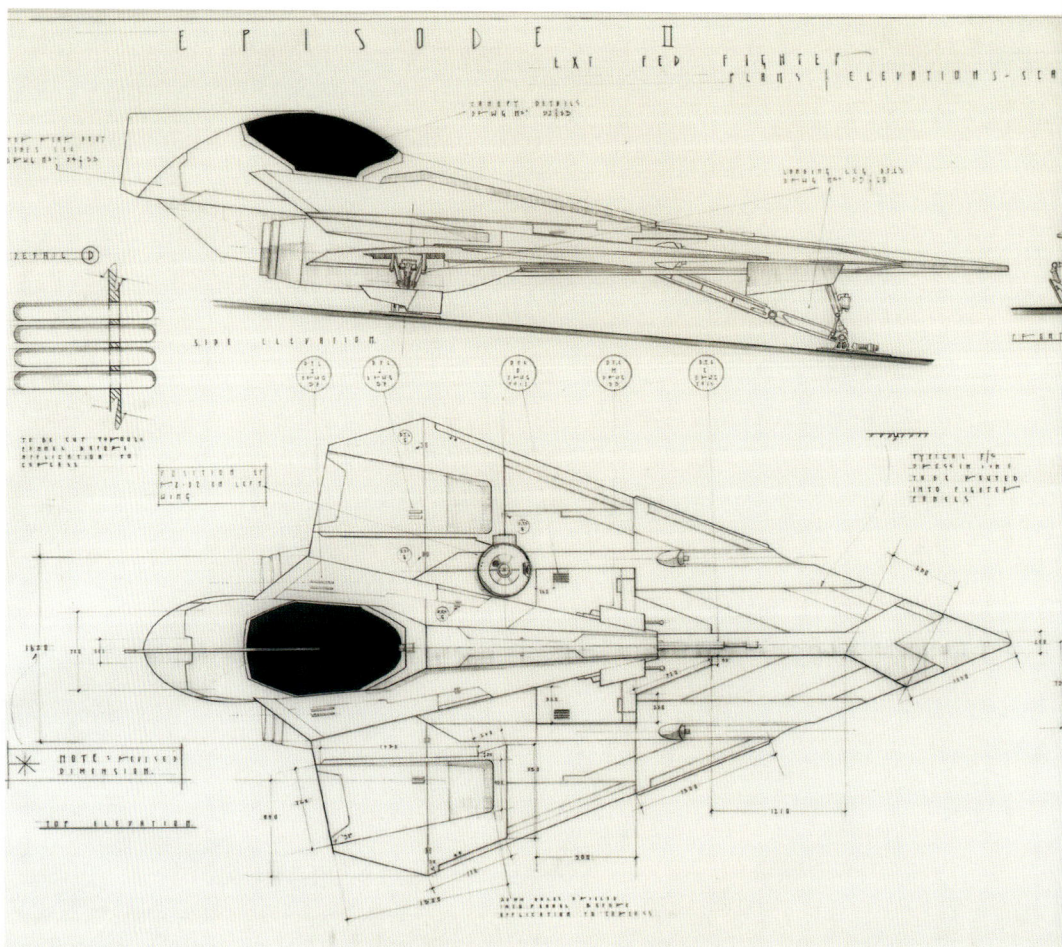

→ Mistakenly marked as a "Fed Fighter," the Jedi fighter's main body was to be dressed with suitable found objects.

SET	JEDI FIGHTER
DETAIL	PLAN & ELEVATIONS
DRG. NO.	56
DATE	MARCH 28 2000
DRAWN BY	MARK BARTHOLOMEW

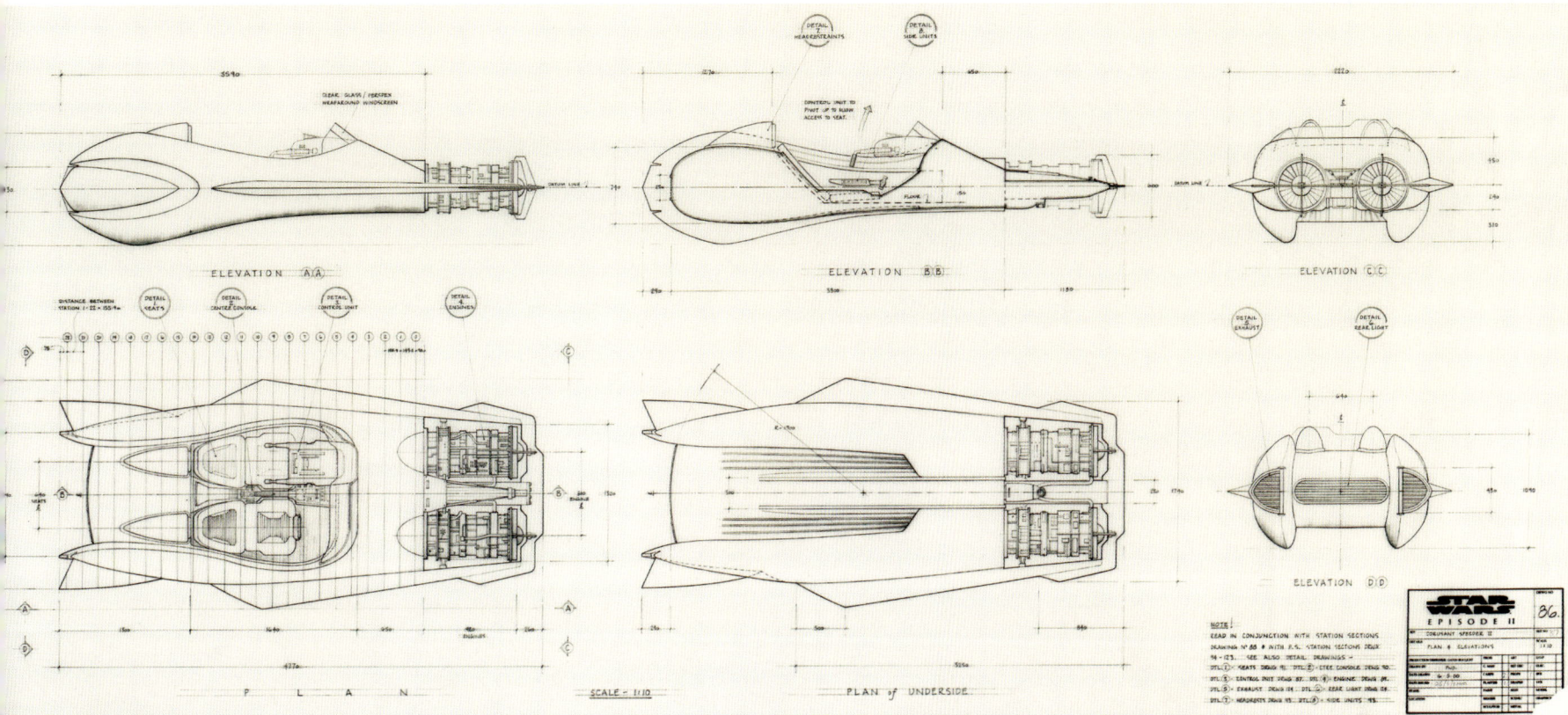

SET	CORUSCANT SPEEDER II (ANAKIN'S)
DETAIL	PLAN & ELEVATIONS
DRG. NO.	86
DATE	MAY 26 2000
DRAWN BY	PETER N. DORME

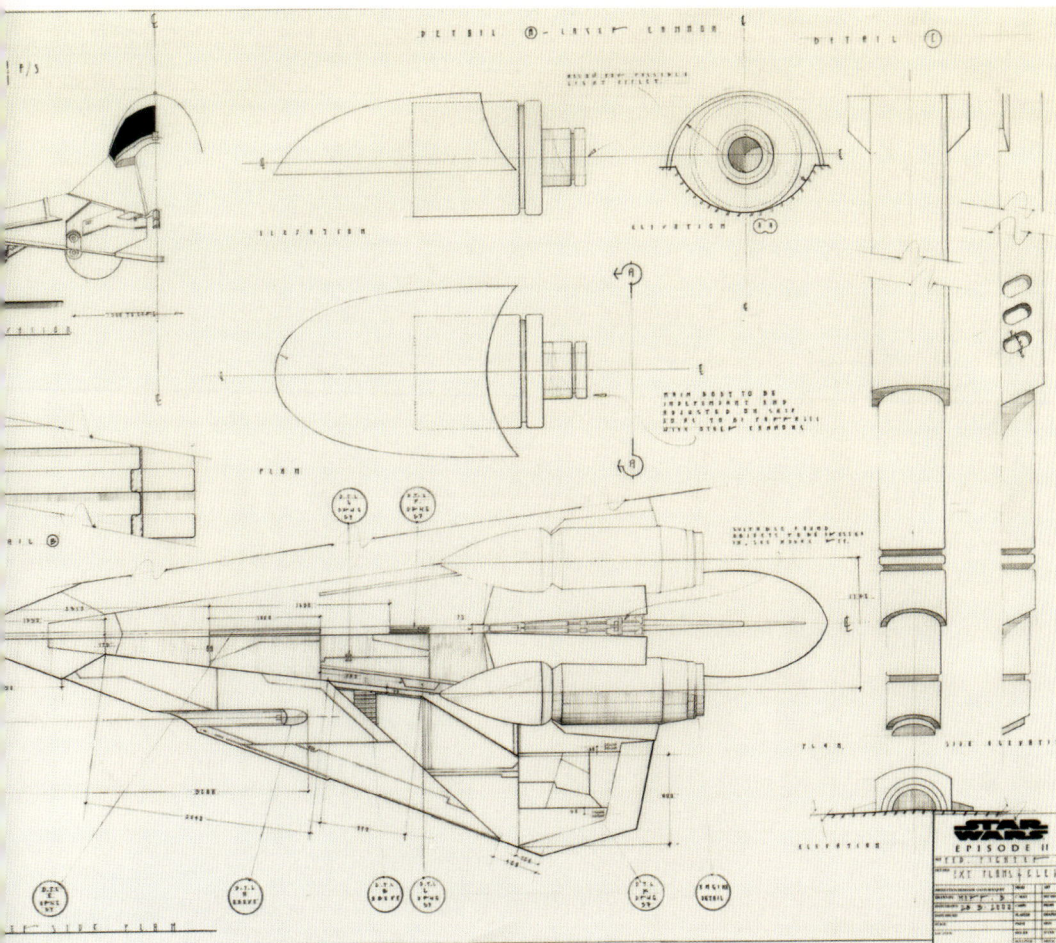

In fact, in the Archives there exist several blueprints of the Jedi starfighter, which was built as a full-sized, partially dressed ship, and as a fully detailed cockpit for close-ups.

"The threshold seems to be the Episode II fighter," added Russell. "Because straight after that you've got the Solar Sailer [no. 483 on page 254], which was expressed as a digital drawing. Jacinta Leong is one of the top draftspeople in Australia and she's a very good exponent of that particular technique."

Also built as a full-sized set, the Solar Sailer would nevertheless undergo changes in post when its cockpit bubble was moved digitally so it abutted against the body of the ship. Otherwise, it would've looked like Count Dooku, after boarding, had to crawl through an impossibly narrow portion of the ship.

↑ The full-sized Jedi starfighter prop is in construction at Fox Studios, Sydney, Australia, spring 2000.

← Concept art of the Jedi starfighter is by Jay Shuster, 2000.

↑ Doug Chiang completed this starfighter concept in November 1999.

→ This enhanced final frame depicts the starfighter being attacked by Jango Fett in his Firespray ship.

SIDE ELEVATION
SCALE 1:20

PLAN
SCALE 1:20

COCKPIT BUBBLE

↓ The full-sized sailer prop is at Fox Studios, Sydney, on Stage 6, where filming took place in August 2000.

12 13 14 15 16 17 18 19 20 21 22 23 24 25 26 27 28 29 30

17000

CANOPY

① CANOPY

② REAR DOOR
486

③ RAMP
487

LANDING GEAR ④
and setback mechanicals

approximate line
of LEVEL GROUND

LANDING GEAR (SKID) in front - refer
to detail on separate sheet.

12 13 14 15 16 17 18 19 20 21 22 23 24 25 26 27 28 29 30

R19520

CANOPY

RAMP

STAR WARS
EPISODE II

DRWG NO.
483

SET: SOLAR SAILER (in HANGAR)   SET NO: 35

DETAILS: PLAN,   SCALE:
SIDE ELEVATION   1:20

PRODUCTION DESIGNER: GAVIN BOCQUET	PROD.	ART	D.O.P.
DRAWN BY: JACINTA LEONG	C.MAN	SET DEC	ELEC.
DATE DRAWN: 06 JUN 00	CARPS	PROPS	SFX
DATE ISSUED: 07 JUN 00	PLASTER	DRAPES	VFX
STAGE: 2	PAINT	SIGN	MODEL
LOCATION	RIGGER	SCENIC	GRAPHICS
	SCULPTOR	METAL	COMPUTER

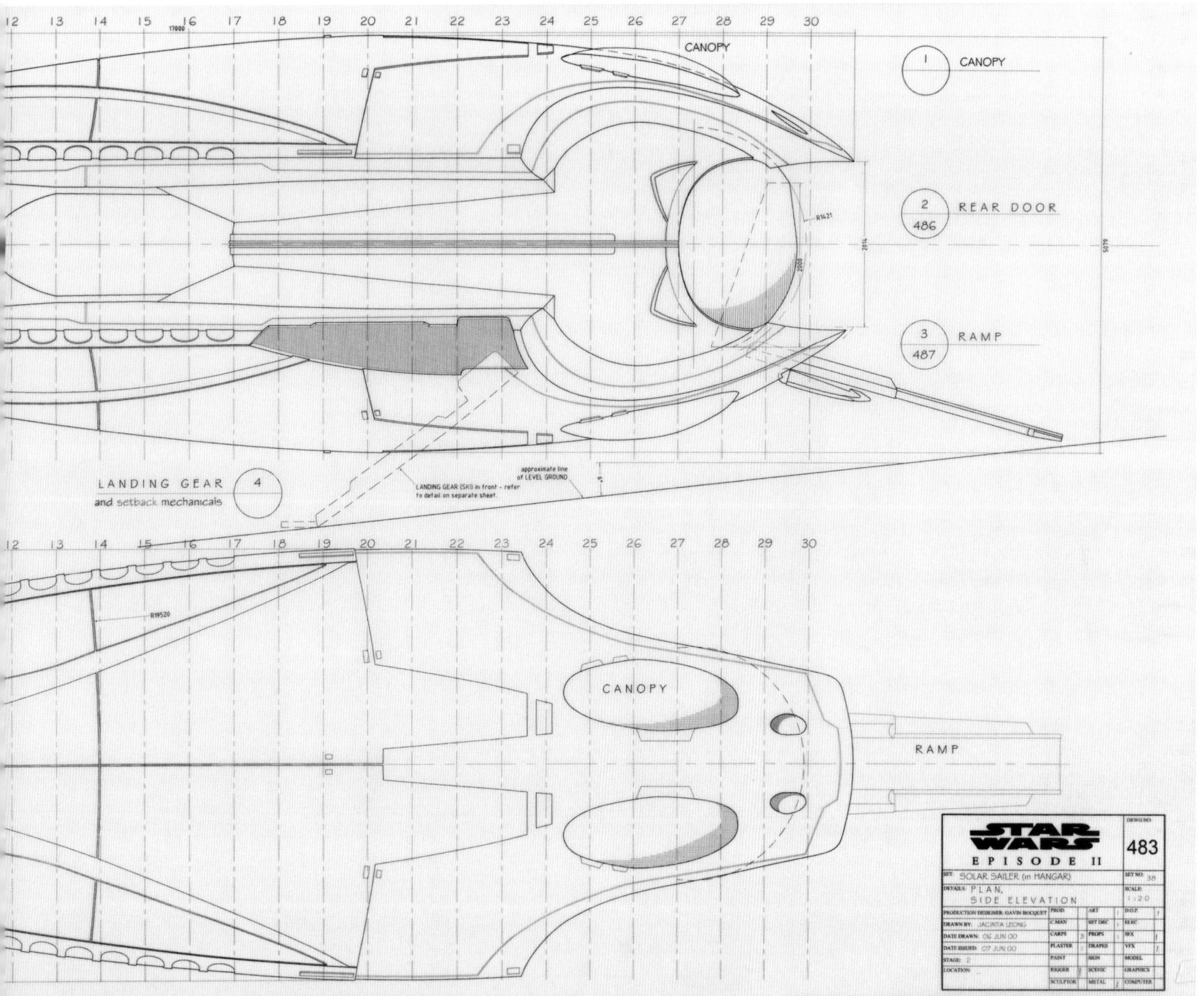

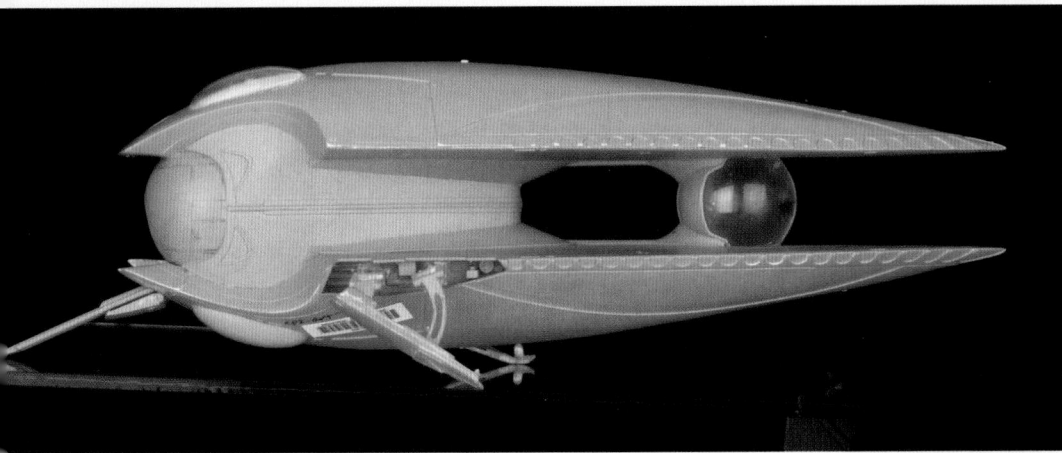

SET	SOLAR SAILER (IN HANGAR)
DETAIL	PLAN, SIDE ELEVATION
DRG. NO.	483
DATE	JUNE 6 2000
DRAWN BY	JACINTA LEONG

↑ A concept model at ILM
depicts Count Dooku's
Solar Sailer.

→ The Solar Sailer is
under construction.

JEDI STARFIGHTER

Production transitioned easily into *Star Wars: Episode III Revenge of the Sith*. It was recorded in the same studio by the same crew in the same country, with many of the same actors. Although three years separated the two shoots, for most of the cast and crew it felt like they had taken a short break and everyone soon fell into old routines after a couple of weeks. Once again, set decorating, props, construction, paint, fiberglass, and other departments—about 400 people strong—were overseen by production designer Gavin Bocquet.

The third chapter of the prequel trilogy opens with a spectacular shot of two Jedi starfighters flying through an epic aerial conflict. As one might expect, the art department in Sydney built only one full-sized starfighter, which was repainted from yellow to red for each respective Jedi pilot. In addition, only one separate cockpit was built for close-ups; Ewan McGregor (Obi-Wan) did his scenes, the set was slightly redressed, then Hayden Christensen (Anakin) performed his lines.

The art department was located in Building 48 at the far eastern end of the Fox Studios lot. During the summer of 2003, the Jedi starfighter, an airspeeder, and couches were located downstairs. Upstairs, in a series of rooms forming a U-like mezzanine around the periphery of the hangar-like building, was Bocquet, his art directors, draftspeople, and set model builders. One room on the ground floor was entirely dedicated to blueprints, hundreds of which hung from racks.

Jacinta Leong executed her two blueprints (no. 142 and 143 on pages 256 and 258) for the starfighter exteriors using a CAD program. "Jacinta's drawing is a great example of how that type of modeling and drafting technology really did help us to create very complex intersections and shapes very accurately," said Russell. "One could export the drawing directly to a computer cutter, for instance, and that component could be created by a machine and arrive ready for assembly."

"CAD is a little more functional in its presentation," said Bocquet, "but has the advantages of speed, versatility, flexibility, and also being able to work in 3D."

"On Episode I, nearly all the drafting was done manually on drawing boards, but by the time you get to Episode III, a serious percentage was being done electronically using various CAD drawing systems," added Russell. "It was probably even a 60 to 40 ratio on a show like *Star Wars*, where you're dealing with a lot of spaceships and high-end interiors. If you look at the progression of blueprints, it's quite interesting that it charts, historically, the change of styles."

"Both technical drawing methods, CAD and the pencil-on-paper technique, are totally valid in today's digital world," Boquets said. "But if CAD does become the more common technique over the coming few years, it is never going to take away the importance of technical drawing itself, however it is done. It still has to be treated with great respect and importance."

FUSELAGE ①   ⓪①②③④⑤⑥⑦

MAIN ENGINE ④
⑩ REAR LEG

STARBOARD
scale 1:10

PORTSIDE ELEV
scale 1:10

↓ A painter touches up the Jedi starfighter at Fox Studios, Sydney.

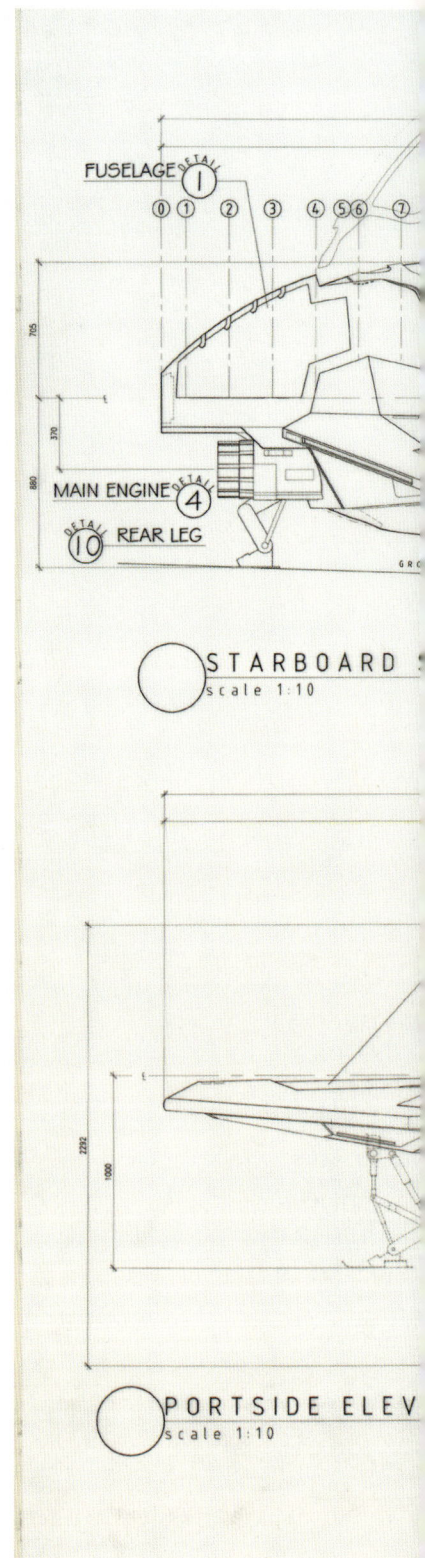

↑ The completed green paint job was for Anakin's ship as it travels to Mustafar; Anakin's fighter would be painted yellow for the opening scenes.

ELEVATION

⑦ DETAIL WINDOW

② DETAIL WING

⑧ DETAIL FRONT LEGS

5470 OVERALL

4285
WING SPAN

1160
FUSELAGE

300°

① DETAIL FUSELAGE

⑤ DETAIL CANNON

② DETAIL WING

⑦ DETAIL WINDOW

⑧ DETAIL FRONT LEGS

③ DETAIL WING FIN & HINGE

NOTE:
UNDERSIDE PLANT ONS to WING
illustrated for completeness of
design only. ILM to use this
information as required.
Read this drawing in conjunction
with drawing separate image, which
indicates extent of build by
CONSTRUCTION.

FRONT ELEVATION
scale 1:10

5470 OVERALL

4825

1530

645

⑬ ⑭ ⑫ ⑪ ⑩ ⑨ ⑧ ⑦ ⑥⑤④ ③ ② ① ⓪

② DETAIL

⑪ DETAIL

280

MAIN ENGINE ④ DETAIL

WING FIN & HINGE ③ DETAIL

PRACTICAL HINGED WING FINS illustrated for completeness of
design only. ILM to use this information as required.
Read this drawing in conjunction with drawing separate image,
which indicates extent of build by CONSTRUCTION.

...ON - with WING FINS OPEN

4285
WING SPAN

1160
FUSELAGE

① DETAIL FUSELAGE

② DETAIL WING

1420

483

470°

517

MAIN ENGINE ④ DETAIL

⑩ DETAIL REAR LEG

1705

370

880

REAR ELEVATION
scale 1:10

STARFIGHTER
ELEVATIONS

NOTE
SOFTEN ALL EDGES with PENCIL ROUNDS.

DRWG NO
142

STAR WARS
EPISODE III

SET	STARFIGHTER		SET NO.	01
DETAILS	GENERAL ARRANGEMENT FRONT, REAR & SIDE ELEVATIONS		SCALE	1:10
PRODUCTION DESIGNER: GAVIN BOCQUET	PROD.	ART	D.O.P.	
DRAWN BY: JACINTA LEONG	C.MAN	SET DEC	ELEC	
DATE DRAWN: 11 APRIL 2003	CARPS	PROPS	SFX	
DATE ISSUED: 15 APRIL 2003	PLASTER	DRAPES	VFX	
STAGE: 04	PAINT	STUDY	MODEL	
LOCATION:	RIGGER	SCENIC	GRAPHICS	
	SCULPTOR	METAL	COMPUTER	

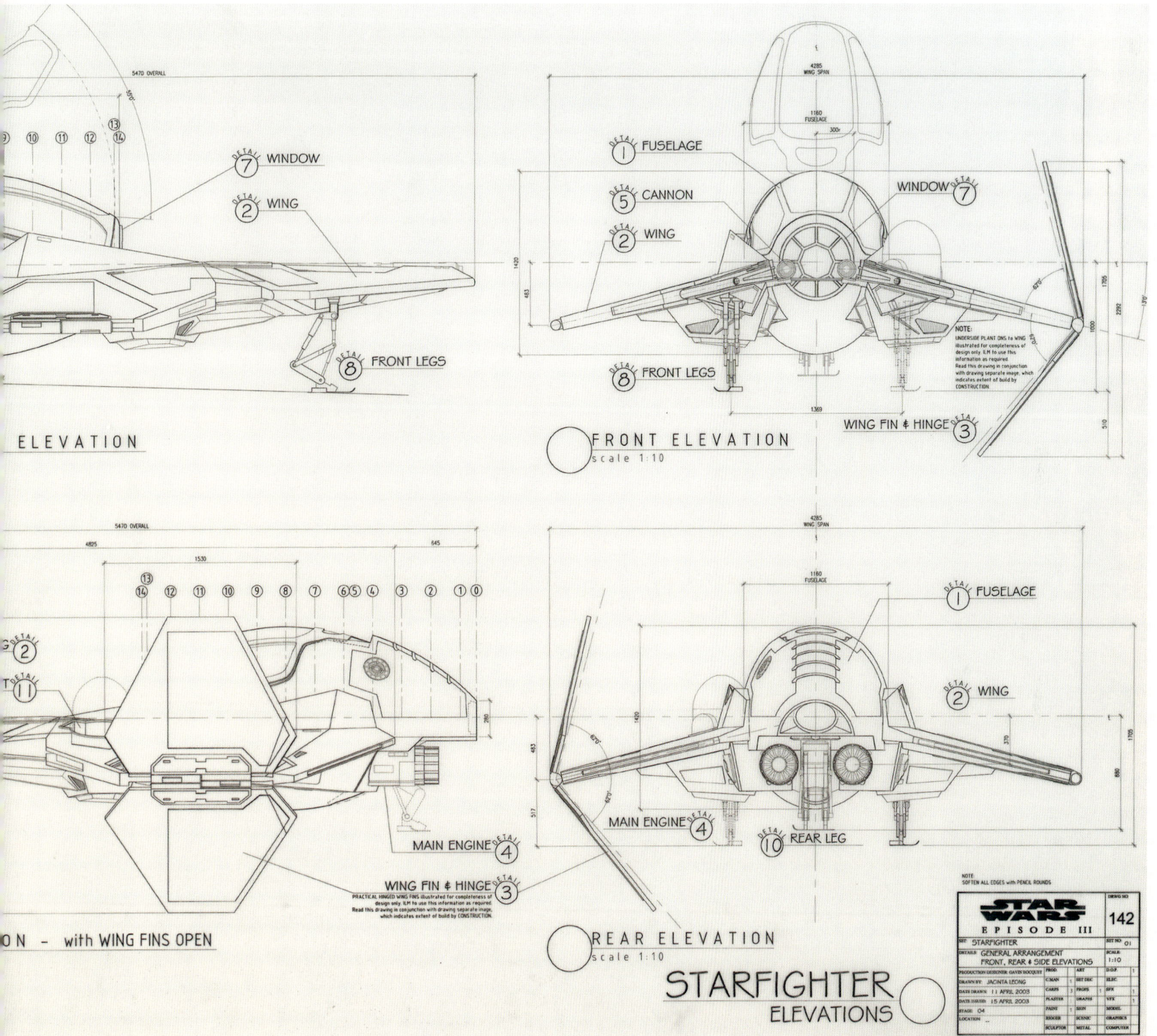

SET	STARFIGHTER
DETAIL	GEN. ARRANGEMENT: FRONT, REAR, & SIDE ELEV.
DRG. NO.	142
DATE	APRIL 11 2003
DRAWN BY	JACINTA LEONG

➜ Concept art
is of the Jedi
starfighter
(version 5) by
Ryan Church.

WING FIN & HINGE ③

WING ②

R2 UNIT ①①

FUSELAGE ①

FIN OPEN

WINDOW ⑦

CANNON ⑤

FIN CLOSED

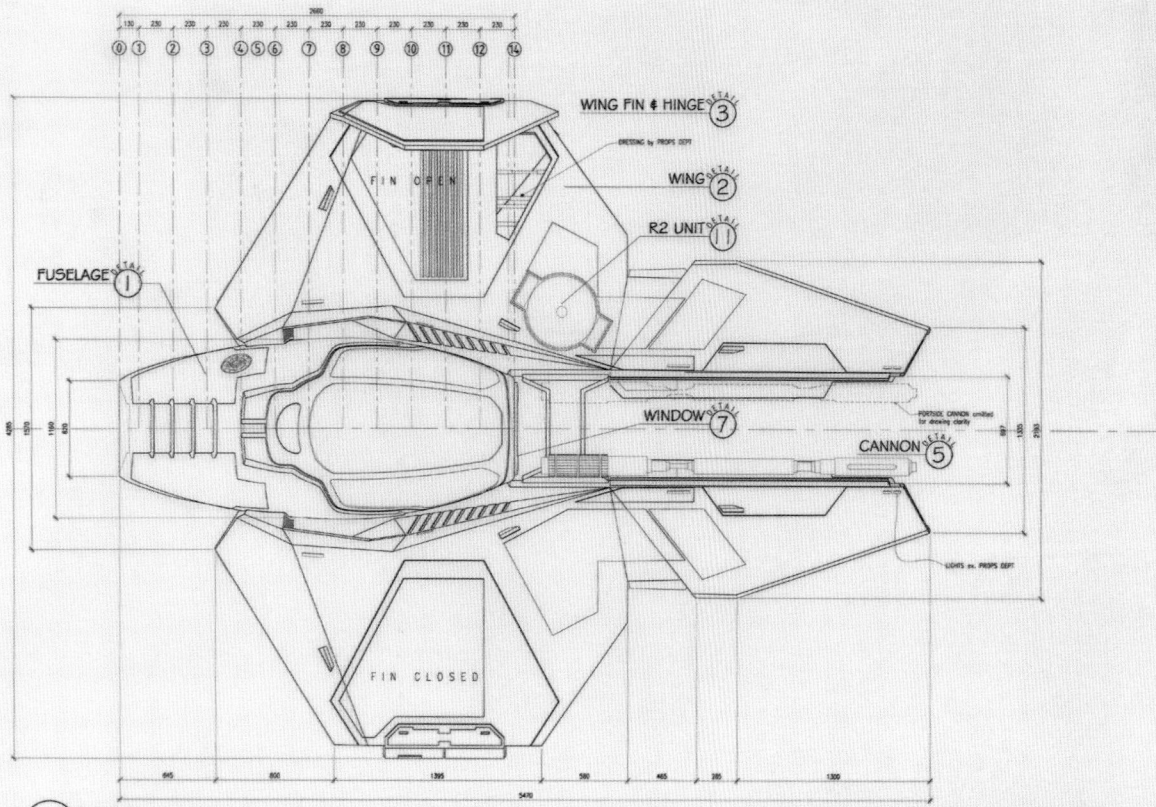

◯ PLAN
scale 1:10

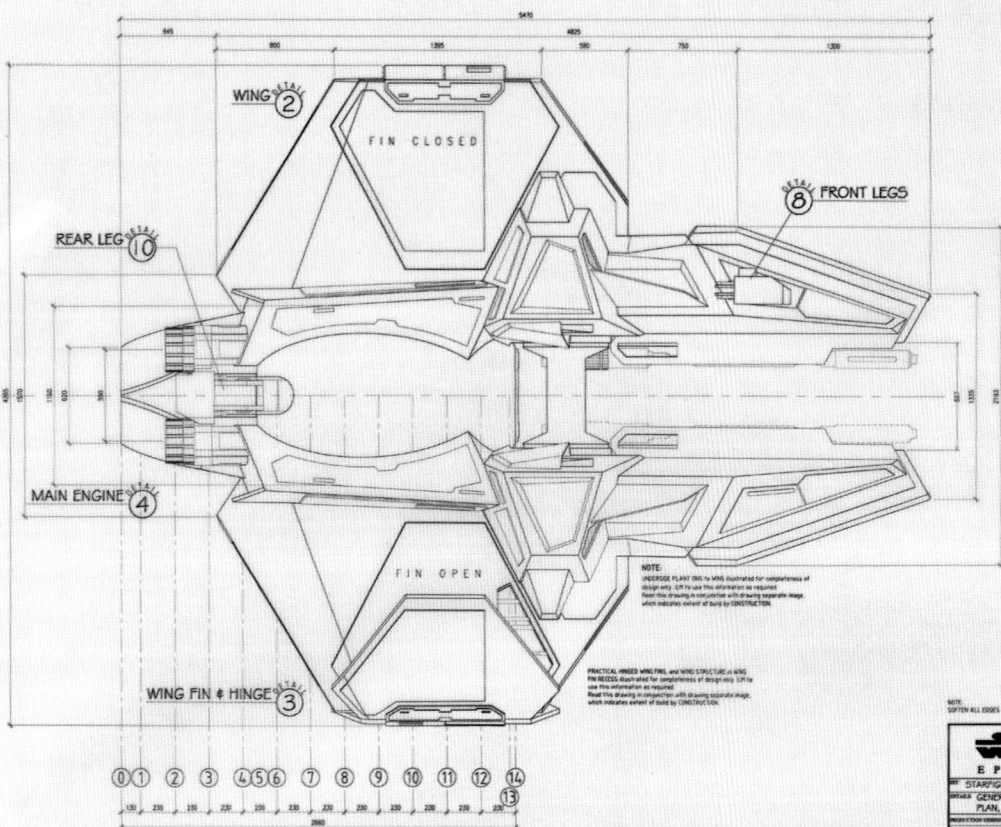

WING ②

FIN CLOSED

FRONT LEGS ⑧

REAR LEG ⑩

MAIN ENGINE ④

FIN OPEN

WING FIN & HINGE ③

◯ UNDERSIDE
scale 1:10

STARFIGHTER
PLANS

STAR WARS		143
EPISODE III		

STARFIGHTER
GENERAL ARRANGEMENT
PLAN, UNDERSIDE PLAN

DRAWN BY: JACINTA LEONG

SET	STARFIGHTER
DETAIL	GEN. ARGT., PLAN & UNDERSIDE PLAN
DRG. NO.	143
DATE	APRIL 11 2003
DRAWN BY	JACINTA LEONG

↑ An enhanced final frame shows Anakin's yellow starfighter and Obi-Wan's red one, both digital recreations of the full-size craft.

↓ Reference photography shows the dressed starfighter prop.

REHABILITATION CHAMBER

For the moment that audiences had been waiting for throughout the prequel trilogy—when Anakin Skywalker is physically transformed into Darth Vader—the art department took concept art by Erik Tiemens and others to create the Rehabilitation Chamber table and floor. The blueprint reveals that the floor grill was to be removable for access and lit from beneath and that the table was designed to rotate from horizontal to vertical positions and would be dressed with myriad greeblies.

"A good old physical drawing of one of those big moments in the film is the Rehabilitation table," remembered Russell. "We all knew that was a big part coming up, and I remember the Chamber soundstage was packed when we shot the scene. There was a lot of worry and angst about what the scene was going to be like." And, of course, everyone wanted to get a glimpse of Darth Vader.

While Drew's drawing was done by hand (no. 562 on page 262), Leong's complementary piece was done with CAD (no. 862). "The balance is changing, because people drawing with CAD are getting better," added Russell in a 2010 interview. "Years ago, CAD was great if you were drawing an oil rig; if you were drawing a castle, with all the texture and the anomalies that go into a building like that, it would have been a nightmare to use CAD.

"But we're getting to a stage now where the guys and girls who are using the programs can actually factor that sort of drama into the drawing. Most of our draftspeople use both, so now we would have a

conversation about not only the style and the type of set you're drawing, but where that information is going. Historically, if a drawing was to be issued only to a plasterer, carpenter, or those sorts of workshops, that was simpler; but nowadays, if we know that the drawing will also be sent to visual effects houses, there's also an argument that a digital document, such as a CAD drawing or a model, is more useful."

And, indeed, the Imperial Rehabilitation Chamber was primarily created at ILM, along with the attendant droids, atmosphere, and explosions.

↓ This concept art of the Rehabilitation Chamber was created by Ryan Church in January 2003.

RIGHT AND RIGHT BELOW
A maquette of the Chamber followed the concept art.

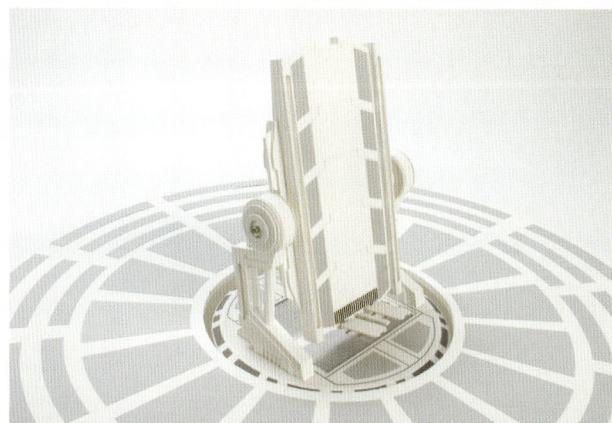

↑ The full-sized operating table was built on Stage 4 as part of the minimal set at Fox Studios and filmed on September 1, 2003.

SECTION A-A
scale 1:10

SET OUT PLAN
scale 1:10

CORUSCANT - IMPERIAL REHAB CHAMBER
SET OUT PLAN

	STAR WARS		862
	EPISODE III		

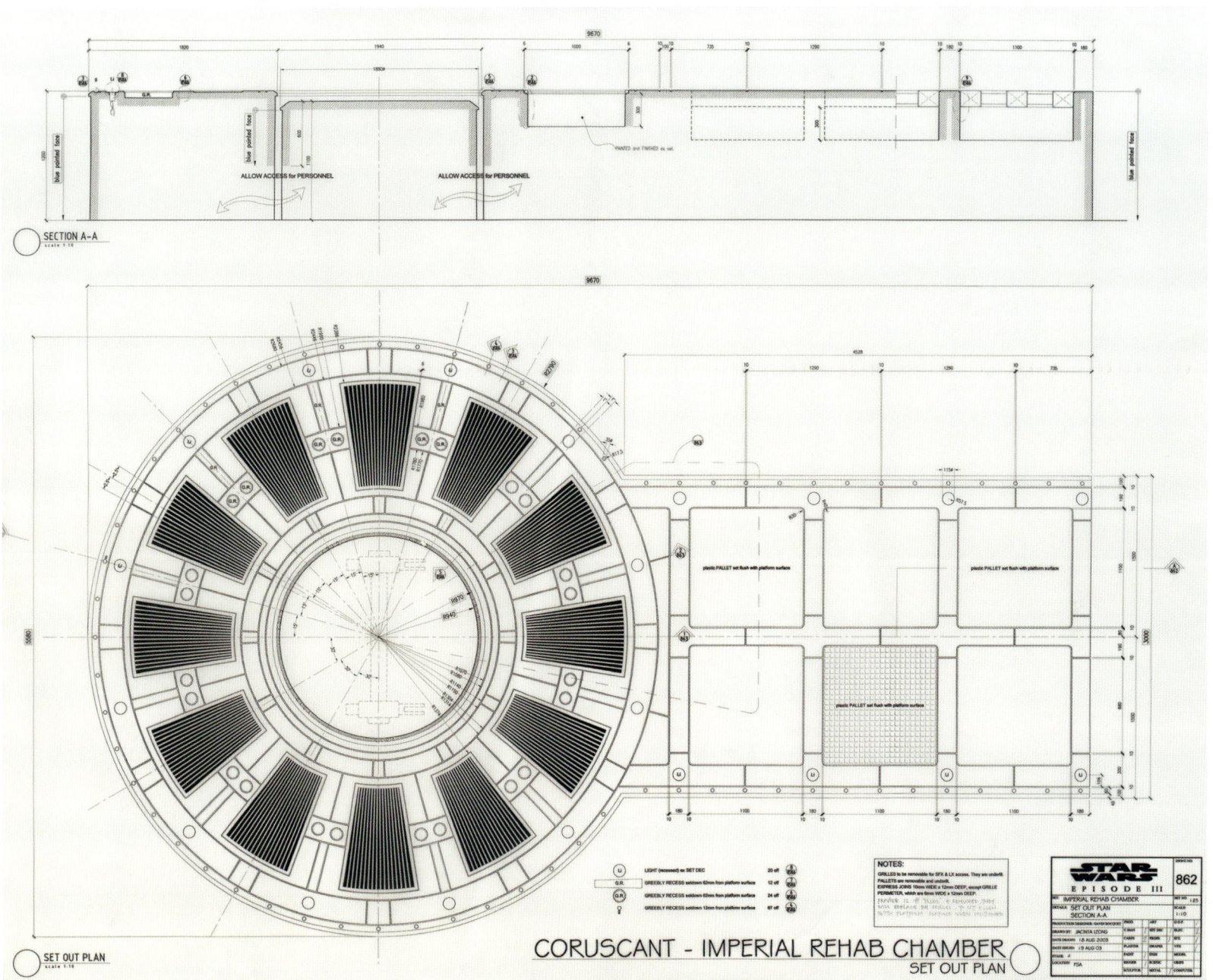

SET	IMPERIAL REHAB CENTER
DETAIL	SET OUT PLAN, SECTION AA
DRG. NO.	862
DATE	AUGUST 18 2003
DRAWN BY	JACINTA LEONG

↓ In this final frame from the Rehabilitation Chamber scene the digital set and assets have been added to the physical one.

↑ The limited build of the Chamber included the table and floor elements, as seen in this reference photo taken on Stage 4.

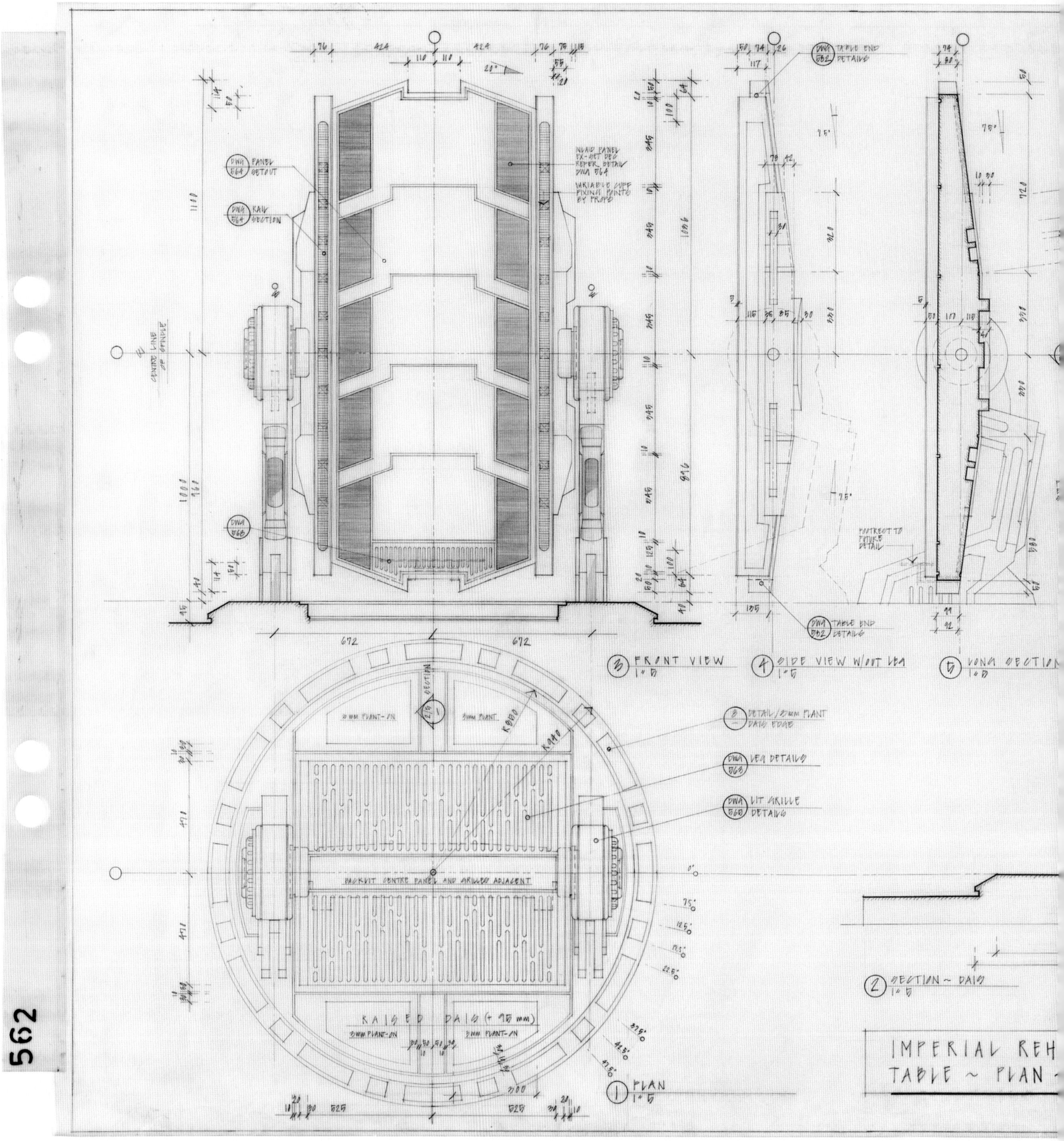

3. FRONT VIEW

4. SIDE VIEW W/OUT LEG

5. LONG SECTION

1. PLAN

2. SECTION ~ DAIS

RAISED DAIS (+ 75mm)

IMPERIAL REH
TABLE ~ PLAN

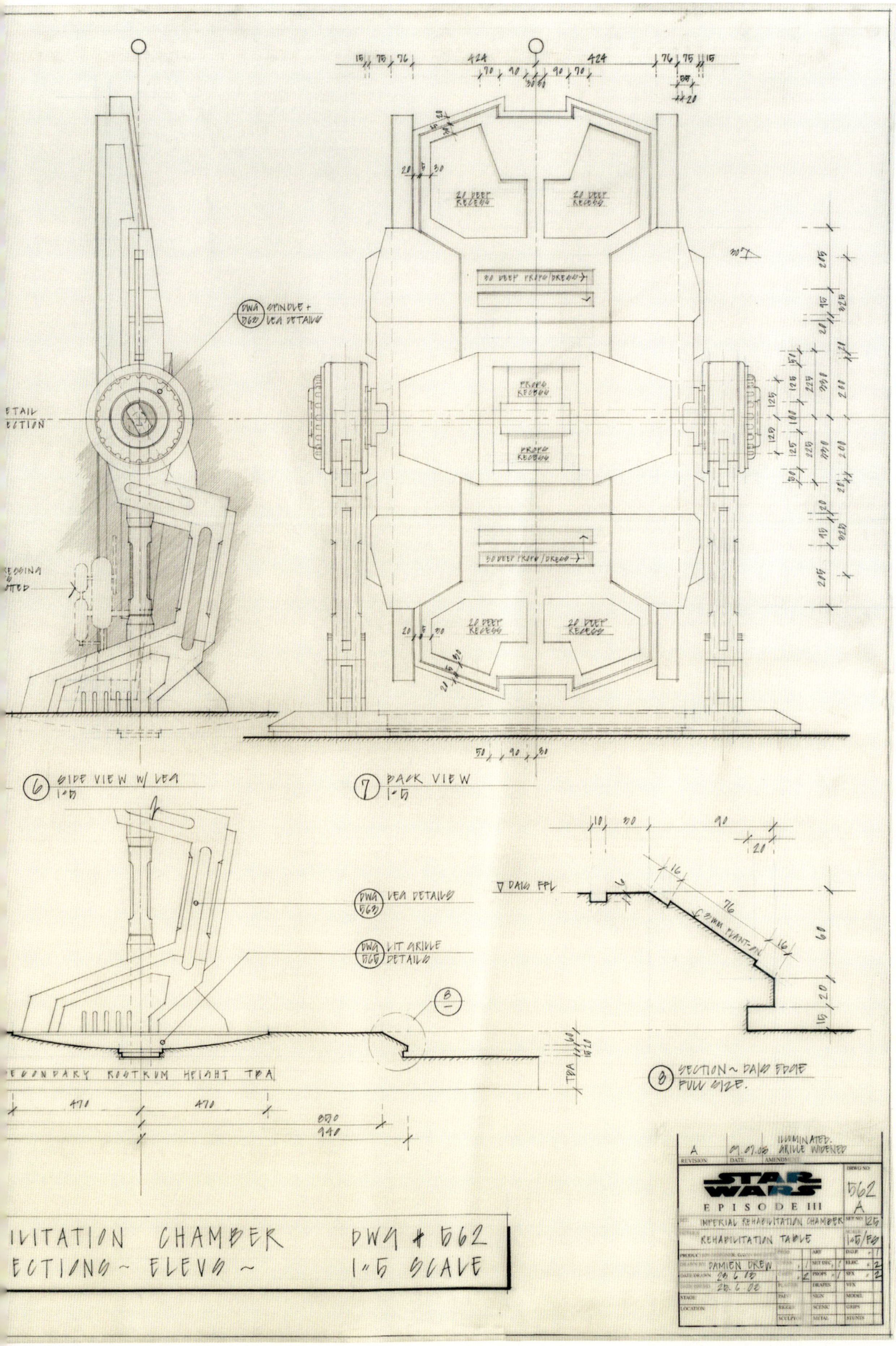

(6) SIDE VIEW W/ VEA
1:5

(7) BACK VIEW
1:5

DWA SPINDLE +
562 VEA DETAILS

DETAIL
SECTION

DWA VEA DETAILS
562

DWG LIT GRILLE
568 DETAILS

B
—

DWA FFL

6MM EVANT-M

SECTION ~ DAW EDGE
FULL SIZE

SECONDARY ROSTRUM HEIGHT TBA

IVITATION CHAMBER   DWG # 562

ECTIONS ~ ELEVS ~   1:5 SCALE

STAR WARS
EPISODE III
IMPERIAL REHABILITATION CHAMBER
REHABILITATION TABLE
DAMIEN DREW
DWG NO. 562 A

SET	IMPERIAL REHABILITATION	DRG. NO.	562
	CHAMBER	DATE	JUNE 23 2003
DETAIL	REHABILITATION TABLE	DRAWN BY	DAMIEN DREW

DIPLOMATIC CRUISER

The blueprint of the Diplomatic cruiser hallway, designated as 001—the first technical drawing executed for Episode III—was another element that brought the prequel trilogy art department full circle to the first drawings created at Elstree. Ironically, though Bocquet's team built exactly the same amount of the L-shaped corridor as Barry's had of the rebel ship, their reference material was limited. "The tricky thing about building this set was that the first film wasn't really archived very well, because nobody knew it was going to be successful," Bocquet said. "So we had to rely much more on photographs; we only had a few drawings to work from."

Harvey's blueprint of the rebuild (no. 001) notes that the wall panels between columns were to float and that several of the doorways were single-sided and non-practical. "The white corridor from the Diplomatic cruiser hallway was fun to do," said Russell. "We were all peering at old DVDs and trying to work out how big it was and how long it was. We couldn't find any useful drawings from the original set, any ones that gave us what we wanted."

In addition to the corridor, the prequel art department constructed a part of the cruiser not seen originally. For the pickups shot at Shepperton Studios, David Lee drew up a blueprint of the ship's cockpit (no. 006). "That was a three-and-a-half-wall little cockpit for a flying scene," said Russell. "George was convinced that ILM could do it with just the seats and blue, but eventually, as a treat, he said, 'No, you can build it.' And that was the last thing we built and shot."

SET	ALDERAAN CRUISER COCKPIT
DETAIL	PLANS & ELEVATIONS
DRG. NO.	006
DATE	JULY 28 2004
DRAWN BY	DAVID LEE

↑ R2-D2 is in the original corridor.

SET	DIPLOMATIC CRUISER HALLWAY
DETAIL	PLAN & ELEVATIONS
DRG. NO.	001
DATE	FEBRUARY 24 2003
DRAWN BY	PHIL D. HARVEY

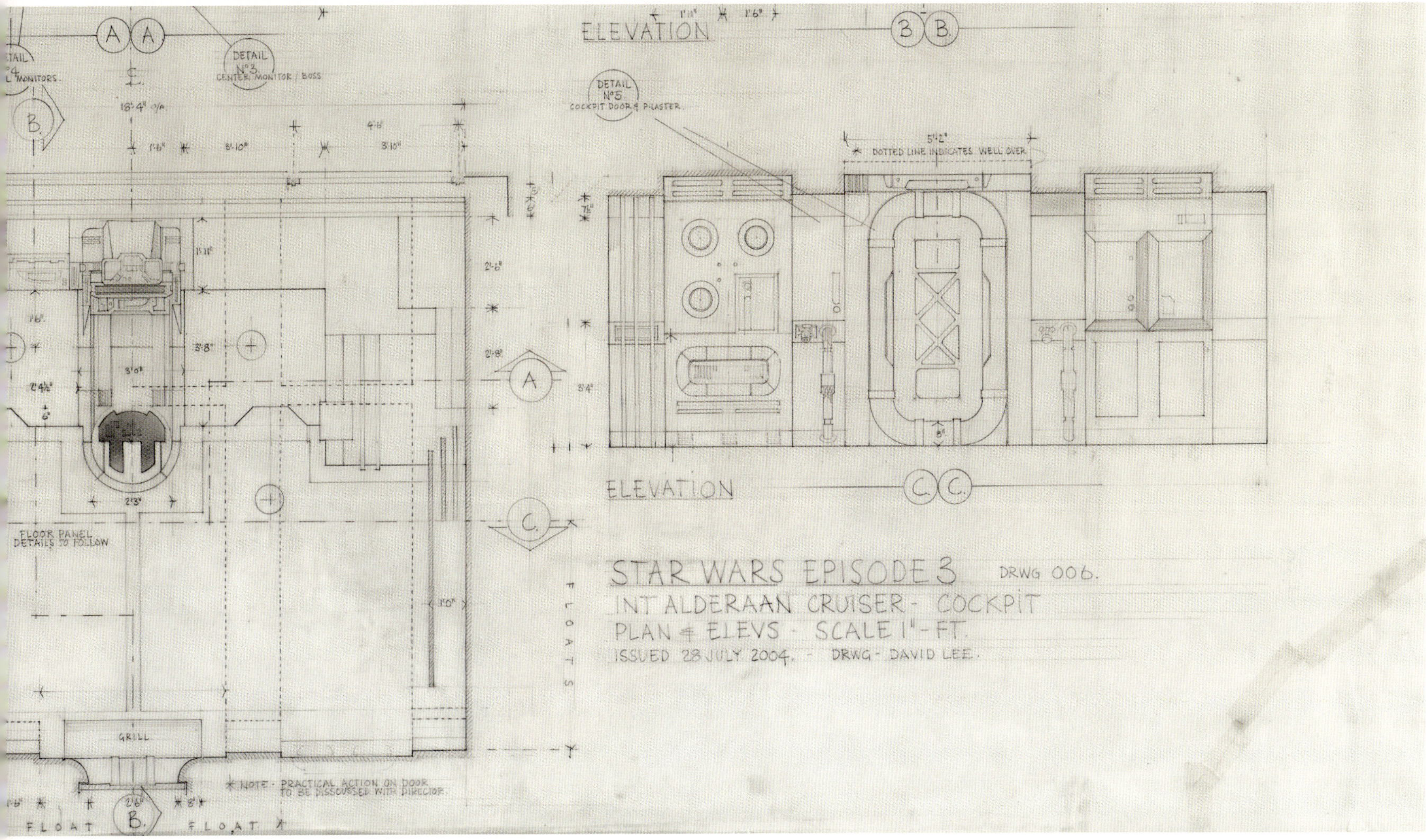

ELEVATION

DETAIL
Nº 3
CENTER MONITOR / BOSS

DETAIL
Nº 5
COCKPIT DOOR & PILASTER

DOTTED LINE INDICATES WELL OVER.

ELEVATION

FLOOR PANEL
DETAILS TO FOLLOW

GRILL

FLOAT B. FLOAT

STAR WARS EPISODE 3   DRWG 006.
INT ALDERAAN CRUISER - COCKPIT
PLAN & ELEVS - SCALE 1" = FT.
ISSUED 28 JULY 2004. - DRWG - DAVID LEE.

✳ NOTE · PRACTICAL ACTION ON DOOR
TO BE DISCUSSED WITH DIRECTOR.

ANTI ROOM.
SEE SEPERATE DWG.

EDGE OF COLUMN INTO FLOOR

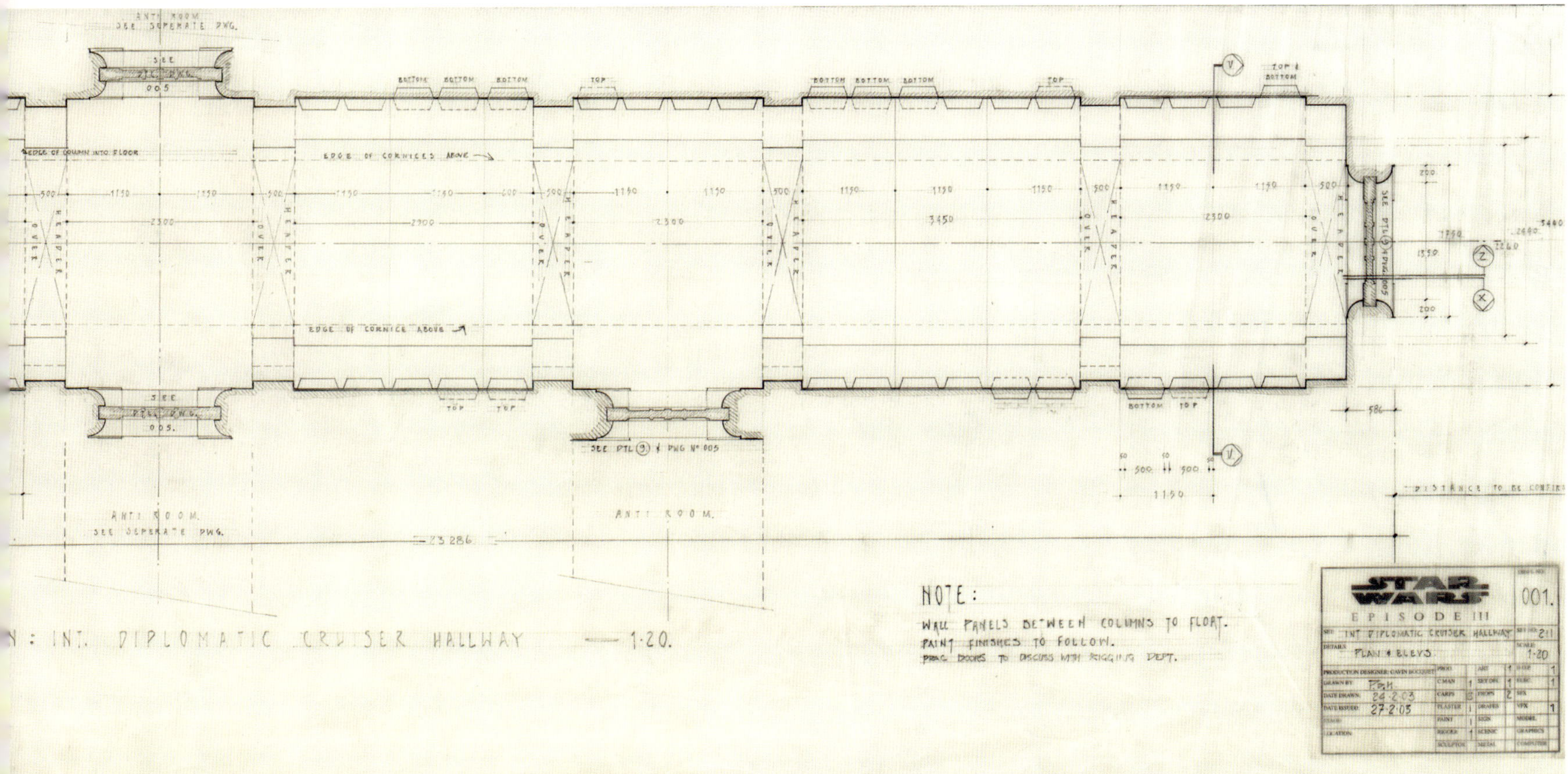

EDGE OF CORNICES ABOVE

EDGE OF CORNICE ABOVE

ANTI ROOM.
SEE SEPERATE DWG.

ANTI ROOM.

N: INT. DIPLOMATIC CRUISER HALLWAY   1·20.

NOTE:
WALL PANELS BETWEEN COLUMNS TO FLOAT.
PAINT FINISHES TO FOLLOW.
DWG DOORS TO DISCUSS WITH RIGGING DEPT.

STAR WARS   001.
EPISODE III
INT DIPLOMATIC CRUISER HALLWAY
PLAN & ELEVS

INTRODUCTION
EPISODES VII, VIII, IX: THE SEQUEL TRILOGY

George Lucas had talked about retirement since the first *Star Wars* movie was completed in 1977. But by early 2012, he began making concrete plans and, in secrecy, initiated a process. First, he hired producing legend Kathleen Kennedy to head up Lucasfilm. Then he crafted springboards for stories that could become new *Star Wars* movies. These treatments would become the carrot to offer an interested buyer, for Lucas planned also to sell his company, its creative works, and its constituent divisions. With the allure of a revived *Star Wars* franchise, the Walt Disney Company announced its acquisition of Lucasfilm on October 30, 2012.

Restarting the live-action production machine of *Star Wars*, which had laid dormant since *Star Wars: Revenge of the Sith* in 2005, was no small task. Kennedy had earned her producing pedigree over decades of close collaboration with such cinematic titans as Steven Spielberg, Robert Zemeckis, Martin Scorsese, and Clint Eastwood. Now she recruited equally acclaimed talent in the form of Rick Carter, production designer on *Back to the Future Parts II* (1989) and *III* (1990), *Jurassic Park* (1993), *Avatar* (2009), and *Lincoln* (2012). "George started the idea that you could begin conceptualizing well in advance, and we took that to heart," said Kennedy.

"I offered to be an advisor, to help guide the direction, and see where it took us," said Carter.

It was still early days—the story had yet to evolve from the few pages of a treatment into a fully fledged screenplay. Carter led concept artists at Lucasfilm and Industrial Light & Magic (ILM) through a blue-sky phase of unbridled exploration and imagination—the so-called "visualist" process. At this stage, the story was undergoing refinement from screenwriters Michael Arndt, Lawrence Kasdan, and Simon Kinberg, with Lucas visiting on occasion and offering his thoughts.

Even before a director joined the production, Kennedy had tasked Jason McGatlin, Lucasfilm's new head of physical production, with finding studio space in England for the film. In many ways, *Star Wars* was returning to its roots, including its geographic origins as a UK production. With the assistance of unit production manager Simon Emanuel, Lucasfilm scored a lengthy commitment from Pinewood Studios—the storied stages that had long hosted the James Bond franchise.

"We found three stages at Pinewood," said McGatlin. "A 30,000 square foot stage, known as the Richard Attenborough, and two 18,000 square foot stages. We had no director, but I started hiring crew. Kathy said, 'I want A-listers on this movie. I want London's best and brightest.'"

A looming 2015 release date accelerated the development process. When J.J. Abrams came aboard as director and co-screenwriter, he brought with him the talents and track record of his successful Bad Robot production company. Abrams, working closely with veteran scribe Kasdan, would craft a *Star Wars* story that would invoke the spirit of the original trilogy while propelling the franchise into a 21st century direction. As a lifelong *Star Wars* fan, Abrams was keen to emulate the processes that imbued the films with their timeless and deceptively effortless charm. His filmmaking process would blend "practical" approaches with cutting-edge techniques.

"When I first heard that this was up and going, I starting making calls on the outside chance I could worm my way into some office somewhere," said Darren Gilford, who had production designer credits on such boldly visual films as *Tron: Legacy* (2010) and *Oblivion* (2015). Gilford would, with Carter, be credited as production designer on Episode VII, code-named "AVCO" in Abrams' nod to the Avco movie theater in Westwood, California, where he had first seen the original *Star Wars*.

"J.J.'s mandate from Day One was to be authentic and true to the original flair of the first three movies," explained Gilford. "He wanted to channel their aesthetic, simplicity, and techniques."

With the storyline now taking a new, sharper shape in screenplay drafts by Abrams and Kasdan, the worlds required for construction also came into focus. The film crews being assembled at Pinewood included descendants of crew members who had worked on the original *Star Wars* and *Indiana Jones* films. "All the Brits secretly feel the UK is the home of *Star Wars*," said producer Simon Emanuel. Art director Alan Tomkins' son, Gary, would serve in the same role as his father on the new film. Props art director Mark Harris, who had worked on *Star Wars: The Empire Strikes Back* (1980), would bring his expertise to AVCO. Scenic artist Matt Walker followed in the footsteps of his father, Bob Walker, who was a décor and lettering artist on *Empire* and *Star Wars: Return of the Jedi* (1983). Production designer Neil Lamont is the son of Peter Lamont, who had worked on several Bond movies at Pinewood and is the nephew of Michael Lamont, an assistant art director on *Empire, Jedi,* and *Raiders of the Lost Ark* (1981). *Star Wars* would continue to be a bond between generations, this time behind the camera.

As Episode VII went before cameras, Rian Johnson had already signed up for the next chapter.

← Early concept art by Iain McCaig shows Rey (then called "Thea") exploring a junkyard filled with scrap from the last great war.

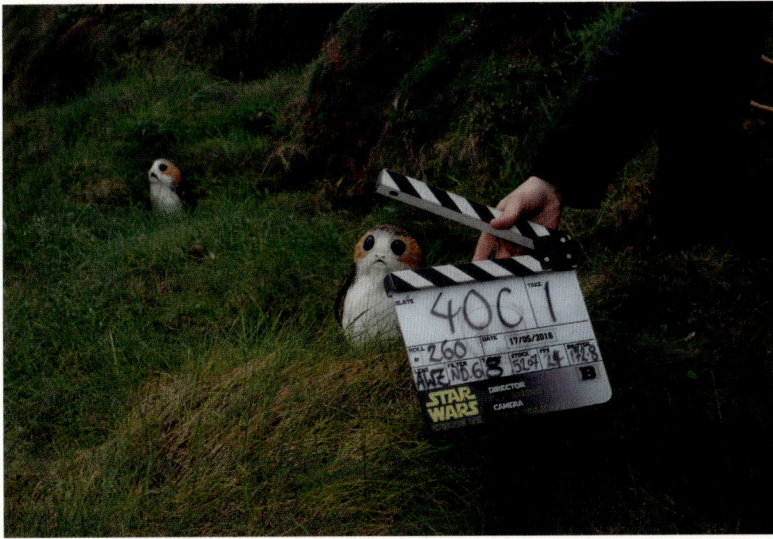

↑ Life-size porg puppets await action on location in the wild, craggy headlands of Loop Head, located north of Dingle in southwestern Ireland, during the production of *The Last Jedi*.

↑ Brian Herring (BB-8 puppeteer), Anthony Daniels (C-3PO), Joonas Suotamo (Chewbacca), Daisy Ridley (Rey), and John Boyega (Finn) are pictured on location in Wadi Rum in Jordan for *The Rise of Skywalker*.

He would write his installment after reading the AVCO script and closely watching footage come in from that production. While it would take a few more months for *Star Wars: The Force Awakens* (2015) to be named, Johnson came to the page with a title in mind: *Star Wars: The Last Jedi* (2017).

While activity in Pinewood shifted to the first standalone movie, *Rogue One: A Star Wars Story* (2016), Johnson's Episode VIII began to take shape. For his production designer, Johnson tapped Rick Heinrichs, whose credits include *The Big Lebowski* (1998), *Pirates of the Caribbean: Dead Man's Chest* (2006) and *At World's End* (2007), and *Captain America: The First Avenger* (2011).

"There's an expectation and desire to have this be part of the world of *Star Wars* and to continue a story that the audience is already familiar with," said Heinrich. "And yet, we want to introduce people to new environments and new looks at the same time."

Much like the classic locations of the original trilogy, the bulk of the settings in *The Force Awakens* were remote outposts exposed to the elements—the deserts of Jakku, the forests abutting Maz's Castle, the snow-capped wilderness of Starkiller Base. In contrast, *The Last Jedi* would draw inspiration from the prequels in showcasing an elegant, cosmopolitan environment in the realization of Canto Bight, the Monte Carlo of the far-away galaxy. The rest of the movie would bounce between the corridors of huge starships, including a Resistance cruiser and the immense *Mega*-class Star Destroyer, and organic, ancient Ahch-To, site of the first Jedi temple. The final act of the movie would be Crait, an otherworldly environment inspired by the world's largest salt flat, Salar de Uyuni in Bolivia.

"We had a huge number of sets," said Heinrichs. "At one point we counted one hundred and forty. But we combined them and figured out how to be smart and efficient. It was a massive challenge to be able to deliver sets to this voracious production company day-by-day, but we were doing it."

Much like Johnson observed Abrams from afar as he awaited his turn in the director's chair, Colin Trevorrow, who directed *Safety Not Guaranteed* (2012) and *Jurassic World* (2015), began development of the movie that would conclude the saga when *The Last Jedi* entered production. His working title, "Black Diamond"—named for the most difficult class of ski slope—was a nod to the challenge of the task ahead. Alex McDowell, whose credits include *Minority Report* (2002) and *Watchmen* (2009), would join as production designer, while the story would be written by Trevorrow and Derek Connolly, writer of *Safety Not Guaranteed* (2012) and cowriter of *Kong: Skull Island* (2017).

This version of Episode IX was not to be. A combination of setbacks—the most heart-breaking being the sudden death of Carrie Fisher on December 27, 2016—threw an insurmountable obstacle on the continuation of the storyline as Trevorrow had intended. A major rethink would be required, although the intended release date of December 2019 could not move. As Trevorrow exited the project, an experienced hand would be required to pick up the baton. On September 12, 2017, Lucasfilm announced J.J. Abrams would return.

Under Abrams' direction, Episode IX would take some very big narrative swings in its goal of ending the Skywalker Saga as dramatically as it had been restarted. To craft the finale, Abrams joined

with screenwriter Chris Terrio and art director Kevin Jenkins, who, with Rick Carter, filled the co-production designer role.

"I worked for ILM, so I have a background in visual effects as well as in art direction of physical productions," said Jenkins. "I was an art director on *The Force Awakens*. I was one of the first artists, if not the first artist, to work on Episode VIII. Then I was one of the last artists pulled off Episode VIII, seguing into Episode IX. The last six years of my life has been nothing but this trilogy."

Star Wars: The Rise of Skywalker (2019)— code-named "Trixie" during production, with emphasis on the central "ix" letters (for Episode IX), in a whimsical logo—would include some of the biggest, most complex sets in a *Star Wars* production to date, from the sprawling mountaintop city of Kijimi to the enormous blockade runner dominating the center of the Resistance base. It would be a mix of new environs and painstaking recreations of what had come before—such as the Emperor's Throne Room, after decades of battering from tempestuous ocean waves, or the iconic Lars Homestead half-buried in the sand. "It's not much sleep to be had," said Jenkins of the workload. "I'll put it that way. It is what it is: It's *Star Wars* Episode IX, and it deserves what it needs to have."

"The most important thing that I contribute is a sense of where this has come from," said Carter, philosophically. "Not just with *The Force Awakens*, but going all the way back to the 1970s, because that's when I started filmmaking. I was doing films before *Star Wars* even came out. So, there's an aspect to this which is about generations handing off to the new generation. That's why I got involved."

FIRST ORDER TRANSPORTER

The action in *The Force Awakens* starts with a group of ominous, boxy transport ships flitting across a night sky, invading the tranquility of a Jakku village. A cut to the inside of one of the craft shows it filled with stormtroopers, the iconic white soldiers reimagined from the Imperial era into a sleek new First Order design.

Inspiration for the transporter came from the landing craft, vehicle, personnel (LCVP), or Higgins boats (so-named for their US designer, Andrew Higgins), that carried Allied troops onto the D-Day beaches of Normandy in World War II. James Clyne developed the concept in the summer of 2013, and it would be one of the first designs approved by J.J. Abrams on the project. By February of 2014, Clyne would relocate to Pinewood Studios to help supervise the initial construction of the physical realization of his design. The production code name for the vehicle was "White Delivery Van," not for the hue of its hull but for the color of its armored cargo.

Art director Andrew Palmer drew up the plans and Chris Corbould's special effects team built the nearly 40-foot-long front section, complete with steam effects and an operational ramp that could support the weight of 20 charging troopers. The aft section was a CG extension containing the engines and stand-up pilot module.

The First Order Transporter entry ramp would cleverly be repurposed as the Resistance transport seen delivering General Leia Organa to the aftermath of the battle at Maz's castle on Takodana. It saw further recycling as the entry ramp section of the Imperial cargo shuttle that the rebels steal from Eadu to infiltrate Scarif in *Rogue One*. A partial build of only about half the extent of the original "White Delivery Van" construction was used for the transporter's return in *The Rise of Skywalker*, where it had the more gruesome production nickname of "Meat Wagon."

↑ The full-scale but partially built prow and entry ramp of the First Order transport stands at Pinewood Studios.

↑ A fully detailed interior of the troop transporter is created for a 360-degree field of camera view.

AVCO EXT WHITE DELIVERY VAN - PLANS & ELEVATIONS - SHEET 2 OF 3.

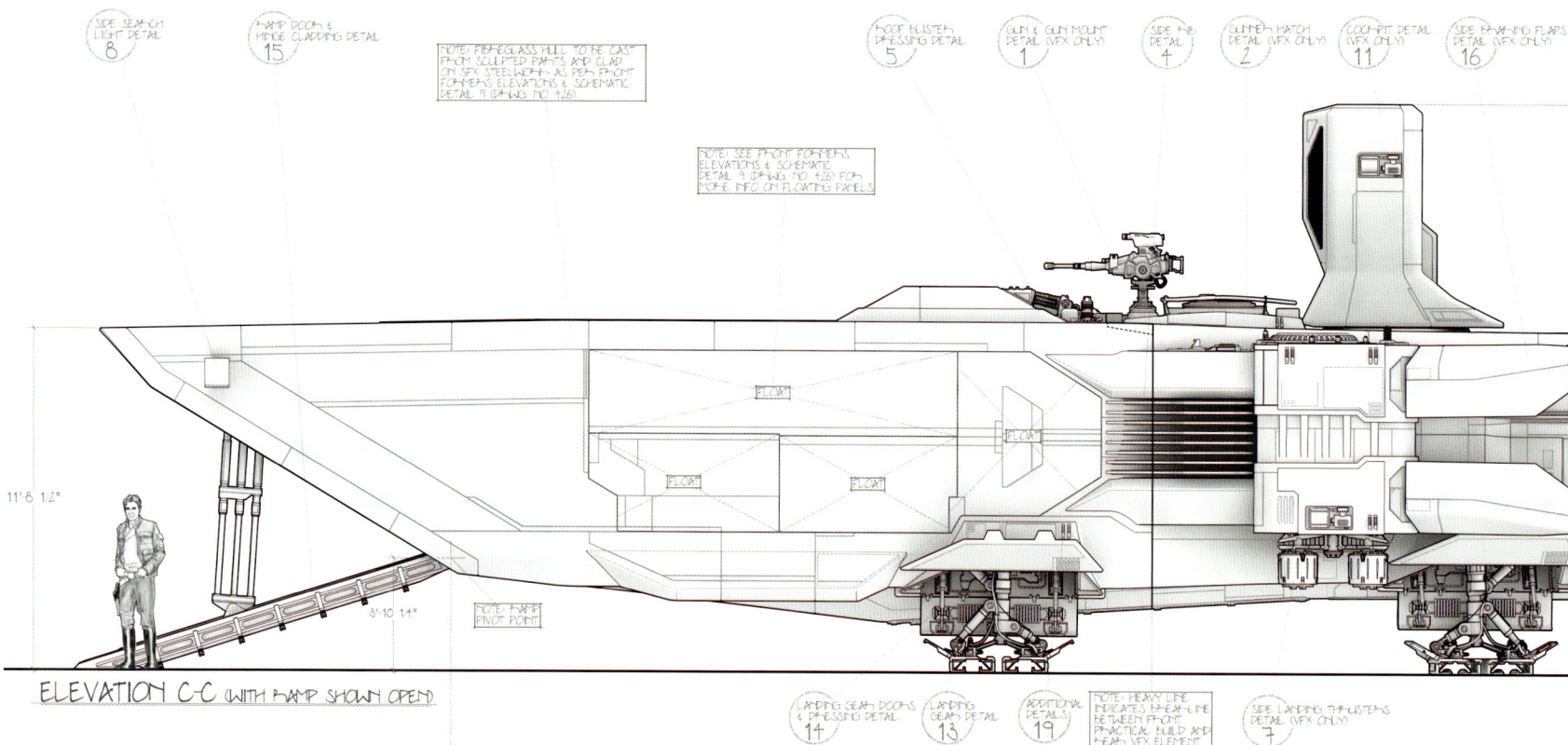

ELEVATION C-C (WITH RAMP SHOWN OPEN)

AVCO - SET 060 - WHITE DELIVERY VAN-EXT / GUN & GUN MOUNT DETAIL 01 / SHEET 01
3"=1'-0" @ A0 / 20.11.13

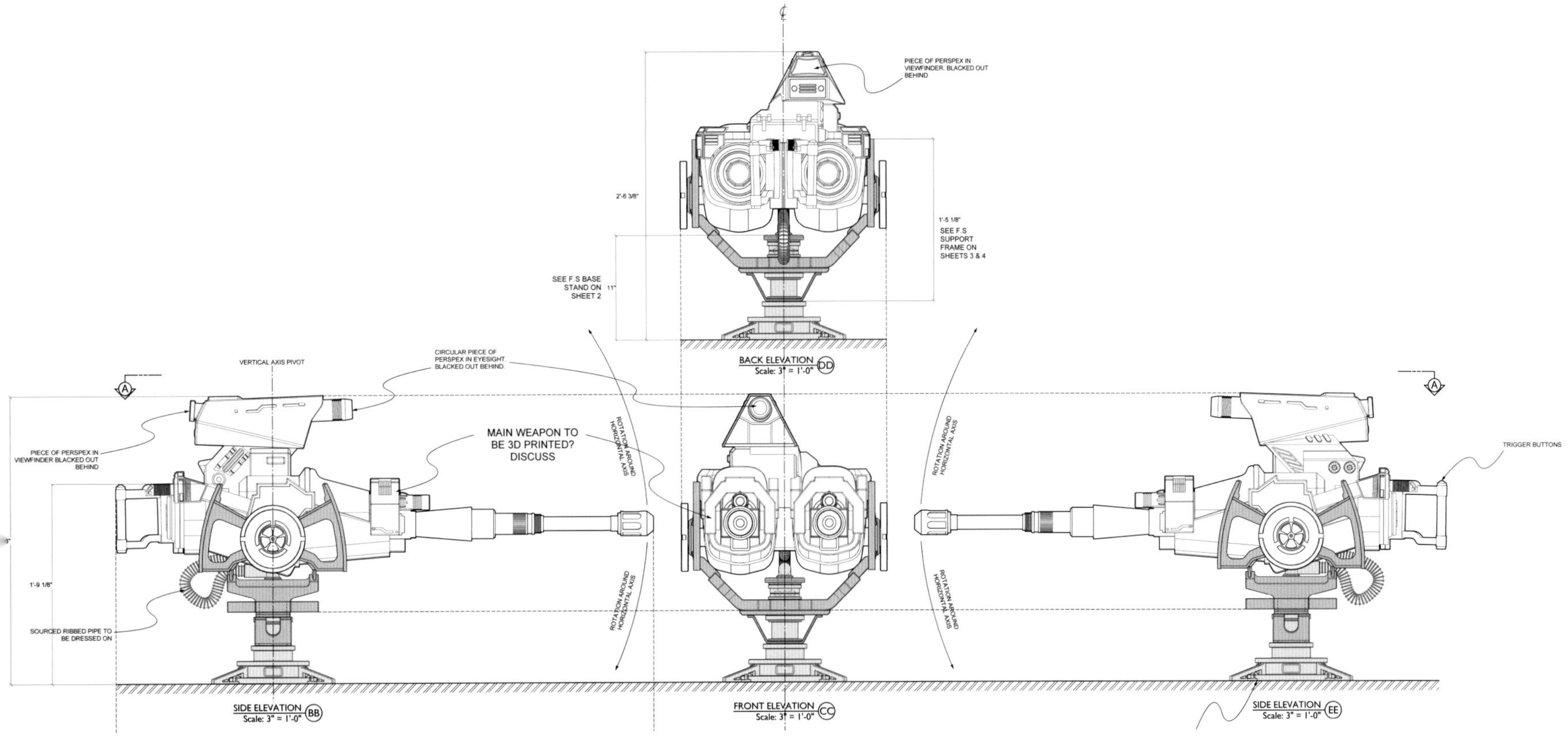

PIECE OF PERSPEX IN VIEWFINDER. BLACKED OUT BEHIND

2'-6 3/8"

1'-5 1/8"
SEE F.S
SUPPORT
FRAME ON
SHEETS 3 & 4

SEE F.S BASE
STAND ON
SHEET 2

BACK ELEVATION DD
Scale: 3" = 1'-0"

VERTICAL AXIS PIVOT

CIRCULAR PIECE OF
PERSPEX IN EYESIGHT
BLACKED OUT BEHIND

PIECE OF PERSPEX IN
VIEWFINDER BLACKED OUT
BEHIND

MAIN WEAPON TO
BE 3D PRINTED?
DISCUSS

TRIGGER BUTTONS

1'-9 1/8"

SOURCED RIBBED PIPE TO
BE DRESSED ON

ROTATION AROUND
HORIZONTAL AXIS

SIDE ELEVATION BB
Scale: 3" = 1'-0"

FRONT ELEVATION CC
Scale: 3" = 1'-0"

SIDE ELEVATION EE
Scale: 3" = 1'-0"

SET	WHITE DELIVERY VAN
DETAIL	GUN & GUN MOUNT DETAIL 01
DRG NO.	350
DATE	NOVEMBER 20 2013
DRAWN BY	RICH HARDY

↑ The detailed illustration shows the trooper-operated gun turret on the First Order transporter.

HEAT ENGINE
DETAILS (VFX ONLY)
18

SIDE DRAWING FLAPS
DETAIL (VFX ONLY)
16

GUN & GUN MOUNT
DETAIL (VFX ONLY)
1

COCK-PIT DETAIL
(VFX ONLY)
11

19'-6 3/8"

13'-2 7/8"

12'-0 1/4"

ELEVATION D-D

HEAT DETAILING
(VFX ONLY)
17

HEAT RADIATOR
DETAIL (VFX ONLY)
3

LANDING
GEAR DETAIL
13

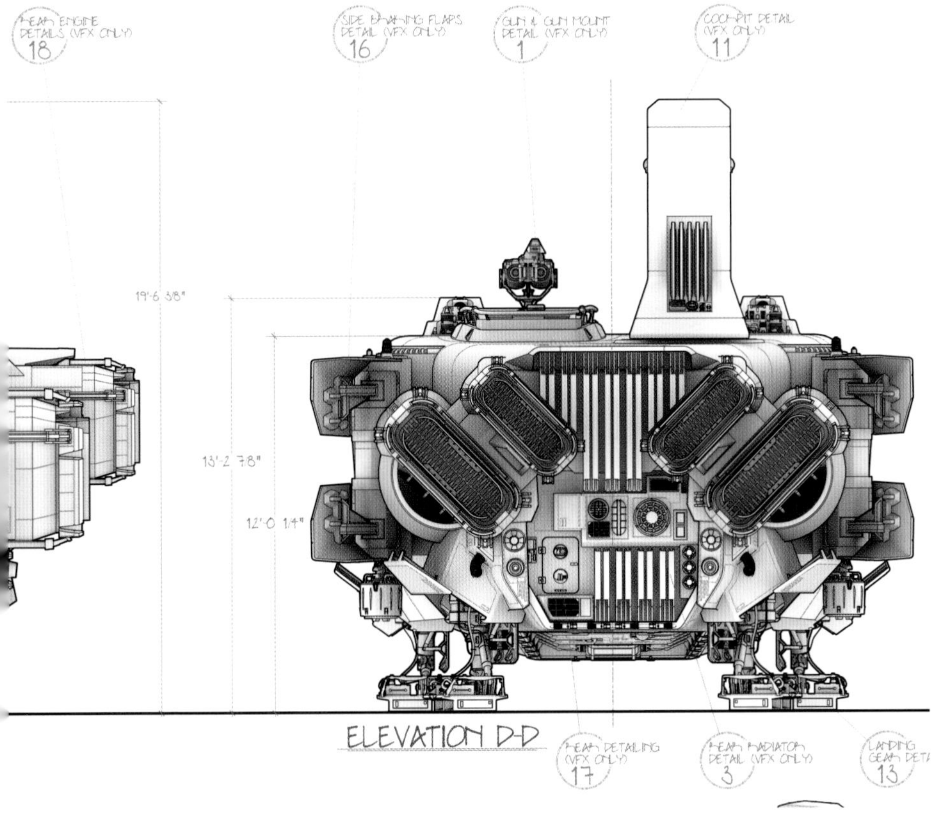

← In these plans and elevations
for the First Order transporter,
a heavy line delineates where
the practical build and rear
VFX element meet.

SET	EXT. WHITE DELIVERY VAN
DETAIL	PLANS & ELEVATIONS
DRG NO.	490
DATE	FEBRUARY 6 2014
DRAWN BY	ANDREW PALMER

REY'S SPEEDER

To traverse the wastes of Jakku and voyage deep into the graveyard of wrecked starships full of valuable salvage, the scavenger Rey pilots a unique speeder that zips across the dunes. A wealth of concept art explored options for this vehicle, with many iterations including a trailer cart for hauling unearthed prizes back into what passes for civilization on this sparsely settled planet.

The speeder was one of Abrams' key concerns—it was as important as Luke Skywalker's landspeeder in *Star Wars: A New Hope* (1977) for establishing just what day-to-day life was like for this desert denizen. Despite many dozens of artworks, nothing was quite landing. "At one point, we were stagnating a little on the speeders and J.J. said, 'Let's have the creature guys take a stab,'" said production designer Darren Gilford. The creature effects (CFX) department, supervised by Neal Scanlan, was also responsible for practical droid designs, so the artists under his purview were well-versed in imbuing technology with distinct personality. In this case, artist Jake Lunt Davies cracked the impasse by finding the shape that would become Rey's speeder.

Eschewing the cargo cart, the successful speeder design instead favored a cargo net that clung to its side without breaking its silhouette. In its distilled essence, it was Luke's landspeeder tilted 90 degrees on its side, with a biker's saddle above its engines. The robust engine section was reminiscent of bulky old agricultural tractors. Though its final hue resembled Luke's landspeeder, the iterative design process would try on a whole spectrum of hues before the speeder's finished look prevailed. Texturally, the final appearance of the speeder benefited from reference photography gathered by Gary Tomkins, which included imagery of weathered helicopters, tractors, and horse saddles in a variety of orange-brown colors.

Two full-sized versions of Rey's speeder would be built, with the weathering carefully replicated. One was a static version, used when Rey climbed aboard or dismounted. The other was motorized, which allowed Abrams to capture as much as possible in-camera when the speeder moved. In the static model, the hatch on the main body would reveal a fictional engine compartment, which ultimately was not needed on-camera. On the mobile model, this hatch revealed where the driver sat.

Special effects supervisor Chris Corbould installed a 1000 cc motorbike engine inside the mobile model, which drove a low-slung, four-wheeled cart. Actor Daisy Ridley rode on top, but an unseen driver steered, braked, and accelerated. "It went pretty fast," said Corbould. "We got it up to seventy miles per hour, but in the desert, with pockets of soft sand, we kept it down to forty."

To complete the illusion, digital artists at ILM and Beijing-based visual effects and animation company Base FX would remove the undercarriage, replacing it with desert landscape and adding more dust effects for a seamless effect. For distant shots of the speeder in motion, there was a fully CG version of it and its rider.

↓ Rey's speeder, shown here in schematics, will be built three times: twice as practical vehicle mounts and once as a static model.

SET	EXT. KIRA'S BUMPER CAR
DETAIL	PLANS & ELEVATIONS
DRG NO.	223
DATE	JANUARY 8 2014
DRAWN BY	ANDREW PALMER

AVCO EXT KIRA'S BUMPER CAR - PLANS

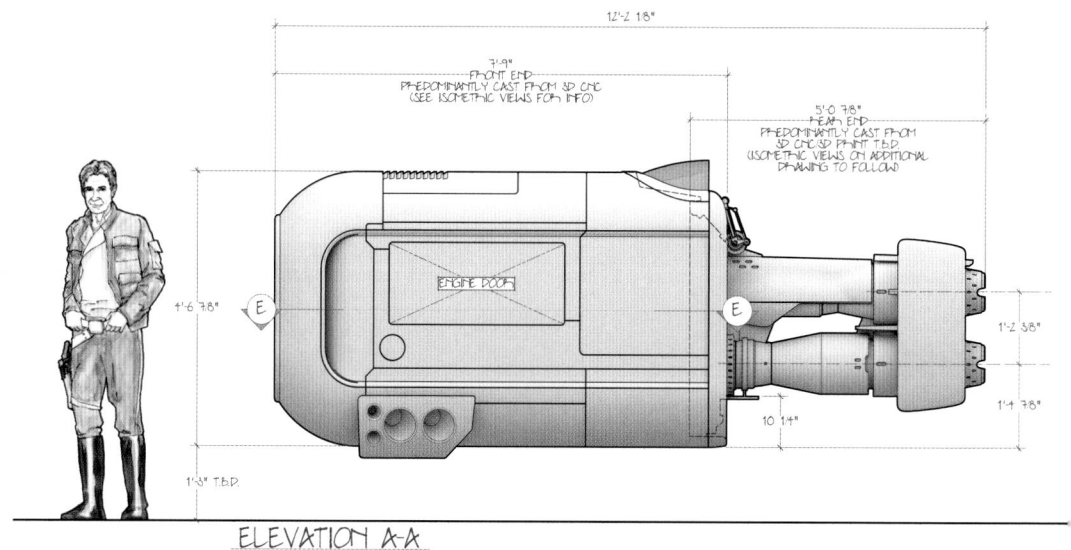

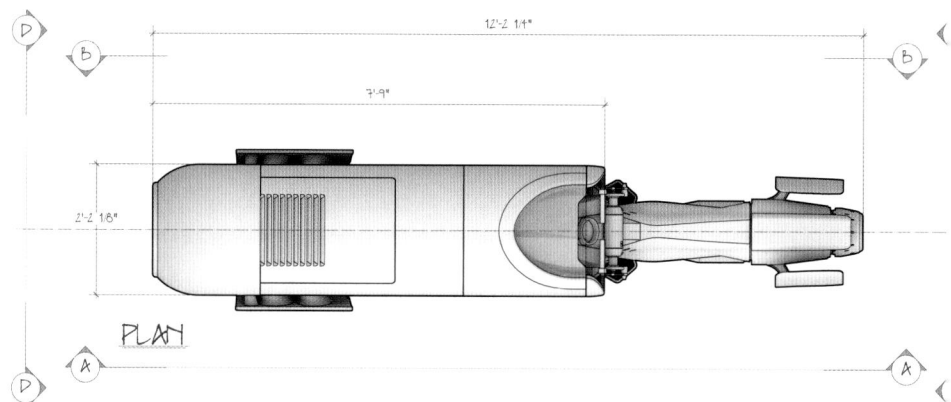

ELEVATION A-A

PLAN

↑ The final practical build of the stationary version of
Rey's speeder dressed with a well-stuffed cargo net.

↓ The plans for Rey's speeder are so detailed that even
the individual vanes that line the inside of the thruster
nozzle ends are delineated.

FRONT ELEVATION OF ENGINE PIECE -
SHOWING INTERIOR PIECES IN POSITON

SET	EXT. KIRA'S BUMPER CAR
DETAIL	PART 24/25 INTERIOR DETAIL PIECES
DRG NO.	275
DATE	JANUARY 21 2014
DRAWN BY	DANNY CLARK

ELEVATIONS

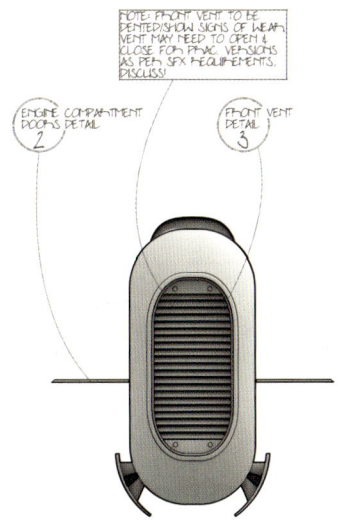

ELEVATION B-B   ELEVATION C-C   ELEVATION D-D

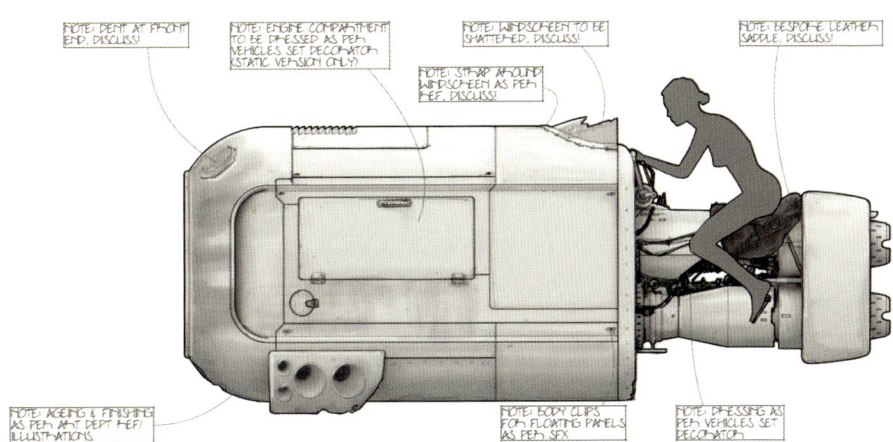

REY'S AT-AT HOME

A variety of early concept artwork for *The Force Awakens* explored the compelling theme of living in the detritus of the Galactic Civil War. This art evolved into the setting of Jakku and, specifically for the movie's protagonist, Rey, her home inside a fallen Imperial walker. "It felt very much like what the movie was about," said Abrams. "We were using remnants of what we knew from the original *Star Wars* trilogy and showing how this material was being used for new things and in new ways."

The concept would require two sets: a partial build of walker legs, which were shot on location in the Liwa Desert outside of Abu Dhabi in the United Arab Emirates, and an interior set of the canted walker, photographed at Pinewood. The walker legs were a generational connection—one of many—for art director Gary Tomkins. His father drew the technical drawings of the original walker for *The Empire Strikes Back*. "When we were proposing to do this in the desert, we got my father's drawing out, redrew it, and built it in Abu Dhabi," said Tomkins. "So, there's a nice symmetry there."

The walker leg-piece also had the notoriety of being the first item to be leaked onto the Internet, as spy photography of the unmistakable foot was rapidly propagated worldwide by a hungry press. "We were just wheeling the foot out from a tent to get it on the truck—but in the two minutes it was exposed, somebody who was camped out by a fence-line with a long telephoto lens got a picture," said Darren Gilford.

The interior of Rey's desert dwelling in the walker was better concealed, tucked away on the L Stage at Pinewood. The confined space was realized as a set built with a deliberate tilt. "I ended up hanging all the set dressing from the ceiling so it felt perpendicular to the floor," said set decorator Lee Sandales. "I exaggerated the tilt of the set, so Rey's bed is a hammock. It's full of details of her childhood, like a little doll dressed in a rebel jumpsuit that alludes to the *A New Hope* era."

↑ The interior of Rey's walker home was built at a canted angle, as made clear by the drape of the hammock and the tilt of the suspended set dressing.

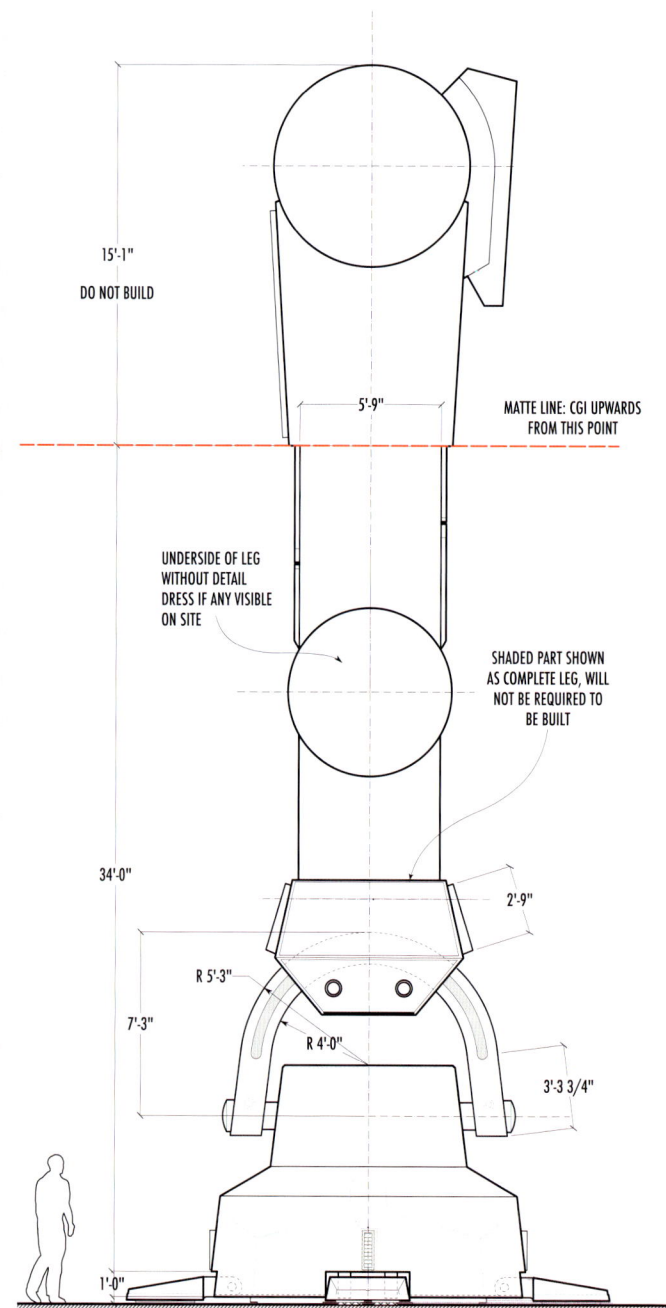

↑ A full-sized walker leg lies in the sands of Jordan. The model was built for direct interaction with Rey, played by Daisy Ridley, who would sit at the foot end while eating and daydreaming.

→ This schematic illustration shows the full-scale walker leg, including demarcation of where the CG would begin. This art benefited from referencing art done by Alan Tomkins and Michael Boone for *The Empire Strikes Back* (see pages 108 and 109).

SET	EXT. KIRA'S HOUSE
DETAIL	OVERALL LEG PLANS AND ELEVATIONS
DRG NO.	546A
DATE	FEBRUARY 6 2014
DRAWN BY	REMO TOZZI

15'-1"
DO NOT BUILD

5'-9"

MATTE LINE: CGI UPWARDS FROM THIS POINT

UNDERSIDE OF LEG WITHOUT DETAIL DRESS IF ANY VISIBLE ON SITE

SHADED PART SHOWN AS COMPLETE LEG, WILL NOT BE REQUIRED TO BE BUILT

34'-0"

2'-9"

R 5'-3"

7'-3"

R 4'-0"

3'-3 3/4"

1'-0"

'AVCO'. EXT KIRA'S HOUSE SETTING OUT BY ANGLE (LEFT HAND HEAD) SCALE = ¼" - 1'-0".

NOTE!
· READ WITH DRAWING NO. 1072,
EXT KIRA'S HOUSE TRIANGULATION
SETTING OUT (LEFT HAND HEAD).

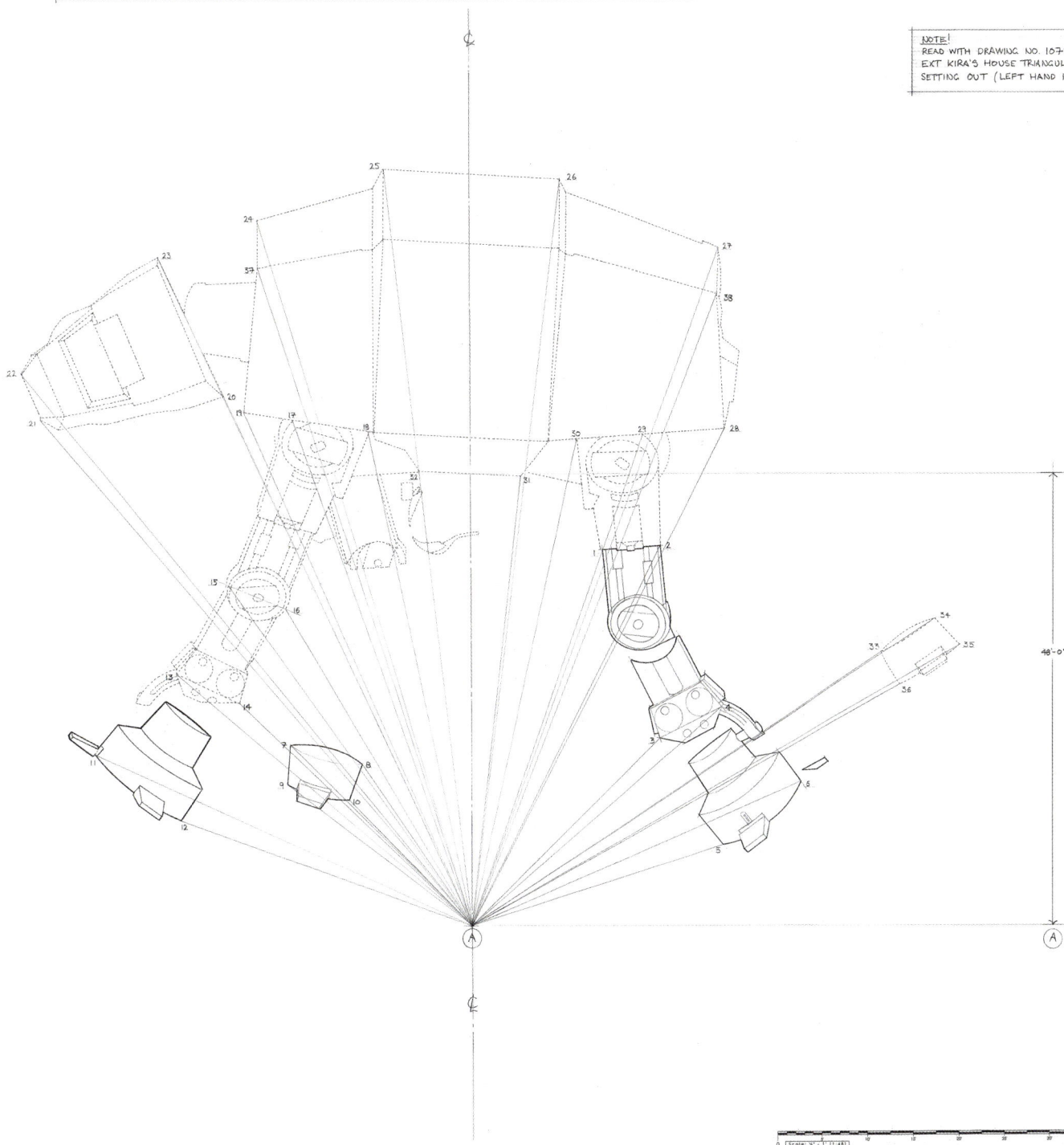

ANGLE KEY

	A	ANGLE
SET BUILD		
1	42'-3"	19.5°
2	46'-3"	27°
3	28'-6"	45.5°
4	35'-9"	49.5°
5	28'-7"	72.5°
6	34'-0"	67°
7	27'-6"	-45.5°
8	20'-11"	-34.5°
9	25'-0"	-53°
10	19'-0"	-45°
11	45'-0"	-66°
12	33'-6"	-70.5°
VFX EXTENSION		
13	44'-10"	-50°
14	54'-6"	-47°
15	45'-0"	-35°
16	39'-6"	-31°
17	57'-6"	-20°
18	53'-9"	-12°
19	60'-0"	-24.5°
20	62'-8"	-25.5°
21	71'-6"	-41°
22	76'-6"	-40°
23	79'-0"	-25.5°
24	78'-9"	-17.5°
25	81'-3"	-7°
26	80'-0"	7°
27	77'-0"	20.5°
28	59'-9"	27.5°
29	55'-6"	19.5°
30	53'-0"	12.5°
31	48'-1"	6°
32	48'-9"	-7°
33	55'-5"	57°
34	60'-3"	57.5°
35	61'-3"	61°
36	53'-6"	61.5°

BODY HEIGHT CO-ORDINATES

	A	ANGLE	HEIGHT
37	74'-0"	-18.5°	24'-9"
38	72'-6"	22°	23'-8"

48'-0"

Ⓐ

AVCO		
SET: KIRA'S HOUSE SETTING OUT BY ANGLE		
(LEFT HAND HEAD)		
DETAIL		
PRODUCTION DESIGNER: RICK CARTER DARREN GILFORD	STAGE: N/A	
SUPERVISING ART DIRECTOR: NEIL LAMONT	LOCATION: DESSERT	
SCALE ¼"-1'-0"	DRAWN BY: SAM R	
DATE DRAWN 22.4.14	DRAWING NO. 1073A	
DATE ISSUED 23.4.14		

2174_Set_KirasHouseExt_140422_SettingOutByAngleLeftHand Head_1073_SR

SET KIRA'S HOUSE SETTING OUT BY ANGLE (LEFT HAND HEAD)
DETAIL N/A
DRG NO. 1073A
DATE APRIL 24 2014
DRAWN BY SAMANTHA REDWOOD

↑ A triangulation illustration defines where the unseen portions of the AT-AT would lie beyond the constructed segments, providing a guide for production to allow for blocking the scene.

→ This final frame from *The Force Awakens* shows the partial set build of Rey's fallen walker home, which has been extended and completed by a digital matte painting.

NIIMA OUTPOST

Except for the nighttime village assault filmed on the backlot at Pinewood Studios, the sparce settlements on Jakku were photographed primarily on location in the deserts of Abu Dhabi. The gathering of structures dubbed Niima Outpost in the script included a tented marketplace called "Main Street" during development. The largest building, where scavengers trade scrap for dehydrated food portions, was the "Concession Stand." A shelter resembling a skeletonized Quonset hut, where scavengers scrub their wares clean, was the "Canteen." Other outlying constructs had functions minimally described in their names ("energy transmitter," "power station," and "pipes"), but these would be background details at most. The outermost structures were built atop flatbed and car carrier trailers for ease of transport and positioning.

Unlike other environs in *Star Wars* movies, Niima Outpost did not get digital set extensions and instead remained sparse. This was part of J.J. Abrams' commitment to capturing this locale practically, in-camera, as much as possible. "If there was any CG, it was something that had been painted out," he said.

The centerpiece of the outpost, the Concession Stand, was a tent-like facility built around the "Gang Boss Structure," the domain of Unkar Plutt, the junk boss. "It was like a circus tent in shape and form, and designed that way so that, as the wind kicks up, it moves all the fabric of the ceiling," said production designer Darren Gilford. Close-ups of Unkar would be picked up at Pinewood, where his shack was rebuilt.

Although the deserts of Jakku appear to be a galaxy away from any body of water, in truth the shooting location was about 140 miles from the Persian Gulf, meaning gusty winds would come in from the coastline. The tent structures appear flimsy on film, but they were built atop steel frames bolted to a foundation of precast concrete blocks sunk into the sand. Stand-by crews stood ready with sewing machines to fix any tears that might appear in the canvas drapery.

Many of the outer structures and additional detailing came courtesy of Stars Poly tankages, a Dubai-based firm that sold massive PVC water-storage drums, which the art department stacked, cut, repainted, and re-dressed as "found object" machinery.

Niima Outpost would occupy the first week of shooting on *The Force Awakens*, and was a baptism of—if not fire, then definitely warm temperatures for the crew. Daytime highs exceeded 115 degrees Fahrenheit, an endurance test for the dozens of costumed alien characters that would populate the outpost.

"We had a bunch of alien characters that Michael Kaplan's costume team suited and booted, and we gave them animatronic heads," said creature effects supervisor Neal Scanlan. "We tried to hold onto the same philosophy as they had in 1977, where people ran out to hardware shops, bought a bunch of stuff, and used their imaginations."

Off to the side of the outpost was a corralled paddock that served as a landing bay for visitors to Jakku, and it was here that CG extensions were required for the few ships parked there, including the beloved *Millennium Falcon*. Entrance to the paddock was through a flared gate based on a design that Ralph McQuarrie had illustrated decades earlier as a concept for Jabba the Hutt's palace. The harried escape from Niima Outpost would be shot with IMAX cameras, demanding exacting detail work for the unyielding visual fidelity of the large-format film.

As Finn, Rey, and BB-8 tear their way past the gate to the ship paddock, special effects supervisor Chris Corbould and his team detonated enormous explosives to simulate the strafing runs of the TIE fighters that would be digitally added to the shot. The neophyte heroes briefly consider taking a quadjumper, a cargo-hauling tug ship, to make their escape, but it explodes in an enormous plume, spewing debris everywhere. The ship would be computer-generated in the final shot, but the explosion was real, consuming a 40-foot-long pyrotechnic "buck"—or shaped stand-in—that would explode in a convincing manner.

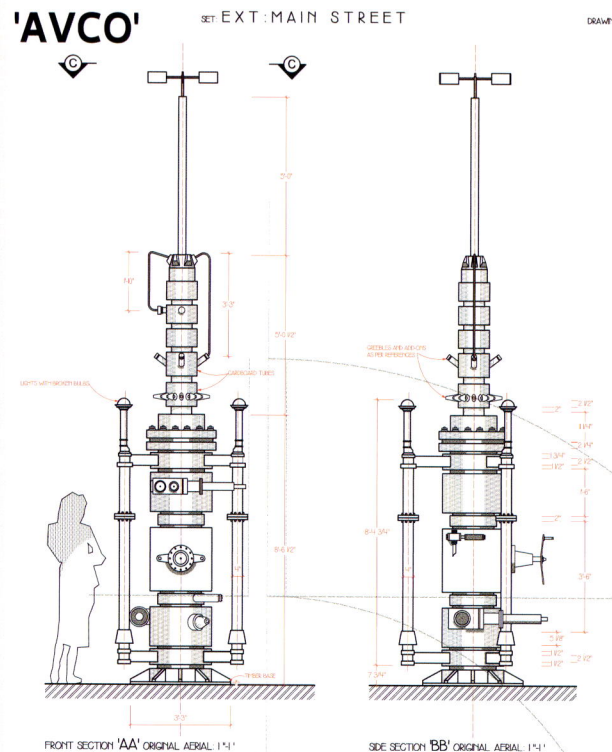

'AVCO'   SET: EXT: MAIN STREET   DRAWING

FRONT SECTION 'AA' ORIGINAL AERIAL 1:4'   SIDE SECTION 'BB' ORIGINAL AERIAL 1:4'

SET	EXT. MAIN STREET
DETAIL	ORIGINAL VAPORATORS FOR SCRAPHEAP
DRG NO.	026
DATE	OCTOBER 8 2013
DRAWN BY	CLAIRE FLEMING

↑ Deserts are common locations in *Star Wars*, so a moisture vaporator styled after the original (see page 26) was an inevitable sight on Jakku. This illustration uses vaporators from the original and prequel trilogies as reference.

↓ The canvas drapes on Niima Outpost not only provided blessed shade, but the natural interaction with the wind helped ground the set as a real on-location environment and not a studio creation.

SET	EXT. MAIN STREET
DETAIL	EXT. CONCESSIONS STAND — PLANS & ELEVATIONS
DRG NO.	490
DATE	NOVEMBER 22 2013
DRAWN BY	SAM LEAKE

→ The "Concessions Stand" structure of Niima outpost is illustrated in a set of blueprints that defines the solid structure as well as the canvas drapery. The illustration includes a Tusken Raider for scale, although the alien's presence at the location is not meant to be taken literally.

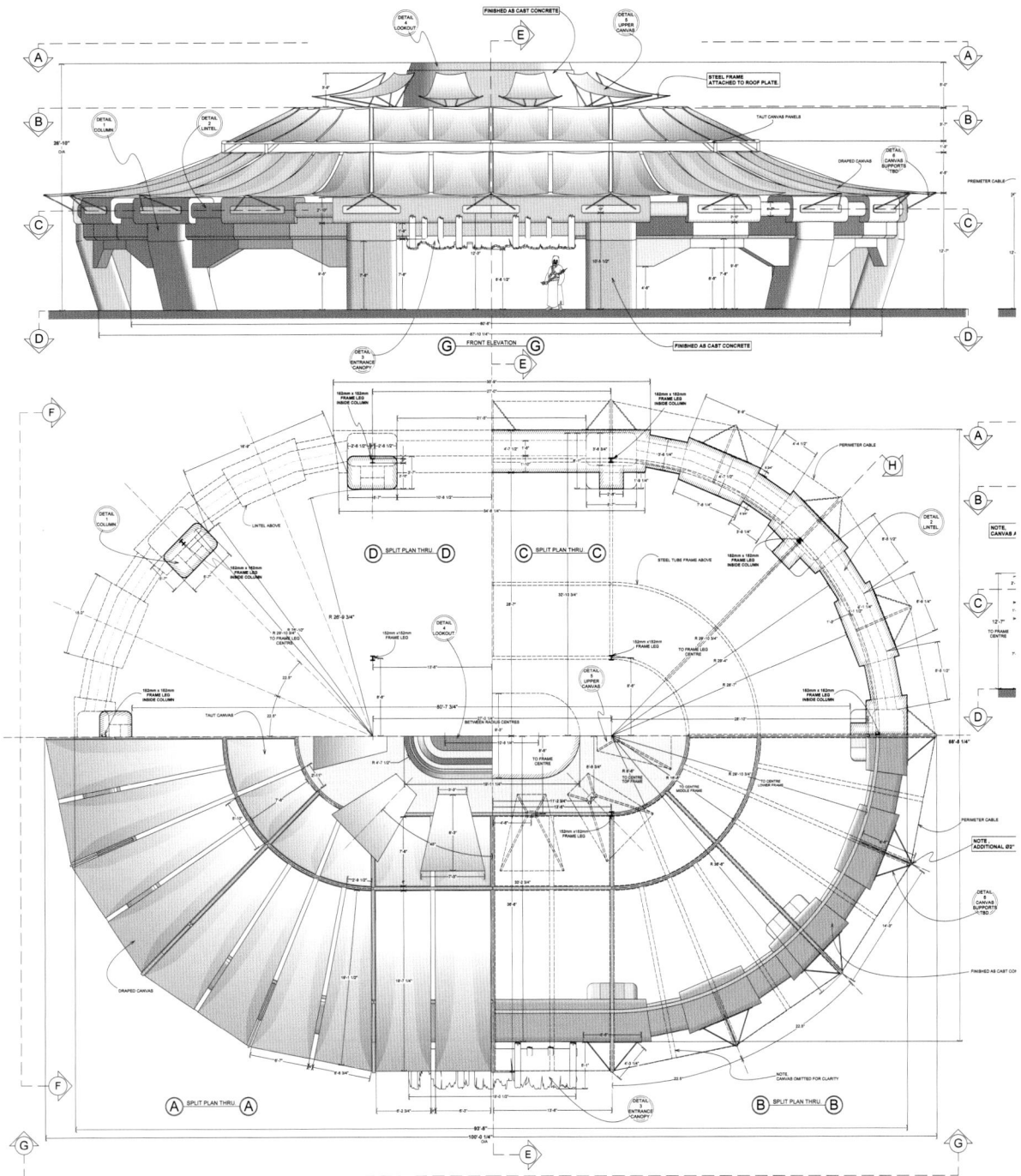

↓ The repeating alien alphanumerics etched into the depot gate are based on Ralph McQuarrie's art of Jabba's palace made for *Return of the Jedi*. These 25 characters would be laser cut from medium-density fiberboard at a height of 1 ft 9 in for each letter.

SET	EXT. MAIN STREET
DETAIL	DEPOT MAIN GATE —
	PERFORATED STEEL ROOF
DRG NO.	219
DATE	JANUARY 8 2014
DRAWN BY	L. S.

MILLENNIUM FALCON

After decades of being grounded, the *Millennium Falcon* was set to soar again. All the iterations of the evolving Episode VII storyline placed the legendary freighter in the thick of the action and, as production readied for the film, every scrap of available reference of Han Solo's battered ship—footage, photography, artwork, and more— underwent diligent scrutiny to help the crew recreate it once again as a movie set.

"The *Falcon* is a character in its own right, as much as Han, Leia, or Luke," said senior art director Gary Tomkins, who led the design work on spacecraft and vehicles. "The audience would welcome it like an old friend. We went through a lot of research and legacy stuff from the Lucasfilm Archives to get all the details correct."

Although some concept art explored add-ons that would change the *Falcon*'s shape, ultimately the call came to realize the ship as a preserved museum piece, exactingly recreated from the original trilogy. Art director Lydia Fry and props art director Mark Harris taped out the *Falcon* floor plan on a stage at Pinewood studios, then mocked up a cockpit and assembled photo research and greeblie details to show Abrams during a visit. "That was when we realized J.J. wanted it to be as accurate as we could possibly make it to the original," Harris said.

"Mark Harris was like a scientist figuring out how the *Falcon* changed from *A New Hope* to *Empire*," Abrams said. "In the second film, the size of the cockpit expanded and the scale of the ship got bigger. We realized that, even with material you thought was canon, big changes were being made."

"Recreating the *Falcon* exactly proved a bit of a challenge, because not only did the ship change between films, but it also changed within each film!" Tomkins noted.

Beginning early in 2014, the rebuilding of the *Falcon* was sometimes a cinematic archeological dig. Mark Harris, a veteran of *The Empire Strikes Back*, combed his memory for first-hand accounts of the creation of the ship for that movie. Fry recalls Harris coming to work one day in triumph, holding a rubber lid from a 1970s coffee jar, the exact kind used to dress the back of the pilot's seat. Other funky found objects that dressed the original *Falcon*, including bubble-wrap packaging, old fuse boxes, and switches, would be replicated in the new construction of the starship.

SET	EXT. CAROUSEL ELEMENTS/INT. FREIGHTER/ PIRATE'S COVE
DETAIL	TOPSIDE PLAN & ELEVATIONS & BASIC HULL STRUCTURE
DRG NO.	817
DATE	MAY 20 2014
DRAWN BY	DANNY CLARK

➜ Danny Clark's illustrations show the "topside Carousel," the segment of the *Millennium Falcon* to be built at full scale. Silhouettes of Chewbacca and Han Solo help define the scale.

➜ The interior of the main compartment set featured in *The Force Awakens* includes the recovery bed, which was only loosely defined in *The Empire Strikes Back*, on a previously unexamined stretch of wall.

For Beak skin detail see 1/2" detail on this sheet and panel detail on sheet 1227

Line indicates centre line of carousel

Extent of cockpit corridor TBD see drawing number 048
19'-8 3/4"

29'-1 3/8"
CENTRE LINE OF COCKPIT

27'-0 1/2"

For radius of carousel hull, see section through on this sheet

73.5 Degrees

68.5 Degrees

Landing gear box side skin

13'-0"

30'-10"
TOP OF DRUM TO CENTRE LINE

4'-5"   4'-9"

Radiused Equator Band shown here for clarity, see detail sheet number 046

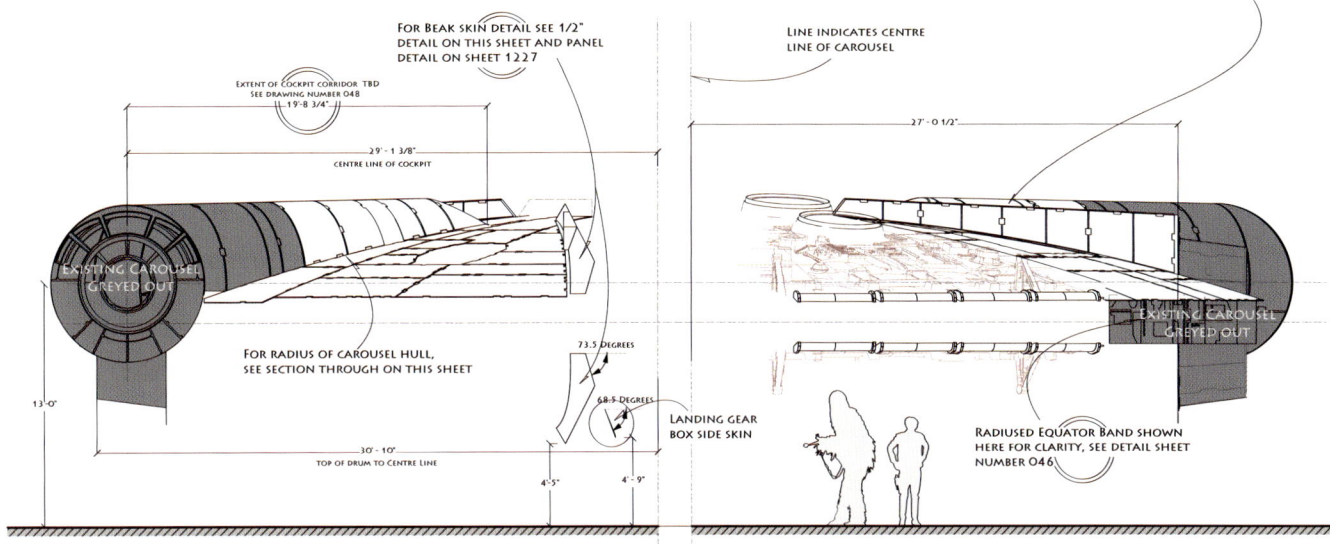

Elevation B - B -
Top Side Carousel
SCALE: 1/4" - 1' - 0"

Elevation C - C -
Top Side Carousel
SCALE: 1/4" - 1' - 0"

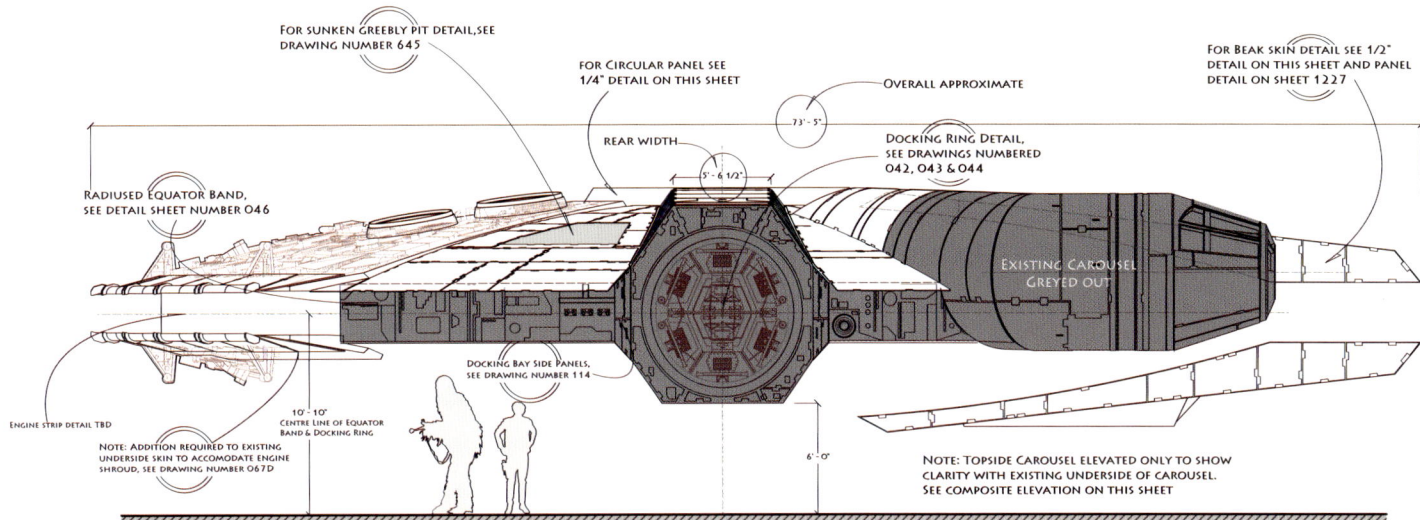

For sunken greebly pit detail, see drawing number 645

For Circular panel see 1/4" detail on this sheet

Overall approximate

For Beak skin detail see 1/2" detail on this sheet and panel detail on sheet 1227

Rear width

73'-5"

Docking Ring Detail, see drawings numbered 042, 043 & 044

Radiused Equator Band, see detail sheet number 046

5'-6 1/2"

Docking Bay Side Panels, see drawing number 114

Engine strip detail TBD

10'-10"
Centre Line of Equator Band & Docking Ring

Note: Addition required to existing underside skin to accommodate engine shroud, see drawing number 067D

6'-0"

Note: Topside carousel elevated only to show clarity with existing underside of carousel. See composite elevation on this sheet

Elevation A - A -
Top Side Carousel
SCALE: 1/4" - 1' - 0"

For Lando's Hatch & Topside docking Bay Panels see drawings numbered: 753, 767, 779 & 796

For docking bay Basic Structure panel details Please see 1" - 1' - 0" drawing on this sheet

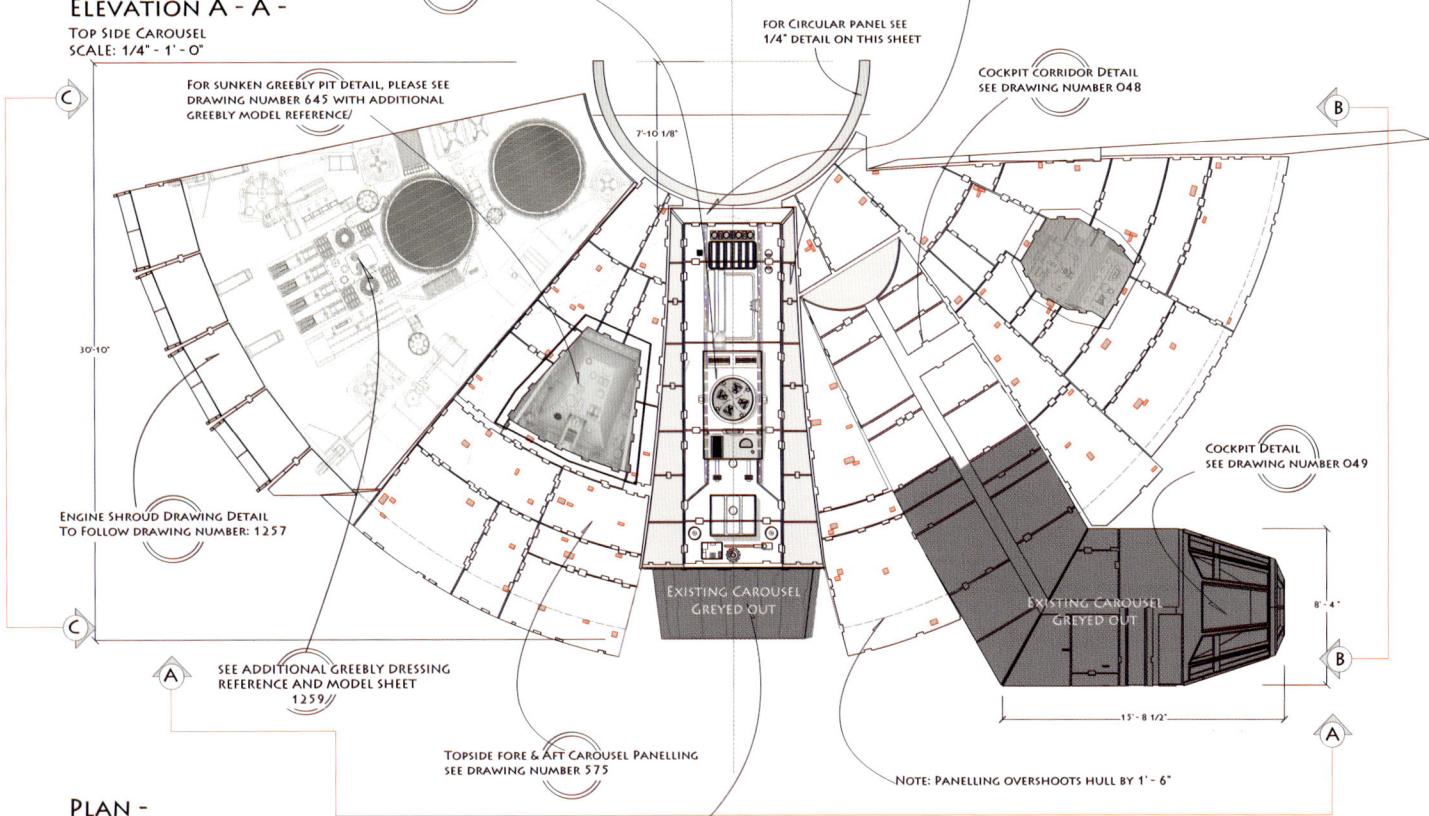

For Circular panel see 1/4" detail on this sheet

For sunken greebly pit detail, please see drawing number 645 with additional greebly model reference/

Cockpit corridor Detail see drawing number 048

7'-10 1/8"

Cockpit Detail see drawing number 049

30'-10"

Engine Shroud Drawing Detail To Follow drawing number: 1257

8'-4"

See additional greebly dressing reference and model sheet 1259

15'-8 1/2"

Topside fore & Aft Carousel Panelling see drawing number 575

Note: Panelling overshoots hull by 1'-6"

PLAN -
Top Side Carousel
SCALE: 1/4" - 1' - 0"

Docking Ring Armour Panels see drawing number 070

"My original intention was to approximate the wall lights with a new found object," Harris explained. "But [asset producer] James Enright said, 'We can model and print them in 3D.' We modeled things like the handles of the control yoke in clay, but we couldn't get the scale right, so we scanned them in 3D and printed them in ten-percent increments to check against real handles, until we got them accurate. I didn't believe we were going to get some things close to the original, but I think we've got them right."

"Since it was thirty years later, we had license to add more dressing," Fry added. "If someone else had taken over the ship, they would have installed things over the years, and run cables and electrics. Adding more texture, aging, dirt, and rust made it live."

"I wanted to build it all," construction coordinator Paul Hayes said. "But the budget meant we cut back. We then only wanted to build the underbelly and the equator band, and we were going to make the cockpit separately. Slowly but surely, we added more—and eventually we almost achieved my goal of making it all. We built about three quarters of the exterior set." The most complete version of the ship was constructed outside the Resistance base at Greenham Common (see pages 288 to 289).

"It was a huge privilege to work on the *Millennium Falcon*, the most iconic spaceship in cinema history," said Fry. "Everyone was excited about it from day one. It was most exciting at the end, when the shooting crew and J.J. and others walked in the first time. They got to experience walking up the ramp, through the circular corridor, straight into the hold or the cockpit, and it meant so much to so many people. Even if you're not a *Star Wars* fan you can't help have a connection and fondness for it."

AVCO CODE NAMES

During the production of *The Force Awakens*, every identifiable character, locale, and vehicle was given a code name. This was to prevent loose documentation from revealing any story beats. Whereas "AVCO" as the umbrella title was a nod to a 1970s movie theater, the vehicles in the film would adopt the names of amusement park rides. The *Millennium Falcon* was the "Carousel," the X-wing was the "Tilt-a-Whirl," the TIE fighter was a "Penny Arcade," and speeders of various types were "Bumper Cars."

↓ The painstakingly recreated interior of the *Millennium Falcon* built to exacting detail from extensive research into the original *Star Wars* trilogy.

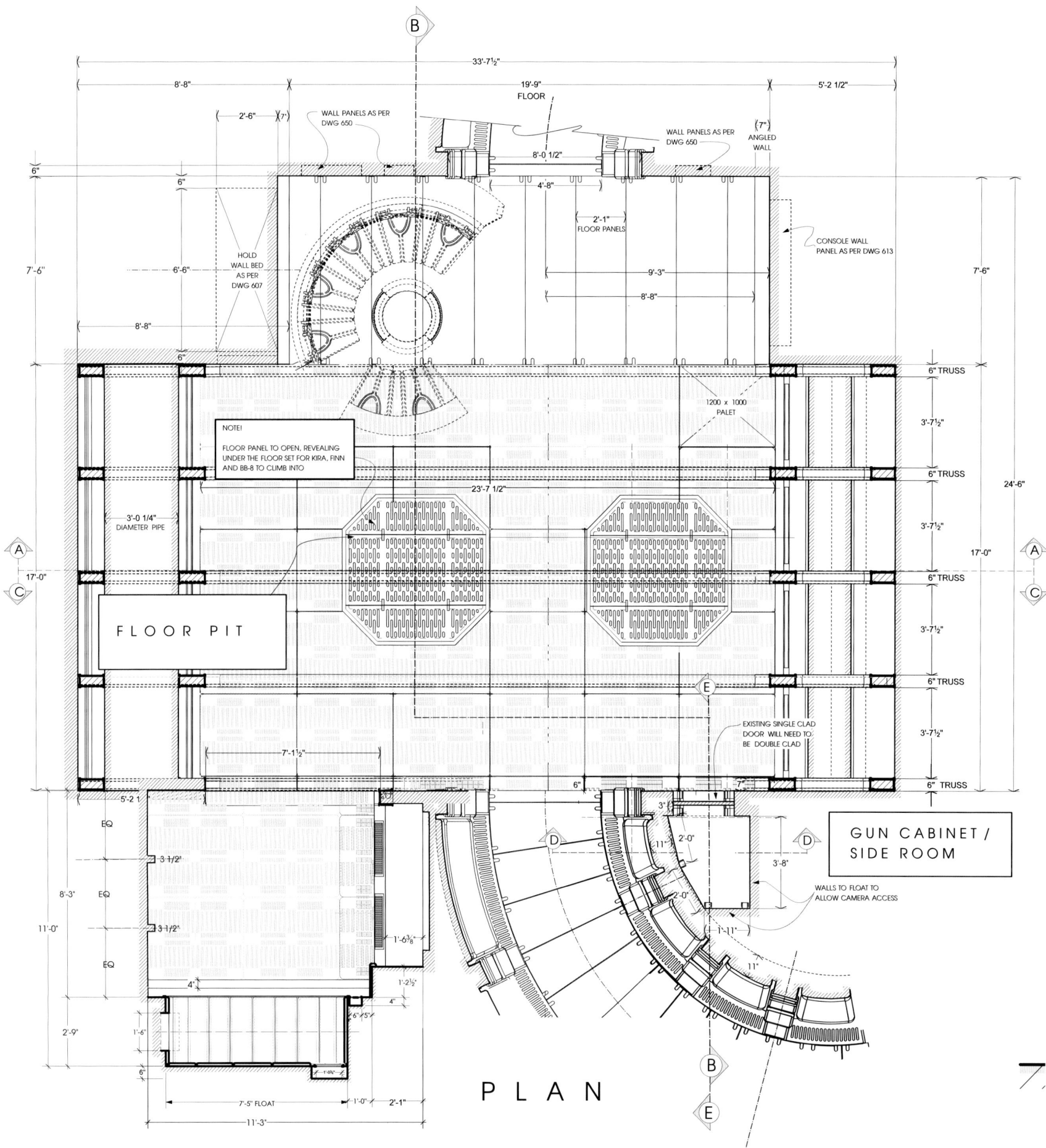

B

33'-7½"

8'-8"

19'-9"
FLOOR

5'-2 1/2"

2'-6"   7'

WALL PANELS AS PER
DWG 650

8'-0 1/2"

WALL PANELS AS PER
DWG 650

(7")
ANGLED
WALL

6"

6"

4'-8"

2'-1"
FLOOR PANELS

CONSOLE WALL
PANEL AS PER DWG 613

7'-6"

HOLD
WALL BED
AS PER
DWG 607

6'-6"

9'-3"

8'-8"

7'-6"

8'-8"

6"

6" TRUSS

1200 x 1000
PALET

3'-7½"

NOTE!

FLOOR PANEL TO OPEN, REVEALING
UNDER THE FLOOR SET FOR KIRA, FINN
AND BB-8 TO CLIMB INTO

6" TRUSS

23'-7 1/2"

3'-7½"

24'-6"

3'-0 1/4"
DIAMETER PIPE

A

A

17'-0"

17'-0"

C

C

6" TRUSS

FLOOR PIT

3'-7½"

E

6" TRUSS

EXISTING SINGLE CLAD
DOOR WILL NEED TO
BE DOUBLE CLAD

7'-1½"

6"

7"

6" TRUSS

5'-2 1

EQ

D

D

3½"

2'-0"

GUN CABINET /
SIDE ROOM

8'-3"

EQ

3'-8"

11'-0"

EQ

3½"

1'-6⅜"

2'-0"

WALLS TO FLOAT TO
ALLOW CAMERA ACCESS

4"

1'-2½"

1'-11"

11"

4"

2'-9"

1'-6"

6" 5"

B

6"

1'-0⅝"

7'-5 FLOAT

1'-0" 2'-1"

P L A N

E

11'-3"

SET	INT. CAROUSEL
DETAIL	PIT & GUN CLOSET
DRG NO.	1644
DATE	AUGUST 28 2014
DRAWN BY	LYDIA FRY

↑ Detail of the "Pit & Gun Closet" plans for the
Millennium Falcon, denoting the maintenance pit where
Rey and Finn hide and the gun closet where Han Solo
retrieves some stashed blasters. The gun closet is
also the place in *The Empire Strikes Back* where Han
and Leia share a memorable kiss.

HAN SOLO'S FREIGHTER

Evidence of their ill fortunes, Han Solo and Chewbacca are flying a decrepit, boxy old freighter that has more in common with a container ship than their former "fastest hunk of junk in the galaxy." The big ship swallows the newly found *Millennium Falcon* whole, like a whale, and within its ramshackle interior, Han has to later face off against two rival gangs of toughs to whom he owes money.

Real-life misfortune impacted the filming of these sequences. Earlier in production, Harrison Ford had injured his leg when a rolling door on the *Falcon* set slammed onto him. As he recovered, the production reorganized its shooting schedule to move up scenes that didn't require Ford, which included the extensive stunt work that would take place aboard the freighter when Solo's monstrous cargo of rathtar creatures runs amok.

This rescheduling meant the freighter set was being constructed on Pinewood's A Stage at the same time as the stunt rehearsals. "We were kind of chasing our tail now, because construction was a little bit behind," explained stunt coordinator Rob Inch.

↓ A preliminary isometric exploration of the corridor set shows one half of the implied cargo modules colored in. The repetitive nature of the structure means that segments of the corridor could be filmed multiple times to suggest an expansive environment.

SET	INT. PILOT'S GARAGE CORRIDORS
DETAIL	ISOMETRIC VIEW
DRG NO.	N/A
DATE	MAY 27 2014
DRAWN BY	SOPHIE BRIDGMAN

AVCO

INT. PILOT'S GARAGE - CORRIDORS

ISOMETRIC VIEW

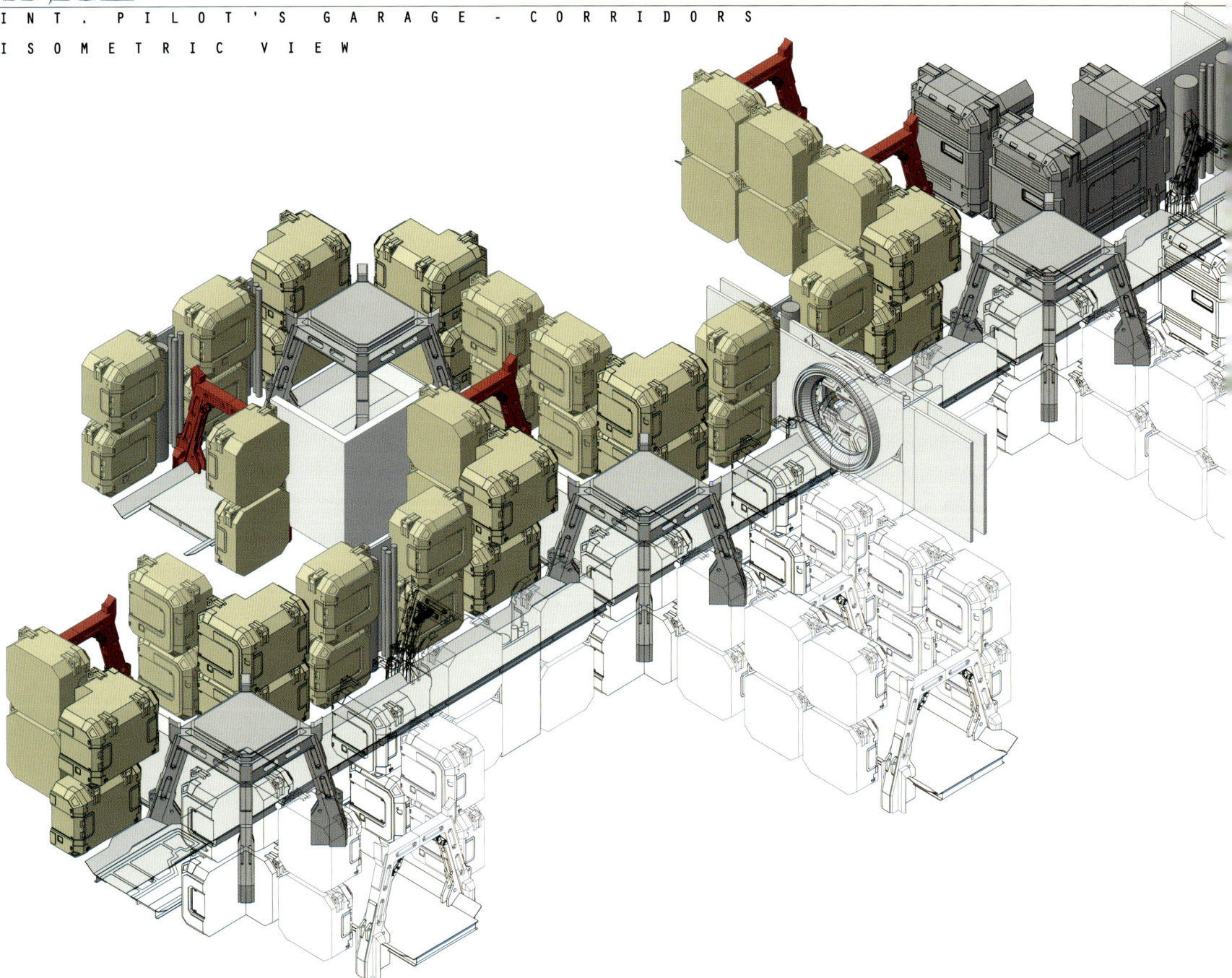

↑ This posed and lit render of the digital model of Han Solo's inelegant freighter was built by ILM.

EXPLODED VIEW
SHOWING STRUCTURE AND FASCIA
COMPONENTS

4 X 2 SFX BOX SECTION STRUCTURE
(ATTACHED TO OUTER RIG AND CHAIN
MECH - OMITTED)

TOP SECTION
LAYER FLUSH WITH
STRUCTURE - 1/4"
OUTSIDE LAYER 3/4"
TOTAL PROJECTION
1" - O/A
1 1/8" INCLUDING
FRAME OF CONTROL PANEL

SFX PADS - 1/8"
X 4 X 2

BOTTOM SECTION - TOTAL
PROJECTION 1"

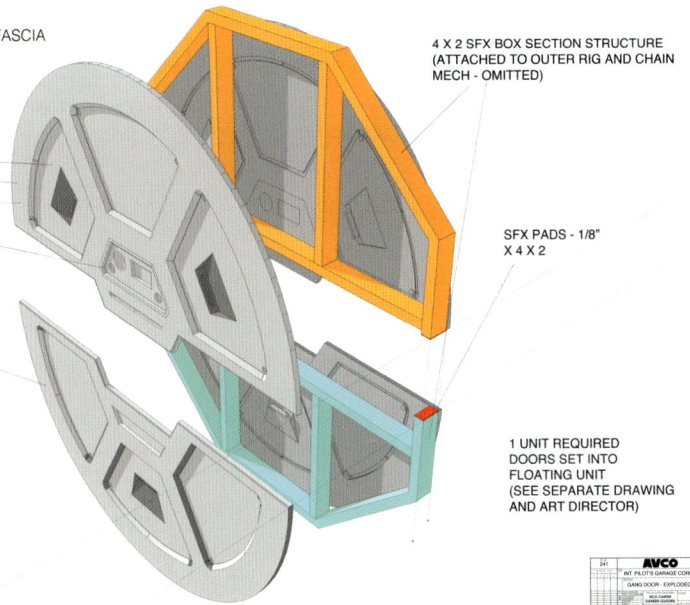

1 UNIT REQUIRED
DOORS SET INTO
FLOATING UNIT
(SEE SEPARATE DRAWING
AND ART DIRECTOR)

AVCO PILOTS FREIGHTER - GANG DOOR / CREATURE CRUSHER
A STAGE BUILD -

CALE - 3/8" : 1'-0"

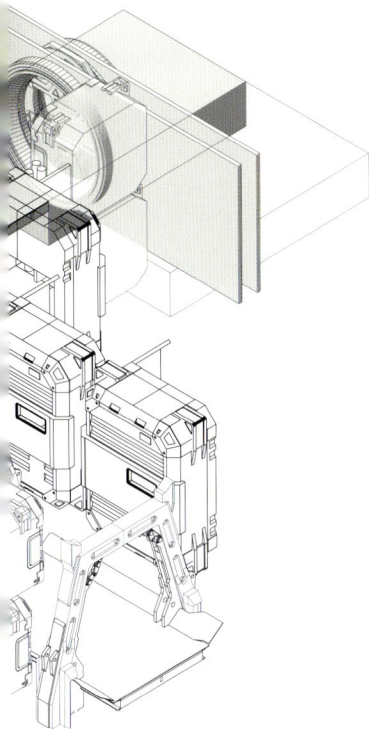

SET	INT. PILOT'S GARAGE CORRIDORS
DETAIL	GANG DOOR — EXPLODED VIEW
DRG NO.	1400
DATE	JUNE 17 2014
DRAWN BY	ROB COWPER

↑ The "creature crusher" door aboard Han's freighter is detailed in this exploded view by Rob Cowper. The colored segments are door structures that will be operated by the SFX team, while the light gray surface cladding is the art-directed, camera-facing exterior.

← An illustration by Jake Lunt Davies puts the fearsome rathtar beast in situ within the corridor set of Han's cargo freighter.

"This meant my team had to work nights for rehearsals. The sequence got brought forward a week, so they were still building the set. We rehearsed in the evening, when it was clearer for us. Everyone and their dog were trying to get their moment on set."

The most involved section of set consisted of a junction of corridors that suggested catwalks connecting cargo modules—these repeated structures could be creatively edited to feel like a larger warren within the freighter. Fully dressed ceilings added to a sense of claustrophobia and could be removed to accommodate the wire rig needed to toss about the rathtar victims. Such work would feature a talented team of Indonesian stunt performers, including Iko Uwais and Yayan Ruhian, who starred in the bone-rattling movies,

The Raid (2011) and *The Raid 2* (2014). "This is a corridor set, really—a ten-foot space," said Inch. "We can grab someone from the floor, smash them up into the ceiling corner, drop them, and drag them along."

The corridor environment also included similarly crisscrossing crawl spaces where Rey and Finn hide from the creature chaos above. "Luckily they had put something on top of the grating, because it was actual grating we were crawling over, and it was seriously sharp," said actor Daisy Ridley, playing Rey.

The rathtar breakout was shot over two days, and later, upon recovery, Harrison Ford was able to film his portions of the sequence. "He returned and was literally running around on this uneven set faster than I've ever run anywhere," marveled Abrams.

MAZ'S CASTLE

Now a united quartet tasked to return BB-8 to the Resistance, Han Solo, Chewbacca, Rey, and Finn land the *Millennium Falcon* on the planet Takodana, next to a serene lake on whose shores stands Maz Kanata's castle. A major location in the film's second act, the environment secured the carnival-themed code name "House of Mirrors," and would be realized through a variety of techniques.

Maz's castle would be the confluence of many different alien cultures and was depicted in early draft iterations like a Western saloon. This, however, made it too much of a callback to the infamous Mos Eisley Cantina of *A New Hope*. "This was clearly our cantina," said Abrams. "It was a nod to the Cantina. It felt like fair game because if you look at *Star Wars*, the notion [is that there are] countless watering holes that exist in various corners of the galaxy. On the one hand, I think cynically you could say, 'Oh, they're just trying to do the Cantina again.' But on the other hand, it's *Star Wars*, and if you don't have a version of one, I would leave feeling like, 'Well, how could they not do the Cantina?' So, the challenge was, how can we do the Cantina—but not *do* the Cantina?"

A new creative prompt for the setting was unlocked when unused concept art from *The Empire Strikes Back* was discovered: a Ralph McQuarrie illustration of what could have been Darth Vader's castle. "Does Maz live in a bar, a ship, a town, a city, or—wait a minute, maybe it can be a *Star Wars* castle!" recounted production designer Rick Carter of the artwork. "We started to riff off it as a place where she could exist. Then we started to make up the story of why she was there…"

"We wanted to develop a whole story about the castle," said set decorator Lee Sandales. "It was a place where people could come to escape and find a home with Maz—a communal place to make deals and plan heists. It was an ancient castle that had an alien history."

→ The "Hall of Mirrors" interior environment, otherwise known as Maz's castle, is defined in these overhead plan and wall elevations.

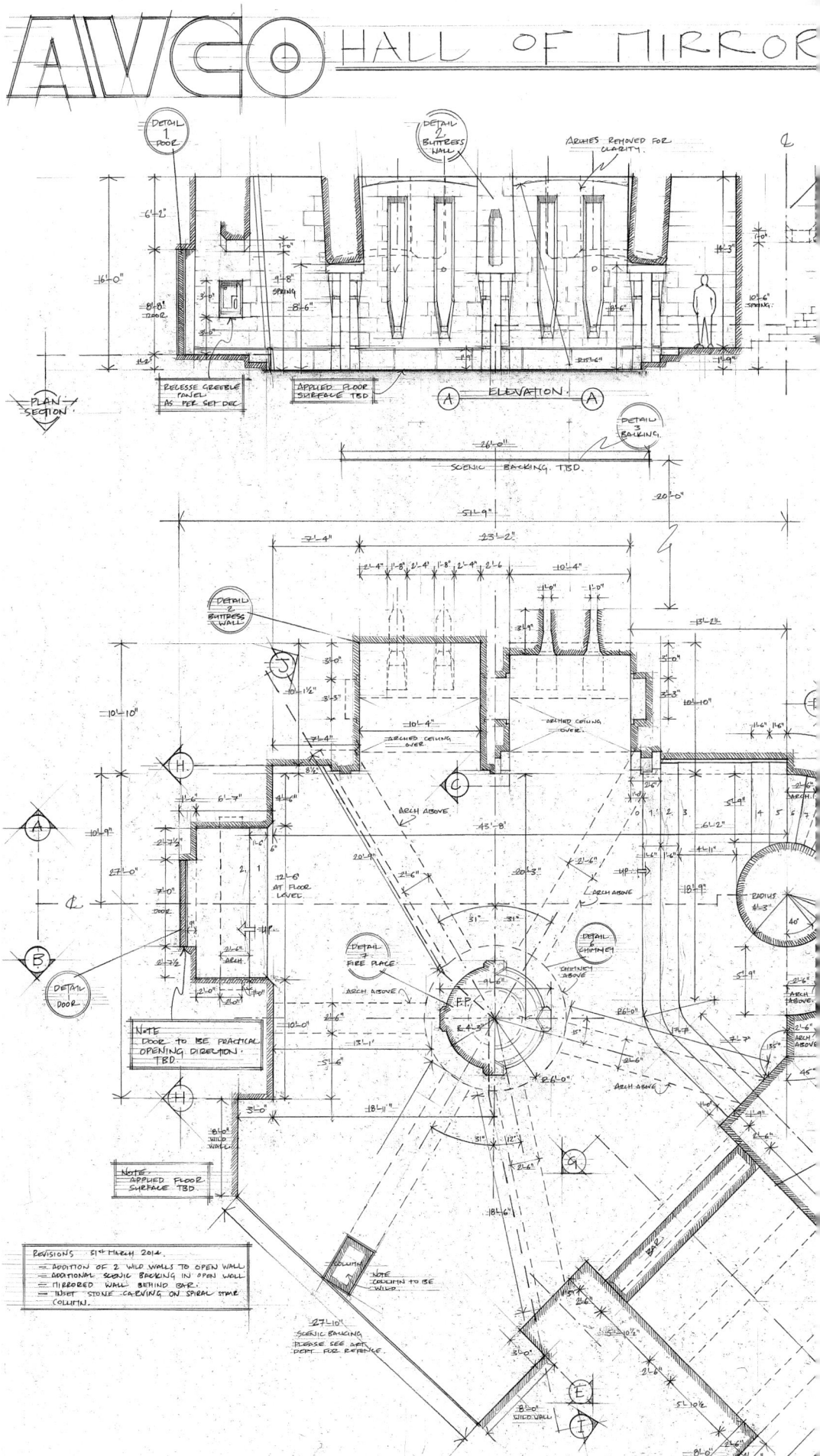

SET	INT. HALL OF MIRRORS
DETAIL	PLANS & ELEVATION
DRG NO.	917A
DATE	MARCH 24 2014
DRAWN BY	SAM LEAKE

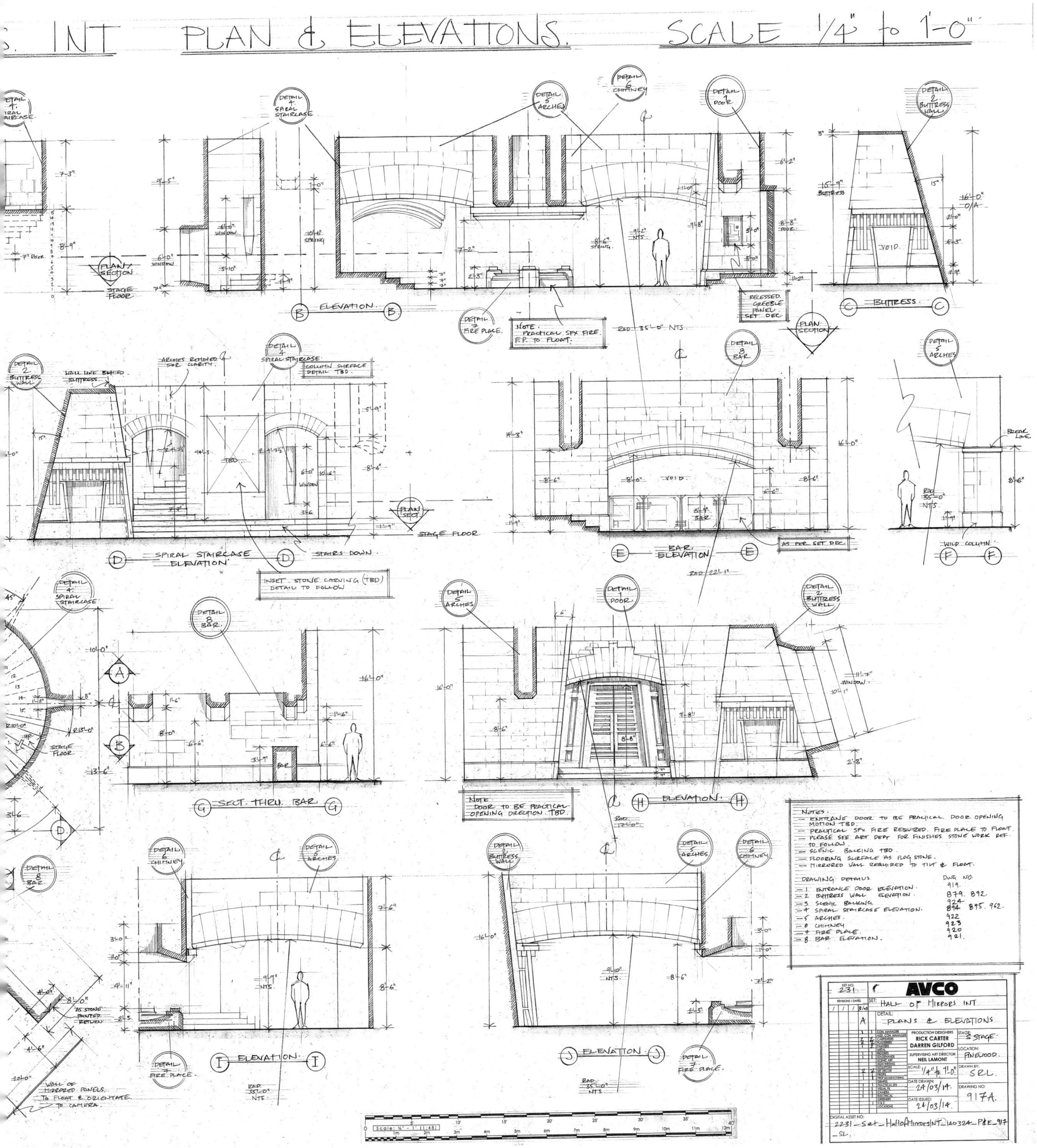

INT PLAN & ELEVATIONS. SCALE 1/4" to 1'-0"

ELEVATION. B

BUTTRESS. C

SPIRAL STAIRCASE ELEVATION. D

BAR. ELEVATION. E

WILD COLUMN. F

SECT. THRU. BAR. G

ELEVATION. H

ELEVATION. I

ELEVATION. J

INSET STONE CARVING (TBD) DETAIL TO FOLLOW

NOTE: PRACTICAL SPX FIRE. F.P. TO FLOAT.

NOTE: DOOR TO BE PRACTICAL OPENING DIRECTION TBD.

WALL OF MIRRORED PANELS. TO FLOAT & ORIENTATE. TO CAMERA.

Notes:
- ENTRANE DOOR TO BE PRACTICAL. DOOR OPENING MOTION TBD.
- PRACTICAL SPX FIRE REQUIRED. FIRE PLACE TO FLOAT.
- PLEASE SEE ART DEPT FOR FINISHES. STONE WORK REF TO FOLLOW
- SCENIC BACKING TBD.
- FLOORING SURFACE AS FLAG STONE.
- MIRRORED WALL REQUIRED TO TILT & FLOAT.

DRAWING DETAILS   DWG NO
1. ENTRANCE DOOR ELEVATION.	919
2. BUTTRESS WALL ELEVATION.	879. 892.
3. SCENIC BACKING.	924
4. SPIRAL STAIRCASE ELEVATION.	894. 895. 962.
5. ARCHES	923
6. CHIMNEY	923
7. FIRE PLACE.	920
8. BAR ELEVATION.	921.

AVCO

SET: HALL OF MIRRORS INT.
DETAIL: PLANS & ELEVATIONS
STAGE: 3 STAGE
LOCATION: PINEWOOD

PRODUCTION DESIGNERS: RICK CARTER / DARREN GILFORD
SUPERVISING ART DIRECTOR: NEIL LAMONT

SCALE: 1/4" = 1'-0"
DRAWN BY: SRL
DATE DRAWN: 24/03/14
DATE ISSUED: 24/03/14
DRAWING NO: 917A

SET NO: 231.

DIGITAL ASSET NO: 231_Set_HallOfMirrors_INT_140324_P&E_917_SRL.

↓ A shattered doorway to the castle is shown in this plans
and elevation view, with a stormtrooper included for
scale. The doorway is designed to be built onto a truck
trailer bed for ease of positioning on the backlot.

6½" CORBEL'S

FOR COLUMN DtL READ
WITH DWG # 830

STONE COURSING T.B.D

APP 6"~1'-2" STONECLAD
WALL & RUBBLE CORE-T.B.D
-SEE ARt DIRECTOR

19'-11"
BUILD EXtENTS

B

R 5'-0"

8'-11"

A

3'-11½"

9"

FRONT ELEVATION

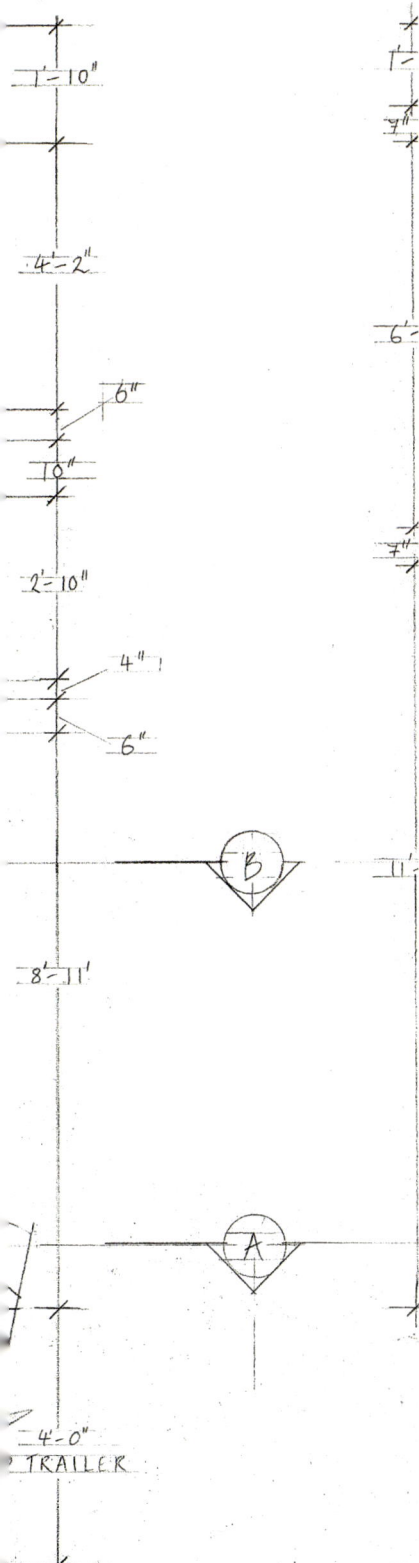

↑ A detail of a final frame from the movie shows Kylo Ren's ominous shuttle coming to land at the crumbling castle. This shot combines the Pinewood backlot construction with digital ruins and extensions.

↑ Kylo Ren (Adam Driver) strides menacingly through the crumbling ruins, shot on the Pinewood South Dock backlot.

The alien-packed watering hole shifted from saloon to medieval mead hall, complete with otherworldly poultry roasting on a spit in one corner, a water well transformed into a large mechanical still to make moonshine, and all sorts of tables to broker business and play games.

"Getting to do a castle in a *Star Wars* environment was a fantastic challenge," said production designer Darren Gilford. "We were working with the English art department, so of course it was in their wheelhouse. It was so wonderful to work with them and tap into the classic construction methodology and skillset. We tried to bring the feel and vibe of a traditional castle, with the quality of brutal, heavy stone, and then add our *Star Wars* details. The team did a great job of finding a blend between medieval castle elements and *Star Wars* vernacular. I could look around and see Ralph's influence: a lamp, the arches, the pit in the middle. I was proud of this McQuarrie-inspired set."

So strong was the influence, Abrams even staged a deliberate homage to McQuarrie's "Cantina" production illustration of March 6, 1975, with new creatures taking the place of devil-tailed demon aliens and a waitress droid standing where a concept-art version of C-3PO stood.

The castle environment consisted of the exterior, which was digitally crafted by ILM, complete with a huge statue of Maz, along with flags and banners representing various allied cultures. The section of entrance courtyard and doorway was built practically outdoors on the Pinewood backlot, while the main interior hall and the cellar storerooms were built on two separate sets on S stage at Pinewood.

"We had the intact castle set and we had a ruined castle set, which got destroyed in a big battle sequence, so we had to make two versions of it," explained Gilford. The Prop Shop crew had to make the rubble, which began with 300 blocks of polystyrene. "It all had to be hand cut into about two thousand pieces," said asset producer and head of digital manufacturing at Prop Shop, James Enright. "We had to paint, age, and finish each piece by hand within two weeks. Then set dressers dressed the set."

The action spills from the backlot ruins into the forests where Kylo Ren finally confronts Rey. This was photographed on location in Puzzlewood, an area of stark natural beauty in the Forest of Dean near the border with Wales. The setting brought a strong mythological resonance to this moment in the film.

"Now you've got castles so you're in a fable," said Carter. "You're with a dark knight in the forest. You are much more grounded, and oriented towards a sense of 'I've heard or seen this story before.'"

SET — EXT. HALL OF MIRRORS
DETAIL — 3D TRAILER 01 — ARCH 'A'
DRG NO. — 829
DATE — MARCH 14 2014
DRAWN BY — LUKE SANDERS

FOR RUBBLE DRESSING PLEASE SEE SET DEC

RESISTANCE BASE

The symbolism entrenched in the military factions of the original trilogy continues in this new film: the heroes have organic shapes, earthly colors, and a lived-in aesthetic, while the villains are typified by harsh mechanical brutalism and rectilinear shapes with jagged edges. The challenge for production designer Darren Gilford was to keep the Resistance and First Order aesthetics separate but also moved on from past designs.

"We wanted to see what the rebel bases, technology, ships, and that whole world had evolved into," Gilford said. "We went back and studied all the sets, ships, and language, and asked how do we progress that by 30 years in our timeline and not take it so far out there that we're just doing something brand new. Again, it had to be grounded and rooted in the original films."

For the Resistance—commonly called "rebels" in production—these roots would be quite visible, as their base would be hidden in the natural world, with early artwork depicting it deep within primordial jungles. This overgrowth was scaled back when Greenham Common surfaced as a possible filming location. A former Royal Air Force base located a mere hour from Pinewood Studios, the scale of the decommissioned Cold War-era cruise missile bunkers proved irresistible to Abrams. "J.J. saw that place and couldn't believe it existed so close to the studio," said Gilford.

↓ An illustration details the root system that permeates the Resistance base set.

SET	INT. PIRATE'S COVE MASTER
DETAIL	ROOT SCHEMATIC
DRG NO.	1136
DATE	MAY 14 2006
DRAWN BY	KATRINA MACKAY

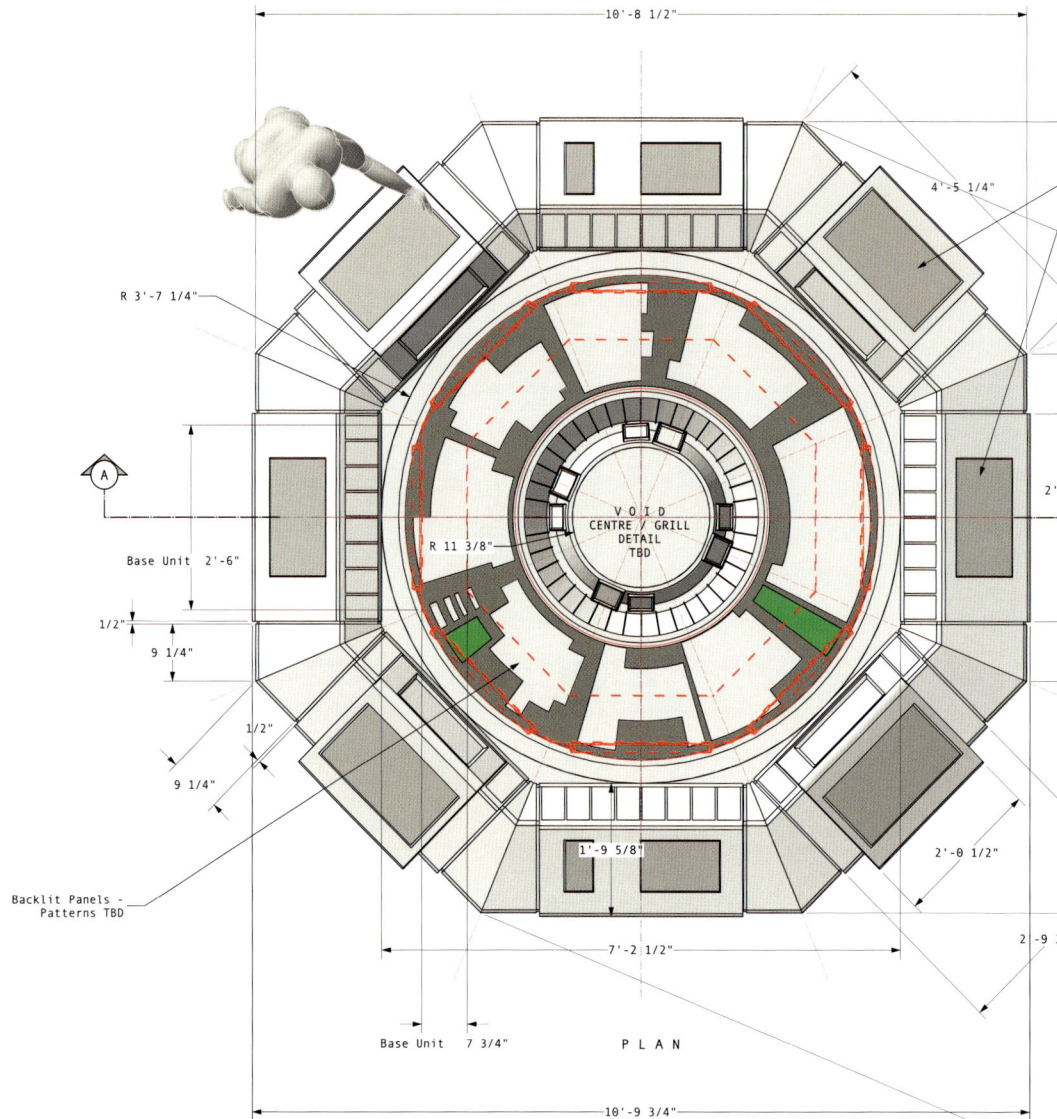

PLAN

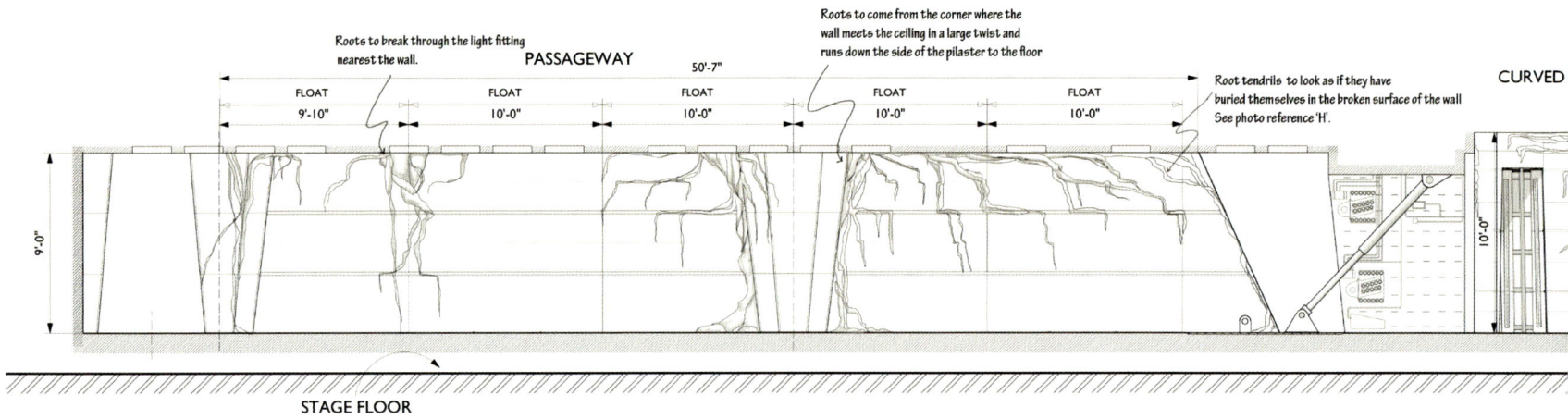

PASSAGEWAY

STAGE FLOOR

CURVED

The production briefly explored the idea of Greenham Common as the site of Maz's base of operations, or perhaps even the fabled Jedi temple which Luke Skywalker had found, but it instead won out as the Resistance Base on the planet D'Qar. "We had already designed the interior set, but then we found this new exterior location," explained Gilford, "which drove a redesign of the interior."

"We had to change our architecture to a military style, rather than big stone blocks with ancient carvings," said art director Al Bullock. The large-scale modelmaking work that had explored a more primeval base setting was instead repurposed to plan out Maz's castle. "These designs aren't always lost when a set goes in a different direction," added Bullock.

"The idea of the roots was something that I loved so much, feeling that it was really underground," explained Abrams of the base interior built out as a large set in Pinewood's E and H stages. "Part of it is obviously the kinship with the original *Star Wars* jungle base. We have vines and roots intertwined with cables." Banks of consoles displayed graphics designed with a '70s vector aesthetic, while real plant life was supplied by the greens department. "The [Resistance] base, technically and aesthetically, was one of the hardest sets to crack," set decorator Lee Sandales said. "You're trying to create something from the 1970s, so it has an almost retro feel to it, particularly with the color and lighting."

← The "Pirate Holographic Table," a build that will be enhanced with panels and displays furnished by the Set Dec team, is shown in this technical illustration.

SET	INT. PIRATE'S COVE
DETAIL	PIRATE HOLOGRAPHIC TABLE
DRG NO.	054
DATE	FEBRUARY 28 2013
DRAWN BY	JULIA DEHOFF

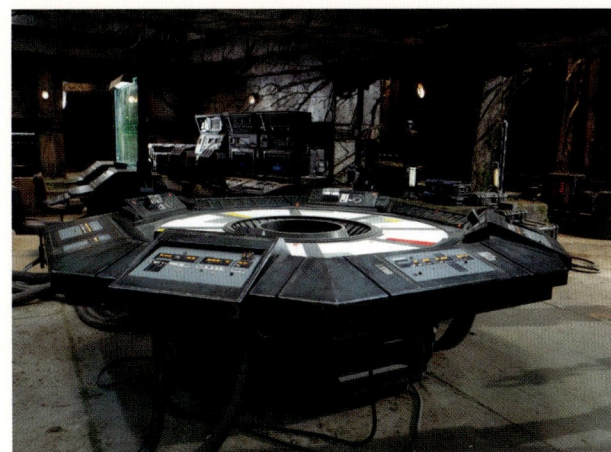

This 1970s approach was also true for the exterior at Greenham, which favored in-camera solutions and leveraged a scant four X-wings on the ground. They included two full-sized X-wings built for production— Poe Dameron's black fighter and the standard Resistance blue one—as well as two full-scale 2D cutouts painted by scenic artist Matt Walker.

"We were inspired by looking at how they did the original hangar at Yavin 4 in *A New Hope*," said Gilford, who was informed of the use of cutouts by Lucasfilm researcher Phil Szostak. "The cutouts were so successful, falling off in darkness—how simple but powerful they were! I made sure that when J.J. first arrived, his vantage point was looking down the gauntlet of the tarmac and runways at the practical X-wings and 2D cutouts."

"We approached [the hangar] as if we were shooting in 1977," said visual effects supervisor and second unit director Roger Guyett. "We didn't want to do giant image-tiled shots of a million X-wings."

In the end, ILM added in a few flying CG X-wings, as well as some mountains to the distant background to better set D'Qar into a faraway galaxy.

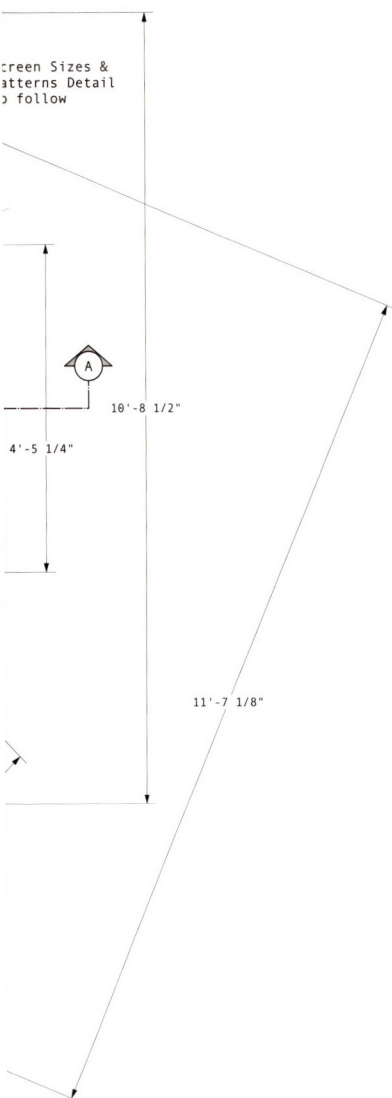

↑ The completed holographic display table in the Resistance base provided the setting for a crucial briefing discussing the strengths and weaknesses of Starkiller Base as a prelude to the film's final act.

screen Sizes &
atterns Detail
follow

A

10'-8 1/2"

4'-5 1/4"

11'-7 1/8"

MAP ROOM   Some join and separate again. See reference 'C'   PIER

IDOR

8'-0"

8'-0"

9'-0"

9'-0"

18'-0"

20'-0"

3'-0"

STARKILLER BASE

The finale of *The Force Awakens* brings the action to the First Order's unthinkable new weapon, the planet-smashing Starkiller Base. Its function and details would evolve through the drafts—at one point it was an elaborate "neutron bomb" kind of device meant to assist the villains in the capture of the New Republic fleet. Its final form was spurred by a suggestion from ILM creative consultant Dennis Muren about the antagonists in the film literally crushing the light, which led to its evolution into a star-gobbling hyperspace laser cannon. The name "Starkiller" dates to George Lucas' early draft scripts of *Star Wars*, repurposed here and suggesting the weapon's ominous nature.

"[Creating] Starkiller Base is basically designing an entire planet," said production designer Darren Gilford of the assignment. "In one of the first briefs, when we see the base holistically as the *Falcon* approaches it, J.J. described it a 'hacked planet.' When you first come across it, you're not sure what its purpose is, but you know it's been manipulated and altered in a severe way. One of J.J.'s favorite references was Luke's training ball, which he uses in the *Falcon* when he first trains with Obi-Wan Kenobi. So, we studied the graphic nature of that ball and the repetitive details, the spacing of them. That was the first place we started with the planet."

For an environment as expansive as an entire planet, the production focused on two dozen sets of varying sizes that would be realized through a practical construction. The final visual appearance of the Starkiller Base would involve combining these sets into background plates, which Roger Guyett would photograph in Iceland, while numerous digital matte paintings and CG environments were used to determine the look of its firing effect. "There was still a lot of design to do at Lucasfilm in postproduction, because J.J. wanted that flexibility as he cut and pieced elements together," said Gilford. "It wouldn't have been prudent to lock in the design at this point. We knew what the sets were, the interiors and exteriors, and how the edges would be blended in. But there was still a lot to do in VFX [visual effects] to finalize the look of the planet."

"It was an iterative development with the base itself because we tackled it from the inside instead of the outside first," said ILM art director Kevin Jenkins. "We knew what it does, but the design for the outside had come along a lot later due to needing to get sets in front of cameras. We took the hacked planet description and put that back onto what's on the inside. We made a lot of very industrial spaces, like a living machine. It wasn't neat and orderly like the Death Star had been. There were pockets of hack all over the planet."

SET	INT. EVIL CASTLE HALLWAYS
DETAIL	PLANS & ELEVATIONS
DRG NO.	1582
DATE	OCTOBER 3 2014
DRAWN BY	PETER DORME

'AVCO'

INT. EVIL CASTLE HALLWAYS
PLAN & ELEVATIONS A-A to H-H   SCALE - 1/4" = 1'-0"

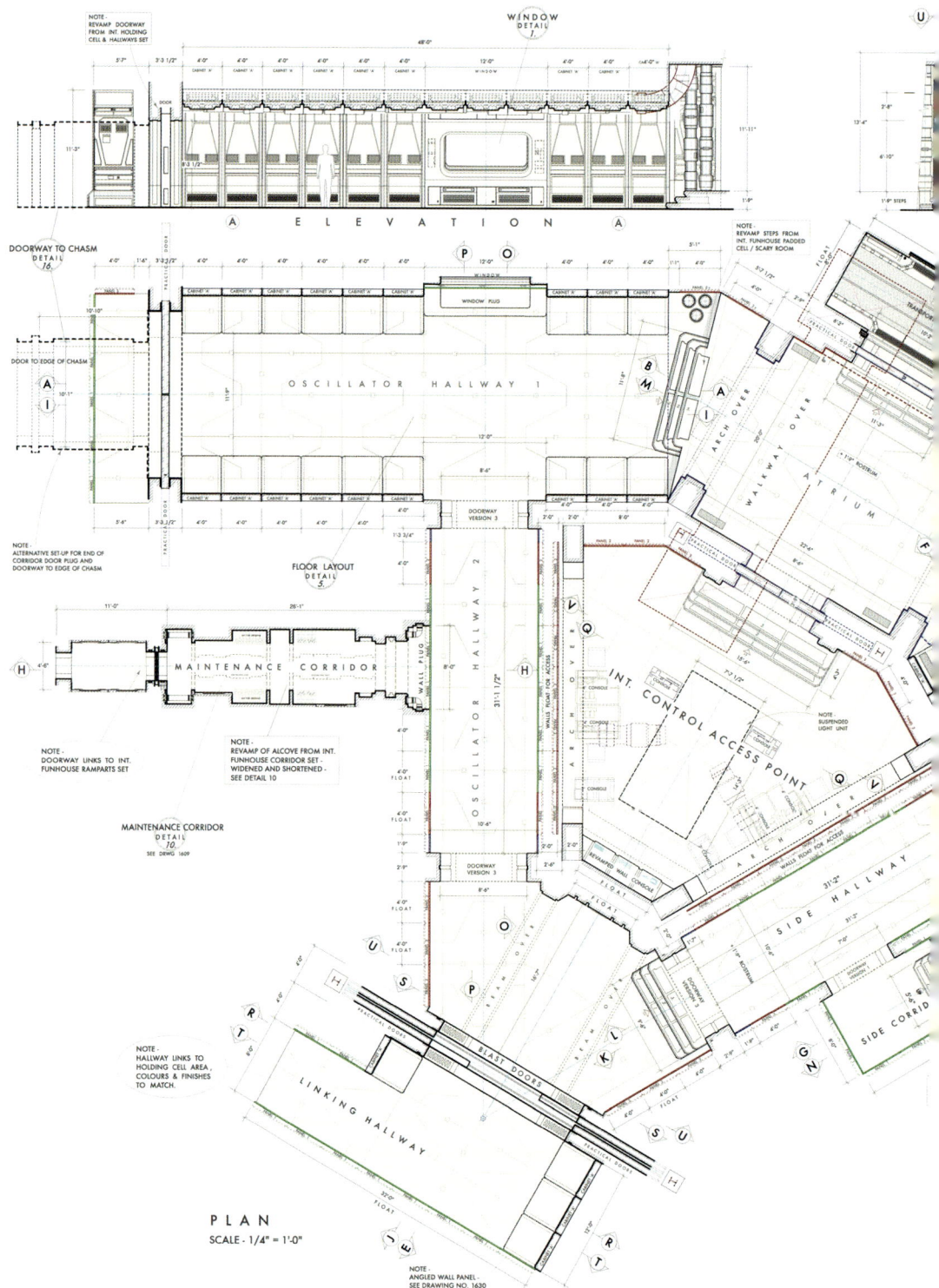

PLAN
SCALE - 1/4" = 1'-0"

↓ The Starkiller Base corridors were inspired by the layout of the original Death Star sets. They connect in a circuitous layout that allows for extensive reuse as different parts of the enormous stronghold.

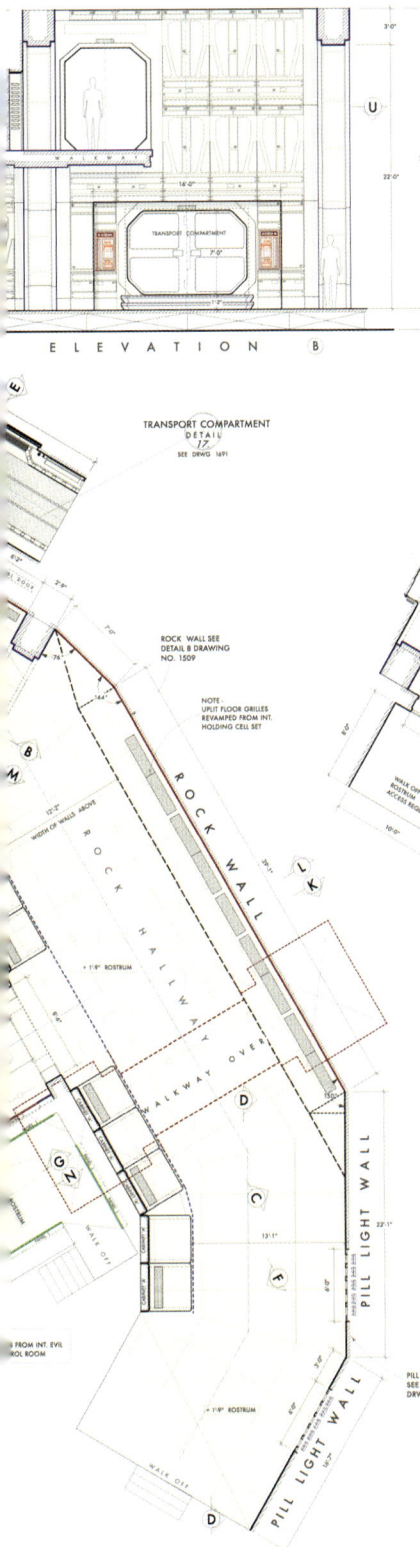

ELEVATION   B

TRANSPORT COMPARTMENT
DETAIL
17.
SEE DRWG 1691

ROCK WALL SEE
DETAIL B DRAWING
NO. 1509

NOTE:
UPLIT FLOOR GRILLES
REVAMPED FROM INT.
HOLDING CELL SET

ROCK WALL

PILL LIGHT WALL

PILL LIGHT WALL

The interior sets carried and amplified the classic Imperial aesthetic, with trapezoidal and angular corridors of oppressive black and gray, red highlights, and the parallel "pill" lights that adorn many a wall and corner. Simulated exposed rock differentiated the design from shipboard corridors, although both the Star Destroyer bridge and the Star Destroyer hangar would be repurposed and re-dressed to represent Starkiller environments: respectively, the gunnery control room and the backdrop to the catwalk where Han Solo meets his fate.

"This set is one of my favorites in the movie," said Abrams of a particular cluster of intersecting Starkiller Base corridors. "It was built, designed by Rick [Carter] and Darren [Gilford], in order to get maximum flexibility and multiple locations from essentially one set. So, every time you're in corridors in Starkiller Base, you're on [this] set. But we always shot from different angles so it felt you were in different areas of the base."

John Barry and Norman Reynolds employed the same approach for their construction of Death Star corridors in *A New Hope*, extracting maximum production value out of a subset of hallways to suggest an entire space station. "I think the interior Starkiller Base set is a perfect example of where everyone was searching for the DNA of *Star Wars*, its architecture, lighting, and cinematic language," said executive producer Kathleen Kennedy. "At the very beginning, we looked at what George had done in *A New Hope*. But with the crispness of how we shoot today, you can't get away with a lot of what he was doing, where you have something like painted plywood. You have to take it a step further. But then the question becomes, how much further can you go without it starting to feel slick and not *Star Wars*? And that's a very complicated thing to get right."

Daytime exteriors of Starkiller Base included pieces photographed on the Pinewood backlot. An entry point, where Han Solo and Finn debate on how to infiltrate the base, was shot on the North Lot, in the same location where the Jakku village was razed by First Order stormtroopers. Scenic snow, Han's parka, and some performative shivers helped sell the subzero temperatures of the world, but it was in fact a warm summer day.

On the Paddock Tank lot, against a huge blue screen wall, a set was built for the parade grounds of Starkiller Base, where General Hux addresses an assembly of troopers prior to the cannon's inaugural firing upon the New Republic. "It's a very Third Reich connotation—quite a sinister scene," said senior art director Al Bullock. "We built a platform twenty-two feet in the air." ILM would expand the setting to consist of over 26,000 assembled First Order stormtroopers.

The final duel between Rey and Kylo Ren in the snowy forests of the planet was not shot on the backlot, but rather indoors on Q stage. "This was an entire interior set built on stage with a background painted by remarkable artists," said Abrams. "It was a very tricky thing to light, but [cinematographer] Dan Mindel and his team figured out a way to do it."

"They used real tree trunks to build the set on the largest soundstage available," said Pat Tubach, ILM visual effects supervisor. "J.J. and his crew shot that set from every conceivable angle. It was like old Hollywood visual effects, where it felt like filmmakers could create anything in a soundstage." ILM would extend the trees and perform some digital paint-out of lighting rigs on some angles. "Occasionally we added trees at the very back," said Tubach. "In most cases, the mist and trees on set were all it needed."

↓ Dulling down the ordinarily reflective surfaces and filling in the sunken crew pit effectively disguise the reused First Order Star Destroyer bridge as a Starkiller Base location.

RESISTANCE CRUISER

Home One, also known as the Headquarters Frigate, under the command of Admiral Ackbar in *Return of the Jedi*, was the first true depiction of a Rebel Alliance capital warship. The Mon Calamari veteran would return to his memorable articulated command chair, as *The Last Jedi* would feature a massive Resistance Star Cruiser of similar pedigree.

"One of the things we've been able to do is extract our understanding of what the central design aesthetic is for the rebel fleet and apply that to the Resistance," said production designer Rick Heinrechs of the evolution of battleships. "It's not just a case of, 'Let's make it bigger.' That's not going to do the trick. It's a question of shape. There are some simple, descriptive form elements that Lucas used from the beginning."

The compound, rounded shapes established for the Rebel Alliance would continue for the Resistance, as art director Kevin Jenkins described. "Everything is a 'time frame iteration.' We took forward what we knew about the Rebel Alliance, and riffed off what Norman Reynolds and the team did on the original trilogy. Working on the Resistance corridors, the ships, the hangars, it's like, you have the same company. It's like looking at a Mercedez Benz in 1940 and seeing one now. You view the same language, and it just moves through the time periods."

"The bridge sets are absolutely inspired by the *Home One* sets from *Jedi* but with our own spin on things," said Heinrichs. Larger in size and with more "interactive" areas—consoles and display boards—the command bridge built on D stage had viewports sloped outward to reinforce the idea that it sat in a dominant position on top of the vessel. Later, when this bridge is destroyed by a First Order warhead, the crew must use a temporary bridge—built on A stage—with windows canted inward to suggest its inferior position far below.

"The temp bridge is in the underbelly of the ship, and we called it the engineering bridge," said Heinrichs. "There was this engine room with all these pipes and gack going on back there. It was a much more industrial space, as opposed to high-tech. It had a nice contrast."

A sunken circle of benches became a briefing area where the assembled crew hears the dire news of the relentless First Order pursuit. It also functioned as a rehearsal space. "After a day of shooting with other actors, I would come and sit with the script with Oscar Isaac and Laura Dern. We would sit on these benches that go around the set and go through their scenes and work them out in the space," said director Rian Johnson.

The spine of the movie's plot involves the Resistance Star Cruiser being harried by the pursuing First Order fleet, meaning much time would be spent aboard the vessel within a wide variety of interior spaces. "It's always a surprise to a director when you actually tell them how many sets they have in their script, because they don't sit and count them," said Heinrichs. "And neither should they. That's a practical concern that we figure out and manage."

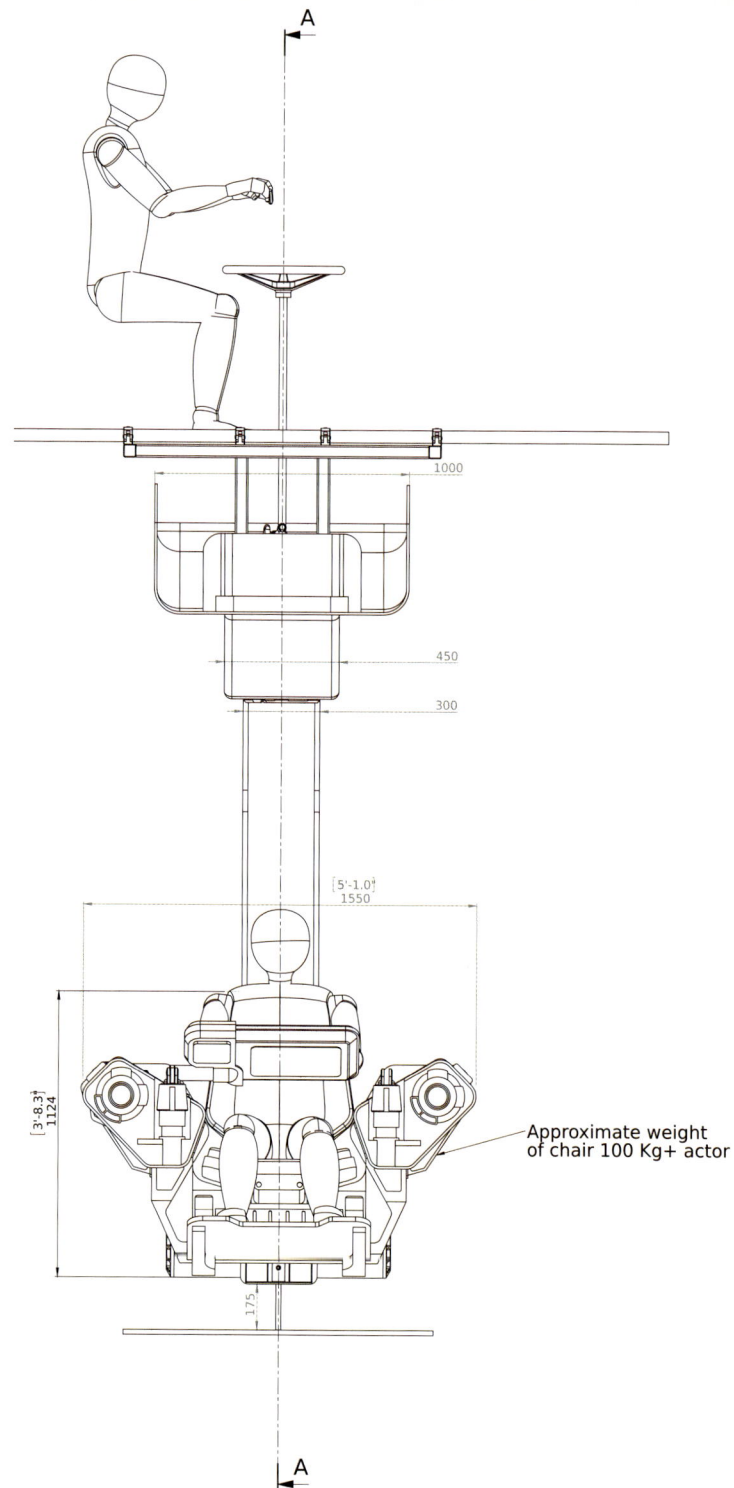

A

1000

450

300

[5'-1.0"]
1550

[3'-8.3"]
1124

Approximate weight
of chair 100 Kg+ actor

175

A

→ Concept artwork by Rodolfo Damaggio illustrates the cruiser's temporary bridge with its arm-mounted chair. This interior was conceived as a more confined area than the main bridge.

SET	INT. RESISTANCE CRUISER — TEMPORARY BRIDGE
DETAIL	PILOT CHAIR MAIN DRAWING
DRG NO.	175
DATE	SEPTEMBER 29 2015
DRAWN BY	CRISSY JO HOWES

↑ A schematic details the suspended pilot chair found in the temporary bridge of the Resistance cruiser. The figure at the top is above the ceiling line of the set, representing the grip who would operate the chair's rotation off-camera.

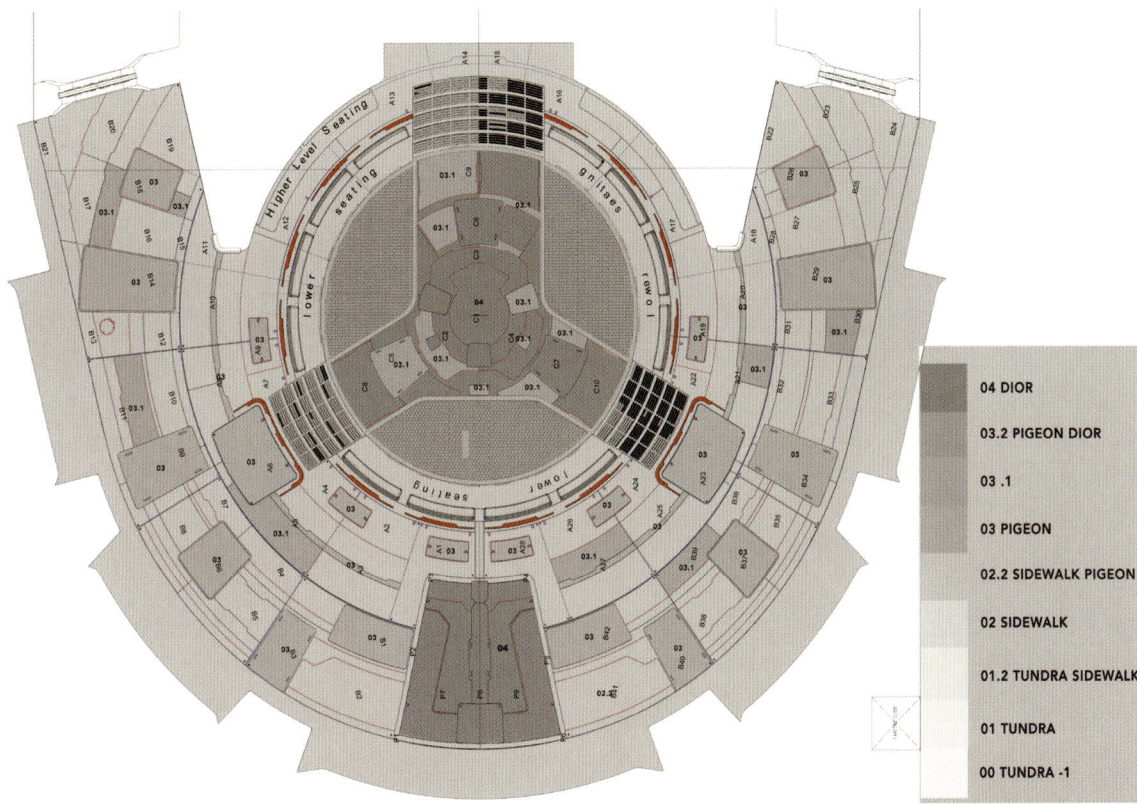

← This floor panel paint guide for the Resistance cruiser temporary bridge denotes a spectrum of grays from "Dior" and "Sidewalk Pigeon" to "Tundra-1."

04 DIOR

03.2 PIGEON DIOR

03 .1

03 PIGEON

02.2 SIDEWALK PIGEON

02 SIDEWALK

01.2 TUNDRA SIDEWALK

01 TUNDRA

00 TUNDRA -1

↓ A 3D layout depicts the damaged Resistance cruiser bridge. The core structures to be built are in red, while blue indicates dressing added to emphasize the damage.

SET	INT. RESISTANCE CRUISER— TEMPORARY BRIDGE
DETAIL	FLOOR PANEL PAINT REFERENCE
DRG NO.	19
DATE	DECEMBER 2 2015
DRAWN BY	DENISE BALL

The Q stage at Pinewood would be home to an evolving series of sets that could be reconfigured or modified efficiently. "We started with the [Resistance] bomber first on Q Stage, and then we had the Resistance cruiser hallways," said Heinrichs. "Then it became the transport hangar. Then it became the medical frigate hallways and hangars. And finally it was the [cruiser] fighter hangar. We were able to reuse hallways and walls and turn things around for all of those."

Other environments built for the cruiser included the industrial-looking escape pod, brig, and engineering section where Rose Tico first appears. Built on L stage, this space had visual elements heavily inspired by the innards of the rebel blockade runner from the beginning of *A New Hope*. Finn's makeshift medical recovery area was a relatively small room on A stage; Leia's recovery chamber was on B stage.

"That was one of the first things we shot," said Heinrichs. "We had this idea of a round shape with these bays off of it and a window. And as we got into it, I remembered in *Empire* there was this area of the *Falcon* with Luke in it that had this feel: inset bunks with a skylight nearby. I always loved the shapes that [art director and production designer] Norman Reynolds had put into it. So, we wanted to riff a bit on that and yet keep it in our world as well."

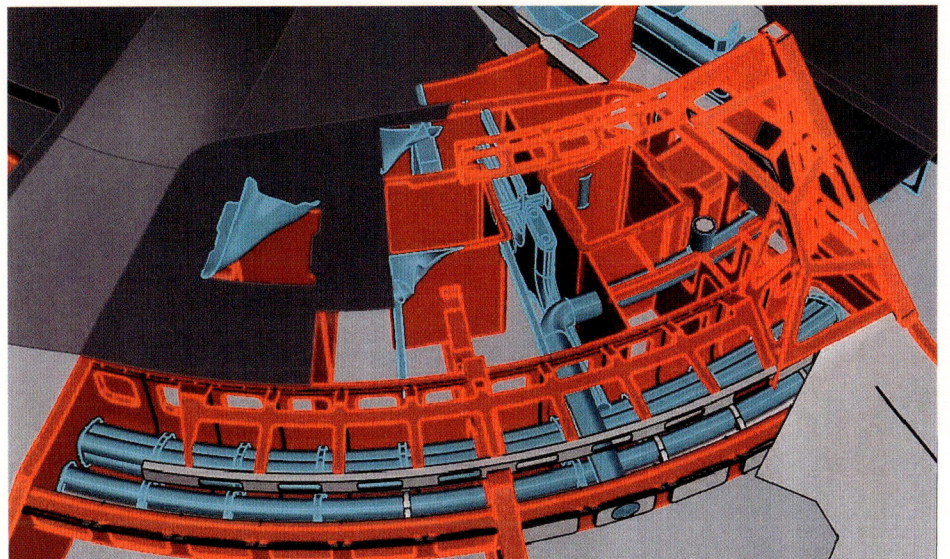

CODE NAMES

Although Rian Johnson had the title *The Last Jedi* in mind from his earliest drafts of the film, the production operated under the whimsical coded title of "Space Bear," with a logo depicting a panda in an astronaut helmet. This naming convention spread internally across characters, locations, and vehicles. Call sheets or documentation would be filled with ursine monikers, including Goldilocks (Rey), Polar Bear (Leia), Smokey Bear (Poe), Ted (Finn), Grizzly (Kylo), and Paddington (Hux). BB-8 was Boo Boo and the stormtroopers were Sugar Cubes. Luke Skywalker was the titular Space Bear. The code names for set environments included:

The Honey Pot (Resistance cruiser)
Honey Bee (A-wing fighter)
Honey Pot Dropper (Resistance bomber)
Bear Island (Ahch-To)
Platinum Bear Ship (the *Libertine*)
1,000 Acre Wood (Mega-Destroyer)
Bee Hive Land (Crait)

RESISTANCE A-WING FIGHTER

Crucial elements of the flight mission that begins the movie are the swift fighter escorts that must protect the heavier, less maneuverable bombers. That task fell to the storied X-wing fighters that had already been showcased in *The Force Awakens*, now accompanied by an updated iteration of another classic design—the wedge-shaped A-wing fighter first introduced in *Return of the Jedi*.

"It's going to be almost disappointingly easy to describe what we did for this one," chuckled production designer Kevin Jenkins. "In *The Force Awakens*, we returned to the Ralph McQuarrie version of an X-wing fighter, one of the pre-designs before the final model was made. Well, we were flicking through, looking at Ralph's art for the A-wing, and there's this blue-lined, white triangle version in a production painting he did for *Return of the Jedi*, and we just said, 'Let's use that.'"

The McQuarrie imagery smoothed out some of the harder angles in the finished A-wing design, which the Resistance model would inherit. Although the final design did not sport the triangle livery, the blue hue did indeed decorate the featured A-wing that would serve as pilot Tallie's vessel. Rather than just construct acockpit—as was done for *Return of the Jedi*—the whole ship was built as a contained vehicle set.

"You know what was thrilling? To see a full-size A-wing on the stage. Not just one, but two," said production designer Rick Heinrichs. "It is a great design, but it never got built full-size before. The size is great. Everything about it is really wonderful."

EXT TALLIE'S A-WING PAINT SCHEMATIC - TALLIE'S - FIGHTER HANGAR & GIMBAL A-WING

PLAN VIEW

↑ A colored overlay on Tallie's A-wing fighter defines the blue paint scheme and red detailing that distinguishes her craft.

SET	EXT. TALLIE'S A-WING FIGHTER
DETAIL	PAINT SCHEMATIC
DRG NO.	8
DATE	MARCH 15 2016
DRAWN BY	RICK HEINRICHS/OLIVER VAN DER VIJVER

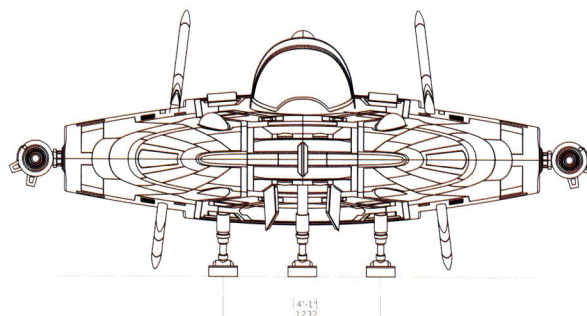

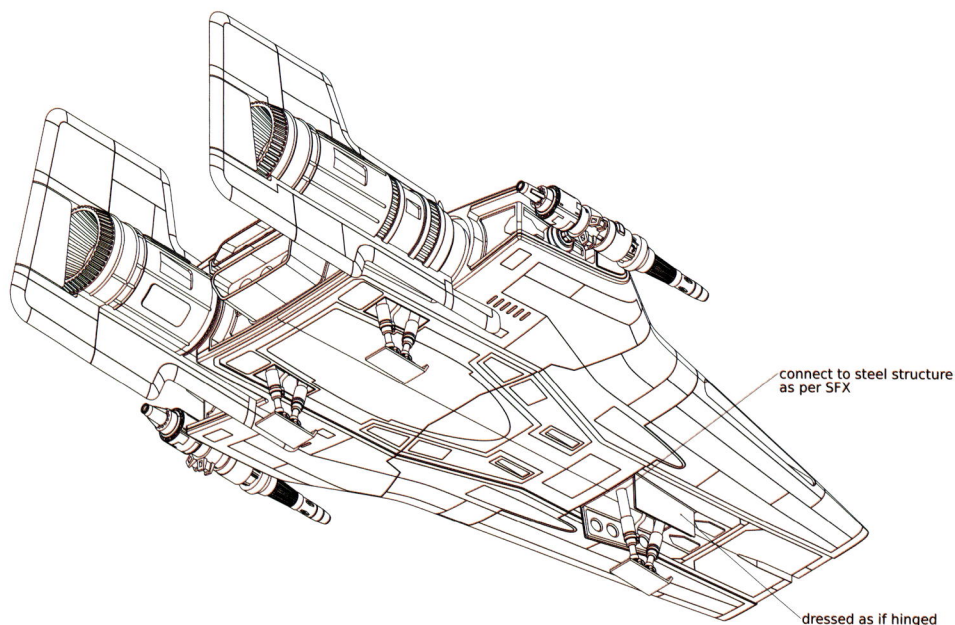

connect to steel structure as per SFX

dressed as if hinged

→ This schematic illustration of Tallie's A-wing fighter provides a detailed view of the craft's landing gear and landing-gear retaining door.

SET	INT./EXT. TALLIE'S A-WING
DETAIL	A-WING LANDING GEAR
DRG NO.	164
DATE	OCTOBER 12 2015
DRAWN BY	CRISSY JO HOWES

Chair Padding to be done by
Drapes based on aluminium
frame provided by Set Dec.

Dressing to match
existing film

Canopy and cockpit hole as per Construction

Hinge and mechanism as per SFX
Requested to open and close in shot

(If possible SFX actuators can
be a visible part of the dressing)

track mechanism as per SFX
Requested to move in shot

Add foot rests

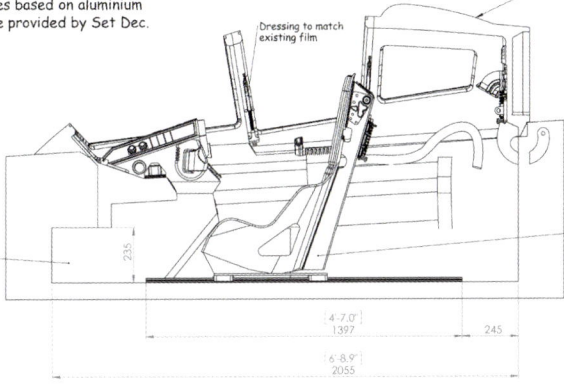

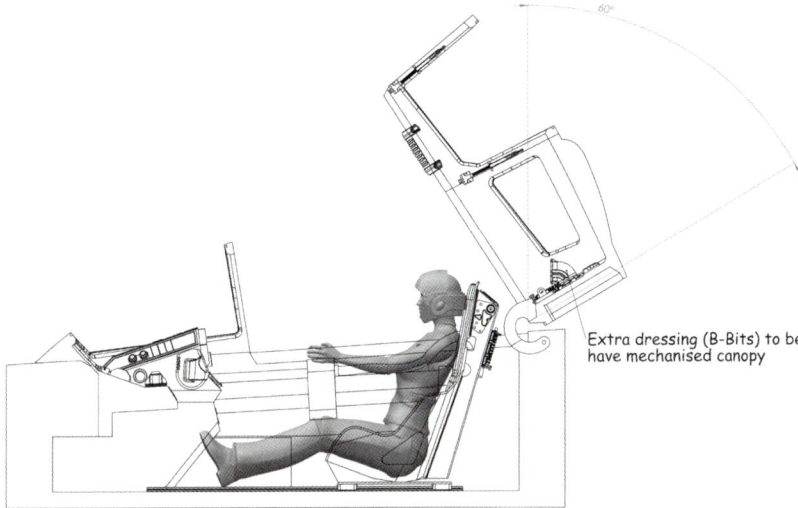

60°

Extra dressing (B-Bits) to be done after SFX
have mechanised canopy

SET	A-WING
DETAIL	COCKPIT DETAIL
DRG NO.	164
DATE	SEPTEMBER 1 2015
DRAWN BY	CRISSY JO HOWES

← The A-wing cockpit and canopy is visualized in this illustration. As noted, the hinge and chair mechanisms would be handled by the SFX crew, while the chair padding was to be finished by the drapes department on a frame provided by Set Dec.

↑ A camera glides across the surface of the full A-wing build. The canopy glass will be added as a digital effect.

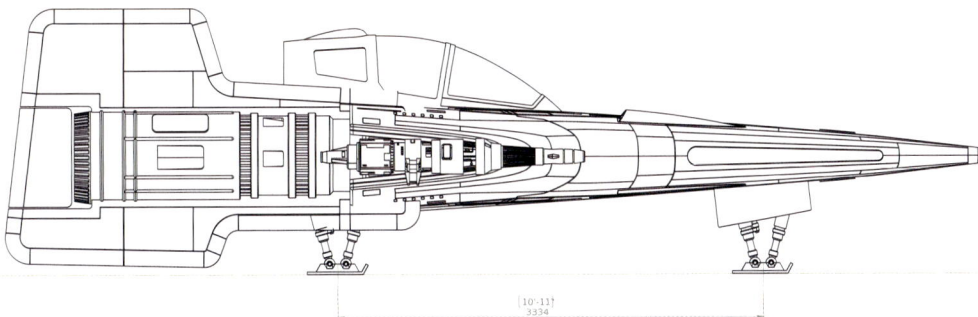

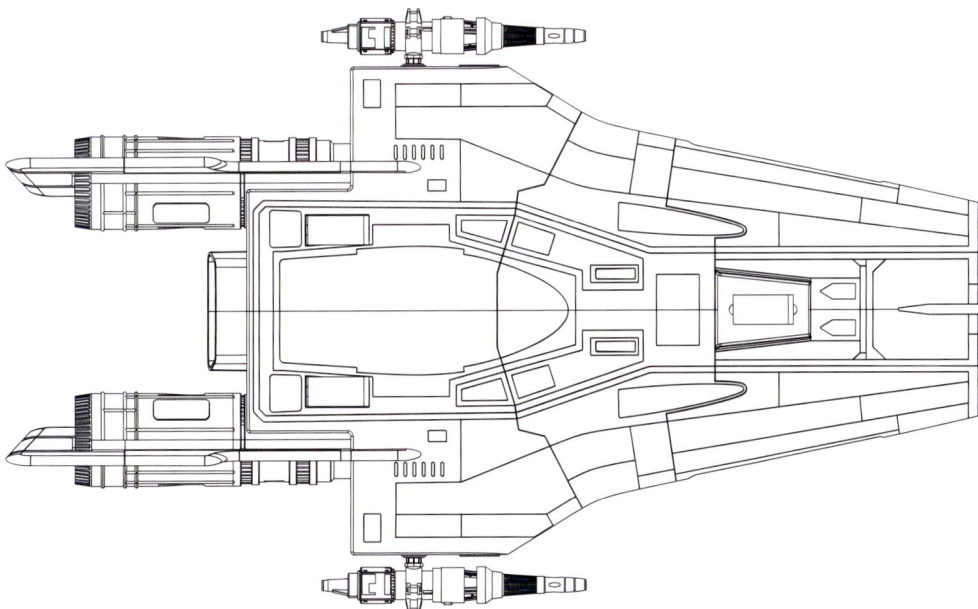

Although some of the preliminary illustrations suggested cutting away sections of the forward hull to accommodate closer camera views of the cockpit, the final version did not feature such segmentation. The entire craft was built around a steel frame that could be mounted onto an articulated gimbal for truly dynamic pilot simulations and camera interactions. A camera on a snorkel-like mount was able to traverse unobstructed across the hull and get in close to the pilot, who could be viewed through the bubble canopy. For such shots, the plastic window was removed from the frame and added back digitally, with reflections created by ILM.

Tallie's A-wing was the blue vehicle, while the second full-sized version had the same brick-red-colored striping sported by the *Return of the Jedi* model. Although the red vehicle wasn't a hero ship operated by a named pilot in the film, it did have the notable distinction of carrying real-world royalty. On April 19, 2016, Prince William and Prince Harry visited the set at Pinewood, and Prince Harry sat within the cockpit of the red A-wing as it rested on Q stage.

RESISTANCE BOMBER

As Rian Johnson began writing *The Last Jedi*, he found inspiration within the research library at Skywalker Ranch. A book titled *Vertical Warfare*, written by Francis Vivian Drake, detailed the bombing missions of the USAF and RAF during World War II. He also screened a selection of films in an ongoing "movie camp" with the Lucasfilm team of development executives to illustrate the inspirations and goals within his coalescing story. The movies included *Twelve O'Clock High* (1949), directed by Henry King and starring Gregory Peck, which focused on wartime B-17 bomber missions. "That ended up leading to the opening sequence of a bombing run," said Johnson.

"I've never quite worked with a director that has so much initial clarity," said art director Kevin Jenkins. "I remember doing one of the first images of the bomber and Rian looked at it and said, 'Can I give you feedback? It's only about seventeen feet wide and only about six feet this way, and the person's not that big, and there needs to be this and this and this.' That's how much Rian had thought about what he was doing."

Jenkins' design resulted in a cumbersome, pistol-shaped craft with a tall bomb bay extending from a barrel-shaped hull. This would then be realized as a series of sets to depict the bomber interior very much inspired by the World War II aesthetic, with exposed bulkheads, visible airframe, grated floors, and cramped spaces. The bomb bay, or "clip," was on Q stage, the fuselage on D stage, and the gun turret operated by Paige Tico (played by Veronica Ngo) on E stage.

"Rian wanted a slow-flying cow," said Jenkins. "It's essentially a B-17 bomber. That's what it represents. It's a slow, vulnerable vehicle. If you think about it, a bomber in a science-fiction world doesn't make much sense [because bombs can't be "dropped" in the zero-gravity of space], but that brings back the analog-ness to the world."

The stacks of hundreds of spherical explosives that fill out the bomb bay were practical, individual constructions designed to "fall" in sequence, propelled out of the bomber by the artificial gravity within, in a satisfying denouement to the bombing sequence. "Our amazing practical effects team built a rig where the bombs actually were on runners that could slide down the ends. And so that shot, where we boom up and all those bombs fall down around us, those aren't digital bombs; they are actually real props that were sliding down," said Johnson.

"The bomb bay went up about forty feet," explained special effects supervisor Chris Corbould. "Within that, we built twenty racks, each containing around ten or twelve bombs, in two layers. We triggered the bombs to drop sequentially and curved the bomb tracks ninety degrees outward, so the bombs disappeared from view as the camera was looking down." As the orbs leave the bay, they transition into computer-generated bombs that continue their downward trajectory toward the First Order dreadnaught far below.

ABOVE TOP The finished Resistance bomber fuselage set, looking towards the front of the craft and the cockpit.

ABOVE The Resistance attack force of A-wings, X-wings, and bombers was built, animated, and rendered by ILM and is shown here in a final frame from *The Last Jedi*.

SET	INT. R. C. – BOMBER HANGAR – GANTRY WALKWAY
DETAIL	PLANS & ELEVATIONS
DRG NO.	01
DATE	DECEMBER 9 2015
DRAWN BY	HUGH MCCLELLAND

→ Ultimately not built or seen in the film, this section of the Resistance cruiser hangar would have housed the bombers. Hugh McClelland's illustration also shows a gantry that allows crewers to enter the docked bomber.

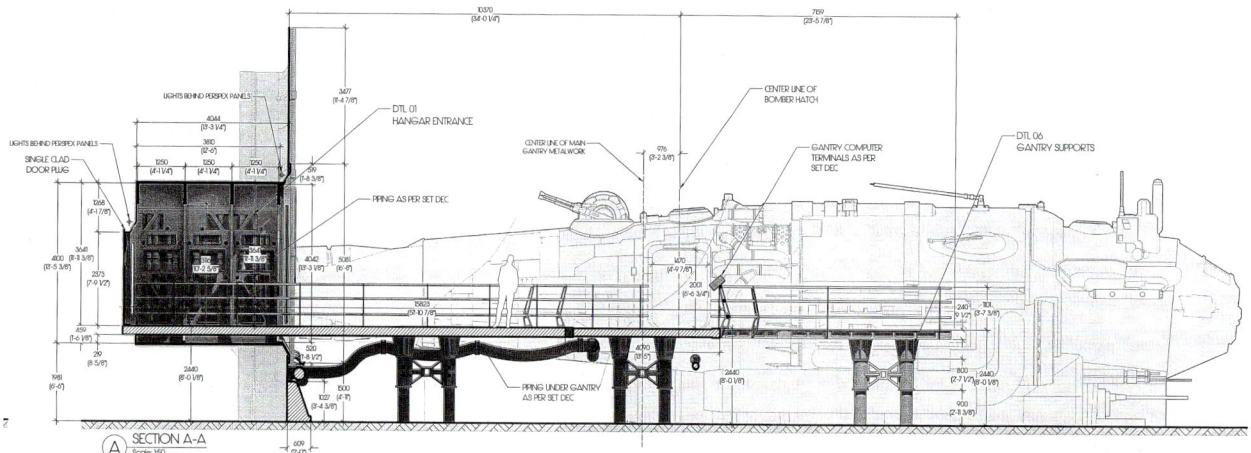

SPACE BEAR   INT. RESISTANCE BOMBER - PAIGE'S GUN TURRET

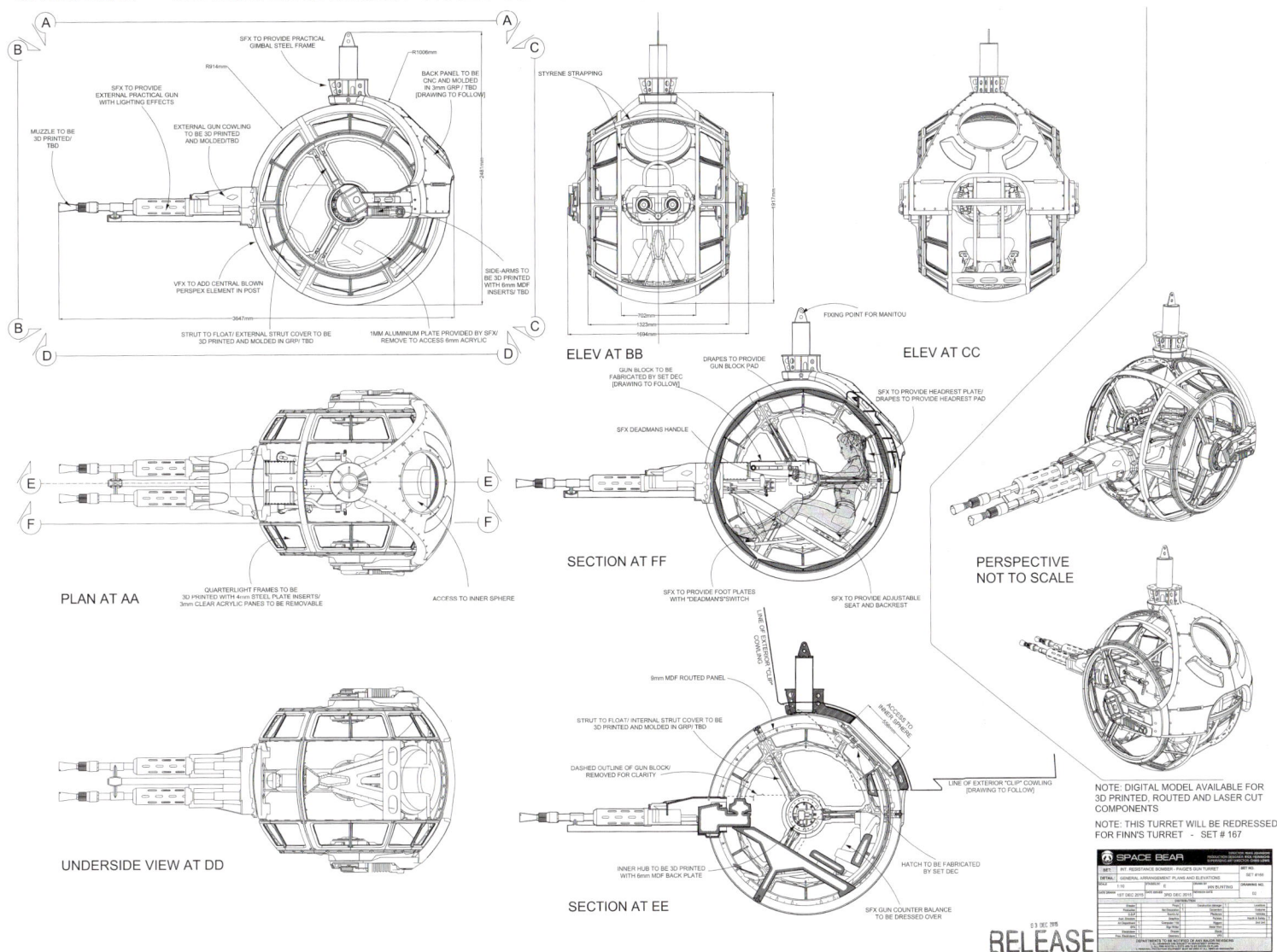

PLAN AT AA

UNDERSIDE VIEW AT DD

ELEV AT BB

ELEV AT CC

SECTION AT FF

SECTION AT EE

PERSPECTIVE
NOT TO SCALE

NOTE: DIGITAL MODEL AVAILABLE FOR
3D PRINTED, ROUTED AND LASER CUT
COMPONENTS

NOTE: THIS TURRET WILL BE REDRESSED
FOR FINN'S TURRET - SET # 167

RELEASE

SET	INT. RESISTANCE BOMBER – PAIGE'S GUN TURRET
DETAIL	GENERAL ARRANGEMENT PLANS & ELEVATIONS
DRG NO.	02
DATE	DECEMBER 1 2015
DRAWN BY	IAN BUNTING

↑ SFX would provide the functional gimbal steel frame, which is clad in detail. A notes explains that the turret will be redressed for Finn, reflecting an earlier incarnation of the story where he was part of the bombing mission.

→ Veronica Ngo as Paige Tico sits in the practical bomber turret and was filmed in front of a green screen background.

AHCH-TO ISLAND

In the final moments of *The Force Awakens*, Rey tracks down Luke Skywalker on Ahch-To, an oceanic world dotted with islands, including one wind-swept refuge that was the site of the first Jedi Temple. Such a location carries historic and dramatic weight in the context of the new trilogy, but also in the wider *Star Wars* mythos.

"If you imagine a place where the Jedi Order could have actually first emerged, that's what led me to Skellig Island," said production designer Rick Carter. "Because this is a place that emerged in 600 CE as a Christian retreat in the world."

The island, off the western coast of Ireland, was considered during recces for a possible Resistance base location in Episode VII, and supervising art director Neil Lamont remembered the historic site as a location that had been considered but rejected for use in the Harry Potter films. Lamont showed an image of the island to J.J. Abrams, who proclaimed it "perfect."

Skellig was ideal in look and feel, but proved a difficult filming location. Its status as a UNESCO World Heritage site meant it could not be altered in any way, and access to it was carefully controlled. Furthermore, the weather and seas could be unpredictably turbulent. "Sometimes you couldn't get on the island; sometimes you couldn't get off," said producer Tommy Harper. "I remember seeing those images and being totally excited—and totally scared. I've got a whole company to bring here to shoot. How are we going to pull this off?"

The AVCO (*The Force Awakens*) production sent a small crew to Skellig during the hiatus in shooting incurred by Harrison Ford's injury. "Only fifty people could go to the island; it's very small," said Abrams. "There were some six hundred or so steps to the top—and everything had to be brought up by hand." Mark Hamill felt a spiritual connection similar to the one he experienced during the production of *A New Hope*, when he stared off into the stark desert landscape of Tunisia. "There's the history of the island, a tranquility and inner peace that comes upon you," Hamill said. "Of course, it helps that you're in ceremonial robes and you imagine the scenario. I'd always thought that, after *Jedi*, Luke would wind up very much like Obi-Wan, a hermit."

Two shooting days in July 2014 captured the fateful meeting of Rey and Luke, and then, in September 2015, Rian Johnson led a small crew to continue this scene for *The Last Jedi*. "We shot on Skellig Michael [the larger of the two Skellig islands] for three days," said Ben Morris, visual effects supervisor on Episode VIII. "It was about three months before principal photography, and our primary goal was to continue the sequence that J.J. had established. We shot pickups, with characters walking around staircases, and a scene where Rey spars with a rock formation—which was a real ancient rock [on the island], 'The Wailing Woman,' so we had to be careful with that."

With Skellig having defined the look of Ahch-To, the extended time spent there in *The Last Jedi* would require the construction of sets that expanded its look, but under controllable conditions. "Not being able to shoot at Skellig was a challenge," said production director Rick Heinrichs, who used tools such as Google Earth to virtually scout nearby and find a suitable site. "I wanted somewhere that looked like Skellig, so we started on the west coast of Ireland and we found a place within eyesight of Skellig. It ended up having the right look. It had to be a combination of dramatic cliff, a certain orientation to the sun and the cliff itself—so you could shoot within our set and also see how dramatic the environment was—and have a view of the ocean at the same time. We settled on this spot after quite a bit of searching up and down the coast."

The location was Sybil Head, near the town of Dingle on the southwestern coast of Ireland. It became the construction site of the Jedi Village set, a recreation and expansion of the ancient "beehive" stone huts found at the monastery site on Skellig. But the location would have to wait, as the weather conditions stipulated in the script demanded the production start in a more local setting.

ABOVE TOP A convincing and practical cinematic illusion blends the foreground Jedi village set and the background water and cliffs of Sybil Head, Ireland.

ABOVE MIDDLE The Jedi village set was built twice during production: first, at the North Lot at Pinewood where conditions could be controlled (seen here), and then on location, cantilevered over a precipitous cliff at Sybil Head in Ireland.

ABOVE On the Richard Attenborough Stage at Pinewood Studios, wooden scaffolding frames a shape that will become a naturalistic rocky interior. This construction will define not only the ancient first Jedi Temple but also the inside of the mirror cave.

SET	EXT. JEDI VILLAGE #02
DETAIL	HUT 4 TYPE C P & E
DRG NO.	007
DATE	OCTOBER 26 2015
DRAWN BY	ALFREDO LUPO

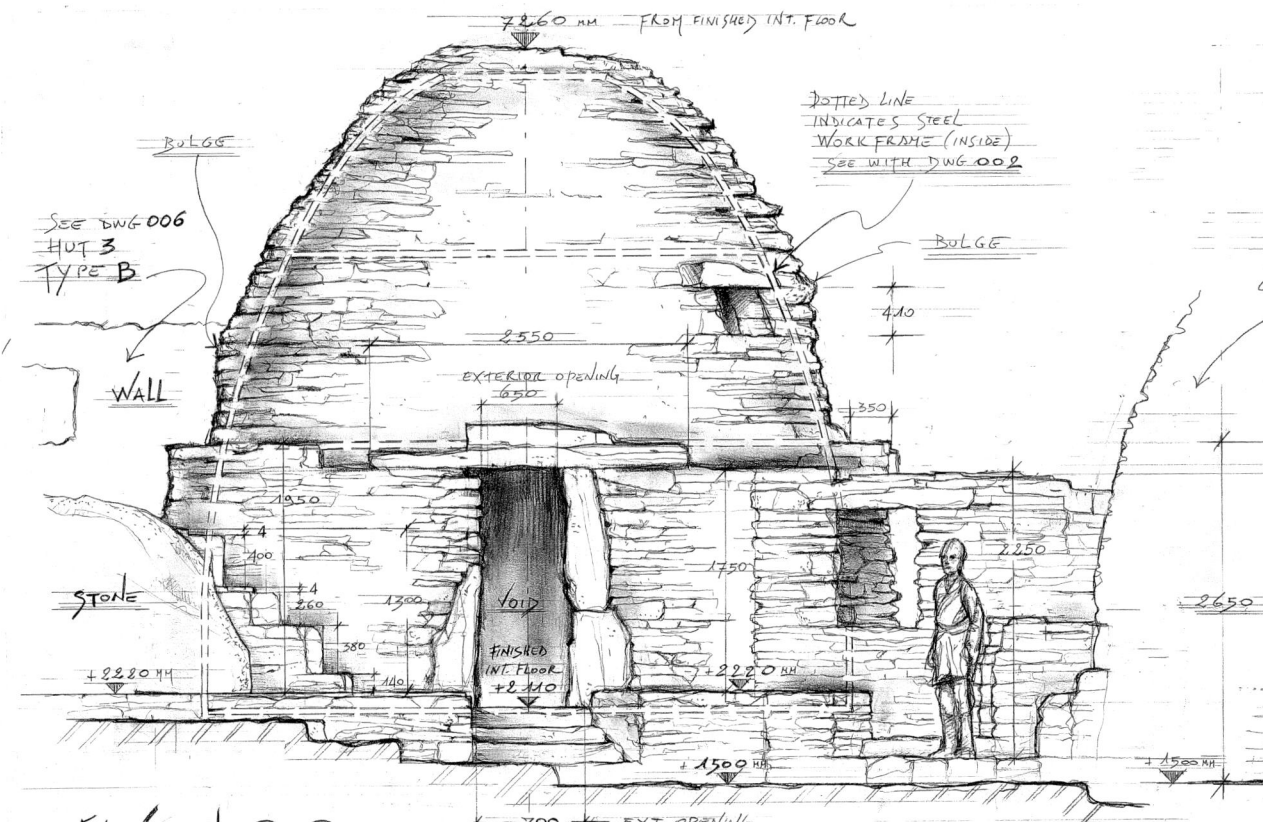

7260 MM   FROM FINISHED INT. FLOOR

DOTTED LINE
INDICATES STEEL
WORK FRAME (INSIDE)
SEE WITH DWG 002

BULGE

BULGE

SEE DWG 006
HUT 3
TYPE B

410

WALL

2550

EXTERIOR OPENING
650

350

1950

2250

STONE

1750

2650

VOID

+4
400

1300

FINISHED
INT. FLOOR
+2 110

+4
260

380

140

+2220 MM

+2220 MM

+1500 MM

+1500 MM

ELEVATION (A) (A)   (D)   700   EXT. OPENING
HUT TYPE C

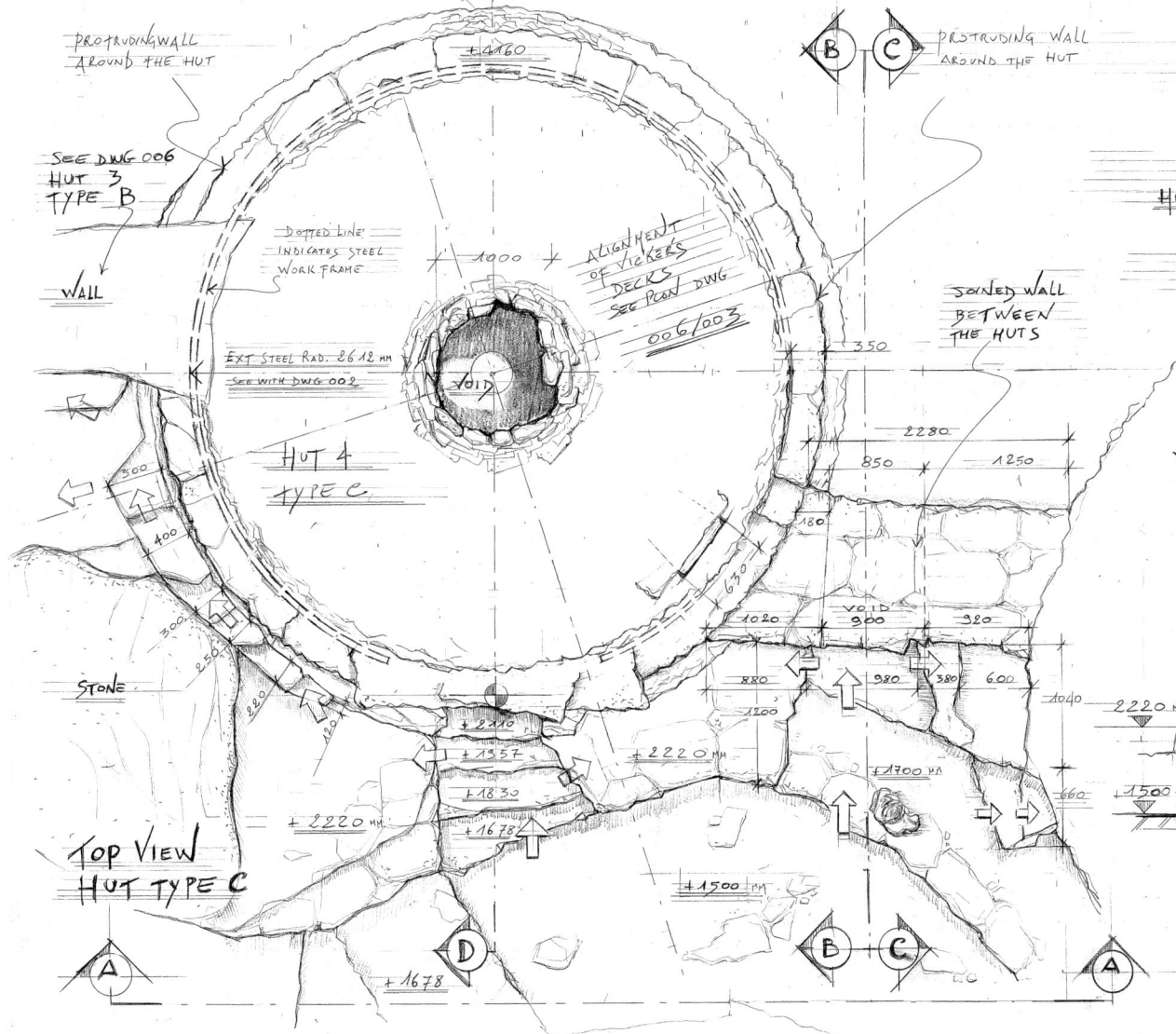

PROTRUDING WALL
AROUND THE HUT

(B) (C)   PROTRUDING WALL
AROUND THE HUT

+4160

SEE DWG 006
HUT 3
TYPE B

DOTTED LINE
INDICATES STEEL
WORK FRAME

1000

ALIGNMENT
OF VICKERS
DECKS
SEE PLAN DWG
006/003

JOINED WALL
BETWEEN
THE HUTS

WALL

350

EXT STEEL RAD. 2612 MM
SEE WITH DWG 002

VOID

HUT 4
TYPE C

2280

850   1250

180

500

690

400

1020   VOID   980
         900

STONE

300

880   980   380   600

250

1200

1040

2220 MM

380

+2210

120

+1357

+2220 MM

+1700 MM

660

1500

+2220 MM

+1830

+1678

TOP VIEW   (D)
HUT TYPE C

+1500 MM

(A)   (D)   (B) (C)   (A)

+1678

← This hand-drawn illustration visualizes one of the corbeled "beehive" huts that comprise the Ahch-To Jedi village. These huts are based on real-world structures on Skellig Michael that could not be filmed due to their protected status as archaeological relics.

"We had to build the Jedi Village a couple of times," said Heinrichs. "There was a night rain sequence that would not only have been difficult [at Sybil Head], but also quite dangerous. That was filmed at Pinewood and, because of scheduling, was shot first. So the crew was familiar with the set by the time we arrived at Sybil Head."

The Pinewood shoot included the complex practical special-effects build of Luke tearing apart a stone hut with the Force to interrupt a connection shared by Rey and Kylo. "It's all in-camera," marveled Heinrichs of the elaborate wire work that sent the fragments of hut hurtling forward. "There is a difference in what you get with Mark Hamill standing there and the rocks really going by him and not feeling like it's a visual effect."

"We decided we'd build the Jedi Village at Pinewood in February and shoot night sequences in the dark months, then take it down and rebuilt it on the edge of a cliff in Dingle for the summer months of May," explained supervising art director Christopher Lowe. "That was deemed doable by our construction manager team and financially doable by Lucasfilm and Disney. Logically, it's complete lunacy. Filmically, it's probably one of the best things we've ever done."

"Sybil Head had sheer vertical cliffs that felt like the Skellig rocks, and we cantilevered a Jedi Village set off those cliffs. It was one of the most spectacular sets I've been involved with," said Ben Morris. The camera angles blended the constructed elements into the cliff-face and included the ocean vistas within the shot, too.

"We assembled Ahch-To from a lot of disparate elements, going all the way to the northern end of Ireland as well," said Heinrichs of the shoots that included Malin Head and Brow Head, respectively the most northerly and southerly points of mainland Ireland. "It really does need to have that comprehensive feel. Is it all going to add up to one place? Yes, it will. But it's going to feel like we're stretching the boundaries of what that island looks like, for sure."

Skellig is naturally treeless, so Ahch-To is similarly barren save for a secluded grove wherein rests a single, ancient, forked tree hollowed out by millennia. Within the tree are secured the sacred foundational texts of the original Jedi Order. Late in the movie, the spectral form of Yoda appears to Luke at the tree to admonish Skywalker on his shortsightedness.

"We went on location to find this first," said Heinrichs. "We found the perfect place to construct our tree—in Iceland. But there were just too many logistical challenges. The final nail in the coffin for going on location was all the specific puppeteering needs that arose from having a certain character there."

"Yoda is only about two feet, three inches tall, but there are thirteen people underneath him," said Lowe.

NORTH LOT   SPACE BEAR - EXT JEDI V
SCALE · 1:50 · PINEWOOD NOR
III REV

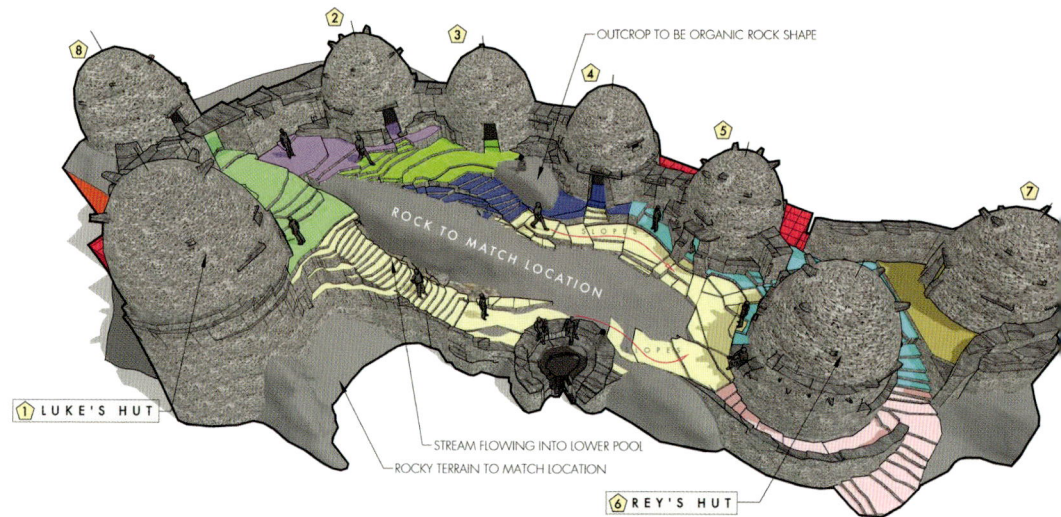

— OUTCROP TO BE ORGANIC ROCK SHAPE
ROCK TO MATCH LOCATION
1 LUKE'S HUT
— STREAM FLOWING INTO LOWER POOL
ROCKY TERRAIN TO MATCH LOCATION
6 REY'S HUT

⬆ VIEW OF NORTHLOT BUILD WITH COLOUR CODED LEVELS ⬆

⬇ PLAN OF PATHWAYS AND BASES FOR HUTS
[VICKERS DECKS OVERLAYED WITH 600mm GRID · TERRAIN OMITTED FOR

NB. COLOUR CODING SHOWS VARYING HUT HEIGHTS IN RELATION TO CONNECTED NEARBY ROSTRA THAT IS ON THE SAME LEVEL OR HIGHER

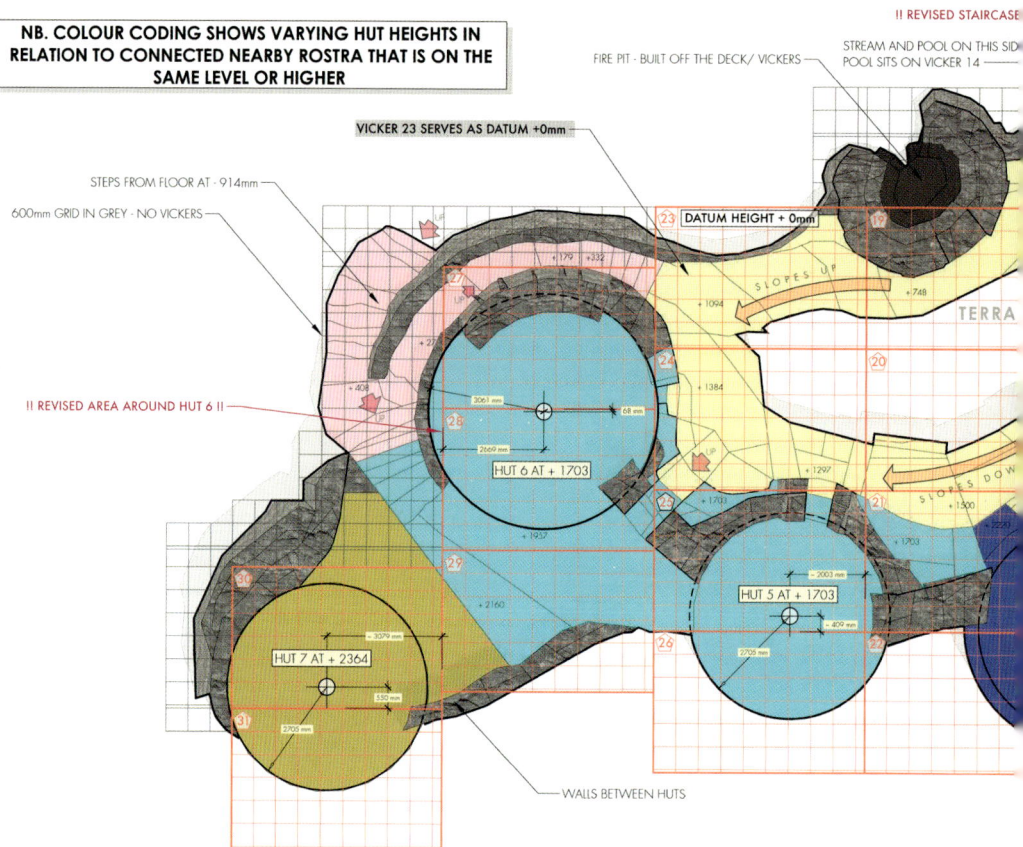

!! REVISED STAIRCASE
STREAM AND POOL ON THIS SID
POOL SITS ON VICKER 14
FIRE PIT - BUILT OFF THE DECK/ VICKERS

VICKER 23 SERVES AS DATUM +0mm
STEPS FROM FLOOR AT · 914mm
23 DATUM HEIGHT + 0mm
600mm GRID IN GREY - NO VICKERS
TERRA
!! REVISED AREA AROUND HUT 6 !!
HUT 6 AT + 1703
HUT 5 AT + 1703
HUT 7 AT + 2364
WALLS BETWEEN HUTS

"Yoda's not the problem; it's squeezing everyone else into the underside of the mountain that is difficult to achieve. Yoda's a lovely character, but when you have Frank Oz—who is six feet, two inches—underneath him with his arm in the air, and other performers servicing Frank and operating ears and eyes, the whole thing becomes a giant hole underneath the tree to puppeteer him."

AGE #2 · PATHWAYS AND HUT BASE LAYOUT
LOT · 16TH OCT 2015 · DWG 006 / 003A
D · 4 NOVEMBER !!!

↓ VIEW OF NORTHLOT BUILD WITH NO HUTS OR TERRAIN ↓

VICKERS DECKS
+ 4284
+ 3390
+ 2110
+ 1703
+ 4162
+ 2364
+ 1703

HUT 1 IS THE ONLY HUT WITH A PACKED UP INTERNAL FLOOR
WALL MARKING EDGE OF VILLAGE
RITY]
SLOPING WALLS
9 REMOVED
HUT 1 AT + 4162 [INT FLOOR AT + 4312]
!! REVISED AREA AROUND HUT 8 !!
HUT 8 AT + 5074
REVISED STEPS OUTSIDE HUT 1
POOL
HALF HUT
THIS WHITE VOID AREA ED FOR CLARITY
NO PATHWAY BETWEEN HALF HUT & VILLAGE - TERRAIN ONLY
HUT 2 AT + 4284
VICKERS DECKS SHOWN AS ORANGE GRID
WALLS BETWEEN HUTS
HUT 3 AT + 3390

REVISIONS SHOW:
1. NEW SIZE OF HUT 6 EFFECTING SURROUNDING STEPS
2. NEW STEP LAYOUT OUTSIDE HUT 1
3. NEW STEP LAYOUT OUTSIDE HUT 4

ORGANIC ROCK OUTCROP DRESSED HERE
INNER LINE MARKS TYPICAL HUT BASE
OUTER LINE MARKS OUTER POINT OF THICKER LOWER WALL

SPACE BEAR
REVISED

SET	EXT. JEDI VILLAGE
DETAIL	PATHWAYS & HUT BASE LAYOUT
DRG NO.	003A
DATE	OCTOBER 16 2015
DRAWN BY	DEAN CLEGG

↑ A color-coded illustration shows the pathways and hut base layout of the Jedi village. The colors indicate varying elevations in the environment, from the lowest steps in pink to the highest hut in green.

An exterior lot at Longcross Film Studios, west of London, became the site of the set. "The place was originally a defense plant," said Heinrichs of the former site of the Military Vehicles and Engineering Establishment (MVEE), a British military research unit. "They would test tanks on slopes underneath [the site of] this set. We're utilizing the hillside as part of the island. The biggest challenge was to create something organic and believable. No part of this was architecture. The trick was to make it feel right and natural, and have continuity with our other locations. Rian was skeptical about being able to achieve that, but this spurred us on in our efforts to make it as real-feeling as possible."

"The tree came about because Rian wanted it to represent the Resistance or rebel logo," said visual effects art director designer Kevin Jenkins. "It makes the same shape as the crest on Luke's helmet in the original *Star Wars* films."

The tree interior was an enclosed set that would not accommodate dolly tracks, requiring photography inside to be accomplished with wide lenses and Steadicam.

THE JEDI TEMPLE

"We came up with this concept of a very Zen Buddhist approach to the Jedi, in balance with nature," said production designer Rick Heinrichs, describing the look of the first Jedi temple. "Nature shapes itself, so we didn't just plunk a building down in the middle of a beautiful island. Our Jedi temple became a cave that [the production] had carved out, with an incredible ledge. You're not sure where the craftmanship ended and nature began, and vice versa."

The environment included a tiled mosaic of the first Jedi at the bottom of a reflecting pool. An exit leads to a meditation ledge, which overlooks the island; in reality this would be green screen backing that ILM would replace with plates of skies and ocean views from Skellig. "It's a space that feels holy. It's a place to commune. You can sit."

To efficiently cut down on the number of sets required, the temple also doubled for the entrance to the mirror cave sequence, where Rey plummets into a grotto during her exploration of the island. "We just filled it up with water and it also served as that set," said Johnson.

CANTO BIGHT

To crack the secret of the First Order's tracking technology, Resistance heroes Finn and Rose Tico need the help of a scoundrel who could only be found in one of the most opulent and extravagant retreats for the rich and powerful in the galaxy: the casinos of Canto Bight.

"The notion of doing a very glamorous, Monte Carlo-inspired *Star Wars* city, where the one-percenters come, came very early in the writing process," said Rian Johnson. "I thought it would be interesting."

"Canto Bight and the casino were the biggest challenges for us, concept wise, from the beginning of the film," said production designer Rick Heinrichs. "As we were immersing ourselves in the DNA of *Star Wars*, they didn't quite fit any preconceived notions of anything I had seen. Rian wanted to shoot elements on location, but I was unsure how we'd take the architecture of real environments and [make them] part of this galaxy."

A concerted online search and scout revealed Dubrovnik, a coastal city in Croatia. "It's a walled medieval city. It was a great blank canvas for us, with a texture that would feel familiar from some of the other *Star Wars* films. Going back to the original *Star Wars*, you have the really cool idea of how Luke's underground place was set in Tunisia. It was very organic to its environment. We were looking for something similar."

Dubrovnik grounded the design of the casino as its interior set at Pinewood began to take shape. "This was a fabulous set to walk onto," said Heinrichs. "Neal Scanlan's creature work and all the props and set dressing were just amazing. We pretty much filled the 007 Stage at Pinewood. We wanted it to have scale. The point wasn't to build the biggest sets in the world. But when you need scale, you need scale. It has to look opulent and over-the-top. If you tried to squeeze this scene into a set the size of the Cantina [in *A New Hope*], it wouldn't have worked. It had to be what it was. It had to unfold the way it did."

"The casino is an excellent example of how you integrate all the departments together," said supervising art director Christopher Lowe. "We had stunts pulling the gaming tables; creatures working, with puppeteers underneath the tables; lighting effects; camera effects; a large wire camera. It was an amalgamation of every department. Visual effects got involved; green screens were used at the end to extend the set. Communication between departments had to be spot-on."

The 007 Stage encompassed the main casino hall and entrance vestibule, with green screen extension and clever placement of mirrors to make the already massive environment appear bigger on-screen. At Longcross Studios, production constructed the exterior casino

← Concept art by Kevin Jenkins visualizes the Canto Bight casino exterior building from a distance.

entrance driveway, where sleek speeders would deliver the gamblers. "A luxury version of *Star Wars* is very hard [to achieve]," said visual effects art director Kevin Jenkins. "It makes people feel uncomfortable because we like our dirt in *Star Wars*; our rust, our grime. It makes it all feel very believable."

The action then moves to the police station in Canto Bight after Rose and Finn fall afoul of law enforcement, shot on M stage at Pinewood. "Since this jail is part of the casino, I wanted it to look and feel kind of like it too, and use the same curves," said Heinrichs. "It's high security, but it's not a dungeon by any means. It's a drunk-tank for the casino."

"This set was a fun example of doing a lot with a little," said Johnson of the jail set. "This was basically just one hallway, shot in a bunch of ways to really stretch it out—the way they did on the original films."

Rose and Finn make their escape via a maintenance hole to arrive at the fathier stables, a set also built at Longcross and which served as a contrast to the jail set. "The fathiers are truly in the dungeon, and they are maligned, mistreated, and abused," said Heinrichs.

Freeing the fathiers from the stables and creating a stampede through the streets of Canto Bight and the casino is the major action set piece of this sequence of the film. The luxury of the casino would come crashing down thanks to the work of Chris Corbould and his special effects team. "I have no problem smashing and blowing things up," said Lowe. "We build [these things] to smash up, so that's good."

A specific section of the stampede would depict the fathiers tearing through a café, built on A stage, and sections of the main hall, on the 007 stage. "We had a static fathier 'buck' behind the casino window," said Corbould. "It was just a rigid form of the fathier's shape and height, so Ben [Morris, visual effects supervisor at ILM] could add animated creatures. We fired it through the glass and knocked tables and bar stools flying. We then rigged tables with snatch cables and worked out

PLEASE NOTE!

PLEASE SEE ART DEPT FOR ALL TEXTURES AND FINISHES AND ANY ADDITIONAL REFERENCES.

RIGS MAY BE REQUIRED VIA SFX FOR CREATURES TBD!

PLEASE REFER TO PADDOCK SITE PLAN FOR POSITION OF SET PIECE SHOWING EXTENT OF REQUIRED BLUE / GREEN SCREENS AS PER VFX REQUIREMENTS.

SET NO : 65   EXT - CANTO BIGHT - SIDE OF CASINO EXTENT OF BUILD STILL TO BE DECIDED

PLEASE REFER TO SITE PLAN FOR EXTENT OF GROUND WORKS REQUIRED TO COVER ALL WIDE SHOTS.

PLEASE SEE VEHICLES ART DIRECTOR AND SFX FOR ADVISE ON ANY PRE BUILD RIGS REQUIRED FOR THE ENTRANCE AREA FOR THE 5 PROPOSED ACTION VECHICLES PARKED IN FRONT.

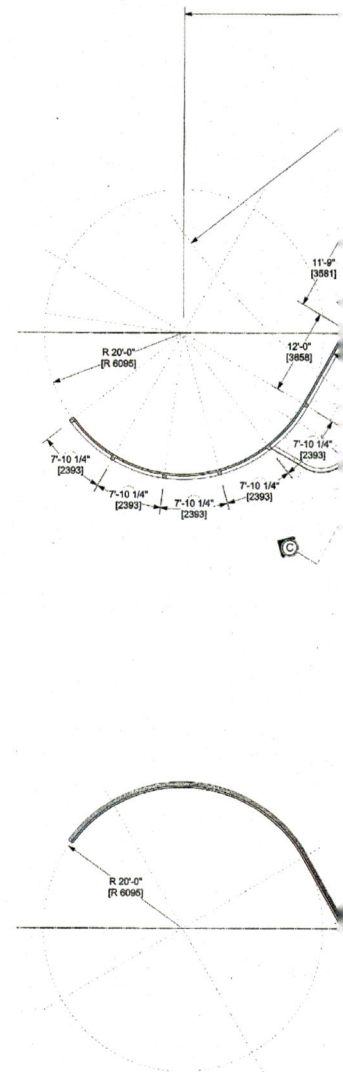

SET	EXT. CANTO BIGHT — LUXSPEEDERS
DETAIL	PLANS & ELEVATIONS
DRG NO.	003
DATE	NOVEMBER 23 2015
DRAWN BY	PHIL SIMMS

↓ The "Alpha Romeo Carabo"-style luxury speeder found on Canto Bight is depicted in a left elevation view.

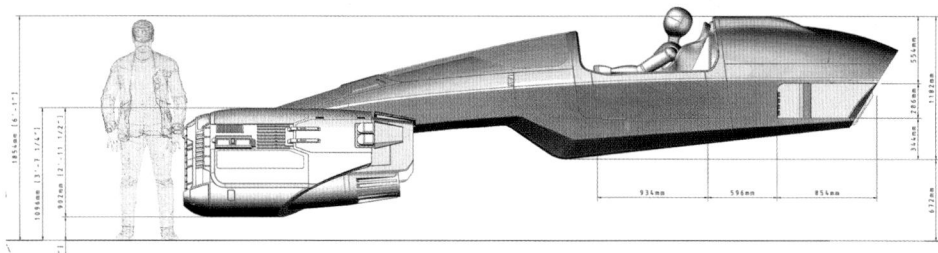

F R O N T   E L E V A T I O N

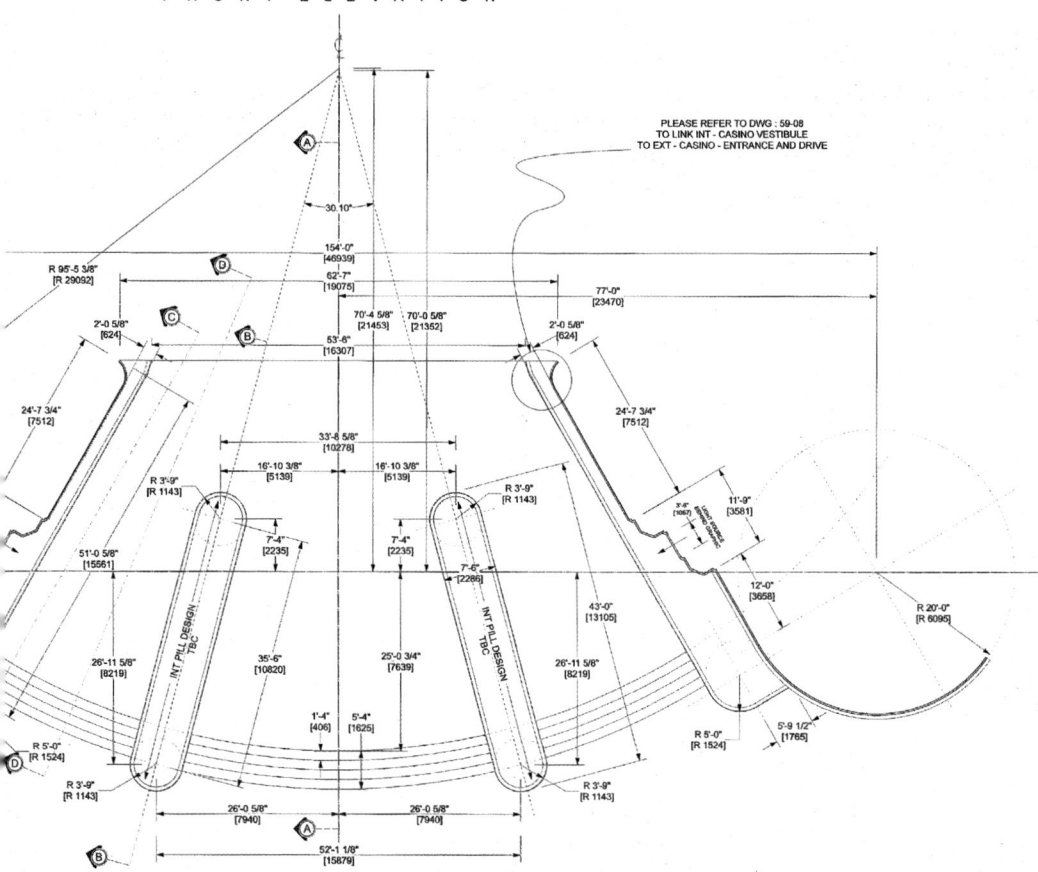

PLEASE REFER TO DWG : 59-08
TO LINK INT - CASINO VESTIBULE
TO EXT - CASINO - ENTRANCE AND DRIVE

P L A N   S E C T I O N   T H R U   (E)(E)

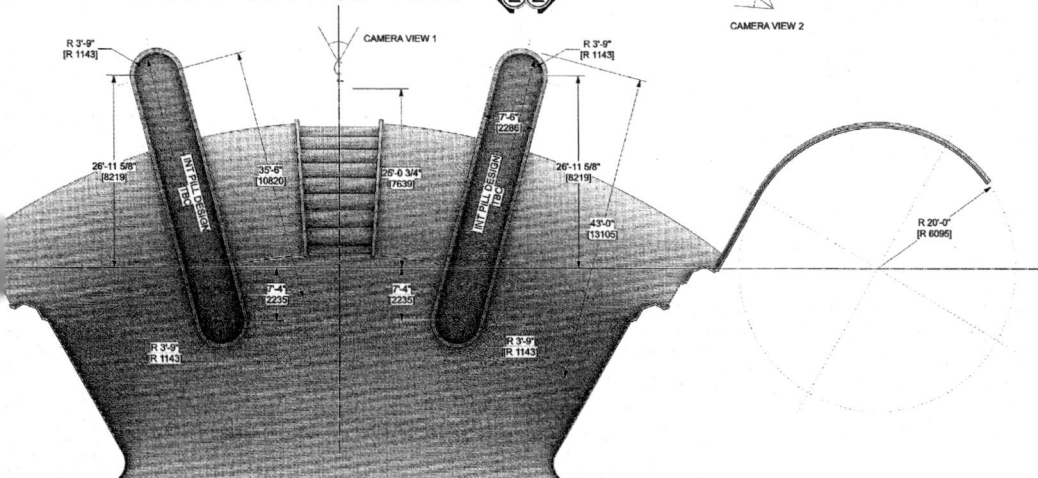

CAMERA VIEW 1

CAMERA VIEW 2

EFLECTED   C E I L I N G   P L A N   T H R U   (F)(F)

how to make them fly as fathiers charged through. They ran a cable-flown camera through that to simulate the fathier's point of view, and we triggered tables electronically from that camera motion."

The stampede spills outdoors, photographed in the streets of Dubrovnik, where many of the medieval buildings were made of polished limestone. "What I've always loved about Dubrovnik is there's a kind of gleam to the streets," said Heinrichs. "It feels like there's a sheen to it, a surface to it, that is very welcoming, luxurious, and exotic. One of the things we tried to do is make everything pretty organic to the existing look and feel of Dubrovnik, but with our own *Star Wars* slant to it. So we added doorways, buttresses, and light fixtures to make up the *Star Wars* language."

"The location dressing was fantastic, but they could only dress eight feet above street level," said Mike Mulholland, visual effects supervisor. "We used that as a reference, building everything up vertically while keeping most of the floor-level location."

"Cities are not snapshots where everything was built at the same exact moment of time and in exactly the same materials," said Heinrichs. "We came up with a concept of older and newer areas of the city. It felt layered in a way that we hadn't seen in a *Star Wars* film. Going back to Lucas' own words and his own instincts, I think one of the problems you have with science fiction movies is it's so clear that somebody had to make that up because it never existed before. And this was the opposite of that. You want to feel like it's always been there, that a team of artists didn't sit down and design it."

The luxury speeders take a pounding as the fathiers race out of the city, with the vehicular destruction delivered by Corbould and his team. "We did a speeder that got knocked up against a wall, slid along, hit a lamppost, and let off sparks," he said. "We had another that was stamped on and broke, another that was hit and flipped onto a parked vehicle. We had speeders on wheels, some on the snatch rigs, another on a track like a little rollercoaster. That started stationary and when it was hit, it launched on its rails and went up a wall."

The last part of the fathier escape were grasslands and a cliff ledge shot at Pinewood's Paddock Tank.

← The Canto Bight casino entrance and driveway is defined in this illustration. The extent of the exterior wall would be 30 feet high.

SET	EXT. CANTO BIGHT — CASINO ENTRANCE & DRIVE (SET #58)
DETAIL	PLANS & ELEVATIONS
DRG NO.	02B
DATE	OCTOBER 20 2015
DRAWN BY	ANDREW BENNETT

THE *LIBERTINE*

To escape Canto Bight, Finn, Rose, and BB-8 hitch a ride with Benicio Del Toro's character DJ, an unscrupulous, amoral hacker who appropriates a sleek sports ship, later identified as the *Libertine*. Coming midway through production, the build for this ship on C stage at Pinewood consisted of its cockpit and lounge, featuring anodized silver, blue, and nickel finishings, along with red and silver leatherette upholstery.

"The ship went through quite a few versions," explained visual effects art director Kevin Jenkins. "Rian said, 'I really need this to feel fast, cool, and sporty.' And because we're all of a certain age and we think back to what we loved as kids, I came back to a white turbo Lotus Esprit." Such a design famously featured in the 1977 James Bond movie, *The Spy Who Loved Me*. "Then, because this film is Flash Gordon- and Buck Rogers-esque, I just put two giant rocket pods on the side of it and a big spoiler on the back."

The telescoping spiral staircase which extends from the bottom of the craft was built on R Stage. "Rian wanted a dramatic way for DJ and BB-8 to appear as they come up over the cliff and rescue Finn and Rose," said Jenkins. "We talked about that great scene in *Indiana Jones and the Last Crusade* [1989] where Sean Connery leans back on the chair and rolls down a spiral staircase as it unfolds."

← The extending spiral staircase beneath the sleek ship is illustrated here in technical drawings and Set Dec plans.

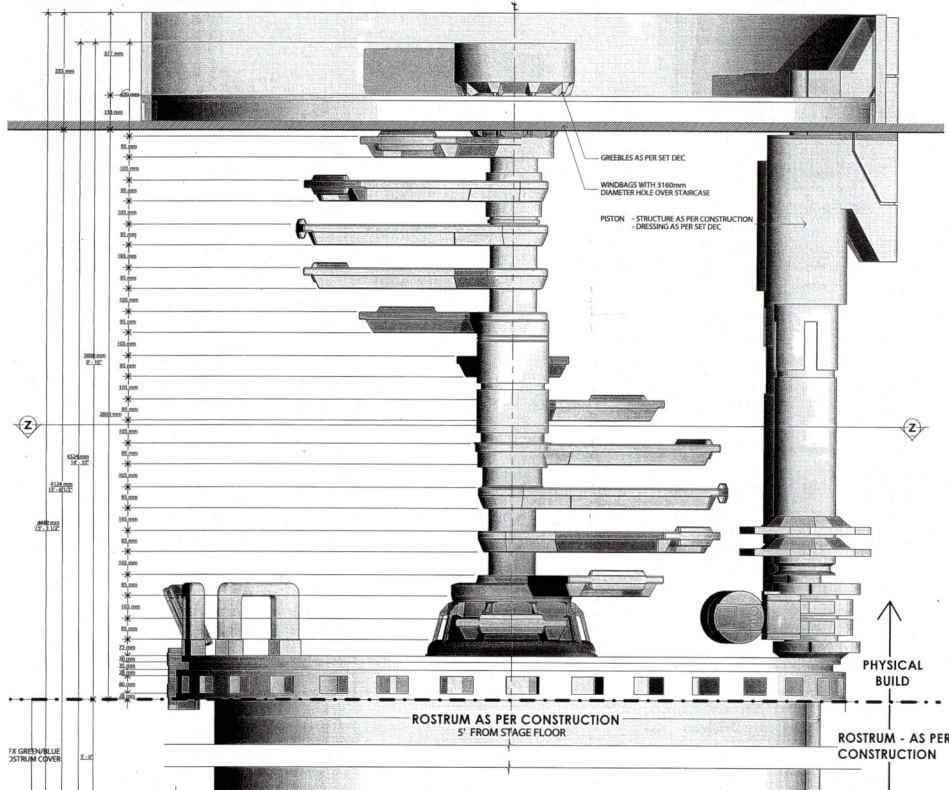

SET	EXT. SLEEK SHIP — SPIRAL STAIRCASE
DETAIL	PLANS & ELEVATIONS — SHOWING SET DEC ITEMS
DRG NO.	01
DATE	DECEMBER 8 2015
DRAWN BY	MATT SIMS/HAZEL KEAN

→ The cockpit of the stolen ship is shown in this set interior photograph.

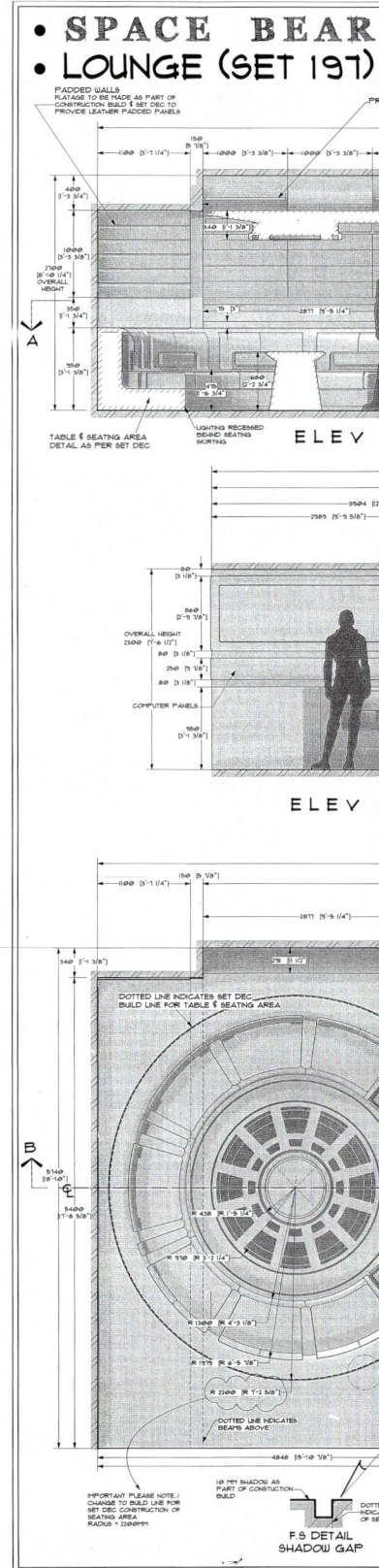

- **SPACE BEAR**
- **LOUNGE (SET 197)**

→ The burnished interior lounge of the sleek ship is illustrated in concept art by Roberto Fernandez Castro.

↓ Set 197 is the sleek ship lounge, represented here in plans drawn by Teri Fairhurst.

SET	INT. SLEEK SHIP — LOUNGE (SET 197)
DETAIL	PLANS & ELEVATIONS — LOUNGE (SET 197)
	REVISION C
DRG NO.	02C
DATE	FEBRUARY 9 2016
DRAWN BY	TERI FAIRHURST

INT SLEEK SHIP • COCKPIT (SET 196) & LOUNGE (SET 197) • PLAN & ELEV'S •
SCALE = 1 : 20 (REVISION C)

SECTION BB

SECTION CC

PRESPECTIVE VIEW OF RECESS BETWEEN SEATING AREA & CUPBOARD

PERSPECTIVE VIEW OF SLEEK LOUNGE AREA

ELEV/SECTION DD

REVISION A :-
- CHANGE TO BUILD LINE FOR SET DEC CONSTRUCTION OF SEATING AREA RADIUS = 1200MM
- EXTRA DETAILS TO FOLLOW ON CEILING PANELS

REVISION B :-
- ADDITION OF FLATAGE AND CEILING PLAN FOR THE TRANSITION BETWEEN LOUNGE AREA TO STAIRCASE & COCKPIT THE LENGHT OF PLATEAGE HAS TO YET TBC..!!!
- 19MM SHADOW GAP BETWEEN THE SET DEC BUILD AND THE CONSTRUCTION BUILD
- CUPBOARD, SLEDGE DETAILS TO BE TAKEN ON BOARD BY CONSTRUCTION
- LENGHT OF CUPBOARD IN ELEV DD IS NOW LONGER

REVISION C :-
- LENGHT OF FLATAGE HAS INCREASED IN SECTION DD BY 3 1/4" (81 MM) THIS BECAUSE OF THE BULLNOSE OF COCKPIT. PLEASE ALSO BE AWARE THAT THE CABINET LENGHT ON THE SIDE ELEVATION HAS INCREASED TOO..!!

IMPORTANT NOTES !!
- ALL FURNITURE PIECES TABLE & SEATING PLUS SLEDGE, CUPBOARD & LIGHTING UNIT AS PER SET DEC DETAILS
- ALL FINISHES & COLOURS AS PER ART DIRECTORS REQUIREMENTS

PLAN SECTION AA
SCALE = 1 : 20

REFLECTED CEILING PLAN

REVISED

SPACE BEAR

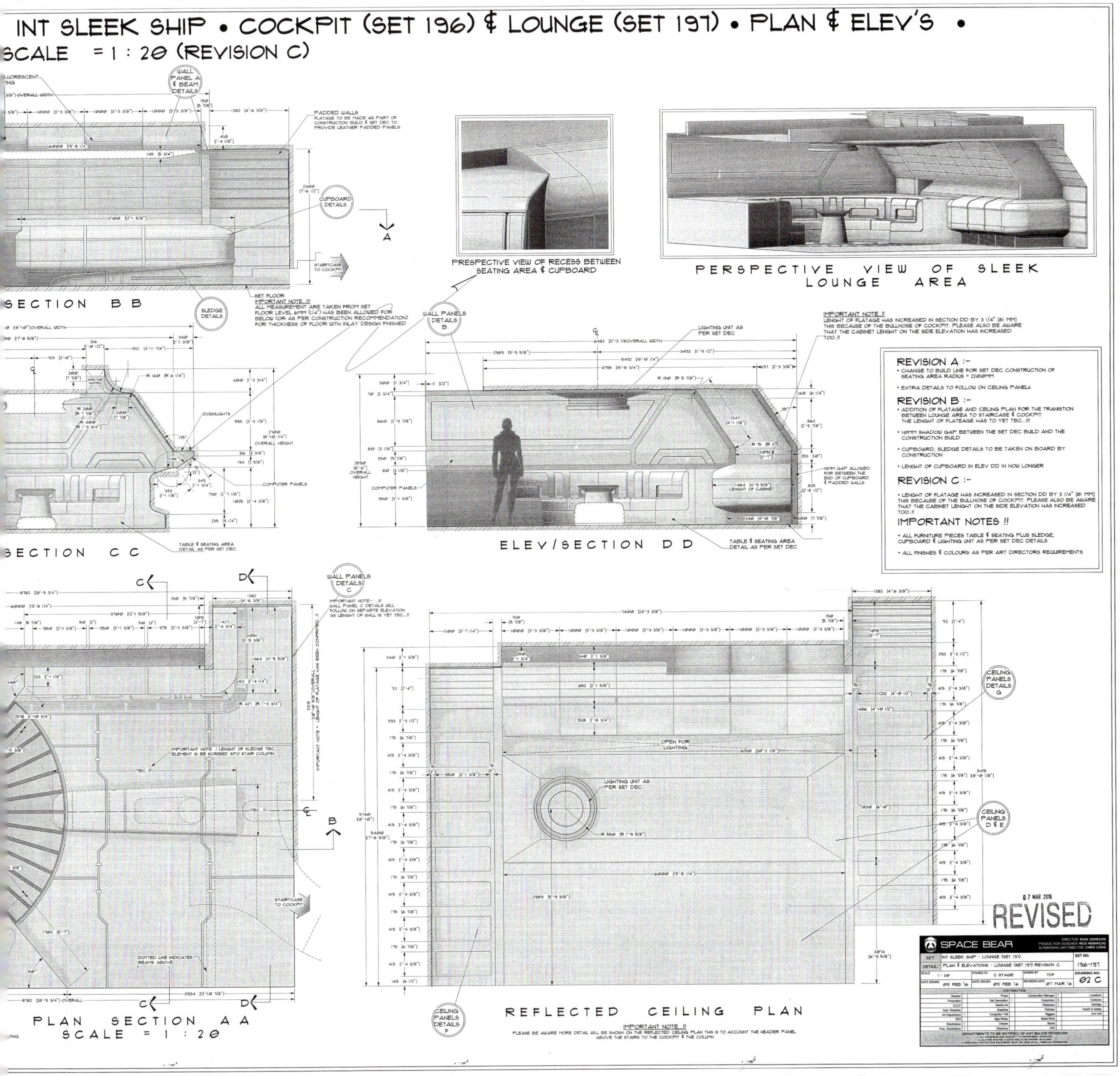

MILLENNIUM FALCON ESCAPE POD

When Rey surrenders to the First Order in a bid to turn Kylo away from the dark side, she enters the Mega-Destroyer in an escape pod jettisoned from the *Millennium Falcon*. This required the construction of the pod itself and an entry chamber.

"We didn't want to say exactly where we were in the *Falcon* so people didn't get too crazy," laughed production designer Rick Heinrichs. "It was very exciting to be involved with a little expansion of the ship's interior." Although production was initially reticent, the Lucasfilm story group's team of *Falcon* experts sketched out where in the ship's structure the entry chamber was and also where the pod ejected from.

"I kept pushing them to make the design feel like a coffin," said Rian Johnson. "There was something about that image. There's a C.S. Lewis book called *Perelandra*, which I was really into when I was in high school; it's part of his Space Trilogy. The main character travels through space in a coffin. Maybe that's it."

↑ The full-sized, coffin-like escape pod is shown as a final construction, with the background removed.

PLEASE NOTE:
CONSTRUCTION TO ARRANGE EXISTING SET PIECES & MAKE BACK WALL FOR POD ONLY
NEW POD ELEMENTS TO BE MADE BY PROP MAKING / PROPS

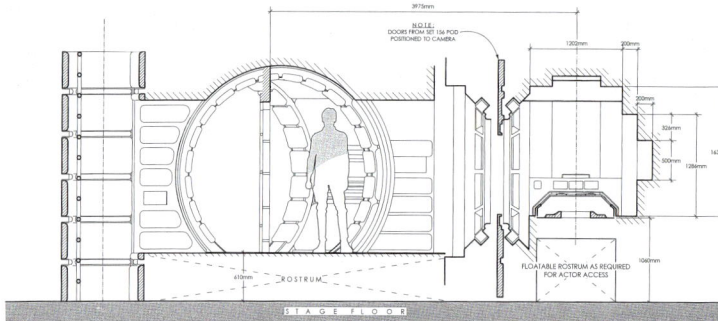

SECTION THRU'
X - X

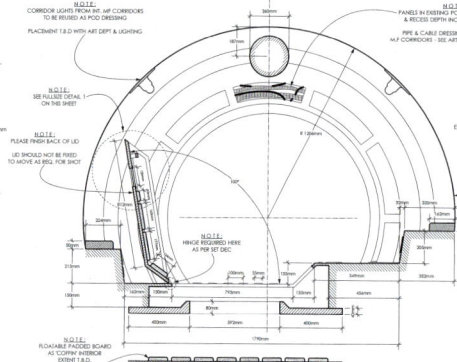

SECTION A-A

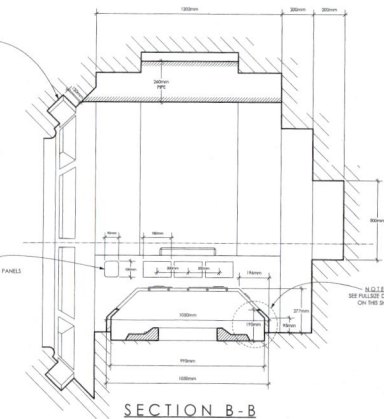

SECTION B-B

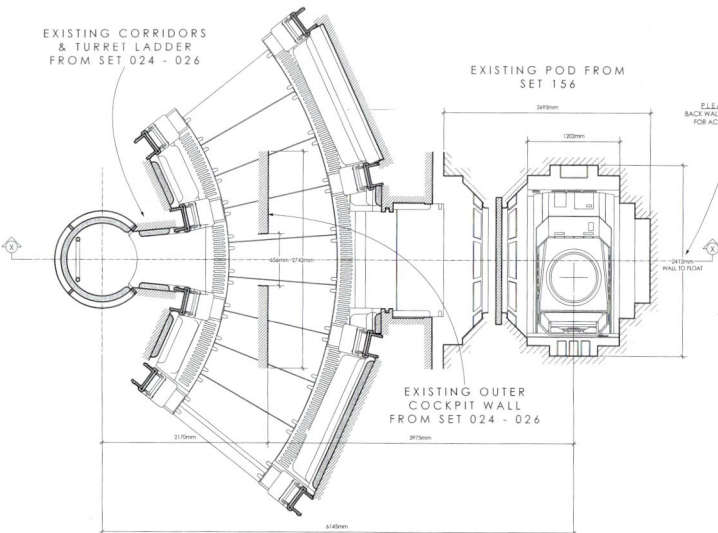

OVERALL PLAN
@ 1:20

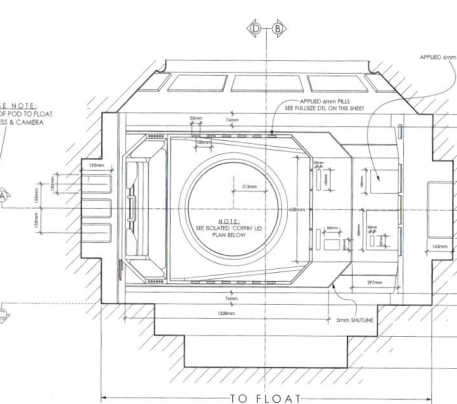

PLAN @ 1:10

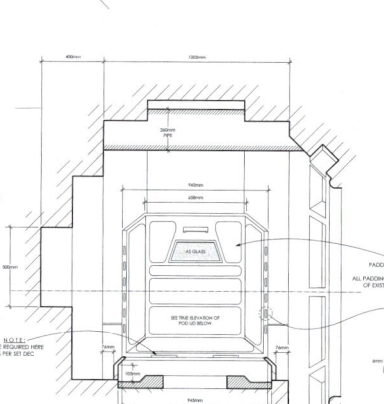

SECTION D-D

FULLSIZE LOCK
PILL DETAIL

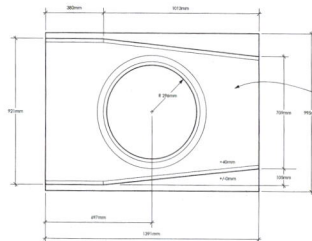

NOTE:
ESCAPE POD LID IS A 110% PARTIAL REPLICA OF THE ORIGINAL

ESCAPE POD LID
ISOLATED PLAN
1:10

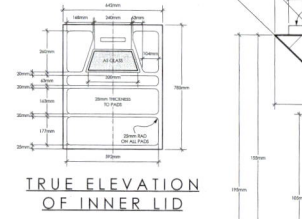

TRUE ELEVATION
OF INNER LID

FULLSI

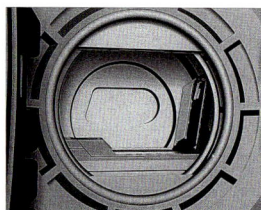

PERSPECTIVE VIEWS OF SET
NTS

SET   FIRST ORDER M. D. — HANGAR 1
DETAIL   COFFIN REVISED
DRG NO.   124
DATE   APRIL 6 2016
DRAWN BY   CRISSY JO HOWES

↓ A perspective illustration of the *Millennium Falcon* escape pod shows the hatch closed and open.

shot as known

dress hero sides only

removable for access

SECTION C-C

NOTE:
IONAL PIPE DRESSING ON CEILING
AS PER SET DEC

NOTE:
CONSTRUCTION TO MAKE NEW BACK WALL ELEMENT

NOTE:
DRESSING TO BE APPLIED TO BACK WALL
SEE ART DEPT. FOR REFERENCE

NOTE:
HANDLE AS PER SET DEC

NOTE:
ALL PADDING TO MATCH
FINISH & AGING OF EXISTING
MF CORRIDOR PADS

FULLSIZE DETAIL ①

NOTES:
• CONSTRUCTION TO ARRANGE EXISTING SET PIECES & MAKE POD BACK WALL
• PROP MAKING / PROPS TO MAKE NEW POD ELEMENTS
• SEE ART DEPT. FOR ALL FINISHES - 3D MODEL AVAILABLE FROM ART DEPT.

RELEASE
DETAIL ②

← The hitherto unseen escape pod bay in a new section of the *Millennium Falcon* is illustrated in this abbreviated set build for a pick up.

SPACE BEAR
SET: INT. MF 'COFFIN' POD BAY   SET NO. 47
DETAIL: PLAN & ELEVATIONS
DRAWING NO. 01

SET   INT. M. F. 'COFFIN' POD BAY
DETAIL   PLANS & ELEVATIONS
DRG NO.   01
DATE   JUNE 10 2016
DRAWN BY   LIAM GEORGENSEN

In the script, the pod is described as being inscribed with the words, "PROPERTY OF HAN SOLO," though in the *Star Wars* galaxy such text would not be in legible English. Rather than opt for the workhorse Aurebesh font usually used to convey textual information, Rian Johnson tasked VFX art director James Clyne to create a new set of hand-drawn characters that would become "Clyne-ese." The need for the inscription fell by the wayside when a shot showing the pod launch directly from the *Falcon* made its origins clear.

MEGA-DESTROYER

Emerging from hyperspace to dwarf even the First Order Star Destroyers pursuing the ragtag Resistance fleet, Supreme Leader Snoke's Mega-Destroyer is unfeasibly huge. "Snoke's ship was thirty-seven miles wide [in the film]," said visual effects supervisor Ben Morris. "Rian wanted to see First Order Star Destroyers hovering like tiny remora around this massive manta ray."

Interior sets for this environment followed the established First Order aesthetic, but on a scale suiting the Supreme Leader's outsized authority. However, the radically different shape of the ship—a giant wing rather than the triangular dagger of a regular Star Destroyer—made it impossible to reuse the Star Destroyer bridge that had already served double duty as the bridge of the Siege Dreadnought seen earlier in the film.

"Rather than the compact conning tower that you have on a Star Destroyer, this ship's bridge is very wide. So, when you look left and right, the view just goes on," said visual effects art director Kevin Jenkins. "We hadn't seen a bridge like that. When you cut to different places and you want the audience immediately to understand where they are, you find certain motifs. For the Mega, everything was going widthwise."

The bridge occupied A stage at Pinewood, while E stage hosted other interior spaces, including a network of main and utility corridors. The medical chamber, where Kylo reveals the scarring from his encounter with Rey in *The Force Awakens*, was built and photographed on F stage, and would later double as Ren's quarters. "We repurposed the medical chamber set and added a few extra elements," said Johnson. "A concept drawing [by Roberto Fernandez Cortez] had a real *Blade Runner* [1982] vibe, and I thought it would really be fun to see."

The chamber containing the hyperspace tracker—a device partially inspired by the look of the flux capacitor in the *Back to the Future* movies—was built on E stage. "We had the worst time trying to keep our reflective floors from getting messed up by people walking on them," said production designer Rick Heinrichs. "That was the bane of my existence for a long period: people would step off a set, walk around outside, and then come back. We were polishing the floor all day long."

THE THRONE ROOM

The standout environment was Supreme Leader Snoke's Throne Room on Q stage. "I think this was maybe my favorite set. It was extraordinary," said Johnson. "I knew I wanted big, theatrical, red curtains that were going to burn away later in the scene, but we couldn't quite visually figure out how to make them work. At some

point, I remembered a beautiful production of *Madam Butterfly* that the late, great Anthony Minghella directed [in 2005]. There was a visual in it that I showed to the team. The pure field of red and the reflective black floor is very much a nod to that."

Heinrichs recalls other sources of inspiration as well. "The red color was one of the elements that were inspired by *Twin Peaks* [1990–91]" he said. "Although I think the most important inspiration for it was a Ralph McQuarrie drawing of Vader in [metaphorical] hell. We've taken the essential organic characteristics of his image and refined them into a much more polished and ceremonial space that is more *Wizard of Oz* [1939]."

"I put my heart and soul into the Throne Room," said Jenkins. "I worked on it for six months."

The Throne Room set needed to accommodate the complex action within, including an extended fight sequence between Rey, Kylo, and the Praetorian Guards. It also had to include the motion-capture array that would digitally record Andy Serkis' performance as Snoke, as Serkis was present on set to interact with the other actors. "We actually had to remove elements of our set for the stunt rig and then reassemble them," said Heinrichs. "We were working crews on the overnight during this whole period. This was definitely a very challenging set to properly service."

OTHER INTERIORS

Several other interiors for the Mega-Destroyer were constructed, including a hangar—which, in the context of the film, was intended to look large enough to contain Star Destroyers. It was housed on Pinewood's D stage, though its construction was cursory—mainly patterned flooring. "The Mega hangar set had a fairly small footprint," said Ben Morris. "The majority of the environment ended up being CG extensions."

"The Mega-Destroyer hangar was a gigantic space. We experimented with putting a Star Destroyer inside. It didn't quite fit, but it was close," explained visual effects supervisor Dan Seddon.

The E stage at Pinewood saw the construction of the laundry room, with its memorable gag shot of a clothes iron descending like a starship—a nod to a similar ship in the 1978 fan parody film *Hardware Wars*.

An immense common room, with seemingly endless banks of work cubicles inspired by the office full of desks in the 1960 Billy Wilder movie *The Apartment*, was built on S stage, although it was edited out of the final film.

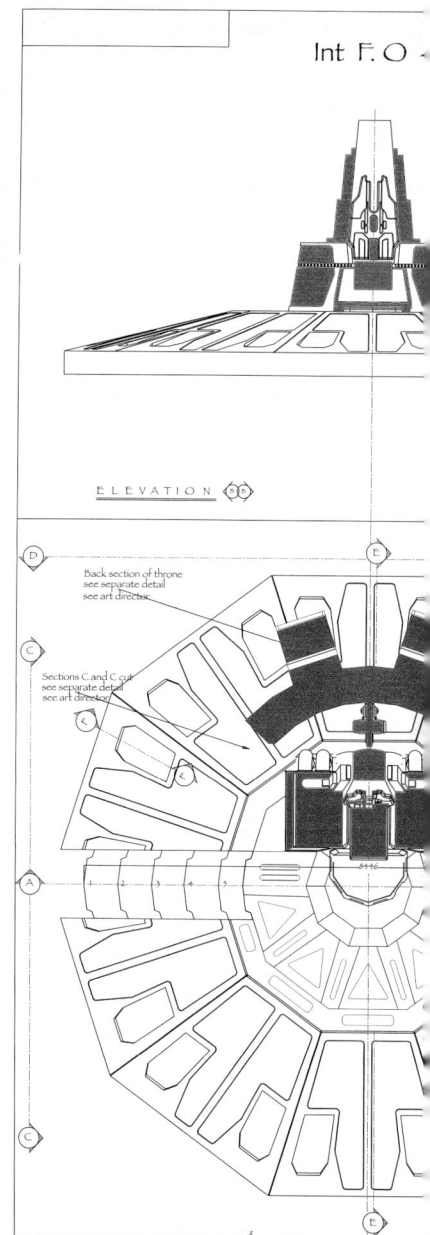

↑ Snoke's Throne Room dais is detailed in this illustration. Figures approximating Kylo and Rey's heights are included for scale.

nt Snoke's Throne room - Throne Dias - Detail #4

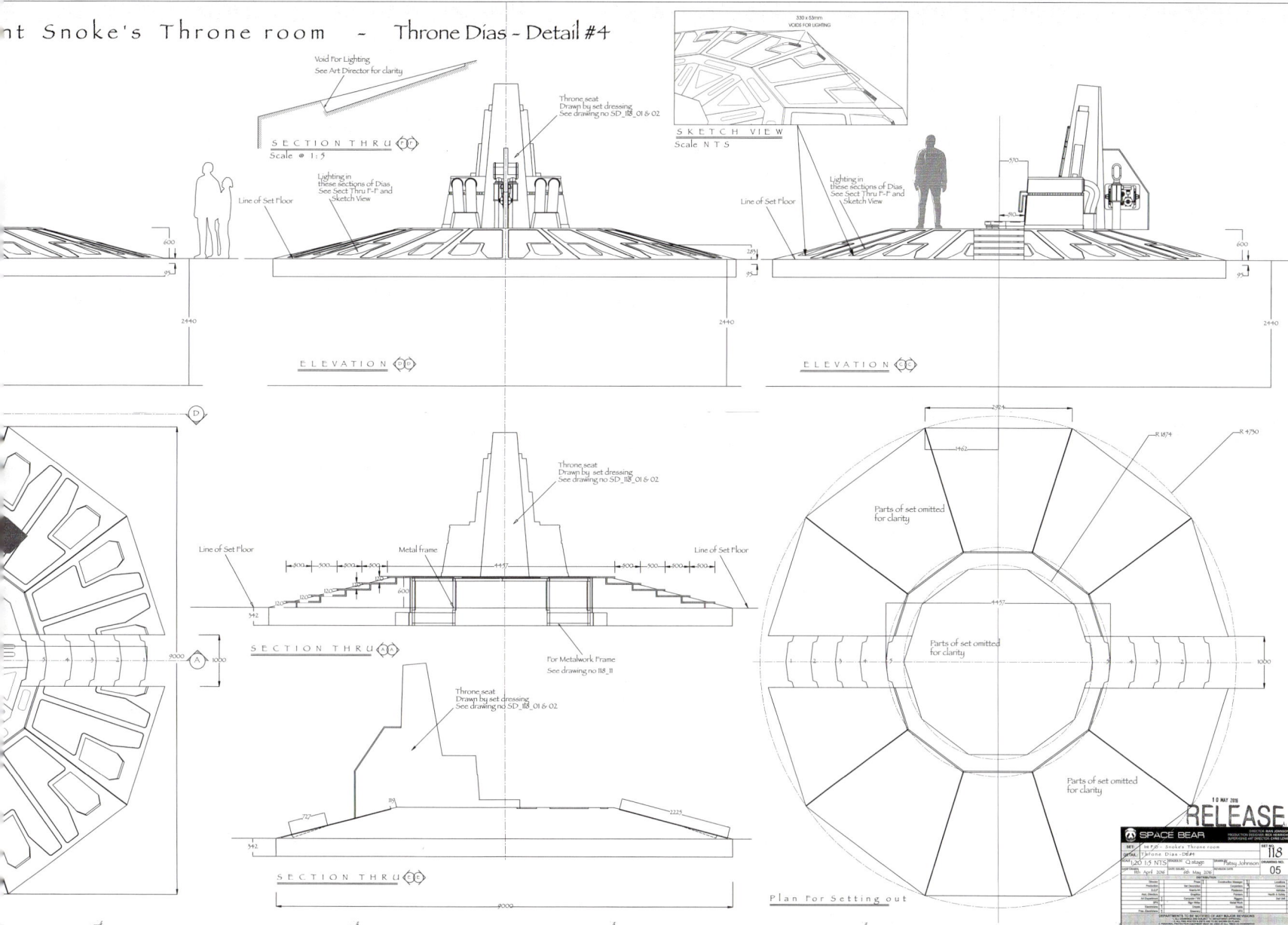

Void For Lighting
See Art Director for clarity

Throne seat
Drawn by set dressing
See drawing no SD_118_01 & 02

330 x 65mm
VOIDS FOR LIGHTING

S K E T C H   V I E W
Scale N T S

S E C T I O N   T H R U
Scale @ 1 : 5

Lighting in
these sections of Dias,
See Sect Thru P-P and
Sketch View

Line of Set Floor

Lighting in
these sections of Dias,
See Sect Thru P-P and
Sketch View

Line of Set Floor

570

600

600

2440

2440

E L E V A T I O N

E L E V A T I O N

Throne seat
Drawn by set dressing
See drawing no SD_118_01 & 02

Line of Set Floor

Metal frame

Line of Set Floor

For Metalwork Frame
See drawing no 118_11

S E C T I O N   T H R U

Throne seat
Drawn by set dressing
See drawing no SD_118_01 & 02

S E C T I O N   T H R U

Parts of set omitted
for clarity

Parts of set omitted
for clarity

Parts of set omitted
for clarity

1000

Plan For Setting out

RELEASE

SPACE BEAR

05

118

SET	INT. F. O. — SNOKE'S THRONE ROOM
DETAIL	THRONE DIAS — D. T. L. #4
DRG NO.	05
DATE	APRIL 11 2016
DRAWN BY	PATSY JOHNSON

➔ In this set photograph,
Snoke's Throne Room is
draped in a dramatic
red curtain.

CRAIT

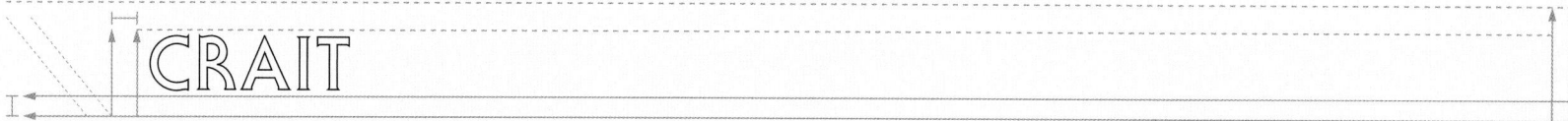

The salty mineral surface of the planet Crait was one of the first visual concepts that writer/director Rian Johnson envisioned for *The Last Jedi*. The crimson mineral that would become increasingly exposed during a battle scene would serve as a grim metaphor in the otherwise mostly bloodless conflict depicted in *Star Wars* movies. Visual effects art director Kevin Jenkins said, "Rian asked me, 'Can you try a salt flat with red underneath?' I sketched a ship crashing into some Resistance troopers on a salt plain, with red exploding upward. He said, 'Yeah, that's going to work,' and that's where it all started. Red meant death. We talked about those ideas a lot. All our designs have symbolic properties in the *Star Wars* universe."

During his research phase at the Skywalker Ranch library in 2014, production designer Rick Heinrichs was drawn to aerial photography of exotic environments in a book titled *Desert Air*. "This location was a salt flat and I didn't really register that until we discovered that we were going to go to the world's largest salt flat, in Bolivia. The photo from the book was that same salt flat. The image that I discovered in the Lucas library in the fall of 2014 was the place we were going to shoot the location. It was meant to be."

"We looked at all the salt plains in the world," said visual effects supervisor Ben Morris. "They included Bonneville Flats in Utah, others in China and Europe, and some in Bolivia, which are the biggest. They're hard to get around, at twelve-thousand feet above sea level, but they are just gigantic. We decided to go there at the end of the filming to shoot as many background plates as possible. That helped us understand the lighting and structure of salt flats, which are covered in strange hexagonal ridges. We took a small crew, a camera truck, and helicopters, and we spent about four days gathering as much visual reference as possible, swooping along at seventy to eighty miles per hour."

The set build for the Crait exteriors would include trenches and gun emplacements at Pinewood's Paddock Tank, a large crater on S stage, and a crevasse on the North Lot. "We hired a company called Snow Business to help us put down paper and magnesium sulfate—salt—to dress it out," said Heinrichs. "We also laid down the fractals, which occur in salt flats when the water dies out and evaporation cracks the surface of the earth, and which create a texture throughout the surface."

→ The Richard Attenborough Stage housed the Crait tunnels, as depicted in this illustration, which shows specific zones of action (as well as some Ahch-To locations).

SET	INT. CHOICE & BOULDER CAVES
DETAIL	MAIN PLAN SHOWING ZONAL BREAKDOWN
DRG NO.	01A
DATE	MAY 28 2016
DRAWN BY	NEAL CALLOW AND DEAN CLEGG

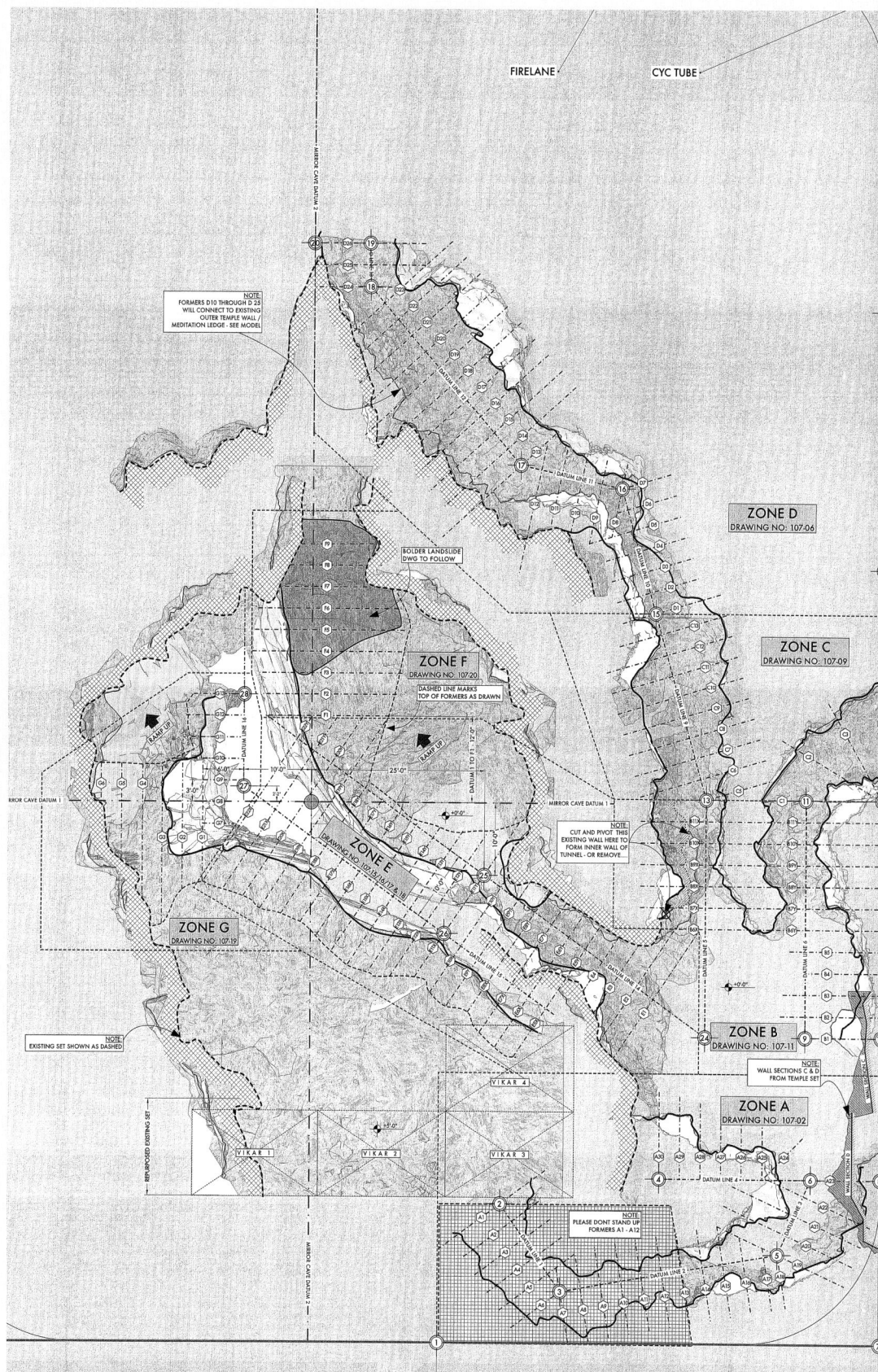

EXT/INT RESISTANCE MINE- SKI SPEEDER - (Hero, Intact, Full Built Cockpit) - P&E's OVERALL DIMENSIONS SHOWING CONSTRUCTION & SET DEC PARTS (ORANGE) - SCALE 1/15

FRONT VIEW
Scale: 1/15

Cockpit to be used on gimbal. See Art Dirctor

Practical breakaway panel to reveal pilot's foot.

PORT
Scale: 1/15

STARBOARD
Scale: 1/15

SET	EXT./INT. SKI SPEEDER – COCKPIT (183)
DETAIL	SKI SPEEDER – P & ES CONSTRUCTION & SET DEC PARTS
DRG NO.	001
DATE	FEBRUARY 3 2016
DRAWN BY	GREG FANGEAUX

↑ A ski speeder illustration depicts overall dimensions, construction, and Set Dec parts. A rendering of Poe Dameron (Oscar Isaac) is included for scale.

↓ A final frame from the end battle of *The Last Jedi* centers on a Resistance ski speeder carving up the salt plains of Crait, as built, animated, and rendered by ILM.

Chris Corbould's special effects team experimented with the explosive techniques that would best emulate the desired graphic impact of red crystalline dust marring the white landscape. "We tried all sorts of red powders, red paper, and red dust, and ended up using coarse red paper," he said. For the Battle of Crait, production built full-sized open cockpits for the ski speeders that the Resistance uses to defend its base. The teams ensured that the speeders had the rickety, jalopy feel that Johnson wanted in order to further emphasize the David versus Goliath nature of the fight against the First Order.

The interior of the Crait base took up large sections of the 007 Stage floor, with a blasted door fissure, the cavern walls, an escape transport from the Resistance cruiser, a drill tank, and a crashed shuttle filling the space. "We did build quite a bit of the crashed shuttle," said Heinrichs. "Special effects had it running in and dragging through, so it comes to a halt at the end. It was another one of those mandates from the director to do as much in camera as possible."

Also on the 007 Stage, as a sort of set within a set, was the mine control center, where the Resistance hunkers down during the First Order assault, and Luke Skywalker suddenly appears to say a farewell to General Leia before leaving to confront Kylo. "This set was just kind of a little box," said Johnson. "I was very frustrated when we started setting up shots in this set, because it didn't feel like there was geography to really move around in. But I ended up working with Steve [Yedlin, director of photography] and ended up being really happy with the choreography we had in here."

As the Resistance survivors trek deeper into the old mines, they go into rocky tunnels strewn with boulders, creating an opportunity for the production to find some efficiencies in reuse. "One of our 'brilliant' ideas was to turn the rock sets around," said Heinrichs. "The rock set is initially the mirror cave on the island [Ahch-To]. Using as much of it as possible, we turned that into the meditation cave. Then the meditation cave became the back of the Crait mine, with tunnels and boulders. What it allowed us to do was to efficiently turn things around. These are not cheap things to build in the first place. So, if there's any way to amortize the cost of constructing it and building it… that's what we did there."

BLOCKADE RUNNER

After scattering from the planet Crait at the end of *The Last Jedi*, the Resistance returns in *The Rise of Skywalker,* sequestered on the jungle world of Ajan Kloss. In the interests of differentiating this base from superficially similar ones that had come before—namely Yavin 4 and D'Qar—Kevin Jenkins, now co-production designer on the film, proposed a new twist.

"I asked, 'What if there's no base? What if a ship is the base? What if there's all these cables coming out and it powers the machines as if that's their generator, their home, their everything? And it's just sitting in a cave. That's all they've got.'"

Director J.J. Abrams enthusiastically approved the idea, and the ship at the heart of the base took on added significance as it also became a proxy for someone dearly departed. Carrie Fisher had died between the productions of Episode VIII and IX, and her absence would loom large over this final installment of the *Star Wars* saga. The ship at the center of the rebuilt Resistance base would be Princess Leia's blockade runner, the ship seen in the first *Star Wars* film, *A New Hope*. "As a tribute to [Carrie], let's go back to the very place that this all started, to the point where we even designed in the correct missing escape pods on our blockade runner," said Jenkins. "It was trying to link this last film all the way back with the very first film by saying, 'This is how we've introduced her, and this is how we finish her journey within *Star Wars*.'"

In the original trilogy, the ship itself had only ever existed as a model, with no exterior build defining its size. To show the vessel on land and have it occupy a space filled with people meant the crew had to deliver a large-scale construction, which would fill a large portion of Stage 5 at Pinewood. "The blockade runner is significantly larger than even a larger stage," said supervising art director Paul Ingles. This necessitated some low-tech movie magic.

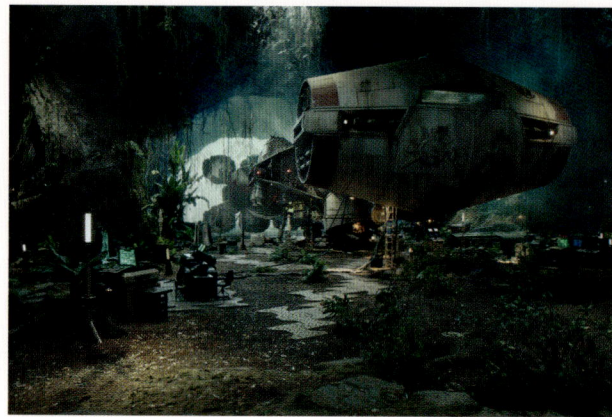

↑ In this scene, the blockade runner is nestled in a large cave system on Ajan Kloss. It returns to fight evil for one final time.

↓ These illustrations of the blockade runner's main body concentrate on the section behind the "hammerhead" bridge module, with specific detail of the landing gear and escape pod bays.

SET	HONOLULU COMPOSITE SET
DETAIL	HAMMERHEAD MAIN BODY – PLAN & ELEVATIONS
DRG NO.	018
DATE	APRIL 25 2018
DRAWN BY	LIZZIE OSBORNE

TRIXIE | HONOLULU COMPOSITE SET | EXT. HAMMERHEAD | MAIN BODY | PLAN & ELEVATIONS

ALL DIMENSIONS ARE TO STRUCTURAL SURFACES

102 018

TRIXIE HONOLULU COMPOSITE - HAMMER HEAD. PLANS AND ELEVATIONS. - 1:50 - 13TH APRIL 2018.

SIDE ELEVATION

FRONT ELEVATION

SECTION A-A

PLAN

UNDERSIDE

WING - TRUE PLAN

SET	HONOLULU COMPOSITE
DETAIL	HAMMERHEAD PLANS & ELEVATIONS
DRG NO.	002
DATE	APRIL 13 2018
DRAWN BY	MATT WYNNE

↑ The illustrations of a section of the blockade runner define the elevated and planar (two-dimensional) views of this ambitious build. The "wings" of the ship are drawn both with proper topside perspective and true planar views to avoid misrepresentation from distortion.

"When they did the original *Star Wars* film, with Mark Hamill and Alec Guinness walking into Docking Bay 94, they only made half the *Falcon* against the wall and then the rest kind of fell off into darkness," explained Jenkins. "We've taken that thought process where we've got as much as we need to see, and then the distance and depths of where you care just covers the rest of it."

Only the first third or so of the blockade runner is a dimensional build, spanning over 96 feet in length. It then terminates in a scenic painting that, when viewed from the front of the craft, continues the final two thirds of the superstructure in perspective. The painting has vines trailing from the engines and hull. "It's audacious and crazy, but it works. It's really an illusion," said co-production designer Rick Carter.

To best sell the scale, Abrams insisted that there should be constant human contact with the ship. Technicians scurry in hatchways, and rappel from the top of the hull. "We watched very closely what Irvin Kershner did [in *The Empire Strikes Back*], placing people on top of the *Falcon*."

"We built a good chunk of [the blockade runner] at extremely high detail," said Inglis. "The interiors included a corridor and a cockpit."

So how does Princess Leia's blockade runner go from being captured by Darth Vader's Star Destroyer at the start of *A New Hope* to being back with the Resistance in *The Rise of Skywalker*? "I don't know where they found it," admitted Jenkins. "But that's the fun of *Star Wars*. There's a story in my mind that wonders about it, but I don't really want anyone to ever tell me."

PASAANA

On the trail for answers to questions regarding her origins and to investigate mysterious reports of an arcane darkness that has returned to the galaxy, Rey travels to Pasaana with her compatriots. An already familiar biome in *Star Wars*—that of a desert planet—is freshened with the spirit of celebration, as the heroes arrive when a festival is teeming with thousands of celebrating Aki-Aki aliens. Reflective of such scenes of jubilation, the production code name for Pasaana was "Louisiana" and the festival grounds were code-named "New Orleans Downtown."

"What you're seeing is a galaxy that is worth fighting for," said co-production designer Rick Carter. "The way it comes across, the majesty of the environment and color, is that it's worth it. It's why we care. That's the message."

Initial concepts for the festival had the locals venerating a god, but the probing of divinity in *Star Wars* raised more questions than could comfortably be answered in the time and pace allotted by the storyline of Episode IX. So, rather than worship a deity, the Aki-Aki locals would instead celebrate their ancestors. "That ended up being interpreted by all kinds of toys, masks, mobiles, puppets, and any number of objects we made," said set decorator Rosemary Brandenburg.

"Originally, we were going to make a seventy-five-foot-tall deity, but that became these little necklaces of one-and-a-half-inch corn husk dolls, which ended up being the strongest expression of that idea in the film."

For the Festival of the Ancestors, construction wasn't focused on sets, as it was largely the natural environment of the Wadi Rum desert in Jordan that would provide the backdrop to the gathering. Instead, creating the infrastructure to shoot on location drew the larger effort. "There were no roads there. There were no facilities. There was no power. There was no food. There was no potable drinking water. No Wi-Fi. No internet. There were no buildings there," described executive producer Callum Greene.

"We had to build a small town in support of the filmmakers," said Martin Joy, production manager in Jordan. The production brought in water, plumbing, catering, portable offices, first aid, and other essentials for the 600 or so visiting UK crew members and 20 locals. "It was almost a civil engineering project for us."

The Royal Jordanian Film Commission supported the effort with military, ambulance, fire, and logistical services, all with a careful eye toward environmental care and sustainability. While the 450 or so extras portraying

'TRIXIE' LOUISIANA VILLAGE TENTS PLAN - OPTION 1

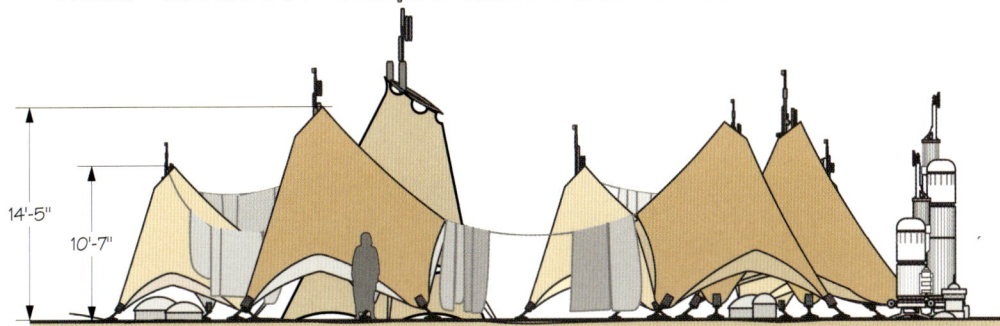

14'-5"
10'-7"

A-A

58'-3"
[18m]

14'-0"
[4m]

TYPE B

TYPE A

12'-2"

TYPE A

B

OTHER TECH
ELMENTS

B

TYPE A

53'-4'

TYPE A

VAPORATOR

16'-6"

OTHER TECH
ELMENTS

TYPE A

TYPE A

A

PLAN @ 1/8" TO 1 FT

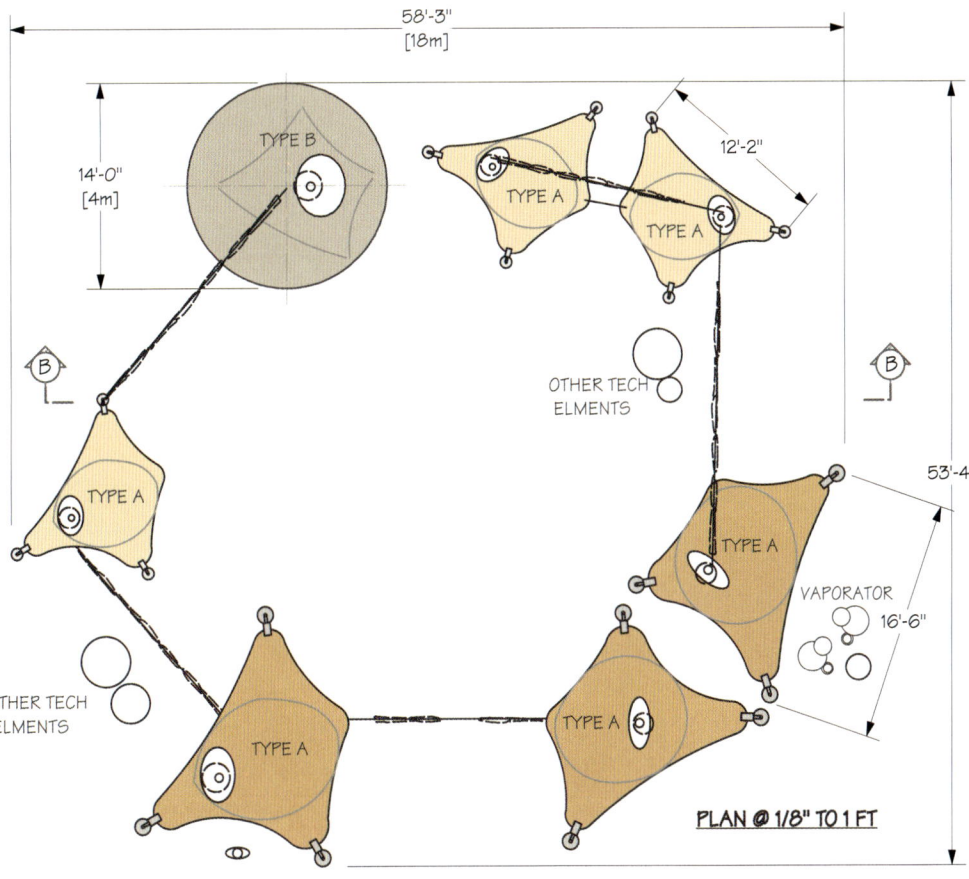

↑ These work-in-progress
options show the layout
and distribution of
Pasaana tent structures
to be crafted by the Set
Dec team.

SET	LOUISIANA
DETAIL	VILLAGE TENTS PLAN – OPTION 1
DRG NO.	N/A
DATE	APRIL 16 2018
DRAWN BY	CLARA GOMEZ DEL MORAL

the Aki-Aki represented the enormous bulk of the festival, it was the set decoration (Set Dec) team that formed the shape of the gathering.

"When we first went [to Wadi Rum] in April 2018, there was nothing there," said art director Claire Fleming. "We scanned the whole area and ILM helped put together a virtual version so that J.J. could walk around with the headset, back in the UK." Based on the placement of clusters of tents in the virtual environment, the Set Dec got to work building out the tents in the UK for eventual shipment to Jordan.

"We designed and fabricated a series of custom tents that involved steelwork and an enormous drapery job," said Brandenburg. "We used some fifteen thousand yards of custom-dyed fabrics imported from India, which we brought over and then over-dyed. We had vendors, drinks, refreshments, a band, and flags floating in the wind all out in the Wadi Rum desert."

Once the tents were placed as per the approved layout, Jenkins worked to add some "noise" to the tidiness. "There was a certain neatness to it all, that felt like an army had put these things up," he said. "We were trying to mess it up because, as people put up tents, some are very good and some are very bad. We just needed to bring the reality to it."

"We were out in the middle of the desert and the wind had been quite tough," said Brandenburg. "You're dealing with tents, which tend to get blown down. When we put things up, it created shade and the little creepy crawlies like the shade so we had to be a bit careful in the mornings. I saw little scorpions—the really poisonous ones that are clear."

The creature department dug a trench to fit nearly 30 puppeteers under the ground level to operate the Aki-Aki children who have gathered to watch a puppet show at the festival. "They would do a sweep for

↓ A concept artwork by Jon McCoy and Adam Brockbank shows an iteration of the Pasaana festival wherein the locals venerated their god.

SET	EXT. NEW ORLEANS DOWNTOWN
DETAIL	50' DEITY PLANS & ELEVATIONS
	(30' BUILT & V. F. X.)
DRG NO.	SD 51
DATE	SEPTEMBER 9 2018
DRAWN BY	CLARA GOMEZ DEL MORAL

← This illustration shows the Aki-Aki deity effigy that was to dominate the celebration on Pasaana before the gathering was reworked to be a Festival of the Ancestors. The base of the 50-foot structure was to be practical, with the alien's head to be determined through visual effects.

scorpions first thing in the morning before we got down there, and scare them all away," said puppeteer Mike Quinn.

The creature shop delivered the hundreds of Aki-Aki masks required for the scene, and these, too, had their numbers bolstered by scenic art. Some 500 hand-painted cutouts of Aki-Akis with varying degrees of details filled out the distance. "Some were really detailed; those became the ones that were closer up, and they also got a bit of costume added," said Brandenburg. "Then there was the next stage where they were slightly detailed, but not enough. And then further back, they were purely two or three colors, but you couldn't tell from the distance that they were lightly painted."

The Pasaana festival required a 16-day shoot to capture. Pickups for the sequence were shot on Stage 4 at Pinewood, with a small 20-foot by 20-foot spot of sand and a kiosk tent standing in for the expansive environment as Rey undergoes a Force connection with Kylo Ren.

THE TREADABLE

Used as a transport by Lando Calrissian, the treadable is a simple, self-propelled track of caterpillar treads that chugs along the sands of Pasaana. It was an Episode VII design that was salvaged from the discard pile: during early exploration on that film, concept artist Thom Tenery illustrated a craft referred to as a "sand vehicle."

"Originally, J.J. said it was going to be something like a sandcrawler," recalled Kevin Jenkins. "Ryan Church did some very cool designs, but J.J. always loved Thom's version."

Jenkins described the treaded vehicle as a "big cassette" because its shape evokes the center of an audio cassette tape—the section with two sprocketed rollers on either side of a rectangular window.

In Episode VII, the treadable was to feature in the Force-back sequence: a scavenger riding within the treaded vehicle would have retrieved Luke's lightsaber from its long and winding journey across the galaxy.

For Episode IX, the vehicle was code-named the "Carnival Float." It consisted of two set builds. An interior set photographed on Stage 4 at Pinewood would be filled with set decoration to suggest a storied hauler of exotic junk, while a rotating drive shaft would line the ceiling. The exterior set—which would be transported to Jordan—represented the fully dressed entrance hatch the actors would interact with, while the rest of the tread assembly was to be computer generated by ILM.

"We tried adding loads of colors like it was a 'jingle truck' [an elaborately decorated delivery vehicle] from South Asia," described Jenkins. "But it all got to be too much. In the end, we chose a version that's red and white."

↑ Industrial Light & Magic created this posed and lit render of the all-digital treadable, aka the "Carnival Float." This model includes an alternate roof rack that was not seen in the finished production.

↓ This schematic view of the treadable indicates the extent of the build atop a trailer bed.

SET	EXT. CARNIVAL FLOAT
DETAIL	PLANS, ELEVATIONS, & ISOMETRIC
DRG NO.	01
DATE	JUNE 6 2018
DRAWN BY	MADHAV KIDAO

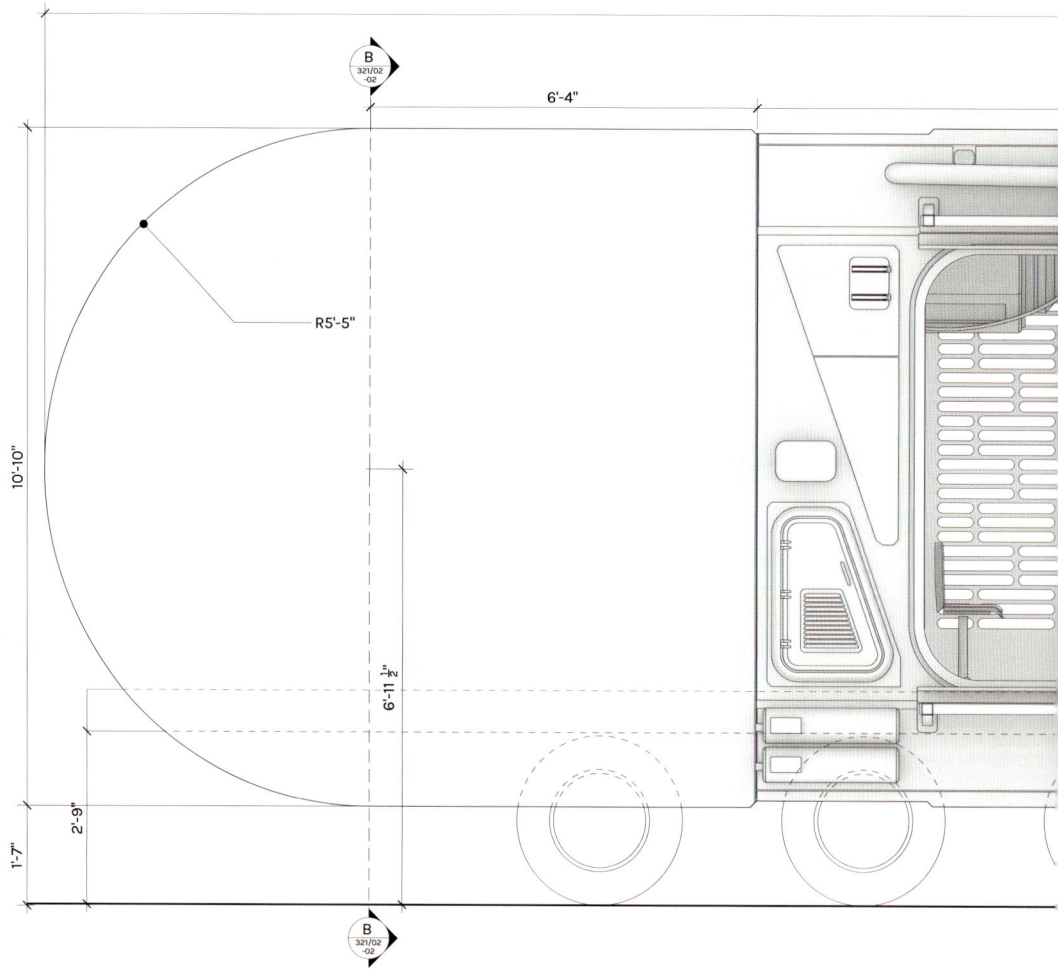

01/ STARBOARD ELEVATION

TRIXIE   Louisiana Taxi — Jaz's — Paint Schematic

↑ Oli van der Vijver's illustration shows the paint schematic for Rey's Pasaana speeder, code-named "Louisiana Taxi."

SET	LOUISIANA TAXI
DETAIL	PAINT SCHEMATIC
DRG NO.	09
DATE	AUGUST 3 2018
DRAWN BY	OLI VAN DER VIJVER

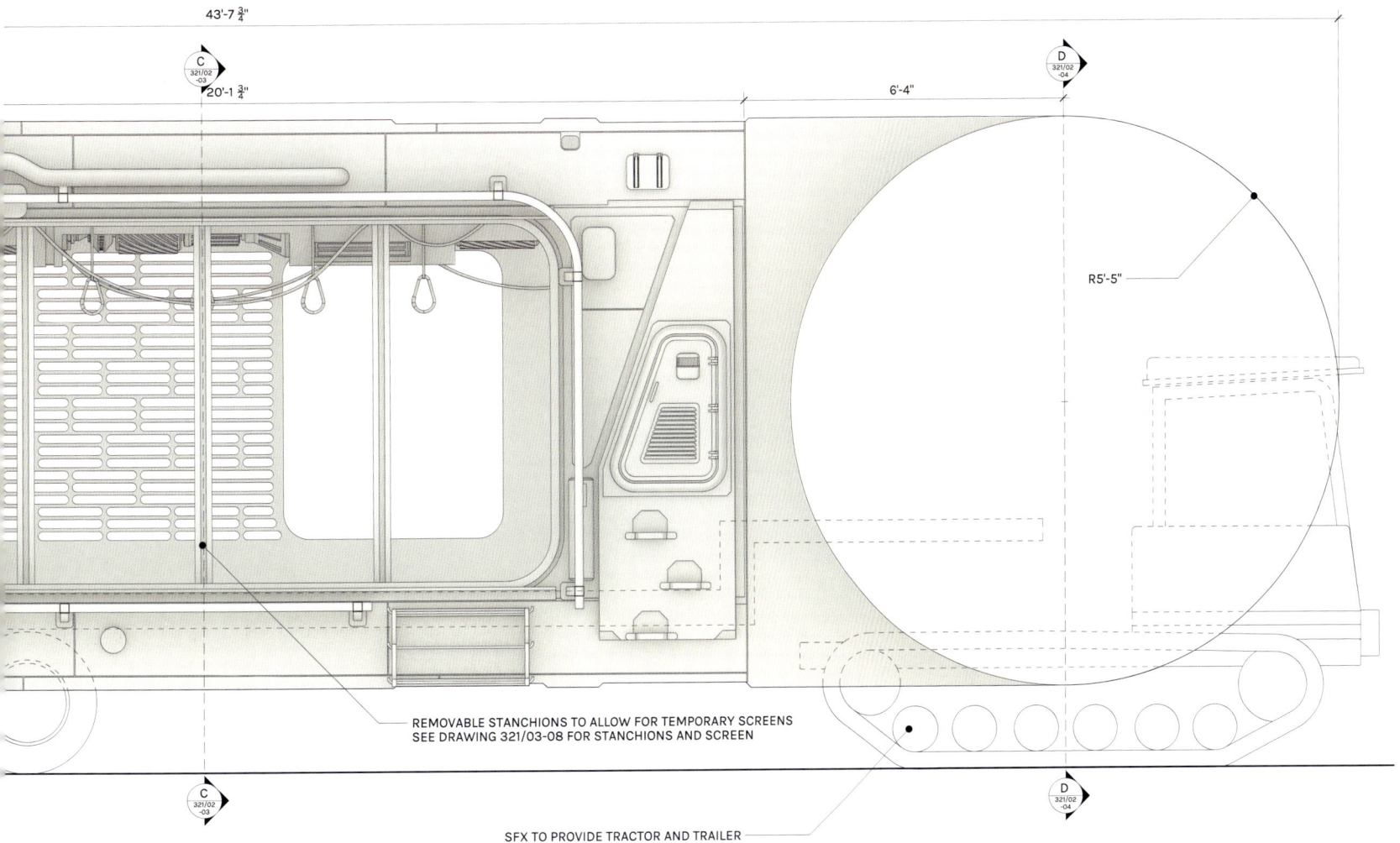

43'-7 ¾"

20'-1 ¾"

6'-4"

R5'-5"

REMOVABLE STANCHIONS TO ALLOW FOR TEMPORARY SCREENS
SEE DRAWING 321/03-08 FOR STANCHIONS AND SCREEN

SFX TO PROVIDE TRACTOR AND TRAILER

3/4" = 1' 0"

OCHI'S SHIP

Resting on a bluff on Pasaana, untouched for nearly two decades, is a ship first glimpsed as a fleeting image in Rey's powerful Force-fueled flashback sequence in *The Force Awakens*. In Rey's nightmarish vision, the ship rises into the skies of Jakku, stranding her as a young girl on the miserable desert world. Now reunited with the vessel, revealed to belong to the late Ochi of Bestoon, Rey begins getting answers to the jumbled mystery of her past.

"Ochi was a Jedi hunter, who was loyal to the Emperor since the days of the Empire. He's an evil character, who essentially functions as an assassin," said co-screenwriter Chris Terrio. "And so, in the course of the film, Rey ends up aboard the very ship where her parents were killed."

During the production of *The Force Awakens*, a small construction of the ship was made: a section of landing gear and an entry staircase. Code-named the "Station Wagon," the design was intended to feature in a moment where Rey glimpses a family departing Jakku in the present, prompting a pang of loss in the lonely scavenger. This sequence was cut from the film, and a distant shot of a CG "Station Wagon" instead became a vessel carrying her family in the Force-driven flashback sequence. Co-production designer Kevin Jenkins referenced this design when defining the new iteration of the vessel, now code-named the "Mayflower."

"J.J. said it had to link back to Episode VII," said Jenkins. "The back end of that ship and our ship match exactly. I got the Episode VII ship back to me from ILM, turned it around, and said, 'We can make ours work.'"

Knowing the ship to be of a past vintage, Jenkins leaned into his retro 1970s sensibilities in both design and construction approach. "We have louvers for the windows; they're even inside and on the landing legs. I wanted it to look like a big

↑ A detail of a final frame shows stormtroopers inspecting Ochi's starship, which has landed within the hangar of a First Order Star Destroyer. ILM has digitally extended the set build to represent the whole ship.

SET	EXT. MAYFLOWER
DETAIL	PAINT SCHEMATIC
DRG NO.	029
DATE	SEPTEMBER 18 2018
DRAWN BY	OLIVER VAN DER VIJVER

MAYFLOWER EXT - PAINT SCHEMATIC   344 - 029

NOTE:
Vehicle has been sat unused in desert for 10+ years. Now seen after first flight so layers of fresh oil, hydraulic fluids over initial rusty, sand blasted age.

→ The paint schematic for the "Mayflower" entry ramp includes a note that this ship has sat "unused in [the] desert for 10-plus years." The paint guide mentions areas that are "heavily aged" with "rust & oil."

KEY:
WHITE AREAS –
CATALINA DESERT WRECK.
GUN METAL/WHITE/BLUE/RUST

BLUE AREAS –
BARE METAL/RUST + OIL

GREEN AREAS –
UPHOLSTERED, NO PAINT REQ

PINK AREAS –
INT OFF WHITE WALLS
HEAVILY AGED

TRIXIE		PRODUCTION DESIGNERS: RICK CARTER & KEVIN JENKINS	DIRECTOR: J.J. ABRAMS SUPERVISING ART DIRECTOR: PAUL INGLIS
SET:	MAYFLOWER EXT		SET No.
DETAIL:	PAINT SCHEMATIC		344
SCALE NTS	STAGE/LOC 3	DRAWN BY OV	DRAWING No.
DATE DRAWN 18/09/18	DATE ISSUED	REVISION DATE	029

'TRIXIE' SET: INT. MAYFLOWER DRAWING: COCKPIT CENTRAL CONSOLE - SCALE: 1:5 AND 1:2

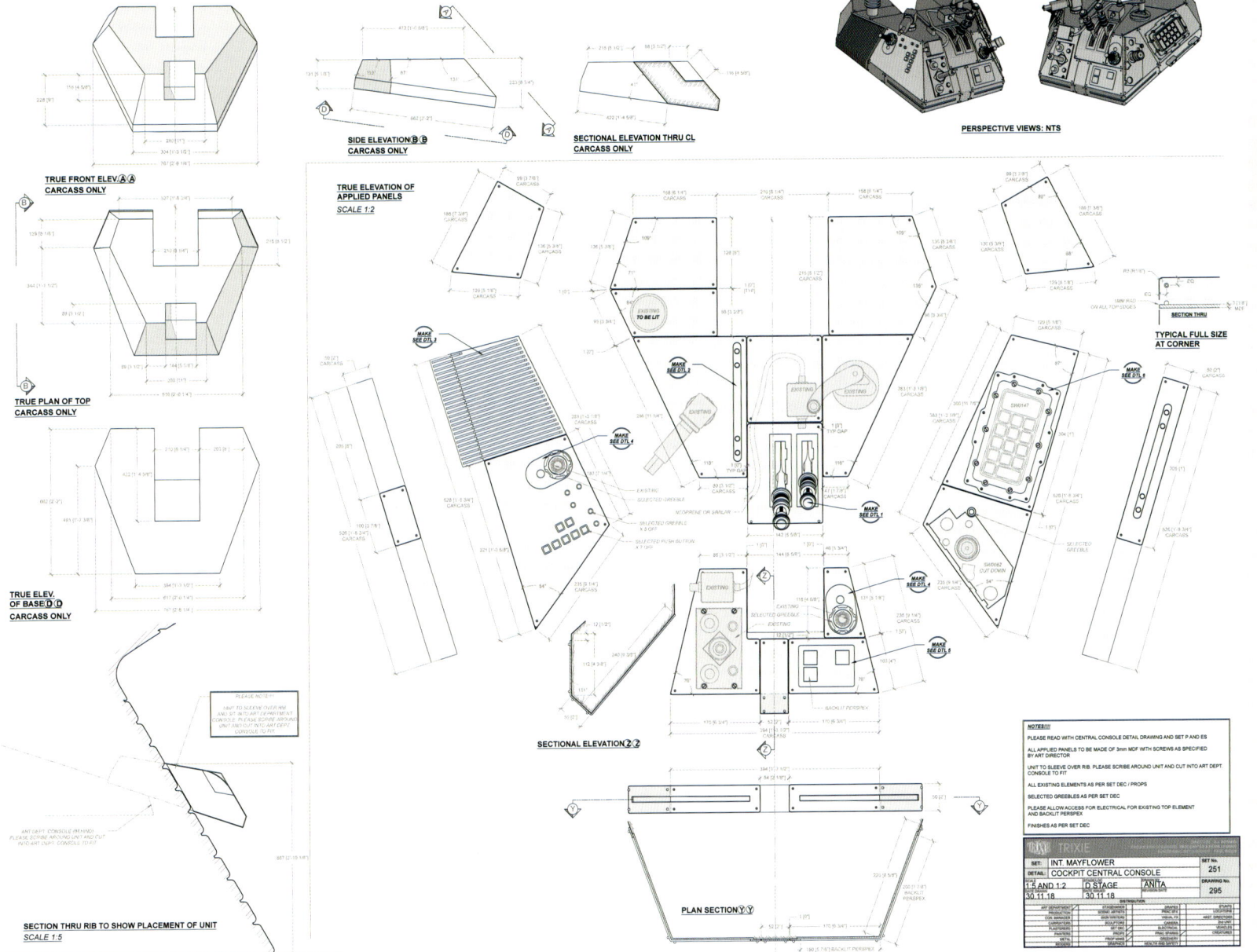

TRUE FRONT ELEV.(A)(A)
CARCASS ONLY

SIDE ELEVATION (B)(B)
CARCASS ONLY

SECTIONAL ELEVATION THRU CL
CARCASS ONLY

PERSPECTIVE VIEWS: NTS

TRUE ELEVATION OF
APPLIED PANELS
SCALE 1:2

TRUE PLAN OF TOP
CARCASS ONLY

MAKE
SEE DTL 1

EXISTING
TO BE LIT

MAKE
SEE DTL 5

MAKE
SEE DTL 4

EXISTING

EXISTING

MAKE
SEE DTL 5

EXISTING

SECTION THRU

TYPICAL FULL SIZE
AT CORNER

TRUE ELEV.
OF BASE (D)(D)
CARCASS ONLY

MAKE
SEE DTL 4

EXISTING

MAKE
SEE DTL 8

EXISTING
SELECTED GREEBLE

SELECTED GREEBLE
K-8 (DIFF)

SELECTED PUSH BUTTON
X-7 (DIFF)

EXISTING

MAKE
SEE DTL 8

SELECTED
GREEBLE

EXISTING

SHROUD
CUT DOWN

EXISTING

BACKLIT PERSPEX

NOTES!!!!
PLEASE READ WITH CENTRAL CONSOLE DETAIL DRAWING AND SET P AND ES

ALL APPLIED PANELS TO BE MADE OF 3mm MDF WITH SCREWS AS SPECIFIED
BY ART DIRECTOR

UNIT TO SLEEVE OVER RIB. PLEASE SCRIBE AROUND UNIT AND CUT INTO ART DEPT.
CONSOLE TO FIT

ALL EXISTING ELEMENTS AS PER SET DEC / PROPS

SELECTED GREEBLES AS PER SET DEC

PLEASE ALLOW ACCESS FOR ELECTRICAL FOR EXISTING TOP ELEMENT
AND BACKLIT PERSPEX

FINISHES AS PER SET DEC

SECTIONAL ELEVATION (Z)(Z)

SECTION THRU RIB TO SHOW PLACEMENT OF UNIT
SCALE 1:5

PLAN SECTION (Y)(Y)

BACKLIT
PERSPEX

TRIXIE			
SET:	INT. MAYFLOWER		SET No.
DETAIL:	COCKPIT CENTRAL CONSOLE		251
SCALE 1:5 AND 1:2	STAGE D STAGE	DRAWN ANITA	DRAWING No.
DATE 30.11.18	30.11.18		295

SET	INT. MAYFLOWER
DETAIL	COCKPIT CENTRAL CONSOLE
DRG NO.	295
DATE	NOVEMBER 30 2018
DRAWN BY	ANITA RAJKUMAR

↑ These illustrations show cockpit schematics and central console specifics for Ochi's starship.

↑ An on-set photograph of the cockpit of Ochi's starship shows dust-covered consoles and seats and the vehicle's distinctive louvered windows

model kit, scratch-built from the films of the 1970s and early 1980s, like [Peter Hyams' 1981 science-fiction thriller] *Outland* and that kind of stuff."

Jenkins imagined the ship to be of a similar era as the *Millennium Falcon*, though he took care not to use designs that would confuse audiences into thinking they were seeing a version of that classic vessel. The color palette of the interior helped make Ochi's vessel distinct. "I was looking a lot at the original Eagle lander from NASA, and I found this lovely picture that had yellows and teals—strange colors from the kitchen in my house in 1975 where my mom was cooking," he said. "These two colors are very hard to use as an artist and a painter, let alone on a set. If you get the wrong kind of yellow, it just looks sort of lemony or wrong. They're hard colors to play with."

Another page from Jenkins' childhood memories helped inform the hitherto unseen front of the ship. "I always loved [1978 TV series] *Battlestar Galactica*," he said, recalling the cockpit of the Cylon raider, "a cube with louvered windows," as designed by Ralph McQuarrie. When presented with the concept, J.J. Abrams was excited by the idea of lighting up the interior of the dusty ship with louvered light from the Pasaana desert.

KIJIMI

In keeping with the *Star Wars* tradition of visually distinct settings, the planet-hopping action jumps from the searing dunes of Pasaana to Kijimi, a frosty world with a mountaintop city. Informally called the "Snowy City" in production, the expansive set also bore the code name "Anchorage Main Street."

"This is one of the first places we got around to designing," said co-production designer Kevin Jenkins. "The main influence was [Akira] Kurosawa's [1958 movie] *The Hidden Fortress*."

The classic Japanese period film was a seminal influence on the original *Star Wars*, with George Lucas' early treatment from 1973 being largely a reframing of the plot of *The Hidden Fortress* as a space movie. Kurosawa's lead actor, Toshiro Mifune, was an inspiration for the Jedi and the hapless peasants who tag along with Kurosawa's heroes would evolve into C-3PO and R2-D2.

Visually, Kurosawa's approach of "immaculate reality"—capturing real, lived-in places that had a sense of weight and history—influenced Lucas' concept of a "used future." For the Episode IX team, too, the visuals of Kurosawa's titular fortress stood out when they were in search of Kijimi. "There was this wonderful shot of the heroes walking up the steps of the main fortress, with these lovely, beautiful, angled walls and massive, Japanese flagstones," said Jenkins.

For Kijimi, the production set out to investigate real-world sites, not only for inspiration, but also for potential filming locations. "We sent scouts to Ravenna and Matera [in Italy]," said supervising art director Paul Inglis. "A lot of topography—staircases, passageways—and much of the feeling of up and down came from those scouts, seeing these real places. Then it got put through the *Star Wars* filter, and it was a case of trying to simplify it, trying to break it down to just a few details, to find the language that they would have applied in the late 1970s to turn it from Kurosawa's Japan to their version of science fiction."

It became clear that Snowy City would be a large set build, and concept art and maquette models began defining the extent of the construction. "There was an earlier version of Snowy City that was a much larger model," said Jenkins. "All of a sudden, we decided to take a third of it off because we needed to be rational, and we couldn't just spend imaginary money. Sometimes the constrictions of making a more restrictive set can be helpful and force you to be cleverer."

"There's working out how much set we actually need to build," added Inglis. "What kind of opportunities are there? How can we be as clever as possible with the reuse

of different views. We had sixteen weeks from an empty site to a finished set, which wasn't very long. It was two weeks shorter than we had hoped."

The North Lot at Pinewood Studios—a 4.3-acre hard-standing, outdoor backlot—would be the construction site for Kijimi, with heavy equipment breaking ground. "The first thing we had to do onsite was actual excavation," said Inglis. "We didn't just build up;

SET	SNOWY CITY
DETAIL	DOOR VERSIONS
DRG NO.	N/A
DATE	MARCH 6 2018
DRAWN BY	CHARLOTTE LEATHERLAND

↓ This assortment of door designs were intended to help establish the character of Kijimi.

VERS. 1   VERS. 2

VERS. 5   VERS. 6

VERS. 9   VERS 10

SNOWY CITY DOOR VERS'S.
CRTL   SCALE ½"-1'0"   6·3·18

↑ An on-set photograph captures the steps on the expansive Kijimi set. The angled sections along the middle serve as smooth runways for droids like BB-8 and D-O.

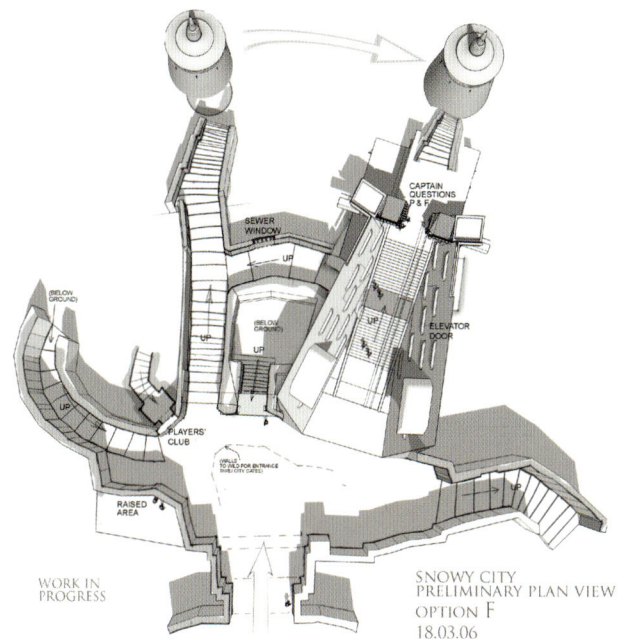

WORK IN PROGRESS

SNOWY CITY
PRELIMINARY PLAN VIEW
OPTION F
18.03.06

SET	SNOWY CITY
DETAIL	PRELIMINARY PLAN VIEW — OPTION F
DRG NO.	N/A
DATE	MARCH 18 2006
DRAWN BY	JIM BARR

↑ This early option for the Kijimi city layout includes demarcated areas for a First Order captain to question Finn and a "players' club".

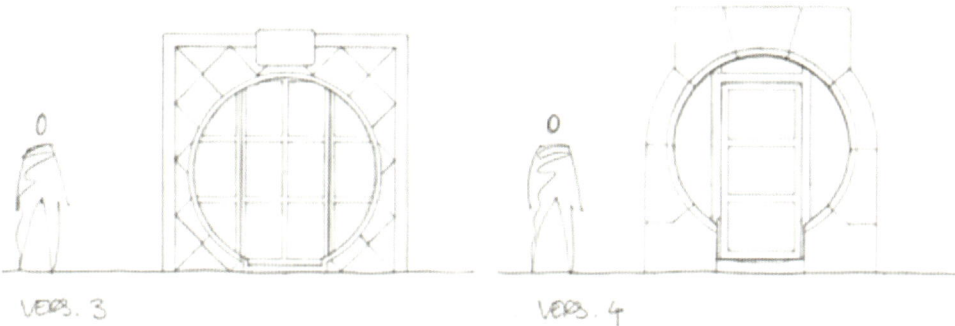

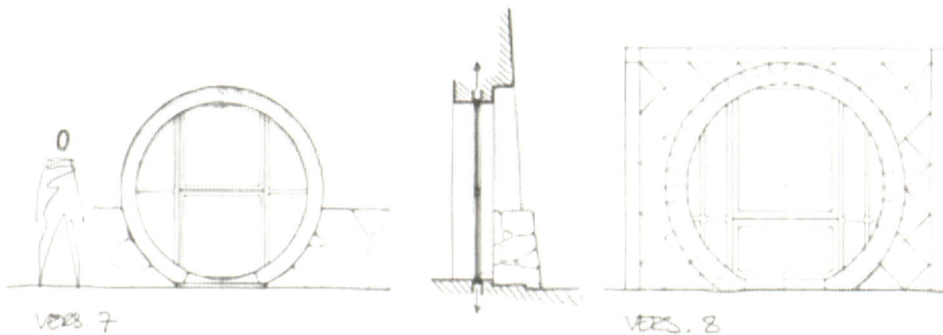

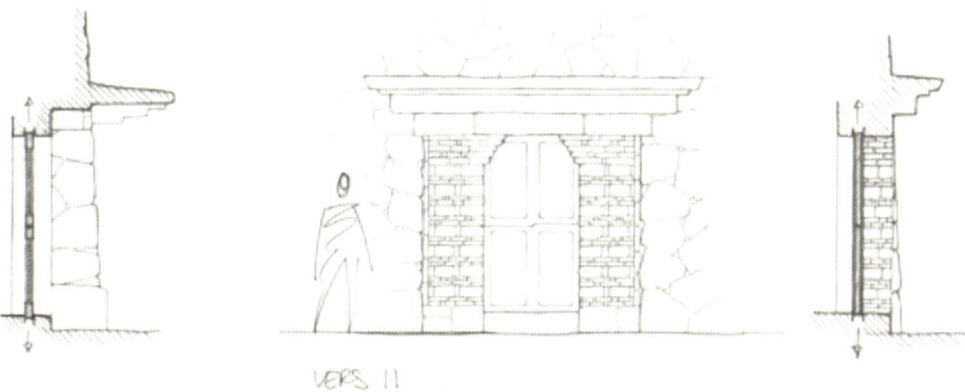

VERS. 3

VERS. 4

VERS. 7

VERS. 8

VERS. 11

we built down as well. We had to put drainage in. We had to set up all the different levels."

Translating the traditional Japanese rooftop into a Kijimi equivalent proved a vexing challenge. "There are not many square roofs in *Star Wars*," said Jenkins. "It took months and months to get right, because you don't want people to notice them. They needed to feel very natural, and they also needed to feel like they were very much in a *Star Wars* film."

Jenkins had long studied and appreciated Ralph McQuarrie's work, developing a shorthand in understanding otherwise unstated rules of design. "There are thousands of drawings, but you can tell why they used them or why they didn't. There are certain rules. A [sense of] proportion that he would have because of his natural style. He had what we call the 'gak band,' where you get a certain percentage of wall and you have a line of *Star Wars* gak [nondescript set dressings] in it. It's that line that makes it *Star Wars*. You take it out and it's just a wall. You put it in, and it's *Star Wars*."

The set would be frosted with scenic snow and ice, and included systems that could create true precipitation. "The special-effects team were putting out snow, which was made out of Epson salts, and then we had snow flurries falling, and that was actual snow," said Rosemary Brandenburg, as she led the effort of decorating the enormous set. "We had pots, sleds, benches, street dressing, doorway dressing, lighting fixtures, pipes, entryway panels, and *Star Wars* gak that's in every city."

BABU FRIK'S SHOP

C-3PO's stringent protocol will not allow him to access certain data from his mind, so to unlock it the heroes must seek out the best droid mechanic on Kijimi, a diminutive alien named Babu Frik. His shop, code-named the "Anchorage Store," would bypass the traditional concept-art stage for a more hands-on approach to development.

"Rather than try to create concept art to define what the space was, we literally marked out a section of the floor and made the set out of giant blocks of foam and bits of set dressing," said co-production designer Kevin Jenkins. "We made full-scale mock-ups of the set as concept, just to see. We could move in the walls, lower the ceiling, and define the space as we were going to shoot it, which was more efficient."

The set decoration and props department (Set Dec) filled the set, constructed on Pinewood's B stage, with all manner of droid detritus and tools scaled to Babu Frik's size. "He could fix anything," explained set decorator Rosemary Brandenburg. "He had workstations and a special robotic surgery table. He had every style of robot known to the galaxy, and almost every one of them was on display here. We had everything from the 'clown droid' [CZ-1 secretary droid from *A New Hope*], to R2 units, to humanoid bots. We made hundreds of robot parts in Set Dec, but in order to augment the environment, we also borrowed them from our friends in Costumes and Creatures, and just put in part after part."

Among the droids crowded into the shop was a recreation of the logo of J.J. Abrams' production company Bad Robot and—specifically at Abrams' request—a replica of the Episode I battle droid. "The vibe that J.J. gave us was it's like Mr. Wing's antique shop in *Gremlins* [1984] where Gizmo was bought: crowded with trinkets and all sorts of things," said Jenkins.

↓ Babu Frik's droid table, workbench, and pivoting footrest are delineated in a detail view. The illustration includes notes about the use of a puppeteered version of C-3PO that would allow for a performance with an open cranium.

SET	INT. ANCHORAGE STORE
DETAIL	DROID WORK BENCH — PLANS & ELEVATIONS
DRG NO.	198
DATE	OCTOBER 3 2018
DRAWN BY	CLARA GOMEZ DEL MORAL

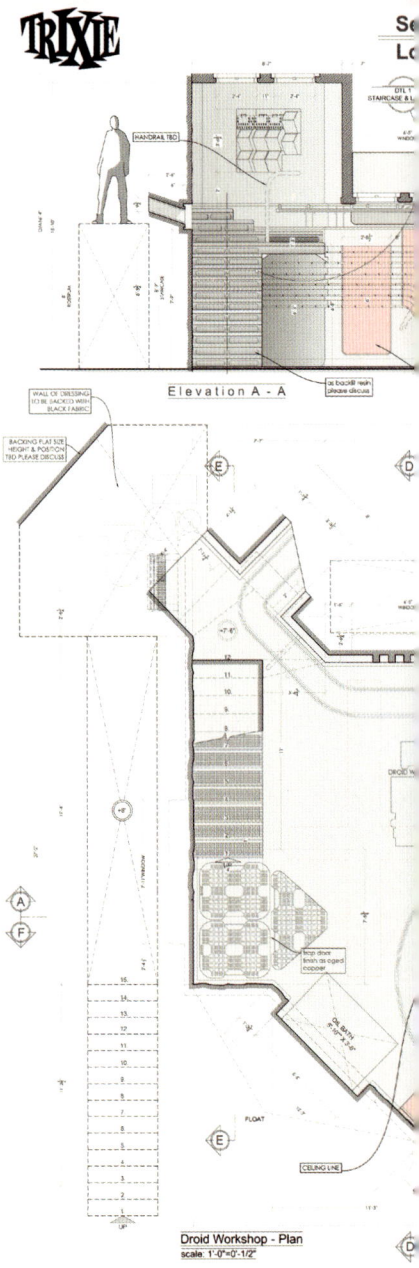

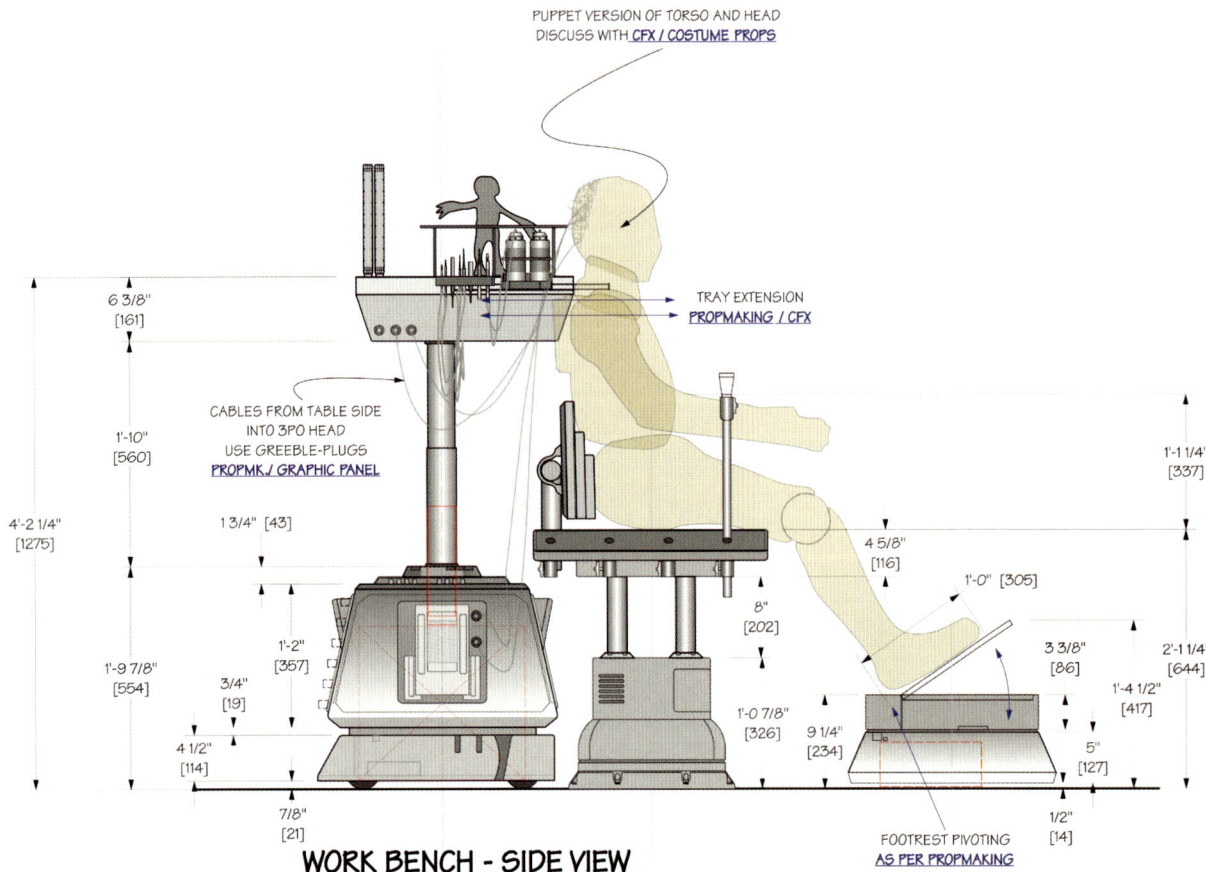

Elevation A - A

Droid Workshop - Plan
scale: 1'-0"=0'-1/2"

PUPPET VERSION OF TORSO AND HEAD
DISCUSS WITH CFX / COSTUME PROPS

TRAY EXTENSION
PROPMAKING / CFX

CABLES FROM TABLE SIDE
INTO 3PO HEAD
USE GREEBLE-PLUGS
PROPMK./ GRAPHIC PANEL

WORK BENCH - SIDE VIEW

FOOTREST PIVOTING
AS PER PROPMAKING

↓ The basic layout of Babu Frik's workshop is defined before the added clutter from Set Dec in this illustration.

SET	INT. ANCHORAGE STORE
DETAIL	PLANS & ELEVATIONS
DRG NO.	001
DATE	JUNE 11 2018
DRAWN BY	SARA TADDEI

7 - Int. Anchorage Store - Plans and Elevations: 1' - 0" = 0' - 1/2" @ A0+ WIP

on: Pinewood STAGE: B

137_001E

Elevation B - B

WALL OF CABLES

Finish as rough spread see art dep for reference

Elevation C - C

ALCOVE TO FLOAT

FINISH AS METAL

FINISH AS CRACKED AND BROKEN SPREAD OVER STONEWORK

Elevation D - D

Floor scooped up wall

FINISH AS CRACKED AND BROKEN SPREAD OVER STONEWORK

Elevation E - E

FLOOR AS AGED AND PITTED POLISHED CONCRETE

FLOAT

FINISH AS CRACKED AND BROKEN SPREAD OVER STONEWORK

FLOAT CAGE AT THIS POINT

DESK

SLIDING DOOR

Elevation F - F

NOTES

All measurements given in feet and inches unless stated otherwise

1. Furniture placement indicitave, final dressing layout as per set dec.
2. For all finishes please see art department for reference
3. All floating walls indicated to be confirmed. PLEASE DISCUSS
4. Internal heights are all given from finished floor level currently 1.5' thick - PLEASE DISCUSS FLOOR THICKNESS
5. Scooped skirting where floor meets wall.

DRAWINGS TO FOLLOW:

DTL 1: Staircase	137_002
DTL 2: Ceiling	137_003
DTL 3: Tracking	137_004
DTL 4: Grooved Wall	137_005
DTL 5: Practical Door Detail	137_006
DTL 6: Windows	137_007
DTL 7: Cage	137_012&13
DTL 8: Escape Tunnel	137_0015
DTL 9: Metal Panels	137_010
DTL 10: Metal Rails in Floor	137_011

REVISION NOTES

SEE REV CLOUD

TRIXIE

SET:	INT. ANCHORAGE STORE	SET No	2137
DETAIL:	PLANS AND ELEVATIONS		
	STAGE B		DRAWING No.
			001D

ESCAPE TUNNEL

NOTE ALL AREAS HIGHLIGHTED IN PINK TO FLOAT

↑ In the finished film, C-3PO reclines but does not relax under the administrations of Babu Frik.

↑ Set photography shows the shadowy corners of Babu Frik's workshop. Lurking among the detritus is a constructed incarnation of the illustrated Bad Robot logo.

THE DEATH STAR RUINS

"One of the ideas J.J. Abrams brought to Episode IX, which he had initially thought of in the early days of Episode VII, was to visit a crashed piece of the Death Star," said producer Michelle Rejwan. Early concept art on *The Force Awakens* explored images of a surviving Death Star, both literal and illusory. They included the battle station inexplicably rising from the desert and incredibly prescient images of "Kira," the prototypical Rey, swimming through underwater Death Star ruins to the Emperor's throne room, where she uncovers a map to Luke Skywalker.

This idea returned in Episode IX with the creation of Kef Bir, an oceanic moon of Endor. Code-named "Big Sur" during production, Kef Bir had an enormous chunk of the Death Star sunken into its waters, an environment that would draw from the carnival-themed code names used on *The Force Awakens* and be known as "Abandoned Funhouse." Aboard the battle station ruins, Rey would uncover a wayfinder device that could point the way to Exegol, a hidden Sith world. Also, she would confront Kylo Ren in the wreckage of the Emperor's throne room.

↓ The Throne Room ruins set, extensively researched from the *Return of the Jedi* blueprints (see pages 206 to 213), is illustrated here.

SET	FUNHOUSE
DETAIL	CONTROL ROOM
DRG NO.	001
DATE	SEPTEMBER 24 2018
DRAWN BY	LAURA MILLER

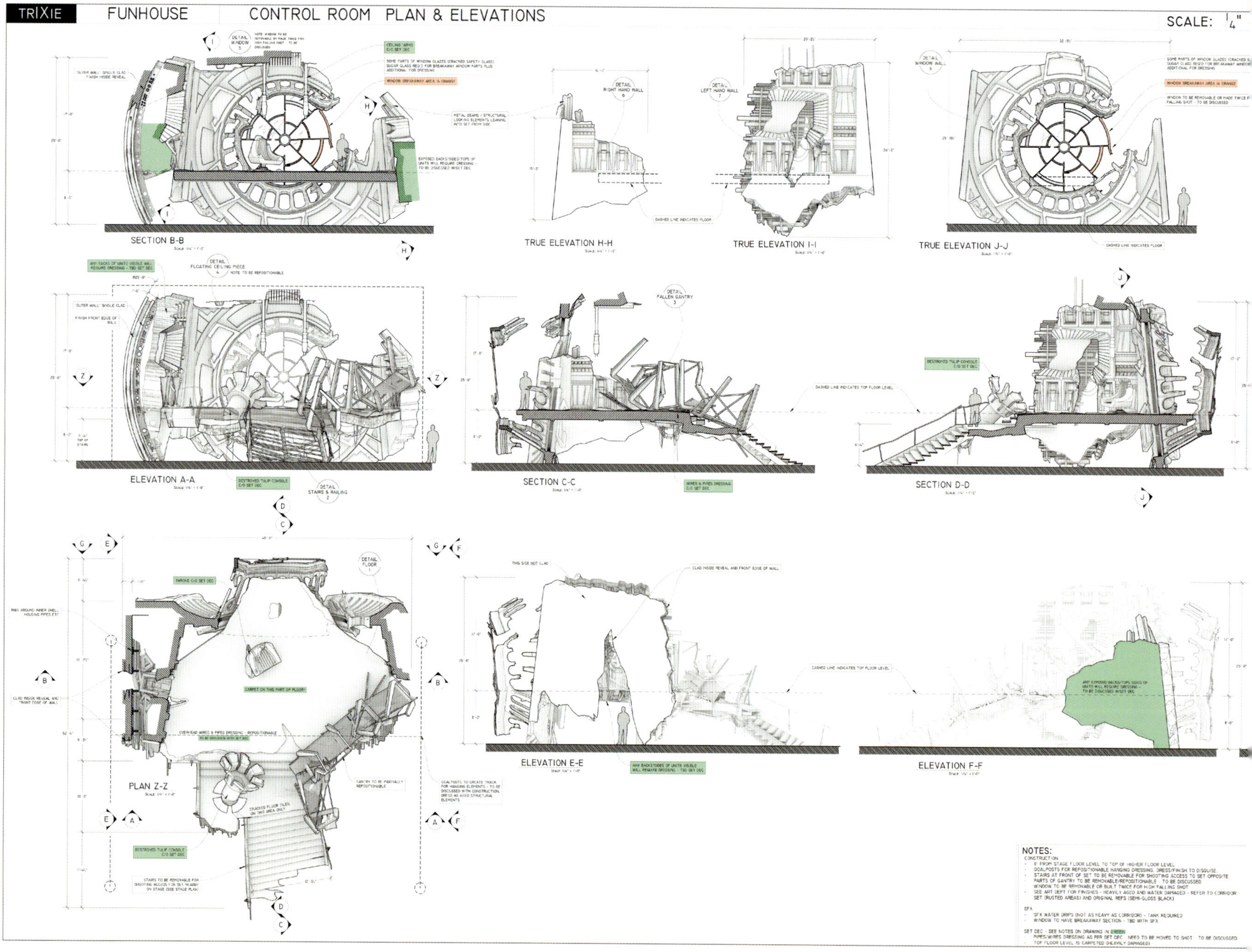

TRIXIE   FUNHOUSE   CONTROL ROOM PLAN & ELEVATIONS   SCALE: ¼"

↑ Final set photography records the ruins of the Emperor's throne room aboard the second Death Star, with extensions and blue screen removal by ILM.

"What more fitting place for Rey and Ren to have their meeting than literally in the ruins of the war that came before? We thought, well, surely the place that they have to meet in is the throne room, which involves both of their grandfathers and their shared history," said cowriter Chris Terrio.

"It involved building it all pristine from the original blueprints and then destroying it," said assistant art director Laura Miller. "We managed to fish out of the Archives some of the blueprints and original drawings from the original set build. From this, I was able to recreate it in 3D, so we created complete models of the original Throne Room." Based on that starting point, the art department began adding damage. Built on a canted floor on Stage 4 at Pinewood, the recreation of the Throne Room required extensive weathering and distressing on the surfaces to convincingly depict decades of saltwater corrosion. Set Dec details included the Emperor's broken throne and damaged "tulip"-style workstations, which had been seen in *Return of the Jedi*. A hitherto unseen door led to the Emperor's secret vault, where he has stored his wayfinder device. "We took the liberty of suggesting it was always there, but you just didn't notice it," said Miller.

As Kylo and Rey begin their duel, the action spills outside—both onscreen and off, as the combatants land on stretches of waterlogged Death Star hull buffeted by crashing waves. These scenes were shot in the Paddock Tank at Pinewood atop a 60-foot-long stretch of set. Surrounding the tank were 24 water cannons capable of firing 1,600 gallons of water 50 feet in the air. "Within ten minutes, we could reload and go again," said special effects supervisor Dominic Tuohy. Actors Daisy Ridley and Adam Driver not only had to contend with complex lightsaber fight choreography, but also with getting thoroughly drenched by water in November in the UK.

3D VIEW

ELEVATION G-G

TAILS:
STEPPED FLOOR
STAIRS & RAILING
FALLEN GANTRY
FLOATING CEILING PIECE
WINDOW
LEFT HAND WALL
RIGHT HAND WALL
WINDOW WALL

INVERTED PYRAMID TO BE HANGING **CHAINED** FOR ADJUSTABLE POSITION NO CEILING PIECE ON SET!!

PYRAMID 1: TO HAVE **MIRROR** BEHING RESING CLADDING ON **FACE A**

PYRAMID 1: TO HAVE **MIRROR** BEHING RESING CLADDING ON **FACE B**

A-A

B-B

MAKE x 2 PYRAMIDS
-1 SATNDING ON FLOOR
-1 HANGING FROM CHAIN
-SEE DRAWING FOR MIRROR CLADDING ON EACH PYRAMID
-BOTH MUST BE READY TO BE HANG ON CHAIN AND HAVE SPACE FOR WAYFINDER BATERY BOX HIDDEN INSIDE

V2: SHOWING DOTTED RED LINE TO MAKE INTERNAL TIMBER BOX

PLAN
SCALE 1:10

↑ The wayfinder holder in the "Funhouse Vault," a secret chamber within the Death Star ruins where Rey experiences a dark vision, is depicted in this illustration. Texture notes on the plans describe the holder as having a "black mirror slate" finish.

SET	INT. FUNHOUSE VAULT
DETAIL	WAYFINDER HOLDER
DRG NO.	SD 287
DATE	NOVEMBER 25 2018
DRAWN BY	CLARA GOMEZ

EXEGOL

The final act of *The Rise of Skywalker* is the revelation of a diabolical plot untold years in the making: the sinister culmination of a Sith Lord's determination to conquer death. Early in the film, Kylo Ren follows clues to the mastermind behind the First Order's most guarded machinations. The quest takes him to the darkest, most *eldritch* world conjured for the screen in a *Star Wars* movie: the shadowy planet of Exegol. By the film's end, both Ren and Rey would be drawn into this darkness to confront a resurrected Emperor Palpatine.

"We knew from the beginning that the movie's structure would be inspired by [Joseph Conrad's 1899 novella] *Heart of Darkness*, and this would be about Rey's journey to the darkest place both in the galaxy and for her. But we had to work a lot to figure out exactly what that was, what it meant, how the past would come into the story, and how the present and future would interact with that past," said cowriter Chris Terrio.

"When we were in Jordan, we took a location scout off to the side and visited Petra," said co-production designer Rick Carter. "There's an ancient civilization there, and that sparked the idea that there's a place where, maybe, the Sith really began in the very beginning, tapping into something that was dark and had power to it."

"I considered it like ancient Egypt or Sumer, five thousand years ago," said co-production designer Kevin Jenkins. "We were going back to the birthplace of an ancient civilization, so the sets were very different to what we've done before. It's an abandoned, dead planet."

The truncated schedule of Episode IX meant work on the look of Exegol continued well into production, though ideas of ancient statuary were present from the inception. The final construction of the Exegol sets would require extensive digital augmentation and blue screen work, but the foundational elements, which would be physically built, had an ancient heft and size.

"One thing J.J. impressed upon me was that Rey must feel small," said Jenkins. "We must feel like little people in a massive world. We talked about [1963 movie] *Jason and the Argonauts*, of walking past a giant statue. We had massive flagstones with giant grout lines."

The production code name for all things Exegol was "Detroit." The sets marked for physical construction included "Detroit Central Station Exterior" on Stage A, which was an expanse of dry, dead rock and soil extending beneath a floating monolith, of which a lower portion, casting an imposing shadow, would be built. On Stage 3, the next stop in the descent into the Sith undercroft is the "Detroit Central Station Elevator" and "Lower Level Interior." Both Ren and Rey would

descend via a "Force pad," a floating stone platform marked by the newly designed, dagger-shaped Sith escutcheon. While an appropriate Sith symbol was being developed, earlier iterations of the pad used the cog-shaped Imperial emblem from *A New Hope* instead.

Next stop in this dark tour was "Detroit Central Station Platform INT—Lab" on Stage 3, where the dark sciences sustaining the undead Emperor came into focus. "We made low, hanging tanks for the lab area. It was kind of a Frankenstein lab, where he's been rebuilding himself for the last thirty years," said Jenkins. The fusing of biology and dark mysticism has preserved Palpatine's withered soul in a rapidly decaying cloned body. The Sith Lord is fragmented and unstable and seeks the power to make himself whole again.

"When Kylo meets him, Palpatine is not fully formed, and he relies on tubes and mechanics, moving around this Sith laboratory on mechanisms that Kevin Jenkins designed," said visual effects supervisor Roger Guyett. "He has the spirit of the Sith, but is trapped in a body that is incomplete."

Ian McDiarmid, the actor who originally played Palpatine, reprised his villainous role, which would now require the added physicality of fitting into a life-sustaining apparatus. It was essential to the *Star Wars* mythology that Palpatine's unnatural, greedy clinging onto life comes at an appalling cost, a lesson already well established by Darth Vader's gruesome cybernetic transformation in the earlier films.

"We had discussions on how we could suspend Palpatine in the scene," said special effects supervisor Dominic Tuohy. "It was so secret, I didn't know who the actor would be, and then I found out it was going to be a seventy-five-year-old gentleman who would have to be nearly twenty feet in the air. It was quite a challenge to hold Ian up that high and make it comfortable for him to

← The resurrected Emperor (Ian McDiarmid) lurks among vital pipes and tubing in this finished set photograph.

TRIXIE ~ INT. DETROIT ROOFTOP ~ THRONE ~ P+E's, VER 4 ~ SCALE 1/4"

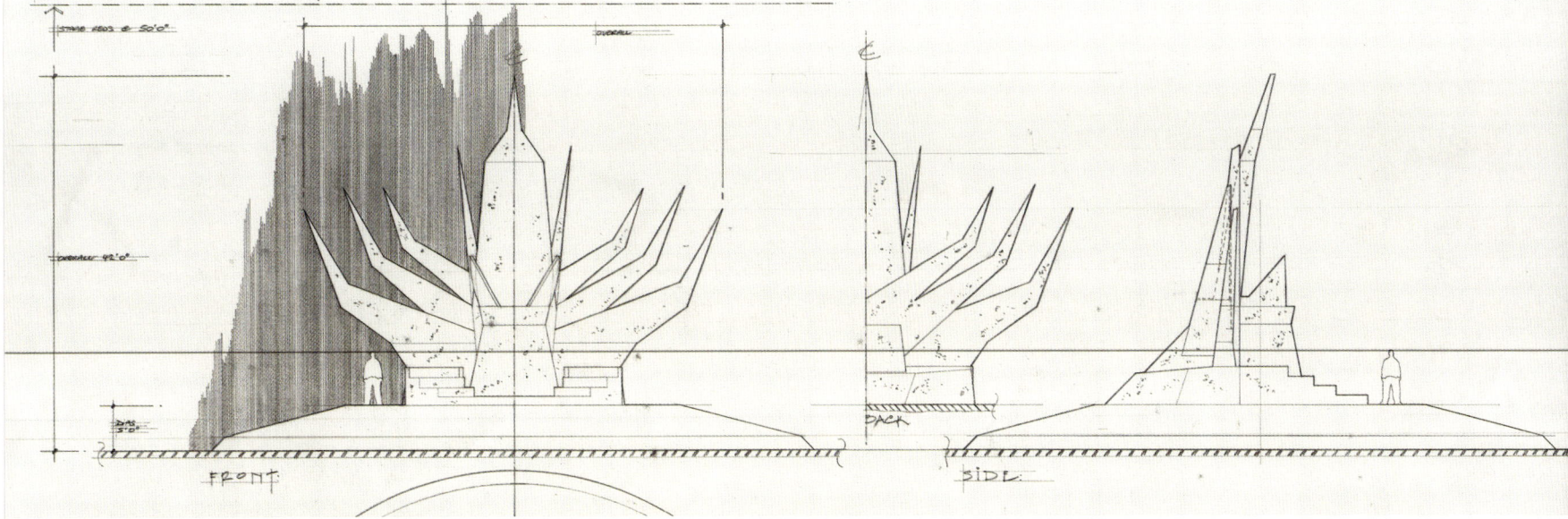

SET	INT. DETROIT ROOFTOP — THRONE
DETAIL	PLANS & ELEVATIONS, VERSION 4
DRG NO.	N/A
DATE	N/A
DRAWN BY	MIKE STALLION

↑ The Throne of the Sith, originally sketched by Ralph McQuarrie for early explorations on *Return of the Jedi*, gets further definition in this artwork of the "Detroit Rooftop — Throne".

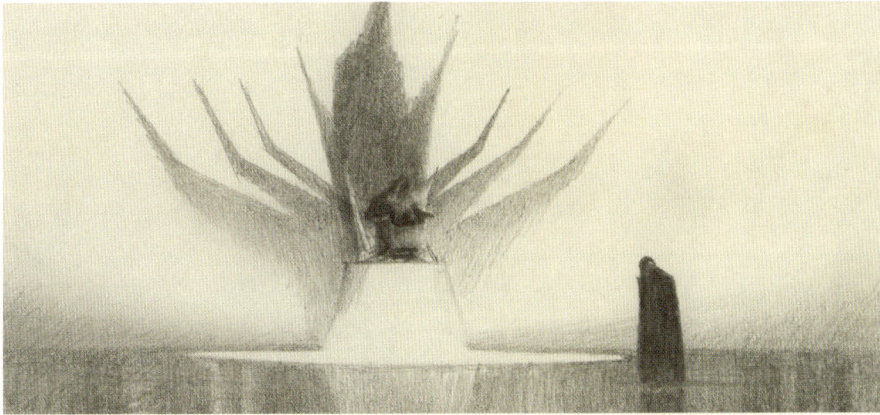

↑ A McQuarrie drawing of the original throne room from *Return of the Jedi*

→ Set photography with visual effects extensions of the Throne of the Sith, found on the sepulchral world of Exegol.

ART DEPARTMENT CREDITS BY FILM

A New Hope **(1977)**
Elstree Studios, United Kingdom
Production designer: John Barry
Art director: Norman Reynolds
Art director: Les Dilley
Set dresser: Roger Christian
Sketch artists: Ivor Beddoes, Harry Lange
Draftspeople: Ted Ambrose, Reg Bream, Peter J. Childs, Alan Roderick-Jones, Peter Shields
Scenic artists: Bill Beavis, Gillian Noyes, Ernie Smith
Modelers: Liz Moore, Brian Muir, Arthur Healey
Art department runner: Stephen (Steve) Cooper
Prop maker: Rodger Shaw
Prop buyers: George Noonan, Edward Rodrigo
Construction manager: Bill Welch
Property master: Frank Bruton
Head of department, carpentry: George Gunning
Head of department, painters: Ben Fensham
Head of department, plasterers: Herbert Rodwell

Industrial Light & Magic, United States
Production illustrator: Ralph McQuarrie
Special effects illustrator & designer: Joe Johnston
Orthographic blueprints & model builder: Steve Gawley

The Empire Strikes Back **(1980)**
Elstree Studios, United Kingdom
Production designer: Norman Reynolds
Design consultant & conceptual artist: Ralph McQuarrie
Art directors: Harry Lange, Alan Tomkins
Assistant art directors: Fred Hole, Michael Lamont
Set dresser: Mike Ford
Sketch artist: Ivor Beddoes
Draftspeople: Ted Ambrose, Michael Boone, Reg Bream, Stephen (Steve) Cooper, Richard J. Dawking
Art department assistants: Stephen Bream, Sharon Cartwright
Décor & lettering artist: Bob Walker
Modelers: Fred Evans, Allan Moss, Jan Stevens
Pattern maker: Brian Archer
Chief buyer: Edward Rodrigo
Buyer: Ian Giladjian
Construction manager: Bill Welch
Master plasterer: Ken Clarke

Industrial Light & Magic, United States
Visual effects art director: Joe Johnston
Assistant art director: Nilo Rodis-Jamero

Return of the Jedi **(1983)**
Elstree Studios, United Kingdom
Production designer: Norman Reynolds
Art director: Fred Hole
Set decorators: Michael Ford, Harry Lange
Assistant art directors: Michael Lamont, John Fenner, Richard J. Dawking
Assistant set decorator: Sharon Cartwright
Set dresser: Doug Von Koss
Assistant set dresser: Chuck Ray
Sketch artist: Roy Carnon
Scenic artist: Ted Michell
Assistant scenic artist: Steven Sallybanks
Décor and lettering artists: Bob Walker, Brian Smith
Set draftspeople: Reg Bream, George Djurkovic, Gavin Bocquet, Kevin Phipps
Production buyers: David Lusby, Ian Giladjian
Model maker supervisor: Brian Archer
Art department junior: Neil Lamont
Art department secretary: Carol Regan
Construction manager: Bill Welch
Master carpenter: Bert Long
Master plasterer: Ken Clarke
Paint foreman: Gary Clark
Master painter: Eric Shirtcliffe

Industrial Light & Magic, United States
Art director: James Schoppe
Effects art director: Joe Johnston
Assistant effects art director: Nilo Rodis-Jamero
Set draftspeople: Mark Billerman, Chris Campbell
Illustrator: George Jensen
Conceptual artist: Ralph McQuarrie

The Phantom Menace **(1999)**
Leavesden Studios, United Kingdom
Production designer: Gavin Bocquet
Supervising art director: Peter Russell
Art directors: Fred Hole, John King, Rod McLean, Phil Harvey
Art director (Tunisia): Ben Scott
Draftspeople: Paul Cross, Neil Morfitt, Gary Tomkins, Toad Tozer, Julie Philpott, Jane Clark Pearce, Philip Elton, Mike Bishop, Lucy Richardson
Scenic artist: James Gemmill
UK concept artists: Tony Wright, Kun Chang
UK art department Coordinator: Laura Burrows
Junior draftspeople: Helen Xenopoulos, Remo Tozzi
Sculptors: Eddie Butler, Tessa Harrison, Richard Mills, Keith Short, Richard Smith
UK art department assistants: Christopher Challoner, Iain Mcfayden, Claire Nia Richards, Emma Tauber

Concept Art Department, Skywalker Ranch, United States
Design director: Doug Chiang
Concept artists: Iain McCaig, Terryl Whitlatch, Jay Shuster, Ed Natividad, Kurt Kaufman, Marc Gabbana
Storyboard artist: Benton Jew
Concept sculptors: Tony Mcvey, Mark Siegel, Richard Miller, Robert Barnes
Concept model makers: John Goodson, John Duncan, Ellen Lee
3-D computer modelers: Caine Dickinson, Simon Dunsdon
Art department coordinators: Jill Jurkowitz, Blake Tucker
Art department assistant: Tom Barratt

Attack of the Clones **(2002)**
Fox Studios, Australia
Production designer: Gavin Bocquet
Supervising art director: Peter Russell
Art directors: Jonathan Lee, Ian Gracie, Phil Harvey, Michelle McGahey, Fred Hole
Assistant art directors: Jacinta Leong, Clive Memmott
Art department coordinator: Colette Birrell
Draftspeople: Andrew Powell, Edward Cotton, Peter Milton, Damien Drew
Junior draftspeople: Mark Bartholomew, Andrew Chan, Cindi Knapton, Paul Ocolisan
Set model makers: Ben Collins, Kerryanne Jensen, Michael Kelm,
Graphics/3-D modeler: Pheng Sisopha
Art department runners: Roderick England, Chris Penn

Concept Art Department, Skywalker Ranch, United States
Concept design supervisors: Doug Chiang, Erik Tiemens, Ryan Church
Art department Supervisor: Fay David
Concept artists: Iain McCaig, Dermot Power, Jay Shuster, Ed Natividad, Marc Gabbana, Kurt Kaufman, Phil Shearer, Ravi Bansal
Storyboard artists: Mark Sexton, Rodolfo Damaggio
Sculptor: Tony Lees
Concept sculptors: Robert E. Barnes, Michael Patrick Murnane, Tony McVey
Concept model makers: John Goodson, John Duncan, Carol Bauman, R. Kim Smith
Art department assistants: Bethwyn Garswood, Ryan Mendoza, Roel Robles, Matthew Saxon, Michael Smale

Revenge of the Sith **(2005)**
Fox Studios, Australia
Production designer: Gavin Bocquet
Supervising art director: Peter Russell
Art directors: Ian Gracie, Phil Harvey
Assistant art directors: Jacinta Leong, Damien Drew, Karen Murphy, Clive Memmott
Art department coordinator: Colette Birrell
Senior draftspeople: Edward Cotton, Cindi Knapton, Andrew Chan, Kristen Anderson, Andrew Powell
Junior draftspeople: Simon Elsey, Katie Carter
Concept draftsperson: Matt Saxon
3-D animator: Lizzie Burt
Art department runner: Dianne Hardman
Art department assistants: Christopher Tangney, Nicholas Tory, Chris Penn, Charlie Cobb

Concept Art Department, Skywalker Ranch, United States
Concept design supervisors: Ryan Church, Erik Tiemens
Art department coordinator: Fay David
Concept artists: Sang Jun Lee, Feng Zhu, T.J. Frame, Derek Thompson, Iain McCaig, Warren Fu, Stian Dahlslett, Gert Stevens
Concept sculptors: Robert E. Barnes, Michael Patrick Murnane
Art department assistant: Stephanie Lostimolo

The Force Awakens **(2015)**
Pinewood Studios, United Kingdom
Production designers: Rick Carter and Darren Gilford
Supervising art director: Neil Lamont
Senior art director: Al Bullock
Art directors: James Clyne, James Collins, Rob Cowper, Peter Dorme, Hayley Easton-Street, Jo Finkel, Mark Harris, Kevin Jenkins, Ashley Lamont, Mary Mackenzie, Andrew Palmer, Oliver Roberts, Stuart Rose, Stephen Swain
Assistant art directors: Andrew Borland, Sophie Bridgman, Claire Fleming, Lydia Fry, Robert Hochstoeger, Katrina Mackay, Remo Tozzi
Art department coordinator: Polly Seath
Senior illustrators: Fausto De Martini, Thomas Tenery
Draftspeople: Alexander Baily, Gavin Dean, Julia Dehoff-Bourne, Liam Georgensen, Sarah Ginn, Jake Hall, Richard Hardy, Matthew Kerly, Sam Leake, Daniel Nussbaumer, Andrew Proctor, Luke Sanders, Emma Vane, Ketan Waikar, Catherine Whiting
Junior draftspeople: Danny Clark, Alfredo Lupo, Anita Rajkumar, Elicia Scales, Rebecca White
Storyboard artists: Simon Duric, Steve Forrest-Smith, Kurt Van Ber Basch
Modelmaking assistants: Laura Barden, Theofano Pitsillidou
Props 3D modeler: Ian Bunting
Specialist researchers: Nicola Barnes, Celia Barnett
Digital asset manager: Kyle Wetton
Digital asset PAs: Paul Purnell, Eren Ramadan
Art department modelmaker: Alex Hutchings
Art department assistants: Helen Dawson, Will Houghton-Connell, Olivia Muggleton, Chris Vincent
Senior art director vehicles: Gary Tomkins
Vehicles assistant: Samantha Redwood
Set decorator: Lee Sandales
Lead assistant set decorator: Ben Barrington-Groves
Assistant set decorators: Stella Fox, Julie Pitt
Production buyer: Kate Venner
Assistant buyer: Lucie Ryan
Petty cash buyers: Guy Mount, Alice Phelps
Set dec PA: Hannah Kons
Lead graphic designer: Laura Dishington
Graphic designer: Dominic Sikking
Vehicles buyer: Harriet Orman

Concept Art Department, United States & United Kingdom
Lucasfilm head of design: Doug Chiang
Concept artists: Matt Allsopp, Christian Alzmann, Chris Baker, Tim Browing, Ryan Church, Seth Engstrom, Will Htay, Iain McCaig, Lee Oliver, Matthew Savage, Erik Tiemens, Dan Walker, Andree Wallin
Concept modelmaker: Neil Ellis
Visual effects art director: Yanick Dusseault
Visual effects concept artists: Christopher Bonura, Luis Carrasco, Ryan Drue, Luis Guggenberger, Jason Horley, Alex Jaeger, Karl Lindberg, Thang Le, Brett Northcutt, Michael Sheffels, David Yee, Stephen Zavala
ILM art department: Jennifer Coronado, Nicole Letaw, David Nakabayashi

The Last Jedi **(2017)**
Pinewood Studios, United Kingdom
Production designer: Rick Heinrichs
Supervising art director: Christopher Lowe
Lucasfilm design supervisor: Kevin Jenkins
Senior art directors: Mark Harris, Philip Sims
Art directors: Andrew Bennett, Neal Callow, Dean Clegg, Jason Knox-Johnston, Matthew Wynne
Assistant art directors: Liam Georgensen, Patricia Johnson, Hazel Keane, Charlotte Leatherland, Hugh McClelland
Art director - action vehicles: Oliver Van Der Vijver
Assistant art director - action vehicles: Richard Campling
Standby art director: Ben Munro
Storyboard artists: David Allcock, Martin Asbury, Kurt Van Der Basch
Lead concept artist: Kim Frederiksen
Concept artists: Adam Brockbank, Timothy Browning, Paul Catling, Paul Chandler, Roberto Fernandez-Castro
Draftspeople: Roxi Alexandru, Denise Ball, Ian Bunting, Gavin Dean, Teri Fairhurst, Mary Pike, Quinn Robinson, Matt Sims
Junior draftspeople: Olivia Muggleton, Alfredo Lupo, Paul Savulescu
Specialist researcher: Celia Barnett
Art department coordinator: Jennifer Lewicki
Art department assistant coordinator: Daniel Willis
3D CAD modeler: Greg Fangeaux
Digital asset managers: Oliver Rayner, Jason Brown
Digital asset assistant: Christina Manlises
Art department modelmakers: Rob Jose, Lisa Royle, Jack Cave
Art department assistants: Charlotte Anthony, Amy Battey, Isobel Mackenzie
Set decorator: Richard Roberts
Assistant set decorators: Charlotte Crosbie, Georgia Somary
Production buyer: John O'Shaughnessy
Set dec coordinator: Roxanna Stapleton
Set dec junior assistant: Connor O'Hara
Assistant buyers: Clare Gosnold, Daniel Pitt
Petty cash buyer: Tom Marriott
Lead graphic designer: Laura Grant
Set dec draftspeople: Alice Biddle, Sandra Phillips
Set dec concept artists: Nick Ainsworth, Chris Rosewarne
Supervising painter: Rob Channon
Senior CAD Designer: Chrissy Howes
Sculptor: Conrad Lindley-Thompson
Graphic designer: Chris Kitisakkul
Assistant modeler: Lisa Royle
Lead modeler: Robert Jose
Junior modeler: Jack Cave
Set designers: Roxana Alexandru, Denise Ball, Gavin Dean, Mary Pike, Quinn Robinson
3D Set designers: Ian Bunting, Robert Hochstoeger, Matthew Sims
Junior set designer: Georgina Goldman

Concept Art Department, United States
Supervising art director: Todd Cherniawsky
Concept artists: James Clyne, Aaron McBride
Art director: John Dexter
Digital asset managers, Lucasfilm: Genna Elkin, Nicole Letaw
Art department coordinator: Andrea Carter
Assistant art coordinator: Alex Gustaveson
Art department assistant: Chris Arnold
Researcher: Priscilla Elliot
Illustrators: Mauro Borelli, Jim Carson, Rodolfo Damaggio, Seth Engstrom, Jamie Jones, Tani Kunitake, Daniel Simon, Justin Sweet
Visual effects art directors: Jason Horley, Yanick Dusseault
Visual effects concept artists: Julien Gauthier, Luis Guggenberger, Brett Northcutt, Timothy Rodriguez, Eric Tobiason, Chris Voy, David Yee, Stephen Zavala

The Rise of Skywalker **(2019)**
Pinewood Studios, United Kingdom
Production designers: Rick Carter, Kevin Jenkins
Supervising art director: Paul Inglis
Set decorator: Rosemary Brandenburg
Senior art director: Philip Sims
Art directors: Matt Wynne, Jim Barr, Claire Fleming, Liam Georgensen, Patrick Harris, Ashley Lamont, Mike Stallion

Liam Georgensen, Patrick Harris, Ashley Lamont, Mike Stallion
Additional conceptual designs: Darren Gilford
Art department manager: Fliss Jaine
Storyboard artist: David Allcock
Standby art director: Peter James
Art director (action vehicles): Oliver Van Der Vijver
Assistant art directors (action vehicles): Madhav Kidao, Matt Sims
Art director (action vehicles workshop): Richard Campling
Assistant art directors: Roxana Alexandru, Petra Balogh, Jake Hall, Charlotte Leatherland, Hugh McClelland, Laura Miller, Kristen Maloney
Draftspeople: Georgina Goldman, Lizzie Osborne, Johanna Sansom, Sara Taddei, Andrew Tilhoo, Chris Vincent, Antia Rajkumar, Kate Pickthall, Helen Dawson, Andy Proctor
Junior draftspeople: Charlotte Anthony, Matt Francis, Georgia Grant, Hannah Weissler Leas
Lead modeler: Robert Jose
Concept modelmakers: Colin Armitage, Mark O'Kane
3D Set Designers: Rebekah Bukhbinder, Ian Bunting

Modelmaker: Lisa Royle
Assistant modelmaker: Jack Cave
Art department coordinator: Louise Dobson
Specialist researcher: Gina De Ferrer
Senior digital asset manager: Kyle Wtton
Digital asset managers: Genevieve Ferrier, Craig Skerry
Asset archivist: Sarah Sanderson
Assistant digital assets: Pavel Kvatch
BFI art department assistant: Isla Bousfield-Donohoe
Art department intern: Henry Abrams
Art department assistants: Madeleine Dymond, Matthew Geldard, Emma Graveling
Location set decorator: Andrew McCarthy
Production buyer: Corina Floyd
Assistant set decorator: Samantha Redwood, Chloe James
Assistant buyers: Lucie Bourgeau, Helen Player
Art directors – props (set dec): Oliver Roberts, Lydia Fry, Daniel Nussbaumer
Assistant art directors – props (set dec): Clara Gomez Del Moral
Lead graphic designer: Dan Burke

Graphic designers: Hannah Kons, Dominic Sikking
Assistant graphic designer: Josie Kealy
Set dec assistants: Joseph Sanchez, Hannah Gautrey
Set dec coordinator: Eleanor Bailey
Drapesmaster: Jesse Jones
Drapesmen: Alex Lewry, Chris Lewry, Daniel O'Brien, Davis Scott, Cleo Nethersole
Supervising painter – set dec: Carl Wildman
Supervising carpenter – set dec: Jim McNeil
Chargehand carpenter – set dec: Duncan McNeil
Chargehand painters – set dec: Tim Lee, Ben Carty, Kevin McNeil
Painters – set dec: Jamie Hall, Andrew Hampshire, Tony Romero, Philip Hawley
Craft painters: Robert West, Richard Lancaster, Peter Rhodes, Keziah Armstrong
Researcher: Nicola Barnes

Concept art department, United States and United Kingdom
Lucasfilm design supervisor: James Clyne
VP & head of design: Doug Chiang
Concept artists: Adam Brockbank, Bob Cheshire, Jon McCoy, Stephen Tappin, Christian

Alzmann, Ryan Church, Rodolfo Damagio, Yanick Dusseault, Sean Hargreaves, Phil Saunders, Erik Tiemens, Adam Baines, Andrée Wallin, Richard Lim
Art department production manager: Genevieve Elkin
Art department associate production manager: Jennifer Hsyu
Art department coordinator: Darnie Galloway
Art department assistant: Madeleine Sandrolini
Concept modeler: Colie Wertz
Practical modelmaker: John Goodson
Researcher: Phil Szostak
Visual effects art directors: Stephen Tappin, Chris Voy
Visual effects concept artists: Amy Beth Christenson, Adam Ely, Brett Northcutt, Bianca Scurtu, Michael Sheffels, Stephen Zavala
ILM art department: Ashley Bradford, Jennifer Coronado, Alexander Gustaveson, David Nakabayashi

INTERVIEWS

Production designer John Barry interviewed by Charlie Lippincott, May 17, 1976 and November 19, 1977

The following new interviews by J. W. Rinzler are listed in chronological order, all from 2010; those of Muren, Knoll, and Peterson were conducted in the Lucasfilm Archives, Skywalker Ranch; all others were conducted by phone or Skype.

ILM Visual effects supervisor Dennis Muren, September 2
ILM Visual effects supervisor John Knoll, September 3
ILM Model shop foreman Lorne Peterson, September 17
Production designer Norman Reynolds, October 19, 20, and 26
Senior draftsman Ted Ambrose, October 27
Draftsman Michael Boone, October 28
Set dresser and second unit director Roger Christian, November 2
Master plasterer Ken Clark, November 3
Art director Alan Tomkins, November 4
Production designer Gavin Bocquet, November 5
Supervising art director Peter Russell, November 5
Producer Robert Watts, December 3
Draftsman Steven Cole, December 3
Draftsman Peter Childs, December 15
Art director Les Dilley, January 19, 2011
Production designer Rick Carter, August 12, 2013

The following interviews were conducted by the Lucasfilm Video Production team during the making of the Sequel Trilogy.

Production designer Darren Gilford, February 24, May 21, September 4, 2014
Creature effects supervisor Neal Scanlan, February 24, 27, May 25, 2014
Set decorator Lee Sandales, February 26, 2014

Production designer Rick Carter, April 4, 2013; March 27, August 28, 2014; June 24, October 1, 2018
Production designer Kevin Jenkins, June 26, 2014; September 23, 2015; August 11, 2016; June 24, July 24, August 10, 29, September 4, 10, 24, 25, October 10, 19, November 14, 26, December 7, 17, 2018; January 9, 15, 29, February 12, 2019
Assistant art director Lydia Fry, June 26, 2014
Production designer Rick Heinrichs, March 7, 13, 31, May 6, July 7, 13, 2016
Supervising art director Chris Lowe, July 6, 2016
Art director Claire Fleming, October 19, 2018
Set decorator Rosemary Brandenburg, November 14, 15, 23, 2018; January 31, 2019
Supervising art director Paul Inglis, November 26, December 18, 2018; January 9, 31, February 14, 2019

The following interviews were conducted by Mark Cotta Vaz during the making of *The Force Awakens*.

Visual effects supervisor Roger Guyett, June 24, 2014
Neal Scanlan, June 26, September 16, 2014
Stunt coordinator Rob Inch, July 1,3, 2014
Asset producer James Enright, July 2, 2014
Senior art director Gary Tomkins, July 1, September 15, 22, 2014
Director J.J. Abrams, July 1, September 27, 2014; March 17, 2015
Lee Sandales, September 27, 2014
Art director Mark Harris, September 30, 2014
Construction manager Paul J. Hayes, October 2, 2014

The following interviews were conducted by Phil Szostak.

Kevin Jenkins, October 13, 2014; November 30, 2018
Darren Gilford, November 21, December 12, 2014
Rick Heinrichs, July 14, 2016
Rick Carter, November 29, 2018

BIBLIOGRAPHY

Arnold, Alan, *Once Upon a Galaxy: A Journal of the Making of The Empire Strikes Back*, Ballantine Books, 1980

Bergan, Ronald, *Irvin Kershner Obituary*, Guardian.co.uk; http://www.guardian.co.uk/film/2010/nov/29/irvin-kershner-obituary

Christian, Roger, e-mails to J. W. Rinzler, November and December 2010

Ford, Michael, notes and e-mails to J. W. Rinzler, December 2010

Hole, Fred, typed notes, to J. W. Rinzler, November 10, 2010

Knoll, John & J. W. Rinzler, *Creating the Worlds of Star Wars: 365 Days*, Abrams, 2005
Lange, Harry, official website: http://www.harry-lange.org.uk

Peecher, John Phillip, *The Making of Star Wars: Return of the Jedi*, Ballantine Books, 1983

Reiff, Chris & Chris Trevas, *Set Pieces* was an ongoing department in *Star Wars Insider*, Wizards of the Coast and Paizo Publishing, 1997–1999
Reynolds, Norman, e-mails to J. W. Rinzler, November and December 2010

Riley, John, "Harry Lange: Oscar-Nominated Film Designer," *The Independent*, Thursday, August 21, 2008
Rinzler, J. W., *The Making of Star Wars*: Episode III *Revenge of the Sith*, Ballantine Books, 2005

The Making of Star Wars, Ballantine Books, 2007
The Making of Star Wars: The Empire Strikes Back, Ballantine Books, 2010
Cloud City Changes, Star Wars Insider, Titan Publishing, 2010

Welch, Brenda, handwritten notes concerning her husband, Bill Welch, to J. W. Rinzler, December 2010

The Director and the Jedi. Directed by Anthony Wonke, Lucasfilm Ltd. 2018

Fordham, Joe. "The Spirit of '77" *Cinefex* #145, February 2016

Fordham, Joe. "Force Strong" *Cinefex* #157, February 2018

Fordham, Joe. "The Long Goodbye" *Cinefex* #169, February 2020

The Skywalker Legacy. Directed by Debs Paterson, Lucasfilm Ltd. 2020

Star Wars: The Force Awakens: A Cinematic Journey. Directed by Laurent Bouzereau, Lucasfilm Ltd. 2016

Szostak, Phil, *The Art of Star Wars: The Force Awakens*, Abrams Books, 2015
The Art of Star Wars: The Last Jedi, Abrams Books, 2019
The Art of Star Wars: The Rise of Skywalker, Abrams Books, 2019

INDEX

PHOTO CREDITS

Sue Adler, Richard Blanshard, Sean Casey, Terry Chostner, Albert Clarke, Murray Close, Frank Connor, Douglas Dawson, Richard Edlund, Jonathan Fisher, Lynn Goldsmith, Keith Hamshere, Jules Heath, Tom Hilton, David James, John Jay, Giles Keyte, Irvin Kershner, Shannon Kirbie, Gary Kurtz, Long Photography, Meghan Marshall, Roberto McGrath, Ralph Nelson Jr., Kerry Nordquist, Jonathan Olley, David Owen, Mark Sennet, Chris Spitale, Paul Tiller, Knut Vadreth, Charles Wessler, Giles Westley, George Whitear, John Wilson

Blueprint photography by Sam Hoffman and JP Jespersen of LightSource. Special thanks to Tina Mills, Stacey Leong, and Matthew Azeveda at the Lucasfilm Image Archives.

BIOGRAPHIES

J.W. Rinzler, former executive editor at Lucasfilm Ltd., is the author of the *New York Times* bestseller *The Making of Star Wars*, as well as multiple other books, including the London *Times* bestseller *The Complete Making of Indiana Jones* and his original novel, *All Up*. Rinzler passed away in 2021.

Pablo Hidalgo has been writing professionally about *Star Wars* since 1995. In 2000, he joined Lucasfilm to become a full-time *Star Wars* authority, first as a StarWars.com writer, and now as a director of franchise story development. He has written or co-written several authoritative *Star Wars* reference books, including DK's best-selling *Star Wars: The Force Awakens The Visual Dictionary, Star Wars: Rogue One The Ultimate Visual Guide*, and *Star Wars: The Last Jedi Visual Dictionary*. He lives in San Francisco.